opposing viewpoints

SOURCES

chemical dependency

opposing viewpoints

chemical dependency

vol. 1

David L. Bender, *Publisher*
Bruno Leone, *Executive Editor*
Bonnie Szumski, *Senior Editor*
Janelle Rohr, *Senior Editor*
Susan Bursell, *Editor*
William Dudley, *Editor*
Robert Anderson, *Assistant Editor*
Karin Swisher, *Assistant Editor*

Scott Davis, Ph.D., *Consulting Editor*
*Instructor in the Chemical Dependency Specialist
Training Program at Minneapolis Community College
in Minneapolis, Minnesota*

greenhaven press, inc.

P.O. Box 289009
San Diego, CA 92128-9009

© 1989 by Greenhaven Press, Inc.

ISBN 0-89908-543-1

ISSN 1042-315X

''Congress shall make no law . . . abridging the freedom of speech, or of the press.''

First amendment to the US Constitution

contents

foreword

"It is better to debate a question without settling it than to settle a question without debating it."

Joseph Joubert (1754-1824)

The purpose of Opposing Viewpoints SOURCES is to present balanced, and often difficult to find, opposing points of view on complex and sensitive issues.

Probably the best way to become informed is to analyze the positions of those who are regarded as experts and well studied on issues. It is important to consider every variety of opinion in an attempt to determine the truth. Opinions from the mainstream of society should be examined. But also important are opinions that are considered radical, reactionary, or minority as well as those stigmatized by some other uncomplimentary label. An important lesson of history is the eventual acceptance of many unpopular and even despised opinions. The ideas of Socrates, Jesus, and Galileo are good examples of this.

Readers will approach this anthology with their own opinions on the issues debated within it. However, to have a good grasp of one's own viewpoint, it is necessary to understand the arguments of those with whom one disagrees. It can be said that those who do not completely understand their adversary's point of view do not fully understand their own.

A persuasive case for considering opposing viewpoints has been presented by John Stuart Mill in his work *On Liberty*. When examining controversial issues it may be helpful to reflect on his suggestion:

> The only way in which a human being can make some approach to knowing the whole of a subject, is by hearing what can be said about it by persons of every variety of opinion, and studying all modes in which it can be looked at by every character of mind. No wise man ever acquired his wisdom in any mode but this.

Analyzing Sources of Information

Opposing Viewpoints SOURCES include diverse materials taken from magazines, journals, books, and newspapers, as well as statements and position papers from a wide range of individuals, organizations, and governments. This broad spectrum of sources helps to develop patterns of thinking which are open to the consideration of a variety of opinions.

Pitfalls To Avoid

A pitfall to avoid in considering opposing points of view is that of regarding one's own opinion as being common sense and the most rational stance and the point of view of others as being only opinion and naturally wrong. It may be that another's opinion is correct and one's own is in error.

Another pitfall to avoid is that of closing one's mind to the opinions of those with whom one disagrees. The best way to approach a dialogue is to make one's primary purpose that of understanding the mind and arguments of the other person and not that of enlightening him or her with one's own solutions. More can be learned by listening than speaking.

It is my hope that after reading this anthology the reader will have a deeper understanding of the issues debated and will appreciate the complexity of even seemingly simple issues on which good and honest people disagree. This awareness is particularly important in a democratic society such as ours where people enter into public debate to determine the common good. Those with whom one disagrees should not necessarily be regarded as enemies, but perhaps simply as people who suggest different paths to a common goal.

The Format of SOURCES

In this anthology, carefully chosen opposing viewpoints are purposely placed back to back to create a running debate; each viewpoint is preceded by a short quotation that best expresses the author's main argument. This format instantly plunges the reader into the midst of a controversial issue and greatly aids that reader in mastering the basic skill of recognizing an author's point of view. In addition, the table of contents gives a brief description of each viewpoint, allowing the reader to identify quickly the point of view for which he or she is searching.

Each section of this anthology debates an issue, and the sections build on one another so that the anthology as a whole debates a larger issue. By using this step-by-step, section-by-section approach to understanding separate facets of a topic, the reader will have a solid background upon which to base his or her opinions. Each year a supplement of twenty-five opposing viewpoints will be added to this anthology, enabling the reader to keep abreast of annual developments.

This volume of Opposing Viewpoints SOURCES does not advocate a particular point of view. Quite the contrary! The very nature of the anthology leaves it to the reader to formulate the opinions he or she finds most suitable. My purpose as publisher is to see that this is made possible by offering a wide range of viewpoints that are fairly presented.

David L. Bender
Publisher

introduction

*"Exploring strange life situations,
revolting against parental authority,
and experimenting with sex and drugs
has been going on for thousands of years."*

Alfred Burger

Editor's note: The use and abuse of mind-altering drugs has occurred in all human societies since prehistoric times. Curiosity, rebellion, and a search for pleasure are some of the desires that lead humans to experiment with drugs. Chemical Dependency: Opposing Viewpoints SOURCES *offers a broad range of viewpoints on the multitude of issues in chemical dependency.*

The following excerpt is from Drugs and People *by Alfred Burger, a professor emeritus of chemistry at the University of Virginia. Burger's overview of the use of drugs through the ages makes a unique and informative complement to this volume of opposing viewpoints.*

Ever since alcohol, opium, cannabis (marijuana, hashish), tobacco, and peyote began to be used by humans, medicines that alter mental states have been regarded with awe, fear, disgust, and other emotions. Some of these substances cause detachment and withdrawal or result in sleep or indifference to outside influences. For centuries surgeons used alcohol and opium to blunt the intolerable pain of amputations and other operations. Some drugs were used in religious or orgiastic rites where the participants wanted to communicate with imaginary deities or to shed restrictions taught by their societies. In lower doses than those causing drunkenness or completely drugged behavior, alcohol and marijuana improve sociability and provide a feeling of success. A sniff of ether may produce overexcitement, and barbiturates and other hypnotics sedate, making animals and humans go to sleep. Such sedative-hypnotics are thought to be the earliest drugs used for depressing brain activity. At the other end of the spectrum, cocaine, amphetamine, and to some extent, ephedrine were

Alfred Burger, *Drugs and People: Medications, Their History and Origins, and the Way They Act.* Charlottesville, VA: The University Press of Virginia, 1986. Reprinted with permission.

among the early brain stimulants that could overcome sleepiness, increase wakeful awareness, and improve the ability to perform complex tasks. . . .

Drugs in Prehistory

When early man tried out every kind of food he could find in fields and forests, he encountered mushrooms and other plants that made him feel peculiar. Later on, brews stewed from such vegetation produced similar feelings. This happened in Central and South America, in India and in Siberia, and probably all over the earth. In that way primitive people learned about plants that would raise their moods to unexpected heights or throw them into depths of fear and despair that they believed was punishment for toying with the secrets of Nature. For better or for worse they experienced strange visions they had not experienced before and glimpsed unknown insights into their "souls." In the language of today's drug abusers, they had good trips or bad trips. We must admire their persistent searching to find such plants among the inexhaustible variety of the vegetable kingdom.

Priests and witch doctors of old soon gathered these plants for their own purposes. They used them themselves and gave them to their followers at times to induce detachment but also religious frenzy or abject fear of their deities. The plants and their decoctions were also used in celebrations, to cause stupor or drunkenness, warlike excitement, and indifference to danger. In English-speaking countries the drugs contained in these plants are sometimes called psychedelic, meaning mind-manifesting. Since some of the effects they produce resemble serious mental conditions or psychoses, the name psychotomimetics is used for the group. The drugs change perception and mood, disturb the autonomic nervous system that controls normal mood, and in high doses, often cause hallucinations. Obviously physicians want to avoid these reactions, which are regarded as unwanted and feared side effects. Such drugs are therefore not used to treat patients.

We know now that natural products from the plant kingdom—and a few animal sources such as toad skins—are not the only sources of mind-tampering drugs. Many synthetic compounds, spearheaded by heroin and LSD, behave the same way. These compounds have given "drugs" such a bad name that many people overlook the value of most drugs for entirely different medicinal purposes. This negative reaction comes from the unhappiness, misery, crime, and death that have resulted when psychotomimetics are abused. Millions of young and old folk all over the world have fallen into this trap from which addiction and personality weakness often bar their escape. . . .

Soma and Marijuana

One of the oldest psychotomimetic drugs was soma, a concoction of unknown botanical origin used in India thousands of years ago. Sanskrit manuscripts say that it made one feel like a god. Similarly, ancient religious oracles and cults like the ones at Delphi and Eleusis in Greece drugged priestesses to visionary incoherence.

The hemp plant, *Cannabis sativa*, dates back at least to the time before Herodotus (2500 Before Present), who wrote that the Scythians on the Caspian Sea used it for self-intoxication. The crusaders encountered hashish in the Middle East made from cannabis. It was used by terrorists sent on missions of assassination. The name *hashish* means assassinate. This drug spread to high society in Europe as a means of escaping boredom, and its sinister threat culminated in this country around 1955, when millions of younger men and women began to smoke the resin of the plant. A more diluted version is called marijuana. It is not a narcotic-hallucinatory drug, but it depresses the brain, causing intellectual indifference, ineffectiveness, listlessness, and loss of productivity. Prolonged use can destroy positive personality traits. The ease of growing and harvesting hemp and the ability of Colombian, South American, and South Asian smugglers to export marijuana to America and Europe has made control of this drug virtually impossible.

The mind-affecting constituents of cannabis are the tetrahydrocannabinols. When isolated, these compounds produce a peculiar sedation of the central nervous system at very low doses. They have helped some asthmatics and have quelled nausea for some taking anticancer drugs. Fiber from hemp is used in making certain kinds of rope.

Central America has supplied more mind-upsetting plants than any other part of the world, probably because Mexican and Peruvian jungles have been more accessible than African or Malayan tropical regions until recent times. Also the Aztecs, Otomacs, and South American Indians as well as those of New Mexico and Arizona have kept up religious cults and ceremonies in which plants play a role despite centuries of attempts to convert them to various Christian sects. This type of social culture has helped botanists to locate sources of such plants.

One of the first magic drugs discovered in Mexico and the American Southwest was *Lophophora williamsii*, also called *Anhalonium lewinii*. The parts of this spherical cactus above ground (mescal buttons) contain a number of alkaloids related to dopamine. The Indians prepare a drink from the cactus called peyote or peyotl. The drink itself, as well as mescaline and other alkaloids isolated from the cactus, have powerful mental effects and produce vivid color visions. Mescaline is a totally disorienting drug that causes long-lasting and frightening psychotic episodes. Physicians can bring them under control slowly with tranquilizing (neuroleptic) drugs. Mescaline and many of its chemical cousins have been repeatedly synthesized and tested.

Another plant still used by several Mexican tribes is ololiuqui, an herb with long white flowers and round seeds. Botanically it is called *Rivea corymbosa*, but it has a number of common names: snake plant, herb of the Virgin, and many others. The crushed seeds, or an alcoholic beverage prepared from them, induce delirium, visions, satanic hallucinations, or a narcotic type of sleep not unlike twilight sleep. The psychotomimetic substances in this plant are ergot alkaloids. Such compounds had been previously isolated from ergot, a mold growing on rye. Rye bread contaminated with ergot caused havoc in the Middle Ages in Europe, ranging from epidemics of abortions from uterine contractions to hallucinations called Saint Vitus' dance (chorea). Albert Hofmann, a Swiss biochemist, cleared up the chemistry of the new and different alkaloids from ololiuqui.

Mushrooms and LSD

A plant called *teonanacatl* ("sacred mushroom") was regarded as a god by Mexican Indians and as the devil by Christian missionaries after the conquest of Mexico by Cortez. This mushroom contains two compounds that affect the mind, psilocin and psilocybin. Chemically they are related to the neurohormone 5-HT (serotonin). Chemists have synthesized these fairly simple compounds, and psychiatrists have tried to use them as aids to psychoanalysis and psychotherapy. The very ancient cult of the mushroom is based on colorful and unreal visions that occur as the mushroom is eaten. . . .

LSD, or LSD-25, is chemically named *d*-lysergic acid diethylamide tartrate. It is the most powerful and most specific psychotomimetic known. It is a synthetic compound, made by laboratory procedures, and—alas—has been at one time or another one of the most widely abused mind-altering drugs. Other amides of lysergic acid occur in the old Mexican magic plant ololiuqui and in ergot. LSD-25 was the result of standardized practice in medicinal chemistry. . . .

Since the first days of the research on the classical mind-altering drugs, many other substances have been found that cause profound psychic changes. Almost all of them have side effects on the autonomic nervous system, and therefore the mental effects are accompanied by changes in heart rate, intestinal irregularities, difficulties in breathing, abrupt changes in blood pressure, etc. This all adds up to making persons very sick who set out only to "expand their minds" without understanding or believing the horrors and pains that result from taking these drugs of ill repute.

Artificial Drugs

The newer horror drugs have chemical names that the users, often school dropouts, cannot pronounce, so they give them an assortment of alphabet-soup initials, which are also used to refer to them in the press and on TV. They are compounds made experimentally that have been smuggled out of research laboratories. In one case a drug had been tested as a general anesthetic before it was appropriated by abusers.

Some of these newer agents have been called synthetic heroin or designer drugs, although they are chemically unrelated to heroin and have not been designed. Two of them were side products in the manufacture of the analgesic meperidine. Others are synthetic compounds tried out by addicts in the hope that they might give them a new mental high. The most dangerous of these materials are 3-methylfentanyl and MDMA, a relative of methamphetamine. Both produce dangerous damage to the general health of the users and cause heroinlike addiction at unbelievably low doses.

Different Kinds of Addiction

These tragic experiences with the abuse of drugs raise questions of what can be done to curb abuse and whether it should be punished or allowed to disappear like other manifestations of a temporary culture. In considering whether drug abuse should be controlled and prevented, a detached scientific point of view will require judging each situation on its own merits or demerits rather than lumping unlike problems together indiscriminately. The abuses of heroin, cocaine, and marijuana can serve as examples. Heroin is an addictive narcotic; cocaine is an addictive stimulant; marijuana is a nonaddictive minor depressant of the central nervous system; with no actions that reach into the narcotic stage. Heroin causes an uncompromising craving for renewal of the narcotic dose; it is unreasonably expensive, its price being driven up by

criminal suppliers and distributors who should be punished unmercifully. This holds true also for cocaine merchants and smugglers, although the addicted victims present a picture different from heroin addicts. Cocaine addicts can quit only with difficulty, but without the dread withdrawal symptoms of the morphine-heroin type. Marijuana users can quit most easily, without any more physical discomfort than that felt by chronic tobacco smokers or coffee drinkers. At the bottom of the failure to stop using this drug is psychological weakness and lack of stamina—insufficient will to lead a drug-free life. Heroin withdrawal requires medical assistance; marijuana withdrawal requires a strong personality. Cocaine withdrawal is between these two.

No legislation will prevent people from experimenting with drugs, not even in a police state. Exploring strange life situations, revolting against parental authority, and experimenting with sex and drugs has been going on for thousands of years. We happen to live near the crest of a wave of drug abuse, as has happened before in other times and places. The danger is that widespread drug abuse—apart from its criminal aspects—may lead to lassitude, social indifference, loss of initiative, and other factors that damage the virility of a civilization. China before Mao had sunk into a state of lowered stamina, not only because of undernourishment of the population, but because of widespread use of opium and hashish and the ensuing improverishment of the users and their families. The Roman Empire crumbled perhaps because malaria weakened many of its peoples, but more likely because of drug abuse. These examples should be a warning to Americans, who—because of their wealth and geographical nearness to drug-producing countries—are the easiest target for drug dealers.

"The United States and much of the rest of the world have experienced an unprecedented drug abuse epidemic."

Addiction Is Epidemic

Robert L. DuPont Jr.

One of the lessons I learned early in my medical training was suggested by the words of the old-time bank robber, Willie Sutton. When the cops finally caught up with him, they asked him why he robbed the banks. "Because," said Willie, "that's where the money is." Now, if we are asking ourselves, "Where is the 'health bank' of this country?" we might well paraphrase Willie's words a bit and say, "Youth is where it's at." If we are seeking ways to improve the health and prolong the lives of the young, we should realize that the payoff has much to do with lifestyles. While the teenage years are not the only years during which decisions involving lifestyles threaten an individual's health, they are the years when lifestyles—and hence health-preserving or life-destroying habits—are established in ways destined to affect all the days of each person's time on earth. During the teenage years, to cite but one example, people make lasting decisions about what they are going to do about the use of tobacco, alcohol, and other drugs. In fact, it is unusual (though not quite rare) for a person to begin drug use before the age of 12 years or after the age of 20.

Primarily, here, we are talking about vulnerability between the ages of 12 and 20—a uniquely vulnerable opening stage between childhood and adulthood. Standing in this opening, often with unseeing eyes, young people make personal decisions about the use of alcohol and other drugs that will deeply affect the rest of their lives. After the age of about 20, the vulnerability dramatically falls. New drug use after the age of 20 is almost as uncommon as it was before age 12.

Once, someone who heard me speak on these matters asked, "Do you mean that if we stop smoking, if we stop drinking, if we end our overeating and start exercising, then we may live

longer?" "Yes," I said, "you got my message." "Well," he said, "I'm not sure whether I would live longer if I did all that, but I know it would *seem* a lot longer." Subtract the humor and you are left with a sense of sadness for the flippant cynicism that covers the close-to-the-surface fears of the young and the not-so-young among us: the awareness, often avoided, that when it comes to avoiding illness and premature death, we are usually our own worst enemy.

Some Specifics

Look for a moment at some of the specifics of drug use and the extent to which it pervades the lifestyles and the health of young Americans. From Table 1 (Annual Drug Use: 1972-1982), we see both the extent of the current use of various drugs and the trends over the last decade. Here we see the percentages of all Americans who reported use of each particular drug during the year prior to the taking of the annual survey. Overall, the table covers 11 classes of drugs, including alcohol and tobacco. From it, certain conclusions are readily apparent. All drug use is highly *age-related*, with peaks of use of all drugs (including tobacco and alcohol) occurring between the ages of 18 and 25 years. Only three drugs—alcohol, tobacco, and marijuana—are used by massive segments of the American population. The drug that is now making a strong move on the leaders, and which is presently in fourth place, is cocaine.

Use of drugs other than tobacco and alcohol was uncommon, if not rare, prior to 1960. The last two decades, however, saw an unprecedented rise in the use of such drugs as LSD, cocaine, heroin, and marijuana. Indeed, the drug abuse epidemic occurred during this two-decade era. Centered on America's youth (some of whom are no longer young), this epidemic is powerfully related to a variety of other lifestyle problems: teenage crime,

Robert L. DuPont Jr., *Getting Tough on Gateway Drugs*. Washington, DC: American Psychiatric Press, 1984. Reprinted with permission.

teenage suicide, teenage sexually transmitted disease, and early teenage pregnancy. These problems are all results of loss of self-control and of family and community control of impulsive, pleasure-seeking behavior.

While there is no easy answer as to why this epidemic has occurred during the last two decades, there are several reasonable and mutually reinforcing explanations. When we understand these reasons, we can more clearly understand what has caused the epidemic and what needs to be done to end it.

TABLE 1. Annual Drug Use: 1972-1982

Age group, drug	1972	1974	1976	1977	1979	1982
Youth (12-17)						
Marijuana	...	18.5%	18.4%	22.3%	24.1%	20.7%
Hallucinogens	3.6%	4.3	2.8	3.1	4.7	3.6
Cocaine	1.5	2.7	2.3	2.6	4.2	4.3
Heroin	< 0.5	< 0.5	< 0.5	0.6	< 0.5	< 0.5
Nonmedical Use of						
Stimulants	...	3.0	2.2	3.7	2.9	5.5
Sedatives	...	2.0	1.2	2.0	2.2	3.6
Tranquilizers	...	2.0	1.8	2.9	2.7	3.0
Analgesics	...	...	...	...	2.2	3.8
Any Nonmedical Use	...	...	...	...	5.8	8.2
Alcohol	...	51.0	49.3	47.5	53.6	46.9
Cigarettes	...	...	...	...	13.3	14.2
Young Adults (18-25)						
Marijuana	...	34.2	35.0	38.7	46.9	40.7
Hallucinogens	...	6.1	6.0	6.4	9.9	7.3
Cocaine	...	8.1	7.0	10.2	19.6	19.5
Heroin	...	0.8	0.6	1.2	0.8	< 0.5
Nonmedical Use of						
Stimulants	...	8.0	8.8	10.4	10.1	11.0
Sedatives	...	4.2	5.7	8.2	7.3	8.4
Tranquilizers	...	4.6	6.2	7.8	7.1	5.9
Analgesics	...	...	...	...	5.2	4.6
Any Nonmedical Use	...	...	...	...	16.3	16.1
Alcohol	...	77.1	77.9	79.8	86.6	83.5
Cigarettes	...	...	...	...	46.7	41.1
Older Adults (26+)						
Marijuana	...	3.8	5.4	6.4	9.0	10.8
Hallucinogens	...	< 0.5	< 0.5	< 0.5	0.5	0.8
Cocaine	...	< 0.5	0.6	0.9	2.0	3.9
Heroin	...	< 0.5	< 0.5	< 0.5	< 0.5	< 0.5
Nonmedical Use of						
Stimulants	...	< 0.5	0.8	0.8	1.3	1.8
Sedatives	...	< 0.5	0.8	< 0.5	0.8	1.4
Tranquilizers	...	< 0.5	1.2	1.1	0.9	1.1
Analgesics	...	...	...	...	0.5	1.0
Any Nonmedical Use	...	...	...	...	2.3	3.0
Alcohol	...	62.7	64.2	65.8	72.4	68.5
Cigarettes	...	...	...	...	39.7	37.3

Note: Numbers are percentages based on any reported use of the listed drugs during the preceding year in repeated national surveys; ... indicates "data not available."
Source: National Household Survey on Drug Abuse, 1982. National Institute on Drug Abuse.

The period 1960 to 1980 was a time of many changes in the United States. The most fateful for the drug epidemic was the rise in the number of youths in the population. The last two decades saw the post-World War II Baby Boom pass through adolescence.

Other changes occurred, although many of them were derived from, or at least reinforced by, this demographic tidal wave. We saw the flowering of the "youth culture," which all but overturned the traditional forces restraining the reckless behavior that has long been characteristic of adolescence. Virtually all of the "reforms" of the last two decades were reductions in controls over individual and group behavior and also reductions in expectations for youths. This was the era of reduced requirements in schools and at home and reduced limitations on what was previously considered deviant behavior (including the lowering of the drinking age in many states during the 1970s). There was a widespread, romantic belief that went something like: "Let the kids have fun. They'll figure it out for themselves." Parents, teachers, and employers were everywhere in retreat as the onslaught of the "youth culture" peaked in the mid-1970s.

Note that I have placed the words "youth culture" and "reforms" in quotation marks. I am not suggesting that all of the changes in America during the last two decades, let alone all aspects of changed roles for youth, have been dangerous. Rather, I am calling your attention to several specific aspects of these changes, aspects that are almost a caricature of many truly positive changes that have occurred. These specific aspects have had a profoundly negative impact on American youth.

The 'Me Generation'

The "Me Generation" flowered beyond youth. Adults were caught up in the winds of change and began to ask, "What about me?" The more traditional expectations and responsibilities of each of us were undercut, and we wondered, "When do I get mine?" Job changes, divorce, and alternate lifestyles were "in." Adults who, for generations, were convinced they had the answers to the problems of their children, over the last two decades grew suddenly hesitant. The Vietnam War, the Civil Rights Movement, the War on Poverty, and the Women's Movement all raised serious questions about the wisdom of the "older generation" and traditional guidelines for individual behavior. It seemed that the new generation had little to learn from their elders, except not to live the way they did. What rules youth needed they would, it seemed, "learn for themselves." "Problems" were not the fault of youth or of the pursuit of pleasure, but of the "no-saying authorities."

What an irony that the generation whose values were crystallized in the austerity of the Great Depression and the sacrifices of World War II and who were so remarkably successful in providing material comforts and quality education for their children (often beyond their most optimistic hopes) discovered that many of their children rejected these prized values, seeking instead the self-gratifications of personal and frequently reckless pleasure.

There is another dimension to this personal pursuit of pleasure. One of the principal characteristics of the "youth culture" is the focus on the present tense. If it is not *now*, it is not, period. That was one of the essential messages of the last two decades. For American youth, earlier ideas about delay of gratification—doing something unpleasant now so that at some later time one could feel good—became as unfashionable as it was to do something "for someone else." Any attempt to suppress personal, present-tense pleasure was seen, in this view, as a "cop-out," a failure of courage or as hypocritical and "other directed."

Drug-Induced Pleasure

Drugs fit nicely into this value scheme since the drug-induced pleasure is *now* and the drug-caused problems tend to come later on—often years after the drug use has become habitual. Similarly, since intoxicating drugs tend to obscure the drug user's critical judgment as an early and characteristic effect, the drug user's own self-awareness of drug-caused problems was restricted.

"A whole generation followed the advice of the self-appointed high priest of drugs, Timothy Leary."

Over this period of 20 years, the legitimacy of *others* in controlling personal behavior was progressively eroded. Whether these others were rooted in religion, law, school, work, or the family, they were all seen as irrelevant or even hostile to the pursuit of personal needs. This, too, fueled the drug epidemic. One poignant aspect of this historical experience is that these others were often acting in the best interests of the youth themselves: they were essentially saying "No" to dangerous but pleasure-producing behaviors because they were concerned not about the pleasure but about the youth.

One of the long-term, painful consequences of this historical process is the difficulty now experienced by many young people between the ages of 20 and 35 in making commitments and even, paradoxically, in finding pleasure in many everyday activities of life, from work and sex to raising a family and participating in religious activities. As the expectation for pleasure rose, as the restraints on pleasure-producing behavior were seen ever more negatively, as intense drug-induced pleasures became the standard against which all pleasure was measured by many in this generation, the "normal" pleasures seemed like "work," and they seemed,

somehow, insufficient. Sex, for example, once it became cheap, lost a lot of its excitement. While previous generations complained about impotence and frigidity (often associated with viewing pleasure as bad), young people between 20 and 35 now complained most often of a total lack of interest in sex (often associated with early, extensive sexual activity).

The national economy, too, played a role in the drug epidemic. Throughout the 1960s and the early 1970s, the sustained, unprecedented prosperity made it seem as if material plenty was an entitlement rather than a reward to be earned by hard work. For children of the middle and upper economic classes, growing up in the 1960s and 1970s was accompanied by a shower of economic plenty given to them by their well-meaning, depression-surviving parents. The earlier values of planning for the future, and even sacrificing one's comfort for the opportunities of one's children, became old-fashioned or, even worse, ridiculous. Indeed, such values were rapidly replaced by the new *now* values. "If it feels good now, do it now" became the new motto. To many Americans, young and old, it seemed that the era of the proverbial "free lunch" had arrived.

There were other factors at work, as well—many of which specifically affected the family life of teenagers. There was an unprecedented rise in divorce, producing a ballooning number of single-parent families. Women entered the work force in unprecedented numbers, thus further eroding the effective parenting power in millions of homes. For the young especially, travel and communications became all but universal. Behaviors and experiences—including drug use—which heretofore had been relatively isolated by time, space, and cultural barriers, were suddenly and easily available to huge numbers of American young people. To a greater or lesser extent, a whole generation followed the advice of the self-appointed high priest of drugs, Timothy Leary: "Turn on, Tune in, Drop out!" Although this advice was given initially about hallucinogens, it rapidly was generalized to all illegal drugs.

The Electronic Revolution

The Electronic Revolution—instant communication, instant excitement, instant everything, seemingly made possible by the advent of television—profoundly reinforced and extended these trends. This drug-using youth population, born after World War II, was the first generation raised on television. What exists between TV viewing and drug use is no accidental relationship. Television-watching has many elements in common with drug-taking. Both tend to be mindless, passive, and ultimately isolating. Fascination with a television screen, like fascination with a drug, can produce a dependence requiring someone else—a nonuser—to set limits on the user. Television can be, in fact, a plug-in drug.

And the ''Contagion'' Will Spread ...

In the United States during the last two decades, many things changed, not all of them bad and not all of them permanent. The hula hoop came and went. Hair styles changed as many a youth concluded, ''If you can see his ears, you can't trust him.'' The more optimistic among the oldsters comforted themselves by saying, ''Not to worry. These things are mere fads.''

Drug use, however, is not like a passing fad: once a person becomes dependent on any drug, that person is likely to have a long and painful experience either in living with or living without the drug. This confusion, especially in the minds of many youths, about the unique seriousness of decisions concerning drug use played a central role in the sweeping drug epidemic.

Playing an almost equally important role is the inescapable fact that drug use in a population acts like a contagious disease. The new drug user tends to proselytize or recruit nonusers, thereby spreading drug-taking behavior. This chain reaction, this epidemic spread of drug use, was encouraged in the United States by the large demographic and social changes described. Many observers of these trends, having had no experience with drug use, even now fail to judge accurately the seriousness and persistence of drug-using behavior. This failure is surprising in view of the increasingly widespread recognition among public health experts of the devastating social and health impact of alcohol and tobacco use by Americans. The so-called newer drugs, while once thought to be less likely to produce long-term harm to health and/or less likely to produce dependence, are now increasingly understood to have all the negative effects of alcohol and tobacco, plus many additional problems unique to themselves.

''Playing an almost equally important role is the inescapable fact that drug use in a population acts like a contagious disease.''

Another factor often overlooked by observers of the drug epidemic is that all drug use is *linked.* Those who use one drug are *more* likely to use each of the other drugs and are not, as many earlier observers assumed, *less* likely to use other drugs. Thus, the same epidemic that carried marijuana and cocaine, as well as LSD and PCP, to unprecedented new levels of use in the United States also produced a sharp rise in the use of tobacco and alcohol among our youth population. Many early observers thought marijuana, for example, might displace alcohol or, in more recent years, that the rise in alcohol use might lead to falling levels of marijuana use. The facts proved to be exactly the opposite: *rising marijuana use leads to rising alcohol use and vice versa.* ...

The Significant Fact

Finally, we must not overlook the significant fact that all drug use is positively correlated with each of the other problems—including delinquency, unwanted pregnancy, murder, and suicide—experienced by young people at unprecedentedly high rates during the last two decades. All of these problems, most noticeably those involving drug use, were both the direct and the indirect results of reductions in the societal, familial, and personal control over the pleasure-producing behaviors of the young. ...

During the last two decades, the United States and much of the rest of the world have experienced an unprecedented drug abuse epidemic. It has uniquely affected Americans who were teenagers during these years. This group, the drug epidemic generation, is now 16 to 35 years old.

The factors which caused this epidemic include the huge increase in the youth population—the post-World War II Baby Boom hitting adolescence—plus complex and mutually reinforcing cultural forces such as a reduced respect for authority and an increased reliance on self-determination of personal behavior. Additional causes of the current drug epidemic were increased communication and travel, as well as the remarkable economic prosperity during the beginning decade of the epidemic.

The safe-seeming drugs, particularly alcohol, marijuana, and cocaine, became the GATEWAY DRUGS for American youth entering into drug dependence. These are all dangerous addicting drugs, despite their popular images. Although there is evidence of a leveling off of drug use in recent years for most dependence-producing drugs, the drug epidemic is continuing on an historically unprecedented scale.

Robert L. DuPont Jr. has worked in the field of drug abuse prevention since the 1960s. He was the first Director of the National Institute on Drug Abuse. He was the chairperson for the section on Drug and Alcohol Abuse for the World Psychiatric Association. He currently directs the Center for Behavioral Medicine and is the vice-president of Bensinger, DuPont, and Associates, a drug abuse prevention consultation firm.

"The overwhelming majority of drug users are 'normal' people free from illness."

Addiction Is Exaggerated

Abbie Hoffman and Jonathan Silvers

With vast quantities of chemicals being consumed by millions of Americans, it's common sense to look at the different categories of drug use. Serious clinicians recognize classification as the first step in any cohesive study. The mass media conveniently avoids such distinctions. In the thirties, during the first major drug hysteria, a person had only to smoke one marijuana joint to earn the label "junkie." Not much has changed fifty years later. A professional athlete today admitting occasional cocaine use (after getting caught) gets lambasted as "an extremely sick person." He gets lumped in with, say, Dennis Hopper, who admitted to using $1,000 worth of cocaine a day for stretches. (He characterized this decline as, "going from *Easy Rider* to *Scarface*.") If everyone using illegal drugs, as well as those abusing legal drugs, were considered in need of treatment, every hotel and ballpark in America would have to be refitted as a rehabilitation center.

The concept of the Undifferentiated Continuum of Drug Use is central to our discussion. It is an imaginary line spanning the spectrum of user personalities. The end points can be thought of as health and sickness, although this somewhat oversimplifies the complex nature of each individual. There are two primary distinctions. Free-choice risk-takers have no compulsion to take drugs. Not-so-free-choice risk-takers are dependent. At one extreme there are the *enlightened*—that is, the people for whom drug consumption is a cathartic, enhancing creativity. Aldous Huxley, Gertrude Stein, and William Burroughs are only a few who made maximum use of the drug trade-offs. After the enlightened come *users*, the majority of consumers who find drugs pleasurable, consciousness-altering,

or medicinal. *Drug dependents* (the habituated), meaning those who practice unconscious consumption as second nature, follow. *Allergics* are the next category, one that has been little studied. Then come *abusers*, the largest category, which consists of persons taking not-so-free-choice risks. (Occasionally the words "abuser" and "abuse" are used more generally.) *Addicts* are those who exhibit extremely hazardous consumption, where there is no creativity or pleasure, only compulsion. There are scores of subcategories in between.

You can get a better idea of the total user/abuser population by reading the chart. The figures are based on what you'd call an educated guess. In defining the total use population, some choices had to be made to make general points. Half of the drug-dependent group, where the biggest risk-taking begins, is on long-term medication prescribed by doctors. There are many more than 5 million people in this category, but several long-term medications do not have bad interactions with psychoactive drugs. The point is, if you are in a long-term program for any illness, you obviously have built up a trust relationship with your doctor and his or her advice. The allergic group is an arbitrary classification, since little research exists in this area. Allergics are individuals for whom a particular drug is harmful because of damaging metabolic or psychosomatic effects. Total alcohol consumption was halved to account for overlap with other substance use. Nicotine was excluded since use and abuse are uniquely close and impossible to distinguish between. Some abusers fall into the addict category while others lean toward drug dependency.

Abstention or Moderation

Pregnant women are not factored into the chart. Because of so much hormonal, enzymatic, and endogenic activity taking place inside a woman's body, drugs are not a good idea, especially in the third trimester. When in doubt, abstention or moderation makes common sense.

UNDIFFERENTIATED CONTINUUM OF DRUG USE

Free Choice Risk-Takers:

Enlightened	1 Million
Users	68 Million
Drug Dependents	3 Million
	72

Not-so-free Choice Risk-Takers:

Addicts	5 Million
Abusers	15 Million
Allergics	1 Million
Drug Dependents	7 Million
	28
Total	100 Million

These figures are estimates only.
Nicotine use/abuse is excluded.
Total alcohol consumption was reduced by half to compensate for overlap.
The Allergic category is somewhat arbitrary.
Drug dependency can be equated with habituation.

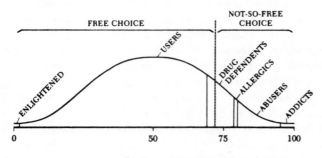

Assuming a normally distributed population, a bell curve would show the relative frequency of each drug-use category on the continuum. The categories are by no means exact, and show only relative frequency. "Undifferentiated" means there are no rigid categories. Adjacent personalities blend into one another.

Here's a personal example illustrating how categorization works. Since my initiation at age seven, I was a cancerette smoker, *habituated* to nicotine. Nineteen years ago, I quit smoking cigarettes. There were about thirty mind-wrenching days, automatic cigarette ticks, and a tendency to let my eyes follow any line of smoke from tail pipes or nearby smokers. Eventually the fantasies and cravings tapered off. I stopped completely and haven't yet resumed. Today, I would no sooner smoke a cigarette than a candle. Close friends, even one who quit with me in a buddy-reinforcement situation, had quite different experiences: "Not a day goes by when I don't think of lighting up upon waking or after sex or a good meal." At moments of great stress, some give in and puff their little

resolutions away, demonstrating their addiction. *Addiction and habituation look very similar when the drug is used, and even share withdrawal symptoms.* The long-term picture is quite different. Habituation is broken more easily than addiction.

Addictive Personalities

My guiding principle in quitting was to make an unconscious act conscious. Habituated users respond successfully to short periods (thirty days or less) of treatment and walk away from any drug if the cycle is broken. Even addictive personalities can develop or be taught coping techniques to lengthen their periods of non-use, limit the cravings. The trick is never to slide into unconscious behavior patterns. Be aware of each puff on each cigarette. Count yourself into consciousness and out of the pattern.

Clinical studies suggest that, for some, addiction fades or mysteriously stops as a person ages. However, in most cases it is long-term, probably lifelong. Free of treatment-center propaganda, true recidivism rates vary from 65 percent to 90 percent, depending upon the study and the drugs examined. Any in-house study claiming near-perfect "success"—0 percent recidivism—should be considered suspect. Reliable follow-up is difficult and costly, given the noncompliance and mobility of former treatment participants.

True addiction, the most serious form of abuse on the continuum, is a small category, but five million is still a lot of people. From the newspapers, you'd think it comprised 90 percent of all usage. Distortions are common, especially if celebrities are involved. Drug-*related* deaths are reported as drug-*caused* deaths. In everyday gossip about addicts or bad experiences, stories of serious abuse get told and retold because they are more dramatic and also because they toe the National Party Line. *A minority of sufferers have a disproportionately high impact on the full range of drug usage.*

Addiction prejudice isn't restricted to the tabloids. The scientific community can be equally biased. Medical journals, conferences, and "experts" invariably discuss addiction while excluding "popular" use. Research grants are awarded to topics unlikely to challenge the National Party Line. Federal funds have been denied to studies of illicit drugs which may confirm beneficial usage. This is hardly unusual in science. Try getting government money to study organic farming or pest control using fewer chemicals. You run up against powerful trans-national corporations who lobby against such funding. The Drug Industrial Complex does exactly the same with regard to research that could prove competitive.

This situation is analogous to, perhaps worse than, when the Freudian school ruled psychoanalysis. Freud spent his life studying very sick people, the ones confined to the darkest wards. His prognoses and theories about general humanity were based on these worst-case scenarios. After some initial skepticism, the scientific community flocked to Vienna. The result: the view of humanity reflected in psychoanalysis was for decades based upon those unfortunate sufferers. Sure, there were healthy people, but that was only because their defenses were strong enough to contain inner chaotic forces of libido and death. In a way, they were faking. Why bother with healthy people? Though there might have been some scientific truths to be discovered, there was no money in it. So the Freudians got the grants, got the big salaries, won the awards, and were invited on all the talk shows.

Not until psychologists like Abraham Maslow, Erich Fromm, and other self-actualization advocates attacked Freud's basically pessimistic view of human nature did another relatively strong school emerge—the Human Potential Movement. Here, theories and therapies were based on the idea that lots of people were satisfactorily coping with life (the normal). Some even achieved mental health and happiness to the extent that they actualized creative and altruistic potentials within themselves. They reached a plateau of enlightenment. Maslow (who was my teacher) and his school of thought are today very acceptable, but forty years ago they were considered kooky and radical.

Running on Empty

Here is probably the most famous example of the research system running on empty. In 1974 at Tulane University, a scientist demonstrated that dead brain cells in rhesus monkeys were "caused" by marijuana. Then California Governor Ronald Reagan, a scholar of renown, cited this study when he told the Los Angeles *Times*, "The most reliable scientific sources say permanent brain damage is one of the inevitable results of the use of marijuana."

The methodology was veiled in secrecy, not subject to independent verification. The media did not question its conclusions. Potheads flocked to get brain scans as "chromosome damage" became a new and frightening trade-off. In 1980, using the Freedom of Information Act (since federal funds were involved), lawyers from NORML [National Organization for the Reform of Marijuana Laws] and the Playboy Foundation publicized the research procedures. The rhesus monkeys had been strapped into a chair, and a gas mask was attached to their heads. Thirty joints were passed through the gas mask directly into the monkeys *in five minutes*! No smoke was lost; the monkeys inhaled it all. Not surprisingly, within ninety days, death occurred. Adjustments for body weight always have to be made in small-animal drug studies before leaping to conclusions about humans (as Reagan did). That would put daily human marijuana intake at well over one hundred average strength "reefers" a day.

Carbon monoxide poisoning and oxygen deprivation were probably more to blame for the loss of brain cells than THC [Tetrahydrocannabinol]. Dr. Heath, who conducted the study, was later criticized for his conclusions and methodology. There were other serious errors, but the Tulane study survives as "fact" in many political arguments. An average pot smoker would take longer than a year to consume one hundred reefers, perhaps two or three. An abuser or misuser would have to push their limits to manage that much inhalation in six months. Not even a Lower East Side regular I knew named "Chimney" Brown could have matched one of those little monkeys in a week. ("Chimney" is today a computer engineer who gave up pot ten years ago: "I got bored with it!")

"Addiction and habituation look very similar when the drug is used, and even share withdrawal symptoms."

Don't deduce from the debunking of this study that marijuana smoking is a harmless activity. Common sense would indicate that inhaling any hot smoke with contaminant particles presents *some* danger. Obviously moderation is a major element of responsible use.

Responsible drug education—education which recognizes drug use as a permanent fixture and tries to mitigate potential damage—is extremely controversial, a distant voice in today's scientific community. It wins no grants or status, and it doesn't help in research departments or funding $2,000-per-diem country-club treatment facilities or slum methadone-addiction dispensaries. When was the last time an advertisement suggested taking no medication for headache? In the seventies marijuana was officially cited as alleviating the side effects of glaucoma. Not today.

It's important to emphasize and re-emphasize that the overwhelming majority of drug users are "normal" people free from illness.

Drug *users* can be recognized by their ambivalence, a take it or leave it attitude. Common expressions they use are "I rarely buy," "It's a social experience," or "Drugs are fun on a Caribbean vacation." There is no compulsion, no frantic search for some misplaced roach or pill. They more often accept a drug than offer one. And they just say no when the occasion is wrong.

Drugs are seen as an unexpected source of pleasure, in the same league as good food, music, art, sex. Dangerous aspects of drug use are recognized and respected. Users differentiate between drugs (head drugs include pot, mushrooms, hallucinogens; body drugs are stimulants and depressants), and between good and bad highs.

Most important, the user cultivates a personal relationship with a drug. What to take, how much, how long the experience lasts, how to "ride out" or "bring down" a bad experience, or where to get help are all known quantities. And it *is* almost always a social experience with friends or lovers. Users feel no need to increase the dosage and frequency, certainly not to the point where they lose complete control.

Users are not prone to wrecking lives. Aware of the trade-offs, they enjoy the experience and don't present a burden to themselves or society. Within limits, their genetic, biochemical, or personality structure is such that it allows them to escape abuse.

We should briefly mention *misuse*—that is the behavior of a user who *occasionally* exhibits the wrong relationship to a drug. The dosage is too high, the setting bad, the mood wrong. Perhaps you took a drug to forget about a bad experience only to find yourself focusing on it more intensely. If you drink to forget a heartbreak, you only become more miserable after the first ten rounds. Try not to be alone, try to be with someone you trust where you can talk about the experience. Some drugs facilitate dialogue, but no one has a dialogue *with* a drug.

Not surprisingly, users are the easiest to treat. If "addiction" were forced upon them, they could successfully treat both the physical and psychological symptoms of temporary body habituation. The record shows that users randomly pressured into heroin experimentation quit with comparative ease. Pregnant women, fearful about the effects of drugs on their fetus, can just stop. People treated with psychiatric medication and asked by their doctor to refrain because of unpredictable side effects can stop or certainly cut back. Anyone taking temporary medication should not be afraid to ask their doctors about the effects of recreational drugs, unless you mistrust the opinion. There are other doctors.

"Use is not abuse, and habituation is not addiction. Confusing one for the other leads to distortions and bad conclusions."

Moving along the continuum, we come to a drug-dependent class. Habituation, physical and psychological, is an easy trap to fall into. Marijuana, a drug considered not to be physically addicting, is nonetheless habit-forming, simply through psychological stimulus-response associations with pleasure, other emotions or circumstances. A traveling salesperson might find sleeping on the road difficult, use sleeping pills over a few weeks or months, and then find it hard to get to sleep without them. Breaking the need can be done by gradually reducing the dosage or going "cold turkey," ending the pill cycle. After two or three restless nights, sleep without pills (which is a healthier, deeper sleep) can resume. If self-discipline fails, therapists can help with support or with chemicals to speed up the termination of withdrawal symptoms.

Symptom Elimination

Contrary to what you might think, symptom elimination is the easy part. Because of the drama, the physical intensity (tremors, fits), and the perceived power of the drug to "hook," withdrawal symptoms get more attention than they deserve. Perhaps this is why a famous athlete caught by a test or a snitch and ushered into a treatment program can walk away after being pronounced "cured." He probably never had an abuser illness to begin with. This works out very nicely for the fancy treatment facility (which can rake in $60,000 for one month's care), the team, the league, the player who is willing to parrot anything (who wouldn't, with a multimillion-dollar career on the line?), sports, the kids, the country, and, of course, the National Party Line. Nothing's wrong with it unless you care about privacy, civil liberties, truth, and honest medical practice.

Use is not abuse, and habituation is not addiction. Confusing one for the other leads to distortions and bad conclusions. In a way, the oft-repeated miracle cure is the opposite of "faith healing." In faith healing, there's lots of faith, but no healing, unless you consider temporary remission a cure. It's very easy to repent and have "faith" in NPL tactics when there was no addiction to cure in the first place. . . .

A Word of Advice to Parents

Drug abusers ruin lives—their own and others. They are a constant source of irritation: the drunk falling down at parties, the coworker bending your ear about some new hotshot chemical, or your kid coming home in a spacy, scary state, often in trouble at school or with the law.

Abusers are not happy people. They have a need for treatment and counseling that they themselves don't recognize, certainly not in the beginning. The general deception central to drug abuse includes self-deception. Like any serious illness, there is a strong tendency to reject and deny reality.

To penetrate this denial, you must be a firm, responsible ally, not one ready to label all use as abuse, not one ready to "blame yourself" for bringing up a "junkie" when your kid might only be experimenting with some substance and will soon stop.

I know this isn't easy, but it's also not impossible. I have three kids of my own. All have experienced drugs at one time in their lives. None are abusers, but there were moments of misuse—in my own experience as well—which were just as frightening to each kid as they are for us parents.

If your relationship is open, chances are good your kid will seek guidance on these points. *Be ready for the bad drug experience to broach the subject if other times seem awkward.* It works better if your kids bring up the subject, easing into it at their own pace.

Increased drug use and other patterns leading to misuse and/or abuse are in great part unconscious acts. They must be accepted and made conscious before they can be corrected. It takes a good deal of love and patience to break through the defenses of any abuser and reach a common reality. Often it means self-examination of the parents' behavior and a willingness to see the problem not in isolation but as part of a complex family social pattern.

Parents should not leap to conclusions just because a kid sleeps late, does poorly in some subjects, or spray-paints "Life's a bitch, then you die!" on the family dog. Don't follow the PTA approach to search your kid's hiding places for strange pills and roach clips. The privacy of citizens extends to kid citizens as well. When Meese successfully pushed the Supreme Court to exempt school lockers from warrantless searches, kids were denied their Fourth Amendment rights. Spying only increases suspicions and makes a difficult dialogue even more difficult.

Hypocrisy and information that comes from suspect sources or a false heart will not bridge the communication gap. Lay the groundwork by establishing trust. . . .

All my kids discuss drugs with their parents, but it would be the height of arrogance to declare flat out the formula for raising kids. One clue I've picked up because of my "unusual" lifestyle and because at colleges and high school speeches I've met so many young people: bringing up parents isn't all that easy for kids, either.

Abbie Hoffman is a political activist who rose to fame during the social turmoil of the 1960s. Hoffman's causes include ending US involvement in Central America, halting CIA recruitment on college campuses, and preserving the environment. Jonathan Silvers is a New York City writer.

"The drug problem . . . is the scourge of our country."

viewpoint 3

Drug Addiction Is a Crisis

William F. Alden

You may have read in the papers that the President signed a National Security Directive, which now, for the first time, defines drug trafficking as a national security issue. I'll be explaining a little bit about our national strategy to address the problem of drug trafficking, at which time I'll describe for you the "whats and whos" of DEA [Drug Enforcement Administration]. To let you know what we, as the lead Federal agency for drug enforcement, can and can *not* do. This will lead me right into, what I hope will be a discussion and not a lecture, about what our respective roles are—our corporate roles and our individual responsibilites—to do something about the drug problem that is the scourge of our country.

To put the problem in perspective, I'd like to start out by sketching the demographics of drug trafficking and abuse—where the drugs are coming from and to what extent they're being abused in the U.S. Of course, it's important, at the outset, to recognize that this is a very fluid business, and the demographics are always changing.

I'll start with dangerous drugs because this is a category of drug abuse that everyone is least familiar with. Actually, this is a two or three part problem depending on how you look at it.

First, is the problem of *legally prescribed drugs*. It may startle you to know that over half of the emergency room admissions in the U.S. relating to drug abuse are related to legally prescribed drugs. In fact, over the past decade until very recently, the number one drug mentioned was Valium, not heroin or cocaine.

Overall, we are talking 20 million Americans using legally prescribed drugs for nonmedical reasons. Millions of dosage units of these drugs are diverted to the illicit market from legitimate sources, most

William F. Alden, "The Scope of the Drug Problem," a speech given to the American Society of Industrial Security in Orlando, Florida on June 24, 1986.

often by the occasional unethical doctor or pharmacist who has forgotten his Hippocratic oath and who is motivated by greed.

The legally manufactured drugs also enter the market through in-transit theft and losses, computer fraud, relaxed security at plants and pharmacies that permit internal pilferage, and similar unintentional or deliberately lax controls as the drugs move through the manufacturing and distribution process.

The other aspect of the dangerous drug problem are *illegally manufactured drugs*. Some of these, like methamphetamine, known on the street as "speed," which can have some legitimate medical uses, are produced in clandestine labs simply to meet the demand of the black market. Other drugs, like the hallucinogens PCP and LSD, have no medicinal value. And although you may not have heard a lot about PCP and LSD lately, in some areas of the country, they still present a very serious problem.

The third component of the dangerous drug problem are the controlled substance analogs—which are what the media has tagged, *"designer drugs."* At DEA, we don't like that name, because usually when you say, "designer" it has a positive connotation, and these drugs are so potent, so dangerous, the last thing we need to do is to try to glamorize them.

When the Congress wrote the drug laws they controlled substances by specifying their molecular structure. What these unscrupulous illicit drug manufacturers do is to alter a drug's molecular structure very slightly, maybe by one molecule, thereby creating a legal drug with a similar effect as the one that is controlled. Except that in changing the structure, they also change the potency.

One Grain of Salt

To help you understand the potency, imagine that a heroin dose is the size of an aspirin tablet. To get an equivalent dosage of the synthetic heroin analog called fentanyl you need less than one grain of salt!

Fentanyl can be between 150 to 1,000 times stronger than heroin.

One of these analogs leaves its victims with all of the symptoms of Parkinson's Disease. Young people are literally frozen in their own bodies. And, for right now, there is no cure.

Turning to another drug of abuse, marijuana, we're also looking at about 20 million regular users, which makes marijuana the most commonly used illicit drug in the country. We can look at some successes here. Daily marijuana use by high school seniors was half in 1985 what it was in 1978. But that still means that 5 percent are still smoking *daily*, we're talking about 1 in 18 students, sitting "stoned" in class.

"Turning to another drug of abuse, marijuana, we're also looking at about 20 million regular users, which makes marijuana the most commonly used illicit drug."

[Since the early 1980s], we've seen a lot of shifts in where the marijuana comes from. Colombia, Jamaica, and Belize are now doing their part to eradicate the cannabis crop. Unfortunately, production in Mexico and Thailand has increased to make up for less production elsewhere.

And, we can't forget domestic production, which now accounts for around 12–15 percent of the marijuana consumed in this country. We have an extensive marijuana eradication program, going on in the U.S.—all 50 states are involved. . . .

But, it seems that the traffickers try to stay ahead of us. When they realized that their fields were being identified from the air, they moved to greenhouses and hydroponics. Then, we started looking for and seizing greenhouses. Now there's a new wrinkle. In Houston, we took down an underground marijuana growing area that was being built under a horse stable. We got over 5,000 plants. If they had finished building the facility, it could have sustained over 100,000 plants. When we debriefed one of the growers, he said that over $300,000 had been invested into the underground facility alone.

Let's switch to heroin. The only encouraging news is that the level of abuse has been stable for about 5 years. That is, we have had about the same number of addicts, about one-half million, [from 1981–1985]. Through our household surveys, we are charting the aging of these addicts. That is, we aren't seeing a lot of new heroin users.

The largest problem we have with heroin right now is an infusion, or a resurgence of a type of heroin from Mexico called *black tar*. It's called that because of its consistency; it's gummy, like a tootsie roll. So far, we've seen this very potent form of heroin in 27 states. We believe that this black tar heroin is responsible for the 104 percent increase we've seen in heroin-related emergency room admissions.

Speaking of problems, what about cocaine? I'd like to digress for a moment and tell a little war story, the story of *Tranquilandia*. [In March 1984], based on a long-term investigation by DEA, we were able to go deep, and I mean deep, into the Colombian jungle with the Colombian National Police to take down a major cocaine processing refinery. There were scores of arrests, although many escaped along the river. Shoot-outs, seizures of arms, heavy equipment, generators, barrel upon barrel of essential chemicals to manufacture the cocaine from the raw material. It was an entire complex spread over acres, with housing and everything else needed for a major encampment and cocaine processing laboratory.

We seized 10 tons of cocaine. 10 tons. One-fifth of what we estimated was then being imported into the U.S. that year. Our Administrator was making speeches, congratulating the Colombians, congratulating the DEA personnel involved. We videotaped the seizure and we showed the tape everywhere. We were confident that, finally, we had made a major breakthrough.

The Lesson

Guess what? It didn't make a dent in the traffic. The price didn't go up. In fact, it has been continuing to go down. The purity at both the wholesale and retail levels didn't go down either. Instead, purity has continued to go up.

The lesson of Tranquilandia hit me soon thereafter. That's when I first realized the depth of the cocaine problem. When I realized that it's going to take a lot more than enforcement activity to make a dent in drug trafficking and abuse in this country. We are up against some "heavy duty odds" in the war against cocaine. And, quite frankly, right now we are not winning.

The cocaine problem in this country is extremely serious. We've seen cocaine-related deaths increase 325 percent since 1980. Consumption rose 11 percent in one year. Since the price has been dropping, cocaine is no longer the drug of just the elite and wealthy. Cocaine abuse now pervades every element of society—even school-age children— our kids. Seventeen percent of high school seniors try cocaine before they graduate. Seven percent now use cocaine on a monthly basis.

And, as the cover story of *Newsweek* pointed out, "crack" cocaine is readily available. Crack is a highly potent form of cocaine that is smoked, rather than inhaled or injected. And with its very low cost—as little as $5 or $10 for a "dose"—it is extremely popular with junior and senior high school students.

I'd like to throw a lot of numbers at you very quickly. This data is all drawn from the research conducted by a national cocaine hotline, called 800-COCAINE, which was founded by Dr. Mark Gold and some associates. When he started the hotline in 1983, Dr. Gold wanted to help cocaine addicts, steer them towards treatment, and at the same time, get from them some basic information about the scope of cocaine abuse in this country. Dr. Gold expected to get 10,000 calls the first year. He gets about 1,200 a day. Day in. Day out. . . .

—In the first survey three years ago, 66 percent of the callers were male. In follow-up surveys, it was more evenly split. In the first surveys, the average caller was 30 years old. In follow-ups, the average age declined by several years.

—76 percent are employed and about 2/3 earn less than $25,000. In earlier surveys, most earned over $25,000.

—Estimates of weekly use ranged from 1–32 grams. At an average of between $100–125 a gram, the average amount spent on cocaine was $637 a week.

—Over 80 percent reported that they were unable to refuse cocaine when it was available. 75 percent said they lost control of their cocaine use. 66 percent defined themselves as addicted.

—Over 90 percent reported adverse physical, psychological, and social/financial consequences, including:

—Over 70 percent said cocaine was more important than family or friends; about 25 percent were divorced as a result.

—56 percent had used up at least half of their savings, half were in debt, and 42 percent had lost all their monetary assets.

—38 percent sold cocaine to support their habit.

—38 percent thought about suicide; 9 percent actually tried.

Before I discuss a separate profile of higher income cocaine users, here's what is happening with the *adolescent cocaine abuser:*

—Just over 1/2 are male, with an average age of 17. Most were consuming between 1–4 grams weekly, an average expense of $440 a month.

—42 percent became dealers to support their habits. 43 percent were in debt. 38 percent had stolen money or property as a direct result of cocaine use.

—20 percent had been arrested for a cocaine related crime.

—33 percent suffered school problems. 18 percent were suspended or expelled or fired from a part-time job.

—65 percent felt addicted to cocaine; 85 percent were unable to turn cocaine down if it were available.

—60 percent preferred cocaine to food.
—50 percent preferred cocaine to friends.
—68 percent preferred cocaine to family.
—35 percent preferred cocaine to sex.

In short, as Dr. Gold says, "In the absence of pre-existing family and school problems, regular cocaine use can lead to serious psychosocial dysfunction characterized by dealing drugs, stealing and other criminal activity, poor academic performance and suspension, loss of peer relationships and isolation from families. This can lead to permanent life changes.

"Drug use is an identity, lifestyle and 24-hour-a-day job."

Drug use is an identity, lifestyle and 24-hour-a-day job. At best, psychosocial dwarfism or failure to develop or being 'frozen in time' is the result."

What about those who should know better? Our society's elite, wealthy, powerful, decision makers? The *affluent* fare no better, in fact, it's worse. The sample showed 82 percent males, an average age of 31, an annual income of $83,000.

—The affluent used an average of 15 grams a week, at an average cost of $100 per gram.

—Despite high incomes, 19 percent were dealing cocaine and 18 percent stealing from work. 5 percent had been arrested for dealing or possession.

—13 percent lost their job due to cocaine.

—21 percent were involved in auto accidents.

—19 percent experienced cocaine-induced brain seizures with loss of consciousness.

Among the Affluent

Dr. Gold explains about cocaine among the affluent, particularly in the workplace, "Not only is there increased exposure to cocaine, but excessive use is encouraged due to the absence of social sanctions. . . . Many are in work situations where they can maintain a facade of adequate functioning so as to avoid discovery of their problem and confrontation by others. As compared to the average user, they are typically not as accountable for their time or whereabouts and are often able to shift responsibilities to associates or employees to compensate for their own drug-related dysfunction."

One more survey from Dr. Gold. He specifically examined *drug use*, all drugs, *on the job.* As it turned out, cocaine was the most often used drug, used by 83 percent of the callers. I'll explain this in a moment.

—75 percent of the callers reported using drugs on the job.

—92 percent performed their jobs under the influence.

—64 percent admitted their work performance suffered and that the quality of the product or service provided was adversely affected.

—39 percent said a promotion or raise would increase their use of drugs.

—25 percent used drugs on a daily basis; 45 percent on a weekly basis.

—64 percent believed that the availability of drugs at work increased their use.

—48 percent sold or distributed drugs at work.

—75 percent admitted to being late or absent because of drugs.

—18 percent reported on-the-job accidents attributed to drug use.

—26 percent said they lost their jobs because of drugs.

As this and other surveys show, cocaine is one of the most popular drugs in the work environment because it meets the drug users' criteria. First, they are looking for a drug that is readily available. It must be easy to obtain, easy to conceal. Cocaine obviously passes this test. Ease of obtaining the euphoria is important. Cocaine is quick acting and requires little paraphernalia.

Also important to the drug users, they are looking for a drug that does not exaggerate their behavior or demeanor. Cocaine use amplifies characteristics of the user, but does not render him "out of it," so that anyone could attribute a change to cocaine or other drug use. The intoxication state doesn't have a tell-tale smell or other physical signs of intoxication, like dilated pupils.

Now you know why cocaine has gained such popularity. The estimates of the cost of drug abuse to industry range considerably, but all are in the billions of dollars. A conservative estimate is around $50 billion annually. These are lost profits. The costs show up in lost efficiency, lost productivity, accidents on the job, claims for workmen's compensation, medical and insurance expenses, absenteeism, and crime costs due to drug use.

"For too long, too many of us have had our heads in the sand, have refused to recognize the drug abuse problem for what it is."

One study has shown that:

—Drug users are 3.5 times more likely to be in a plant accident.

—Drug users are 5 times more likely to file a workmen's compensation claim.

—Drug users receive 3 times the average level of sick benefits.

—Drug users function at 67 percent of their work potential.

In our country, about 1 in 10 are drug users and somewhere between 3 and 7 percent use an illegal drug on a daily basis. . . .

We have got a long way to go. For too long, too many of us have had our heads in the sand, have refused to recognize the drug abuse problem for what it is. A major problem in our society has been our acute lack of awareness of the scope of the problem, a lack of understanding of the health implications of drug use, and an unwillingness to address the drug problem in every environment—our homes, our schools, and our places of business.

Recognize Yourself

Can you recognize yourself here? Emory University Medical School released a study where they polled high school students and their parents. When asked whether their child had used marijuana in the past 30 days, 3 percent of the parents acknowledged yes, their son or daughter had used marijuana. Their children were polled and 28 percent admitted smoking dope. Fully 25 percent of those parents polled had no idea their child was using marijuana. They don't see the problem.

Incidentally, one of the other questions the poll asked was, "In whom would you confide about drug abuse?" More than 50 percent of the parents answered that their child would come to them. But, only 20 percent of the seniors said they would go to their parents; most would go to their friends—the great bastion of misinformation about drug abuse and treatment.

I can't stress how important it is for each of us to understand the scope of the drug problem and to recognize that each of us—everyone in the room here—is responsible for the solution.

William F. Alden is the chief of the Office of Congressional and Public Affairs in the Drug Enforcement Agency.

"The statistics do not show that more people are doing drugs."

The Drug Addiction Crisis Is Media Hype

Adam Paul Weisman

In the national news business, there's nothing unethical about "running with a hot item." Even "milking something for all it's worth" can be justified if the story has serious implications for a broad cross section of the population. It's hard to make people care about the toxic waste problem in New Jersey unless they happen to live in New Jersey, but it is reasonable to point out that there are toxic waste dumps in other states and that the lawless people who dump waste in New Jersey probably wouldn't hesitate to dump some in the reader's own backyard if they knew he wasn't looking. What journalists, unlike politicians, do universally condemn is the practice of cooking figures and using alarmist headlines and prose to make it sound as if the toxic waste were already in your backyard, when they know damn well it isn't. But that is exactly what happened with the long-running melodrama known as "the drug crisis in America."

For a reporter at a national news organization, the drug crisis in America is more than a story, it's an addiction—and a dangerous one. Some, but not all, of us feel mighty guilty for having tried to convince readers that practically everyone they know is addicted to crack, and that they too are likely to be addicted soon. We know the rush that comes from supporting these claims with a variety of questionable figures, graphs, and charts, and often we enjoy it. Blatant sensationalism is a high.

A Sober Family

Now, I was brought up in a sober family where we were instilled with a strong Judeo-Christian sense of news value at a young age. Mom was a journalist and Dad was a liberal-minded lawyer. Sure, Mom would occasionally take a shot of *Cosmo* or *Vogue*

after a hard day's work, but who doesn't? After all, it's not illegal. Dad never touched the stuff. For him it was the *New York Times* in the morning, the *New Yorker* at night. Because of my upbringing, I was considered a bit of a square on my high school and college newspapers. While my colleagues sat around the newsroom in a haze of sensationalism, passing clips from the tabloids, I sat alone, reading the trades.

I'll never forget the first time I took a hit of irresponsible journalism. My editor suggested that I use G. Gordon Liddy in a feature I was writing. I knew it was wrong. I knew Liddy was a crook and a man who didn't deserve to be in a feature story, but the temptation was too great. I called Liddy. I hesitate to admit it, but the experience was fantastic! I can only describe the feeling as a journalistic orgasm in my brain. There I was, talking to one of the most infamous figures of our time, and I kept on talking to him long after I got the quotes I needed. I just couldn't get enough.

I came down fast after the Liddy piece went to print, and I hit really hard. Richard Cohen savaged my feature in his column in the *Washington Post*. I became depressed. My productivity declined. Then my editor called me in and offered me authorship of a story on drug abuse in America. He gave me the angle, told me the points we wanted to make and how he wanted it to conclude. Again, I tried to resist. This wasn't back-of-the-book recreational sensationalism. This was the hard stuff: a cover story.

I'd seen what irresponsible drug stories had done to other magazines, reducing them to four-color zombies, begging readers from the tabloids and drooping off the supermarket racks without a shred of journalistic integrity left in their spines. Then I thought, hey, maybe it can be done responsibly. Nancy Reagan talks about drugs and still stands tall,

Adam Paul Weisman, "I Was a Drug-Hype Junkie," *The New Republic*, October 6, 1986. Reprinted by permission of THE NEW REPUBLIC, © 1986, The New Republic, Inc.

so does Jesse Jackson. I made the classic mistake. I thought: "It won't happen to me."

Negative Reputation

I called the National Institute on Drug Abuse (NIDA) for their statistics, made some calls to well-known doctors, and ordered clips up from the library. Everything I read and everybody I talked to made drugs sound really bad, and I began to become intoxicated by the overwhelmingly negative reputation they have. What I didn't realize was that I was losing track of the facts and slipping into a journalistic dream world where the writer is free to write almost anything he chooses because nobody is going to call him on it. Nobody, but nobody was going to defend drug abuse in America, least of all the people who use drugs every day. In a way, it was the perfect cover story: sensational, colorful, gruesome, alarmist, with a veneer of social responsibility. Unfortunately, it just wasn't true.

"I was selectively writing only the facts I uncovered that made drug abuse sound like an ever-increasing problem."

Let me say flat out that drug abuse in America is not a good thing, and that people who do drugs have become more messed up in recent years as drugs have become cheaper, more plentiful, and more potent. The problem is, the statistics do not show that more people are doing drugs. That doesn't mean drug abuse isn't a major problem. It is. But it is not, as *Newsweek* would have it, an epidemic "as pervasive and as dangerous in its way as the plagues of medieval times." Nor are drugs, as *U.S. News and World Report* puts it, "the nation's No. 1 menace." Not while we still have poverty, unemployment, illiteracy, malnutrition, murder, and the Soviet Union.

But here's how it looked to you folks at home. The *Atlantic* was first and best, publishing a thorough, non-alarmist cover story about cocaine in January [1986]. Starting in March, *Newsweek* did three covers on drug abuse within five months. *Time* used drugs on the cover twice, in March and September, and gave them a cover line in between. *U.S. News and World Report* devoted a cover to drugs on July 28, [1986]. Ted Koppel chatted with his video monitors about it.

All of the network news shows covered it ad nauseum and reductio ad absurdum in their nightly reports. CBS iced the cake September 2, [1986] with a "news" documentary called "48 Hours on Crack Street." According to the Nielsen ratings, "Crack Street" earned the highest rating for any news documentary on any network in more than five-and-a-half years, delivering almost 15 million news addicts to its advertisers—three times the highest estimate for the number of regular cocaine users in America. Three days later, NBC ran its cocaine special, "Cocaine Country." In Tom Shales's (negative) review in the *Washington Post* of Brokaw and Company's effort, he asked a pertinent question: "If the problem is as critical as they keep saying, why does this broadcast seem so listless?"

Now I'll make the call. Based on NIDA's figures for 1985, 17 percent of all high school seniors have tried cocaine at least once in their life. That's a whopping increase of one percent from 1984. Between 1982 and 1984, the percentage held steady at 16.

An upward trend? Sorry. In 1981, 17 percent said they had tried the white stuff. Yes, the percentage did go up in 1985, but it has been hovering around the 16 percent mark for almost seven years. Wouldn't it be more accurate to refer to the '84 to '85 increase as a fluctuation? If we were talking about the stock market, would a one percent increase four years after a one percent decrease and a three-year period of stability be cover-story material? Not on your life. Maybe that's the point. We're talking about human lives here, not meaningless statistics based on cold, hard cash. Fair enough. But it doesn't make for hot news. "Use of cocaine among high school seniors increased one percent in 1985, according to statistics released today by the National Institute on Drug Abuse. At a press conference in Washington, D.C., a spokesman for NIDA said . . ." Look for that item on page 23 of your local paper in the capsule news column.

Here are some other drug abuse trends. According to NIDA, among 1985 high school seniors, one-time-minimum use of marijuana is down. So is the use of inhalants, hallucinogens, stimulants, sedatives, barbiturates, alcohol, and cigarettes. What's up, other than cocaine? Nothing. Several categories have held steady, including amyl and butyl nitrates, LSD, PCP, heroin, opiates other than heroin, and tranquilizers.

Now put yourself in my position. Are you alarmed by NIDA's statistics? Not particularly. Do you believe them? They're probably as good as any statistics you're going to find. What about the most alarming category, daily use? It remains unalarmingly low, less than one percent. Are you concerned about drug abuse in America? Yes. Do you believe your readers need to be given hard statistical evidence that substances conclusively proven to be bad in most every way constitute the greatest known threat to American society? Of course not.

The Plethora of Circumstances

Do I feel bad coming right out in a national magazine and saying something that will probably be misinterpreted by many people as a dismissal of the drug abuse problem in America, and a tacit admission that drugs are OK? Yes, I do, but not half as bad as I felt when I was selectively writing only the facts I uncovered that made drug abuse sound like an ever-increasing problem, while leaving out the plethora of equally legitimate mitigating circumstances.

I've given you the real numbers. Now let's look at the facts. Just about every expert I interviewed, from Dr. Charles Schuster, the director of NIDA, to Dr. Carlton Turner, director of the White House Drug Abuse Policy Office, agrees that the No. 1 drug threat in America today is alcohol. But you already knew that, and besides, it's boring, so let's move on to something sexier.

"The percentage of high school seniors who have used heroin at least once in their lives has been the same since 1979: one percent."

The percentage of high school seniors who have used heroin at least once in their lives has been the same since 1979: one percent. Deaths from heroin overdoses, on the other hand, are increasing, according to the Drug Abuse Warning Network (DAWN). . . . Still, heroin is only No. 2 in terms of overdose deaths. Alcohol in combination with other drugs is still No. 1 (1,131 deaths in 1984), and alcohol alone contributes to as many as 100,000 deaths annually. But let's overlook that fact, because it makes alcohol sound worse than heroin.

Now, cocaine is bad stuff. It contributed to 613 overdose fatalities [in 1985]. *Newsweek* says in its August 11, [1986] issue that there are five million "regular" coke users. Other drug stories have quoted similar figures, all attributed to NIDA. I have most of NIDA's publications in my files, and the only source for that figure I can find is a report that reads "between three and five million used cocaine during the last month."

OK, the media took the high end of the estimate. They have to go sit in the corner. But NIDA, in most of its surveys, uses four categories to establish the pervasiveness of drug abuse: "ever used," "used in last year," "used in past month," and "daily users." Lots of people experiment with lots of things at least once in their life. Clearly, one is more suspect if he or she has experimented with a drug in the last month, but there is an inherent fallacy in using such a figure to imply regular behavior and therefore addiction. *Time* recognized this in its September 15, [1986] cover story, where it cited figures from the same NIDA survey but referred to seniors who used cocaine in the past month as "current users," not "regular users."

Maybe I'm being picky here, but we're talking about statistics, not opinions, so we have to be precise. People who used cocaine in the past month are not necessarily regular users. People who use cocaine daily are regular users. In the report being discussed, NIDA does not offer an updated figure for daily use, so the media had to fudge their numbers. When in doubt, scare the reader. Remember, *Newsweek* is the magazine that said unmarried 40-year-old women have a better chance of being killed by a terrorist than of finding a husband.

How about PCP? "Angel Dust" gets a lot of press. Because it kills a lot of people? Not really. According to DAWN, Angel Dust killed 194 people [in 1985], and the numbers have been declining steadily since 1983. The number of high school seniors who have tried PCP is down substantially from its peak in 1979. Experts who work in drug enforcement and rehabilitation make it clear that PCP use is almost exclusively limited to the inner city, and they pinpoint Los Angeles and Washington, D.C., as the only hotbeds. In their opinion, the PCP craze of the 1970s has already come and gone, leaving behind it (as drug crazes always do) a sad but relatively small group of people who can't stop using it. They also point out that most people who try PCP do not like it and don't use it a second time. It is just not accurate to include PCP with cocaine and marijuana in an enlightened analysis of the pervasiveness of drug abuse any more than it would be accurate to include banging your head against the wall in a survey of popular leisure activities. Sure, some people do it, but most people who try it once never do it again.

Designer Drugs

Let's talk about designer drugs. It is true that many designer drugs, or "synthetic analogues," as they are called by experts, are easy to make. They are equally easy to outlaw, which the DEA [Drug Enforcement Agency] does as soon as it finds an analogue on the street. How easy do you think it is for someone with a college background in chemistry to discover new analogues? Not very. Analogues are sold as the drug they mimic (heroin). Since it's so easy to get heroin, nobody needs designer drugs. So the story isn't how pervasive the use of designer drugs is. (Dr. Darryl Inaba, director of the drug detox project at San Francisco's Haight-Ashbury Free Clinic, told me he had seen a pronounced "lull" in their use, and California was considered the center of designer drug abuse.) The story isn't that designer drugs are legal. So what is the story? As far as I can tell, there is no story. . . .

To say that marijuana has assumed a unique place in the drug culture—and in American culture at large—is an understatement. It is still America's most popular illicit drug (54 percent of high school seniors have tried it), though its popularity has been declining slowly but surely since 1981. The idea that marijuana is harmless to the body and mind has gone the way of the Edsel. Research has proven that heavy use depresses production of sperm, contributes to lung cancer, and causes heavy users to suffer that unique form of lethargic depression known as "burnout." Still, NIDA agrees with the National Organization for the Reform of Marijuana Laws that lowered sperm production and burnout can both be reversed if one stops smoking pot.

"The story isn't that designer drugs are legal. So what is the story? As far as I can tell, there is no story."

The battle that was waged in the 1960s and '70s to keep people from smoking pot would seem to have been lost. Marijuana is entrenched, socially and economically. Still, that hasn't stopped people from trying to get other people to stop smoking it. In fact, a new wave of anti-drug organizations led by the National Parents' Resource Institute for Drug Education (PRIDE) has stepped up its efforts and is rallying around a central theme, which is—stop me if you've heard this one before—marijuana leads to harder stuff. As PRIDE explains it: "Ten years of national surveys now reinforce the public's perception that marijuana is the gateway into further illegal-drug usage."

In fact, PRIDE offers little new evidence to back up this assertion. Its pamphlet states conclusively: "Certainly many casual experimenters do *not* try other drugs, but among pot-smokers, a shocking 60 percent do progress to 'harder' drugs. Conversely, if young people do *not* smoke pot, the odds are 98-to-1 that they will *ever* try any other illicit drug." Such an argument proves little more than that people who are inclined to do drugs are inclined to do drugs. It makes little headway against NIDA statistics that show the number of 13-year-olds who tried marijuana between 1978 and 1982 (15.2 million) tripling from the period between 1968 and 1972. The fact is, marijuana is so available that experimentation among young teenagers has become an entrenched adolescent institution. But if teenage use is not increasing overall, it is obvious that these young experimenters are not sinking into Reefer Madness or going on to harder drugs.

I don't have a survey handy, but I think it has been pretty well proven that young people will try almost *anything* that is available to them, especially under pressure from their peers. This is a tough set of circumstances for any organization to combat, but PRIDE's best bet is drug and health education, what experts call "primary prevention." As Chauncey Veatch III, director of California's drug and alcohol programs, told me, "This country has embraced a better living through chemistry lifestyle. The only way to fight it is to start educating with the *youngest* child." To its credit, PRIDE is a prime mover in the struggle to educate young people about drugs. Its efforts aren't much helped by the hype cum glamorization of the media. Six months ago, crack was a street-corner drug in a handful of big cities. Thanks to the media, everyone everywhere knows about it—and wants to try it. "We haven't come across it yet," one law enforcement official from rural Michigan told the *New York Times*. "But I think just because there's cocaine available, it will surface here sometime."

Everyman's Drug

Now for everyman's drug: alcohol. Like heroin and cocaine, alcohol is a dependence-forming psychoactive drug. Unlike heroin and cocaine, it killed 98,186 people in 1980. For years the medical community has been urging that alcohol be included in any analysis of drug abuse. While public concern about alcoholism, drunk driving, and teenage drinking has been rising, the press still tends toward separate discussion of drugs and alcohol. Ostensibly, the difference is that alcohol is legal, but really it is because alcohol use and abuse gets people too close to where they live: the corner tavern, the Super Bowl party, the 19th hole. You've heard it before, and I hate to be the one to say it again, but 92 percent of high school seniors have tried booze. The National Institute on Alcohol Abuse (NIAA) estimates that two-thirds of all adults are drinkers. There are nearly 18 million alcoholics and alcohol abusers in the United States today, and 28 million young people (seven million of them under the age of 18) are the children of problem drinkers. If we really believe new and draconian laws are going to stop drug abuse, we should first reconsider our permissive laws governing alcohol.

Not only do the figures for alcohol abuse dwarf those of all illicit drugs, they reduce to high comedy the flap over "legal" designer drugs. Alcohol is truly legal, and nothing could be more "designer" than a tall, frosty glass topped with a pink parasol. And talk about a threat to society. Alcohol was involved in 50 percent of all car accidents [in 1985]. For people between the ages of 15 and 24, alcohol-related automobile fatalities are the No. 1 cause of death. In 1983 our country spent an estimated $116.7 billion taking care of and rehabilitating its alcoholics, paying for their early mortality and making amends for their reduced productivity and the crimes they committed.

An Alcohol Problem

It should be noted that even in places like Harlem or the South Bronx, where Dr. Benny Primm's clinics have fought drug abuse since 1966, alcohol is still the most severe problem, and it is a complex one. Primm points out that 30 to 40 percent of his methadone maintenance patients are also alcoholics. "I can't regulate their blood pressure on methadone if they're drinking," laments Primm. "Alcohol is the main reason I lose methadone patients."

No wonder Bill Gregory, the spokesman for the NIAA who is in charge of relating alcohol abuse figures to the press, sounds so depressed on the phone. He fields a lot of calls, but almost never gets quoted in the press because he doesn't "give good copy." Here's the pithiest thing he said to me: "Alcohol is our nation's No. 1 drug abuse problem." That's not going to stop the presses.

Is there a real drug story? I think there is, but I'm not going to spill a whole lot of ink over it. I refer readers to *Time*'s June 2, [1986] story, "Crack." Again, you will see the inaccurate figures and the gruesome pictures and read the prose dripping with fear and loathing, but you will also get a more reasonable three-page feeling for why it is worth worrying about this highly potent, highly addictive form of cocaine.

"If teenage [drug] use is not increasing overall, it is obvious that these young experimenters are not sinking into Reefer Madness."

And why is that? Because crack has hit No. 1 with a bullet on the drug charts. Crack has become a focus of national attention and has captured the imagination of the many silly and fewer not-so-silly people who are willing to put dangerous things into their bodies. The reason for crack's notoriety is the reason for Madonna's: the media. True, the media have helped crack achieve national prominence (you can tune in CBS in Montana more easily than you can buy crack), but you can't blame crack use on reporters any more than you can blame it on the pushers in Washington Heights. Like the pushers, the media just gives the people what they want.

I'm not an expert on drug abuse. Thanks to the assignment thrust on me, I just know a good deal more about the subject than most people and a lot more than I care to. I'm clean now but I've seen the depths of drug journalism depravity. A little education has helped me kick the habit that once threatened to ruin my career. Now I hope that I can help others avoid making the same mistake I did. So if someone offers you drugs or the opportunity to write a cover story about them, take a tip from Nancy Reagan: just say no.

Adam Paul Weisman is a Washington journalist.

"Drugs abridge the freedom of the individual by enslaving him in a habit which he may no longer control."

Illicit Drugs Are Inherently Addictive

Gabriel G. Nahas

In its 1984 annual report, the International Narcotics Control Board of the United Nations states that the illicit traffic and consumption of dependence producing drugs has markedly increased in the major consuming countries of Western Europe, North America, Australia, and in the producing nations of Africa, South America, and Southeast and Southwest Asia. Seizures of heroin have increased by 23%, of cocaine by 50%, of hashish and marijuana by 30%, over those of the preceding year which had already reached an all time high. Such figures may be considered as the barometer of the increasing penetration of these drugs in the consuming countries which seem to offer an ever-expanding market with millions of consumers in spite of the many counter-measures which have been taken.

In contrast to the drug producing or consuming countries of the "Western" sphere of influence, the U.S.S.R. and its allies, as well as mainland China, have kept the consumption of these illicit drugs under control by using very harsh methods of repression against traffickers and addicts alike.

New Solutions

In its concluding remarks the International Narcotics Control Board calls for *new* and global solutions which should "decrease supply as well as demand of illicit dependence producing drugs." The "new" solutions need not refer to strictly repressive methods, which are actually ancient and prevail in the Communist countries, but rather to more recent ones formulated by the World Health Organization (W.H.O.). This advisory body to the United Nations states that since there is no medical cure for drug dependence, the only effective measure is to suppress the drug as much as possible, treating it

like an infectious agent, and to rehabilitate the addict through quarantine until he is able to lead a drug-free life.

Over the past two decades such measures have been successfully implemented in Japan, Taiwan, and Singapore, where a national consensus has supported a social taboo against illicit use of drugs designated by the United Nations Single Convention on Narcotic Drugs (cannabis, cocaine, opiates) and the Vienna Convention on Psychotropic Drugs (newer dependence producing drugs such as LSD, barbiturates, amphetamines).

Such policies have enabled Japan and Singapore to roll back *major* epidemics of amphetamine and of heroin addiction in the past decade. By contrast, the United States and Western countries have failed to follow the W.H.O. and United Nations' recommendations or have ignored the success story of the Asian democracies and have not succeeded in curtailing their epidemics of illicit drug use. Instead their drug policies have been influenced by the views of social theoreticians who have committed three major errors of judgement which have contributed to the spread of the epidemic.

Three Major Errors

1. Illicit, addictive drugs (mainly cannabis, cocaine, opiates) are not bad in themselves. They are just substances like any other and may be used for good or evil purposes. Illicit drugs are no more dangerous than licit ones such as alcohol or tobacco. There are no bad drugs, just bad drug users. One should distinguish between "recreational" and "excessive" drug use. **Such assumptions underestimate the inherent damaging and addictive properties of illicit dependence producing drugs.**

2. A person may be taught through proper information and education to use addictive drugs in a responsible fashion. Drug addiction is a disease which may be treated as such. **Such assumptions**

Gabriel G. Nahas, *A Drug Policy for Our Times—1985*. Atlanta, GA: National Parents' Resource Institute for Drug Education, 1985. Reprinted with permission.

overestimate man's ability to control the use of dependence producing drugs and the overall effectiveness of the "medical treatment" of drug addiction.

3. A progressive society should legalize the sale of illicit addictive drugs according to the model now used for the sale of licit drugs, tobacco and alcohol. Such a measure would take the crime out of the corrupting drug traffic. **This assumption minimizes the individual and social cost associated with the legitimate commercial availability of presently illicit dependence producing drugs,** as illustrated by scientific studies.

Let us now examine in greater detail these erroneous assumptions:

1. **Underestimating the inherent properties of dependence producing drugs.** According to the current permissive theory on drug addiction, the dangers to mental and physical health caused by illicit, addictive drugs have been greatly exaggerated. These drugs act primarily on the mind, and the mind can control their use to take advantage of their redeeming value. Indeed an addictive drug should be considered as a substance like any other. According to one psychiatrist, there is little difference between heroin and sugar, both white crystalline powders which produce addiction. . . . The same theoreticians claim that marijuana is a "soft" drug, less dangerous than tobacco and alcohol, and that its sale should be legalized or at least "decriminalized," which in effect increases social acceptance and consumption. Cocaine was even considered with benign neglect.

Two professors of psychiatry wrote in *Scientific American* (April 1983) that cocaine is no more addictive than peanuts or potato chips! A specialized organization created by major foundations to study drug abuse prevention methods claimed in 1980 that cocaine use produced few adverse effects and did not lead to dependence.

These theoreticians also minimize the long term damaging physical and mental effect of illicit addictive drugs when they are absorbed frequently.

Trusting Reason

2. **Overestimating man's ability to control the use of dependence producing drugs.** According to this trend in thinking, the modern American man or woman should be considered as a rational and mature individual. Each has inherent rights, as defined by John Stuart Mill, "over himself; over his own body and mind, the individual is sovereign." For government or society to prevent an individual from using the drug of his choice is felt to be an invasion of privacy and an infringement of individual freedom. Man's reason, it is assumed, will ultimately prevail over his craving for pleasure inducing drugs and most individuals are able to control their use of drugs, including opium and cocaine, without abusing them. According to this

assumption, experimentation with drugs is a basic feature of man's behavior; therefore, drug education of school children should consist of teaching them how to use drugs in a "responsible" fashion. Children should be taught how to develop "good relationships with drugs," or how to "get intoxicated without getting into trouble;" and those who get into trouble will be treated by a "drug abuse specialist." The same theoreticians also claim that drug dependent people have a psychological profile that triggers their addiction. This has never been scientifically proven. All individuals are susceptible to the addictive power of the major illicit dependence producing drugs.

> *"All individuals are susceptible to the addictive power of the major illicit dependence producing drugs."*

Other sociologists have stated that drug addicts are the victims of a repressive society that must relax its anti-drug policies in order to deal more effectively with drug addiction. History indicates clearly that the opposite is true. A number of drug abuse professionals have also expressed an over-optimistic view on the treatment and recovery of confirmed addicts, despite the fact **there is no medical cure for drug addiction.** Abstinence is the only cure.

Underestimating Costs

3. **Underestimating the social and individual cost of legalizing the use of presently illicit, dependence producing drugs.** The same social philosophers claim that because drugs are more and more available, their prohibition in a free and democratic society does not work, no more than does the prohibition of alcohol. Any prohibition is counterproductive and compounds the problem by breeding crime and more addiction. Instead, man should learn "chemical survival," that is to say, how to live with drugs, how to use them for pleasure in a responsible fashion, without abusing them. The increased availability of drugs is to be accompanied by a massive educational program to teach people how to use them in moderation. But none of these theoreticians has ever projected the individual and social damage which would be caused by the commercial availability of presently illicit drugs. By the most conservative estimates, such damage would be infinitely greater than that associated with present use of alcohol and tobacco.

All these erroneous assumptions have been widely disseminated for two decades through the popular media and they have inspired hundreds of books and articles which have flooded libraries. They have also permeated popular thinking and encouraged a greater tolerance towards the use of dependence producing drugs, which has resulted in their greater and greater social acceptance.

The results have been disastrous. American society is in the throes of an epidemic of drug dependency unprecedented in the history of mankind, and which is threatening the fabric of its democratic institutions. It is time to reassess all of these erroneous theories about drug dependence, in order to chart a new course based on current scientific knowledge. Indeed there is no sound basis for the assumptions just enumerated. It is now time to formulate the scientific and rational basis on which an effective policy of drug addiction prevention can be built.

The Lessons of Science

1. **What does science tell us about dependence producing drugs?** Science tells us that these drugs may be defined by four main properties which distinguish them from other substances.

a) First, these drugs produce a pleasurable feeling, a "reward" because of their action on the pleasure centers of the brain. As a result, a person who has consumed one of these dependence producing drugs will have a tendency to take it again in order to obtain the initial pleasurable sensation. These drugs will also dissipate unpleasant feelings, decrease anxiety, produce detachment from the world, and alter the state of consciousness.

"Drugs produce a temporary impairment of brain function."

b) Secondly, these drugs produce a temporary impairment of brain function (neuropsychotoxicity) or an inability to interpret the outside world as it really is. An intoxicated brain cannot process the millions of signals which keep an individual alert and functional in his environment. Psychological and psychomotor performance will be impaired. Science tells us also that some addictive drugs such as nicotine, caffeine (in moderate amounts) and alcohol (in small doses) do not induce neuropsychotoxicity. That is why their use has been tolerated for adults in many societies, despite their inherent potential for abuse. All these societies, however, do emphasize that tobacco and alcohol need to be restricted to adults, controlled by law, and that intoxication with alcohol is a deviant behavior which in many instances has to be penalized.

c) Thirdly, while consumption of addictive drugs provides a pleasurable feeling, abstinence from these drugs results in unpleasant and painful reactions— "the withdrawal symptoms." Therefore a drug dependent person is caught between the urge to take a drug for pleasure and the desire to avoid the unpleasantness and difficulties that occur when no

longer under its influence. (There are withdrawal symptoms from all dependence producing drugs, including tobacco, a highly addictive substance.)

d) Fourthly, the use of these drugs is associated with tolerance, that is, the necessity of increasing dosage in order to obtain the initial pleasant effect. Tolerance accentuates the problems of drug supply and the need for frequent readministration.

The combined factors of pleasure and reward, the dream state of neuropsychotoxicity, withdrawal symptoms, and tolerance lead to drug seeking behavior and to compulsive, frequent, daily self-administration. Addiction is characterized by major preoccupation with securing the drug and a high tendency to relapse after discontinuing usage. Medical science also tells us that the regular use of all dependence producing drugs is associated with a high incidence of mental and physical ailments. This holds true for marijuana, which should no longer be called a "soft" drug because it impairs the lung, the brain, and the immune and reproductive systems. The science of epidemiology tells us that because of these inherent properties of illicit addictive drugs and their effects on man's brain, their use will spread in an epidemic pattern when social circumstances are favorable. These drug epidemics are especially contagious because the individual victim will seek out the drug, whereas he will try to avoid the contaminating agent in an epidemic of infectious disease.

Drugs Abridge Freedom

2. **What does science tell us about man's primary reaction to dependence producing drugs?** Science tells us that man has a limited power to control the intake of these drugs once he has been exposed to their use. The principal target of these drugs is a group of nerve cells which have been identified with the pleasure reward centers, located in the old primitive brain.

Nature has endowed the brain with these pleasure/reward centers for a specific purpose: to favor those behaviors essential for the survival of the individual and the species in order to insure the continuation of the dominant activities of nutrition and reproduction. The functional integrity of these pleasure/reward centers is even more crucial today, in order to survive in our demanding technological society.

However, the rapid production of pleasure through chemical stimulation of the brain by dependence producing drugs, has remained throughout history a profound desire of man. This is particularly true in the young person who is very vulnerable to dependence producing drugs: his brain functions are in the process of integration and development, and the dominant pleasure centers tend to orient his behavior towards immediate fulfillment of the desire for fun. Only through training the "new brain"—that is, the "neocortex" that covers the old brain—will reason develop so that the individual will be willing and able to forego immediate satisfaction in order to obtain long lasting rewards. That is what education is all about.

Man, because of the very nature of his brain, has a natural propensity to consume pleasurable dependence producing drugs. It is now clear that these drugs **abridge the freedom of the individual** by enslaving him in a habit which he may no longer control. Indeed science tells us, that whatever method is used, rehabilitation of a confirmed addict to a drug free life is hard, long, and often disappointing with a success rate of 50% at best.

Drugs in Different Societies

3. **What does science tell us about the consumption of dependence producing drugs in different societies?** Science tells us that in societies where dependence producing drugs are socially acceptable and easily available, they are widely consumed, and their usage is associated with a high incidence of individual and social damage.

"The abuse potential of marijuana is seven times that of alcohol."

The lessons of history are clear: in 1858, the British imposed by force of arms the legal trade of opium in China. By 1900, 75 million Chinese were addicted to the drug. It took a national revival and 50 years of very coercive measures for the country to become opium free. In the 1920s, the unrestricted commercial availability of cocaine and heroin in Egypt resulted in a massive epidemic which was curtailed by similar restrictive methods. In our Western society, recent studies have documented in a statistical fashion the relationship between alcohol consumption and the occurrence of alcoholism. The French mathematician, Sully Ledermann, after extensive investigations in France and other countries reported that the more there were consumers of alcohol in a society, the more there were alcoholics, and problems associated with alcoholism. This observation seems to derive from common sense but Ledermann gave it a mathematical formulation. His general conclusion was that in order to decrease the incidence of alcoholism and related damage, one had to attempt to decrease the overall consumption of alcohol in a given population. For instance, if it is desirable to decrease the casualties among eighteen-year-olds in alcohol-related road accidents, then raising the legal drinking age to 20 is an effective measure. What is being done, in fact, is to decrease the overall consumption of alcohol in that vulnerable age group.

Ledermann also observed that in a given population within a given time period the percentage of the consumers of alcohol who consume excessively corresponds to about 7% of the drinking population, which in France represents two million alcoholics and in the United States over twelve million.

A similar analysis may be applied to the population of marijuana smokers among high school students in the United States. In the population of high school seniors who reported smoking marijuana during a period of one year, 18% of them used the drug daily. And yet this drug was an illicit one, not readily available. Other surveys of marijuana consumption were made in three Jamaican villages where the drug is freely available and socially acceptable. In these villages 64% of the villagers who consume marijuana smoke an equivalent of ten joints a day (i.e., are intoxicated daily).

Another survey made among a population of coca leaf chewers in the Bolivian Andes where this habit is an inherent part of the local culture, is even more striking. Out of the population which chewed the coca leaf, 90% used it daily in large amounts, equivalent to 300–500 mg of cocaine a day, which is an intoxicating dose. In the United States, the major constraint on cocaine use is its high price which limits its availability. And it is common knowledge that heroin addicts have to consume their drug of choice everyday.

Such surveys indicate that the percentage of excessive consumers of these illicit, dependence producing drugs is related to their respective addictive properties. It is now appropriate to conclude that their abuse potential (their compulsive daily usage associated with intoxication) is *much* higher than that of alcohol.

From the surveys which we have reported, one may conclude that the abuse potential of marijuana is seven times that of alcohol, and the abuse potential of cocaine and heroin fourteen times higher, when these drugs are socially acceptable and easily available.

Gabriel G. Nahas is a professor of anesthesiology at Columbia University in New York City and narcotics consultant to the United Nations Commission.

"Any drug can be used successfully, no matter how bad its reputation, and any drug can be abused, no matter how accepted it is."

Drugs Are Not Inherently Addictive

Andrew Weil and Winifred Rosen

Most people would agree that heroin is a drug. It is a white powder that produces striking changes in the body and mind in tiny doses. But is sugar a drug? Sugar is also a white powder that strongly affects the body, and some experts say it affects mental function and mood as well. Like heroin, it can be addicting. How about chocolate? Most people think of it as a food or flavor, but it contains a chemical related to caffeine, is a stimulant, and can also be addicting. Is salt a drug? Many people think they cannot live without it, and it has dramatic effects on the body.

What Is a Drug?

A common definition of the word *drug* is any substance that in small amounts produces significant changes in the body, mind, or both. This definition does not clearly distinguish drugs from some foods. The difference between a drug and a poison is also unclear. All drugs become poisons in high enough doses, and many poisons are useful drugs in low enough doses. Is alcohol a food, a drug, or a poison? The body can burn it as a fuel, just like sugar or starch, but it causes intoxication and can kill in overdose. Many people who drink alcohol crusade against drug abuse, never acknowledging that they themselves are involved with a powerful drug. In the same way, many cigarette addicts have no idea that tobacco is a very strong drug, and few people who drink coffee realize the true nature of that beverage.

The decision to call some substances drugs and others not is often arbitrary. In the case of medical drugs—substances such as penicillin, used only to treat physical illness—the distinction may be easier to make. But talking about psychoactive drugs— substances that affect mood, perception, and thought—is tricky.

In the first place, foods, drugs, and poisons are not clear-cut categories. Second, people have strong emotional reactions to them. Food is good. Poison is bad. Drugs may be good or bad, and whether they are seen as good or bad depends on who is looking at them. Many people agree that drugs are good when doctors give them to patients in order to make them better. Some religious groups, such as Christian Scientists, do not share that view, however. They believe that God intends us to deal with illness without drugs.

When people take psychoactive drugs on their own, in order to change their mood or feel pleasure, the question of good or bad gets even thornier. The whole subject of pleasure triggers intense controversy. Should pleasure come as a reward for work or suffering? Should people feel guilty if they experience pleasure without suffering for it in some way? Should work itself be unpleasant? These questions are very important to us, but they do not have easy answers. Different people and different cultures answer them in different ways.

Society and Drugs

Drug use is universal. Every human culture in every age of history has used one or more psychoactive drugs. (The one exception is the Eskimos, who were unable to grow drug plants and had to wait for white men to bring them alcohol.) In fact, drug-taking is so common that it seems to be a basic human activity. Societies must come to terms with people's fascination with drugs. Usually the use of certain drugs is approved and integrated into the life of a tribe, community, or nation, sometimes in formal rituals and ceremonies. The approval of some drugs for some purposes usually goes hand in hand with the disapproval of other drugs for other purposes. For example, some early Muslim sects encouraged the use of coffee in religious rites, but had strict prohibitions against alcohol. On the other hand, when coffee came to Europe in the seventeenth century, the Roman Catholic Church opposed it as an evil drug but continued to regard wine as a traditional sacrament.

Everybody is willing to call certain drugs bad, but there is little agreement from one culture to the next as to which these are. In our own society, all nonmedical drugs other than alcohol, tobacco, and caffeine are viewed with suspicion by the majority. There are subgroups within our society, however, that hold very different opinions. . . .

Furthermore, attitudes about which drugs are good or bad tend to change over time within a given culture. When tobacco first came to Europe from the New World it provoked such strong opposition that authorities in some countries tried to stamp it out by imposing the death penalty for users. But within a century its use was accepted and even encouraged in the belief that it made people work more efficiently. In this century Americans' attitudes toward alcohol have shifted from nonchalant tolerance to antagonism strong enough to result in national prohibition, and back to near-universal acceptance. The current bitter debate over marijuana is mostly a conflict between an older generation that views the drug as evil and a younger generation that finds it preferable to alcohol. . . .

What Is Drug Abuse?

The desire to call some drugs good and others bad has recently given rise to the term *drugs of abuse.* Government officials and medical doctors frequently talk about drugs of abuse, by which they usually mean all illegal substances. In their view, anyone using them is automatically guilty of drug abuse.

"Any drug can be used in a nonabusive fashion, even if it is illegal or disapproved."

But what is drug abuse? To say that it is the use of a drug of abuse is circular and meaningless. We think that the use of *any* drug becomes abusive when it threatens a person's health or impairs social or economic functioning. Cigarette smokers with lung disease who continue to smoke are clearly abusing tobacco. Students who cannot concentrate on classroom activities because they are stoned are abusing marijuana. Alcoholics who are unable to hold down jobs are abusers of alcohol. Junkies who must steal to support their habits are abusers of heroin. On the other hand, any drug can be used in a nonabusive fashion, even if it is illegal or disapproved. There are many people who consume tobacco, marijuana, alcohol, and heroin without abusing them; that is, they remain healthy and fulfill

their social and economic obligations. Drug abuse is not simply a matter of what drug a person chooses to consume; rather, it depends on the relationship an individual forms with that drug.

Many factors determine relationships with drugs. Obviously, the drug itself is one important factor; there is a whole science, pharmacology, devoted to finding out what drugs do.

The Effects of Drugs

Unfortunately, effects of drugs are difficult to specify. Different people show different responses to the same dose of the same drug, probably because people differ in biochemistry, just as they do in appearance. Even the same person may respond differently to the same dose of the same drug at different times. Pharmacologists attempt to minimize these variations by giving drugs to animals and people under controlled laboratory conditions. The results of these experiments enable them to classify drugs into different categories. For example, they can show most psychoactive drugs to be either stimulants or depressants of the nervous system.

Laboratory experiments also show us that the dose of a drug is a crucial variable. High doses of a substance may produce very different effects from low doses. Moderate doses of alcohol will give many people feelings of well-being and relaxation; high doses may cause incoordination, confusion, and sickness.

The way a drug is put into the body also shapes its effects. When you take a drug by mouth it enters the bloodstream slowly, and its influence on the nervous system is less intense than when you bypass the gastrointestinal tract by sniffing, smoking, or injecting it. High doses of drugs introduced by one of these more direct routes are likely to be more harmful and more addicting over time.

These pharmacological facts can explain some of the variations we see in the relationships people form with drugs. For instance, South American Indians who chew coca leaves swallow low doses of cocaine and do not seem to become abusers of that stimulant. People who put much larger doses of refined cocaine in their noses are much more likely to develop medical, social, and psychological problems. The abuse potential of snorting coke is far greater than the abuse potential of chewing coca. In other words, people are more likely to form good relationships with coca than with cocaine, and this difference clearly has some basis in pharmacology.

Set and Setting

However, the laboratory is not the real world, and pharmacology can only explain certain aspects of human relationships with drugs. When people take drugs in the real world their experiences are often not what pharmacologists would predict. The reason is that outside the laboratory other factors can completely change the effects of drugs. One such factor is called *set*; set is what a person expects to happen when he or she takes a drug. Expectation is shaped by all of past experience—what a person has heard about the drug, read about it, seen of it, thought about it, and wants it to do. Sometimes it is not easy to find out what people expect of a drug because their real feelings might be hidden from themselves. A teen-age boy smoking marijuana for the first time may think he is eager to have a new experience, whereas unconsciously he may be terrified of losing his mind or getting so stoned he will never come down. Such unconscious fears can determine reactions to marijuana more than the actual effect of the drug.

"The fact that effects of psychoactive drugs can change so much from person to person . . . points up the folly of calling any drug good or bad."

Set can also be as important as pharmacology in shaping long-term relationships with drugs. For example, some people expect marijuana to make them relaxed and tired and so will use it only occasionally at bedtime to help fall asleep, whereas others, who feel that pot reduces their anxiety and makes it easier to relate to people, use it so frequently throughout the day that they become dependent on it.

Setting is another factor that modifies pharmacology. Setting is the environment in which a drug is used—not just the physical environment but also the social and cultural environment. During the Vietnam War many American soldiers got into the habit of smoking large amounts of the high-grade heroin that was cheap and easily available to them in Southeast Asia. They rolled it into cigarettes with tobacco or marijuana and used it primarily to escape boredom, because for many American soldiers Vietnam was, more than anything else, boring, and because heroin seems to make time pass more quickly. Pharmacologists would have predicted that most of these soldiers would become heroin addicts, but in fact, most of them stopped using opiates as soon as they came home. It was the special setting of army life in Vietnam that shaped this pattern of drug use, and when people left that setting most of them stopped easily.

Set and setting together can modify pharmacology drastically. Therefore, talking about the effects of drugs in the real world is not so simple. Effects of drugs are relative to particular people, places, and times. In ancient India, marijuana was eaten for religious purposes; people used it for its effects on consciousness in socially accepted ways. In England

and America during the nineteenth century, doctors gave tincture of marijuana to sick people as a remedy, and most patients never reported getting high on it, probably because they did not expect to and so ignored the psychoactive effects. In the United States in the 1920s, members of certain subcultures began smoking marijuana to feel high—a practice regarded as deviant by the dominant culture. Many early marijuana smokers freaked out and some even committed acts of violence under its influence. Today, the smoking of marijuana is accepted in many circles, and users think it decreases aggression and hostility.

The fact that effects of psychoactive drugs can change so much from person to person, from culture to culture, and from age to age points up the folly of calling any drug good or bad. But if there is no such thing as a drug of abuse, still there *is* drug abuse, and learning to recognize it is important. Only in analyzing people's relationships with drugs can *good* and *bad* have meaning. Some people may be upset by the notion that you can have a good relationship with a drug, but chances are they fail to acknowledge that many socially accepted substances are, in fact, drugs.

Good Relationships

Good relationships with drugs have four common characteristics:

1. *Recognition that the substance you are using is a drug and awareness of what it does to your body.* People who wind up in the worst relationships with drugs often have little understanding of the substances they use. They think coffee is just a beverage, marijuana an herb, and diet pills just "appetite suppressants." *All drugs have the potential to cause trouble unless people take care not to let their use of them get out of control.* A necessary first step is to acknowledge the nature of the substances in use and to understand their effects.

2. *Experience of a useful effect of the drug over time.* People who begin to use drugs regularly often find that their early experiences with them are the best; as they use the drugs more and more frequently, the effects they like seem to diminish. People in the worst relationships with drugs often use them very heavily but get the least out of them. This curious pattern happens with all drugs and can be very frustrating. Frequency of use is the critical factor in determining whether the effect of a drug will last over time. If the experience you like from a drug begins to fade, that is a sign you are using too much too often. If you ignore the warning and continue consuming the drug at the same frequency, you will begin to slide into a worse and worse relationship with it.

3. *Ease of separation from use of the drug.* One of the more striking features of a bad relationship with a drug is dependence: it controls you more than you

control it. People in good relationships with drugs can take them or leave them.

4. *Freedom from adverse effects on health or behavior.* People vary in their susceptibility to the adverse effects of drugs. Some individuals can smoke cigarettes all their lives and never develop lung disease. Some people can snort cocaine frequently and remain physically and psychologically healthy and socially productive. Others cannot. Using drugs in ways that produce adverse effects on health and behavior and continuing their use in spite of these effects is the defining characteristic of drug abuse.

No Good or Bad Drugs

Whether a drug is legal or illegal, approved or disapproved, obtained from a physician or bought on the black market, if the user is aware of its nature, can maintain a useful effect from it over time, can easily separate himself or herself from it, and can remain free from adverse effects, that is a good relationship with the drug.

"There are no good or bad drugs; there are only good and bad relationships with drugs."

Bad relationships with drugs begin with ignorance of the nature of the substance and loss of the desired effect with increasing frequency of use, and progress to difficulty in leaving the drug alone, with eventual impairment of health or social functioning.

Any drug can be used successfully, no matter how bad its reputation, and any drug can be abused, no matter how accepted it is. There are no good or bad drugs; there are only good and bad relationships with drugs.

Andrew Weil is an adjunct professor at the University of Arizona, and has researched and written about drugs and alternative medicine. Winifred Rosen is an author of books for young people.

Drug Addiction Should Be Treated as a Disease

Eric A. Voth and Kathleen Cahill Tsubata

Editor's note: The following viewpoint is in two parts. Part I is by Eric A. Voth. Part II is by Kathleen Cahill Tsubata.

I

Since the recognition of addiction as a primary disease, a variety of opinions have emerged on the subject. This [viewpoint] will clarify the primary disease of addiction from the perspective of the parents' movement, and it will hopefully clear the air on the subject. Unfortunately, some prefer for whatever reason, to look at addiction as some type of moral issue or character deficit, which it is not.

A disease is a disorder which results in the disruption of normal body function (in this case psychological or physiological function). Most diseases have identifiable signs and symptoms as well as one or more known causes. Many, however, have no known cause.

Heart disease for example, is a prototype disease. It is known that genetics, the environment, personality, and noxious stimuli are factors which may cause heart disease. A person who has a family history but makes an effort at controlling other elements such as diet and smoking may not develop heart disease. On the other hand, a person with no family history but who has a bad diet, smokes, and is under heavy stress may develop the disease. Conscious control of lifestyle early in life can help arrest the disease whether or not there is a genetic predisposition.

Addiction is very similar. It is a chronic, progressive, yet treatable disease with a variety of signs and symptoms. Family history of addiction produces a genetic risk which may increase the risk

of subsequent relatives becoming addicted if the right conditions exist.

Even though heavy emphasis is placed on genetic predisposition toward addiction, we should not forget that children at risk were generally raised in impaired families in which addiction existed. The learning of interpersonal skills may become disrupted in such an atmosphere (environmental stress). Other examples of the environment include schools, peer groups and the entertainment media. Any may have positive or negative influences.

Personality Effects

Personality has some effect as well. Some individuals are extremely resilient to genetic, environmental, or other risks. Others may fall prey to addiction easily. Evidence exists that fostering early refusal skills while bolstering self-image helps to buttress an individual's ability to resist problems.

Last, but certainly not least is the exposure to noxious stimuli (drugs and alcohol). By exposure to mood altering substances alone, addiction may be precipitated. Most addicts intended to originally use recreationally or to self-medicate. They all originally believed that they could somehow control their use.

This is the great danger of recreational drug use. Any drug abused, from cocaine at one end of the spectrum to caffeine at the other, is addictive. Furthermore, the evidence is clear that the earlier the exposure to mind-altering drugs, the greater the risk of subsequent problems. Thus, no mind-altering substance should be used in adolescence.

The symptoms of addiction have been well described elsewhere. In general, a compulsion for mind-alteration is the hallmark. As the disease progresses, mood-changes, interest in school or work slides, and in general performance suffers. As interpersonal relationships fail, families and friends will bear a great burden. It is generally easy to recognize late addiction, but early addiction may be

Eric A. Voth, "Addiction as a Primary Disease," *Drug Awareness Information Newsletter,* September 1987. Reprinted with permission. Kathleen Cahill Tsubata, "The Low-Down on Addiction," *The World & I.* This article appeared in the November 1988 issue and is reprinted with permission from *The World & I,* a publication of *The Washington Times Corporation,* copyright © 1988.

far more subtle. Early addiction may be manifested as repetitive intoxication despite admonishments to the contrary. Recognizing resistance to maintaining sobriety is the key to early recognition. Excuses and promises of the addict always cloud the issue.

Many attempts have been made to characterize the stages of addiction. I have found the Johnson Institute model very helpful. Although these stages are represented to different ways, the most helpful that I have found are:

1. learning the high
2. seeking the high
3. early dependency
4. late dependency or burnout

So many people only think of addiction as late stage 3 or 4. Actually the behaviors of stage 1 and 2 set up the individual for true dependency. In stage 1 the individual has just become exposed to the experience of getting high or intoxicated. There may be rapid progression to stage 2 in which the individual actively, and knowingly seeks intoxication. In this stage the ability to give up the drug at will may still exist, but it is lost in stage 3. Once true dependency has begun, generally drug rehabilitation and treatment is the only successful approach to treatment. This is definitely the case in stage 4, where the user requires much more vigorous treatment.

Addictionology

Addictionology is the practice of the treatment of drug and alcohol addiction. A wide range of attitudes exists within this field as to whether "responsible drug use" is a real entity. I maintain that those who support the notion of responsible use are short-sighted and do not fully understand the disease of addiction. Some physicians in this field also support the more typical psychiatric orientation that drug use is always secondary to other problems. This is not the case. Certainly drug use may either be the cause of psychiatric problems or be caused by them. Overall however, drug abuse and addiction is a primary disease. If psychiatric problems co-exist, the addiction must be treated before there is any hope of controlling the psychiatric elements.

"Drug abuse and addiction is a primary disease."

Unfortunately, the disease concept has been abused by many people for a variety of reasons. Some individuals wrongly believe that no matter what stage of addiction the individual is in, he can "get well" if he exerts enough willpower. This attitude has been used as a weapon against the addict to ostracize him. It has been used to label the addict as someone morally weak or unworthy. These attitudes are only counterproductive, and are particularly destructive to an individual who is trying to recover from addiction.

The converse of this is that the addict may hide behind the disease by contending that he cannot be held responsible for his actions "because he is sick." The addict does however, have the responsibility for working on and maintaining a recovery program no matter how rocky the road is. A person with heart disease may have even caused his own disease by his lifestyle, but he may be able to control his disease if he controls his lifestyle in a healthy manner.

One of the most destructive misapplications of the disease model has been to try to justify "responsible drug use." Proponents of responsible use contend that "careful use" in people who have no genetic predisposition toward addiction is relatively safe. The problem is that what may be careful use to one person is abuse to another. Alcohol may be a problem for some people; cocaine or marijuana for others. There is no effective way to predict who will become impaired or addicted. Drug use is like Russian roulette, and the earlier that an individual is exposed to mind-altering chemicals, the greater risk of addiction. I have yet to meet an addict who intended to become addicted when he started using drugs or alcohol.

The disease of addiction is more effectively handled through a combined approach of prevention, intervention, and rehabilitation. This is the goal of the parents' movement. We must give our children a set of values and good self-esteem; we must teach them how and why to "say no" and be certain that they do.

II

Michael Keaton snorts a line of coke at the beginning of the movie *Clean and Sober*. "Here, get your heart started," he urges the woman he has met the night before as he puts some cocaine on her pillow. But as he runs his hands over her still body, he finds that her heart actually *has* stopped—completely. With nowhere to run, he checks into a rehabilitation center, and we watch him continue to destroy his life and then struggle to retrieve it.

Addiction (including compulsive eating, gambling, and "sex addiction,") is not just a subject of interest to moviegoers, but has a real impact upon many of our lives. Soaring crime figures are directly related to addiction. A January 1988 Justice Department study found drug traces in the urine of nearly 80 percent of arrestees nationwide. Nine out of ten suspects charged with serious crimes like murder, rape, and burglary tested positive for drugs. Alcohol is America's most abused drug, the misuse of which costs the nation an estimated $120 billion a year. Alcohol-related accidents cause twenty thousand American deaths a year, and an additional one hundred thousand individuals die annually from alcohol-related health problems. An estimated nineteen million Americans are defined as "heavy drinkers," and fetal alcohol syndrome has become the third leading cause of birth defects in newborns. The most common excuse given for abusers is, "I just can't stop."

And in fact they can't. *Intervention* is a treatment process growing in popularity. Through this method counselors can help the family, employer, and friends of an addict to lovingly confront him with the seriousness of the situation and strongly urge treatment. In most cases, the arrangements are made in advance so the patient can go immediately into a treatment facility.

This is a modification of the traditional view that an addict has to "hit bottom" before he can admit he is helpless and seek to change. Studies indicate that the further the addictive disease has progressed, the more drastic the withdrawal, and the higher the likelihood that the addict may die before hitting bottom.

"Interventions are risky," says Bob, a recovering alcoholic and counselor. "But the percentage of success is high if done properly. That means using a trained counselor, having all the interested parties in the addict's life there, rehearsing a couple of times, and surveying the leverages—the threats which you are prepared to carry out if the person refuses to go into treatment."

Typical Intervention

Involved in a typical intervention might be the boss, the coworker, the best friend, the spouse, and the children of an addict. The participants read letters explaining their experiences with the addict and the feelings that led them to conclude that he or she needs treatment. If the addict is reluctant to comply, they have a "bottom line" prepared. This might be: "If you don't go into treatment, I have to fire you," from the boss. Or "You can't come home," from the spouse, or "I will not allow you to visit my home," from the friend. Whatever the bottom line is, a participant must be prepared to carry it out absolutely.

Even if the addict refuses to get help, the individual will find himself "hitting bottom" if everyone sticks to their promises. "It's a way to force the bottom up," says Bob. "They don't have to take the elevator all the way down before they reach bottom. This brings the bottom up to them.

"No one really voluntarily goes into treatment," says Bob. "Everyone has a footprint on their rear somewhere."

Going into treatment is a first step toward learning "how to cut off the three heads of the addiction dragon—physical, emotional, and spiritual" explains Bob. "If you try to cut only one or two off, the dragon still lives."

Addiction to many substances includes a physical dependence and consequent unpleasant withdrawal symptoms such as nausea, tremors, or hallucinations. The dependence also causes preoccupation with ensuring access to the substance, which eventually overrides every other emotional need. The user's focus narrows to himself and his need. Sensitivity to others declines, as do ethical or moral concerns. This is the spiritual side of the illness.

Weak Willpower

For many years laymen, health professionals, and addicts believed that weak willpower was the culprit. The logical corollary was that the addict should and could exert willpower, stop using the substance, and thus return to a nonaddicted state.

But research into the physiology of addiction has shown that certain people are physically predisposed to react abnormally to certain substances such as alcohol.

"The disease of addiction is more effectively handled through a combined approach of prevention, intervention, and rehabilitation."

"The accidental discovery of heroin-like substances existing in the brain tissue of alcoholics sparked a chain reaction of scientific revelations about the differences in metabolic processes between the alcoholic and nonalcoholic," says Dr. David L. Ohlms.

According to Dr. Charles Lieber of the Mount Sinai Alcohol Research Center in New York, the liver enzymes that convert alcohol into acetaldehyde, a toxic intermediate to its eventual conversion into acetic acid, or vinegar, are initially underproduced in the alcoholic's body. The liver cells multiply to meet the demands for increased enzyme production. This in turn creates an abnormal reaction, in which a certain amount of alcohol *must* be consumed in order to prevent the unpleasant reactions of the enzymatic action that is triggered.

Another anomaly differentiating the alcoholic from the nonalcoholic shows up in the parts of each cell responsible for metabolizing nutrients for the cell. These parts, called mitochondria, transform themselves to make more use of the quick energy produced by alcohol, eventually becoming misshapen and useless for normal metabolic processing. The cell membranes of an alcoholic become similarly modified. Toughened, they become inefficient in their function of letting nutrients into the cell and letting out the toxic waste products of cell metabolism. Instead, they let in poisons and let out vital substances, causing widespread cell breakdown.

In the brain, reports Ohlms, a portion of the acetaldehyde is metabolized into a powerful morphine-like substance called tetrahydro-isoquanaline, or THIQ. Experiments with monkeys indicate that THIQ remains in the brain tissue for years. Rats that previously shunned alcohol, when injected with minute quantities of THIQ, suddenly choose alcohol over water, becoming instant alcoholics.

"Addiction to many substances includes a physical dependence and consequent unpleasant withdrawal symptoms such as nausea, tremors, or hallucinations."

Lieber theorizes that THIQ accounts for the progressiveness of the disease; an alcoholic who has been sober for years will revert to the exact stage of consumption that took him decades to progress to—within a few days or weeks of resuming drinking.

Alcoholics have a high level of the enzyme dopamine betahydroxylase (DBH), which has been linked by researcher John Ewing to the lift and stimulation that alcoholics experience from drinking, as opposed to the sedation and melancholy that nonalcoholics report. More than one thousand such studies led the American Medical Society on Alcoholism to publish a definition in 1976:

"Alcoholism is a chronic, progressive and potentially fatal disease. It is characterized by: tolerance and physical dependency, pathological organ changes or both—all of which are the direct or indirect consequences of the alcohol ingested."

Other drugs mimic brain chemistry. Cocaine, heroin, morphine, barbiturates, and amphetamines all imitate naturally produced substances such as adrenalin, endorphins, and others. The ability of the drug to simulate extremely pleasurable sensations is what makes it so alluring. "Take the pleasure you experience in sex, and multiply it fifteen or twenty times or so, and you get an idea of the rush from cocaine," says a former user.

Artificially Low

The downside is that many of the drugs block the body's natural pleasure mechanisms. Thus, without the drug, the person is not only not "high" but artificially "low." The consequences of stopping drug use, according to treatment professionals, may range from emotional problems (depression, anxiety, preoccupation) to physical problems (sweats, tremors, nausea, sleeplessness, circulatory and respiratory changes, unconsciousness, and convulsions) to mental problems (hallucinations, vivid dreaming, paranoia, and psychotic episodes).

Since 1970, more than six hundred scientific papers have detailed the harmful effects of marijuana use. Psychiatrists Harold Kolansky and William Moore found that in a group of habitual marijuana users with no previous emotional disorders and no other drug use, a variety of symptoms were found, including problems with social judgment, attention span, concentration, and speech, and a high level of confusion, anxiety, depression, apathy, passivity, paranoia, and inability to construct thoughts. Significantly, they found that these symptoms were present even when the users were not intoxicated on the drug.

This bears out other physiological data. The cannabinoids that are the active ingredients in marijuana are fat-soluble, depositing themselves in the fatty tissues of the body. From there, they are doled out into the bloodstream in continual doses over long periods of time. The chief repositories for the 421 chemicals of the cannabinoids are the reproductive organs and the brain.

Many people look for quick-fix solutions. Some of the chemical solutions have proven helpful when used with a total treatment plan, but as a "magic bullet" that hits the addictive bull's-eye, none has been successful. Antabuse (disulfiram), first used in the 1940s, interferes with the liver's metabolism of alcohol, making the drinker violently ill. When taken daily, this was thought to be effective in conditioning alcoholics to associate drinking with horrible consequences, ensuring that the alcoholic would not drink.

But recent studies have linked antabuse with side effects such as psychosis, seizures, fetal deformities, cardiovascular disease, nerve deterioration, and intolerance for certain foods.

Synthetic Drugs

Methadone, which blocks the desire for heroin without imparting a "high," is a synthetic opiate being used to treat seventy thousand addicts in the United States. Although methadone enables the user to get off the merry-go-round of using, it is itself addictive; withdrawal from it can take several months, much longer than the week-long withdrawal from heroin.

Naltrexone, or trexan, is a synthetic drug that blocks the opiate effect. After taking this, an addict will feel no effect from heroin or any opiate, in any dosage, for seventy-two hours. It is not addictive, gives no "high," and can be used by anyone except those with liver problems or hepatitis. The problem with this treatment is that the user can always stop using it in order to get high again when the need becomes great.

Some treatments use only psychoanalysis or hypnotism to prod the addict into recovery. Yet experts in the field feel that treating addiction as a psychological aberration both ignores the physiological base of the problem and falsely defines it as a mental health problem. Numerous studies have shown that sample populations of addicts and nonaddicts have nearly identical cross-sections of mental health indicators.

Additionally, the mental illness approach loses credibility when one considers that less than 10 percent of alcoholics under psychiatric care are cured. Harvard psychiatrist George Valliant studied 202 subjects for thirty-five years, publishing his findings in 1977. His conclusion: "Alcohol is the antithesis of a tranquilizer and the average alcoholic does not drink because his childhood was unhappy; he is unhappy because he drinks."

For this reasons, counselors now focus on the primary goal—getting the addict off the drug—before evaluating any suspected underlying personality disorder. In most cases, when the addiction is not active, the "psychological problems" disappear.

AA Success

Nearly every successful treatment for addiction follows the pattern originally set by the two alcoholics in the 1930s who formed Alcoholics Anonymous. AA has succeeded where scientists have failed, and has inspired a number of similar programs for other addictions: Narcotics Anonymous, Cocaine Anonymous, Overeaters Anonymous, and others. For the families and friends of the addicts arose the support groups aimed at healing their problems, such as Al-Anon, Adult Children of Alcoholics, Naranon, Cocanon, Alateen, and Families Anonymous.

Many addicts need to first withdraw from their substance before beginning the Twelve Steps process of AA. One in five alcoholics will have convulsions in withdrawal, if untreated; 8 percent will have delirium tremens, the auditory and visual hallucinations accompanied by hyperactivity of the cardiovascular, respiratory, and nervous systems, which is fatal in 20 percent of its victims.

The detoxification portion of treatment programs involves administering decreasing amounts of sedatives, monitoring vital functions, and taking vitamin and nutritional supplements. Detoxification may vary somewhat, but usually follows the same basic pattern. Most medical insurance plans cover such treatment today, another indication that addiction has been accepted by medical professionals as an actual disease, not a lack of willpower.

Once "dried out," the patient usually goes through a twenty-eight-day program involving group meetings, writing assignments, therapeutic exercise, responsible activities, and individual meditation. In a typical treatment program, the addict will go through the first five of the Twelve Steps. The dynamic of the group discussions keeps the focus on honesty, support, and growth. The counselors challenge the participants, direct discussion, and give assignments, including some unorthodox ones tailored to individual needs.

Patients are brought to local AA meetings to acquaint them with its methods. After treatment, they are encouraged to attend meetings to maintain their sobriety: The recommendation is ninety meetings in the first ninety days.

"Addiction is a fatal illness, if not treated."

To those who aver that treatment has a low success rate—some 40 percent—Bob answers: "Addiction is a fatal illness, if not treated. In the arena of fatal diseases, we are not doing that badly. Look at the statistics. After treatment, 40 percent never use again. Another 40 percent use again, but their lives improve. Twenty percent die of the addiction. That means 80 percent of people who would have died had a reversal and improvement.

"Some people may not believe they are powerless (over alcohol or drugs) until they have a relapse and have 'just one drink.' Only when they find out how that one drink affects them can they really understand what being powerless is. So that guy may become one of the totally abstinent the next time he goes into treatment.

"On the other hand," Bob continues, "once an addict knows he has the disease, he can't abdicate responsibility for using again."

Eric A. Voth is the medical director of the Chemical Dependency Treatment Center at St. Francis Hospital in Topeka, Kansas. Kathleen Cahill Tsubata is a free-lance writer in the Washington, DC area.

Drug Addiction Should Be Treated as a Chemical Imbalance

Lynne Lohmeier

The continuous coffee drinker, the hard-core heroin addict, the alcoholic, and the closet binge eater seemingly have very different problems. But according to Janice Keller Phelps, M.D., they're actually suffering from the same condition—an in-born physiological hunger for addictive substances. Phelps says that it makes no difference if the substance is nicotine, prescription drugs, sugar, cocaine, or caffeine. Addiction is addiction, and in one form or another, it strikes four out of every ten people. If Phelps's radical ideas about addiction are true—and there's recent research as well as her own experience treating addicts, that indicate they are—she could be in the process of revolutionizing the treatment of addiction.

Co-author of *The Hidden Addiction* and *How to Get Free* (Little, Brown and Co., 1986), Phelps has treated over 5,000 cases of addiction since founding her Seattle-based clinic Alternatives in Medicine almost ten years ago. A conventionally trained physician who's expanded into holistic health care, Phelps treats addiction like any other physiological disorder which attacks both body and mind—by readjusting the body biochemically and teaching the patient how to properly maintain this internal balance.

A self-described pediatrician gone astray, Phelps's concept of addiction grew out of her clinical experience treating addicted individuals of all ages. As medical director of a children's correctional institution in the early 1970s, she saw the usual cases of "real" addiction, those involving hard drugs. But for every kid hooked on illegal street drugs, she saw many more who couldn't handle common chemicals, primarily sugar.

In 1977 she became director of Seattle's Center for Addiction Services, and it was here that she began to suspect all addictions are essentially the same. She watched addicts readily substitute one drug for another if their drug of choice were unavailable: tranquilizers for alcohol, alcohol instead of narcotics, and so on. She also observed that addicts of every kind seem to have a problem with sugar metabolism. Heroin addicts gorge on sugar to stave off withdrawal symptoms, for example. Recovering alcoholics crave sugar (and then relapse), and bulimics often fall into a drug-like euphoria after a sugar binge. From observations like these, Phelps suspected early on that addictiveness is somehow related to a biochemical disturbance in the metabolism of simple carbohydrates.

But sugar is only half the story. Phelps had also identified an underlying, often subtle depression in almost all her patients. Some had been vaguely depressed all their lives. Others hadn't recognized depression for what it was, but described themselves as always feeling a little down, subject to mood swings, chronically fatigued, tearful, or anxious. She realized all these individuals use addictive chemicals for the same reason—to temporarily alleviate their inner discomfort. And it works fairly well, at first. Eventually, however, continued use of addicting chemicals no longer eliminates depression, and in fact actually exacerbates it. But by this time, the user's no longer drawn to the substance for its "high." He or she is using it, often unknowingly, in an attempt just to feel normal and to keep withdrawal symptoms at bay.

Dismal Results

Phelps had seen the dismal results of conventional treatment for various addictions. In many cases, the only outcome is a change in drug use. Heroin addicts becoming hooked on methadone and Valium addicts switching to Xanax doesn't seem like much of an improvement. Moreover, she was struck by the degree of compulsion shown by addicts. They arrange their whole lives around their addiction.

One way or another, they always find a way to fulfill their needs, even if it means hurting their loved ones or breaking their personal moral codes. Parting with orthodox thinking at the time, Phelps concluded that such obsessive behavior can't simply be the result of stress, an addictive personality, lack of will power, or a "weak" character. There has to be something far more powerful stimulating the addict's appetite.

She carefully examined the family histories of her patients and discovered a strong genetic predisposition toward addictiveness. Children of alcoholics, for example, are frequently staunch teetotalers, yet they're easily addicted to prescription or street drugs, sugar, and nicotine. Furthermore, even the most conservative mental health professionals now recognize that heredity plays an important role in depression, and Phelps is convinced the depression seen in addictive people isn't just your garden variety case of the blues. It's a genetic, biochemical, and pervasive depression which blocks one's ability to experience normal, natural joy, and it must be treated before an addict of any kind can truly recover.

Addiction, Phelps concluded, is a matter of biochemistry and genetics, and her working definition clearly includes more than recreational drugs and liquor: "An addiction is the compulsive and out-of-control use of any chemical substance that can produce recognizable and identifiable unpleasant withdrawal symptoms when use of the substance is stopped. Such addiction is driven by an inborn physiological hunger in the addictive person, and is frequently intimately related to depression." Note this definition excludes the use of chemicals by *nonaddictive* people. Phelps has found that people born nonaddictive simply don't become hooked on anything. They may partake of addicting substances occasionally, but they don't use them to relieve an in-born depression as do addictive people.

"Endorphins, the natural morphine-like chemicals produced by the brain, are also implicated in both addiction and depression."

It's not clear exactly how sugar dysmetabolism and genetic depression combine to create a physiological vulnerability to addictiveness. Neither Phelps nor anyone else completely understands the complicated process of carbohydrate metabolism, although everyone agrees that the hormones of the hypothalamus, pituitary, and adrenal glands are involved. Cortisol (one of the major stress hormones) from the adrenal cortex, for example, is an important regulator of sugar levels, and Phelps suspects

addictive people suffer from adrenal insufficiency. The neurotransmitter serotonin controls our subjective desire for carbohydrates and is linked to some forms of depression. Researchers at MIT [Massachusetts Institute of Technology] and elsewhere have recently shown that irregularities in serotonin secretion alter both our appetite for sweets and our emotional stability.

Endorphins

Endorphins, the natural morphine-like chemicals produced by the brain, are also implicated in both addiction and depression. (These are responsible for the "high" of vigorous exercise, and recent work at Johns Hopkins University suggests that eating sweets also stimulates endorphin production.) Phelps has identified a handful of people in her practice whose blood profiles indicate that they normally produce almost no endorphins. Not surprisingly, they're constantly miserable. They have headaches and their muscles hurt. They're anxious, depressed, and rarely experience any real joy. Understandably, they easily become addicted to anything which makes them feel better. For one of these patients, a physician, several hours of strenuous daily exercise apparently produces enough endorphins to make his life bearable. For others, only tranquilizers or narcotics give them any relief and combat the potential risk of suicide.

Phelps doesn't claim to understand the biochemical intricacies of addictiveness, and her concept of addiction isn't written in granite. She's more than willing to modify it if and when new data come to light. But she's also quick to point out that her working model is just that—it's working. It fits the characteristics seen in addictive patients; it allows her to identify addictive people; and most importantly, it enables her to treat addicts successfully. She conservatively estimates her *long term* (six to eight years after treatment) "cure" rate at over 50 percent. Conventional in-patient treatment centers succeed with maybe 25 percent of their clients over the long haul. According to Phelps, the 70 to 90 percent success rates often claimed by these centers fail to include long-term follow-up studies, and as any addictive person knows, addiction is by nature a disease of relapse.

Dr. Phelps's clinic has been treating addictions of every kind and degree since 1978, but it wasn't until several years later that she faced her own alcoholism. Today she recognizes that she had been a practicing alcoholic for thirty years, yet she fit the profile of a typical social drinker. She drank only in the evenings, never lost control, didn't have hangovers, miss work, or wreck cars. But while studying alcoholism and ways to treat it in 1980, the experts kept telling her that alcohol distorts the emotions, feelings, and thinking, *even when* there's no alcohol in the bloodstream. Although skeptical, she decided to quit for a couple of months just to prove to herself her thinking wasn't distorted. She hasn't had a drink since.

Drinking Years

Although Phelps was a functioning professional, wife, and mother throughout her drinking years, she says today that she wasn't really "present" during that period. She wasn't fully participating in life, or able to grow emotionally and spiritually. She describes her hard won freedom from alcohol as "fighting her way back to reality. It was like being under deep water and coming out into the sun and the air and the flowers."

"An addict who understands the physiological basis for her problem can take steps to correct it."

Phelps kicked alcoholism the conventional way, relying only on her own determination and Alcoholics Anonymous (A.A.) as a support system. She says now she wishes her own treatment plan had been available to help her. Getting sober was the hardest thing she ever did and a major reason she's worked so hard to develop a program which prevents much of the agony and fear she experienced. Although A.A., Narcotics Anonymous (N.A.), and counseling are an important part of her program, Phelps's approach to treating addiction encompasses more than moral support. She treats both the physical and emotional ravages of addiction. In explaining her philosophy, she's fond of an analogy involving cancer treatment: Suppose you had cancer and joined a patient support group where you all sat around and discussed your mutual concerns. Undoubtedly, at the end of each meeting, you would go home feeling better. But what if that were the *only* treatment you received? What if there were no medical treatment for your disease? That's the situation faced by most addicts receiving conventional therapy.

So how does the Phelps program work? First comes education. It's imperative that patients understand what's wrong with them. They must be freed of the guilt-invoking misconceptions that make them feel shameful or inferior. Phelps has found that when clients understand that their problem is a biochemical one, and they're not weak or lazy people, much of their guilt and fear dissipates. Additionally, the knowledge that addictiveness is a *highly treatable* biochemical imbalance allows patients to take responsibility for their own recovery. Much like a diabetic who has learned to control her health by diet and lifestyle, an addict who understands the physiological basis for her problem can take steps to correct it.

Hand-in-hand with education comes abstinence. The patient must make an honest commitment to stop using addictive substances immediately and completely. This means abstinence not only from the drug of choice but to *all* addicting chemicals—caffeine, alcohol, sugar, the entire spectrum. Frequently patients trying to beat one addiction will turn to another legal or more socially acceptable chemical for relief from withdrawal symptoms. (A.A. meetings are famous for their smoking, coffee, and donuts!) Phelps, unlike most professionals in the field, feels such substitutions defeat the purpose of abstinence and lead to relapse. She believes any and all chemicals which satisfy the physiological hunger of addictive people must be avoided so the body has a chance to return to its proper internal balance.

New clients often resist this step. Some have been coerced into treatment by their families and don't really want help. Many just want to cut down on their drug use but not quit entirely (for example, limit drinking to the weekends). Others want to eliminate only certain habits (kick the cocaine, but keep the marijuana). Phelps makes these people a hard to refuse offer: "Give me thirty days of total abstinence to get your body back in balance. After that, you can go back to using any drug you wish." They usually don't.

During this first thirty days of treatment, any similarity between Phelps's program and conventional therapy ends because, Phelps contends, the latter fails to provide the vital medical treatment needed during detoxification and withdrawal. The first step Phelps takes with every new patient, regardless of the drug involved, is getting them physically capable of enduring the initial period of abstinence. To detoxify the body of all addicting chemicals, she precribes 4,000 mg of vitamin C every two or three hours while awake during the detox period (usually two to seven days). This flushes toxins from the system and modifies cravings. In addition, she designs a high intensity nutritional program individualized for each patient—vitamins/minerals, protein supplements, adrenal cortical extract, liver detoxifiers, etc. She asks patients to take small feedings of high-protein foods (excluding all refined carbohydrates) about six times a day. And for specific problems, she outlines the use of various supplements: the amino acid glutamine for alcohol craving, tyrosine and niacinamide for depression, calcium plus magnesium for anxiety, and a long list of others.

Antidepressant Drugs

An integral part of Phelps's program is the use of nonaddicting antidepressant drugs for those who need them, a practice that's elicited criticism from her more conservative colleagues. Not only do most patients exhibit signs of genetic depression (which helped lure them into addiction in the first place), but the early detox period itself frequently brings on depressive episodes. She's found that if patients get depressed, they're going to use, which in turn makes them more depressed, so they use again . . . which means, of course, starting all over again. Consequently, she treats depression aggressively right from the start.

During the early, sometimes difficult detoxification period, Phelps sees or speaks with the patient daily. If necessary, she administers large doses of vitamin C by intravenous infusion once or more each day to relieve particularly unpleasant withdrawal symptoms. In some cases of opiate addiction (morphine, heroin, Demerol), she prescribes specific nonaddicting drugs for a short period to alleviate severe discomfort.

Concurrent with medical treatment, Phelps and her staff counsel the client, ideally with family members, and as soon as patients feel ready for it, she starts them on a daily exercise regimen and recommends (but doesn't require) enlisting the aid of A.A., N.A., church/spiritual groups, or any other support system. She believes the most important part of her program is treating each patient as a unique individual; what works for one patient may be useless or even detrimental to another. In fact, her major criticism of conventional in-patient centers is that they treat everyone in exactly the same manner. Phelps's clinic offers a wide range of services in addition to basic medical care and counseling—hypno-therapy, massage, acupuncture, and other alternative approaches to wellness. If something helps a particular patient, it's incorporated into his or her individual program. If a treatment doesn't work, or if a patient feels uncomfortable with it, it's simply discarded. Phelps calls this pragmatic, broad-based approach "complementary medicine"—the best of both conventional and holistic health care.

"People drug-free for perhaps the first time in years need to learn ways of replacing drug-induced highs with the reality-based gratifications of daily life."

Recovery for some is quick and relatively painless. One patient, owner and manager of her own corporation, was reduced to total nonfunction due to a heavy sugar/caffeine addiction. Convinced she was going crazy, she couldn't work, drive, get the mail, or answer the phone. Thirty-six hours after entering Dr. Phelps's office, she felt fine and remains so today. A college professor who drank before classes simply wanted to cut down on the drinking so his students wouldn't complain about his alcoholic breath. Phelps offered him the thirty-day abstinence deal, and a week later he was back in her office

feeling better than he ever had. Harry, a heroin/methadone addict, felt well enough on the third day of withdrawal to take a ten-minute walk. He attended his first N.A. meeting on the fifth day, and by the second week, he was making plans to return to work.

Relapse a Threat

Recovery for others is far more difficult, and for many it lasts a lifetime. Relapse is always a threat, and recovering addicts must continue to follow a vigorous nutrition/exercise program which excludes *all* addicting chemicals. But beyond this, people drug-free for perhaps the first time in years need to learn ways of replacing drug-induced highs with the reality-based gratifications of daily life. An advocate of Robert Fritz's DMA self-development concepts, Phelps shows her patients new and positive ways of creating joy in their lives, and eventually they begin to get in touch with the biochemical sensation of natural pleasure as opposed to that of depression.

Finally, Phelps seems to have an unusual amount of patience and compassion for her patients (after all, she's been there). "We're sensitive to the patients' needs," she says. "We treat them uniquely, and we treat them with love and dignity. I've never seen a person who doesn't respond to love and dignity." Even her advice to other physicians on this subject is clear cut: "[Your patients] need love and understanding, not scoldings and dire predictions. The fact that their addiction is harming their health is not enough to get them to abstain. If you cannot show loving patience with this disease, let someone else treat it. Then take some continuing education workshops on addiction."

People from all over the country trek to Phelps's clinic where the cost of treatment is one-tenth to one-fourth as much as conventional in-patient programs. For those who can't manage a trip to Seattle, *The Hidden Addiction* includes her Individual Addictiveness Profile, which helps identify addictiveness and genetic depression. For readers who realize they have a problem and are ready to make some changes, she's included a comprehensive step-by-step self-help program for those who want to go it alone. She's also included a chapter for physicians and hopes to begin training clinicians throughout the country in the near future. Lauded by health authorities such as Linus Pauling and Lendon Smith, Phelps's work has generally been well received by the conventional medical community. Probably the major criticism of her approach is that it's too simplistic, based too heavily on commonsense ideas. To this she responds, "Yes, that's true, but they work. Why go to something more complicated when something simple works?"

Dr. Lynne Lohmeier is a zoologist and free-lance writer in Mississippi.

"I believe that to hold people responsible for their behavior is the most moral and effective 'treatment' we can administer."

viewpoint 9

Drug Addiction Should Be Treated as a Lack of Self-Discipline

William L. Wilbanks

There is an emerging philosophy that strikes at the very core of the concepts of the all powerful human will, self-discipline, and responsibility. I refer to this growing danger as the New Obscenity. I do not refer to any 4-letter word but to a philosophy that is summarized by a phrase of 4-words. This 4-word phrase is obscene because it is offensive to the core concept of humanity. The phrase in fact denies the very quality that makes us human and not simply animals. The phrase might appear innocuous and even scientific but it is obscene. The 4 words are: "I cannot help myself."

We are hearing it more and more. Sometimes it comes from respectable scientists. Perhaps you saw the *60 Minutes* segment a couple of years ago on the San Antonio rapist. The rapist was caught after he broke into the house of a 26-year old woman and raped her for the third time over a period of three months. He confessed but told a San Antonio jury that he was the victim of a high testosterone level (i.e., a hormonal defect) that increased his sexual appetite to the point that he couldn't help himself. . . .

The problem is that the advocates of the New Obscenity have no concept of what has historically been called "temptation." The belief in temptation is viewed as being moralistic, religious and unscientific. The human mind is viewed by many scientists in mechanistic terms as a simple arbitrator of competing forces. In this mechanistic view the stronger force wins the battle and thus there is little room for choice. There is certainly no room for the belief that certain of these alternative choices or forces are "temptations" and that they can and should be resisted. In the words of Dr. Thomas Szasz: "Temptation—resisted or indulged—has been

supplanted by drives, instincts and impulses— satisfied or frustrated. Virtue and vice have been transformed into health and illness."

The medicalization of deviance has no place for the concept of temptation. Solutions to human problems are not seen as moral (i.e., resisting temptation) but as technical and medical. Is it any wonder that the medical model of misbehavior completely ignores the idea of moral choice and resistance to temptation. The peddlers of the New Obscenity assume that if a person commits rape, or drinks excessively, or abuses drugs, etc., he is the victim of impulses or forces he could not control. As a naive high school senior you might ask, "But isn't it possible that the behavior was not uncontrollable but simply uncontrolled (i.e., isn't it possible that the 'actor' simply chose to give in to temptation)?" Let's take the examples of alcoholism and drug addiction to illustrate the abandonment of the concept of temptation.

Lost Control

We are told that there are as many as 15 million "alcoholics" in this country who have been overpowered by the craving for alcohol to the point that they have "lost control"—there is another obscenity. And yet the idea that alcoholism is a "disease" which is characterized by the loss of control was only endorsed by the American Medical Association in 1956. Critics argue that the acceptance of the disease model of alcoholism represented not a triumph of scientific evidence over myth but a political and ideological statement by the medical profession.

There is no good scientific evidence that alcoholics have "lost control." Critics suggest that problem drinking is a *habit* in which the so-called alcoholic simply has decided that the benefits of drinking outweigh the liabilities. There is no evidence that the will of the drinker has been overpowered. But,

William Wilbanks, "The New Obscenity," a Baccalaureate address at Belton High School in Texas on May 29, 1988. Reprinted with permission.

of course, the worst thing society can do is to tell a person who is tempted to drink and get drunk that he really has no control over these "physical urges." The New Obscenity of "you can't help yourself" only convinces the person so tempted to give up on a hopeless task. If we encourage the drinker to believe that he will reach a point in his drinking where he can't help himself we are peddling obscenity. This obscenity is more than demeaning to the concept of humanity—it is untrue and it produces the very kind of problem behavior it attempts to explain.

But Dr. Wilbanks, don't you know that some alcoholics have a biological predisposition for their disease? I am aware of that claim and I am aware that the "inherited predisposition" claim has largely been discredited. But even the most ardent supporters of the disease model of alcoholism do not believe that all those with a biological predisposition to alcoholism become alcoholics. How does one explain why those with the predisposition never become "addicted"? Could it be that they overcome that obstacle or "biological temptation" by will-power? Granted that biological predisposition—if it exists—may make the battle of temptation more difficult. But the battle is still winnable.

"I believe that we can control our own behavior—if we believe that we can and exercise self-discipline."

Professor, you sound so uncaring and harsh. Why blame the alcoholic for something he can't help? I maintain that he can help himself and I maintain that I am not blaming the alcoholic so much as I am advocating that we hold him responsible. I believe that to hold people responsible for their behavior is the most moral and effective "treatment" we can administer. And in the long run it is the most caring approach because it restores to the so-called alcoholic a sense of dignity in that it confirms his humanity—it says you have free-will.

One of the most common myths I run across in my classes is the near unanimous belief of my students in what is known as the "disinhibition thesis." Most people—probably most of you in the audience—believe that alcohol, by virtue of its toxic assault upon "the higher brain centers," renders the drinker temporarily immune to the internalized restraints or inhibitions that normally serve to control one's behavior. In other words, the "disinhibition thesis" assumes that alcohol "unleashes our more primitive urges" by removing inner constraints of conscience.

The problem with this view is that there is no empirical evidence to support it. Our

"comportment" when drunk is a product of learning. We learn from our culture how drunk people behave and when we are drunk we mimic the drunken comportment we have seen in others. Some of us have learned to be aggressive when drunk, some have learned to be depressed, some have learned to be the life of the party. Drunks have not lost control but the problem is that most drunks believe they have lost control and use that loss of control to excuse inappropriate behavior.

Cultural Belief

One sociologist has suggested that those who beat their wives when drunk do so not because alcohol has disinhibited their inhibitions but because society has provided the cultural belief—or excuse—that one is not in control when drunk. The wife-beater does not beat his wife when sober because he would feel guilty but when he gets angry he then goes out and gets drunk and then beats his wife saying, "I can't help myself"—it's the alcohol. The belief in a loss of control thus serves as a "time-out from acceptable behavior." Thus the belief in the loss of control, not the chemical properties of alcohol, produces the aggressive behavior.

The belief that alcohol controls us rather than that we control alcohol is part of the New Obscenity. It is obscene because it rejects the very idea of humanity—that we are not simply animals controlled by our instincts and impulses. I believe in the uniqueness of humans. I believe that we can control our own behavior—if we believe that we can and exercise self-discipline.

This is not to suggest that support for the person trying to quit is not helpful but it is to say the first step to cure is not to state that one cannot control himself—a requirement for those entering AA. It is possible that the very act of turning oneself over to a treatment program is antagonistic to the personal belief in self-sufficiency and control that is needed for a "cure."

Perhaps the ultimate obscenity with respect to control over drinking is the TV commercial which suggested that anyone who tried to cure his own alcoholism was like a person trying to operate on himself. It should be noted that there is evidence that the self-cure rate for alcoholics is as good as the rate for medical treatment programs or Alcoholics Anonymous. Many critics question the "hospital cure" approach and suggest that the health profession has a vested financial interest in the disease model of alcoholism since this designation allows treatment costs for alcoholics in hospital treatment programs to be paid by medical insurance policies.

Approximately 20 percent of the U.S. adult population smokes. Most of that number are said to be "addicted" to cigarettes. Unfortunately, the term addiction suggests that smokers have "lost control" and cannot help themselves. However, we know that 30 million Americans quit smoking from 1965-1975. The vast majority of those who quit did so without any official treatment program. They simply decided to quit smoking and did so.

Acts of Will

But if they were addicted how could they quit by a simple act of will? Isn't addiction by definition a state in which the individual has lost control and can't help himself? Cigarette smoking is a *habit*, not an addiction, and the habit can be broken by the smoker without "therapy." But you say, aren't we quibbling over words and definitions? What's wrong with saying smokers are addicted to cigarettes? The problem is that the term addiction connotes a loss of control and a need for therapy when in fact the smoker never loses control and doesn't require help to quit. The real question is how many smokers give up trying to quit because they have been brainwashed by the New Obscenity that tells them they are addicted and have lost control? Why try to quit if you are addicted and the effort is futile? The self-cure rate would surely be greater if more of the 20 percent of Americans who smoke rejected the addiction obscenity.

"I view the concept of addiction as obscene in that it offends the concept of humanity."

Another common example of the New Obscenity— "he can't help himself"—is in discussions over anger and violence. How many times have you heard the Obscenity, "he lost control." There is no such thing as losing control when speaking of anger. No one makes us angry—we decide to be angry. It is a strategy, not an instinct. Carol Tavris, who has written the most authoritative book on anger, points out that we "decide to be angry" when we interpret some frustration as being unjustified. She views aggression not as a biological inevitability but as an acquired or learned strategy for dealing with anger.

There are many strategies for dealing with anger— suppress it, talk about it, shout and yell or become physically violent. We choose the strategy that has proven effective for us in the past. For example, when dealing with strangers, men rather than women are more likely to fight when someone "makes them angry" while women are more likely to talk. It appears that men fear being labeled as a "wimp" or "chicken" if they don't fight when angered while women fear being labeled a "bitch" if they do fight (or yell and scream). In other words, we learn anger habits or strategies that get us social approval.

The idea that we "lose control" is a convenient fiction that justifies the failure to resist the temptation to become angry and to act violently. Have you ever noticed that we seldom "lose control" when frustrated by our boss but often do so when frustrated by our friends or family? We don't decide to be angry and/or violent against our boss because that strategy will prove counterproductive.

America is a very violent nation in part because we are an angry people. Violence is certainly endemic where I live—Miami, Florida. One talk show host who lived in Miami and many other cities suggested to me that of all the places he had lived he found those who lived in Miami to be the most angry. Everyone who called his talk show seemed to be angry. And, of course, many people who "decide to be angry" express that anger via violence. I have noted that I am more likely since I have lived in Miami to "decide to be angry" when I am frustrated by someone who doesn't know how to drive an automobile. I got into the anger habit of honking at such "jerks" until I was threatened with a machete by a person who "decided to be angry" at me when I indicated displeasure with his driving behavior. That experience cured my "loss of control." I simply decided not to get angry at jerks who can't drive. I decided that the anger/honking strategy that I had learned was counterproductive—and dangerous. . . .

America's most respected criminologist, James Q. Wilson of Harvard University, says that our increased crime rate is largely due to the cultural support given to the shift from a value system that emphasized self-control and self-restraint to a value system that emphasizes self-expression. The highest crime rate in U.S. history appears to have been in the 1830's when the nation began to industrialize and urbanize. Religious and civil authorities, concerned about the growing problem of crime and disorder, launched a campaign to change American values so that impulse control and self-restraint would become the most cherished values in American society.

The social reformers involved in such efforts as the Temperance Movement and religious revivals succeeded and by the opening of the twentieth century "character" in American society was measured by such qualities as self-restraint and self-discipline. Unfortunately, beginning in the 1920's our culture began to devalue self-discipline and to glorify those involved in self-expression and even self-indulgence. Wilson suggests that we continue to pay the price for that shift in the core value of our culture. . . .

New Obscenity

But surely the most commonly heard example of the New Obscenity is the statement that someone is "addicted" to drugs. I view the concept of addiction as obscene in that it offends the concept of humanity. It suggests that drugs have the power of control over the human will to the point that those who use drugs "lose control" and "can't help themselves." It may surprise you to learn that the concept of addiction is very much under attack.

The popular notion of drug addiction to such hard drugs as heroin and cocaine says that those who take such drugs will inevitably increase their intake until they reach a point where the craving for the drug high and the fear of withdrawal causes them to lose control. The loss of control is evidenced by the willingness to sacrifice all—to the point of self-destruction—to ingest the drug. This popular belief in addiction is buttressed by animal research that allegedly shows that monkeys will press a lever to get more cocaine until they kill themselves. The monkeys cannot help themselves because the addictive power of cocaine is so great. The popular idea of addiction is perhaps best represented by the statement of the cocaine addict who said that while he was addicted his greatest fear was that he would win the million dollar state lottery. He knew that if he had a million dollars he would buy and consume cocaine continuously until he died.

Critics dispute the "monkey model" of addiction. Other research suggests that animals will not choose drugs when they have a choice and when studied in a natural environment. Furthermore the view that addiction is the automatic result of a biological process is contradicted by millions of "controlled" users of such drugs as alcohol, marijuana, amphetamines and even cocaine and heroin. The controlled users regulate their intake of drugs because their self-image, value system and self-discipline keep them from descending to the "depths of addiction" as it is commonly perceived. The controlled users simply decide to limit their intake of drugs.

"Addiction is basically a moral problem. People choose to become addicted."

Thousands of American soldiers in Vietnam became "addicted" to hard drugs but only 14 percent remained "addicted" upon their return to the U.S. The 86 percent who quit simply decided that they did not want to get involved in the American drug culture. Their value system and self-discipline helped them to "Say No." The problem with the popular notion of addiction is that it is shaped by a biased sample. Those who ask for treatment are those who did not control their drug habit. They are the losers in the battle of drug temptation. They say they couldn't help themselves and their therapists buy this self-deception and rationalization.

Perhaps this study of addicts in treatment is similar to a criminologist attempting to determine why people sink to a life of crime by interviewing men in prison. The inmates tell the interviewer that the attraction of crime was overpowering and that they had uncontrollable impulses to rape, steal and kill. I think you would agree that before I accept that rationalization I should go and speak with people who have faced similar "temptations" but who appear to have won the battle since they are law-abiding. If the law-abiding overcame similar circumstances and temptations maybe the claim of the inmates that they couldn't help themselves is a self-deception.

Consider another important fact. Look at those who appear to have reached the point in their drug use that they are considered addicted. They are not a random sample of those who experiment with and use drugs. Literally millions of people in this country have used or are using cocaine. A small percentage of that number are "addicted." And have you noticed that the vast majority of these were already "losers" in the sense that they were already criminals or were alienated from meaningful social contacts or were losers in the financial rat race?

Note also that most of the addict population is also addicted to alcohol, cigarettes, gambling, illicit sexual affairs, etc. They are simply people who are not self-disciplined. But they blame their failure on drugs. "The devil (drugs) made me do it." If I hear another criminal use that excuse I think I will throw up. You would think they were Mother Teresa's mirror image before they became addicted to drugs.

No Experimentation

Don't misunderstand me. I do not favor experimentation with drugs. I do not use drugs and I do not approve of or associate with those who use drugs. But the focus on the overpowering and addictive nature of drugs has led us to ignore the issue of values and self-discipline. Sure, drugs represent a tremendous temptation in that they provide a high that is often (but not always) pleasurable. But the vast majority of Americans simply say no to drugs because addiction is inconsistent with their self-image and their value system and they exercise their power of self-discipline to reject drugs.

We will continue to lose the War on Drugs as long as we view addiction as a medical problem. Addiction is basically a moral problem. People choose to become addicted. Why do we think we can take the stereotypical street addict and place him in a hospital setting and cure the moral and discipline defects that he has? Not only do many such programs not address the problem of temptation but they confirm the addict's view that he can't help himself. Is it any wonder that the relapse rate for treatment programs is worse than the rate of "spontaneous remission"?

We will not solve the drug problem until we begin blaming those who take drugs and holding them responsible. We must stop viewing the drug addict as a victim while placing all the blame on the "pusher" and the drug. There are many people in this country who have acquaintances who use cocaine but who would never think of directly confronting or criticizing those acquaintances. After all maybe they can't help themselves. And yet the same people may call for the death penalty for pushers. Let's start blaming the people who are responsible for the drug problem—the users. Let's confront the users of cocaine with the moral dilemma that thousands of people are dying in this country because they and people like them use the drug. Let's tell them drug abuse is a bad habit and not an addiction.

The idea that drugs have the power to overwhelm the human will is a myth. Such a suggestion is obscene as human beings have a mind and they can and do decide to totally abstain after experimenting with drugs, or they limit their use, or they decide after excessive use to simply quit taking drugs.

Drugs do provide a kind of "high" that many people find to be very pleasurable. But there is no evidence that any drug provides a psychological or physiological high that overwhelms the human will. For example, the euphoria of cocaine might be viewed as a kind of physiological temptation. But the temptation is one that can be and often is controlled by the human will. And by the way, whatever happened to the concept of temptation?

Many of those who discontinue the use of drugs find as much pleasure in the drug as do "addicts" but they decide that excessive use of drugs is inconsistent with their values and self-image. They may not want to disappoint their friends and family, they might fear the reaction of their employer, or they might fear a fatal overdose, etc. But for whatever reason they simply decide that they discontinue the use of drugs. It is incorrect to say that they never became "addicted" as no one is addicted to drugs. Many people have a drug *habit* in that they continue to take drugs because they like the good feelings that the drugs provide and they find insufficient reasons to forego those pleasures. In short, they decide, whether consciously or unconsciously, to continue drug use because they are more concerned with the drug high than the negative reaction to their drug use by others.

Obscene Phrase

The next time you hear someone use the obscene phrase, "drug addict," why don't you stop them and say, "Don't you mean drug 'habit' rather than drug 'addiction'?" Remind those who use the term addiction that the uncontrolled use of drugs is not evidence of the inability to control the use of drugs. And ask those who insist on using the term "drug addiction" whether they believe that there are those who can control their use but simply decide not to do so. How do we tell the difference between uncontrolled use and uncontrollable use? You cannot tell the difference and neither can those who claim to be experts on drug use.

"The uncontrolled use of drugs is not evidence of the inability to control the use of drugs."

It seems to me the worst thing we can do is tell those who are greatly tempted to continue the use of drugs that they will reach a point where they will lose control and can't help themselves. That message erodes their effort toward self-control. Those who study the psychology of control tell us that a belief in the ability to control is needed to ensure maximum effort toward self-control. The message that one has lost control may contribute to "learned helplessness" and greatly erode the ability to exercise self-control.

Also, the message of loss of control through addiction demeans the concept of humanity and free-will. The notion of drug addiction might also be seen as blasphemous in that it suggests that God would allow a person to be tempted with a substance so powerful that even the God-given power of human free-will is overwhelmed.

The "medicalization of deviance" has gone so far that we are now hearing from scientists that many people are "compulsive" gamblers or "addicted" to gambling. A new organization—Gamblers Anonymous—has appeared that is devoted to the concept that compulsive gambling is a disease and that those afflicted with this disease have an uncontrollable compulsion to gamble that can only be overcome when the "victims" of the disease state publicly that they have "lost control" and seek help from God and the Gamblers Anonymous support group.

Unlike the case with alcoholism and drug addiction, there is no claim that there is any physiological base to the addiction to gambling. Rather the argument is that gamblers become so enamored with gambling that they develop a psychological craving for gambling that eventually overpowers their ability to control. Those who have sunk to the point where they borrow money to gamble or steal money to gamble and neglect their family and jobs are said to be addicted to gambling.

But again, how do we differentiate between a gambling habit and a gambling addiction? How do we distinguish between uncontrolled gambling and uncontrollable gambling? The "professionals" in this field have an easy answer. If someone reaches a point where the gambling appears to be uncontrolled the assumption is made that the gambler has lost control. If there was ever a case of circular reasoning or tautology surely this is it. The observer tries to explain deviant behavior ("excessive" gambling) by inferring that the cause of the deviance is an uncontrollable compulsion to gamble but the only evidence we have of this uncontrollable compulsion is the excessive gambling. There is no independent evidence of the alleged "addiction" other than the behavior itself. . . .

"The term addiction incorrectly suggests that a drug has greater power than the human will."

First, DON'T BELIEVE IT. When you are tempted to abuse alcohol or drugs, or to get angry, or to have an extra-marital affair remember that the greatest power in this world is the power of the human will. There is no power that is greater than you. But Professor Wilbanks, don't you believe in the power of alcohol, cocaine, sex, anger, etc? I BELIEVE IN YOU! If you believe in yourself you can overcome any temptation. Remember all of the people who do exercise self-discipline and who triumph over alcohol, cocaine, sex, etc. Don't listen to those who would point only to the "losers" in the Battle of Temptation. You will be told that those losers are addicted. It's a lie! They are quitters—they quit the battle of self-control because they didn't want to win or because they didn't believe they had a chance to win. Many of the losers believed the obscenity that suggested they couldn't help themselves.

But perhaps you are asking, Dr. Wilbanks, what if you are wrong and many of those with drug (or other) habits are actually addicted and have really lost control? Psychologists tell us that the illusion of control is actually helpful as the illusion only makes us work harder at self-control. Thus my message could only help the addict. But let's ask the reverse question: What if I am right? If I and other critics of the concept of addiction are correct, then those who tell "addicts" that they have lost control are eroding their ability to exercise self-control and undermining the only effective cure.

Battle Winnable

Second, TEACH YOUR CHILDREN THAT THE BATTLE OF SELF-DISCIPLINE IS ALWAYS WINNABLE. As young parents you will often be afraid to send your children out into a world with so many temptations. You may think that the best course of action is to shield your children from those temptations. I want to suggest that the best course of action is to teach your children about the process of temptation and fortify them with the values to resist those temptations and with the self-confidence that they can win the battle. Give them the kind of values and self-image that will enable them to say, "I am not the kind of person who abuses alcohol or drugs." . . .

Third, WHEN YOU HEAR SOMEONE UTTER THE NEW OBSCENITY, CHALLENGE THEM. If someone tells you they are addicted to drugs or cigarettes or anything else, break into the conversation and say something like,

> There is no such thing as addiction. Many people have a drug or cigarette habit but uncontrolled behavior is not the same as uncontrollable behavior. I believe in the power of the human will and I believe that the concept of addiction is an obscenity.

If that statement doesn't generate a debate I don't know what will.

But if you are not confident in your debating techniques or are hesitant to confront anyone who utters the New Obscenity I have a backup suggestion. Send them—anonymously if you wish—a little note that will alert them to the character of and the dangers of the New Obscenity. Write something like:

> Recently I heard you use the term "drug addiction." I wonder if you realize that there are many people, including some drug experts, who believe there is no such thing as an "addiction." The term addiction incorrectly suggests that a drug has greater power than the human will. The vast majority of people who use drugs regulate and control their use because uncontrolled drug use is inconsistent with their value system and because they are persons who value self-discipline. The minority who do not exercise control and who develop a drug habit are not addicted but are simply people who have made a choice—to continue their drug habit.

I hope you will join me in challenging the New Obscenity.

Dr. William Wilbanks is professor of criminal justice in the Department of Criminal Justice, School of Public Affairs at Florida International University.

"Doctors...say a disease is something that is primary, progressive, *and* chronic. *Alcoholism meets all these standards."*

Alcoholism Is a Disease

Mary Ellen Pinkham

The disease of chemical dependency is the addictive, abusive, and (eventually) destructive intake of mood-altering chemicals. The chemical of choice may be alcohol, it may be a drug (anything from sleeping pills to heroin), or it may be both alcohol and drugs. Soda isn't the only thing alcoholics are mixing into their cocktails. They're combining alcohol with amphetamines, meperidine, methylphenidate, and all sorts of other drugs. Many of the people I went through treatment with had dual addictions. They may have started out alcoholic, but eventually moved on to prescribed medications and wound up drug dependent. Today there are fewer "pure" alcoholics going through treatment centers than ever before, but more people are addicted to alcohol than to everything else combined.

Anyone who drinks is a potential alcoholic. Still, only a very small percentage turn into the stereotyped derelict. And an even smaller percentage are the headline grabbers, the rich and famous who all seem to be coming out of the closet these days and revealing their chemical addictions.

While that's good for raising public awareness, I think it may also be creating another kind of confusion. Punk rockers and movie stars haven't cornered the market on being chemically dependent. Most alcoholics are nice, middle- to upper-middle class people who are in the house doing the laundry, taking care of their kids as best they can, getting their jobs done. Some of them can be very successful (plenty of chief executive officers are alcoholics), but basically they're just regular folks who happen to have a serious problem that is interfering with the whole of their lives. They're suffering from a disease and they are probably unaware that they have it.

In 1956, the American Medical Association recognized that alcoholism was a disease. This was enormously helpful because it meant that alcoholics could at last get help in a hospital setting. It should also have helped to change public opinion and end the moral issue that historically has clouded the subject. Because alcoholism was viewed as a moral problem, few people could find help to recover; and because so few did, others assumed that people who drank excessively were lacking in character. They believed that by simply diagnosing the problem— "You're an alcoholic"—they could expect the afflicted person to recover spontaneously or cure himself.

Information Available

Yet despite the fact that information about the disease of alcoholism is widely available today and that a great deal of effort is spent disseminating that information, most people still don't seem to know that alcoholism is a disease—or they simply can't believe it. That's because we tend to think of a disease as something that's caused by a germ (like flu) or that's the result of some system in the body that has gone berserk (as in diabetes or cancer).

Doctors, however, take a different approach. They say a disease is something that is *primary, progressive,* and *chronic.* Alcoholism meets all these standards. So it doesn't matter what your mother has to say or what your friend's opinion is; if the person you care about is alcoholic, he is suffering from a *disease.* It's as likely to afflict you or the guy next door as a rock singer, a movie star, or a President's wife. Therefore you have the right and the obligation to be just as concerned about the person and just as caring as if he or she had cancer.

By *primary,* doctors mean that the alcoholism is a disease itself rather than a symptom of some greater social, emotional, or physical problem. Now, a lot of psychologists and psychiatrists who should know better still ignore this fact. Their attitude is, "Before a person can get help with his drinking or his alcoholism, we have to discuss what his problems are."

One of my friends experienced this attitude when she went for psychological help. On the form he gave her, the doctor asked that she list five reasons for being there. The first she listed was stress. The second was problems with her husband. The third was business problems, and the fourth problems with her son. She finally got around to her drinking—in fifth place. She knew that drinking was the real reason she'd come, but she couldn't own up to it.

"If the person you care about is alcoholic, he is suffering from a disease."

She never had to, either. Two thousand dollars' worth of talk later, the psychologist had still never addressed the fact that she had a chemical abuse problem. Of course, my friend knows now that she couldn't stop the drinking problem by working on the marriage or her son's behavior. The drinking was causing the other problems. Any solution that doesn't deal with the alcoholism itself is no solution at all—it's like wrapping a blanket around someone who's got a chill and believing that you're treating the fever. It's unreasonable to treat the symptoms of alcoholism and think you're curing the disease.

Insanity or Death

By *progressive*, doctors mean that the problem's going to get worse. The fact is, it will inevitably lead to insanity or death. Oh, you may not see the word "alcoholism" on the death certificate, but 97 percent of alcoholics die of alcoholism (via alcoholism-related diseases or accidents while under the influence). Only about 3 percent get help. According to the National Council on Alcoholism, it's the direct or indirect cause of about 95,000 deaths a year. Cirrhosis of the liver alone causes 30,000 deaths.

My own dad died of alcoholism when he was forty-eight years old, but in his case they called it heart failure. Since that's what my mom would prefer to believe, she's convinced herself it was so. A few years ago she told my brother he ought to be very careful about his cholesterol because there was heart disease in the family. What he really has to be careful about, of course, is drinking.

Other serious diseases associated with chronic alcohol abuse are cancer of the liver, larynx, esophagus, stomach, colon and breast, and malignant melanoma. It also leads to high blood pressure, stroke, and heart attack; damage to the brain, pancreas, and kidney; stomach and duodenal ulcers,

colitis, and irritable colon; birth defects and fetal alcohol syndrome.

Chronic alcohol abuse also may be a cause of impotence and infertility, premature aging, and other problems such as muscle cramps, lowered immunity, sleep disturbances, and edema.

After I'd been in recovery a while, a friend of mine who didn't know that I had an alcohol problem said to me, "Mary Ellen, you know, you're not as sick as often as you used to be." Until he pointed this out, I hadn't even realized how often I'd complained of being ill when I was drinking. My brother, who as a recovering alcoholic knew the real nature of my problem, later said that he'd never met a woman who had her period as often as I did. Every week I complained of "cramps"—my coverup for hangovers. Even if I wasn't hung over, most of the time I really didn't feel well. And I was one of the lucky ones: I stopped drinking before I developed any serious problems.

Alcohol-Related Diseases

I've read in National Council on Alcoholism literature that alcohol-related diseases account for about 20 percent of national expenditures for hospital care, and in the *New York Times Sunday Magazine* that 30 to 50 percent of all hospital admissions are alcohol-related. Doctors estimate that chemically dependent persons will die fourteen years before their normal life expectancy. If they don't die prematurely, they'll go insane because of damage to the brain cells. While the death of a person you love usually causes great pain, I think you sometimes suffer more when you have to watch him or her slowly disintegrate, either physically or mentally.

The progress of alcoholism isn't always steady. Very few people become full-blown alcoholics the moment they start drinking. I suffered few consequences—other than hangovers and some embarrassing behavior that seemed minor compared to the rewards of drinking—until I was really into heavy drinking. In my case, the switch came quickly. There's no pattern to it. You don't wake up one day and say, "Today is the day I think I'll screw up my life with alcohol," and start on the downward spiral. Usually, in fact, an alcoholic follows an up and down pattern—some good periods interspersed with some bad.

It may take five years or it may take fifty, but eventually it will happen: The alcoholic will hit bottom.

By *chronic*, doctors mean exactly what you would expect. There is no known cure for the disease. You can, however, control it. Alcoholism is the most treatable—and yet the most untreated—disease that exists. With help, an alcoholic may lead a happy, meaningful, and fulfilling life. I'm proof that it can be done. And there are many recovering alcoholics like me.

I think that those afflicted, and the people around them, deny that alcoholism is a disease because it's not unlike being diagnosed as having cancer or any serious illness. The first reaction is usually denial. Everyone feels that if he ignores the facts, the problem will go away.

With chemical dependency, shame is also part of the picture. Like the cancer patient, the alcoholic may think, if only I'd taken care of myself, this wouldn't have happened. The alcoholic's family circle takes on blame as well: Dad and Mom believe they weren't good parents, the wife thinks she hasn't been loving enough, the kids feel they haven't been dutiful.

Ignoring the Disease Potential

I also think that people want to protect their own social drinking by ignoring the disease potential, just as smokers like to deny the evidence and point out that at ninety George Burns is still smoking cigars. It's generally acknowledged that smoking causes lung cancer and other diseases, and it's foolish to continue the habit. Similarly, if you acknowledge that drinking can lead to alcoholism, it's kind of foolish to keep using alcohol. But drinking is a habit few people want to give up.

The staff at Families in Crisis counsels people who say, "I'm a professor," "I'm a doctor," "I'm a lawyer," "How did this happen to me?" "I should have known better." Once you accept that alcoholism is a disease, you have to acknowledge something else. A disease is very democratic. It does not respect age, sex, race, color, creed, or class.

Nobody knows exactly what kind of environmental or psychological facts send you over the line from social drinking to alcoholism. Some experts believe that research will eventually reveal that there is no distinction (a "heavy drinker" is just an alcoholic at an earlier stage), and I tend to agree with them.

No one has ever been able to pinpoint a "typical" alcoholic personality, but everyone seems to agree that metabolically, alcoholics are different from non-alcoholics. The difference is due either to genetic predisposition or just to the effects of heavy drinking.

"Alcoholism is the most treatable—and yet the most untreated—disease that exists."

I don't like scientific language any better than you do, but I think it's important that you understand a few specific things about the way the disease works in the body of an alcoholic. Personally, I found this information amazing.

In a pamphlet called "The Disease Concept of Alcoholism," Dr. David L. Ohlms explains that a Houston, Texas, scientist doing brain research just a decade ago was one of the first to note the different way in which alcohol affects alcoholics. In order to get fresh tissue for her studies, the scientist made arrangements through the local police to study the brains of derelicts who had died the night before.

In the course of her work, she happened to mention to her colleagues that she was surprised to discover that the derelicts were also heroin users. She based this assumption on the fact that in the brains of these chronic alcoholics she'd found certain substances closely related to heroin.

Her colleagues pointed out that the derelicts, who could barely afford a bottle of cheap wine, were extremely unlikely to be using drugs. That realization tipped the researcher off to a new area of investigation, and she began to explore the effects of alcohol on the brain.

A Toxic Substance

She discovered that in the bodies of normal drinkers, alcohol breaks down into a toxic substance called acetaldehyde. Then it breaks down into carbon dioxide and water, both of which are passed off as waste products.

In alcoholics, the system doesn't function as well. Not only does the alcoholic's liver produce more acetaldehyde, but also, according to Dr. Charles Lieber of the Mount Sinai Alcohol Research Center in New York City, it doesn't produce enough of an enzyme that eliminates acetaldehyde in the normal drinker.

When it remains in the body, acetaldehyde travels to the brain, where, according to some animal experiments, it becomes a powerful, morphine-like substance called THIQ. This substance has some interesting properties. THIQ occurs only in the brain of an alcoholic drinker. THIQ is so potent that when it was tested for use as a painkiller during World War II, it was rejected as being too addictive.

Certain strains of rat that refuse to drink anything alcoholic even in the most diluted form immediately prefer alcohol to water when injected with a minute quantity of THIQ. You might say that they become instant alcoholics. Dr. Ohlms reports that when THIQ is injected into a monkey's brain, it remains there for years. He links this fact to the progressiveness of the disease. It may explain why someone who's been sober for years suddenly starts drinking again at the same intensity and with the same behavior patterns as years before. The THIQ level in his brain has remained constant.

Why do some people's bodies deal differently with alcohol? Test results on animals and humans seem to indicate that a malfunctioning enzyme system precedes the onset of alcoholism. Such a chemical flaw might be inherited and might explain the fact that children of alcoholics, according to various studies, are three to five times as likely to be alcoholics as the general population.

Another possible genetic link has been explored by a researcher who discovered that even after months of sobriety, some 80 percent of alcoholics tested had abnormal brain waves. These resulted in memory impairments and a condition called anhedonia—an inability to experience pleasure and to respond appropriately.

Abnormal Brain Waves

This researcher suspected the problem might predate the alcoholism. He tested children of alcoholics, boys who'd never been exposed to alcohol even in utero, and confirmed that they had a higher incidence of these abnormal brain waves than the general population.

I met an alcoholic who was adopted and who could only start making progress toward his recovery when he'd traced his biological parents and discovered they were both alcoholics. At that point, he could accept the fact that he was the victim of a disease.

"Everyone seems to agree that metabolically, alcoholics are different from non-alcoholics."

Another friend whose parents don't have a drinking problem became an alcoholic himself. When he started recovering, he thought back to the stories he'd heard about his grandparents and realized they'd both died of alcoholism. No one acknowledged Grandpa was an alcoholic. What they said was "Grandpa worked real hard. He had a real good job. Oh, every once in a while he beat up Grandma, but you know, she kind of deserved it because she got 'mouthy.'" They didn't talk about how much he drank.

Some alcoholics with no family history of alcoholism may develop the disease, possibly later in life than people with alcoholic relatives. Researchers suspect that these people are born with deficient levels of endorphins, opiates that the body produces naturally. They may be predisposed to drink in order to feel normally good.

Other research indicates that some alcoholics have a metabolic irregularity that causes alcohol to stimulate pleasure more than in normal people (so they become dependent) or that they may be neurologically supersensitive and so use alcohol as a protection. . . .

The first time I broke into the liquor cabinet with my friends, I was starting what specialists in the field call the *learning* phase of alcohol abuse. This happens either as a result of experimentation (as in my case) or accidentally, as when a doctor's

prescription hooks someone on a drug habit. I learned that alcohol worked for me. It was as though it had been waiting for me. Once we connected, we became close buddies.

"The Feeling Disease"

Experts call alcoholism "the feeling disease," since it progressively affects the emotional life of anyone dependent on it. They explain that the range of human feelings goes from pain to euphoria, with normal feeling in the middle. In the learning stage, you feel euphoria while you're using alcohol, and after use you return to normal.

When I went into what they call the *seeking* stage, I started to look forward to alcohol. At this stage, you're not really upset if you can't get to your chemical of choice, and you still return to normal after the euphoria of using. Lots of drinkers stay at this stage. But the conservative estimate is that one in ten will become an alcoholic at this point.

When you get to the next stage, you've crossed over the line from social drinking into *dependency*. You're hooked. You begin to display the classic signs of alcoholism. You escalate from feeling euphoric to going out of control. Instead of feeling normal after drinking, you may begin to feel some pain.

If you don't get help, you go right to the last stage—*drinking to feel normal*. You start drinking when you're in pain (which, because of all the other problems that have cropped up in your life by now, is virtually all of the time). Afterward, you're in pain once again. If you're confronted about your alcoholism, you'll rationalize your use (blaming it on other problems), project unpleasant feelings (you hate yourself, so you turn that hate on others), and deny that you have a problem with alcohol.

From what I understand, it normally takes from ten to fifteen years to pass through the different stages. You use (or learn) anywhere from six months to five to seven years, abuse (or seek) for three to five. It takes only about two years of dependency until you cross right over to the last stage. When they can speak truthfully, people close to the alcoholic, particularly the spouse, say they suspected the problem was alcoholism for at least seven years before they reached out for help or could even admit the situation.

I have read another description of the stages of drinking which includes many of the same milestones, although it groups them slightly differently. According to this description, the early stages (most typically the person affected is twenty to twenty-five) are characterized by blackouts, increasing tolerance, sneaking of drinks, and guilty feelings.

The middle stage, in which the drinker is perhaps twenty-five to thirty-five, finds him still trying to keep a grip on his career, social life, and family, but seeing deterioriation in all those areas. He begins to experience loss of control, becomes preoccupied with drinking, and often winds up hospitalized for alcohol or an alcohol-related disease.

The hospitalization may precede the chronic phase, which includes obsessive drinking, deterioration of moral and ethical behavior, and physical symptoms such as psychomotor problems, (i.e., being unable to tie his shoes).

Tricky Manipulation

Occasionally, someone with a drinking problem will come right out and admit, "Yeah, I'm an alcoholic." This is the trickiest of all manipulations. This admission keeps you, and the alcoholic, completely stuck. Diagnosing the problem doesn't make it go away. No one will be cured without help.

More typically, alcoholics (and the people close to them) try to convince themselves they're just social drinkers. Either they don't admit the amount of alcohol they drink or they convince themselves they're in control of it. Even if they've read and heard that it's a disease, even if they *believe* that it's a disease, they don't want the "alcoholic" label. For one thing, it would require them to deal with it—by stopping drinking.

"Even if they've read and heard that it's a disease, even if they believe *that it's a disease, they don't want the 'alcoholic' label."*

To me the definition of a social drinker is someone who decides she wants a martini, goes to mix the drink, discovers there's no olive, and decides to forget the whole thing. It's someone who goes to a party whether or not there will be liquor. If you *must* have a drink to be social, you're not a "social drinker."

But the final criterion is that when people are just social drinkers, alcohol isn't causing problems for them or the people around them. . . .

It is generally acknowledged that alcoholism is characterized by four main symptoms, all of which have become evident by the dependent stage. These symptoms are the only characteristics common to all alcoholics.

Preoccupation. This includes the anticipation of drinking at certain times of the day (watching the clock for lunch break, waiting for the end of the work day to go home and drink), and/or as the primary factor in other kinds of activities (for example, waiting for a party or weekend when a lot of drinking will take place, or planning a vacation that is anticipated as a drinking binge). It also means the growing need for alcohol during times of stress, whether it's work or family-related, or times of celebration. It includes taking precautions never to run out of a supply of alcohol.

Rigidity around use. The alcoholic will have set times during the day or week for drinking. I was a binge drinker, and Wednesday was my big day. Some people never drink on workdays, so they don't believe they have a problem. Some people binge only one month of the year. What is important is that if they're alcoholic, they won't tolerate interference with their drinking. If the original reason for drinking doesn't materialize (a party is canceled), the alcoholic will find another way to drink at that particular time. . . .

Drinking Alone

Because of his rigidity, the alcoholic will limit his social activities only to those that involve drinking. He won't go anywhere where he might be without a supply. If he doesn't have sufficient opportunity to drink his "quota" in public, he may begin to drink alone.

Growing tolerance. Alcoholics develop the well-known "wooden leg" syndrome, and are able to hold liquor without showing it. As the disease progresses, they need more and more to get the euphoric effect, of course. So they also find ways to take in larger amounts without being obvious. They may gulp drinks, order stiffer drinks, order the next round before the present one is finished, act as the bartender at parties, drink before a social engagement, buy alcohol in greater quantities. They begin to use alcohol medicinally.

Loss of control. This includes everything from morning to binge drinking, drinking more than planned, and increased blackouts. The loss of control due to repeated chemical use results in harmful consequences. The alcoholic may drive while drunk, drink while pregnant, subject others to verbal or physical abuse, and violate his or her own moral standards with actions such as adultery or stealing. . . .

By the fourth phase—drinking to feel normal—tolerance is usually reduced. Your body is in such poor physical condition that it can't handle large amounts anymore. But all the other symptoms are present and heightened. The alcoholic has lost all power over his use, becomes paranoid, guilt-ridden, self-hating, lonely, possibly even suicidal. If you can see many obvious signs that he's in trouble, you can help him before he gets to this point.

Mary Ellen Pinkham is a columnist for Family Circle *and* The Star.

"What seems compassion when done in the name of 'disease' turns out . . . to subvert the drinker's autonomy and will to change."

Alcoholism Is Not a Disease

Herbert Fingarette

The idea that alcoholism is a disease is a myth, and a harmful myth at that. The phrase itself—"alcoholism is a disease"—is a slogan. It lacks definite medical meaning and therefore precludes one from taking any scientific attitude toward it, pro or con. But the slogan has political potency. And it is associated in the public consciousness with a number of beliefs about heavy drinking that do have meaning, and do have important consequences for the treatment of individuals and for social policy. These beliefs lack a scientific foundation; most have been decisively refuted by the scientific evidence.

This assertion obviously conflicts with the barrage of pronouncements in support of alcoholism's classification as a disease by health professionals and organizations such as the American Medical Association, by the explosively proliferating treatment programs, and by innumerable public-service organizations. So it may seem that a sweeping challenge to the disease concept can only be hyperbole, the sensationalist exaggeration of a few partial truths and a few minor doubts.

To the contrary: the public has been profoundly misled, and is still being actively misled. Credulous media articles have featured so many dramatic human-interest anecdotes by "recovering alcoholics," so many "scientific" pronouncements about medical opinion and new discoveries, that it is no wonder the lay public responds with trusting belief.

Public Unaware

Yet this much is unambiguous and incontrovertible: the public has been kept unaware of a mass of scientific evidence accumulated over the past couple of decades, evidence familiar to researchers in the field, which radically challenges each major belief generally associated in the public mind with the phrase, "alcoholism is a disease." I refer not to isolated experiments or off-beat theories but to massive, accumulated, mainstream scientific work by leading authorities, published in recognized journals. If the barrage of "public service" announcements leaves the public wholly unaware of this contrary evidence, shouldn't this in itself raise grave questions about the credibility of those who assure the public that alcoholism has now been scientifically demonstrated to be a disease?

One may wonder why it is important whether or not alcoholism is a disease. To begin with, "disease" is the word that triggers provision of health-insurance payments, employment benefits such as paid leave and workmen's compensation, and other government benefits. The direct cost of treatment for the "disease" of alcoholism is rapidly rising, already exceeding a billion dollars annually. Add in all related health costs and other kinds of benefits, and the dollar figure is well into the tens of billions annually. Alcoholism is, of course, profoundly harmful, both to the drinkers themselves and to others. But if it ceased to be characterized as a disease, all the disease-oriented methods of treatment and resulting expenditures would be threatened; this in turn would threaten the material interests of hundreds of thousands of alcoholics and treatment staffers who receive these billions in funds. The other side of the coin would be many billions in savings for taxpayers and those who pay insurance premiums.

It is not surprising that the disease concept of alcoholism is now vigorously promoted by a vast network of lobbies, national and local, professional and volunteer, ranging from the most prestigious medical associations to the most crassly commercial private, profit-making providers of treatment. This is big politics and big business.

Use of the word "disease" also shapes the values and attitudes of society. The selling of the disease

Herbert Fingarette, "Alcoholism: The Mythical Disease," *The Public Interest*, Spring 1988. Reprinted with the author's permission.

concept of alcoholism has led courts, legislatures, and the populace generally to view damage caused by heavy drinkers as a product of "the disease and not the drinker." The public remains ambivalent about this, and the criminal law continues to resist excusing alcoholics for criminal acts. But the pressure is there, and, of more practical importance, the civil law has largely given in. Civil law now often mandates leniency or complete absolution for the alcoholic from the rules, regulations, and moral norms to which non-diseased persons are held legally or morally accountable. Such is the thrust of a current appeal to the U.S. Supreme Court by two veterans, who are claiming certain benefits in spite of their having failed to apply for them at any time during the legally specified ten-year period after discharge from the army. Their excuse: alcoholism, and the claim that their persistent heavy drinking was a disease entitling them to exemption from the regulations. The Court's decision could be a bellwether.

"Our current disease-oriented policies have not reduced the scale of the problem; in fact, the number of chronic heavy drinkers reported keeps rising."

What seems compassion when done in the name of "disease" turns out, when the facts are confronted, to subvert the drinker's autonomy and will to change, and to exacerbate a serious social problem. This is because the excuses and benefits offered heavy drinkers work psychologically as incentives to continue drinking. The doctrine that the alcoholic is "helpless" delivers the message that he might as well drink, since he lacks the ability to refrain. As for the expensive treatments, they do no real good. Certainly our current disease-oriented policies have not reduced the scale of the problem; in fact, the number of chronic heavy drinkers reported keeps rising. (It is currently somewhere in the range of ten to twenty million, depending on the definitions one uses.) . . .

Conventional Wisdom

Science, according to the conventional view, has established that there is a specific disease that is triggered by drinking alcoholic beverages. Not everyone is susceptible; most people are not. But (the argument continues) a significant minority of the population has a distinctive biological vulnerability, an "allergy" to alcohol. For these people, to start drinking is to start down a fatal road. The stages are well-defined and develop in regular order, as with any disease, with the symptoms accumulating and becoming increasingly disabling and demoralizing. First comes what looks like normal social drinking, but then, insidiously and inevitably, come heavier and more frequent drinking, drunken bouts, secret drinking, morning drinking, and, after a while, "blackouts" of memory from the night before. It begins to take more and more liquor to get the same effect—physical "tolerance" develops—and any attempt to stop drinking brings on the unbearable and potentially life-threatening "withdrawal" symptoms. Eventually, the crucial symptom develops: "loss of control." At that point, whenever the person takes a drink, the alcohol automatically triggers an inability to control the drinking, and drunken bouts become the rule. There follows an inevitable, deepening slavery to alcohol, which wrecks social life, brings ruin, and culminates in death. The only escape—according to this elaborate myth—is appropriate medical treatment for the disease.

The myth offers the false hope that as a result of recent "breakthroughs" in science we now basically understand what causes the disease—a genetic and neurophysiological defect. But fortunately, it is claimed, medical treatment is available, and generally produces excellent results. However, the argument continues, even after successful treatment the alcoholic can never drink again. The "allergy" is never cured; the disease is in remission, but the danger remains. The lifelong truth for the alcoholic is, as the saying goes, "one drink—one drunk." The possibility of a normal life depends on complete abstinence from alcohol. There are no "cured" alcoholics, only "recovering" ones.

That is the classical disease concept of alcoholism. As I have said, just about every statement in it is either known to be false or (at a minimum) lacks scientific foundation. . . .

Even if the disease concept lacks a scientific foundation, mightn't it nevertheless be a useful social "white lie," since it causes alcoholics to enter treatment? This common—and plausible—argument suffers from two fatal flaws.

First, it disregards the effects of this doctrine on the large number of heavy drinkers who do not plan to enter treatment. Many of these heavy drinkers see themselves (often correctly) as not fitting the criteria of "alcoholism" under some current diagnostic formula. The inference they draw is that they are therefore not ill, and thus have no cause for concern. Their inclination to deny their problems is thus encouraged. This can be disastrous, since persistent heavy drinking is physically, mentally, and often socially destructive.

No Treatment

Furthermore, since most people diagnosable as alcoholics today do not enter treatment, the disease concept insidiously provides an incentive to keep drinking heavily. For those many alcoholics who do not enter treatment and who (by definition) want very much to have a drink, the disease doctrine assures them that they might as well do so, since an effort to refrain is doomed anyway.

Moreover, a major implication of the disease concept, and a motive for promoting it, is that what is labeled "disease" is held to be excusable because involuntary. Special benefits are provided alcoholics in employment, health, and civil-rights law. The motivation behind this may be humane and compassionate, but what it does functionally is to reward people who continue to drink heavily. This is insidious: the only known way to have the drinker stop drinking is to establish circumstances that provide a motivation to stop drinking, not an excuse to continue. The U.S. Supreme Court currently faces this issue in two cases before it. And the criminal courts have thus far resisted excusing alcoholics from criminal responsibility for their misconduct. But it's difficult to hold this line when the AMA insists the misconduct is involuntary.

The second flaw in the social "white lie" argument is the mistaken assumption that use of the word "disease" leads alcoholics to seek a medical treatment that works. In fact, medical treatment for alcoholism is ineffective. Medical authority has been abused for the purpose of enlisting public faith in a useless treatment for which Americans have paid more than a billion dollars. To understand why the treatment does no good, we should recall that many different kinds of studies of alcoholics have shown substantial rates of so-called "natural" improvement. As a 1986 report concludes, "the vast majority of [addicted] persons who change do so on their own." This "natural" rate of improvement, which varies according to class, age, socioeconomic status, and certain other psychological and social variables, lends credibility to the claims of success made by programs that "treat" the "disease" of alcoholism.

Many of the clients—and, in the expensive programs, almost all of the clients—are middle-class, middle-aged people, who are intensely motivated to change, and whose families and social relations are still intact. Many, often most, are much improved by the time they complete the program. They are, of course, delighted with the change; they paid money and went through an emotional ordeal, and now receive renewed affection and respect from their family, friends, and co-workers. They had been continually told during treatment that they were helpless, and that only treatment could save them. Many of them fervently believe that they could never have been cured without the treatment.

The Sound and the Fury

The sound and the fury signify nothing, however; for the rates of improvement in these disease-oriented treatment programs do not significantly differ from the natural rates of improvement for comparable but untreated demographic groups. That

is to say, these expensive programs (which cost between $5,000 and $20,000) contribute little or nothing to the improvement. Even so, the claims that patients leave their programs improved are true; to the layman such claims are impressive. The reality, however, is less impressive, since over half a dozen major studies in the past two decades have concluded that the money, time, and trust expended on these treatments are badly spent.

"Alcoholism is not a disease; the assumption of personal responsibility, however, is a sign of health, while needless submission to spurious medical authority is a pathology."

There is some disagreement about the effectiveness of more modest forms of treatment. Some reports—for example, a major study done by Leonard Saxe and his colleagues for the Congressional Office of Technology Assessment—conclude that no single method of treatment is superior to any other (a judgment made by all the major studies). But according to the Saxe study, the data appear to show that "treatment seems better than no treatment." That is, some help-oriented intervention of any kind—it doesn't matter which—may contribute modestly to improvement. The now classic British experiment led by Griffith Edwards showed that an hour or so of firm and sensible advice produced overall results as good as those produced by a full year of the most complete and sophisticated treatment procedures in a first-class alcoholism hospital and clinic. Such conclusions have led a number of authorities (including a World Health Organization committee in 1980) to argue for brief informal counseling on an outpatient basis as the preferred method in most cases.

Note, however, that what is now recommended is not really *medical* treatment. Physicians may still control it, and the institutional setting may be "outpatient," but the assistance provided is merely brief, informal, common-sense advice. The medical setting merely adds unnecessary expense.

So much for the optimistic view about "treatment." A British report concludes that "it seems likely that treatment may often be quite puny in its powers in comparison to the sum of [non-treatment] forces."

The more pessimistic reading of the treatment-outcome data is that these elaborate treatments for alcoholism as a disease have no measurable impact at all. In a review of a number of different long-term studies of treatment programs, George Vaillant states that "there is compelling evidence that the results of our treatment were no better than the natural history of the disease." Reviewing other major treatment programs with long-term follow-ups, he remarks that the best that can be said is that these programs do no harm.

New Approaches

In recent years, early evaluation studies have been reexamined from a non-disease perspective, which has produced interesting results. For example, it appears that the heaviest and longest-term drinkers improve more than would be expected "naturally" when they are removed from their daily routine and relocated, with complete abstinence as their goal. This group is only a small subset of those diagnosable as alcoholics, of course. The important point, though, is that it is helpful to abandon the one-disease, one-treatment approach, and to differentiate among the many different patterns of drinking, reasons for drinking, and modes of helping drinkers.

Indeed, when we abandon the single-entity disease approach and view alcoholism pluralistically, many new insights and strategies emerge. For example, much depends on the criteria of success that are used. The disease concept focuses attention on only one criterion—total, permanent abstinence. Only a small percentage of alcoholics ever achieve this abolitionist goal. But a pluralistic view encourages us to value other achievements, and to measure success by other standards. Thus, marked improvement is quite common when one takes as measures of success additional days on the job, fewer days in the hospital, smaller quantities of alcohol drunk, more moderate drinking on any one occasion, and fewer alcohol-related domestic problems or police incidents. The Rand Report found that about 42 percent of heavy drinkers with withdrawal symptoms had reverted to somewhat more moderate drinking with no associated problems at the end of four years. Yet, as non-abstainers, they would count as failures from the disease-concept standpoint.

The newer perspective also suggests a different conception of the road to improvement. Instead of hoping for a medical magic bullet that will cure the disease, the goal here is to change the way drinkers live. One should learn from one's mistakes, rather than viewing any one mistake as a proof of failure or a sign of doom. Also consistent with the newer pluralistic, non-disease approach is the selection of specific strategies and tactics for helping different sorts of drinkers; methods and goals are tailored to the individual in ways that leave the one-disease, one-treatment approach far behind. . . .

In any case, the goal of total abstinence insisted upon by advocates of the disease concept is not a proven successful alternative, since only a small minority achieves it. If doubt remains as to whether the controversy over controlled drinking is fueled by non-scientific factors, that doubt can be dispelled by realizing that opposition to controlled drinking (like support for the disease concept of alcoholism) is largely confined to the U.S. and to countries dominated by American intellectual influence. Most physicians in Britain, for example, do not adhere to the disease concept of alcoholism. And the goal of controlled drinking—used selectively but extensively—is widely favored in Canada and the United Kingdom. British physicians have little professional or financial incentive to bring problem drinkers into their consulting rooms or hospitals. American physicians, in contrast, defend an enormous growth in institutional power and fee-for-service income. The selling of the term "disease" has been the key to this vast expansion of medical power and wealth in the United States.

"Instead of hoping for a medical magic bullet that will cure the disease, the goal here is to change the way drinkers live."

What should our attitude be, then, to the long-term heavy drinker? Alcoholics do not knowingly make the wicked choice to be drunkards. Righteous condemnation and punitive moralism are therefore inappropriate. Compassion, not abuse, should be shown toward any human being launched upon a destructive way of life. But compassion must be realistic: it is not compassionate to encourage drinkers to deny their power to change, to assure them that they are helpless and dependent on others, to excuse them legally and give them special government benefits that foster a refusal to confront the need to change. Alcoholics are not helpless; they can take control of their lives. In the last analysis, alcoholics must *want* to change and *choose* to change. To do so they must make many difficult daily choices. We can help them by offering moral support and good advice, and by assisting them in dealing with their genuine physical ailments and social needs. But we must also make it clear that heavy drinkers must take responsibility for their own lives. Alcoholism is not a disease; the assumption of personal responsibility, however, is a sign of health, while needless submission to spurious medical authority is a pathology.

Herbert Fingarette is a philosopher at the University of California at Santa Barbara.

viewpoint **12**

Alcoholism Should Be Treated as a Disease

G. Douglas Talbott

Alcohol is a drug, and if you are addicted to alcohol, you are an alcoholic. Alcohol is a compound—C_2H_5OH—an etherlike substance, a sedative hypnotic drug. At the Ridgeview Institute I don't let the nurses talk about anybody being drunk or intoxicated. They have to say, "Dr. Talbott, you have a drug O.D. out front."

Your brain has no more idea than a pussycat's does whether you O.D.'d on alcohol, meprobamate, Miltown, Equanil, Phenobarbital, Valium, Librium, or any one of dozens of other sedative hypnotic drugs. The brain gets the same message from sleeping pills and tranquilizers as it does from the beverage alcohol. But America isn't ready to look at that yet.

If you take a bottle of beer or wine or any kind of alcoholic beverage—scotch, bourbon, after-dinner liqueurs, gin, vodka—whatever alcoholic beverage you want—take away the color and the taste, stick in a spigot, and drip off the water, you have ether. The body and the brain have no idea whether you're in an operating room, breathing ether from a mask on your face, or in a field drinking beer. The chemical message to the body and brain is the same.

The majority of Americans drink because America's culture is a drinking one. Probably 140 to 150 million people in this country drink.

Approximately 22 million Americans, one out of seven, are drinking alcoholically. This figure is based on my own research with the Baltimore Alcohol Program and our research at the Ridgeview Institute. Other studies agree with this figure.

The old figure was 10 million alcoholics. I was interested in where that figure came from and found it was thought up one night in Washington when the first alcohol support bill was presented to Congress.

Senator Harold Hughes asked his staff what a good number was. They said 10 million, and that figure got frozen into literature. It is way beyond that now, and, as far as we are concerned, 22 million people have an alcohol problem related to the disease of alcoholism.

An alcoholic is an individual who compulsively uses alcohol as it destroys his or her life and who displays other symptoms, such as withdrawal, blackouts, and changing tolerance.

The ultimate consequences for a drinking alcoholic are these three: he or she will end up in a jail, in a hospital, or in a graveyard. These consequences will always threaten.

Alcoholism is a chronic, progressive disease, the same way that tuberculosis and diabetes are chronic, progressive diseases. We talk of alcoholism in four stages: first using, then abusing, then crossing the wall, then developing the disease.

The disease is manifested by the compulsion to use even as the using destroys your life. In this country, it normally takes anywhere from ten to fifteen years to go through the stages. People generally use for five or seven years, abuse for three to five years, and take two years to cross the wall.

You can't become an alcoholic overnight any more than you can contract any of the other progressive diseases overnight. A person with rheumatoid arthritis doesn't end up in a wheelchair a week after developing some vague pains in the joints. It may take years. The loss of control that signals alcoholism may start when a person overdrinks at one party and then continues to do that for several years.

Imposing Limits

In their early teens, people begin to go to parties and make plans for the next day. They realize the next morning that they can't pursue those plans because they drank more than they meant to. So, for the first time, they begin to impose limits on themselves: "I'm not going to drink as much tonight because I couldn't go to the movie today."

They try to impose limits on themselves, but they are not successful. They try to impose tighter and tighter limits, saying such things as, "I'm not going to drink whiskey, I'm just going to drink beer." As they continue to try to put constraints on their drinking, it doesn't work. Therefore, they begin to lie about their drinking. They lie first to themselves and then to other people. At the same time, they begin to develop feelings of shame and embarrassment. They begin to hide their drinking. They do such things as drinking before going to parties, so that people won't realize they're drinking so much. The lying, the hiding, the shame—the phenomenon of denial begins to creep in. They begin to change brands and pretty soon they go to extremes of subterfuge and deceit, hiding their liquor.

"As the disease progresses it produces blackouts, which are true drug amnesia."

Now they begin to feel really guilty about their drinking. By this time, the progression, which may have taken place over months or years, is finished. The full-blown feelings of the alcoholic are present, predominantly feelings of loneliness and loss of self-respect and self-worth.

There aren't any lonelier people in the world than alcoholics. Lots of them have pain from the physical trauma of minor falls, which result in broken bones or from withdrawal, but there is no pain more devastating, more excruciating than the pain of loneliness and loss of self-respect. I can remember reading Saint-Exupéry's *Little Prince* a thousand times because I, too, felt as if I was wandering on a desert.

At that point the disease usually manifests itself in a way that begins to affect the individual's life. It begins to affect his family. Unlike heart disease and cancer, which are our two greatest killers, this disease affects the family tremendously. I've never seen an alcoholic without a spousaholic or childaholics or parentaholics. So the family begins to get terribly sick. As the disease progresses it produces blackouts, which are true drug amnesia. The impact on the kids, wife, husband, parents is just tremendous. Very soon it will begin to affect the community. The alcoholic will draw away from the church. The disease will begin to affect the job through absenteeism, injury, or lack of quality work. The individual will begin to fall behind in performance. He may be affected to the point of being fired. This is what I call the target syndrome.

Show me an alcoholic, and I'll show you an individual who has the target syndrome. I named this after the .22 target I used to fire at when I was a child. Regard a target as the skins of an onion. Alcoholics begin to peel off layers. First goes the activity in the church; second goes the activity in the community; third goes the activity with friends, the hobbies and leisure-time activity; fourth goes the activity with peers, people at work, fellow housewives, and so on—people the alcoholic interacts with during an average work day; fifth goes the distant family; sixth goes the nuclear family. Then, suddenly, the alcoholic is in the middle of the target, completely isolated. The only friend he or she can rely on is the bottle. Standing in the center of that target, he is completely de-peoplized. He has layered off every person around like skins off an onion and he is alone. The alcoholic continues to drink because of compulsivity and he fails to recognize the presence of the disease or the consequences of his drinking because of denial. Denial is part of the disease. Denying is different from lying. Denial is self-deception brought about by the lack of self-respect and self-growth. Alcoholics cannot see the nature of the disease as long as denial is there, and the disease itself presents the dilemma that it does because of the compulsion. They continue to drink and the denial gets worse. The combination of the biogenetic compulsion to drink along with the denial, keeps them in the center of the target. Alcoholics drive other people away because the hostility and anger and fear they project won't permit people to come near them. They continually isolate themselves.

The Disease of Loneliness

Alcoholism is the disease of loneliness, the disease of aloneness, and until you get the alcoholic out of the center of that target, he or she is never going to recover. Recovery, of course, is not merely taking away the drug. You have to start there. You take away the drug and lead the alcoholic out of the target syndrome. There is no longer any question that the most effective modality of treatment is not treatment centers. Treatment centers are important, detoxification is important, physicians are important, and nurses are important, but the most therapeutic weapon we've got was started fifty years ago by a physician and a stockbroker and it's called Alcoholics Anonymous (AA). The blueprint to recovery is in the Twelve Steps of AA. There's a pathway spelled out there that helps the alcoholic to come out of the target syndrome, to re-peoplize, and to live in peace and serenity without drugs.

A Re-peoplization Blueprint

There is almost no way to move out of the center of the target without re-peoplization. The Twelve Steps of AA are a re-peoplization blueprint.

What is recovery from alcoholism or drug addiction? It's three things: honesty, sharing, and love. These deal with re-peoplization, and to recover from alcoholism and other drug addictions you have to trust people, be honest with people, share with people, and love people. That will get you away from chemical dependence and give you personal accountability.

Whether you become an alcoholic or not depends on genetic predisposition. We know the reason the compulsivity exists is because of a change in the endorphin and cephalin systems in a primitive portion of the brain. The reason for the disturbance in the biochemistry of the primitive brain is a predisposition. Nobody talks any longer about becoming an alcoholic. You don't become an alcoholic—you are born an alcoholic. You're an alcoholic the day you get out of the uterus. You are like the *Titanic*, waiting till time and circumstance present the iceberg, and then you sink. The days that the alcoholic with the genetic predisposition abuses start his journey toward that iceberg.

It's the genetic predisposition that, if stimulated, causes the compulsion—not volume, dose, or duration of drinking.

It is probably not a single gene that is responsible, but a number of genes. We don't know at this point. America does not look on alcohol as a drug—a lethal addictive drug—and it certainly does not look on alcoholism as a disease. It looks on it as a bad habit, something caused by a lack of will power, a moral or ethical issue. At best, it is seen as symptomatic of an underlying emotional or psychiatric disorder.

But to say that alcoholism is a symptom of an underlying disorder is simply not true. Alcoholics do have severe secondary emotional problems. Of the thousands I've seen, I have practically never seen one who didn't have depression, who didn't have anxiety, anger, grief, who wasn't very lonely, who didn't have tremendous nervousness and insomnia—a tapestry of emotional feelings. But many studies utilizing exquisite psychiatric triage have shown that 90 percent of alcoholics do not have underlying psychiatric disease. We no longer hold to the premise that people who drink too much do so because of underlying psychiatric disorder. Just the opposite is true. Alcoholism is a primary biogenetic disease, and psychiatrists over the past fifty years have traditionally done very badly with it.

An Abnormal State

Disease is an abnormal state of health characterized by specific signs and symptoms. Alcoholism has that. Disease has a chronic, progressive course. Alcoholism has that. We don't know the causes of alcoholism yet. We don't know the causes of heart attacks, diabetes, or cancer, either, but we call them diseases. These diseases cause biochemical and anatomical changes.

Alcoholism does that. It is a primary symptom, not a secondary one. We know that to be true. When anybody says, "Well, disease is a cop-out, it's not really a disease," then I say, "Fine. Let's have it your way and say it's not a disease. Here at Ridgeview Institute for Impaired Physicians, I have five psychiatrists as patients, as alcoholics. Tell me why those five psychiatrists continued to drink compulsively as it destroyed their lives. I can assure you that those five psychiatrists have exquisitely normal psychiatric profiles and yet they continued to drink. Now tell me why. You say it's not a disease and I'm saying, O.K. it's not a disease. Then give me a reason. There has to be one. If not, then they're bad, dumb, evil, weak. Of course, none of those fit."

"It's the genetic predisposition that, if stimulated, causes the compulsion—not volume, dose, or duration of drinking."

Endorphin and cephalin metabolism in the hypothalamic primitive brain center is responsible for the compulsive drinking. Alcoholism is a biogenetic disease with a psychosocial background. Of course you have to abuse. That is where the emotional psychosocial factors come into the disease, but the disease itself is biogenetic.

The medical profession has not recognized alcoholism as a disease until very recently. I had only an hour's lecture on alcoholism in my entire medical school career. We're just getting it into the medical school curriculum. The rate of alcoholism is thirty-five times higher among medical people than among laymen. If you choose to be a physician, dentist, pharmacist, or nurse, it's an occupational hazard. So there is an element of denial in the medical profession. We're talking about ignorance of the disease, denial that it exists. The medical professional has been threatened by AA, even though a physician cofounded the organization. We're trying to educate the medical profession about the importance of using AA as a treatment modality. Because alcoholism is a medical disease, we need physicians to be involved *and* we need detoxification centers. We often need churches, too, because it's important to have a strong spiritual program. We need treatment facilities and holistic treatment teams. We need to use all of the modalities that we can to help bring about recovery.

Alcoholism is the most treatable untreated disease in this country.

Dr. G. Douglas Talbott is the director of the Ridgeview Institute Alcohol and Drug Program in Smyrna, Georgia.

"The disease conception of alcoholism doesn't withstand scientific or philosophical scrutiny."

Alcoholism Should Not Be Treated as a Disease

Robert Wright

"He's a sick person," says Jane Wyman of Ray Milland. "It's as though there were something wrong with his heart or his lungs." The movie is *The Lost Weekend*, and Milland is Don Birnam, an aspiring writer whose potential is stifled only by his perennial willingness to pawn anything, including his typewriter, for enough money to drink himself unconscious. Wyman, Birnam's aspiring fiancée, is explaining why he deserves forgiveness and patience. It's not as though his disintegration were his fault, she's saying; the man has a disease.

The movie, released in 1945, could hardly have been better timed. For the previous ten years, Alcoholics Anonymous had been pushing the idea that alcoholism is a disease, and in 1946, about the time *The Lost Weekend* was winning a fistful of Academy Awards, the idea received the imprimatur of science with the publication of E. M. Jellinek's "Phases in the Drinking History of Alcoholics." Jellinek (who, perhaps not coincidentally, based his study on questionnaires designed and distributed by AA) found that alcoholism follows a roughly predictable pattern, from social drinking through various stages of excess, culminating in secret drinking, blackouts, and other symptoms. For the true alcoholic, Jellinek found, this grim cycle is virtually inexorable, and once he is in its grip, a single drink can destroy all self-control. Salvation lies in accepting that he has a disease—that he will never be able to drink like other people, and complete abstinence is his only alternative to a squalid, perhaps short, life.

With the help of AA (not to mention Jane Wyman), Jellinek's model took root. Today a huge majority of Americans—and of the psychologists, physicians, and other therapists who treat alcoholics—consider alcoholism a disease.

Robert Wright, "Alcohol and Free Will," *The New Republic*, December 14, 1987. Reprinted by permission of THE NEW REPUBLIC, © 1987, The New Republic, Inc.

Still, when this idea's implications are made explicit, the average citizen's enthusiasm for it may cool. Should the insurance premiums of teetotalers and moderate drinkers go to pay for other people's excesses, as they must in the numerous states whose legislatures have dictated that group health insurance cover alcoholism? Should Veterans Administration hospitals and Medicare, amid present fiscal pressures, spend tax dollars on people who can't stay off the bottle? And what is the import of the Federal Rehabilitation Act, which defines alcoholism as a handicap and prohibits federal agencies and federally subsidized institutions from discriminating against the handicapped? . . .

Jellinek's Paper

The rationale for considering alcoholism a disease has evolved since Jellinek's landmark paper. In the forthcoming book *Heavy Drinking*, a formidable critique of alcoholism as a disease, Herbert Fingarette, a philosopher at the University of California, Santa Barbara, shows that research in recent decades has painted a more complex picture than the common phrase "alcohol dependence syndrome" implies. Studies suggest that alcoholics do not, in fact, all follow the same route to dissolution, and that some can even learn to drink moderately; alcoholism, Fingarette argues, is not a single, binary condition whose course is predictable, but a grab bag of different kinds of problems.

In response, defenders of the disease concept say that there may be several kinds of disease under the rubric of alcoholism, just as there are various strains of flu. And, they add, some problem drinkers whose patterns diverge from the norm aren't "real" alcoholics anyway. Still, even as they dismiss Fingarette's criticisms, these people are also doing some strategic repositioning. They are staking their case less to the supposed clinical coherence of alcoholic behavior and more to fresh evidence of that behavior's biological underpinnings.

For instance, some people appear to be genetically predisposed to problem drinking. Alcoholics' children who are adopted by non-alcoholics are several times more likely to become alcoholic than the adopted children of non-alcoholic parents. And studies of identical twins reared apart also point to a genetic factor. Further, there are physiological abnormalities—in biochemistry, and in brain wave patterns under certain laboratory conditions—that occur disproportionately in alcoholics. In fact, some occur disproportionately in the children of alcoholics, even children who have never had a drink. All of this, the argument goes, underscores the soundness of the disease label and the fallacy of blaming alcoholics for their problems. Since the biological deck is stacked against them, it is wrong, as one researcher at the National Council of Alcoholism put it, to label them "moral weaklings."

It is hard to attack this line of argument, because it is hard to discern it clearly in the first place. Some alcoholism-as-disease advocates talk as if the physiological correlates of alcoholism might be causes of the disease, whereas others seem to view them more as biological labels, identifying alcoholics as fundamentally different from the rest of us. To the extent that a unifying theme exists, it is the belief that the more "biological" a given behavior is, the less control the behaver has over it.

This belief does not exactly belong along the frontiers of modern thought. To talk as if some behaviors (the free-will kind) have a purely psychological basis while others (the disease kind) have a partly physiological basis is like distinguishing between election victories due to a candidate's popular support and victories due to the number of votes received. It is a basic, if usually unspoken, tenet of modern behavioral science that physiological and psychological processes are not alternative explanations of behavior but parallel explanations. We presume that all aspects of subjective experience—ideas, emotions, epiphanies, cravings—have physiological counterparts; that every behavior, while explicable in terms of thoughts and feelings, could also be explained as the result of a particular flow of neuronal, hormonal, and other biochemical information; that all behavior is in the deepest sense physically compelled. This is just an assumption, of course, but it is an assumption central to science, and research in neurology, psychology, and genetics has tended to substantiate it.

Indeed, so has the very fact that many alcoholics have a characteristic brain-wave pattern; they have characteristic patterns of behavior and sensation, so any good scientific materialist would suspect the existence of characteristic physiological patterns. Granted, if the physiological patterns were neater and cleaner than the behavioral patterns, then the

alcoholism-as-disease crowd could take heart; if there were a physiological abnormality that all alcoholics and no non-alcoholics possessed, then the claim that alcoholism is a single, coherent syndrome would be in some measure strengthened. But so far the physiological evidence is fragmented, just like the behavioral evidence: some alcoholics have this unusual trait, others have that one, and others have none. And all of these physiological traits can be found, with less frequency, in the non-alcoholic population.

> "To say that alcoholism has a heritable component is not to say that alcoholism is ever preordained by the genes."

Alcoholism-as-disease proponents may think this sermon about the philosophy of behavioral science pedantic and beside the point. The point, they will say, is that the physiological correlates of alcoholism, like the alcoholic behaviors themselves, appear to be, in some cases, hereditary. Alcoholics, in other words, are born, not made. Strictly speaking, of course, this isn't true. To say that alcoholism has a heritable component is not to say that alcoholism is ever preordained by the genes. It is to say that some people who inherit alcoholics' genes have a genetic predisposition toward heavy drinking, that the range of circumstances that will lead to alcoholism is broader for them than for most people.

Deepen Compassion

Now, it may be that this fact should deepen our compassion for alcoholics. But if it qualifies them as disease victims, and leaves them blameless for their behavior, then for the sake of consistency we are going to have to begin cutting down on the use of blame generally—and of credit. For there is now evidence that genes can similarly predispose people toward violent behavior, stellar intellectual achievement, and various other things. So should we consider violence a "disease" and exonerate murderers? Should we withhold praise from great mathematicians because their genes gave them a head start?

And these questions are just the beginning of the trouble. Science appears to be on the verge of perceiving a host of obscure connections between genes and behavior. Fingernail biting, reading pulp novels, altruism, entrepreneurship—thousands of such behaviors, some trivial and some consequential, may well turn out to vary according to genes. And even those behaviors not linked in this way will turn out to be under short-term physiological control, as the complex network of biochemical influences comes into focus. So if we are going to follow the alcoholism-as-disease logic, and equate genetic inclinations and physiological influences with the surrendering of volition, then we are going to have to give up on the concept of volition altogether. It is redundantly true that the more we understand about the mechanics of behavior, the more deterministic behavior will seem. (And it is worth noting that, notwithstanding the aversion of free-will aficionados to genetic explanations of behavior, it won't really matter whether the determinism appears to be mostly genetic or mostly environmental. When it comes to the question of free will, determinism is determinism is determinism.)

The alcoholism-as-disease advocates sometimes show encouraging signs of understanding all this, but they never seem to grasp its generality. . . . The National Council of Alcoholism argues, ''Whether any particular individual who drinks will become an alcoholic is largely the result of forces beyond his or her control. Extensive research has demonstrated that the disease of alcoholism is produced by a confluence of genetic/biochemical, environmental, and sociocultural factors.'' Can anyone think of a behavior that doesn't fit that description?

My point is not that we should abandon the concepts of blame and credit. Whatever science seems to say about the deterministic nature of human behavior, the inescapable fact is that no society can function well without holding people responsible for their actions. This is one of life's four or five great ironies: we are all victims of (or beneficiaries of) an extremely complex conspiracy between our genes and our environment, yet all of us must be held accountable for the results; otherwise, things fall apart. So, as the march of science yields more and more evidence that people are basically machines, we are going to have to get used to the idea of blaming robots for their malfunctions. It feels strange at first, but you get used to it after a while.

Useful Fiction

There are those who concede that the disease conception of alcoholism doesn't withstand scientific or philosophical scrutiny yet insist on preserving it as a ''useful fiction.'' They say that (a) by absolving alcoholics of blame, this fiction keeps them from being saddled with ''irrational guilt feelings,'' and (b) the word ''disease'' underscores the importance of abstinence. The obvious responses are: (a) What's so irrational about feeling guilty when you're flushing your life down the toilet and bringing your family along for the ride? For every alcoholic who is immobilized by guilt, there are probably several who use the ''disease'' idea to insulate themselves from the guilt that might otherwise incite a recovery; (b) People have been known to abstain completely from things—coffee, for example—without first concluding that they had a disease. AA could drop the word

''disease'' without appreciably altering its prescription for recovery.

Perhaps the most common ''useful fiction'' argument is that the disease conception of alcoholism keeps the treatment funds (now totaling an estimated $1 billion a year) flowing—from the government, from health insurance companies, from paternalistic corporations. Of course, the people most vociferously advancing this argument pay their rent with these funds, thus casting some doubt on their objectivity. Moreover, in *Heavy Drinking*, Fingarette shows that the efficacy of treatment programs remains unclear; because many treatment centers deal with precisely those patients who are most likely to recover on their own—the affluent, employed, and well-educated—seemingly impressive recovery statistics often mean less than meets the eye.

''For every alcoholic who is immobilized by guilt, there are probably several who use the 'disease' idea to insulate themselves from the guilt.''

None of this is to say that corporations and insurance companies should stop pouring money into alcoholism treatment, or that alcoholic veterans shouldn't receive free therapy. Perhaps objective analysis—that is, analysis performed by someone other than the treatment industry's hired guns— would show that, given the costs and the benefits, it's often cheaper in the long run to subsidize certain kinds of treatment. (And certainly a socially inexpensive effort like AA is worth the trouble.) But this analysis shouldn't be short-circuited by the groundless presupposition that alcoholism is a disease in the sense that cancer is or a handicap in the sense that blindness is.

The treatment-industry spokesmen who are always waving around those suspiciously large estimates of the societal costs of untreated alcoholism like to maintain that they're not trying to tug at anyone's heartstrings. ''We're talking dollars and cents,'' the director of the National Association of Addiction Treatment Providers told me. ''We want to get beyond the compassion issue.'' Well, fine; let's get beyond it. The first step is to quit using the word ''disease''—which, all told, is just a crutch.

Robert Wright is the editor of New Republic Books.

The Case for Alcoholics Anonymous

Alcoholics Anonymous

We in A.A. are men and women who have discovered, and admitted, that we cannot control alcohol. We have learned that we must live without it if we are to avoid disaster for ourselves and those close to us.

With local groups in thousands of communities, we are part of an informal international fellowship, which now has members in 110 countries. We have but one primary purpose: to stay sober ourselves and to help others who may turn to us for help in achieving sobriety.

We are not reformers, and we are not allied with any group, cause, or religious denomination. We have no wish to dry up the world. We do not recruit new members, but do welcome them. We do not impose our experience with problem drinking on others, but we do share it when we are asked to do so.

Within our membership may be found men and women of all ages and many different social, economic, and cultural backgrounds. Some of us drank for many years before coming to the realization we could not handle alcohol. Others were fortunate enough to appreciate, early in life or in their drinking careers, that alcohol had become unmanageable.

The consequences of our alcoholic drinking have also varied. A few of us had become derelicts before turning to A.A. for help. Some had lost family, possessions, and self-respect. We had been on skid row in many cities. Some of us had been hospitalized or jailed times without number. We had committed grave offenses—against society, our families, our employers, and ourselves.

Others among us have never been jailed or hospitalized. Nor had we lost jobs or families through drinking. But we finally came to a point

Alcoholics Anonymous, *This is A.A.* New York: Alcoholics Anonymous Publishing Inc., 1984. Reprinted with permission of Alcoholics Anonymous World Services, Inc.

where we realized that alcohol was interfering with normal living. When we discovered that we could not live without alcohol, we, too, sought help through A.A.

All the great faiths are represented in our Fellowship, and many religious leaders have encouraged our growth. There are even a few self-proclaimed atheists and agnostics among us. Belief in, or adherence to, a formal creed is not a condition of membership.

We are united by our common problem, alcohol. Meeting and talking and helping other alcoholics *together*, we are somehow able to stay sober and to lose the compulsion to drink, once a dominant force in our lives.

We do not think we are the only people who have the answer to problem drinking. We know that the A.A. program works for us, and we have seen it work for every newcomer, almost without exception, who honestly and sincerely wanted to quit drinking.

Through A.A., we have learned a number of things about alcoholism and about ourselves. We try to keep these facts fresh in our thinking at all times, because they seem to be the key to our sobriety. For us, sobriety must always come first.

What We Have Learned About Alcoholism

While there is no formal "A.A. definition" of alcoholism, most of us agree that, for us, it could be described as a *physical compulsion, coupled with a mental obsession.* We mean that we had a distinct physical desire to consume alcohol beyond our capacity to control it, and in defiance of all rules of common sense. We not only had an abnormal craving for alcohol, but we frequently yielded to it at the worst possible times. We did not know when (or how) to stop drinking. Often, we did not seem to have sense enough to know when not to begin.

As alcoholics, we have learned the hard way that willpower alone, however strong in other respects, was not enough to keep us sober. We have tried going on the wagon for specified periods. We have taken solemn pledges. We have switched brands and beverages. We have tried drinking only during certain hours. But none of our plans worked. We always wound up, sooner or later, by getting drunk when we not only wanted to stay sober, but had every rational incentive for staying sober.

We have gone through stages of dark despair when we were sure that there was something wrong with us mentally. We came to hate ourselves for wasting the talents with which we had been endowed and for the trouble we were causing our families and others. Frequently, we indulged in self-pity and proclaimed that nothing could ever help us.

We can smile at those recollections now, but at the time they were grim, unpleasant experiences.

Alcoholism a Disease

Today we are willing to accept the idea that, as far as we are concerned, alcoholism is an illness, a progressive illness which can never be "cured," but which, like some other illnesses, *can* be arrested. We agree that there is nothing shameful about having an illness, provided we face the problem honestly and try to do something about it. We are perfectly willing to admit that we are allergic to alcohol and that it is simply common sense to stay away from the source of our allergy.

A.A. has a way of expressing this: "For an alcoholic, one drink is too many and a thousand are not enough."

Another thing that many of us learned during our drinking days was that enforced sobriety was generally not a very pleasant experience. Some of us were able to stay sober, occasionally, for periods of days, weeks, and even years. But we did not enjoy our sobriety. We felt like martyrs. We became irritable, difficult to live and work with. We persisted in looking forward to the time when we might be able to drink again.

Now that we are in A.A., we have a new outlook on sobriety. We enjoy a sense of release, a feeling of freedom from even the desire to drink. Since we cannot expect to drink normally at any time in the future, we concentrate on living a full life without alcohol *today*. There is not a thing we can do about yesterday. And tomorrow never comes. Today is the only day we have to worry about. And we know from experience that even the "worst" drunks can go twenty-four hours without a drink. They may need to postpone that next drink to the next hour, even the next minute—but they learn that it *can* be put off for a period of time.

When we first heard about A.A., it seemed miraculous that anyone who had really been an uncontrolled drinker could ever achieve and maintain the kind of sobriety that older A.A. members talked about. Some of us were inclined to think that ours was a special kind of drinking, that our experiences had been "different," that A.A. might work for others, but that it could do nothing for us. Others among us, who had not yet been hurt seriously by our drinking, reasoned that A.A. might be fine for the skid row drunks, but that we could probably handle the problem by ourselves.

"The A.A. recovery program works for any alcoholic who honestly wants it to work."

Our experience in A.A. has taught us two important things. First, all alcoholics face the same basic problems, whether they are panhandling for the price of a short beer or holding down an executive position in a big corporation. Second, we now appreciate that the A.A. recovery program works for almost *any* alcoholic who honestly wants it to work, no matter what the individual's background or particular drinking pattern may have been.

We Made a Decision

All of us now in A.A. had to make one crucial decision before we felt secure in the new program of life without alcohol. We had to face the facts about ourselves and our drinking realistically and honestly. *We had to admit* that we were powerless over alcohol. For some of us, this was the toughest proposition we had ever faced.

We did not know too much about alcoholism. We had our own idea about the word "alcoholic." We tied it up with the down-and-out derelict. We thought it surely meant weakness of will, weakness of character. Some of us fought off the step of admitting that we were alcoholics. Others only partially admitted it.

Most of us, however, were relieved when it was explained to us that alcoholism was an illness. We saw the common sense of doing something about an illness that threatened to destroy us. We quit trying to deceive others—and ourselves—into thinking that we could handle alcohol when all the facts pointed the other way.

We were assured from the beginning that no one could tell us we were alcoholics. The admission had to come from us—not from a doctor or minister or wife or husband. It had to be based on facts which we ourselves knew. Our friends might understand the nature of our problem, but we were the only ones who could tell for sure whether or not our drinking was out of control. . . .

We began to wonder what we had to do to stay sober, what membership in A.A. would cost, and who ran the organization, locally and worldwide. We soon discovered that there are no musts in A.A., that no one is required to follow any formal ritual or pattern of living. We learned also that A.A. has no dues or fees of any kind; expenses of meeting rooms, refreshments, and literature are met by passing the hat. But even contributions of this kind are not a requirement for membership.

It soon became apparent to us that A.A. has only a minimum of organization and has nobody giving orders. Arrangements for meetings are handled by group officers who move on regularly to make room for new people. This "rotation" system is very popular in A.A.

How, then, do we manage to stay sober in such an informal, loosely knit fellowship?

The answer is that, once having achieved sobriety, we try to preserve it by observing and following the successful experience of those who have preceded us in A.A.

Their experience provides certain "tools" and guides which we are free to accept or reject, as we may choose. Because our sobriety is the most important thing in our lives today, we think it wise to follow the patterns suggested by those who have already demonstrated that the A.A. recovery program really works. . . .

'Twelve Steps'

Early in our association with A.A. we heard about the "Twelve Steps" of recovery from alcoholism. We learned that these Steps represented an attempt by the first members to record their own progress from uncontrolled drinking to sobriety. We discovered that a key factor in this progress seemed to be humility, coupled with reliance upon a Power greater than ourselves. While some members prefer to call this Power "God," we were told that this was purely a matter of personal interpretation; we could conceive of the Power in any terms we thought fit. Since alcohol had obviously been a power greater than ourselves during our drinking days, we had to admit that perhaps we could not run the whole show ourselves and that it made sense to turn elsewhere for help. As we have grown in A.A., our concept of a greater Power has usually become more mature. But it has always been our own personal concept; no one has forced it upon us.

"No one is required to follow any formal ritual or pattern of living."

Finally, we noted from the Twelfth Step and from the experience of older members, that work with other alcoholics who turned to A.A. for help was an effective way of strengthening our own sobriety. Whenever possible, we tried to do our share, always keeping in mind that the other person was the only

one who could determine whether or not he or she was an alcoholic. . . .

Will A.A. Work for Everyone?

The A.A. program of recovery from alcoholism, we believe, will work for almost anyone who has a desire to stop drinking. It may work even for those who feel they are being prodded in the direction of A.A. Many of us made our first contact with A.A. because of social or job pressures. Later, we made our own decision.

We have seen some alcoholics stumble for a while before "getting" the program. We have seen others who made only token efforts to follow the tested principles through which over a million of us now maintain our sobriety; token efforts are generally not enough.

But, no matter how down-and-out an alcoholic may be, or how high he or she may be on the social and economic scales, we know from experience and observation that A.A. offers a sober way out of the squirrel cage of confused problem drinking. Most of us have found it an easy way.

When we first turned to A.A., many of us had a number of serious problems—problems involving money, family, job, and our own personalities. We soon discovered that our immediate central problem was alcohol. Once we had that problem under control, we were able to make successful approaches to the other problems. Solutions to these problems have not always come easily, but we have been able to cope with them far more effectively when sober than we were able to do during our drinking days.

'A New Dimension'

There was a time when many of us believed that alcohol was the only thing that made life bearable. We could not even dream of a life without drinking. Today, through the A.A. program, we do not feel that we have been *deprived* of anything. Rather, we have been *freed* and find that a new dimension has been added to our lives. We have new friends, new horizons, and new attitudes. After years of despair and frustration, many of us feel that we have really begun to live for the first time. We enjoy sharing that new life with anyone who is still suffering from alcoholism, as we once suffered, and who seeks a way out of the darkness and into the light.

Alcoholics Anonymous (AA) is an alcoholic recovery program based on group meetings and a program called the Twelve Steps of recovery which includes admitting powerlessness over alcohol, admitting past failures, and then rectifying those failures. AA is a non-profit, non-denominational group begun in the mid-1930s.

"To argue that A.A. does not require religious convictions is ludicrous."

The Case Against Alcoholics Anonymous

James Christopher

The alcohol/chemical addiction problem in this country is statistically astronomical, and certainly it is tragic. Lives are being wasted all across the land. All sorts of people suffer from these addictions; their relatives, friends, and colleagues are battered emotionally and sometimes physically as well. This cannot be denied; it is our situation, here and now.

Over fifty years ago when two men (an ex-stockbroker and a medical doctor, both alcoholics) started what was to become Alcoholics Anonymous, they brought to light what previously had been shoved under the national rug. They openly acknowledged the problem, ending what had previously amounted to massive collective denial, and offered an answer, a real solution. And for that they deserve applause from all those affected, directly or indirectly, by alcoholism/addiction— applause to the point of bringing blood to the palms. And those affected include just about everyone in the United States and around the globe.

One of these men, Bill Wilson, was inspired by the then soon-to-be-defunct ultra-rigid religious organization called the Oxford Group. He had dropped his personal agnostic stance because of the sudden and powerful religious experience he had there, though he eventually broke away from the group.

Because in those days society viewed alcoholics as pariahs, Bill and "Dr. Bob" built A.A. on a first-name-only basis. The literature of A.A. reflects the widespread belief that the causes of alcoholism are character defects and an unknown factor. The theory was basically this: Put the plug in the jug, turn your will and your life over to the care of God as you understand Him, work on your character defects through A.A.'s twelve-step spiritual program, and carry the message to other alcoholics. Unlike the Oxford Group, members of A.A. did not strive for spiritual perfection. Instead, more realistic spiritual progress was their goal: "We are not saints," reads the Big Book of A.A.

Today, though its founders are deceased, Alcoholics Anonymous remains alive and well—fortunately. However, A.A. is religious (or "spiritual") requiring belief in a mythical higher power, which is a meaningless concept to many free thinkers. Let's face it folks, its founding fathers based the group on their beliefs and, although A.A. apologists try to get around it, A.A. remains a spiritual movement. And that's fine for spiritual people.

The Twelve Steps

Here are the famous twelve steps of Alcoholics Anonymous:

1. We admitted we were powerless over alcohol— that our lives had become unmanageable.
2. Came to believe that a Power greater than ourselves could restore us to sanity.
3. Made a decision to turn our will and our lives over to the care of God as we understand Him.
4. Made a searching and fearless moral inventory of ourselves.
5. Admitted to God, to ourselves, and to another human being the exact nature of our wrongs.
6. Were entirely ready to have God remove all these defects of character.
7. Humbly asked Him to remove our shortcomings.
8. Made a list of all persons we had harmed, and became willing to make amends to them all.
9. Made direct amends to such people wherever possible, except when to do so would injure them or others.
10. Continued to take personal inventory and when we were wrong, promptly admitted it.
11. Sought through prayer and meditation to improve our conscious contact with God as we understand Him, praying only for knowledge of His will for us and the power to carry that out.
12. Having had a spiritual awakening as a result of these steps, we tried to carry this message to alcoholics, and to practice these principles in all our affairs.

Reprinted from *How to Stay Sober: Recovery Without Religion* by James Christopher with permission of Prometheus Books, Buffalo, New York.

My personal thoughts, feelings, and experiences within Alcoholics Anonymous were suppressed on a number of occasions, and A.A. was not particularly fulfilling or supportive to me as an alcoholic free thinker. I had to "go it alone" for many years. But through it all, I kept my sobriety through prioritizing it on a day-to-day basis. There is no higher power keeping me sober. I make this choice and reacknowledge it daily. No one can do it for me.

Many nonreligious persons feel as I do. We are secularists and we choose life over an alcoholic existence that usually culminates in an alcohol-related death. We support each other while realizing that each of us is responsible for his or her own sobriety *no matter what*. Through having experienced years of full-blown alcoholism, our addiction potential is etched in our brains; active physiological addiction can remain arrested as long as we do not ingest mind-altering chemicals.

"A.A. was not particularly fulfilling or supportive to me as an alcoholic free thinker."

Grass-roots Secular Sobriety Groups offer an alternative or supplement to Alcoholics Anonymous, though both speak to this country's undisputed need for solutions to the lightning-speed growth of alcoholism and chemical dependency.

I had been sober almost nine years when I began to seriously consider the need for alternative secular groups that would utilize the sobriety priority rather than dependence upon a mystical higher power as the means to achieve and retain sobriety.

Free Inquiry magazine published an article in which I expressed my frustrations with A.A.'s religiosity and my belief that the needs of free thinkers are not being met there. My article received positive responses from alcoholic secularists across America. So I called my local parks-and-recreation department to inquire about the cost of renting a room one night a week. . . .

Meanwhile, *Free Inquiry*, after receiving favorable responses from around the nation regarding my article, published a piece by Donald Simmermacher entitled "A Humanistic Alternative to Alcoholics Anonymous." Portions of his article follow:

"Sobriety Without Superstition" by James Christopher (FI, Summer 1985) was a refreshing disclosure. As a civilian social worker for the U.S. Air Force Substance Abuse Rehabilitation Program, I am frequently involved with clients who share this view.

Alcoholics Anonymous (A.A.) is religious in nature, and its emphasis on public confession, acts of contrition, and divine intervention is well documented. Most who espouse the A.A. philosophy openly thwart any efforts to introduce more humanistic or secular approaches to the substance-abuse field.

. . . One of my greatest concerns is that A.A., as a religious organization, is being imposed upon individuals as a condition of substance-abuse treatment and rehabilitation. Mandatory attendance at A.A. meetings has become a common practice in treatment programs across the country.

. . . I have witnessed numerous cases in which A.A. has been imposed as a mandatory condition of alcohol-abuse rehabilitation. In one case, an individual was considered to have failed his treatment because of his resistance to attending A.A. and was removed from the Air Force. His prognosis was considered unfavorable because, as stated in the medical summary, "he was unable to find his *Higher Power*" (emphasis mine).

These cases represent just the tip of the iceberg. There are thousands of people forced to attend A.A. even though they do not respond to the religious approach of this self-help group.

. . . The *American Heritage Dictionary* defines "religion" as follows: "The expression of man's belief in a reverence for a superhuman *power* recognized as the creator and governor of the universe . . . the spiritual or emotional attitude of one who recognizes the existence of a superhuman *power* or *powers*" (emphasis mine).

The A.A. process is guided by twelve steps. Six of the twelve clearly refer to the surrender to, or the dependency on, an external higher power.

. . . Anyone who has ever attended A.A. meetings is aware of the "Serenity Prayer" that is said at the beginning of each meeting. The prayer begins with the word "God." Acknowledgement of the existence of God requires belief in a superhuman or supernatural power. The second word of the prayer is "grant," which implies the belief that this *higher power* is a supernatural being or power who can bestow or give to lesser beings.

The Big Book

The book *Alcoholics Anonymous*, or the so-called Big Book, makes frequent reference to the need to believe in God, or a higher power, as a condition of maintaining sobriety and alcohol-abuse recovery.

Many other examples could be given to show that A.A. is indeed religious in nature. Its literature refers to "God," "Him," and "Higher Power." To argue, therefore, that A.A. does not require religious convictions is ludicrous.

. . . A.A. membership is estimated to be somewhere between half a million and one million members. Since there are an estimated ten to twelve million alcoholics in the United States, of them, many may be in need of an alternative recovery program.

. . . A.A. participants are not encouraged to become self-supporting or self-reliant. Their social life is often limited to making friends only with other alcoholics. Some disagree with the concept that members can never move beyond the A.A. group. It can be viewed as the substitution of chemicals for another kind of dependency—the continual A.A. group meeting that becomes a way of life.

. . . Since not all alcoholics or other *drug-abusers may respond favorably to A.A., there is a need to develop secular support groups that can act as alternatives for those who may not be religious*. . . . [Emphasis added.]

I was soon asked to write a second article for *Free Inquiry*, describing the S.S.G. meetings as a secular alternative to A.A. I began to receive many phone calls and letters, all in support of S.S.G. What follows are quotes gleaned from those responses:

I'm an alcoholic. And I was downright joyful to read the article about the Secular Sobriety Groups in *Free Inquiry*. . . . My secular humanism is a commitment that is hardwon and a very serious part of my own belief system, and the "humanist" A.A. meetings were actually more upsetting to me than just to stay home and apply the valid points of the A.A. program to myself for sobriety . . . I don't want to sit and listen to some good-intentioned sober person tell me about how I should just use the A.A. group as a higher power. I'm not interested in any higher power!!! I'm only interested in staying sober as a humanist, *not* as a theist, and I find all the religiously oriented regimens of A.A. meetings very disturbing and counterproductive to my own program of sobriety. . . . Most mainstream A.A. members are convinced one cannot stay sober and enjoy life without being some variety of Christian or believer. The *Free Inquiry* article and news of S.S.G. gives me new hope.

Seeking Sobriety

I am an "active" alcoholic who has been half-heartedly seeking sobriety through A.A. drug treatment centers (with mandatory A.A. attendance). . . . I don't know what I am . . . except a drunk who wishes he were sober. A.A. acquaintances assure me that it's simply a question of my not having hit whatever my "bottom" is to be and that when, inevitably, I do, adherence to the precepts of A.A. will come easily and naturally. Perhaps they are right, but it terrifies me to contemplate how much further down I will have to sink before this occurs . . . and that my "bottom" might be death or irrevocable insanity. . . .

I am not a believer in God or any other higher power in the A.A. sense, and that fact has caused me a *lot* of trouble in A.A., so much so [that] at times the difficulty and the feeling that "I don't fit" in A.A. have jeopardized the little sobriety I have. Despite the A.A. disclaimers, it seems to me that those (such as myself) who do not believe in a higher power as a necessity for sobriety do not fit well in Alcoholics Anonymous. Nevertheless, it almost seems as if A.A. is "the only game in town" for those of us who perceive the [need] for a recovery support group.

I am a secular humanist and I am also an alcoholic. I have nine years of sobriety. But it has been a hard go. I tried A.A. off and on for years and years. But I was very frustrated with all of their higher-power philosophy. I would stay sober for long periods of time, then I would go to an A.A. meeting, and right after these meetings I would go out and get drunk. So A.A. was really worse for me than nothing at all.

I have been concerned about a family member's drinking for some time, but have never before found any support group or treatment center I could even suggest. This person feels very strongly about the mysticism associated with any religon, and I know this person would not have anything to do with A.A.

I am very impressed with the rational intelligence and ethical sensitivity of S.S.G.'s approach. "Ahh, at last, minds I could communicate with, people whose judgment I could respect." Since repudiating Christian religiosity was a primary act of self-liberation and ethical choice in adolescence, I found A.A. so offensive as to be unusable—not even a port in a storm. I've never felt more alienated in my life than at their meetings or when trying to communicate my objections to the twelve-step program to a counselor trained to work hand-in-glove with A.A.

As a humanist I strongly believe in the strengths of the individual. I firmly believe in the resources of the *informed* person against addiction. I certainly understand that the condition (and it is a disease process, *not* an outcome of failures of moral development) *can* reach the point where people need outside help even to realize what has been happening to them and break the cycle. However, once people get help, recognize the illness, I believe that reason, persistence—all the tools of the mind—used to actively search out and find whatever helps the individual— not blindly following someone else's X-step program—will work. In any case it's been working for me this last year and a half.

In one of your articles you mentioned the difficulty of breaking away from A.A. (the grateful syndrome), or questioning, dissenting within A.A. It's not surprising that that's hard to do. The program *teaches* learned helplessness, dependency, a non-questioning (humble) cast of mind.

What I would tell people is "Yes, you have developed this illness. This addictive condition will always be a potential risk for you. Your body needs treatment and support. Your life may have to be put back in order, but there are people who will support you, and many, many things you can do to help yourself. *You* have resources. You're *not* helpless and you're *not* guilty." . . .

"A.A. was really worse for me than nothing at all."

The bottom line for alcoholics is staying sober. Growth is important too, however; alcoholics and nonalcoholics alike must strive to become better, happier persons, lead more fruitful lives, choose more fulfilling (and less destructive) behaviors, and deal with emotions without superstition, emerging from the existentialist void with our reasoning muscles flexed and our intimacy bondings balanced. All this makes for clearer perspectives toward the realities of living.

Hypothetical Scenarios

To illustrate what a Secular Sobriety Group meeting is like, in contrast to the more traditional A.A. meeting, I offer two hypothetical scenarios:

Believer's Version, Including Higher Power

"Hi, I'm Sally and I'm an alcoholic."
Group responds: "Hi, Sally!"
Sally continues: "I really didn't want to come here tonight, but I guess my Higher Power felt I needed a meeting, so here I am. I had a really big fight with my boss today. I feel bad about it but I guess I've got

to turn it over to my Higher Power. I've been sober for a little over six months now."

The group applauds and encourages her to continue with "Atta girl, Sally," "Ha! That's it Sally!" etc.

Sally goes on: "You people have really made me realize what love and caring can be. I've been trying to work the steps and haven't got very far yet, but I keep trying. If it weren't for you people and my Higher Power, I know I'd be right back out there again on my face in some bar. I don't have the strength to do it on my own. My Higher Power must be taking care of me, holding me close. Sometimes when I'm alone at night my Higher Power calms me down. It works. These steps and these principles work. I told my A.A. sponsor yesterday that sometimes I doubt—maybe that's not the right word—sometimes I want things too fast, things that my Higher Power feels are not for my own good. I listen to my sponsor, most times. Sometimes I think she's full of it and I want to rebel, go my own way, but I know I need this. I need her help. She's been sober for a long time and I know she knows what she's talking about. I've started going back to my old church. When I was drinking I used to curse God. Now I'm willing to surrender.

"My best thinking got me here. I try not to let my crazy head tell me what to do. I just put one foot in front of the other and take one step at a time, one day at a time. My boyfriend is getting along better now with my little girl. God is disclosing more and more to me each day. It's a relief to just 'let go and let God.' I called my mom two days ago. We cried. She's so pleased that I'm going to church again and that I'm sober now. I wasn't going to share this tonight, but Paul (my boyfriend) keeps insisting that I pack up and move in with him. I don't feel ready for that just yet. I need more time in sobriety. Paul's a nonalcoholic. He says he loves me but when we talk I get confused. He screws around with my thinking. He respects my A.A. program and all, but he's not a believer. My sponsor said I should picture God as I understand him, not punishing and harsh, like I was taught, but caring and loving and powerful. Somehow Paul may come to believe. I know I can't change him, but I think I really love him. Anyway, thank you all for being here and 'keep coming back.'"

The group responds with applause and cheerful hoots.

Heretical Version, Free from Higher Power

"Hi, I'm Sally and I'm an alcoholic."
Group responds: "Hi, Sally!"
Sally continues: "I really didn't want to come here tonight, but I felt I needed a meeting, so here I am. I had a really big fight with my boss today. I feel bad about it. I guess I've got a right to my feelings, but I don't have to dwell on them.

"I've been sober for a little over six month now."
The group applauds and encourges her to continue with "Atta girl, Sally," "Ha! That's it Sally!" etc.

Sally goes on: "You people have really made me realize what love and caring can be. If it weren't for my choosing each day to prioritize my sobriety *no matter what* and the encouragement of you people I know I'd be right back out there again on my face in some bar. Now I'm willing to surrender to the fact that I am an alcoholic and each day I feel a little bit better, and a little bit stronger.

"My boyfriend is getting along better now with my little girl. I called my mom two days ago. We cried. She's proud of me. I feel better about myself, too. I

wasn't going to share this tonight, but Paul (my boyfriend) keeps insisting that I pack up and move in with him. I don't feel ready for that just yet. I need more time in sobriety.

"Paul's a nonalcoholic. He says he loves me but I want to be really sure of my feelings and more secure in myself before making a commitment. I think I really love him. Anyway, thanks for listening."

The group responds with applause and cheerful hoots. . . .

Overreacting to Stress

Heretical Sally, newly sober, is as subject to overreacting to stress as is Believer Sally, but is clear on the fact that when all else goes bananas she still has her sobriety priority, one day at a time. Religion does not get in the way or cloud the issue of her priority. Her Secular Sobriety Group may individually or collectively disappoint her—they might even for some strange reason board a bus for Toledo, leaving no forwarding address. A hurricane may destroy her home, her mother may suddenly go insane, her boyfriend might introduce her to his new boyfriend, but she still has her sobriety, *if* she continues to prioritize it daily. And as time passes, with reasonable effort, she'll develop new coping skills in living sober, unhampered by religious dogma. Believer Sally could come out of the aforementioned events sober also if, in that crisis moment, she puts her sobriety before the whims of her God.

"Religion does not get in the way or cloud the issue."

Which Sally would you lay odds on?

Okay, my argument could be construed as being somewhat slanted. But time and again I have seen free thinkers give in, by their own admission, to bad feelings experienced early on, rather than hanging in there by prioritizing sobriety. After years of being told over and over by A.A. religionists that they must find a higher power to stay sober, many succumb to peer pressure. . . .

Just don't drink. You now have the opportunity to choose to stay sober each day, one day at a time, lifelong. It is not a matter of willpower. Honestly setting your priorities is your key to the sober life.

James Christopher is the founder of Secular Sobriety Group, an alternative to Alcoholics Anonymous. He is also a free-lance writer who has studied alcoholism and chemical dependency.

"During the '80s, nearly 30 states raised their drinking age to 21. They have consistently showed a 10-to-15 percent decrease in nighttime crashes."

Crackdowns on Drunk Driving Are Effective

Ray McAllister

It was 10:55 p.m. Saturday, May 14. The old school bus, headed south on Interstate 71, now was outside Carrolton, Ky. The 63 teen-agers and four adults on board, all members of the First Assembly of God Church in Radcliff, Ky., were returning home from Kings Island amusement park north of Cincinnati.

Coming the other way in a Toyota pickup truck was Larry Mahoney, 34, a chemical worker from Worthville, Ky. He was headed north, but in the southbound lanes, apparently too drunk to realize he was driving the wrong way.

"If it were possible to turn back the clock, we would," Gov. Wallace Wilkinson would say four days later in declaring a day of mourning. "Whatever consolation we can give will never make up for the loss of friends and loved ones."

Mahoney and the bus driver, John Pearman, each tried to brake.

It was too late.

"I just heard a crash, felt the impact of the [truck] and looked up and saw flames," said Wayne Cox, a 14-year-old who survived. "They spread pretty fast. . . . I was pinned. Everything was pretty wild."

An Orange Fireball

The fuel tank of the bus ruptured and exploded in an orange fireball that shot from the front to the back of the bus. Flames engulfed the bus—"Not one part of it was untouched," Carroll County Coroner James Dunn told reporters, "inside, outside."

Twenty-four teen-agers and three adults died when they could not reach the rear exit. Their bodies were burned beyond recognition. Dental records were used because, as Kentucky State Medical Examiner Dr. George Nichols told family members, he did not want the families to view the charred remains.

"The picture . . . of their children in that room,"

Ray McAllister, "The Drunken Driving Crackdown: Is It Working?" Reprinted with permission from the September 1988 *ABA Journal*, The Lawyer's Magazine, published by the American Bar Association.

he explained to reporters later, "is not what they have in their memories or wallets."

Mahoney was charged with 27 counts of murder, and Carroll County Commonwealth's Attorney John Ackman said he would seek the death penalty.

Drunk Driving

Mahoney had driven drunk before. He pleaded guilty in 1984 to drunken driving, was fined $300 plus court costs, and ordered to pay $140 for traffic school. Under the toughened standards of the 1980s, his license also was suspended for six months.

Mahoney's blood-alcohol content level at that time was .16, more than one-and-a-half times the intoxication level. Four years later, his drunkenness was worse.

On May 14, the day he killed 27 people on I-71, his blood-alcohol level was .24. Eleven one-ounce drinks consumed in one hour would yield a level of .24 for a 150-pound person.

The Kentucky crash has prompted renewed looks at the nation's drunken driving problem. Has the legislative and judicial crackdown of the 1980s been a panacea? Has it worked at all?

Following several widely publicized crashes, public attention and debate focused on the issue in the early 1980s.

Everyone could agree that drunken drivers were the enemy. Citizen lobbies—notably Mothers Against Drunk Driving, Students Against Drunk Driving, Remove Intoxicated Drivers—were organized.

Politicians joined in. Law enforcement efforts were increased. State and federal legislators stiffened penalties for drunken driving, made some penalties mandatory, and tied federal funds to others.

As a result, arrests for drunken driving rose by 223 percent from 1970 to 1986, the Bureau of Justice Statistics says. Young drivers, the biggest offenders, were hit hardest. In 1983, the peak year, one of every 39 licensed drivers aged 21 was arrested.

Moreover, through federal inducement, all 50 states raised their drinking ages to 21 (Wyoming, a holdout, became the 50th [in] July [1988]). Most adopted .10 (or even lower) as the per se level of intoxication. Most increased sentences. Many adopted mandatory license loss, at least for repeated driving-under-the-influence offenders.

And judges handed down tougher sentences, in part because they had to. In 1983, according to the Bureau of Justice Statistics survey, the median sentence given to first-time drunken drivers had reached five months in jail. For repeat offenders, the sentences were about twice as long.

What Happened?

So what happened when everyone got tough?

From 1982 to 1985, the U.S. Department of Transportation says, alcohol-related traffic deaths declined by fully 11 percent. It is a bottom line that even skeptics have to consider impressive.

But who gets the credit? The obvious answer isn't necessarily the right one. It's not clear that tougher penalties have been wholly or even largely responsible for the drop.

For instance, a survey of judges in six states—California, Colorado, Georgia, Maryland, Pennsylvania and Wisconsin—raises a question about the effectiveness of mandatory sentencing, a key element in the get-tough legislation across the country.

Critics have long contended that some judges maintain a there-but-for-the-grace-of-God-go-I attitude toward such cases, refusing to implement tough sentences because they drive drunk themselves. An article presenting the survey results was published in the *Judges' Journal* in 1985. It suggests that "the judges' opinions indicated they believe mandatory sentencing makes it less likely that offenders will be sentenced."

"[Administrative license revocation] is simply the single most effective change a state can make."

"Like the old English juries that would not find thieves guilty if this meant hanging them, our modern American judges know that their colleagues and juries may prefer to give no punishment rather than to give one that is excessively harsh."

Dr. Ralph Hingson, chief of social and behavioral sciences at the Boston University School of Public Health, says, "Within the courts, judges vary in their response to laws like per se laws and mandatory penalties that take some of their discretion from them. I would suspect there is a debate within the judicial branch on the utility of these laws."

But Hingson advances the theory that publicity and public debate, and not necessarily the legislative and judicial response, may be more responsible for change, anyway.

"It's a real chicken-and-egg sort of thing," he says. "But there's social process going on in which society is trying to change its norms about what's acceptable in terms of drinking and driving. . . ."

Renewed Publicity

Now, "we are seeing an upswing of interest again," as evidenced by renewed publicity and in new laws that increased to a total of 216 in 45 states in 1987.

Doris C. Aiken, president and founder of the New York-based Remove Intoxicated Drivers, which has chapters in 34 states, sees less of a break in attention paid drunken driving. Even with the recent increase in deaths, "we're not up to where we were before" the law changes. California is an exception, she says.

While she is heartened, Aiken adds that "I think we've done 50 percent of what we have to do." Two major items remain on the agenda: Taking a drunken driver's license immediately upon arrest for a period of 45 (or 90) days. And setting up drunken driving checkpoints. Many states have adopted one, the other, or both.

RID is not alone in wanting to take a drunken driver's license immediately. That administrative act, which is carried out by the arresting police officer before any court conviction, is in use in 23 states and likely will be adopted by more.

"Now that there is 50-state compliance with age 21 as the legal drinking age, probably the No. 1 priority right now is administrative license revocation," says MADD's Russell.

The reason: It is simply the single most effective change a state can make.

Ray McAllister is a reporter for the Richmond Times Dispatch.

"The whole effort to combat drunk driving may be misconceived."

Crackdowns on Drunk Driving are Ineffective

Laurence Ross and Graham Hughes

The United States has one of the lowest rates of fatal road accidents in the Western world, but you might not know it from the publicity generated by organizations like MADD, SADD and RID. In the past five years Mothers Against Drunk Driving, Students Against Driving Drunk and Remove Intoxicated Drivers have had considerable success in drawing public attention to what they see as the havoc wrought by drunk driving. Thanks to their efforts more police resources have been directed against drunk drivers, roadblocks have become a common sight, penalties have been increased and plea-bargaining curtailed in drunk driving cases.

For all its advocates' zeal and good intentions, the campaign will probably not lead to a substantial or permanent reduction in the number of serious traffic accidents. Although drunk driving poses risks to the driver and others, the popular impression of the number of traffic deaths it causes is exaggerated. It is frequently stated that alcohol is responsible for 50 percent of U.S. traffic fatalities, but that statistic has no solid foundation. The figure includes all traffic deaths in which anyone directly involved has consumed any alcohol. That means cases of drunken pedestrians who are killed by sober drivers, or accidents involving a drunk driver properly stopped for a red light and hit by a reckless but sober motorist.

In many cases it is impossible to determine the cause of an accident. Most alcohol-related traffic deaths occur when other important causal factors are present—fatigue, inexperience, poorly lit and badly designed roads. Despite improvements in police reporting, we still have only the murkiest idea of the role alcohol plays in traffic fatalities.

Perhaps the most accurate estimate, from the National Academy of Sciences, attributes roughly 25 percent of fatal accidents to intoxication. That is certainly a substantial number, but it means that a program that reduced drunk driving by 10 percent could diminish deaths in crashes by only 2.5 percent. What's more, there is little reason to believe that criminal law enforcement deters drunk driving over the long run. In 1985 a review of the available studies, published in the *Journal of Studies in Alcohol*, indicated that increasing the penalties for drunk driving was almost totally ineffective. No evidence since then has seriously challenged that assessment. Publicity campaigns and stepped up police activity, combined with harsher punishment, may reduce the amount of drunk driving for a short time. In the long run, however, certainty of punishment is the only true deterrent, and the actual chances of being caught while driving drunk are on the order of one in a thousand such trips.

Huge Expenditures

A serious policy of deterrence would require huge expenditures. More personnel, more vehicles, more training for the police, would all be necessary, and that, in turn, would divert funds and police from other areas. Punishing drunk drivers more severely and taking away their opportunity to engage in plea-bargaining has already increased the need for judges and lawyers. Local jails are horribly overcrowded, and many have been further strained by the rising number of drunk drivers serving sentences. But efforts made so far are only token compared with what might be needed to have a significant impact.

The less visible costs of the campaign against drunk driving may be even higher. The courts have held that the public must be given notice of what is forbidden by criminal law. How does one know when one has drunk too much to drive legally? The concept of intoxication, generally understood in this context as an alcohol-induced condition that substantially impairs the capacity to drive, is vague

Laurence Ross and Graham Hughes, "Drunk Driving: What Not To Do," *The Nation* magazine, December 13, 1986. Copyright 1986 *The Nation* magazine/The Nation Company, Inc.

and difficult to identify except in gross cases. Some states, for example, make it a minor offense to drive with a blood alcohol content of more than .05 percent, although studies indicate that many people can drive safely at that level. . . .

Threat to Rights

The greatest threat to constitutional rights is posed by the recent fad for sobriety checkpoints. The procedure once a car is stopped can involve a close examination of the driver, possibly including waving a breath sensor close to the mouth, perhaps followed by a request that he or she step out and take a "field sobriety test," such as walking a line or counting backward. Every driver is stopped, whether or not there is cause for suspicion. If roadblocks are constitutionally permissible, as many courts have ruled, what would be wrong with street checkpoints at which pedestrians would be patted down for guns or sniffed by trained dogs for drugs? Yet there is no evidence that these road checks are particularly effective in stopping drunk driving.

In any case, the whole effort to combat drunk driving may be misconceived. Even if stricter law enforcement could substantially reduce the general incidence of drunk driving, it would probably not reduce the number of serious accidents caused by alcohol. A large proportion of drunk drivers are alcoholics or problem drinkers, who are likely to be troubled, aggressive or depressed. More than half of those killed in alcohol-related accidents are the drunk drivers themselves, which suggests that some of those deaths are deliberate or half-conscious suicides. Such people are not moved by threats of imprisonment, and they will drive without licenses. The drivers who are scared by stricter drunk driving laws will probably be the least dangerous ones, and making them more careful will lead to a disappointingly small reduction in the number of accidents. This seems to be the case in Norway and Sweden, where the relatively few drunk drivers still cause numerous deaths and serious injuries.

Why has so misguided a policy toward drunk driving developed? Part of the answer lies in the passionate lobbying by the families of the accident victims. Those people understandably perceive all drunk driving as extremely dangerous, although the chance of causing a death has been estimated at one in every 330,000 miles of impaired driving. To the survivors, all drunk drivers are surrogates for the one who killed a relative, and retribution is the only satisfying response. Because nobody wants to defend drunk driving or oppose grieving mothers, there has been virtually no opposition to organizations like MADD.

To interpret social problems solely in terms of individual irresponsibility is in tune with our times. The automobile and liquor industries are delighted to blame accidents on the abuse of their products by a small fraction of consumers, and to join in public relations campaigns to discourage such abuse. How painless that is compared with making safer cars or admitting that alcohol is a dangerous drug.

What would a more effective and economically efficient policy entail? Improved and expanded public transportation might help, but in most places that is not a practical option. A higher drinking age probably saves some lives; a higher driving age would save more, but no politician is going to propose that. . . .

"The drivers who are scared by stricter drunk driving laws will probably be the least dangerous ones."

The most useful policy would focus on all traffic deaths and injuries rather than just on those associated with alcohol, and would intervene in the most cost-effective way. Some remedies are well known; they involve protecting the occupants from the "second collision," the contact, after the crash, between the occupant and the vehicle. Much has been done over the years to reduce this cause of maiming and death, but dangers remain. Only now are most states beginning to require that seat belts be fastened. Mandatory installation of air bags would save thousands of lives a year, but their introduction has been repeatedly postponed and has now been delayed until 1989. Pickup trucks and vans are not covered by many of the structural safety requirements that apply to automobiles.

The dramatic reduction in the death rate on American roads in the past five years had a variety of causes: the reduced speed limit, safer cars, better roads with better lighting, improvements in medical techniques and in the delivery of emergency medical services. Measures against drunk driving have probably played an insignificant part. We should persist in condemning drunk driving and in prosecuting those who are caught. But an obsessive concern with this single phenomenon carries two dangers. It promises much more than it can deliver in terms of public safety, and it diverts attention from the corporations that ignore the harm caused by their products and the government officials who fail to initiate action to correct defects that threaten lives.

Laurence Ross is a professor of sociology at the University of New Mexico. Graham Hughes is a professor of law at New York University.

"During 1985, . . . 18,492 people were treated for the number one drug abuse problem in the U.S.A., the family of tranquilizers and sleeping pills known as the benzodiazepines."

Tranquilizer Addiction Is a Major Problem

Public Citizen Health Research Group

When former National Security Advisor Robert McFarlane recently had to go to the Bethesda Naval Hospital because of a drug abuse problem, it was not surprising that the drug involved was neither heroin nor morphine, nor was it cocaine or crack.

A federally funded program called the Drug Abuse Warning Network (DAWN) collects information from hospital emergency rooms and coroners' offices serving about one-third of the people in the country. During 1985, the latest year for which data are available, 13,501 people went to emergency rooms because of cocaine-related problems, 14,696 for morphine and heroin combined. But 18,492 people were treated for the number one drug abuse problem in the U.S.A., the family of tranquilizers and sleeping pills known as the benzodiazepines.

Although we are now spending hundreds of millions of dollars a year trying to solve the more traditional street-drug problems, the much-easier-to-get legitimate prescription drugs in the benzodiazepine family are taking their toll. The family of 11 drugs includes eight tranquilizers (VALIUM, XANAX, ATIVAN, TRANXENE, LIBRIUM, CENTRAX, SERAX, and PAXIPAM) plus the three sleeping pills (DALMANE, RESTORIL, and HALCION).

The only significant differences between these 11 drugs is how they are pushed in the marketplace, as tranquilizers or sleeping pills, and the amount of time it takes to clear them from the body. As we will discuss later, they can all put someone to sleep, can induce tranquility, at least for a while, and they all share the adverse effects of addiction and other serious problems.

During 1985, Americans, persuaded by their doctors, filled 81 million prescriptions for these drugs, a total purchase of 3.7 billion pills. If every

person in the country were a user, this would be equal to 15 pills per person per year. With the actual number of users being approximately 25 million, however, the average "sale" per person was 148 pills a year. As seen in the table, there were 61 million prescriptions filled for the eight tranquilizers, 20 million for the three sleeping pills.

Sales of Valium have fallen from the record high of 61 million prescriptions in 1975 to 23 million in 1985 (only 38 percent of the earlier year). The other good news is that total benzodiazepine prescriptions—81 million in 1985—are not as high as the record for that total of 98 million, set in 1975 as well, but the family is making a comeback. As doctors and patients have learned about the dangers of Valium, the crafty drug-pushers have put 6 of the 11 benzodiazepines on the market since 1975, "positioning" them as not having the disadvantages, such as the "buzz," of Valium. Through an enormous amount of false and misleading advertising, the sales of the family, having fallen steadily from 1975 to 1981, have been on the rise since. For the tranquilizers, drugs like Xanax and Tranxene have replaced a good portion of lost Valium sales. As we have emphasized before, all of them have the same risks.

Low Probability

Because he was, fortunately, too dumb to realize that the 20 or 25 Valium pills that he swallowed were not likely to kill him, Robert McFarlane is now alive. This low probability of death, even with massive doses, is common to all the benzodiazepines, just as it is for large doses of another well-known central nervous system depressant, alcohol. In all of these cases, the soporific properties of the drugs are likely to induce sleep before too much damage is done, at least in adults. But if Mr. McFarlane had downed a few drinks along with his Valium, (even if he had taken fewer pills) he might well be dead

Public Citizen Health Research Group, "Drug-Induced Tranquility," *Health Letter*, April 1987. Reprinted with the permission of Health Letter, 2000 P St. NW, Washington, DC 20036.

now. This was the fate of 492 benzodiazepine-using people in 1985 who wound up in the coroner's office, most commonly due to the combination of alcohol along with their favorite tranquilizer or sleeping pill. Although many of these unfortunate people were not attempting suicide, many did themselves in unintentionally, having underestimated the fatal properties of benzodiazepines in combination with drugs such as alcohol.

Addicting Benzodiazepines

If you listen to the drug-makers, you might think that the only people who become addicted to benzodiazepines are those with a history of drug abuse or alcohol abuse. This is untrue, as several studies have shown that people without this kind of history often get addicted to members of the family. Another myth spread by the drug industry is that addiction only occurs if you use more than the recommended dose. Again, several studies have now shown that almost half of the people using the doctor-recommended dose of these drugs can become addicted, often after weeks or months of use. After such steady use, suddenly stopping the habit brings on withdrawal symptoms, within hours for the rapidly cleared drugs, in a day or two for the longer-lasting ones such as Valium. The easiest way to remedy the unpleasant nervousness, tremor, agitation, and other withdrawal symptoms is to go back to the drug, a behavior pattern which perpetuates the addictive state.

Benzodiazepine Prescriptions: 1985

Brand Name	(Generic Name)	Prescriptions Filled (Millions)
Tranquilizers		
Valium	(Diazepam)	23
Xanax	(Alprazolam)	11
Ativan	(Lorazepam)	10
Librium	(Chlordiazepoxide)	7
Tranxene	(Chlorazepate)	7
Centrax	(Prazepam)	2
Serax	(Oxazepam)	2
Paxipam	(Halazepam)	< 1
Sleeping Pills		
Dalmane	(Flurazepam)	8
Halcion	(Triazolam)	7
Restoril	(Temazepam)	5

(Source: National Prescription Audit)

The benzodiazepines, considering their addictive properties and other dangers, are weakly regulated by the federal government, with five refills allowed with merely a phone call once the original prescription is filled. Added to this is the often poorly informed patient and doctor who, even after another office visit, may continue rewriting and rewriting prescriptions.

The result of the inadequate government regulation and inadequately informed doctors and patients is a massive amount of chronic, steady, long-term use of these drugs, even though there is no evidence they are effective for such periods of time.

A recent government study found that 2.9 million Americans were taking these drugs every day for at least four months and that 2.1 million of these people were daily users for a year or more. Many of these people are addicted to their benzodiazepines but this risk is not accompanied by any proven benefit.

Risks to Older People

Addiction, death, confusion, memory loss, increased risk of an auto accident, poor coordination, impaired learning ability, and slurred speech can happen to anyone of any age who uses these drugs. But older people are at special risk for several reasons.

As people age, there is a gradual impairment in many of the processes which get rid of drugs after they have been ingested or taken into the body by other routes of administration. As a result, higher levels of many of these drugs occur in older people than in their younger counterparts. Some researchers also think that, in addition, older people may be more sensitive to some of these drugs. Despite this evidence, doctors often give older people the same doses as younger people would get. Another problem resulting in a higher risk for older people who use benzodiazepines is the fact that older people are more likely to get a prescription for these drugs than younger people and, when they do, the prescription is much more likely to last for months, if not years.

Because of these factors, which place older people at greater risk from these drugs, the adverse effects mentioned above occur more commonly and are often more severe in older people. Further aggravating this situation is the fact that many of these "side effects" are easily attributed to growing old rather than being linked to the use of the tranquilizers or sleeping pills. The onset of memory loss, confusion, impaired coordination, or impaired learning in a younger person will more likely prompt an inquiry leading to the drug as culprit. But the same symptoms in an older person, especially if they develop more slowly, may well be attributed to "Well, he (or she) is just growing old, what do you expect?" This lack of suspicion allows the drug to keep doing the damage because the doctor keeps up the prescription.

In view of all of this, the use of benzodiazepines in older people is not a good idea.

A recent well-controlled experiment suggests an important alternative to the use of benzodiazepines, not only in older people but for everyone. Ninety patients, mainly suffering from anxiety, were randomly divided into two groups when they went to see their family doctors. The first group was given the usual dose of one of the benzodiazepines. The people in the other group were given a small dose of a much safer treatment consisting solely of "listening, explanation, advice, and reassurance." The two treatments were equally effective in relieving the anxiety, but those getting the counseling were more satisfied with their treatment than were the others. Of interest was the fact that the doctors did not find that the several minutes they spent interfered with their work schedules.

Some patients with extreme anxiety do not immediately respond to brief counseling and there are some doctors, practicing good, careful medicine, who feel that a small fraction of anxious patients might benefit from a very brief course of treatment with a tranquilizer. But to protect both doctor and patient, the prescription should state "NO REFILL." The size of the prescription should also be limited to one week's treatment. By this time doctor and patient should have begun to understand the cause of the anxiety or sleeplessness, and further progress can occur without the use of more drugs. If the prescribing of these drugs was limited in these ways, the use of benzodiazepines would fall to less than one-tenth of the current levels as would the number of people addicted to, killed by, or otherwise damaged by these powerful drugs.

Helping to bring patients' anxiety down to tolerable levels through conversation is much safer and humane therapy than the current epidemic of 3.7 billion benzodiazepine pills bought each year. Even though they may earn a little less by spending a little more time talking with their patients, American doctors, who take in an average net income after expenses of $108,000 a year, will survive, and patients will be better off.

"Helping to bring patients' anxiety down to tolerable levels through conversation is much safer and humane therapy than the current epidemic of . . . benzodiazepine pills."

We have all heard the phrase, "If you drink, don't drive." The idea is that if you are under the influence of alcohol, your coordination and your decision-making abilities are impaired. Similarly, those who engage in the two- (or one- or three-) martini lunch do not usually have the ability to make important decisions in the afternoon. The same kind of impairment occurs with the benzodiazepines. Part of the problem has to do with the proper weighing of opposing, often conflicting choices you have as you are deciding what to do.

Clear thinking is just that, decision-making unencumbered by alcohol, hard drugs, or benzodiazepines. Whether the decisions have to do with yourself, your family, or your job, including important ones such as National Security Advisor, the outcome is more likely to make sense if the competing tensions are allowed to exist.

The Age of Chemicals

As Aldous Huxley said in *Brave New World Revisited*, written as the age of chemical tranquility was beginning,

> As things now stand, the tranquillizers may prevent some people from giving enough trouble, not only to their rulers, but even to themselves. Too much tension is a disease; but so is too little. There are certain occasions when we ought to be tense, when an excess of tranquillity (and especially of tranquillity imposed from the outside, by a chemical) is entirely inappropriate.

The Public Citizen Health Research Group was co-founded in 1971 by Ralph Nader and Sidney Wolfe as a group working to give consumers more control over health decisions.

"Only a minority of patients on full therapeutic doses of benzodiazepines over extended periods of time develop withdrawal symptoms."

viewpoint **19**

Tranquilizer Addiction Has Been Exaggerated

Sidney Cohen

Benzodiazepine derivates (Valium-type drugs) are widely used as anticonvulsants, antianxiety, anti-insomnia and muscle relaxant medications. Their clinical efficacy is well documented. They have a favorable therapeutic-toxic ratio; in fact, it is difficult to commit suicide when any amount of these agents are consumed alone.

It was well known that prolonged high dose usage could be associated with some abstinence phenomena. More recently, withdrawal effects in patients taking average amounts of these drugs over prolonged periods have been found to result in physical dependence, including withdrawal symptoms if the benzodiazepines were abruptly discontinued. The length of time on the medication seems to be at least as important as the total daily dose consumed. Short half-life benzodiazepine (lorazepam, Ativan, for example) withdrawal has a prompt onset and a more intense, but briefer duration. Long half-life benzodiazepines, diazepam for example, are delayed in onset and tend to have less intense symptomatology but last longer. These differences are due to dissimilar plasma curves for short vs. long half-life compounds.

Gradual Withdrawal

Although only a minority of patients on full therapeutic doses of benzodiazepines over extended periods of time develop withdrawal symptoms, everyone who has been taking any drug in this group should be gradually withdrawn from it. The same procedure is recommended for all sedative-hypnotics, including the barbiturates and meprobamate. Other drugs or drug classes that should be gradually discontinued after prolonged use to avoid withdrawal or rebound symptoms include opioids, stimulants, neuroleptics, antidepressants, beta blockers, corticosteroids, clonidine, ergotamine and the organic nitrates.

Reduction of dosage should be two mg. or less per week in diazepam equivalents. If the patient experiences a number of symptoms mentioned in the table below, the dose reduction program should be discontinued and restarted later.

The anxiety cluster may or may not be a withdrawal effect. Anxiety that increases during the first week after discontinuance or dose reduction and then tends to subside might be a withdrawal-related effect. Anxiety that increases and then stabilizes over weeks or months may constitute re-emergent anxiety that had been suppressed by the benzodiazepine therapy. Further, a current anxiety reaction that had been controlled with the anxiolytic would become worse following its elimination.

Prompt relief of withdrawal symptoms following administration of a dose of the benzodiazepine neither proves nor disproves that the complaints are actual withdrawal or emergent anxiety. In both conditions relief might be obtained by reactivating the use of the drug.

Just why some long-term therapeutic dose level users of benzodiazepines manifest withdrawal effects while many others do not is unclear. A few reports emphasize the possibility of genetic factors, including familial alcoholism.

Personality factors may also be a reason for the emergence or intensity of withdrawal complaints. In this regard, anticipatory withdrawal or pseudowithdrawal has been observed in research studies. When patients are told that their benzodiazepine may be continued, or an identically appearing placebo might be substituted, some patient-subjects will describe withdrawal effects even though they are in the drug group.

The benzodiazepine syndrome is identical to sedative-hypnotic withdrawal states (the DTs). Long-acting hypnosedatives, like phenobarbital, have

Sidney Cohen, "Benzodiazepine Withdrawal," *Drug Abuse and Alcoholism Newsletter*, January 1987. Reprinted with permission.

delayed but protracted withdrawal reactions just as long-acting benzodiazepines do.

The range of possible abstinence symptoms mentioned in the table below is never all reported or seen in any one individual. Inspection of the symptoms and signs reveals that, for the most part, they are identical to the alcohol and sedative-hypnotic withdrawal syndrome with one exception. The sensory excitation cluster of symptoms is reported by patients who have stopped using benzodiazepines more frequently than during alcohol or barbiturate withdrawal.

Table

Possible Benzodiazepine Withdrawal Symptoms
(A variant of the depressant withdrawal syndrome)

1. Anxiety Rebound
   Tension
   Agitation
   Tremulousness
   Insomnia
   Anorexia
2. Autonomic Rebound
   Hypertension
   Tachycardia
   Sweating
   Hyperpyrexia
3. Sensory Excitation
   Paresthesias
   Photophobia
   Hyperacusis
   Illusions

4. Motor Excitation
   Hyper-reflexia
   Tremors
   Myoclonus
   Fasciculations
   Myalgia
   Muscle weakness
   Tonic-clonic convulsions
5. Cognitive Excitation
   Nightmares
   Delirium
   Depersonalization
   Hallucinations

The appearance of withdrawal symptoms does not require that plasma levels of benzodiazepines or their metabolites be zero. A considerable drop in the plasma level is sufficient to induce symptoms of this condition.

An unresolved question is: "Why do long half-life benzodiazepines produce the withdrawal syndrome?" It might be imagined that, since the plasma levels drop relatively gradually, they would have a built-in ability to avoid withdrawal. This is not so, nor is it true for long half-life members of other drug classes like THC, methadone or phenobarbital. The explanation may be that long half-life drugs are still not long enough to prevent a sufficient drop in brain levels to suppress the effects of discontinuing the drug.

A special form of abstinence phenomena is rebound insomnia. Especially the short-acting hypnotic benzodiazepines like triazolam (Halcion) or temazepam (Restoril) are liable to produce insomnia after discontinuing the drug. Daytime anxiety has also been described under these conditions. Long half-life hypnotic benzodiazepines after prolonged use are occasionally known to provoke rebound insomnia. Of course, barbiturates and the non-barbiturate, non-benzodiazepine hypnotics, also can induce withdrawal insomnia.

How Benzodiazepines Work

The antianxiety and anticonvulsant effects of the benzodiazepines are apparently due to their impact upon GABA (gamma-aminobutyric acid) transmission. The amino acid, GABA, is the major inhibitory transmitter in the brain, accounting for about a third of all cerebral neurotransmission. Benzodiazepines facilitate GABA function by increasing the affinity of GABA for its receptor. It does this by displacing an endogenous inhibitor of GABA binding.

Both the GABA receptor and the benzodiazepine receptor exist in close proximity to chloride (Cl-) channels in the neuronal membrane. GABA increases permeability to Cl- ions into the neuron, resulting in hyperpolarization. The membrane is, therefore, unable to discharge, and transmission is inhibited. This results in a decreased excitation of many neuronal systems, diminishing anxiety and hyperalertness and elevating the convulsive threshold.

Abrupt discontinuance of a benzodiazepine would produce a psychophysiologic reaction opposite in direction to the relaxing, anxiety-reducing properties of these drugs. Benzodiazepine receptors would be vacated, GABA activity is reduced, and Cl- channels would close, permitting widespread depolarization and rebound excitation of many neuronal pathways and inducing the clinical symptoms described above.

In addition to the very gradual tapering of benzodiazepine dosages, other measures will help avoid post-withdrawal symptoms. Many anxiety reactions respond to short courses of benzodiazepines, and providing these drugs in average amounts over periods of only weeks or a few months does not appear to lead to physical dependence. When a patient has trait anxiety and is dysfunctional without anxiolytic drugs, a number of options are open. Non-drug techniques to reduce tension or panic feelings could be employed to lower the dose of the benzodiazepine. Giving the drug as needed when anxiety levels are rising, rather than on a regular basis, will reduce the amount necessary to control the situation. When high anxiety levels exist over long periods of time, advantage should be taken of periods of reduced symptomatology to lower or discontinue the benzodiazepine. The lowest effective amount is preferred over larger amounts that could completely obliterate anxiety.

Patients with a pre-existing history of alcohol, sedative or opiate abuse are high-risk candidates for benzodiazepine dependence and their use of anxiolytics should be very carefully supervised. The physician should always look for opportunities to discontinue the anxiolytic in these people.

Now that the furor of the early 1980s has subsided, it is possible to evaluate the benzodiazepine withdrawal controversy somewhat more dispassionately. The excitement about people who discontinued using diazepam or other benzodiazepines and promptly experienced a noxious state was, in good part, a media spectacular. For a while, articles, quasi-documentaries and movies provided stories of people who had undergone the misery of withdrawal or of recrudescent anxiety. Why were we surprised at this development? The lay people had used diazepam almost as though it was not a drug. The medical profession did not classify it as a sedative-hypnotic with many characteristics of this group. It was safe; after all, millions had stopped taking diazepam without adverse consequences. The truth was that the benzodiazepines were not that safe.

> *"The excitement about people who discontinued using diazepam or other benzodiazepines and promptly experienced a noxious state was, in good part, a media spectacular."*

The numbers of major withdrawal events following the withdrawal of therapeutic amounts are not great. But the unexpected occurrence of even a few surprised and unsettled all concerned. Now that we know that we cannot treat the benzodiazepines lightly, and that their discontinuance requires what all hypnosedatives require, namely, slow dosage reduction, it should be possible to use these agents within the context of their capabilities and limitations. Anxiety and its derivative disorders can be incapacitating, and they merit pharmacologic and non-pharmacologic treatment. Once more we have learned the lesson of the New Drug: we learn its efficacy before we learn its complications.

Sidney Cohen is a clinical professor of psychiatry at the Neuropsychiatric Institute at the University of California in Los Angeles. He also edits the Drug Abuse & Alcoholism Newsletter.

"By 1990 generic drugs will have grabbed nearly 50 percent of the prescription drug market."

Generic Drugs: An Overview

Paul Lavrakas

Until recently, consumers buying prescription drugs to treat their ills usually found their choices limited to brand-name products. Now, thanks to federal action aimed at stemming rising health costs, they can pick among an expanding array of less costly generic copies of brand-name drugs. And yet, while no one denies that switching to these generic copies can save money, can we count on them to do the same job as safely and effectively as the familiar standbys they imitate? And will an expanding generic market have any negative effects on research and development of new drugs?

Developing Drugs

Developing a new drug has been compared to breeding pandas in captivity—an expensive, lengthy process with little guarantee of success. Usually thousands of chemicals must be tested before one is found with therapeutic promise, at which time its discoverer obtains a patent giving him sole right to sell the drug for a set term (currently 17 years).

The American Medical Association assigns every new drug a generic name describing its chemical makeup. Since this technical appellation may be a real tongue-twister, the new drug's manufacturer has the right to sell it under an exclusive—and more memorable—brand-name of its own devising (e.g., the top-selling brand-name Dyazide carries the generic title of Hydrochlorothiazide-Triamterene).

Whether a drug ever reaches the market is decided by the Food and Drug Administration (FDA), which first must certify it safe and effective. To earn this stamp of approval, the pioneer drug company conducts on animals and humans exhaustive and costly clinical tests closely monitored by the FDA. At present it can cost more than $90 million to get a new drug over the FDA hurdle and onto the market.

Paul Lavrakas, ''Generic Drugs: What's In a Name?'' *Consumers' Research*, January 1986. Reprinted with permission.

And, as Joseph Williams, chairman of the Pharmaceutical Manufacturers Association (PMA) points out, this FDA review process can chew as much as eight to nine years off a drug's patent term.

The payoff, however, can make the wait worthwhile. Of the more than $18 billion in prescription drugs sold in 1984, the U.S. Department of Commerce reports that an average of 19.1 percent returned as profit, compared with an average 7.1 percent rate for all other industries. It is not uncommon for a patent-protected brand-name drug to gross $200 to $300 million a year. However, in 1985 alone, pharmaceutical manufacturers spent about 15 percent of their sales on existing and new drug research.

Brand-name manufacturers dread the end of a patent term. At that point anyone can copycat their drug and sell it under a generic name at 20 to 80 percent below brand-name cost. Generics cost less because their makers are spared the immense cost of new drug research and development. Moreover, generic competition can be devastating: a brand-name antibiotic, Garamycin, went off patent in 1981 and fell 58 percent in sales in one year.

Over the years, as more and more patents have run out, the generic share of the prescription market has grown to 15 to 20 percent. Interestingly enough, most generics are made by the brand-name companies, essentially because the manufacturing capacity is already in operation. Some put out generic versions of their own patented drugs and call them brand-name generics. The Generic Pharmaceutical Industry Association estimates that only six percent of the prescription market in 1983 went to small, independent firms specializing solely in generic copies.

Background

Until the 1950s, Americans had their prescriptions filled by a local pharmacist mixing bulk generic ingredients. However, World War II battlefield innovations led to the preparation of drugs in prepackaged, premeasured dosages. Taking advantage of this wartime breakthrough, the large pharmaceutical manufacturers swept into the peacetime marketplace with new "miracle" drugs sold under their own labels. Spurred by yearly profit growth of 15 percent, the drug makers entered a golden age, their names—Roche, Ayerst, McNeil, Upjohn, Pfizer—becoming almost as well known as their brand-name products—Valium, Inderal, Tylenol, Motrin, Diabinese. Today, annual prescription drug sales are approaching the $20 billion mark. Prescription drugs have become big business—and with an aging American population, it can only get bigger.

But now generics are beginning to offer big competition. At one time, all 50 states had laws forbidding the substitution of generics for brand-names. In the 1960s, however, consumer groups campaigned to reverse these laws, and today all the states allow substitution.

A roadblock keeping generic copies of many best-selling brand-name drugs off the market was FDA's demand that generics pass the same battery of clinical tests required of the original drug—something independent generic manufacturers could not afford. Although brand-name drugs worth more than $4 billion in yearly sales were to go off patent in the 1980s, this FDA bottleneck promised to sustain brand-name monopolies. In 1984, however, all of this changed, and the generic floodgates opened.

"The FDA insists it is helping cut costs, but not by cutting corners."

In September of that year, Congress unscrambled the logjam at FDA that was keeping many generics out of pharmacies by passing The Drug Price Competition and Patent Term Restoration Act. The law mandates the FDA to process new generic drug applications within 180 days under vastly simplified procedures. (Although specifically tailored to lower drug prices by the infusion of generics, the bill was supported by the brand-name industry in exchange for patent term extensions to compensate for FDA approval delays of new drugs. According to the Act, patent term extensions, depending on the conditions, may not exceed five years, nor may the time from the date of the drug's approval to the termination of the patent extension exceed 14 years.)

Getting FDA Approval

Under the 1984 prescription drug law, instead of conducting lengthy clinical tests, a generic manufacturer need only prove to the FDA that its product is the therapeutic equivalent of the brand-name drug it copies.

The generic drug may differ from the brand-name drug only in superficial ways, such as color or tablet shape. To get FDA approval for public sale of its product, a generic drug manufacturer must show that the drug:

• Contains the same active ingredients;
• Is identical in dosage strength;
• Has the same dosage form (tablet, solution, etc.);
• Has the same route of administration (i.e., by mouth or injection);
• Is used for the same illness;
• Is bioequivalent.

Bioequivalence means that a generic drug gets to its destination in the body in the same amount and at the same rate of speed as the original brand-name does, and that once there it does the same job as effectively.

To prove bioequivalence the generic manufacturer must conduct tests on 20 to 30 normal males (for fear of affecting the female reproductive system) under the age of 40 in order to measure the rate at which the product, after dissolving in the stomach, passes into the bloodstream and is carried throughout the body. (The time it takes for a chemical to reach its destination is referred to as bioavailability.) The FDA insists that the generic must reach its destination as fast and in the same amount as the brand-name product does. To verify this, a head-to-head test is often ordered between the original and its copy.

The FDA insists it is helping cut costs, but not by cutting corners. Defending the FDA's new method of generic approval, Dr. Marvin Seife, head of the FDA's Division of Generic Drugs, says: "These drugs are interchangeable; they are mirror images of each other." Even a spokesman from the PMA, the brand-name industries trade group, admits: "There is no scientific reason a generic drug should not be bioequivalent."

Questioning Generics

The brand-name manufacturers are not reticent, however, about calling generics into question: "All we're saying is that when it comes to a serious or life-threatening disease, you should use a product that you have relied on in the past," says a spokesman for American Home Products (AHP).

Several brand-name companies, including Hoffman-LaRoche and Sandoz, filed petitions with the FDA demanding more extensive tests of generic versions before approval. The FDA has by and large rejected these objections as scientifically groundless. Outside of such petitions, the brand-name manufacturers have no administrative recourse.

Once a drug, whether generic or brand-name, is on the market, the FDA relies on its own post-approval surveillance system, by which health professionals alert them to drugs demonstrating harmful effect on their patients' health. Additionally, the FDA conducts spot checks of pharmaceuticals on the shelf.

Since no drug behaves exactly the same way in any two people, the FDA and industry pharmacologists have over the past three decades developed statistically based guidelines for the allowable variations in the effect a drug may have on individuals. These guidelines apply to both generics and brand-name drugs in the approval process.

To make sure no one is fudging on his new-drug application test data, the FDA tests the active bulk ingredients of a drug and the finished dosage form in its own laboratories. Also, FDA inspectors make on-site visits to plants where the drugs are made to enforce adherence to the agency's manufacturing codes.

To handle the flood of generic applications stimulated by the new approval procedures, the FDA has set up a special team of pharmacological experts. . . .

Four of those approved are copies of Top Ten best-sellers (generic name in parentheses): Inderal (propranolol HCl), an anti-hypertensive; Valium (diazepam), the popular tranquilizer; Motrin (ibuprofen), a general painkiller; and Darvocet (acetaminophen/propoxyphene napsylate), a painkiller. Sales of these four drugs together totaled almost $1.2 billion [in 1985]; on the average their generic equivalents sell for about one-third less.

Today, with only one exception, all Top Ten selling drugs are obtainable in generic form. According to the Generic Pharmaceutical Manufacturers Association, nearly all of the top 50 drugs will have approved generic versions by 1990.

A Competitive Market

The federal government is not alone in encouraging consumers to make the switch to generics. Many insurance companies, following the pioneering example of Blue Cross of Michigan, offer 100 percent reimbursement to policyholders using generic drugs while paying only 50 to 75 percent of brand-name drug costs. Unions, such as the United Auto Workers, are negotiating health plans for their members that insist on generic substitution. Additionally, state-operated Medicaid programs, seeking to reduce copayment of drug costs, are offering incentives for generic use.

Doctors play the key role in making the choice between brand-names and generics. A doctor may block generic use by writing "No substitution" on the prescription form. Knowing this, brand-name manufacturers spend tens of millions annually on advertising and promotions to encourage doctors' loyalty to familiar brands.

A Harvard University study showed doctors more influenced in drug selection by such advertising than by any other factor. Countering this, a Duke University study indicates that doctors will prescribe generics to save their patients money: when informed of savings available from generics, doctors in a test group increased generic prescriptions from 21 to 58 percent.

> "Today, with only one exception, all Top Ten selling drugs are obtainable in generic form."

The new competitive environment is pushing brand-name manufacturers for the first time to target the consumer, along with doctors and druggists, in their advertising campaigns. In 1983, in response to some public-oriented ad campaigns, the FDA slapped a moratorium on drug commercials mentioning a product by name, but lifted it in October of [1985].

Brand-Name Reaction

The brand-name industry is hurting not just from generic competition, but from a scarcity of new products. In the 1980s, they have been introducing only about half as many new drugs annually as they did in the glory days of the preceding two decades. The brand-name companies' response to this double pinch is to accelerate the search for new drugs.

In congressional testimony, Gerald J. Mossinghoff, president of the PMA, in defense of drug price increases, asserted that brand-name firms would spend more than $4 billion in research and development in 1985, a four-fold jump in 10 years. To underwrite this commitment to heavy research investment, most brand-name companies are raising prices despite the increased competition of generics. A *New York Times* business analysis observes: "most [brand-name] companies seem prepared to stick with significantly higher prices . . . despite evidence of consumer interest in generics." And Mossinghoff stated: "The increased investment in pharmaceutical R&D has contributed to higher drug prices today, but will certainly lead to better, even more cost-effective medicine tomorrow."

The major research goal is to develop and market new breakthrough drugs for the treatment of cancer and cardiovascular disease. Spokespersons for both the brand-name and generic industries agree that the introduction of major new patent-protected drugs will encourage brand-name companies to lower prices of existing drugs closer to those of generics. Faced with the FDA obstacle course and the generic market, the big pharmaceutical houses are counting on the profits of such new drugs to pull them through. If this fails, some may bail out altogether.

A PMA representative says: "If it becomes more attractive and financially safer for pharmaceutical houses to invest in mouthwash and toothpaste, they will almost certainly do so."

Uncertain Savings

Changes in the drug industry are too recent for clear predictions, but leading drug industry analyst David F. Saks of Morgan, Olmstad, Kennedy and Gardner projects that by 1990 generic drugs will have grabbed nearly 50 percent of the prescription drug market. Also, generic versus brand-name competition can be expected to generate an unprecedented wave of consumer drug advertising. Price competition is predicted as inevitable, but how much the consumer will actually save remains to be seen.

The fact remains, however: generic drugs cost significantly less than brand-name drugs and will continue to do so into the immediate future.

Paul Lavrakas is a writer in Washington, DC.

"Millions of older persons . . . could save a great deal of money by using generics."

Generic Drugs Are Better Than Brand-Name Drugs

Cyril F. Brickfield

Editor's note: The following viewpoint is an excerpt from a speech Cyril F. Brickfield made at a conference on pharmaceuticals for the elderly.

AARP [American Association of Retired Persons] is the nation's largest organization of Americans age 50 and older, with a membership of more than 21 million. We are a non-profit, non-partisan organization which offers a wide range of membership benefits, legislative representation at federal and state levels, and educational and community service programs through a national network of volunteers and local chapters.

Not incidentally, we represent the primary consumers of pharmaceutical products in this country. As I'm sure you know, some 30 percent of all prescriptions filled in the U.S. are for persons age 65 or older.

We have made remarkable progress in health care during the past 50 years. New technologies, effective research into the causes and treatments of disease, and an increased awareness of what we—ourselves—can do to stay healthy and fit have all contributed to these gains.

But advances in the range and quality of pharmaceutical products have also played an important part in our health care progress. For this, we commend the members of the P.M.A. [Pharmaceutical Manufacturers Association]. I think it is safe to say that AARP might not have achieved its 22-million-member milestone without the vital research and development pioneered by the pharmaceutical industry.

To serve our members, AARP operates the largest private, non-profit mail-order pharmacy in the world. To help them save money, we promote the use of generic drugs. And to insure their safety, we enclose

Cyril F. Brickfield, "Pharmaceutical Industry and the Consumer: Renewing the Trust," a speech delivered to the Conference on Pharmaceuticals for the Elderly in Washington, DC on February 13, 1986.

with most of our prescriptions an informational leaflet which describes the drug and its potential side effects.

It is our concern about costs and misinformation about generic drugs that I wish to underscore.

The High Cost of Prescription Drugs

A recent survey conducted for AARP on the financing of health care for older Americans found that prescription drugs are the second highest out-of-pocket health cost for older Americans, exceeded only by the cost of long term care.

That should come as no surprise. As Henry Waxman, Chairman of the House Health Subcommittee, has said: "Unless one is poor enough to be eligible for Medicaid, sick enough to be sent to the hospital, or lucky enough to belong to one of the few insurance programs that cover drugs, one must pay for prescription drugs out-of-pocket. Unfortunately, only 20 percent of the population falls into one of these categories. Eighty percent must pay from their own pockets."

That's why older Americans—particularly those living at or near the poverty line—are hurt every time prescription prices go up.

It is no secret that drug prices in the U.S. are the highest in the world. Most nations impose price controls on prescription drugs; some have even mandated price reductions on prescriptions. But in this country, drug prices *rose* by 10 percent [in 1985]. And the prices for some products have already been reported to have increased 10, 11 or even 12 percent [in January 1986] alone.

We at AARP do not believe that such sharp price increases can be justified, particularly when they must be paid—in many cases—by the sickest and poorest among us.

For many years, we have been told that the reason drugs cost so much in the U.S. is because of the research and development that goes into them.

Roughly $4 billion was spent [in 1985] on the development of new drugs. We support and commend such important and demanding work. But that R&D figure alone doesn't tell the whole story.

The pharmaceutical industry generally spends 10 percent of its gross sales on research and development. This percentage has remained relatively constant for many years. But despite that stability, and despite the fact that the industry has won from Congress tax credits for R&D and patent term extensions, prescription prices have continued to skyrocket and have far outpaced other producer price indexes. The rate of inflation for pharmaceutical products had been more than twice the rate of increase in the Consumer Price Index since 1981—56 percent for drug prices compared to 23 percent for the C.P.I.

This has created havoc for millions of older Americans in terms of both their finances and their health.

Prescription drugs are a necessity, not a discretionary purchase. Yet individuals sometimes may be forced to choose between having prescriptions filled and paying the rent or mortgage, or the grocery bill, or the doctor bill.

But these inflated pricing practices are doing more than hurting older consumers. I suggest that they are hurting the pharmaceutical industry itself.

"The pharmaceutical industry is hurting itself with its pricing and anti-generic policies."

Until now, older Americans have been reluctant to adopt the attitude of "let the buyer beware," especially when it comes to medicine and health. They have tended to rely on their doctor and pharmacist without question. But I can assure you that this trust is being jeopardized by this continued inflated pricing structure of the drug industry.

When consumers saw the price of Inderal shoot up by 89 percent in the three years before its patent expired, they didn't need a PhD to understand why. And when they see the manufacturer of Inderal leading the campaign against generic drugs, they can easily figure out that concern for consumers may not be the prime motivation.

Blatant Misinformation

AARP is deeply concerned by the increasingly blatant attempts to dissuade American consumers from using equally effective, less costly generic drug products.

We've seen a host of seemingly objective, independent academicians and practitioners speaking out against generic drugs, without disclosing who is paying them to do so. For example, on the NBC "Today" show, a spokesman for a group calling itself "Concern for Understanding of Research in Ethical Pharmaceuticals" questioned the safety and efficacy of generics. He went on to claim that the Food and Drug Administration does not use the same rigorous testing standards for generic drugs as it does for brand-name. . . . That statement is absolutely false. Unfortunately, neither the spokesman nor the "Today" show revealed that his group is supported by Ayerst Laboratories, a brand-name drug manufacturer.

Another group called "Medicine in the Public Interest" is also spreading misinformation and creating fear about the FDA approval process for generics. This so-called "public interest" group is supported by brand-name industry funds and is represented by an attorney who was involved with the "Committee for the Care of Children." That committee, as you may know, was subsidized by industry funds to oppose the placement of Reyes Syndrome warning labels on aspirin. So much for the public interest.

Perhaps the most far-reaching and insidious effort to disparage generic drugs can be found in the continuing anti-generic crusade of a tabloid called the *Medical Tribune*. This magazine, supported entirely by industry funds and published by the owner of an advertising firm representing brand-name companies, is sent to 150,000 doctors. It has little of the scholarly merit attributed to the *New England Journal of Medicine* or the *Journal of the American Medical Association*. And who here really believes that its articles on generics are prompted by scientific rather than economic concerns?

Unfortunately, *Medical Tribune* is apparently succeeding in misinforming some physicians about the inferiority of generics and the incompetency of the FDA. A spokesman for the American Academy of Family Physicians, appearing on the "MacNeil-Lehrer Report", cited *Medical Tribune* articles as "evidence" of the poor quality of generics.

Victimizing the Elderly

This "smear and fear" campaign against generic drugs is of particular concern to us because it is victimizing millions of older persons. They are the primary users of long-term maintenance drugs for chronic conditions and could save a great deal of money by using generics. Yet they are being scared away from generics by those who impugn their safety and efficacy for purely economic reasons.

Most of the customers at AARP's walk-in pharmacy on K Street are living on low or fixed incomes. But when our pharmacists inform them that they can save $10 or more in some cases by having their prescriptions filled generically, many of them refuse. "If it costs less, it can't be good," they tell us. How wrong they are!

We at AARP are not going to sit idly by and let the drug industry's misrepresentations about generics go unchallenged. . . . We plan on using educational efforts to provide needed ammunition to the less well financed side of this struggle for the "hearts and minds" of health care consumers.

We believe that the pharmaceutical industry is hurting itself with its pricing and anti-generic policies. It is most assuredly creating a more cynical group of older consumers. And, I would suggest that it is in danger of losing its long-standing leadership role in scientific research and development and its credibility with policymakers, business leaders and the general public. As industry-watchers have observed, the breakthrough medicines we hear about today are being developed more frequently by researchers or academic institutions, not drug companies.

When a book like Arthur Hailey's *Strong Medicine* stays on the *New York Times* best-seller list for 20 weeks, the pharmaceutical industry should pay attention. The public clearly wants to know more about what the book describes as "the battles between ethics and profits that rage in a business devoted to both."

When the media increasingly devotes space and time to stories about unsafe products and questionable marketing tactics, and when it features a Congressional hearing in which the integrity of research-based companies is openly challenged, the industry should heed the message.

Restoring Public Trust

Clearly, all of us have a large stake in maintaining public confidence in the pharmaceutical industry. If that confidence continues to erode, it will slow our nation's medical progress. Cures for cancer, Alzheimer's Disease and other afflictions may hang in the balance.

With so much at stake, so much risk and so much promise, we cannot afford a continued crisis of confidence. . . . Our shared investment in a healthier future demands nothing less than our commitment to practices that will lead to a restoration of the public trust.

Cyril F. Brickfield is the executive director of the American Association of Retired Persons, the largest senior citizen organization in the US.

"Generic drugs are being approved for marketing that are not in practice therapeutically equivalent to the pioneer products."

Brand-Name Drugs Are Better Than Generic Drugs

Pharmaceutical Manufacturers Association

Companies that apply to the Food and Drug Administration to manufacture generic copies do not have to conduct the exhaustive safety and efficacy studies that the inventor and developer performed on the pioneer product. Since 1984 generic applicants have been required to show only that the product they propose to make is "bioequivalent," meaning that it contains the same active ingredient as the pioneer product *and* that the ingredient is absorbed by the body in approximately the same manner.

Bioavailability

Bioequivalence of two different drug products is determined by comparing their "bioavailabilities." Bioavailability commonly is defined as the *rate* and *extent* to which an active drug ingredient is absorbed from the drug product (tablet, capsule, etc.).

In general, bioavailability is determined by three measurements: (1) the total amount of drug absorbed following administration of a single dose, (2) the maximum concentration achieved in the blood, and (3) the rate or speed of absorption.

To assess whether two products are bioequivalent, one must perform a statistical comparison of their three bioavailability measurements. Currently, FDA typically follows a rule allowing a new generic formulation to vary by up to 20 percent in bioavailability when compared to the original product.

PMA [Pharmaceutical Manufacturers Association] President Gerald J. Mossinghoff summarized the industry position on bioequivalence and generic drugs at a hearing on October 21, 1987, before the Senate Subcommittee on Antitrust, Monopolies and Business Rights, Committee on the Judiciary. The following is from the testimony:

(1) Our way of life in the United States would be unimaginable without the modern medicines discovered and developed by the PMA companies through their research and development. During 1986, PMA companies invested $54.6 billion in R&D, an increase of 12 percent over 1985. People are living longer, healthier and more productive lives as a direct result of that investment. In recent years, the costs of providing health care, and the prices charged, have risen substantially. The same is true for prescription drugs. But modern prescription drugs are a very good value. Prescription drug prices have remained well below the overall Consumer Price Index [CPI] ever since that index was set at 100 in 1967. And drug prices today are less than two-thirds the overall price index for medical care.

Investing in Research and Development

(2) Research and development are the hallmarks of the PMA member companies. Their investment in R&D continues to double every five years. [In 1987] the industry will spend $5 billion in developing new life-saving medicines, at an average cost of $125 million for each new drug. There would, of course, be no generic drugs at all without this huge investment by PMA companies in developing new drugs and in educating physicians and other health-care professionals to use them properly and effectively.

(3) Moreover, the industry is investing an increasingly higher percentage of sales—currently 15 percent—to finance its growing investment in R&D. Measuring increases in R&D expenditures the same way we measure price increases, the "index" for R&D conducted by PMA companies now stands at over 1,000, three and one-half times the prescription drug CPI.

(4) There obviously is a place in the U.S. free-market economy for generic copies of pioneer drugs whose patents have expired. PMA is concerned,

"Generic Drug Equivalence," a position statement published in October 1988 by the Pharmaceutical Manufacturers Association. Reprinted with permission.

however, that generic drugs are being approved for marketing that are not in practice therapeutically equivalent to the pioneer products. Despite the claim of the Food and Drug Administration that it "is not aware of a single documented case of bioinequivalence involving any generic drug product that has been approved by the Agency as bioequivalent," there are many examples where drugs approved as therapeutically equivalent produced different clinical results than the pioneer products. . . .

In one drug-switching example, as reported by a physician in the *Journal of the American Medical Association*, Sept. 4, 1987, a 16-year-old girl who had been stable on the same antiepileptic medication for nine years suffered a dramatic increase in her seizure frequency after being switched to a generic drug. The physician reported that, despite the FDA's claim that it is not aware of a single documented case of bioinequivalence involving any generic drug approved by the Agency as bioequivalent, "our patient provides such a case."

Problems with Switching Drugs

(5) PMA is particularly concerned about the indiscriminate switching of drug products, whether from brand name to generic, generic to brand name or from one generic to another. Patients on maintenance regimens whose daily dosage must be individualized are especially at risk when drug products are changed. Many such drugs are given to elderly patients and patients whose illnesses, such as heart failure or diabetes, can have life-threatening consequences if treatment is inadequate. Many maintenance drugs require dose titration because of factors such as inter-patient variability, steep dose response curve, narrow therapeutic index and variable clinical course. Case reports demonstrate that patients with epilepsy, diabetes, cardiac disease and hyperactive children experienced problems following a switch from one version of a drug to another. In cases where patients resumed taking the original drug, their condition was again controlled.

(6) The FDA itself has acknowledged that, of the approximately 6,000 multisource drug products listed in its *Approved Drug Products with Therapeutic Equivalence Evaluations* (also known as the "Orange Book"), about 20 percent have not been determined by the Agency to be therapeutically equivalent to the pioneer products. Many physicians and pharmacists are unaware that FDA assigns different therapeutic ratings to marketed products, and thus do not use this information in prescribing and dispensing. This obviously raises a serious question as to why more than 1,000 drugs—that have never been tested for safety and efficacy or determined by FDA to be bioequivalent to pioneer products that have been so tested—are allowed to remain on the market.

(7) PMA believes that the process used by the FDA to approve generic drugs needs to be improved. Indeed, the FDA itself has stated that its testing procedures for approving generic drugs can be improved. PMA believes that the FDA should (1) tighten the standards it uses to determine bioequivalence, by repudiating the across-the-board plus-or-minus 20 percent rule in favor of individualized drug-by-drug bioequivalence criteria; (2) use existing FDA surveillance systems to collect and evaluate bioinequivalence data on generic products, and (3) extend FDA's warning about the risks of switching drugs—for drugs approved between 1938 and 1962—to all maintenance drugs approved through bioequivalence testing and include this caution in the product labeling, until such testing is scientifically demonstrated to assure safety and effectiveness. . . .

"The process used by the FDA to approve generic drugs needs to be improved."

As a result of FDA's Fall 1986 public hearing on Bioequivalence of Solid Oral Dosage Forms, a report was issued from the Agency in February of 1988. The report indicates that FDA seriously considered the presentations and viewpoints offered by the research-based pharmaceutical industry, physicians, and academics.

PMA had urged for a more scientific interpretation of bioequivalence data, and we were encouraged by several recommendations presented in FDA's report. For example, the Agency concluded that its system for detecting and evaluating therapeutic failures needs improvement and acknowledged that some drugs or drug classes may require tighter limits than the generally applied ±20% rule.

Obviously, there is still much to be done; some problems identified at the conference and in subsequent discussions remain unresolved—in particular, the validity of bioequivalence testing as an assurance of interchangeability of drug products under all actual conditions of use.

The Washington-based Pharmaceutical Manufacturers Association is a professional organization. The companies belonging to the Association develop pharmaceutical and biological products.

*"Hundreds of thousands of dollars'
worth of unnecessary and even
irrational prescriptions are written every
year by doctors."*

viewpoint **23**

Doctors Are Responsible for Prescription Drug Abuse

Ellen Ruppel Shell

Not long ago, more prescriptions for amphetamine were filled in Michigan than in any other state. The reason for this was not clear, but there was informed speculation that assembly-line workers in the automobile industry were probably involved. Assembly-line work is boring, and uppers are known to make time pass quickly. The pusher in many cases was a certain doctor, whose practice was limited to distributing amphetamine in large quantities to anyone who asked for it. People lined up at his door every morning, and the line was said to stretch around the block. These people were weighed and had their blood pressure taken by a nurse, and were then ushered in, seven or eight at a time, to see the doctor. He told them they were looking fine and gave them each a large packet of pills. Some "patients" went through this ritual daily.

Prescribing for Profit

The Michigan doctor, who has since been arrested and is no longer licensed to practice, is said to have distributed more than a million doses of amphetamine a year. His is an extreme example of a problem that the medical profession has been quietly monitoring, and dealing with, for more than a decade. The federal Drug Enforcement Administration (DEA) estimates that about 17,000 of the nation's 650,000 doctors and a fraction of the 50,000 pharmacies dole out prescription drugs purely for financial gain, a clearly illegal practice. But the vast majority of what is called inappropriate prescribing does not involve these unscrupulous "scrip doctors." Hundreds of thousands of dollars' worth of unnecessary and even irrational prescriptions are written every year by doctors acting in a perfectly legal capacity.

Inappropriate prescription-writing is the most common complaint heard by medical review boards, in some states eclipsing all other complaints combined. "We have found doctors prescribing fifteen drugs, five of which were contraindicated," says John Ulwelling, the executive director of the Oregon Board of Medical Examiners. "There's no doubt that this is the number-one problem facing medical boards across the country."

Of all drug-related emergency-room cases, more than half involve drugs that were legally prescribed. Of all drug-related deaths, 70 percent involve prescription drugs (the percentage of deliberate overdoses is unknown). Although the American Medical Association makes a point of loudly condemning the handful of crooked doctors who write thousands of illegal prescriptions for narcotics and other psychoactive drugs, the crux of the problem lies with honest doctors who simply do not know—or, in some cases, care—that the medication they are recommending for a patient is ineffective, needlessly expensive, or dangerous. "The average American doctor is simply writing too many prescriptions," says Dr. Jerry Avorn, an internist and an associate professor at Harvard Medical School. "And, surprisingly, most of the problem is with non-narcotic drugs."

A classic example, Avorn says, is propoxyphene, a prescription analgesic most commonly known by one of its brand names, Darvon. Propoxyphene is widely prescribed to alleviate mild to moderate pain, yet controlled studies show it to be at best no more effective a pain reliever than aspirin or acetaminophen (Tylenol). The DEA does not consider propoxyphene a particularly dangerous drug, and for that reason many physicians consider it to be relatively benign. But propoxyphene has a number of unpleasant side effects, including dizziness, drowsiness, nausea, and vomiting, and can be dangerous when combined with alcohol. It is also addictive. In a study completed in 1983, overdoses of the drug were blamed for roughly a thousand deaths a year, only about half of which were suicides. Yet doctors continue to prescribe it: Darvocet, a mixture of propoxyphene and another analgesic, is one of the most commonly prescribed drugs in the country.

The Placebo Effect

Ironically, the main reason propoxyphene is sometimes preferred to aspirin is that it is available only by prescription. There is a strong belief among physicians that patients have faith in prescription drugs and will perceive themselves to be better served if they obtain a prescription during an office visit. The placebo effect of prescription drugs is thought to be greater than that of over-the-counter drugs, and this effect is sometimes considered critical in the treatment of things like arthritis, headache, and chronic back pain, which are extremely difficult to treat.

"Some patients won't patronize a doctor unless he prescribes drugs," says Dr. Lial Kofoed, of the Department of Psychiatry at Dartmouth Medical School, in Hanover, New Hampshire. "They feel ripped off if all they get is a talking-to. If you go to dinner with doctors in a big city, you'll hear them complain about competition. They don't want to lose a patient to the doctor who will give out a prescription for the latest drug."

Newer drugs may be perceived as better or safer than older drugs, because they haven't been around long enough for their limitations to show. For example, in the seventies and early eighties doctors widely prescribed Valium (diazepam) for anxiety and tension. Dubbed "mother's little helper" (after a song by the Rolling Stones), the drug was so popular that, doctors reported, patients asked for it by name. But Valium's popularity waned as it became associated with middle-class malaise and as its addictive properties became widely recognized. According to Kofoed, Xanax (alprazolam) is gradually supplanting Valium as the drug of choice for anxiety (Pharmaceutical Data Services reports that Xanax was the fourth most dispensed brand-name drug in 1987). Part of the reason for the change is probably that the patent on the formula for Valium is about to expire, and so Valium is not being heavily advertised in medical journals, whereas Xanax is.

There is now some concern, however, that Xanax is even more addictive than Valium. "One of the best ways to make a temporary problem permanent is to addict a patient to a drug," Kofoed says. "In the case of Valium or Xanax, you get the original anxiety supplemented by withdrawal anxiety"—that is, people are afraid to give up the drug for fear that if they do, their original symptoms will return.

Doctors in large practices prescribe more drugs per patient than do doctors in smaller practices. Writing a prescription has in many cases become a tacit way of indicating that the appointment is over—and the sooner the prescription is written, the sooner the doctor can get on to the next case. "It takes a lot less time to prescribe a drug than to explain to a patient why you won't," Kofoed says. "Also, most doctors want to maintain the image of helper, and some doctors will do almost anything to keep up that image. So they prescribe a pain-killer or a tranquilizer, and the patient is happy."

This compulsion to please patients at almost any cost is made more dangerous by the fact that many doctors don't know all that much about drugs in the first place. Physicians receive surprisingly little formal training about prescription drugs in medical school. They are expected to learn most of what they need to know during their internship and residency and, later, in medical journals and occasional courses. In reality, however, doctors get the vast majority of their information about new drugs from pharmaceutical sales representatives, known in the industry as detail men, or detailers. Detail men meet with doctors in their offices. They offer free samples, to tide patients over until a prescription is filled. As salesmen, the detailers try to promote the latest and most profitable drugs for their companies, not to give the doctor a balanced presentation. At any rate, many salesmen are incapable of giving one, because they lack the facts to do so. Although a few companies, like Eli Lilly, strive to hire pharmacists to fill their sales slots, most do not. Of 27,000 detailers in the industry, only 4,000 hold degrees in pharmacy. According to T. Donald Rucker, a health economist and a professor of pharmacy administration at the University of Illinois at Chicago, most detailers are not scientifically trained.

"Physicians receive surprisingly little formal training about prescription drugs in medical school."

"When hiring a salesman, some companies figure they're better off with an English or music major than with a pharmacist," Rucker says. "If you are trying to bamboozle a physician into thinking a certain drug is the greatest thing since sliced bread, it helps if you don't know anything about the product beyond what your boss has told you. Besides, pharmacists are in demand, and they are expensive—maybe five or ten thousand more a year than a liberal-arts major."

Selling More Drugs

Detailing is an expensive process. A study published [in] November [1987] concluded that drug companies spend an average of $81 for every face-to-face encounter between one of their salesmen and a physician. Yet it appears that this approach is cost-effective—every major drug company in the country uses it. In 1977 a vice-president of marketing for a major drug manufacturer told a reporter for *Sales Marketing and Management* magazine, "Dealing with physicians is the best way to sell drugs. . . . All I can say is that every time we've added salespeople, sales have gone up." It is safe to assume that the number of sick people does not correlate with the number of drug salespeople on the road—more drugs are sold because more physicians have been advised to prescribe them.

Jerry Avorn and his colleague, Stephen B. Soumerai, who has a doctorate in public health, ran a controlled study to see whether doctors' prescribing practices would change if they were provided with unbiased information about particular drugs. In an effort they called academic detailing, they enlisted clinical pharmacists to make office visits and explain the action and limitations of three drugs that are widely considered to be overprescribed: vasodilators, which are prescribed inappropriately for the treatment of senility; cephalexin, an antibiotic that, while effective, is much more expensive than equally effective alternative drugs; and propoxyphene. After spending just over half an hour with a pharmacist, physicians reduced their prescription of these drugs by an average of 13 percent, relative to a control group. Avorn believes that such an outreach program, widely expanded, could reduce the $2.8 billion worth of prescriptions that physicians write each year, and thereby save millions of dollars and many lives. "Nobody's minding the store in academic medicine to systematically inform doctors about drugs," Avorn says. "Industry is very good at this—it does continuing education and marketing that reaches just about every doctor in the country. The bad news is that industry's message is a commercial message. Clearly, industry is not to blame—it's the doctor's fault if this is the only message he listens to, and it is the patient, and society, who is hurt."

"You can't fix senility with a pill. Prescription medications are not a substitute for compassion—or common sense."

Elderly patients are at particularly high risk of being inappropriately medicated. Ordinarily, the liver or kidneys will clear the body of excess drugs, but in the elderly the efficiency of these organs lessens and some drugs can build up to toxic levels. On average, people over age sixty-five take twice as many pills as the rest of us (nursing-home patients typically receive from four to a dozen every day, half of them tranquilizers). Often elderly people go to several physicians, each of whom may prescribe one or more drugs without knowing what drugs the other doctors are prescribing or what over-the-counter medications the patient is taking. Hence the risk of dangerous drug interactions is greatly increased. Side effects of overmedication are particularly hard to detect in older people, because they include the very symptoms associated with "normal" old age: incontinence, tremors, loss of facial expression, depression, agitation, confusion, and falls. Often elderly patients are given a long-lasting drug for a short-term problem, such as occasional sleeplessness, which may linger in their systems for up to three days. The result may be permanent listlessness and what looks like symptoms of depression—symptoms that may prompt the prescription of an antidepressant.

No Substitute for Common Sense

"The problem is that most of us went into medicine because we wanted to help and because we enjoyed science," Avorn says. "Chemical intervention seems to be a scientific way to help people. Drugs represent one of the most effective technologies for ameliorating disease—but they don't always work. You can't fix senility with a pill. Prescription medications are not a substitute for compassion—or common sense."

Ellen Ruppel Shell is a senior writer at Boston's public television station, WGBH. She also writes frequently for the monthly periodical The Atlantic *on science and health issues.*

viewpoint **24**

Patients Are Responsible for Prescription Drug Abuse

Alfred Burger

Drugs are chemical compounds that modify the way the body works. Most people think that these biological activities should help or heal sick people or animals. There is, however, no known drug that is not harmful or even poisonous at high doses, and much of the scientific work on drugs has attempted to widen the gap between effective and toxic doses.

The word *drug* has acquired bad connotations in recent years since the widespread abuse of a few chemicals that affect the central nervous system has become a serious sociological problem. Nevertheless, drugs act on many other organs in the body, can benefit as well as harm the nervous system, and have made possible a revolution in the way modern doctors treat disease.

More Benefits than Drawbacks

Just as there is no health benefit without potential toxicity, there is no absolute goodness about drugs. However, their enormous health benefits outweigh the drawbacks in individual cases. . . .

There are people who pride themselves on "never" taking any drugs whatsoever. This is to be recommended during pregnancy, because some drugs can traverse the placenta and may cause adverse or even dangerous effects in the fetus. In all other conceivable conditions, however, not taking a drug when it might alleviate a disease or discomfort is unjustifiable. Religious fanatics may deny themselves the comfort of medications, but normal, rational individuals should never consider falling into that trap.

The other extreme encompasses people who take too many drugs. Some even take every drug in sight, and others take a drug because it was given to them free or sold as a bargain. This holds not only for vitamins, although they are first in line. One elderly woman we knew lined up twenty-four capsules and tablets on the breakfast table and washed these pretty, multicolored chemicals down with another drug product, coffee. She had collected her medications quite simply. Her physician prescribed three or four for her, but when she bought them she was assailed by doubts. Would they really work? Would it not be better to ask for a second opinion about her condition? Insurance would pay most of her bill, and so she saw a second—and finally a third—physician. These doctors diagnosed the same illness as the first one but prescribed different brands of the same medication. They also recommended a few vitamin capsules, and that is how she ended up with all those pills. The outcome was that she ingested three times the therapeutic dose of each medication. No wonder she landed in a hospital with toxicity symptoms from these overdoses.

Patients and Prescriptions

This case is not unusual. The high cost of visits to a physician drives thousands of patients everywhere to attempt self-medication with over-the-counter, nonprescription drugs. Catastrophic intoxication is avoided only because those over-the-counter drugs are often not very effective anyway. This does not protect sensitive individuals from allergic reactions to the drug. It does not eliminate the danger of overmedication in attempts to commit suicide.

All this illustrates the fact that many patients do not comply with their physician's prescriptions and directions. Some patients just will not take the prescribed drugs at all, for whatever reason—unwillingness to obey orders; adherence to Christian Science, which shuns drugs; or because their bridge partner or beauty parlor operator has warned them of side effects of the drug. Others want to save the expense of buying the prescription—and some drugs are indeed very expensive.

Alfred Burger, *Drugs and People: Medications, Their History and Origins, and the Way They Act*. Charlottesville, VA: The University Press of Virginia, 1986. Reprinted with permission.

Physicians are aware of drug interactions but in years past did not adequately focus on such dangers. The best advice on drug interactions can be obtained from a knowledgeable pharmacist, some of whom now hold a Doctor of Pharmacy degree. A pharmacist who can supply such information can be as important to the patient as a physician.

Drugs may interact with each other by influencing each other's metabolism, absorption, etc. For example, phenobarbital can stimulate the oxidative destruction of several unrelated drugs and thereby make them less long-lasting and less effective. Anticoagulants are made less effective by barbiturates and a spate of other unrelated drugs. When such drugs are used concurrently, blood clotting may occur. It is therefore imperative to follow a physician's careful directions in such cases.

"Drugs, like all the creations of human brains, cannot be expected to be perfect."

Obviously, two drugs that have the same type of activity should not be taken simultaneously unless toxicity from large doses of either of these drugs is to be minimized. Many patients heap one "painkiller" on top of another, which may induce depression and other unwanted side effects. Two drugs that have opposite activity should not be administered together either. Thus, vitamin K, which promotes blood coagulation, will nullify the action of an anticoagulant.

Not all harmful interactions arise from two drugs that interfere with each other; dietary factors also play a role. The most famous case is that of cheddar cheese, red wine, or bananas and the antidepressant monoamine oxidase inhibitors. Those foods contain a biogenic amine called tyramine, which raises the blood pressure. Ordinarily, tyramine is destroyed rapidly by the enzyme monoamine oxidase, but if this enzyme is held in check by the monoamine oxidase inhibitors, tyramine may lead to a dangerous rise in blood pressure. Likewise, while taking an antibiotic or other antibacterial agent, it would be foolish to include vitamins and other nutrients in one's diet that promote the essential life processes of the pathogens. Tetracycline loses its antibacterial activity when taken with milk or other calcium-containing foods.

On the other hand, combination of several drugs in one tablet may not only be convenient but also pharmacologically justified. Many anticancer drugs must be taken in doses verging on overt toxicity if they are to be effective. By mixing lower doses of three anticancer drugs and attacking tumor growth by three different biological routes, some of the toxic

side effects of the individual components of the mixture can be minimized.

Some drugs, when taken in excessive doses or over long periods of time, can induce symptoms of chronic toxicity that may well be called drug-induced diseases. A considerable percentage of patients seeking admission to hospitals are victims of such drug diseases. Reversing the chronic effects of a drug is difficult if not impossible. Since all drugs are tested for chronic toxicity in laboratory animals before being admitted to clinical usage, experienced physicians will be able to adjust prescriptions in a manner that promises to avoid such incidents.

A Physician's Role

The physician is regarded by patients as a dual person. He must be competent in diagnosing and treating the disease and in prescribing the most up-to-date and effective and the least toxic drugs. Most patients require a second quality in their doctor, whether he be a primary family practitioner or a specialist. They want him or her to be a sympathetic, comforting parent figure, emanating professional authority *and* compassion. This is demanding a good deal from a physician who sees and treats twenty and sometimes fifty or more patients every day. However, it is the physician's duty to explain the diagnosis to the patient, prescribe adequate medication, and advise about side effects or even failures of the drug prescribed. The physician should also make it clear when and how long a drug should be taken. Elderly patients, especially those with little education, may stop taking an antibiotic as soon as they are free from fever, and will invite a relapse if they interrupt the treatment before all pathogens have been killed. A factual attitude toward all drugs without prejudice will do much to help in the drug therapy of a disease. This factual attitude should include the hope that a given drug will do the task expected of it, but that the drugs, like all the creations of human brains, cannot be expected to be perfect.

Quackery

The horse-drawn medicine cart, gaily painted and decorated, has been a cherished American tradition in the same league as the circus coming to town. The driver of the cart was a combination comedian, huckster, self-appointed health adviser, and fake. Crowds greeted his visit and men and women alike succumbed to his hard-sell advertising of snake-bite oil, hair tonics for balding heads, rejuvenating nostrums, aphrodisiacs, deworming medicines, and backache liniments.

The blandishments of these unauthorized "doctors" and the ineffectiveness of their medications were the direct cause of the Pure Food and Drug Act that the U.S. Congress passed in 1906. This legislation abolished most, although not all, outright quackery that had been foisted on the public by medical swindlers in a shameless manner for centuries. . . .

The dread of cancer of old has driven desperate patients and their families into the hands of would-be healers and the use of unproven medications. Now that early diagnosis and combination treatment by irradiation therapy, surgery, and chemotherapy has greatly reduced morbidity and mortality from malignancies, this fear should have been replaced by cautious optimism. But two recent incidents of serious quackery do not support such more enlightened attitudes. The first of these incidents was the announcement by two Balkan "healers" about 1952 that they had discovered an anticancer agent in horse serum. They manufactured the product, named it Krebiozen (Krebs is cancer in German), and allied themselves with a prominent physiologist who, in an as yet unexplained delusion, gave the drug respectability. No need to state that Krebiozen was a hoax and did no good.

The second incident was the case of Laetrile. This material was obtained from crushed apricot pits. They were extracted, and the evaporated extract left behind the agent. Chemical studies revealed that it contained a glycoside of mandelonitrile. This known compound can split off highly poisonous hydrogen cyanide, but in very small amounts. Mandelonitrile and its glucoside have no known therapeutic action; hydrogen cyanide is a general cell poison that may have accounted for some of the toxic symptoms caused by Laetrile. Although this information was widely disseminated and supported by a careful study by scientists of the National Institutes of Health (NIH), thousands of deluded cancer patients insisted on taking the "drug." Laetrile was banned in many states, but patients traveled to Mexico, where it remained available. Politicians in several localities were threatened with reprisals if they refused to reintroduce Laetrile. Apart from the deaths directly attributable to the toxicity of Laetrile, patients believing in the power of this agent refused to submit to approved medical methods of cancer treatment and thereby hastened their own demise.

"The barrier to dangerous and counterproductive quackery is education of the lay public."

A curious invitation to quackery has sprung up in scattered groups of mostly young people who are seeking security in an insecure world by retiring to rural communes. There they try to lead a pioneerlike primitive life. Among their habits is the exclusive consumption of "natural" foods, which they grow themselves or buy in health foods stores. As long as these stores offer an often tasteless diet of nuts and vegetables, one might regard their wares as refreshing variations from prepared, prepackaged, and precooked meals offered by supermarkets. But the shelves of health food stores also hold materials promoted as natural drugs and sources of essential nutrients, minerals and vitamins. They are botanical powders, crystals, oils, and extracts, and some of them are indistinguishable from similar products offered in oriental markets. A number of these products, however, are totally worthless. They must have slipped by the inspection of government agencies that watch over truth in advertising. This would not matter if the customers of these stores would have the facts about such products at their fingertips, but many are uneducated and gullible. Such wasted purchases can only be prevented by more effective consumer protection.

Better Science Education

The barrier to dangerous and counterproductive quackery is education of the lay public. Constant reports of suspected cases of quackery, backed by scientific evidence translated into plain English, can dispel superstition and ignorance bordering on voodoo. With a wider emphasis on science in the public schools, the next generation should take a fresh look at beliefs that have come down through the ages, before understanding and searching for the truth had reached the state that we now value. In medicine there is always an outside chance that some natural or synthetic product may turn up as a new and valid therapeutic agent. Until such a claim has been verified by preclinical and approved clinical studies, however, the public should beware and remain skeptical.

Alfred Burger is Professor Emeritus in the chemistry department at the University of Virginia.

"Health benefits and reductions in price suggest that the net benefits of direct consumer advertising of prescription drugs may well exceed the costs."

Prescription Drugs Should Be Advertised

Alison Masson and Paul H. Rubin

Prescription drugs are seldom advertised directly to consumers, partly because of strict regulation by the Food and Drug Administration. In fact, there has been a moratorium on direct consumer advertising since 1983. The two types of consumer advertising permitted as exceptions to the moratorium are circumscribed in such a way as to weaken greatly the incentive to advertise. Even before the moratorium, the requirement that the ads include a "fair balance" of information about effectiveness, side effects, and contraindications made advertising very costly. Thus, public policy has consistently opposed the routine advertising of prescription drugs to consumers.

This policy is remarkably uncontroversial. In our opinion, this is because too little attention has been paid to the potential benefits of such advertising. We cannot offer here a full cost-benefit analysis, but in this essay we emphasize the benefits because others have focused on the costs and because we think that the benefits outweigh the costs.

Opposition to prescription-drug advertising to consumers usually relies on two major arguments, both of which we dispute. The usual health argument is that the restrictions protect the health of consumers, since advertisements would induce consumers to put pressure on physicians to prescribe inappropriately and physicians would respond to this pressure. We suggest that the match between patient and drug could in fact often be improved if consumers were led to bring to the physician's attention information that might otherwise not be included in the prescribing process. The second argument is that there is an "inescapable economic imperative" that prices would have to increase to pay for the cost of advertising. We believe that, on the contrary, prices would probably fall. . . .

Alison Masson and Paul H. Rubin, "Matching Prescription Drugs and Consumers: The Benefits of Direct Advertising," *The New England Journal of Medicine*, Vol. 313, No. 8, pp. 513-515. Reprinted with permission.

Some types of information may not be incorporated into the prescribing process at all unless the patient draws them to the physician's attention, and for that to happen the consumer must be made aware of the relevance of the information. Alternatively, it may simply be more efficient for the information to be drawn into the process at the patient's initiative rather than at the physician's. Sellers have an incentive to provide information of value if they can thereby profit, and this is often true in advertising. The four types of information discussed below, if provided directly to consumers through advertising, might lead to improved matches between patients and drugs. In addition, compliance with prescribed drug regimens might improve as a result of the improved matching.

Experience Symptoms

Consumers may experience the symptoms of a disease without realizing that they are symptoms. An example is the thirst associated with diabetes; this association is one of the messages conveyed by Pfizer's current "institutional" advertising. Institutional advertisements, in which no specific product may be named, are permitted as an exception to the moratorium. It is apparently worthwhile to Pfizer to pay for its institutional advertisements, perhaps because it sells the most frequently prescribed oral hypoglycemic drug. Yet, Pfizer's incentive to undertake this type of informational campaign must be limited, because it must share with other makers of hypoglycemic agents the demand-increasing benefits of the advertising for which Pfizer alone bears the entire cost. If a specific product could be named, the advertiser could benefit from more of the increased sales; the "free-rider" problem would be diminished, and the incentive to advertise therefore enhanced.

Consumers who do not recognize in their physical condition symptoms of a treatable problem will, obviously, not consult a physician. Therefore, physicians are not an efficient substitute for advertising in disseminating this type of information.

Encouraging Treatment

Information about an acceptable form of treatment—for example, a newly developed drug—may lead a person with an already-diagnosed disease to return to a physician to seek treatment. For example, a drug chain in the Washington, D.C., area used newspaper advertisements to inform people who already knew that they had herpes that acyclovir had recently been approved by the FDA for use in alleviating the symptoms of recurrent bouts of herpes.

Similarly, people who know themselves to be particularly susceptible to a disease would value information about the creation of a vaccine for the disease. For two reasons, direct consumer advertising may be superior to reliance on physicians to volunteer or request information. First, healthy people cannot be expected to seek out a physician to ask about a preventive measure if they believe none exists, and second, the cost of advertising targeted to selected susceptible groups may be lower than the cost of physicians asking every patient about a special susceptibility. An example is Merck Sharp and Dohme's advertisements in periodicals whose readers included many homosexuals—a group at special risk of contracting hepatitis B—for a vaccine useful against the disease. This example also underscores the possibility that patients may know better than their physicians that they are at risk for certain diseases.

"Unless patients at least know about the existence of a drug, they cannot request the drug and thus learn whether it conforms with their personal willingness to accept risk."

For many conditions, the physician can choose among several drugs appropriate for treatment—drugs that may vary in side effects. Doctors may not review with each patient all the possible side effects nor explain the alternatives in terms of differences in side effects (and other characteristics). Therefore, patients who experience a side effect may not think of it as possibly drug related, and they may not consider the possibility that an alternative treatment may be available. Advertisements that direct consumers' attention to this possibility could lead to more tolerable courses of treatment, which would be valuable in itself, and to improved compliance as well. For example, sexual dysfunction is not an

unusual side effect of drugs, yet patients may never consider the possibility that the problem could be drug related and may feel embarrassed about mentioning it at all. Their receiving the message directly through advertising would therefore increase the likelihood of physician-patient discussion of the problem. Shortly before the moratorium, Ciba-Geigy unsuccessfully sought approval from the FDA for an advertisement with the message that their antihypertensive drug was less likely than some others to cause impotence.

There is no reason to expect physicians to have the same risk preferences as patients (even putting aside liability issues). The patient may be more or less averse to risk than the physician or may consider physical symptoms to be more or less tolerable than the physician judges them to be. Unless patients at least know about the existence of a drug, they cannot request the drug and thus learn whether it conforms with their personal willingness to accept risk. Even if consumers are held to be sometimes foolhardy, the requirement of a prescription limits the effects of the foolhardiness.

Price Effects

The second argument made by those opposed to direct consumer advertising of prescription drugs is that prices must rise to pay for it. Instead, by increasing competition, advertising may serve to lower prices, and that is what we predict. In fact, even if prices did not fall—indeed, even if there were some increase—consumers might still be better off with advertising than without. Any improvement in the match between consumers and drugs will increase the value of the drugs to patients. Consumers are willing to pay more for products that offer greater satisfaction.

The issue of the effect on prices is ultimately empirical. Since arguments for both the increasing and the decreasing of prices can be put forward, the relative magnitudes of the countervailing effects determine the net effect. A number of empirical studies in other markets confirm that price decreases do sometimes occur when advertising is introduced into a market; it is evident that there is no "inescapable economic imperative" that advertising must always raise prices. The pioneering study by L. Benham found that the prices of eyeglasses were lowered by both retail advertising that was price-oriented and retail advertising that was not. J. Cady found that retail prescription-drug prices were lower in states that permitted price-oriented advertising. Other studies (of such disparate products as gasoline, bicycles, toys, chocolate, soap, and legal services) have similarly found price decreases associated with the practice of advertising. . . .

There are several mechanisms by which prescription-drug prices might be reduced as a result of direct consumer advertising.

Any redirection of prescribing from one brand to an equivalent but lower-priced brand will lower the average prices paid by consumers. There is ample opportunity for such savings; approximately two-thirds of all outpatient prescriptions are for drugs with more than one source, and price differences between brands of the same drug can be substantial. Physicians have been shown to have relatively little knowledge of or interest in drug prices, so it is likely to be at the consumer's urging that a cheaper product is prescribed. For example, Boots Pharmaceuticals advertised to persuade consumers to ask their physicians to prescribe Rufen, Boots' prescription version of ibuprofen, rather than Upjohn's more expensive brand, Motrin. Price-oriented advertising is permitted as an exception to the moratorium, but because no mention may be made of the physical condition for which the drug is used, the audience whose attention will be caught is restricted, and the incentive for this kind of advertising is therefore reduced.

Shifting to Other Drugs

Even if physicians did not change the way the prescription was written, advertising might lead consumers to ask the pharmacist to dispense one brand instead of another. This is possible either when the prescription is written generically, which was the case in about 22 per cent of multisource prescriptions in 1980, or when substitution is legally permitted, as it now is (with constraints) in all states. Although some retailers have advertised lists of paired brand-generic prices, the regulations may deter this type of price advertising as well.

When more than one drug is available for treatment, the relative cost can be an important concern of patients. Differences in efficacy may be small, whereas differences in price are large. . . . Advertising could point this out to consumers.

"Providing consumers with information about drugs can serve to improve the match between drugs and patients."

The increased competition brought about by advertising could be expected to lead to reductions in manufacturers' prices. There is evidence that other, non-advertising forms of competition in prescription-drug markets (for example, the entry of new products) has led to lower prices.

The advertising of retail prices may direct consumers to retailers who have lower prices, lowering the average price paid. Another potential source of reductions in retail prices is the fact that national advertising of brands has been shown to reduce retailers' price-minus-cost margins.

Advertising is expensive, but so is detailing. Relaxation of the constraint on direct consumer advertising would allow manufacturers to allocate their marketing resources more efficiently. Any reduction in total marketing costs could then be reflected in prices.

Important Benefits

The benefits of direct consumer advertising of prescription drugs have been overlooked or understated. Because consumers have knowledge about themselves that prescribers do not have and cannot easily obtain, providing consumers with information about drugs can serve to improve the match between drugs and patients; sellers with an incentive to advertise are practiced in communicating effectively with potential buyers. In addition, advertising is likely to cause drug prices to fall. Evidence from other markets predicts this result, and several price-reducing channels in the pharmaceutical industry itself can be identified. The combination of probable health benefits and reductions in price suggest that the net benefits of direct consumer advertising of prescription drugs may well exceed the costs.

Alison Masson is an economist at the Federal Trade Commission. Paul H. Rubin is associate executive director for economics at the Consumer Product Safety Commission.

"There is an inherent conflict between a promotional advertisement and the provision of adequate and objective drug information."

viewpoint **26**

Prescription Drugs Should Not Be Advertised

Eric P. Cohen

In 1983, Dr. Arthur Hull Hayes, then commissioner of the Food and Drug Administration, discussed direct-to-the-public advertisement of prescription medication in a speech to the Pharmaceutical Advertising Council. He noted that such direct promotion had first been discussed in 1981, that discussion had been initiated by the drug industry, and that the FDA had been involved early on in talks with pharmaceutical manufacturers, advertisers, consumer groups, and Congress. He added that "the FDA has serious reservations about pharmaceutical companies and advertisers moving into this uncharted area. . . ."

The First Ads

After Dr. Hayes' speech, the FDA asked for and obtained a moratorium on direct advertising. During the moratorium, such advertising was evaluated by the FDA, and opposition to it formulated by individuals and such major organizations as the American Medical Association, the American College of Physicians, the American Society for Clinical Pharmacology and Therapeutics, the American Society of Hospital Pharmacists, and the American Association of Retired Persons. Finding current regulations "sufficient," the FDA commissioner ended the moratorium in 1985, all the while restating the FDA's unchanged policy: that direct-to-the-public prescription advertising was not in the public interest. Most drug companies seemed to dislike such advertising, judging it not in their best interest, either. But future direct ads were not ruled out, and in September 1987, ads for an antiallergy drug, Tavist, appeared in *The New York Times*, the Chicago *Tribune*, and other newspapers. The FDA expressed reservations about the content and propriety of these ads and has prevented their

subsequent appearance. Indeed, there is an inherent conflict between a promotional advertisement and the provision of adequate and objective drug information. This ethical conflict and the stated FDA policy should have been sufficient to prevent direct advertising in recent years, but the ads have now appeared and may appear again. Discussion of the issue has been too limited; it deserves a wider audience, and the logical basis of the opposition needs to be further developed.

Direct ads are not specifically forbidden by FDA rules. When they are used, they have to conform to FDA regulatory standards. During the moratorium, the FDA studied the issue and published a report in 1984 summarizing its conclusions. Not surprisingly, the study showed that despite being amply provided with information about risks, test subjects remembered potential benefits much more often than risks. The report concluded that "the degree to which risk information is communicated is related to the way the information is structured in an ad," and that "techniques that might distract attention from the ad or portions of the ad containing risk information were obvious barriers to communicating risks." Television spots lasting 30 or 60 seconds are not conducive to "fair balance," and the carefully worded conclusions of the FDA report confirm this.

Direct advertising would mean that radio, television, print, and other media carrying advertising would become available to the companies making and selling prescription drugs. Ads for antibiotics, antihypertensive medications, corticosteroids, and any other prescription medication could appear, designed to sell and bringing to bear all the slick pressure of which Madison Avenue is capable. These ads would be aimed at the public, even though they might appear to be addressed to doctors, as in the case of the recent Tavist ads. They would attempt, for instance, to push one antihypertensive drug over another,

Eric P. Cohen, "Direct-to-the-Public Advertisement of Prescription Drugs," *The New England Journal of Medicine*, Vol. 318, No. 6, pp. 373-375. Reprinted with permission.

much as one brand of hair spray is advertised as more desirable than the others and better able to help its user realize the American dream.

Now, without much warning, we are very close to widespread direct-to-the-public advertising of prescription medications. Issues of regulation of advertising, cost, competition, public health, and individual well-being need to be carefully examined so that such ads can be effectively opposed and prevented.

Regulation of Advertising

The FDA regulates prescription-drug advertising as it currently appears in professional publications. The large print, graphics, and illustrations used in such advertising must be accompanied by precautions and listings of the product's side effects, toxic effects, and contraindications. This notion of "fair balance" in drug advertisements is embodied in the Federal Food, Drug, and Cosmetic Act. These rules have applied to ads aimed at doctors, who are expected to have sufficient background and experience to evaluate them. Appropriate mention of the negative aspects of medication is thus mandated by law.

"That drugs of lesser benefit require more advertising than those whose benefit is known confirms the premise that advertising seeks to increase sales, not knowledge."

Nonetheless, information about side effects has sometimes been concealed. Such a practice is not a mere aberration. J.S. Yudkin showed that in developing nations (where regulatory laws are limited), serious and even fatal side effects of analgesics, hormones, and antibiotics had been concealed by certain pharmaceutical companies whose drug-promotion efforts, furthermore, did not always coincide with the medical needs of the countries involved. Regulations and oversight are necessary in Western nations, too, as exemplified by the thalidomide calamity. G.W. Mellin and M. Katzenstein aptly summarized this point in 1962:

> The ultimate experimental model is public utilization . . . communication is of the utmost importance. Several correspondents were concerned with the communication mediums of advertising, whereas representatives of the company and another correspondent defended the nature of the advertisement. Neither of the latent toxic effects of thalidomide were first reported to the medical profession by the manufacturer.

Had direct ads been used for thalidomide, the number of injuries due to the drug would surely have increased by orders of magnitude.

Ads for cigarettes are now regulated and must include a statement about the dangers of smoking. In the 15 years since their ads were banned from television and radio, the cigarette advertisers have steadily increased their skill at reducing the visual impact of the required printed warning. Indeed, "fair balance," if it can be said to apply to cigarette ads, has been subverted. Should one expect anything different if the same advertising firms are asked to hawk prescription medications? Side effects, toxic effects, and contraindications, listed in small, unobtrusive print off to the side, would be ignored by the incautious reader as is the warning in the cigarette ads by the smoker.

Dubious nostrums provide a further example. They are publicized to the hilt, until common sense and reason take over. Oil of primrose was promoted as a cure-all until regulators caught up with its vendors. Many Americans bought starch blockers, heavily advertised as providing an easy way to lose weight, until they were debunked and removed from the market. If the ad agencies are willing to promote such nonsense, they may go to any length for legitimate products such as prescription medications. In short, without careful and stringent regulation, deception is not unlikely. . . .

Increasing Sales, Not Knowledge

In their study of current drug advertisements, G.R. Krupka and A.M. Vener found that "great investment in advertising is necessary in order to achieve high levels of sales for drugs such as Valium® (diazepam) which do not have a clear-cut ameliorative effect . . . [and] that saturation advertising would not significantly enhance sales of such drugs as Dyazide® (triamterene and hydrochlorothiazide) because of its well established therapeutic value. . . ." That drugs of lesser benefit require more advertising than those whose benefit is known confirms the premise that advertising seeks to increase sales, not knowledge. It stands to reason that public education belongs in more restrained environments than television or tabloids.

Of real concern is the danger that we may all be misled in areas outside our own expertise. The ads we hear and see every day, for all kinds of consumer products, are predicated on the ability of the ad to persuade, not educate, the public. Indeed, the principles of advertising—those of salesmanship in print—are incompatible with education.

Costs and Competition

Cost-benefit analysis of direct advertising has probably already been undertaken. Indeed, several large drug companies have stated that should a competitor begin direct-to-the-public advertising, they would do likewise. Incentives to provide information would then be overrun by the incentives of profit and market advantage.

Under the threat of competition and reduced income, competing companies may feel forced to advertise. Overall costs would rise, putting upward pressure on consumer prices. The ratio of advertising to sales, already high in the drug industry, would rise still higher. In fact, the projected costs to the company in one case were thought to be prohibitive, although the variables in such a calculation would change if direct advertising became the norm. In that case, the cost of not advertising, and possibly losing one's share of the market, might be greater than the cost of advertising. Finally, to preserve the profit margin, companies would permit these excess costs to trickle down to the consumer.

"If direct advertising should prevail, the use of prescription medication would be warped by misleading commercials and hucksterism."

J.I. Mackowiak and J.P. Gagnon also suggest that promotion may increase only costs, not competition, and that real competition occurs only when new products are developed. Granted, competition may lead to lower prices in a diversified market. The prices of a variety of types of a single generic product may go down as a result of advertising-stimulated competition, as shown by L. Benham for eyeglasses. But the prescription-drug market, although quite diversified in some broad categories, is limited in others. There are, for instance, only two nonsteroidal immunosuppressive agents commonly used in renal transplantation—azathioprine and cyclosporine. Clearly, the introduction of the newer product, cyclosporine, provided "competition" in this case. Advertising had no role here. Moreover, I can think of no argument to support direct advertising of either agent and can easily imagine major doctor-patient conflicts arising from such advertising.

An Overmedicated Society

In addition, in a market with few choices, competition is subverted by advertising, not enhanced, because the use of ads rewards persuasiveness, not efficacy. A successful advertiser whose ads have captured the market can manipulate prices at will.

Direct-to-the-public advertising would be undertaken with the goal of increasing a company's revenues and profits. Even if advertising resulted in lower unit costs for medication, increasing company revenues would then depend on higher overall drug sales—that is, more per capita drug consumption in our already overmedicated society. And regardless of concerns about cost, direct ads by their very promotional nature may lead to more use of medication. Indeed, elderly patients, perhaps most in danger of overmedication, were among the earliest targets of direct advertising. Although we need more effective and less toxic drugs, we don't need to take more drugs. We also don't need the higher insurance premiums and taxes that would accompany such an overall jump in the consumption of prescription drugs. In sum, direct ads are expensive and anticompetitive, and may promote unnecessary drug consumption. The funds and effort devoted to direct advertising may also burden drug companies, limiting important research and development. . . .

In conclusion, if direct advertising should prevail, the use of prescription medication would be warped by misleading commercials and hucksterism. The choice of a patient's medication, even of his or her physician, could then come to depend more on the attractiveness of a full-page spread or prime-time commercial than on medical merit. Another intrusion into the doctor-patient relationship would have gone unchecked, unless the medical profession's stated formal opposition becomes active, informed, and real. Regulators, legislators, and drug-industry officials should be informed of our opposition to direct advertising. They should know that such advertising would serve only the ad makers and the media, and might well harm our patients.

Eric P. Cohen teaches at the Medical College of Wisconsin in Milwaukee.

Cigarette Smoking Is Harmful

American Council on Science and Health

The American Council on Science and Health joins with the U.S. Public Health Service, the World Health Organization, the American Cancer Society, the American Lung Association, the American Heart Association and countless other organizations concerned with public health in condemning cigarette smoking as a major health hazard. The scientific evidence indicates unequivocally that cigarette smoking is the most important single cause of preventable death in the United States, being responsible for more than 300,000 premature deaths each year.

Cigarette smoking is addictive and increases the risk of developing and dying from cancer, heart disease and chronic lung disease. It greatly increases the health risks associated with oral contraceptive use and occupational exposure to certain harmful substances. Smoking during pregnancy poses a significant threat to the unborn child. Smoking is also responsible for increased rates of absenteeism and disability among workers and is the major cause of residential fires. Parents who smoke may jeopardize their children's health.

The American Council on Science and Health warns nonsmokers not to begin smoking and urges smokers to "kick the habit." This is one issue where the choices are clear: smoking *or* health. . . .

It was not until the 20th century that large numbers of people began to use tobacco in a much more deadly form: the cigarette. While cancers of the mouth, lips, throat and nose had already been linked with the use of snuff, cigars and pipes by a few astute physicians, these forms of tobacco did not seriously affect the rest of the body. With the development of the blended cigarette, however, tobacco users were able to inhale smoke into their lungs, exposing the entire body to many of tobacco's harmful substances. . . .

The great 20th century cigarette advertising campaign began right after World War I, capitalizing at first on the patriotism that went along with the war effort. The advertising was clever, original, brazen, alluring and extremely high-pitched. The ads often featured testimonials by movie stars, athletes and even doctors, who went so far as to suggest that good health and good looks were the rewards of smoking. Some cigarette manufacturers made particularly bold health claims for their products, advising that their brand could steady the nerves or even cure smokers' cough.

The advertising campaigns were so effective that by 1939, a *Fortune* survey showed that 53% of adult American men smoked cigarettes. Sixty-six percent of men under 40 smoked cigarettes.

The widespread use of cigarettes among women lagged some 25 to 30 years behind that of men. Although a few daring women had smoked cigarettes even before World War I, women did not take up smoking in large numbers until the 1940s.

The First Clues

Unbeknownst to the smoking public, an impressive amount of speculation—and some hard scientific evidence—linking smoking with disease had appeared in the period between 1920 and 1940. Tobacco companies chose not to acknowledge this evidence and continued to promote cigarettes heavily.

By today's standards, the medical evidence gathered against cigarettes by 1940 would have been enough to stimulate a thorough investigation of the matter and extensive coverage in the popular press. But unfortunately, this was not the case at the time.

Few people were aware of the evidence and those who were did not appear to be overly alarmed by it. This may have been due partially to the fact that

Smoking or Health: It's Your Choice, published in July 1984 by the American Council on Science and Health. Reprinted with permission.

cigarettes had become as common and as all-American as apple pie, so people found it difficult to be suspicious of them. Also, the majority of American men were smokers who were physically and psychologically dependent upon cigarettes, and who didn't want to believe bad news about something which they would have found hard to give up. Finally, the nation had developed a large economic stake in tobacco and thus was resistant to any information which could have jeopardized the industry's viability.

During the 1950s, the evidence became more difficult to ignore. By the middle of the decade there was an impressive amount of solid medical evidence that cigarette smoking increased the risk of lung cancer as well as other diseases. And for the rest of the decade, the data continued to accumulate.

As the data came in, not only was its consistency undeniable, but the list of specific adverse effects of cigarette smoking continued to grow. What had started out as just a ''lung cancer scare'' had become a general ''health scare.''

Although the tobacco industry (and articles in the popular press) continued to assert that there was still controversy over the health effects of smoking, cigarette manufacturers rushed to provide consumers with a ''less harmful'' cigarette. In 1950, about 3% of cigarettes had been filtered. By 1957, more than 50% were.

Regulatory Action in the 1960s

By the early 1960s, the scientific evidence against cigarette smoking was overwhelming. Thus, when the Surgeon General's report was released on January 11, 1964, it merely made official what had been known for some time in the scientific community.

Behind locked doors and surrounded by ''No Smoking'' signs, reporters heard the grim warnings of the nation's chief physician, Dr. Luther Terry, and his 10-member panel of experts. Smokers would have been hard put to find any good news in the 387-page report—except that they could reduce their elevated risks of cancer, heart disease, and emphysema by quitting.

''Smokers are about 10 times more likely to die from lung cancer than are nonsmokers.''

One week after the Surgeon General's report was released, the Federal Trade Commission (FTC) proposed that all cigarette packages and advertising be required to carry a strong warning of the hazards of smoking. Although a watered-down version of the health warning did appear on cigarette packages in 1966, it represented more of a victory for the tobacco industry than for public health. Instead of the explicit warning on cigarette packages and advertising called for by the FTC, the industry orchestrated a Congressional mandate for a wishy-washy ''may be hazardous to your health'' statement on cigarette packages only. (The warning eventually was strengthened slightly, but did not appear on cigarette advertising until several years later.) . . .

What are the long term effects of cigarette smoking?
The long term health risks associated with cigarette smoking are, indeed, overwhelming:

• Cigarette smoking is the most important single cause of preventable death in the United States today.

• Four of the five leading causes of death are related to cigarette smoking.

• Approximately one in six deaths in this country is smoking-related. Each year, at least six times as many Americans die from smoking-related causes as die in automobile accidents.

• Overall, a smoker is 70% more likely to die prematurely than is a comparable nonsmoker. Heavy smokers are nearly 200% more likely to die prematurely than are nonsmokers.

• Male cigarette smokers report 33% more days lost from work than do those who have never smoked. Female cigarette smokers have an absenteeism rate which is 45% greater than that of nonsmokers.

• Men who smoke cigarettes report 14 more days of bed disability than do those who have never smoked. Women who smoke report 17% more days of disability than do nonsmokers.

Lung Cancer

Lung cancer kills more Americans each year than any other form of cancer. It is the most common cause of cancer death among males, and is expected . . . to become the leading cause of cancer death among women. (This has already occurred in California and Washington.)

At least 80% of all lung cancer deaths are caused by cigarette smoking. More than 90,000 Americans died from cigarette-related lung cancer in 1982.

Smokers are about 10 times more likely to die from lung cancer than are nonsmokers. Heavy smokers (2 or more packs per day) are up to 25 times more likely to die of lung cancer than are nonsmokers.

Few people survive lung cancer. Seventy percent of lung cancer patients die within one year of diagnosis. Ninety percent are dead within five years.

Cigarette smoking increases a person's risk of developing cancer of the mouth, pharynx, larynx, esophagus, bladder, kidney and pancreas.

Thirty percent of *all* cancer deaths are tobacco-related.

Overall, cigarette smoking is responsible for 10 times as many cancer deaths as is the next most reliably known cause of cancer. In fact, it is responsible for far more cancer deaths than all other reliably known causes of cancer *combined.*

Heart Disease

Far more smokers die from heart disease which has been caused by cigarettes than die from cancer.

Coronary heart disease is the most common cause of death in the United States; 30% of these deaths are attributable to cigarette smoking. Approximately 170,000 Americans died of heart disease due to cigarette smoking in 1982.

It is estimated that one of every 10 Americans alive today will die prematurely due to cigarette-related heart disease.

Cigarette smoking is the *major* avoidable risk factor for heart disease.

The average smoker is 70% more likely to die from heart disease than is a nonsmoker. Heavy smokers are two to three times more likely to die of heart disease than are nonsmokers.

Smoking significantly increases the chances of a second heart attack in someone who has already had one.

People who quit smoking decrease their risk of dying from heart disease. Ten years after giving up smoking, the risk approaches that of a lifetime nonsmoker.

Smoking is the *major* cause of emphysema and chronic bronchitis.

Eighty-five percent of all chronic bronchitis and emphysema deaths are related to cigarette smoking.

In 1982, there were more than 46,000 smoking-related emphysema and chronic bronchitis deaths.

Smokers have an increased incidence of less serious respiratory problems, such as influenza.

The lung function of smokers is measurably impaired.

Smokers have a peptic ulcer disease death rate which is twice that of nonsmokers.

Evidence suggests that smoking retards the healing of peptic ulcers. . . .

Altogether, how many Americans die each year from cigarette-related causes?

It is estimated that more than 300,000 excess deaths occur each year in the United States due to cigarette smoking.

How is that figure calculated?

This figure is based upon information from studies involving more than 20 million person-years of observation, using the standard epidemiological method of comparing "expected" death rates with "observed" death rates.

By studying samples of nonsmokers, we can determine the number of deaths which we would *expect* in a group of any given size. For example, if we were to study a representative sample of 1,000 nonsmokers, we might find 2 lung cancer deaths. Thus, if cigarette smoking were not related to lung

cancer, we would expect to find the same number of lung cancer deaths among a group of 1,000 smokers. If we actually *observed* 72 lung cancer deaths among the smokers, we could conclude that there were 70 "excess" deaths due to smoking, assuming that other factors were accounted for.

The proportion of excess deaths can be calculated in this way for different smoking-related diseases and applied to the total population to arrive at the number of excess deaths attributable to smoking.

Pregnancy

What are the effects of smoking during pregnancy?

Cigarette smoking during pregnancy poses a well-established threat to pregnancy outcome and to the health of the newborn baby.

Many substances inhaled during cigarette smoking, or their metabolic byproducts, enter the mother's bloodstream and thus reach the fetus. Smoking just one or two cigarettes significantly slows fetal breathing movements and increases fetal heart rate.

Pregnant women who smoke are more likely to spontaneously abort (miscarry) or have stillborn babies than are nonsmoking women. Smoking also increases the risk of several complications of pregnancy, including dangerous bleeding during delivery and premature birth. It is estimated that up to 14% of all premature births in the United States may be attributable to maternal cigarette smoking.

"Pregnant women who smoke are more likely to spontaneously abort (miscarry) or have stillborn babies than are nonsmoking women."

Babies born to smokers weigh an average of 7 ounces less than babies born to comparable nonsmokers. This means that infants of women who smoke are more likely to fall into the low birth weight category. Low birth weight babies face significantly greater health risks than do normal weight newborns.

The more a woman smokes during pregnancy the greater the reduction in infant birth weight. Fortunately, if a woman gives up smoking early in pregnancy, her risk of having a low birth weight infant decreases.

Smoking apparently causes decreased birth weight by slowing down the growth rate of the fetus. There is some evidence that this fetal growth retardation may adversely affect the child's long term growth, intellectual development and behavioral characteristics.

Can other agents interact with cigarette smoking to increase a smoker's risk of disease?

Yes. Heavy drinking of alcoholic beverages,

combined with cigarette smoking, greatly increases the risks of developing cancer of the mouth, larynx and esophagus.

Cigarette smoking enhances the risk of developing heart and circulatory diseases associated with oral contraceptive use. Women who smoke and take oral contraceptives have a much higher risk of heart attack and subarachnoid hemorrhage (a type of stroke) than would be expected by simply adding the two factors together.

Cigarette smoking interacts with the other major heart disease risk factors, hypertension and elevated serum cholesterol, in a synergistic manner to greatly increase the risk of developing coronary heart disease.

Workplace Hazards

Cigarette smoking can also exacerbate the effects of some toxic substances to which certain workers may be exposed on the job.

Perhaps the most dramatic example of the interaction of cigarette smoking with occupational hazards occurs with asbestos. Workers who are exposed to airborne asbestos fibers and who smoke greatly increase their risk of developing lung cancer.

Asbestos workers who do not smoke have about a fivefold greater risk of dying from lung cancer than do people who neither smoke nor are exposed to asbestos.

The risk of dying from lung cancer is increased about tenfold for individuals who smoke, but who have not been exposed to asbestos. When the two are combined, the results are unexpectedly deadly.

Asbestos workers who smoke are 53 times as likely to die of lung cancer as are members of the general population, according to a major study involving several thousand asbestos workers. Asbestos workers who are heavy smokers (more than 20 cigarettes per day) may be 87 times more likely to die of lung cancer than are nonsmoking, non-asbestos workers.

"There are very few people unconnected with the tobacco industry who contend that smoking is not extremely dangerous to one's health."

Cigarette smoking also appears to act synergistically with radiation from radon gas to increase the risk of lung cancer among underground uranium miners. It has been suggested that cigarette smoking may interact with vinyl chloride, nickel and 2-naphthylamine to increase the risk of cancer among workers exposed to these substances.

How well established are the risks of cigarette smoking? Isn't there still some scientific controversy over whether or not smoking is harmful?

References to the "smoking and health controversy" appear almost exclusively in tobacco industry literature. There are very few people unconnected with the tobacco industry who contend that smoking is not extremely dangerous to one's health.

Extensive Studies

Literally thousands of scientific studies have demonstrated that smoking is a major health hazard. Indeed, there are few subjects which have been so thoroughly and extensively investigated—and with such unequivocal results. There is not a single major medical or health organization in the world which denies that smoking poses a significant threat to health.

Nevertheless, the tobacco industry, through its trade and lobbying organization, the Tobacco Institute, claims that there is still some question as to the risks of smoking. Industry spokesmen and writers use a number of ploys in an attempt to discount the evidence. Discussed below are some of their more common arguments, which may sound very convincing to someone untrained in epidemiology, but which are a distortion of scientific fact.

Tobacco industry ploy: The recent increase in lung cancer may be due, not to cigarette smoking, but to improved diagnosis.

Fact: Indeed, techniques for detecting lung cancer have improved but so have techniques for detecting all other cancers. Only for lung cancer, which is the cancer most strongly associated with cigarette smoking, have we seen a dramatic increase during this century (the first in which large numbers of people began to smoke cigarettes). The increase in the lung cancer rate among women lagged behind that of men by about 30 years—as did their widespread adoption of the cigarette smoking habit. Furthermore, lung cancer rates remain low among Mormons and other religious groups who still have low smoking rates and in other countries where smoking is not a widely practiced behavior.

Tobacco industry ploy: The relationship between cigarette smoking and disease is entirely statistical. A statistical association should not be confused with a causal relationship.

Fact: When there is a long period of time between initial exposure to something and its observed effect, statistics are essential in establishing causation. Statistics showed us the association between thalidomide use and birth defects. Through statistics we learned that vaccinations protect us from polio, smallpox and measles. Through statistics, a tobacco company can tell if its new advertising campaign has been successful.

Granted, not every factor found to be associated with disease in an epidemiological study is a cause of that disease (and the Tobacco Institute loves to highlight such examples). Observed associations can be spurious, occurring for example, because of a third factor to which both the disease and its supposed cause are related. On the other hand, many associations *do* point to cause, and such is the case with cigarette smoking and the diseases mentioned previously.

Not only do the data on cigarettes conform to all the accepted criteria for establishing causation, but the association has been demonstrated over and over by thousands of studies. Autopsies and clinical and experimental data also corroborate the epidemiological findings.

Tobacco industry ploy: If cigarette smoking causes cancer, then why don't all smokers get cancer?

Fact: Those warning of the dangers of smoking openly acknowledge that not everyone who smokes will develop cancer, heart disease or chronic lung disease. There are obvious differences in susceptibility to all types of disease. Less than 2% of persons infected with the polio virus develop paralytic polio. Not everyone exposed to the tuberculosis microbe develops the disease. Yet, no one would discount the role of these agents in causing illness.

Not everyone who rides in or drives a car is killed in an auto accident; however, the risk increases depending on the manner of driving, the number of miles and the type of car driven. The same holds true for cigarettes. Not every smoker dies of cancer or heart disease, but the risk increases depending on the manner of smoking and the number and type of cigarettes smoked.

"Cigarettes...are known to kill more than 300,000 Americans each year."

Tobacco industry ploy: If cigarette smoking hasn't been shown to cause disease in animals, then it couldn't cause disease in man.

Fact: Although research has shown that tobacco ''tar'' is carcinogenic when painted on the skin of mice, there are not many data on the effects of actual smoking on animals. Largely, this is due to the fact that it is very difficult to get animals to smoke cigarettes in the same way that humans do. Even so, in one study where researchers trained beagles to ''smoke'' through holes cut in their throats, cancerous lung changes were observed.

It is usually the case that animal data provide leads for epidemiological studies on humans. In the case of cigarettes, we began to see cancer in humans well before there was enough suspicion to begin extensive animal testing. At this point, given what we already know about the effects of smoking on humans, it would seem unnecessary to revert to studying its effects on animals.

Tobacco industry ploy: There are so many health hazards to which we are exposed, why should anyone worry about cigarettes?

Fact: We live in a world where new ''health hazards'' seem to turn up daily. Many of these ''hazards'' are merely hypothetical, overrated, or have been suggested by only one or two studies.

Cigarettes, on the other hand, are known to kill more than 300,000 Americans each year. The risks of cigarette smoking have been demonstrated in thousands of studies and are unquestionably far greater than those associated with most other commonly feared ''health hazards.'' . . .

What are the economic costs of smoking-related disease?

It is estimated that smoking-related illness accounts for nearly 8% of all direct health care costs and more than 11% of the total economic cost of disease (direct and indirect costs) in the United States. (Indirect costs include earnings lost due to smoking-related illness and premature death.)

More than $11 billion were spent in 1980 in medical care costs for smoking-related diseases. Lost earnings due to cigarette smoking amounted to $36 billion in 1980.

Who pays these costs?

All Americans, smokers and nonsmokers alike, pay the costs of smoking. Funds collected from public taxes are used to pay hospital and disability benefits to smokers disabled by smoking-related diseases and to support the survivors of those who die prematurely due to cigarettes.

Health and life insurance companies which charge equal premiums to smokers and nonsmokers also shift the burden of smoking-related disease to nonsmokers. Although smokers and nonsmokers pay equal premiums, smokers and their families are more likely to collect insurance benefits, due to the increased risk of disease and early death.

Smokers also charge their medical hills to nonsmokers through higher prices on consumer goods. In 1980, smokers spent an estimated 150 million more days off the job and 81 million more days in bed than did nonsmokers. Their job-related accident rate is double that of their nonsmoking co-workers. In addition to losses in productivity, employers must bear the expenses of more frequent cleaning and repair of office furnishings and increased costs of air conditioning to filter smoke from the air. The employer, of course, then passes these costs on to all consumers in the form of increased prices. . . .

Unable To Give It Up

Is cigarette smoking addictive?

A 1982 NIDA [National Institute on Drug Abuse] report stated that ''cigarette smoking behavior should be considered a form of addiction and tobacco, in the form of cigarettes, an addicting substance.'' The DSM-III, the standard diagnostic manual of psychiatric disorders, and ICDA-9, the World Health Organization's International Classification of Disease, both categorize tobacco dependence as a drug dependence disorder.

Surveys indicate that 90% of smokers would like to quit. Eighty to 85% of those who have tried, however, say that they have relapsed within three months. These figures indicate that *the majority of smokers smoke, not because they want to, but because they are unable to give it up.*

The American Council on Science and Health is a national consumer health organization that publishes studies on health risks associated with food, chemicals, smoking, and the environment.

"Science does not know what role, if any, smoking may play in production of disease."

Cigarette Smoking May Not Be Harmful

The Tobacco Institute

There *is* a cigarette controversy. The *causal theory*—that cigarette smoking causes or is the cause of the various diseases with which it is reported to be related statistically—is just that, a theory.

That the cause or causes of lung cancer and other diseases has *not* been scientifically proved is supported in the almost 4,000 printed pages of testimony and evidence presented on the cigarette labeling bills of 1982 and 1983 by research workers, government officials, voluntary health association representatives and behavioral experts.

Most supporters of the causal theory acknowledge that the mechanisms by which lung cancer, heart disease, emphysema and perinatal problems occur are unknown. But they have concluded there is sufficient other evidence to determine that cigarette smoke has a causal role.

The allegations about cigarette smoking and disease arose from a number of large-scale epidemiological surveys, or population studies, in the United States and the United Kingdom during the 1950s and 1960s.

In most of these, called *prospective* studies, groups of smokers and nonsmokers, matched for such factors as age and sex, were followed for a number of years and their health monitored. In others, called *retrospective*, researchers looked back at individual causes of death and smoking histories.

As recorded and reviewed in the Surgeon General's reports and presented as evidence to the hearings, these and some subsequent surveys and experimental and clinical studies have led the authors of the Surgeon General's reports to acceptance of the causal theory.

The testimony presented to the congressional committees by scientists who oppose the causal theory also was based on published research results.

It is important to note that neither those scientists nor the tobacco industry made or make any claims other than that *it is not known whether smoking has a role in the development of various diseases,* and that *a great deal more research is needed to uncover the causes and the mechanisms involved in their onset.*

Among the main thrusts of the testimony against the proposals in the bills:

• The authors of reports such as those of the Surgeon General have selected favorable evidence to review and *ignored* the results of studies contrary to their conclusions.

• There were basic flaws in the methods used in the major epidemiological surveys that cast doubts on the accuracy of the claimed correlations.

• Essentially, whole-smoke animal inhalation studies have failed to reproduce the heart and lung diseases in question. Indeed, some smoking animals lived longer than the nonsmoking animals.

• Recent studies have reported other factors associated with lung cancer, heart disease, emphysema and perinatal problems.

• Much more research is needed if the causes of these diseases are to be known.

• Attempting by legislation to resolve the medical controversies surrounding smoking can abuse the cause of science and impede the advancement of knowledge.

Selective Evidence

Scientists testified that conclusions drawn in reports of the Surgeon General were not necessarily valid because the reports were selective reviews.

According to testimony, the authors of the Surgeon General's reports apparently selected and reviewed primarily evidence that supports their case. The committees were provided with examples of contrary evidence that had *not* been reviewed in the reports and that should have been taken into account.

The Cigarette Controversy: Why More Research Is Needed, published by the Tobacco Institute in February 1984. Reprinted with permission.

"The Surgeon General's reports," wrote [Richard J. Hickey, a] widely published biostatistician, "have the characteristics of briefs for the 'prosecution' only; the 'defense' has been largely omitted even though these reports should have been unbiased."

A number of epidemiologists, statisticians and other scientists challenged the validity of inferences drawn from epidemiologic surveys that have reported a correlation between smoking and disease and that form a major part of the case against smoking.

Among the general criticisms of such surveys and use of survey findings:

• Epidemiological surveys can only point out a statistical association between factors, such as smoking and disease, but cannot determine whether the relationship is *causal*.

• Smokers, ex-smokers and nonsmokers have been reported to have different behavioral patterns. Because they made their own decisions about smoking they constitute "self-selected" samples. Both these and other factors can bias an epidemiological study and cast doubt on its conclusions.

• Many factors other than smoking are believed to affect health, including general lifestyle, alcohol consumption, occupational and environmental exposures, genetics, aging and the immune processes. These were not considered adequately in the large-scale surveys. When these factors are examined, results may differ from the findings of the large-scale studies depended on by Surgeon General's reports.

"When other environmental and lifestyle factors are considered, smoking cannot explain the ethnic and geographic patterns of lung cancer mortality."

Many witnesses directed criticism, too, at the methodology of specific epidemiological surveys cited in the Surgeon General's reports. In general, they agreed that methodological flaws in research make indicated correlations uncertain. It is scientifically incorrect, they said, to project disease rates of smokers in surveyed populations to the whole population when the groups studied are not representative of the whole.

The American Cancer Society million-persons study by Hammond in the 1950s and 1960s earned especial attention. Scientists who reexamined the data from this study—on which the conclusions of the Surgeon General's reports have relied strongly— testified that the nonsmoker and smoker populations:

• Were not randomly selected.

• Contained proportionally more smokers than the U.S. population.

• Were not representative of the population in age distribution, education or race.

• Contracted disease at different rates than the U.S. population.

• Lived in only 25 states, which were predominantly urban industrialized, with little rural representation.

• Were interviewed by inexperienced volunteers.

The witnesses were critical, too, of other studies cited in the Surgeon General's reports. One of the experts who testified on scientific non sequiturs in the causal theory, Eleanor J. Macdonald, professor emeritus of epidemiology, University of Texas, has spent her lifetime studying the epidemiology of cancer. This is how she summed up the general view:

> There is a concept widely accepted by public health schools that if many studies, in themselves not based on definable populations, all arrive at the same conclusion, then that conclusion must be valid. *This concept disregards the fact that the same intrinsic error in method might produce the same result.* (Emphasis added.)

Ignored Evidence

Several of the scientists testified about studies that they said raise questions about conclusions from the large-scale surveys. They said many of these studies have not been reviewed by the authors of the Surgeon General's reports.

Among the evidence cited:

• Studies in the U.S. indicate that, when other environmental and lifestyle factors are considered, smoking cannot explain the ethnic and geographic patterns of lung cancer mortality.

• A number of new studies suggest such factors as nutritional and economic status—not smoking—to be strongly correlated with perinatal problems. These confirm the findings of older studies questioned by supporters of the causal theory.

One scientifically accepted step in determining whether a statistical correlation relates to cause and effect is animal experimentation. Such work can present both positive and negative results. *The negative result is as important to the advancement of knowledge as the positive.*

Ten researchers presented evidence on cigarette-smoke inhalation experiments conducted with animals over the last 20 years. They discussed *negative* as well as *positive* findings.

Several had been directly involved in animal experiments seeking to determine if smoking causes lung cancer, heart disease or emphysema.

Among the points made:

• Over the last 20 years, not one experiment that was scientifically acceptable—or that produced the same results when repeated—has shown smoking to produce lung cancer or emphysema.

• Some studies were scientifically unacceptable because the animals were "smoked" at a rate equivalent to man's smoking 600 cigarettes per day. Others were confounded by infection or inhalation by the animals of extraneous material, such as dust.

• Experiments with animal models produced lung cancer or emphysema with *techniques other than tobacco smoke inhalation.*

• In some experiments, the groups of smoking animals contracted less lung cancer or lived longer than the nonsmoking groups.

Thus, according to the testimony, reports of the Surgeon General have ignored or played down the importance of negative animal results. Evidence showed that the reports have also ignored published criticisms of other animal work and relied in their conclusions on experiments that have been challenged by scientific peers of the investigators.

Much evidence was presented to the congressional committees for and against the proposition that smoking is a proven lung cancer cause.

The scientific testimony summarized above underscores the inconclusiveness of the epidemiological and animal work cited by those who accept the causal theory. Other testimony on lung cancer dealt with:

1. Contradictory evidence
2. Disease trends and diagnostic errors
3. Pathological findings
4. Physiological factors

Contradictory Evidence

Fifteen witnesses explained why they consider the hypothesis that cigarette smoking causes lung cancer to be unproven.

They cited results of research to support their conclusions. Among the points mentioned:

• Smoking is neither a sufficient nor a necessary cause of lung cancer. The vast majority of even heavy smokers do not get lung cancer while among those who do contract the disease more than 10 percent are nonsmokers.

• When smoker and nonsmoker lung cancer mortality ratios are compared there are large and significant differences among the populations of different countries—particularly between Caucasians and Asians; between population subgroups within countries—by race as well as by sex; and between urban and rural dwellers and persons in residential and industrialized suburbs.

• Some studies report that factors such as lifestyle and residential and workplace pollution are correlated with lung cancer.

• There is evidence that heredity and genetic factors play an important role in lung cancer incidence.

A number of witnesses examined trends of lung cancer incidence and the claim that cigarette smoking has caused an "epidemic" of the disease.

Here, too, the experts cited evidence from recent studies.

Among the points made:

• In the early part of the century lung cancer was *under*diagnosed, while in recent years it has been *over*diagnosed.

• Changes in the rates of increase of lung cancer diagnosis have occurred simultaneously in men and in women, although, generally, women took up smoking some 30 years later than men.

• Significant increases have occurred recently in the incidence of lung cancer among nonsmokers.

"The vast majority of even heavy smokers do not get lung cancer while among those who do contract the disease more than 10 percent are nonsmokers."

• Changes in the International Classification of Diseases since 1948 have thrown together for the first time in official mortality records cancers that originated in the lung and some of those that had *spread* to the lung from another body site. Major internal cancers frequently metastasize to the lung. Hence combining some secondary and primary lung cancers has resulted in a continued recorded increase in lung cancer while hiding the true incidence of cancers originating elsewhere in the body.

• Combining primary and secondary lung cancer for reporting mortality has made it impossible accurately to establish a statistical relationship of primary lung cancer and *any* agent or factor, including cigarette smoking.

• Persistent errors in diagnosis of lung cancer as recorded on death certificates continue to cast doubt on the validity of statistical correlations in epidemiological studies and of claimed mortality patterns and trends.

Pathological Findings

Cancer research and pathological findings in both humans and animals were discussed by eight scientists.

Dr. Katherine Herrold gave special attention to the relevance of conclusions drawn from epidemiological surveys. Now retired from the U.S. Public Health Service, the pioneering physician was a member of the government team that in 1958 reported results of a survey of 300,000 U.S. veterans, one of the first, and largest, of the prospective studies now used to support the causal theory.

Dr. Herrold subsequently reviewed the clinical and pathological data of the lung cancer patients in the veterans study. She told a congressional committee she found:

• No correlation between various lung cancer cell types and the amount of tobacco smoked.

• No relationship between the age at death and the age at which smoking started, the number of years of smoking or the number of cigarettes smoked per day.

"The relationship between smoking and heart disease is neither strong nor consistent."

Dr. Herrold pointed out that these results were almost identical to the findings, some 10 years earlier, of a British scientist, the late R. D. Passey, and those of Doll and Hill in their study of British doctors in the 1950s and 1960s.

Another witness, Dr. Victor B. Buhler, a pathologist, challenged claims that cell and tissue changes reported in the lungs of smokers are "precancerous," a point made frequently by proponents of the causal theory.

Such changes appear also in nonsmokers, wrote Dr. Buhler. The past president of the College of American Pathologists said his testimony was based on "examination of thousands of lungs in microscopic detail." Despite his long experience, he said, he could not confirm that significant cell changes in the lung occur more frequently in smokers than in nonsmokers.

Dr. Buhler summed up:

> As a pathologist, I find the arguments on 'precancerous' lesions to indict smoking as a cause of lung cancer to be unconvincing and indeed inconsistent with my own clinical observations.

Other research cited by the witnesses included:

• Central European hospitals, which regularly conducted autopsies, found lung cancer as early as the 19th century, when cigarette smoking was practically unknown. The lung cancer incidence reported then was similar to that of today, although the disease was not officially diagnosed in 90 to 95 percent of the cases.

• Errors in the stated cause on death certificates range from 30 percent to 60 percent.

• Except at autopsy, it is not possible to determine whether lung cancer is primary or secondary, and only about 12 percent of deaths in the U.S. from all causes today are autopsied.

Physiological Factors

Two eminent surgeons told why, based on their own clinical observations, they do not accept the causal theory. Among the points made:

• Although both lungs of the cigarette smoker are exposed equally to smoke, lung cancer rarely occurs in both simultaneously. It is also rare for subsequent lung cancer to appear after successful treatment of the first.

• Lung cancer occurs often in the parts of the lung *least* exposed to smoke.

• Cancer of the trachea is rare even though the trachea, or windpipe, is exposed to *all smoke* going into and out of the lungs. Anatomically, embryologically and physiologically, the trachea is identical to the rest of the bronchial airway.

• Cancer of the larynx and tongue is rare. Yet the mouth and voice box are *exposed to at least the same smoke concentration as the lungs*.

• Nonsmokers get a type of lung cancer *identical* to that in smokers.

• The rate of increase of the incidence of lung cancer has *fallen*—as predicted more than 20 years ago—regardless of smoking rates.

In summary, these experts took the position that it is not scientifically possible to state that cigarette smoking causes lung cancer, because of apparent flaws in the basic epidemiologic studies, the failure of animal studies to reproduce lung cancer in animals with whole smoke and recent work that has reported other factors involved in the disease.

The scientific witnesses agree that far more research is needed to find the cause or causes of lung cancer and the mechanisms of the disease.

Coronary Heart Disease

Sixteen scientists questioned evidence presented to the committees on the alleged causal relationship between smoking and coronary heart disease (CHD).

Individually citing their own research or review of the literature, the scientists presented reasons why they cannot support the causal theory.

Among the reasons:

• The relationship between smoking and heart disease is neither *strong* nor *consistent*—among populations of different countries, among those within a country or between men and women. For instance, while a statistical correlation between smoking and CHD has been reported in the U.S. and some other countries, none has been found despite similar scrutiny in Finland, Holland, Yugoslavia, Italy, Greece or Japan.

• The substantial fall in heart disease mortality rates in the U.S. in recent years cannot be explained by smoking patterns.

• While smoking has increased among Swiss women in the last quarter century, the rate of heart disease in women there has declined significantly in the same period.

• The government's ongoing heart study in Framingham, Massachusetts, showed no excess CHD in male smokers over 55 years of age, and no relationship in women of *any* age.

• Other recent studies have reported similar

results and found that *ex*-smokers have less CHD than *non*smokers.

• Although some have claimed women who smoke and take oral contraceptives suffer more strokes and heart attacks, supporting evidence is limited, weak and controversial and the object of severe criticism from impartial experts. Several studies, also subject to controversy, have come to the opposite conclusion.

• Some types of CHD, for instance angina pectoris, are not reported to be statistically correlated with smoking. And pipe and cigar smoking have not been even statistically linked with CHD.

• Other factors, including heredity, emotional stress and environmental exposures and diet, have been reported in recent studies to be related to the incidence of CHD. Studies with identical twins have suggested a strong genetic influence in CHD incidence.

• Perhaps most important of all, no mechanism has been established to explain *how* tobacco smoke might cause CHD.

The testimony of these witnesses may be summed up by the statement of Dr. Carl Seltzer of Harvard, who wrote, "The bill's proposed warning, 'Cigarette smoking is a major cause of Heart Disease,' *is not scientifically valid.*"

"California studies among pregnant women who smoke have indicated neither increased risk of abortion or still-birth nor increased risk of birth defects."

Dr. Seltzer, who has published more than 35 articles on smoking and health research and is a fellow of the American Heart Association's Council on Epidemiology, has consistently called for more research to find the causes of CHD. He was echoed by most of the scientists who opposed the claims about heart disease at the labeling hearings.

Witnesses also questioned the assertion that cigarette smoking causes emphysema in particular and chronic obstructive lung disease (COPD) in general.

Among the points made:

• Many animal inhalation experiments with cigarette smoke have failed to produce emphysema in animals. Emphysema has been induced in animal models with other inhalants.

• Epidemiological studies suggest a number of risk factors are associated with COPD, among them outdoor and indoor pollution, alcohol consumption, previous infections, familial predisposition and genetic susceptibility. Discussion of these in Surgeon General's reports has been minimal.

The conclusion from the testimony was that the causes of COPD have not been established and that the answers will be found only through further research.

Pregnancy

Early epidemiological studies showed a statistical correlation between smoking by mothers and a number of perinatal problems, including low birth weight, fetal growth retardation, perinatal mortality and congenital abnormality. Other studies have reported different findings.

Three scientists who have conducted research in this area submitted testimony on their work.

Among the points made:

• Most studies on smoking and pregnancy problems claimed to support the causal theory do not take into account important biological and social factors that can affect birth weight and perinatal mortality.

• The excess of perinatal mortality reported in mothers who smoke is not found in higher income families but only in poorer families.

• Similarly, a number of studies have reported that when birth weight is adjusted for gestational age, the mother's previous pregnancy experience and the sex of the infant there are no significant differences in the birth weight of babies of smoking and nonsmoking mothers—in wealthier families. *Significant* differences are reported among the poorest families.

• Nutritional deficiency, and low protein intake in particular—not smoking—has been found to be an important factor in fetal growth retardation.

• California studies among pregnant women who smoke have indicated neither increased risk of abortion or still-birth nor increased risk of birth defects.

More Research Needed

The congressional testimony reviewed here represents the considered views of many eminent scientists from universities, teaching hospitals and research institutes in the United States and Europe.

These men and women have spent much of their lives studying smoking related issues or trying to find the causes of lung cancer, heart disease, emphysema and perinatal problems. Citing their own research and reviews of the worldwide scientific literature they explained why they maintain that causes of these diseases are still scientifically unknown.

As each disease was discussed there were strong calls for more research to examine the new leads—and older evidence that may have been discounted or ignored—whether or not contradictory to the causal theory.

The statements of these scientists raise many basic questions that must be answered.

Here are just half a dozen:

1. Why are published criticisms suggesting flaws in often cited research on smoking ignored, while findings of the surveys in question are still treated as valid?

2. When such factors as indoor, outdoor and occupational pollution, nutrition and genetics are examined and significant correlations with the relevant diseases reported, why do the correlations between smoking and those diseases often differ?

3. Why in more than two decades of animal inhalation experiments with whole smoke has no scientist been able, in a scientifically acceptable and repeatable experiment, to reproduce heart and lung diseases reportedly associated with smoking, when these diseases *have* been produced with techniques other than tobacco smoke inhalation?

"Only through much more research can causes and mechanisms be established and the cigarette controversy resolved."

---

4. Why have such *negative* results not received much attention when they are as important to the advancement of knowledge as *positive* results?

5. When smoking rates are controlled, why are there significant differences in the reported incidence of lung cancer and heart disease between Caucasian and Asian peoples, within groups or areas in a single country and between males and females?

6. Why is a correlation between smoking and the incidence of perinatal problems reported primarily among less affluent mothers, and not the wealthy?

Harming the Cause of Science

With such basic questions in mind, it is hardly surprising that many witnesses expressed deep concern that government attempts to resolve scientific uncertainties by legislation and edict can only gravely harm the cause and course of science.

Two dominant themes ran through the testimony of the scientists who opposed acceptance of the causal theory and the proposals of the cigarette labeling bills.

The first is that science does not know what role, if any, smoking may play in production of disease.

The second: Only through much more research can causes and mechanisms be established and the cigarette controversy resolved.

The Tobacco Institute is a national organization of tobacco manufacturers whose goal is to improve public understanding of the tobacco industry.

Cigarettes Are a Primary Factor in Poor Health

Elizabeth M. Whelan

What do the following have in common: dioxin in Missouri; chemical seepage at Love Canal; radioactive contamination at Three Mile Island; saccharin; hairdyes; formaldehyde; coffee; Red Dye #2? All of these topics have been extensively, and emotionally, covered by the media in recent years. All have been indicted as possible causes of cancer, birth defects, and other human maladies.

In recent months, we have witnessed dozens of television documentaries, magazine cover stories, and unsettling headlines focused on the theme, "America, the Poisoned." We have seen a dramatic increase in the use of scare verbs like "ooze," "seep," "brew," and "foul," and scare adjectives like "ominous," "sinister," and "horrific." We have come to believe that there is an environmental time bomb ticking, and that what we see today is only the tip of the iceberg. We are left with a guilt-provoking and anxiety-producing feeling that modern American technology is just now catching up with us, that we will ultimately pay the highest price for the conveniences we now enjoy—environmentally induced premature death.

The Environmental Protection Agency, Consumer Product Safety Commission, Food and Drug Administration, consumer groups, and home owners' associations have responded to—and indeed contributed to—this escalating fear of environmental sources of disease by demanding the banning of pesticides, food additives, urea formaldehyde foam insulation, and other products of modern industrial know-how. In the case of the Love Canal, Pres. Carter went so far as to declare an official state of emergency and order the costly relocation of more than 700 homeowners. In Missouri, the EPA was the subject of bitter criticism, and damning press coverage, for not evacuating families sooner from the dioxin-contaminated areas. . . .

Those topics listed above have something else in common as well. Although in some cases there was suggestive evidence to indicate a *potential* threat to human health, and there was just reason for vigilance, there is no solid evidence that exposure to these substances has caused either deaths or any deleterious long-term impact on human health! In other words, in retrospect, the swell of American anxiety about environmental contaminants, and the apparent mandate for action to control them, is based on very little evidence of the existence of a real problem. . . .

The Real Killer

It is in this context that the cigarette stands out as the ultimate paradox in American society. While magazines, newspapers, and the electronic media focus almost daily on the *hypothetical* risks posed by environmental chemical contamination and the techniques of modern food production and processing, and the American public is demanding that the government "do something" to prevent environmentally induced disease, there is a near complete lack of interest in the leading cause of premature death in the U.S.—the cigarette. *While no one died at Love Canal or Three Mile Island, some 400,000 Americans this year alone will die prematurely from diseases directly associated with cigarette smoke. . . .*

It goes without saying that, if the cigarette were being considered for introduction today, there is no way it would meet the safety criteria of either the Food and Drug Administration or the Consumer Product Safety Commission, the two agencies which would seem most logical for approving and regulating it. Even without the dozens of human studies which we have today, the agencies would reject cigarettes because burned tobacco contains a

Elizabeth M. Whelan, "Big Business vs. Public Health: The Cigarette Dilemma," *USA Today*, May 1984. Copyright 1984 by the Society for the Advancement of Education.

significant number of cancer-causing agents and the immediate effects of tobacco inhalation (increased heart rate, increase in blood carbon monoxide levels, inhibition of stomach contractions) would be sufficient sources for concern. Whether it was the small businessman trying to have cigarettes approved or a large corporation's research department which had come up with this "brainstorm," today, the cigarette would not make its way out of the Federal testing laboratories, and the economic impact of the non-approval of cigarettes would be negligible.

However, the cigarette is *not* just being introduced; it has been around for approximately 100 years. (Tobacco, of course has been used for generations, but it was the invention of the cigarette manufacturing machine in the 1880's which resulted in a new and devastating form of behavior— inhalation of smoke on a regular basis, directly into the lungs.)

"Cigarette smokers are physiological prisoners, their bodies in need of the substances in cigarette smoke in order to perform efficiently."

Through the first 60 years of its 100-year existence, the cigarette and the marketing techniques that went with it represented a stellar success for those who worked hard and cleverly in a free enterprise environment to sell a product that gave pleasure, prestige, and relaxation to millions of eager customers. During the first six decades, there was, of course, "controversy" about cigarettes, and eventually some impressive scientific evidence that cigarettes were hazardous. In general, however, the time period between 1890 and 1950 marked the golden age of the cigarette, the birth of a new symbol of the all-American man and, eventually, the all-American woman. That was the dream: the carefree life; the glamorous ads; the hints that cigarettes might not only be pleasurable, but even healthful; and the development of a major, successful economic base for millions of people, directly or indirectly financially dependent on the production, manufacture, sales, and advertising of cigarettes.

Then, in 1950, the dream became a nightmare. In a near explosion of medical data, smokers and nonsmokers alike were jolted by the reports of the devastating health impact of the pleasure-giving cigarette. The news was, quite decidedly, too frightening to fully digest, and indeed, through much of the 1950's, the most prevalent reaction of the medical profession, the press, and the general public was to downplay the evidence, demand "further data," point to alleged gaps and limitations of the

"statistics," and run as far from the reality as possible. Human innovation had backfired, and people did not know what to do about it. For years, honest, hard-working, enterprising Americans had grown tobacco, manufactured cigarettes, and promoted and distributed the product in a clever (and well-intentioned) manner. The tragedy here is that, by the time the bad news about cigarettes had accumulated, the cigarette had become socially desirable, enormous segments of the economic system—including the U.S. government—were dependent on the cigarette as a source of revenue, and a sizable portion of the American population was physically addicted to the product.

Addiction

Most Americans are well aware of the addictive properties of illegal "recreational" drugs like heroin. Many would be shocked to learn that Dr. Williams Polin, director of the National Institute on Drug Abuse, terms cigarette smoking "the most widespread drug dependence in our country." In general, the number of cigarettes consumed by the average smoker is 30 per day. Each inhaled puff delivers a dose of drug to the brain, resulting in 50,000 to 70,000 such doses per person every year. There is no other form of drug use which occurs with such frequency and regularity.

The evidence on the addictive nature of smoking is evident in national surveys which indicate that 90% of smokers would like to quit and that 85% have tried to quit, but failed. Cigarette smokers are physiological prisoners, their bodies in need of the substances in cigarette smoke in order to perform efficiently. Repeated studies indicate that tobacco is more addictive than heroin, producing very strong physical dependence. Cigarette withdrawal symptoms include significant body changes leading to decrease in heart rate, increase in appetite, disturbances in sleep patterns, anxiety, irritability, and aggressiveness.

When a smoker tells you that he has tried to stop smoking, but just can't, he really means it. Moreover, of those who *are* able to give up smoking, some 70% resume the habit within three months— about the same recidivism rate as heroin. One can not overstate the contribution that this addictive nature has made to the continued use of the cigarette; indeed, it is an essential component of the tobacco industry's recipe for survival.

Psychological Blackout

The survival of the cigarette in the 1980's is a classical testimony to the existence of the psychological mechanisms which protect us from facts with which we cannot cope. The classic response to cognitive dissonance, which occurs when people acquire new information that clashes with their current behavior or firmly held belief, was vividly evident during the 1950's, when retrospective and prospective human epidemiological studies around the world confirmed the extraordinary rates of lung cancer, heart disease, emphysema, and other ailments among smokers. People simply refused to incorporate this new information into their consciousness. During that entire decade, there was enormous resistance on the part of the media, legislators, and even physicians to believe the new findings, and a tendency to dismiss what was unacceptable. During the early 1950's, some 70% of American men from all walks of life smoked, had previously thought it was at worst only slightly harmful, and could not deal with a different assessment.

Today's surveys show that 90% of Americans know cigarette smoking is hazardous to health (although most of them "know" it only in the rhetorical sense, unaware of the specific dangers). The clash here is between the reality of smoking and the evidence available that it is harmful. The two beliefs cannot exist together, so it is the evidence that is repressed and in some cases sublimated. (For example, when the smoker declares his "health consciousness" by joining an exercise club or shopping at a "health food" store.)

In plain English, smokers do not want to talk or think about the dangers of their habit. Currently, public service advertisements about the hazards of smoking are few and far between, so most smokers find it relatively easy to avoid mental dissonance. Cigarette smoking literally becomes an involuntary, automatic form of behavior, with no incentive for the smoker to reevaluate his decision to smoke from week to week. . . .

> "In the 1980's, we should not be moralizing about cigarettes, but . . . asking ourselves, if we really want to win the war against environmental disease, why don't we start by identifying the number-one enemy?"

Part of the psychological cover-up on the subject of smoking might be explained by the human eagerness to blame misfortune on anyone but ourselves. In the case of Third World-feeding practices, the "enemy" was the infant formula manufacturers; in the case of the anxiety about the health effects of dioxin or Red Dye #2, the "villain" was a chemical or a food company; in the case of the cigarette, the "villain" is the smoker or, as the cartoon figure Pogo once said, "We have met the enemy and he is us." It is far easier to focus one's attention and ire on health risks imposed by outside forces than it is to become introspective about one's own role in human disease. . . .

The Number-One Enemy

The cigarette has been maligned by a series of critics through the ages, but, until 30 years ago, the attacks were primarily emotional, with heavy moral overtones. In the 1980's, we should not be moralizing about cigarettes, but simply facing up to the realities and asking ourselves, if we really want to win the war against environmental disease, why don't we start by identifying the number-one enemy?

Elizabeth M. Whelan is the executive director of the American Council on Science and Health, a national consumer group that studies health risks caused by smoking, food, and chemicals.

"The rising hysteria about smoking is a tactic in part designed to divert our attention from the inexorable poisoning of the environment."

Cigarettes Are Not a Primary Factor in Poor Health

Ann Giudici Fettner

"Health for all by the year 2000." This was the declaration of the World Health Organization at its 1976 Alma Alta conference in the Soviet Union. While the health of developing nations continues to grow worse, stern Surgeon General Dr. Edward Koop has co-opted WHO rhetoric in his call for a smoke-free America. Koop's claims of risks to nonsmokers (or "passive smokers") in proximity to smokers is based on evidence so flimsy that even the National Cancer Institute's December 1986 announcement on passive smoking was couched in the most tentative language: "Because environmental tobacco smoke contains many agents that *may* contribute to pulmonary cancer and because constituents of tobacco smoke have been detected in the saliva, blood, and urine of passive smokers, it is *biologically possible* [emphasis added] that a causal relationship exists between passive smoking and lung cancer."

Prevention

In his diatribes about passive smoking, Koop characterizes his proof of lit tobacco's danger to nonsmokers as "inferential, of course." Given his opinion, it is only because the surgeon general's authority doesn't extend further that we have been temporarily spared a new, global kind of Prohibition. The outcry against smoking and smokers addresses an issue of such relative unimportance when compared to other current health concerns that it begs the question: Why is smoking being singled out for wide-ranging social sanctions in the name of health prevention?

"The issues of prevention," writes Dr. Petr Skrabanek of the Department of Community Health at the University of Dublin, "have little to do with science, relative risks, and risk factors. They could

be more profitably debated within the framework to which they belong—ethics, politics and vested interests."

Furthermore, "there are many who wish to believe that premarital sex causes venereal diseases, that homosexuality causes AIDS, and that smoking causes lung cancer. This simply is not true; infectious diseases are caused by an infectious agent and not sinful behavior; in the case of lung cancer, smoking is neither sufficient nor necessary cause," insists Skrabanek.

Nevertheless, proposals coming before Congress include a ban on smoking on all forms of public transportation and in all federal buildings. A number of industries and workplaces have instituted an unofficial policy of not hiring smokers, and have designated smoke-free areas or banned smoking entirely from their premises. And as New York's death knell for smoking is fast approaching, restaurants and other public places are sure to come under the same kind of regulations prohibiting smoking. All this without showing a direct cause and effect relationship between passive smoking and cancer.

Koop's Campaign

Using the unquestioning media to build public alarm to the fever pitch needed to ram through regulations and laws, Koop has turned a personal campaign against smoking into a national program based on a soggy and insubstantial set of criteria. Add to this the recent rush to test urine and blood for other traces of pleasure and it becomes evident that our medical and scientific leaders in government are manipulating data and employing scare tactics to their own ends.

Despite the patent weakness of Koop's arguments—which ignore the inability of the National Academy of Science's select panel on smoking hazards to implicate passive smoke as

Ann Giudicci Fettner, "Where There's Smoke There's Ire," *The Village Voice*, March 31, 1987. Reprinted by permission of the author and The Village Voice.

dangerous to health—little controversy has been generated. And no scientist has come forward to point a finger at flagrantly manipulated numbers, or to demand a public dialogue.

Nor has the press questioned. Much media play was given an article in the *New England Journal*, which reported that merely cutting down on smoking produces no benefit. No note was taken of the *first* article in the same issue describing studies that showed "a reduction of as much as 50 per cent in the relative risk of endometrial cancer among female smokers, confirming previous evidence of a protective effect of cigarette smoking on this disorder." Smoking protects women against endometrial cancer? And no one mentioned it?

In its December 5, 1986, issue, *Science* magazine had an article titled "Age Factors Loom in Parkinsonian Research," which reluctantly stated ". . . these new data seem to add considerable support to the increasingly popular notion that natural Parkinson's disease is caused by some kind of environmental toxin, perhaps by MPTP (an ingredient in the ubiquitous pesticide, paraquat) itself or something very similar to it.

"Wild as it might seem, this latter suggestion just might turn out to be correct. For instance, it has been *known for some time* [emphasis added] that one activity that correlates negatively with the incidence of Parkinson's disease is cigarette smoking, which suggests that there might be something in cigarette smoke that protects the brain against environmental toxins."

"Contrast this speculative 2400 passive smoking deaths to the rate of cancer in farmers and others with high exposure to pesticides . . . and other known and suspected carcinogens."

To call for a national ban of smoking—because that's what is fast approaching—all of the evidence must be factored in and fairly presented and interpreted; in essence, as far as possible to determine, it must be *true*.

So what does a scientific truth consist of? There was a time not so long ago that we were assured masturbation caused madness or, at the very least, made hair grow on the palms of the hands.

Where are the studies of elderly smokers to see if they indeed have a lower incidence of Parkinsonlike brain degeneration? Or those comparing endometrial cancer in female smokers and abstainers? Where's the truth and why aren't we demanding it?

Estimates made at the National Research Council meeting were that "of the 12,000 lung cancer deaths in 1985 among nonsmokers, over 2400 were caused

by environmental tobacco smoke." Do 2400 *estimated* yearly deaths from passive smoking constitute a clarion call for restrictive regulations on the population?

Known Deaths

Contrast this speculative 2400 passive smoking deaths to the rate of cancers in farmers and others with high exposure to pesticides, herbicides, solvents, and other known and suspected carcinogens.

At a basic biological level, we don't know what triggers cells to become cancerous. We can create in animals specific cancers with a variety of substances, and most of them are found in our environment. They are the pesticides, herbicides, and industrial wastes; the levels of radiation and the radon in our homes; the food additives and preservatives.

Again from the NCI, in September 1986 came a report stating that a "striking band of elevated death rates for leukemia ran through counties in the central states from North Dakota to Texas. For non-Hodgkins' lymphoma and multiple myeloma, rates were elevated in the North Central States." In Nebraska, for instance, the NCI epidemiologists found farmers had a 25 per cent greater risk of leukemia than nonfarmers. Wisconsin farmers had rare chronic myeloid leukemia 80 times more frequently than other leukemias.

Kansas farmers who used herbicides had six times the risk of developing non-Hodgkins' lymphoma. Pesticide use in Iowa and Minnesota is associated with a 1.4-fold risk for lymphocytic (white blood cell) lymphoma. Those with leukemia "had more frequently used some pesticides including DDT, ethoprop, methosychlor and nicotine." The studies in just these *four states* included 578 men with leukemia and 622 with lymphomas between 1980 and 1983.

Where is the rush to ban these chemicals, which fill every niche in the environment, leak into the groundwater supplies, wash into the rivers, and are carried in the air?

Other Correlations

Would not, for instance, the likely correlation between Parkinson's and the use of pesticides be reason enough? The pesticide paraquat is implicated, as its chemical make-up resembles that of MPTP, which caused irreversible Parkinson's in young adults who thought they were using heroin. There are others.

• Aldicarb, used liberally in most agricultural states, suppresses the immune systems of mice in doses far lower than the EPA allows. This is the chemical that caused the deaths of 2000 in Bhopal, India, and sickened 142 Union Carbide plant workers [in 1986]. As we well know from AIDS, suppression of the immune system leaves the body open to cancers and infections.

• Airborne dioxins—part of Agent Orange—are reported to cause 330 to 1440 cases of cancer each year per million Americans, according to a report by the Center for the Biology of Natural Systems, directed by Barry Commoner of the Queens College Center.

• Then there's chlordane, a chemical that has been banned for agricultural use but is still being pumped into homes to kill termites. This is a highly carcinogenic substance, thought also to cause aplastic anemia, birth defects, neurological problems, and immune suppression. In use for 20 years, the levels found in hundreds of millions of U.S. homes and the implications of this are still being described by the EPA as "not definitive."

"In the free world, health encompasses as far as is possible self-determination and the freedom to indulge in habits which, though perhaps not health-promoting, are enjoyable."

I would suggest that whether conscious or not, the rising hysteria about smoking is a tactic in part designed to divert our attention from the inexorable poisoning of the environment. And why has the medical profession rushed in so fast to stamp its well-shod foot over passive smoking, while neglecting the known effects of environmental pollutants? One guesses this is an issue that allows physicians to come down on the side of "right." This is a stance they've had a hard time finding recently, what with abortion, teenage pregnancy, and associated infant mortality, Baby Doe regulations, the right to terminate life in the hopelessly moribund elderly and so on, and other issues that have plagued the medical profession with questions few doctors are educationally or intellectually equipped to deal with.

Attacking Real Health Hazards

Health, as defined at Alma Alta, is far more than merely the absence of disease. In the free world, health encompasses as far as is possible self-determination and the freedom to indulge in habits which, though perhaps not health-promoting, are enjoyable. Smoking is merely an easily manipulated paradigm for a futile hope that nevertheless seems to promise if we are "good," we can remain young and beautiful and perfectly healthy forever. What we're really being told is that enjoying ourselves brings retribution. When Dr. Koop and the federal

government turn their attention to the rapidly degenerating environment and the impact it is known to have on our health, and to other clearly preventable causes of death and morbidity, then perhaps there will be leisure to scrutinize the habits of individuals. We are currently under seige by ideologies expressed in scientific terms. Banish smoking on the available evidence? A pipe dream, Dr. Koop.

Writer Ann Giudici Fettner is a regular contributor to The Village Voice, *a weekly New York City newspaper.*

"Involuntary smoking is a cause of disease, including lung cancer, in healthy nonsmokers."

Passive Smoking Is Harmful

C. Everett Koop

Editor's note: The following viewpoint is an excerpt from the Surgeon General's 1986 report on cigarette smoking.

Inhalation of tobacco smoke during active cigarette smoking remains the largest single preventable cause of death and disability for the U.S. population. The health consequences of cigarette smoking and of the use of other tobacco products have been extensively documented in the 17 previous Reports in the health consequences of smoking series issued by the U.S. Public Health Service. Cigarette smoking is a major cause of cancer; it is most strongly associated with cancers of the lung and respiratory tract, but also causes cancers at other sites, including the pancreas and urinary bladder. It is the single greatest cause of chronic obstructive lung diseases. It causes cardiovascular diseases, including coronary heart disease, aortic aneurysm, and atherosclerotic peripheral vascular disease. Maternal cigarette smoking endangers fetal and neonatal health; it contributes to perinatal mortality, low birth weight, and complications during pregnancy. More than 300,000 premature deaths occur in the United States each year that are directly attributable to tobacco use, particularly cigarette smoking.

This Report examines in detail the scientific evidence on involuntary smoking as a potential cause of disease in nonsmokers. Nonsmokers' exposure to environmental tobacco smoke is termed involuntary smoking in this Report because the exposure generally occurs as an unavoidable consequence of being in proximity to smokers, particularly in enclosed indoor environments. The term "passive smoking" is also used throughout the scientific literature to describe this exposure.

The magnitude of the disease risks for active smokers secondary to their "high dose" exposure to tobacco smoke suggests that the "lower dose" exposure to tobacco smoke received by involuntary smokers may also have risks. Although the risks of involuntary smoking are smaller than the risks of active smoking, the number of individuals injured by involuntary smoking is large both in absolute terms and in comparison with the number injured by some other agents in the general environment that are regulated to curtail their potential to cause human illness.

This Report reviews the evidence on the characteristics of mainstream tobacco smoke and of environmental tobacco smoke, on the levels of exposure to environmental tobacco smoke that occur, and on the health effects of involuntary exposure to tobacco smoke. The composition of the tobacco smoke inhaled by active smokers and by involuntary smokers is examined for similarities and differences, and the concentrations of tobacco smoke components that can be measured in a variety of settings are explored, as is smoke deposition and absorption in the respiratory tract. The studies that describe the risks of environmental tobacco smoke exposure for humans are carefully reviewed for their findings and their validity. The evidence on the health effects of involuntary smoking is reviewed for biologic plausibility, and compared with extrapolations of the risks of active smoking to the lower dose of exposure to tobacco smoke found in nonsmokers. . . .

Tobacco Smoke's Toxicity

Important considerations in examining the risks of involuntary smoking are the composition of environmental tobacco smoke (ETS) and its toxicity and carcinogenicity relative to the tobacco smoke inhaled by active smokers. Mainstream cigarette smoke is the smoke drawn through the tobacco into

C. Everett Koop, *The Health Consequences of Involuntary Smoking: A Report of the Surgeon General.* Rockville, MD: U.S. Department of Health and Human Services, 1986.

the smoker's mouth. Sidestream smoke is the smoke emitted by the burning tobacco between puffs. Environmental tobacco smoke results from the combination of sidestream smoke and the fraction of exhaled mainstream smoke not retained by the smoker. In contrast with mainstream smoke, ETS is diluted into a larger volume of air, and it ages prior to inhalation.

The comparison of the chemical composition of the smoke inhaled by active smokers with that inhaled by involuntary smokers suggests that the toxic and carcinogenic effects are qualitatively similar, a similarity that is not too surprising because both mainstream smoke and environmental tobacco smoke result from the combustion of tobacco. Individual mainstream smoke constituents, with appropriate testing, have usually been found in sidestream smoke as well. However, differences between sidestream smoke and mainstream smoke have been well documented. The temperature of combustion during sidestream smoke formation is lower than during mainstream smoke formation. As a result, greater amounts of many of the organic constituents of smoke, including some carcinogens, are generated when tobacco burns and forms sidestream smoke than when mainstream smoke is produced. For example, in contrast with mainstream smoke, sidestream smoke contains greater amounts of ammonia, benzene, carbon monoxide, nicotine, and the carcinogens 2-napthylamine, 4-aminobiphenyl, N-nitrosamine, benz[a]anthracene, and benzo-pyrene per milligram of tobacco burned. Although only limited bioassay data comparing mainstream smoke and sidestream smoke are available, one study has suggested that sidestream smoke may be more carcinogenic.

"Of the epidemiologic studies . . . that have examined the question of involuntary smoking's association with lung cancer, most (11 of 13) have shown a positive association with exposure."

Although sidestream smoke and mainstream smoke differ somewhat qualitatively, the differing quantitative doses of smoke components inhaled by the active smoker and by the involuntary smoker are of greater importance in considering the risks of the two exposures. A number of different markers for tobacco smoke exposure and absorption have been identified for both active and involuntary smoking. No single marker quantifies, with precision, the exposure to each of the smoke constituents over the wide range of environmental settings in which involuntary smoking occurs. However, in environments without other significant sources of

dust, respirable suspended particulate levels can be used as a marker of smoke exposure. Levels of nicotine and its metabolite cotinine in body fluids provide a sensitive and specific indication of recent whole smoke exposure under most conditions.

Widely varying levels of environmental tobacco smoke can be measured in the home and other environments using markers. The time-activity patterns of nonsmokers, which indicate the time spent in environments containing ETS, also vary widely. Thus, the extent of exposure to ETS is probably highly variable among individuals at a given point in time, and little is known about the variation in exposure of the same individual at different points in time.

Lung Cancer

The American Cancer Society estimates that there will be more than 135,000 deaths from lung cancer in the United States in 1986, and 85 percent of these lung cancer deaths are directly attributable to active cigarette smoking. Therefore, even if the number of lung cancer deaths caused by involuntary smoking were much smaller than the number of lung cancer deaths caused by active smoking, the number of lung cancer deaths attributable to involuntary exposure would still represent a problem of sufficient magnitude to warrant substantial public health concern.

Exposure to environmental tobacco smoke has been examined in numerous recent epidemiological studies as a risk factor for lung cancer in nonsmokers. These studies have compared the risks for subjects exposed to ETS at home or at work with the risks for people not reported to be exposed in these environments. Because exposure to ETS is an almost universal experience in the more developed countries, these studies involve comparison of more exposed and less exposed people rather than comparison of exposed and unexposed people. Thus, the studies are inherently conservative in assessing the consequences of exposure to ETS. Interpretation of these studies must consider the extent to which populations with different ETS exposures have been identified, the gradient in ETS exposure from the lower exposure to the higher exposure groups, and the magnitude of the increased lung cancer risk that results from the gradient in ETS exposure.

To date, questionnaires have been used to classify ETS exposure. Quantification of exposure by questionnaire, particularly lifetime exposure, is difficult and has not been validated. However, spousal and parental smoking status identify individuals with different levels of exposure to ETS. Therefore, investigation has focused on the children and nonsmoking spouses of smokers, groups for whom greater ETS exposure would be expected and for whom increased nicotine absorption has been documented relative to the children and nonsmoking spouses of nonsmokers.

Of the epidemiologic studies reviewed in this Report that have examined the question of involuntary smoking's association with lung cancer, most (11 of 13) have shown a positive association with exposure, and in 6 the association reached statistical significance. Given the difficulty in identifying groups with differing ETS exposure, the low-dose range of exposure examined, and the small numbers of subjects in some series, it is not surprising that some studies have found no association and that in others the association did not reach a conventional level of statistical significance. The question is not whether cigarette smoke can cause lung cancer; that question has been answered unequivocally by examining the evidence for active smoking. The question is, rather, can tobacco smoke at a lower dose and through a different mode of exposure cause lung cancer in nonsmokers? The answer must be sought in the coherence and trends of the epidemiologic evidence available on this low-dose exposure to a known human carcinogen. In general, those studies with larger population sizes, more carefully validated diagnosis of lung cancer, and more careful assessment of ETS exposure status have shown statistically significant associations. A number of these studies have demonstrated a dose-response relationship between the level of ETS exposure and lung cancer risk. By using data on nicotine absorption by the nonsmoker, the nonsmoker's risk of developing lung cancer observed in human epidemiologic studies can be compared with the level of risk expected from an extrapolation of the dose-response data for the active smoker. This extrapolation yields estimates of an expected lung cancer risk that approximate the observed lung cancer risk in epidemiologic studies of involuntary smoking.

"Given this abundance of evidence, a clear judgment can now be made: exposure to ETS is a cause of lung cancer."

Cigarette smoke is well established as a human carcinogen. The chemical composition of ETS is qualitatively similar to mainstream smoke and sidestream smoke and also acts as a carcinogen in bioassay systems. For many nonsmokers, the quantitative exposure to ETS is large enough to expect an increased risk of lung cancer to occur, and epidemiologic studies have demonstrated an increased lung cancer risk with involuntary smoking. In examining a low-dose exposure to a known carcinogen, it is rare to have such an abundance of

evidence on which to make a judgment, and given this abundance of evidence, a clear judgment can now be made: exposure to ETS is a cause of lung cancer.

The data presented in this Report establish that a substantial number of the lung cancer deaths that occur among nonsmokers can be attributed to involuntary smoking. However, better data on the extent and variability of ETS exposure are needed to estimate the number of deaths with confidence.

Respiratory Disease

Acute and chronic respiratory diseases have also been linked to involuntary exposure to tobacco smoke; the evidence is strongest in infants. During the first 2 years of life, infants of parents who smoke are more likely than infants of nonsmoking parents to be hospitalized for bronchitis and pneumonia. Children whose parents smoke also develop respiratory symptoms more frequently, and they show small, but measurable, differences on tests of lung function when compared with children of nonsmoking parents.

Respiratory infections in young children represent a direct health burden for the children and their parents; moreover, these infections, and the reductions in pulmonary function found in the school-age children of smokers, may increase susceptibility to develop lung disease as an adult.

Several studies have reported small decrements in the average level of lung function in nonsmoking adults exposed to ETS. These differences may represent a response of the lung to chronic exposure to the irritants in ETS, but it seems unlikely that ETS exposure, by itself, is responsible for a substantial number of cases of clinically significant chronic obstructive lung disease. The small magnitude of the changes associated with ETS exposure suggests that only individuals with unusual susceptibility would be at risk of developing clinically evident disease from ETS exposure alone. However, ETS exposure may be a factor that contributes to the development of clinical disease in individuals with other causes of lung injury.

Cardiovascular Disease

A few studies have examined the relationship between involuntary smoking and cardiovascular disease, but no firm conclusion on the relationship can be made owing to the limited number of deaths in the studies.

Perhaps the most common effect of tobacco smoke exposure is tissue irritation. The eyes appear to be especially sensitive to irritation by ETS, but the nose, throat, and airway may also be affected by smoke exposure. Irritation has been demonstrated to occur at levels that are similar to those found in real-life situations. The level of irritation increases with an increasing concentration of smoke and duration of exposure. In addition, participants in surveys report irritation and annoyance due to smoke in the environment under real-life conditions.

Determining Exposure

Exposure to ETS has been documented to be common in the United States, but additional data on the extent and determinants of exposure are needed to identify individuals within the population who have the highest exposure and are at greatest risk. Studies with biological markers and measurements of ETS components in indoor air confirm that measurable exposure to ETS is widespread. However, within exposed populations, levels of cotinine excretion and presumably ETS exposure vary greatly.

"The children of parents who smoke compared with the children of nonsmoking parents have an increased frequency of respiratory infections."

In a room or other indoor area, the size of the space, the number of smokers, the amount of ventilation, and other factors determine the concentration of tobacco smoke in the air. The technology for the cost-effective filtration of tobacco smoke from the air is not currently available, and because of their small size, the smoke particles remain suspended in the air for long periods of time; thus, the only way to remove smoke from indoor air is to increase the exchange of indoor air with clean outdoor air. The number of air changes per hour required to maintain acceptable indoor air quality is much higher when smoking is allowed than when smoking is prohibited.

Environmental tobacco smoke originates at the lighted tip of the cigarette, and exposure to ETS is greatest in proximity to the smoker. However, the smoke rapidly disseminates throughout any airspace contiguous with the space in which the smoking is taking place. Dissemination of smoke is not uniform, and substantial gradients in ETS levels have been demonstrated in different parts of the same airspace. The time course of tobacco smoke dissemination is rapid enough to ensure the spread of smoke throughout an airspace within an 8-hour workday. In the home, the presence of even one smoker can significantly increase levels of respirable suspended particulates. . . .

Policies Restricting Smoking

Policies regulating cigarette smoking with the objective of reducing explosion or fire risk, or of safeguarding the quality of manufactured products, have been in force in a number of States since the late 1800s. More recently, and with steadily increasing frequency, policies regulating smoking on the basis of the health risk or the irritation of involuntary smoking have been promulgated.

State and local governments have enacted laws and regulations restricting smoking in public places. These policies have been implemented with few problems and at little cost to the respective governments. The public awareness of these policies that results from the media coverage surrounding their implementation probably facilitates their self-enforcement. Public awareness may best be fostered by encouraging the establishment of these changes at the local level.

Policies limiting smoking in the worksite have also become increasingly widespread and more restrictive. However, changes in worksite policies have evolved largely through voluntary rather than governmental action. In a steadily increasing number of worksites, smoking has been prohibited completely or limited to relatively few areas within the worksite. The creation of a smoke-free workplace has proceeded successfully when the policy has been jointly developed by employees, employee organizations, and management; instituted in phases; and accompanied by support and assistance for the smokers to quit smoking.

This trend to protect nonsmokers from ETS exposure may have an added public health benefit—helping those smokers who are attempting to quit to be more successful and not encouraging smoking by people entering the workforce.

The three major conclusions of this report are the following:

1. Involuntary smoking is a cause of disease, including lung cancer, in healthy nonsmokers.

2. The children of parents who smoke compared with the children of nonsmoking parents have an increased frequency of respiratory infections, increased respiratory symptoms, and slightly smaller rates of increase in lung function as the lung matures.

3. The simple separation of smokers and nonsmokers within the same air space may reduce, but does not eliminate, the exposure of nonsmokers to environmental tobacco smoke.

Since becoming Surgeon General of the US Public Health Service, C. Everett Koop has issued several reports on the dangers of cigarette smoking.

"There is no consensus among scientists on the question of whether exposure to ETS [environmental tobacco smoke] can adversely affect the health of nonsmokers."

Passive Smoking May Not Be Harmful

Mark J. Reasor

Recently considerable attention has focused on the question of whether exposure to the smoke exhaled by smokers or emitted by their cigarettes (frequently termed *passive* or *involuntary smoking*) is detrimental to the health of nonsmokers. Because nearly 30 percent of the American population are active smokers, the potential for exposure of nonsmokers, at work and at home, to what is termed environmental tobacco smoke (ETS) is considerable. Since a large number of people may be exposed to ETS, the scientific community must make every effort to determine whether such exposure adversely affects health.

In response to this need, many scientists throughout the world are involved in this effort, and much information on this subject has been collected. This [viewpoint] presents a perspective on the scientific issues relating to whether exposure to ETS adversely affects the health of nonsmokers. It describes ETS and its similarity or dissimilarity to the smoke inhaled by active smokers (mainstream smoke), examines the nature of exposure to ETS, relates what adverse health effects have been reported, describes problems encountered in analyzing existing studies, and considers what types of studies should help obtain the most scientifically sound and definitive answers. . . .

Comparing Smoke

ETS originates principally from the smoke emitted from a cigarette between puffs. The smoke released from the cigarette, termed *sidestream smoke*, consists of particles that are visible and gases that are invisible. Smoke exhaled by the smoker (*exhaled mainstream smoke*) also contributes to ETS but it is

believed to make less of a contribution than sidestream smoke.

As sidestream smoke and exhaled mainstream smoke are released into an indoor environment, a number of processes occur that influence the concentration and composition of the end product, ETS. Overall these events are termed *aging*. The first and most important event from a health perspective is dilution with room air. This will be extensive under most circumstances and will be influenced by a number of factors, including the size of the room and the existing ventilation rate. The concentration of ETS also will depend upon the rate of smoke generation and, hence, the number of smokers in the room. Other important processes affecting the level of ETS include adsorption onto and absorption into materials in the room, such as furniture, drapes, and carpets, as well as chemical and physical reactions that the material undergoes. The types of reactions that occur are not well characterized, but there is some evidence that changes occur that both increase and decrease the presence of potentially toxic substances. In general, the extensive dilution of the smoke materials would be expected to offset or diminish possible health effects resulting from the generation of more toxic species. Although the presence of potentially toxic substances in an environment is cause for concern, exposure to very low levels of a given substance may not result in toxicity even when exposure to a much higher level will.

Because it is much easier to collect freshly generated sidestream smoke in a scientific laboratory than to collect ETS under actual conditions, sidestream smoke has been commonly used as a surrogate for ETS. Although much is known about the chemical composition of undiluted sidestream smoke, serious limitations exist in interpreting the information obtained from such an analysis. When all factors are considered, it becomes apparent that

Reprinted by permission of the publisher, from *Clearing the Air*, edited by Robert D. Tollison. Lexington, MA: Lexington Books, D.C. Heath and Company. Copyright 1988 D.C. Heath and Company.

ETS and sidestream cigarette smoke are quantitatively and, to some extent, qualitatively different.

The composition of ETS has been compared frequently to that of the mainstream smoke inhaled by an active smoker. Constituents found in mainstream smoke are also found in sidestream smoke. Under standardized smoking conditions used in the controlled laboratory setting, higher amounts of most of these materials are present in the undiluted sidestream smoke released from a cigarette than are present in the mainstream smoke generated from the same cigarette. From this type of investigation, it has been reported that sidestream smoke has more toxic potential than mainstream smoke. Although this may be true if the undiluted materials are compared, such a statement is misleading since it is ETS and not undiluted sidestream smoke to which nonsmokers are exposed.

Exposure to ETS

A substance may be toxic at one concentration but not at a much lower concentration. Therefore of primary importance in evaluating the potential health effects of any material, including ETS, is knowledge of the dose, or amount, of the material to which the individual is exposed. Because of difficulties in accurately determining exposure levels, interpretation of purported health effects as a result of exposure to ETS is hampered. To illustrate this problem, it is appropriate to compare exposure to and retention of ETS by a nonsmoker to the inhalation and retention of mainstream smoke by an active smoker.

Nonsmokers inhale ETS almost exclusively through the nose with a normal breathing pattern. Smokers draw mainstream smoke directly into the lungs, often with a deep breath and a pause that allow prolonged contact of the material with the lungs. This difference in respiratory pattern increases the chance for deposition and absorption of material by active smokers. Studies have shown that differences in the physical properties of mainstream smoke and sidestream smoke (used in this case as a surrogate for ETS) result in less retention of sidestream smoke particles in the lungs compared to particles of mainstream smoke. Studies on the retention of particles in ETS have not been reported. It is often said that exposure to ETS is the same as actively smoking cigarettes, the only difference being that the components are more dilute. For the reasons already noted, such extrapolation is scientifically inaccurate and therefore unwarranted.

Certain substances in tobacco smoke have been detected in indoor environments. Unfortunately it has not always been possible to determine the contribution, if any, of ETS to indoor air pollution, principally because a number of the components of ETS are not unique to tobacco. For example,

particulate matter and carbon monoxide have been used as markers for the presence of ETS. Nontobacco-related particles can arise, however, from both indoor and outdoor sources. Indoor sources include coal- and wood-burning fireplaces and general house dust. Particles from outdoor sources can enter homes or buildings under any circumstances and particularly when the structures are near construction sites, agricultural fields, heavily traveled roads, and so on. In spite of these complications, there is good evidence that the level of particulate matter can be higher in homes when smokers are present. Carbon monoxide is a gaseous material that results from the incomplete combustion of organic material and may arise in an indoor environment from sources other than the burning of tobacco—for example, from gas stoves. This chemical can also arise from outdoor sources. An example is in office buildings where fresh air may be drawn in from sites near the generation of automobile exhaust.

"Very little is known about ETS and it is not valid to extrapolate from active smoking to passive smoking because they are markedly different exposure situations."

The most specific marker for ETS appears to be nicotine because tobacco is the only source of this chemical. Nicotine has been measured in indoor environments and has been detected in body fluids (blood, urine, and saliva) of nonsmokers. Nevertheless, the use of nicotine as a marker for ETS has certain limitations. Nicotine in ETS is a gas, so it can serve at best only as a marker for components in the gas phase and not for materials in the particulate phase. Consequently it is not possible to determine how much absorption of other substances has occurred nor can information about the cumulative exposure to ETS and accumulation of materials in the body be derived. Proper characterization of the contribution of ETS to indoor air pollution will require an integrated approach that examines a number of components simultaneously.

There is concern about the possible presence of potential carcinogens in ETS. Such material may exist in minute quantities, compared to nicotine, making their detection in body fluids of nonsmokers very difficult. Ideally it would be desirable to have a marker representing a carcinogenic material that could be used to measure the cumulative exposure to ETS and permit an estimation of carcinogenic risk. At present, such a marker is not available, although scientists are searching for one.

Recently investigators have been looking for the presence of mutagenic substances in the urine of nonsmokers as an indicator of exposure to carcinogens that may be present in ETS. (If a substance causes mutations it is believed to have the potential to cause cancer.) Even if ETS-specific mutagens are found in the urine of nonsmokers, however, the health consequences of their presence would be difficult to interpret.

Health Effects of ETS

Although very little is known about ETS and it is not valid to extrapolate from active smoking to passive smoking because they are markedly different exposure situations, nevertheless there is considerable concern about the effects of ETS exposure on human health. Reports on this topic have been appearing in the scientific literature for well over ten years. Interest has centered on two types of health effects: acute and chronic.

With any substance, acute effects may result from a single exposure and disappear after exposure stops. Chronic effects are those that result when exposure occurs over a longer period of time, generally months or years. Chronic effects may or may not be more severe than acute effects, depending upon the substance and levels of exposure. It is much easier to attribute acute effects to a particular material than it is to attribute chronic effects because chronic effects often appear well after exposure has occurred, making it difficult to identify a causative agent.

Acute Effects

The most common acute responses reported by individuals who are exposed to ETS are detection of unpleasant odors and irritation of eyes, nose, and throat. The perception of an offensive odor may alter a person's sense of well-being and comfort but is generally not considered to be a health effect. Since it can affect attention, attitude, and work performance, however, it warrants concern.

There is little question that some nonsmokers experience irritation of eyes, nose, and throat when exposed to sufficient amounts of ETS, particularly in inadequately ventilated environments. The responses to ETS are variable; some individuals report no irritation, and others claim to be allergic to ETS. It has not been established that such reactions are true allergies, although certain persons do appear to be highly sensitive to the irritative effects of ETS. Although there are reports that individuals with respiratory disorders such as asthma and emphysema have an increased sensitivity to ETS, inadequate scientific evidence exists to confirm this.

Chronic Effects

A number of chronic health effects purportedly resulting from exposure to ETS have been reported in the scientific literature, among them lung cancers and cancers in tissues other than the lung, respiratory disturbances in adults and children, cardiovascular disorders, and certain other adverse effects in children. The studies reporting these effects have been the subject of intense scrutiny in recent years, and there is controversy concerning their conclusions.

"In no study to date is there an accurate or adequate measurement of exposure of any of the subjects to ETS."

In 1986, two major reports on ETS were published, one by the U.S. surgeon general and the other by the National Research Council of the National Academy of Sciences (NAS), both containing an extensive review of the scientific literature by eminent scientists and physicians from throughout the world. They concluded that ETS has not been shown scientifically to increase the risk of cancers in tissues other than the lung or to increase cardiovascular disorders or deficits in respiratory function in adults, although they claimed a positive association between exposure of the nonsmoker to ETS and an increased risk of lung cancer. Additionally, both concluded that young children whose parents smoke have an increased frequency of certain conditions, including ear infections, acute respiratory illness, and respiratory infections in early infancy and an increase in cough, wheezing, and sputum production. Other commentaries and reports have addressed these issues of the risk of lung cancer in nonsmokers and health effects in children, some agreeing with the finding of a positive association and others disagreeing. It is important to examine why this controversy exists.

Epidemiological investigations have been used to examine the relationship between ETS exposure and lung cancer in nonsmokers. It has been reported that nonsmoking wives of men who smoke have an increased risk of about thirty percent in developing lung cancer compared to nonsmoking wives of men who do not smoke. Because of the nature of epidemiological studies, it is very difficult to establish a direct association between exposure and disease and is virtually impossible to establish causality. Critical evaluation clearly shows that a number of deficiencies exist in studies reporting an increased incidence of lung cancer in nonsmokers as well as those reporting no increase.

The most serious problem is the absence of verified exposure information. In no study to date is there an accurate or adequate measurement of exposure of any of the subjects to ETS. Exposure is most frequently estimated from the smoking habits of the spouse, and this information is obtained by questionnaire or interview with the subject. Such methods have serious limitations, not the least of which is the accuracy of respondent recall of facts. Evidence exists that spousal smoking habits may not accurately represent ETS exposure. Additionally the studies suffer from one or more of the following problems: an inadequate number of subjects to permit statistical analysis, inaccurate or unverified information about the subjects, lack of clinical verification of the actual presence of lung cancer, and misclassification of the subjects with regard to their smoking status or exposure conditions. These flaws need to be corrected for in any future epidemiological study before reliable conclusions can be drawn.

"The present data do not show a clear association between ETS and lung cancer."

There are also substantial doubts about the appropriateness of aggregating or combining flawed epidemiologic studies in an effort to reach conclusions that cannot be supported or confirmed by the studies individually. The bringing together of individual studies does not necessarily diminish the importance of the underlying study defects, and the aggregation technique thus may result in spurious conclusions. The overriding need in the area of ETS and lung cancer is the design of better and more rigorously conducted investigations, not the statistical manipulation of studies that already have been conducted.

A Low Concentration

Since sidestream smoke contains carcinogens, it is likely that ETS does also; however, the concentrations of these materials would be expected to be very low in ambient ETS and, if present in the particulate phase, would be even less likely to be retained in the lungs. The important issue is whether nonsmokers are exposed to a sufficient amount of such materials to cause lung cancer. Possibly this question may never be answered definitively. What is clear, however, is that the investigations completed to date have not offered satisfactory answers. It is imperative that research continue on this topic.

Because young children are less able than adults to control their exposure to ETS and because exposure in youth may impair normal development, the issue of whether exposure to ETS results in health problems in this age group is significant. Nicotine and its metabolite have been detected in the body fluids of children of smokers. Since no quantitative cumulative measurements of ETS exposure have been obtained in the studies where health effects have been reported, the extent of exposure cannot be verified. Nevertheless, there are a number of reports that a higher incidence of the disorders described occurs in young children of parents who smoke. Some scientists have questioned, however, whether this is actually due to ETS, since other factors may contribute to these responses. For example, cross-infection from a parent may have been the causative agent rather than ETS. In addition, socioeconomic factors and the possible effects of smoking during pregnancy have not always been considered in these studies. Because of the sensitive nature of this issue and the possible important consequences of the findings, researchers need to design appropriate studies to eliminate these deficiencies.

There is no consensus among scientists on the question of whether exposure to ETS can adversely affect the health of nonsmokers. Further research is needed to determine whether ETS presents health risks. . . .

The present data do not show a clear association between ETS and lung cancer, much less meet the criteria for judging causality. Because of the small increases reported in the risk of lung cancer, it is not likely that causality can ever be established using epidemiological techniques. Consequently new experimental approaches are needed. One approach that warrants attention is the use of laboratory animals for short- and long-term exposure to ETS. Most information on the toxicity of nonmedicinal chemicals has been obtained in animal studies, so it is logical to utilize such an approach in the study of ETS. It should be possible to expose laboratory animals to ETS for periods up to their entire lifetime. Under controlled circumstances, the development of lung cancer in adult animals and the development of respiratory disorders in newborn animals, as well as many other toxicities, can be assessed. Such studies have obvious difficulties, not the least of which is their expense. Additionally although it is important to determine if there is a potential for toxicity, as lifetime exposure to high concentrations of ETS would permit, it is necessary to conduct experiments that simulate realistic conditions of ETS levels and durations of exposure.

A Continuing Quest

As the quest continues to evaluate whether ETS is a health hazard, scientists must strive to conduct carefully designed and appropriate research. Careful scientific evaluation and dispassionate criticism of the studies must occur.

Mark J. Reasor is a professor of pharmacology and toxicity at the West Virginia University Medical Center in Morgantown, West Virginia. He belongs to the Society of Toxicology and American Society of Pharmacology and Experimental Therapeutics.

viewpoint **33**

The Case for Nonsmokers' Rights

William L. Weis and Bruce W. Miller

By 1911, when the mass-produced cigarette was still fairly new, many nonsmokers were aware that "comfort" for smokers meant discomfort for themselves. That year Dr. Charles G. Peace organized the Non-smokers' Protective League, whose purposes he explained in the November 10th issue of the *New York Times*:

> The league does not seek to abridge the personal rights of anyone, but it does seek to awaken the sense of fairness in those who use tobacco and to impress upon them the fact that they have not the right to inflict discomfort and harm upon others.
>
> That tobacco smoke and the odor of tobacco are irritating to normal, unpoisoned respiratory membranes is attested to by the personal experience of thousands of persons who are daily, and in many cases hourly, forced to inhale them. They produce headache, dizziness, nausea, and even fainting; they injure the eyes and lungs, the nervous and alimentary systems, and in other ways they cause harm, discomfort, and pain.

Peace's description still rings true today. But instead of quietly suffering, nonsmokers are saying "No" to smoky environments—in public and at work. Nonsmokers' rights groups are multiplying and have been winning victory after victory to clear the air. City ordinances are being passed to prohibit smoking in public places. And restaurants are being pressed to provide clean air as well as clean food.

Struggle in the Workplace

The most intense struggle is taking place in the smokers' last stronghold: the workplace. Here smokers and nonsmokers must confront each other because they have no choice. Unlike patrons of a restaurant, most workers cannot simply walk out.

That smoking takes its toll on the health of smokers has been obvious for many years. One merely needs to observe a smoker cough or wheeze through the day to see the evidence. But smoking has been such an accepted part of American life that, until recently, few people paid attention to how it hurts nonsmokers.

Nonsmokers today *are* paying attention. We rub our burning eyes—and know that work would be more pleasurable and productive without the smoke. We see cigarette burns in the carpets. We ponder the black ring around the ventilation register that delivers the air we breathe. We wonder whether the salesman who coughs throughout his sales pitch will be the one to service the account. And, when traveling by air, we wonder whether a cigarette butt dropped in the wrong place will spark another airline disaster.

Even with these thoughts, the idea that workplaces should be entirely smoke-free may be uncomfortable to both employees and management—not because they like smoke, but because they fear change. Rather than expend energy solving this problem, many defend or excuse the status quo. Nonsmokers may say, "It's really not that bad." Smokers declare that "smoking gives me something to do during my break." And management decides, "Banning smoking would upset too many people."

Actually, people who think this way are fooling themselves. Do they really believe that keeping unhealthy practices is better than promoting healthier ones? Or that an organization will lose by promoting the health of its employees?

Harmful to Health

The norm *should* be a smoke-free work environment. But, if applicants ask whether smoking is allowed on the job, some employers perceive them as troublemakers. Supporting this view are smokers who claim that banning smoking would infringe on their personal liberty and who turn a deaf ear to the argument that their smoking imposes air pollution on others.

Frank Wetzel, executive editor of the Bellevue (Wash.) *Journal American*, responded wisely to a reporter's concerns that liberties were on the way out when smoking was banned in the newsroom:

> Your comment about the next freedom to go tells me that you have missed the whole point. We aren't dealing with something that "bothers" people, for heaven's sake; we are dealing with something that is harmful to their health.

Whether management likes it or not, the move for nonsmokers' rights is irreversible. The "right" to smoke on the job is no longer unquestioned. What will management do with this new challenge? Ignore the issue and foster resentment by nonsmokers? Fire nonsmokers for their justified objections? Play musical chairs with smokers and nonsmokers? Wait for smokers to quit or die, and hope that no more apply for work? Hope that clean air advocates will find other jobs? Or take the lead in resolving an issue before it gets too hot and interferes with work more than the smoke already does?

The nonsmokers' rights movement is not only raising a moral issue but also calling attention to the high costs of permitting smoking on the job—and of having smokers on the payroll, even if they don't smoke at work. . . .

Why Smoke-Free Workplaces?

"Our policy at Radar Electric was quite simple," explained Warren McPherson, president of Radar Electric in Seattle, Washington, from 1972 to 1983. "We hired only nonsmokers and prohibited smoking on company premises—and that applied to visitors and customers as well as employees."

Why break the time-honored tradition of allowing, and sometimes even encouraging, smoking on the job? For any or all of these reasons:

- to reduce absenteeism
- to increase productivity
- to improve morale
- to improve the health and well-being of employees
- to improve compliance with OSHA's [Occupational Safety and Health Administration] mandate to provide a safe work environment
- to protect the company's investment in human resources
- to protect furniture and equipment
- to reduce maintenance and cleaning costs
- to reduce insurance costs
- to reduce the risk of industrial accidents and fires
- to reduce the cost of ventilation
- to enhance organizational image
- to improve the appearance of the organization's buildings and grounds
- to reduce employee turnover
- to reduce the risk of offending customers.

"Many of these were important fringe benefits of our policy," said McPherson, "but I actually

instituted the policy for personal reasons. You see, my mother had lung cancer, and I wanted to fight back at the enemy that tortured and finally killed her. This policy was my way of doing that. I just wanted my company to be smoke-free."

So add one more reason to be smoke-free:

- to generate personal satisfaction from confronting what Surgeon General Everett Koop has proclaimed "the most important public health issue of our time."

"Every time she struck a match, it was a signal that the time had arrived for another informal—and unauthorized—work break."

Clearly, the effects of smoking are costing organizations a bundle. Those that already forbid smoking on work premises have reported decreased expenditures for cleaning, maintenance, and replacement of furniture, carpeting, and equipment. So it's not surprising that more and more employers are thinking twice about allowing smoking on the job and about hiring smokers.

Reinforcing this trend is the nonsmokers' rights movement, which has increasingly turned its attention toward the workplace. Recent research supports what nonsmokers have known all along: that in addition to being irritating and annoying, smoke can damage the health of nonsmokers. The number of complaints, grievances, worker's compensation claims, and lawsuits filed by nonsmokers is on the increase. Indeed, the number one job-related complaint in the 1980s is a smoky work environment. . . .

Smoking and Productivity

"Not only did her smoking ritual shut down her own work—it shut down half of the office," complained Dale Stephens, vice president for data processing with a major West Coast bank. "Every time she struck a match, it was a signal that the time had arrived for another informal—and unauthorized—work break. Four or five of my staff members would move, in unconscious reflex, toward her desk to begin another 10-minutes of chitchat. Every single cigarette she lit was costing me an hour of lost productivity."

Not any more. Corporate headquarters told Stephens to establish whatever smoking policy he deemed appropriate for his department. So he announced a clear policy that smoking would no longer be tolerated during working hours. . . .

Smoking rituals are often so masterfully executed that most people accept them as a part of the smoker's job description. And let's not forget the time lost looking for a cigarette, which can even take the smoker out of the workplace to buy another pack. Cleaning and fiddling with a pipe is also good for a major break at least twice during the day.

The tobacco industry argues that all workers waste time whether they smoke or not. Even if this is true, it wouldn't justify time lost due to smoking. . . .

A smoking ban is also an effective way to keep break times equal among smokers and nonsmokers—especially when worker morale and productivity are important. Mark Miller is a maintenance man for Lincoln General Hospital in Lincoln, Nebraska. He has reported that his boss criticized him severely for taking a few extra minutes for his break. "The boss said more or less that he wanted me to hurry up and get something done. It's all right for smokers to sit down or stop what they are doing and go have a smoke. Just because I don't smoke I'm getting penalized for taking a little longer on break." Miller says his morale went downhill and that his response is to "do what I have to do and that's it. I don't go out of my way to do anything extra." . . .

Statistical Studies

How much time is actually lost to the smoking ritual? Several businesses and consulting firms have measured the amount of time the average smoker loses to the smoking rituals of lighting, puffing, staring, appearing deep in thought, and enjoying an informal work break. The Major Pool Equipment Company in Clifton, New Jersey, found that smokers lost 2 to 10 percent of their efficiency, depending on how frequently they smoked. The average smoker wasted about 30 minutes a day to the smoking ritual—some 6 percent of the work year. . . .

"Cigarette smoke . . . contains more than 3,000 contaminants that can cause respiratory irritations and serious health problems for nonsmokers as well as smokers."

If we accept the finding that smokers waste 30 minutes a day, workers paid $25,000 per year would waste $1,500 of their employers' money, and 94 nonsmokers could do the same amount of work as 100 smokers. These figures do not include lost productivity of offended nonsmokers or their increased absenteeism. Nor do they include billing time lost when astute clients protest.

While the smoking employee is gazing off into space, the client is still being billed at the usual rate. Occasionally a client will have the opportunity to observe this subtle form of theft and balk at payment, as did the production editor of a business journal. She timed how long the paste-up artist in

the typesetting shop took to light and smoke cigarette after cigarette. Ten minutes of each hour went up in smoke. When she demanded a 6 percent reduction of the artist's bill, she got it. (She should have asked for 16 percent!)

When time lost to smoking is combined with time lost to absenteeism, the average smoker loses 17 days per year—which means that the work done by six smokers could be done by five nonsmokers.

Lower Insurance Rates

Should nonsmokers and smoke-free organizations pay less for health, life, disability, fire, auto, and industrial accident insurance? America's insurance companies understand this. Their data show conclusively that nonsmokers pay more than their share for the smoking habits of others. This amounts to grand larceny!

Ponder these statistics:

• According to health economist Dr. Marvin Kristein, smokers burden the nation's health care system (particularly hospitals) *at least* one and a half times as much as nonsmokers.

• Two other studies cited by Kristein found that industrial accident rates for smokers are twice that of nonsmokers.

• According to a study by State Mutual Life Assurance Co. of America, death rates for smoking policyholders in all age categories are two and a half times more than for nonsmoking policyholders.

• Figures from State Mutual also show that smokers are killed in fatal auto accidents at 2.6 times the rate of nonsmokers.

• Thirty percent of building fires and 97.4 percent of fatalities in structural fires are attributable to careless smoking. . . .

Perhaps you've heard about canaries in coal mines. Those caged birds extended the miners' senses by providing an early warning signal that dangerous gases were flowing through the mine. When the birds dropped dead, the miners scrambled out of the tunnels to avoid a similar fate.

Nonsmokers, however, don't need canaries to learn about the quality of their air at work. Their senses serve that function. Irritated noses and lungs are normal reactions to irritants and poisons in the air. But symptoms like this, which warn that corrective action is needed, often fail to get the attention they deserve. Smokers and management often dismiss these reactions by saying they are personality quirks or that complainers are "hypersensitive." It is true that some nonsmokers are so sensitive that smoke can trigger asthma attacks or other serious problems. But defensive use of the word "hypersensitive" is merely a smokescreen for inaction.

The Costs of Passive Smoking

Group surveys have confirmed what individual nonsmokers have known all along—that smoke in the workplace causes discomfort. For example, a survey of more than 20,000 workers at the Social Security Administration Headquarters in Washington, D.C., found that nonsmokers exposed to tobacco smoke complained about the following: conjunctival irritation (47.7%); nasal discomfort (37.7%); coughing, sore throat, or sneezing (30.3%); and difficulty digesting food (19.4%). . . .

Constant annoyances can create stress and impair a person's ability to work. In the Social Security Administration survey, nonsmokers reported three main responses to smoke: 51.2 percent said they had difficulty working near a smoker; 20.6 percent said they had difficulty concentrating on work; and 13.5 percent said they had difficulty producing work.

"Fired up by burning senses, armed with medical evidence, nonsmokers are speaking up at work, hoping to clear the air."

A nationwide survey sponsored by Honeywell Technalysis and conducted by Public Attitudes of New York found that cigarette smoke bothered 54 percent of the 600 workers surveyed and that 53 percent said that cleaner air would make their organizations more productive. The symptoms mentioned most frequently were: tired or sleepy feelings (56%), nasal congestion (45%), eye irritations (41%), breathing difficulties (40%), and headaches (35%).

According to James E. Woods, Ph.D., senior staff scientist for Honeywell's Corporate Physical Sciences Center: "The most common indoor-air problem is cigarette smoke. It contains more than 3,000 contaminants that can cause respiratory irritations and serious health problems for nonsmokers as well as smokers."

After a comprehensive review of research, Roy J. Shepard concluded in *The Risks of Passive Smoking* [Oxford University Press, New York, 1982] that "eye irritation seems to be the main complaint during passive exposure to cigarette smoke" and that "more annoyance is caused by smouldering cigarettes than by active smoking." . . .

Researchers J. L. Repace and A. H. Lowrey, who reviewed 14 epidemiological studies, found that all but one showed evidence that nonsmokers exposed to cigarette smoke had an elevated risk of cancer. They estimate that ambient smoke causes between 500 and 5,000 lung cancer deaths per year in the United States, and some of the studies suggest that the risk is doubled. They note that mainstream tobacco smoke (the smoke inhaled by the smoker) is a potent carcinogen. They also estimate that mortality from passive smoking is many times that

of cancer-causing chemicals regulated by the Federal Clean Air Act. Researcher Peter Fong says "ambient smoke is estimated to cause an excess of deaths between 50,000 and 10,000 a year in a population of 220,000,000."

Based on data from the R. J. Reynolds Tobacco Company, R. Fritz Hafer, Ph.D., and Floyd Frost, Ph.D., calculated that the average passive smoker inhales between 1/1000 to 1/100 cigarette per hour. Assuming 1/500 cigarette per hour for 12 hours by 73 million passive smokers in the United States, Hafer and Frost figure this "amounts to 1,750,000 cigarettes *per day* 'smoked' by non-smokers . . . Concerns over health effects from passive cigarette smoke are hardly a myth . . . passive cigarette smoke is likely the most dangerous air pollutant we face today."

White and Froeb [in the *New England Journal of Medicine*, March 27, 1980] have concluded that nonsmokers who work in a smoky environment have about the same risk of impairment in the small airways of the lungs as do smokers who do not inhale and smokers who inhale between one and ten cigarettes per day. An earlier study by Snyder and Stellman [in *Cancer Research*, December 1977] concluded that the latter group suffers approximately one-fifth the damage of normal smokers. Each smoker could be increasing an employer's cost for every nonsmoker on the payroll by about $243. Because each smoker puts approximately two nonsmokers at risk, the additional payroll cost to an organization because of nonsmokers' poor health from tobacco smoke would be about $486 per smoker per year. And when smoking-induced absenteeism reduces the number of billable hours per week, the loss can be substantially greater.

Psychological Harm

Nonsmokers suffer not only from physical afflictions attributable to smoke, but from psychological ones as well. In the Social Security Administration survey mentioned above, employees were asked about their mental reactions to smoke. Among nonsmokers, 24.2 percent reported frustration because of the smoky nuisance and 22.3 percent reported hostility toward smokers and management. Consider the morale of this nonsmoker after getting this memorandum from a smoker he had asked not to smoke:

> The very law of dispersion indicates that generally what you are smelling is not tobacco smoke but something else.
>
> There are few times that I enter your den of purity with a foul smelling fag in my grubby paw and in the majority of those times the smoke emitting from my long white stick is dispersed and you are picking up only remnants with your long enduring nose.
>
> It is my hope that only the methane gas reaches and accumulates in your big toe and I am confident that you shall surely die of cancer from this city long before you do from my Marlboro.

These frustrations and hostilities erode employee morale, the desire to do good work, and organizational loyalty. Exactly what percentage of nonsmokers quit their jobs because of smoky working conditions is difficult to assess. But turnover is definitely increased. The nonsmoker who received the memo above quit after nine months on the payroll—after $2,000 in addition to his professional salary was spent for his training. . . .

Indifferent Smokers

Fired up by burning senses, armed with medical evidence, nonsmokers are speaking up at work, hoping to clear the air. Many smokers don't seem to care. When Gary Fox worked at the Boeing Aerospace Center in Kent, Washington, he complained to his boss for a week that smoke bothered him. The boss (a smoker) finally said, "The desk you're working on has always been there. It's always going to be there, and that's where you're going to work." Frustrated, Fox called the Environmental Protection Agency. "I called . . . on a Friday. Monday, they sent two people out. Wednesday, I was transferred to another building," Fox reported. "They just wanted me out of their hair."

Roger Maldonado, a bus driver for Jefferson County Transit, posted a sign in the Port Townsend, Washington, drivers' lounge asking smokers to please clean their ashtrays. The request was usually ignored; to get relief from the resultant odor of smoke, Maldonado emptied the ashtrays himself.

"Until management takes a stand for health and profit, nonsmokers will find ways to express their discomfort and disdain for polluted air."

For some nonsmokers the battle can be long, hard, and frustrating. A few years ago, Janet Schmirler worked for Pacific Bank in Seattle (now called First Interstate). "In the mortgage division I was so physically uncomfortable that it was really difficult to do my work," she has reported. Her smoking co-workers were indifferent and began avoiding her. When appeals to her supervisor did nothing, she wrote to the bank's personnel office.

The official response acknowledged that "some smokers need to be reminded to show consideration for those who may be adversely affected by cigarette smoke." But it did nothing more than refer her back to the supervisor, who, according to Schmirler, was a heavy smoker and unwilling to restrict smoking for fear that other smokers would spend too much time away from the job on "smoke breaks." The lack of a policy to protect nonsmokers at the bank, she heard,

was due to top management's fear of losing middle managers, many of whom smoked.

After three months in the mortgage division, Schmirler secured a transfer to a better ventilated department. But the presence of smoke still bothered her enough that she began looking for a smoke-free job. After a total of 13 months at the bank, she found one and took it. . . .

Infringing on Nonsmokers' Rights

Seattle City Light worker Louise McClellan tried fighting smoke with smoke—by burning incense. For her attempts to sweeten the foul air she received a reprimand from the management.

That smokers can burn tobacco, but nonsmokers can't burn incense, is just one example of how smokers are given "protection," according to Ramona Hensrude, past president of Fresh Air for Nonsmokers, Washington state's nonsmokers' rights coalition. "They are given every possible opportunity to continue their habit without being responsible for the breathing air they pollute for others." When smoky air is imposed on nonsmokers, they can become "demoralized because of the frustration and the delay in making the workplace a healthier environment. Then nonsmokers lose respect for supervisors and co-workers." Hensrude notes further that management's indifference and inertia often occur because they don't understand the issue, taking it personally instead of seeing it as a health issue.

The mental suffering of nonsmokers resulting from a sense of helplessness is not easily remedied. Cornelius J. Peck, professor of law at the University of Washington, says there may be little recourse for nonsmokers who are harassed and taunted by management or co-workers. The employment-at-will doctrine, he explains, allows employers to hire and fire as they please unless union contracts or civil service regulations intervene. Without such protection, vocal nonsmokers run the risk of losing their jobs because the "employer can be just exactly that arbitrary." . . .

Until management takes a stand for health and profit, nonsmokers will find ways to express their discomfort and disdain for polluted air. Adverse reactions to smoke are often perceived by management as mere annoyances that can be ignored. "Mere annoyances" or not, they are real concerns to nonsmokers.

Management and smokers seem to overlook their own culpability in this denial process and the interpersonal problems that ensue. Rather than deal constructively by promoting health, which might entail a ban on smoking, they try to justify their unhealthy behaviors.

When normal reactions to unhealthy conditions are consistently denied and persecuted, employee morale and loyalty fade. Employees unable to leave such an appalling situation may become bitter, inefficient workers, perhaps determined to exact revenge on the employer. Others—very likely the brighter and better workers who want to feel good about what they do—will seek work in a healthy environment. Who loses in the end? The uncaring employer. . . .

Smoking Restrictions Are Accepted

Several years ago Jeanne Weigum, personnel director for Immuno Nuclear Corporation in Stillwater, Minnesota, described her company's strict compliance with the Minnesota Clean Indoor Air Act:

> I did a survey of attitudes toward smoking restrictions. All line personnel participated . . . The survey results indicated 100 percent agreement with smoking restrictions in the workplace . . . A majority of people indicated that smoking restrictions at work were very important to them (as opposed to somewhat important or unimportant).
>
> It would be misleading to give the impression that the company is preoccupied with smoking and smokers. It is not. In fact, it is seldom an issue, and the regulations are a simple and acceptable fact of our workplace.

That message expresses what most smoke-free employers would want to convey to other employers who are apprehensive about restricting or prohibiting smoking: *Most employees favor a no-smoking policy because it helps them work better and feel better about working. Most smokers will support the policy because they, too, acknowledge nonsmokers' rights to clean air.* One or two smokers may object, but as we have seen, complications are rare and likely to be minor. Overall, the results are clearly favorable to both employer and employees.

Managers charged with implementing smoking restrictions may assume that employees, unions, and customers will create a wave of problems. Concern is appropriate; anxiety is not! Policies that are carefully designed and executed run into little or no trouble. . . .

Smokers Need Not Apply

All of us make choices. We choose a red car instead of a blue one. We choose Channel 5 because it has better programs. Choosing can be considered a form of discrimination—of selecting what we want over what we don't. Usually we try to choose what we think is best for ourselves. Sometimes we pick what we think is best for others.

Organizations use a similar process when selecting employees. From a stack of 1,000 job applications, for example, only two are needed to fill two open positions. Which applicants are the best? Developing job-related skills would be a waste of time if employers drew resumes from a hat instead of selecting people whose characteristics appear best for the job.

Such characteristics as race, sex, age, and national origin are beyond individual control and are usually irrelevant to job performance. Discrimination on the basis of such attributes is illegal and, in the opinion of most Americans, is immoral as well. But when it comes to education, most people have control over their choices. Employers have always considered education important for some jobs and have "discriminated" among applicants accordingly. The same reasoning is being applied to smoking as more employers realize that hiring only nonsmokers makes economic sense.

"Hiring nicotine addicts to work in a smoke-free work environment would be like hiring claustrophobics to work in a submarine."

If an organization commits itself to becoming smoke-free, it certainly makes sense to stop hiring smokers—especially heavily addicted ones. Hiring nicotine addicts to work in a smoke-free work environment would be like hiring claustrophobics to work in a submarine. Does it make sense to continue to hire smokers into an environment that may unsettle their nerves? Both logic and good faith seem to say no. Restricting future hiring to nonsmokers (or smokers determined to quit) will ensure in the long run a smoke-free organization without complications. . . .

The "employment-at-will" doctrine, upon which labor laws in the United States are based, frees employers to establish hiring and firing criteria subject only to specific legislative exceptions. This means that private employers may discriminate against job applicants on *any* basis except those specifically prohibited by statute. Those prohibited now include race, color, religion, sex, and national origin (Title VII of the Civil Rights Act of 1964), union membership (National Labor Relations Act), and certain physical handicaps (Rehabilitation Act of 1973). . . .

The world will be more livable when smokers work for employers who don't mind polluted environments and nonsmokers work for employers committed to health and good management practices.

William L. Weis is an associate professor in the department of accounting at Albers School of Business at Seattle University. He is also a health and management consultant with Rosner, Weis, and Lowenburg, Inc., a firm that specializes in developing smoking policies for workplaces. Seattle-based writer Bruce W. Miller has published the Nonsmoker's Assertiveness Guide *and several articles in magazines.*

The Case Against Nonsmokers' Rights

Workers Vanguard

In [1988], New York City's "Clean Indoor Air Act" has outlawed smoking in practically every indoor area imaginable, and a total smoking ban on every domestic airline flight of two hours or less (including segments of longer flights) went into effect, courtesy of the feds. "This is going to be one of the best self-enforced laws in the country," crowed New York's hysteria-mongering mayor, Ed Koch. How grotesque—New York City currently leads the U.S. in carbon monoxide pollution and barely escaped a multimillion-dollar cutoff of federal monies by the notoriously lax Environmental Protection Agency . . . and they want to blame the smoker for the rotten air quality in the Big Apple! In keeping with the spirit of social totalitarianism, no sooner did the NYC ban become operative than commuter vigilantes beat up a smoker in a train station.

Then the Surgeon General of the United States issued a report declaring that smoking is an addiction. They're taking aim at cigarette vending machines, talking about licensing tobacco sellers. This is a move to enforce social conformity. Using the pretext of "secondary smoke" harming others, they're going to treat smokers as legal "addicts." Donald McDonald, Reagan's drug adviser, calls tobacco along with alcohol and marijuana "gateway drugs," the first step to heroin and crack. Who's next on their list? Junk food "junkies," chocolate "freaks," coffee drinkers ("caffeine addicts"), everyone who doesn't do the Jane Fonda Low Impact Workout—you name it, you're on it. Now the Supreme Court okays government snoops rifling your trash. How long before they tell you what to read and what to think?

They're trying to stamp out smoking with the jackboot of the state and the snarling zealotry of "live clean or die" puritans. During the debate over California's sweeping ban on smoking on *all* public transportation one Republican state senator aptly denounced "health fascists." A spokesman for the Bakery Confectionery and Tobacco Workers International Union, Ray Scannell (a nonsmoker), said:

> This is Big Brother. This is Carrie Nation. This is good old-fashioned prohibitionism run rampant. It's an attempt to dictate behavior, and Americans are not very good at having behavior dictated to them, especially by self-righteous moralists who have decided it's not good for you to smoke.
> —*Los Angeles Times*, 14 January, [1988]

(As a matter of fact, during Prohibition nine states banned tobacco as well as booze.) There are powerful interests at work here. Behind Big Brother is Big Business, rubbing its hands in anticipation of a profitable speedup—particularly for the nation's 33 million office workers—backed by the U.S. Surgeon General, the Meese police and yuppie power prudes. . . .

Profits Not Health

Today, volunteer "smokeout" cops are being mobilized around the country for an ideological crusade whose goal is not health but *wholesale regimentation of the workforce*, to increase productivity by any means possible. And these aren't Moral Majority backwoods bigots. You've got the '70s "Me Generation," '80s yuppies and quite a few liberal civil libertarians, who a few years ago were all for legalizing marijuana (we're for it), now in an unholy alliance with the Reagan administration to wipe out the "evil weed," tobacco. Nicotine is being added by the Surgeon General to the list of "addictive drugs." The head of the Federal Office on Smoking and Health said on CBS's *Face the Nation* that smoking should be given "the serious attention that we do for the illicit drugs such as heroin, cocaine, etc." And you know what they do about those.

"Warning: Anti-Smoking Crusade Dangerous to Your Rights," *Workers Vanguard*, May 20, 1988. Reprinted with permission.

Train crash, plane crash—forget about the antiquated signal systems, the overloaded air traffic control, they test the workers for drugs and alcohol, and the merest trace will get the bosses off the hook in the media . . . and out of liability suits. Random urine testing is a great way to cow the workforce, and throw in lie detectors to establish "proper employee morale." Now with the smoking bans, a third of the American population and almost half the industrial proletariat will be turned into "legal addicts." There is a strong class bias to the various anti-smoking laws and regulations—the private office retains its sanctity while those on the shopfloor or in the typing pool have to snuff their butts, or else. And in this racist society, no doubt cigarette bans will feed into discrimination against blacks and Latins, more of whom are smokers.

The bosses' concern is not for our health but for *their balance sheets*. Northwest Airlines, whose ads ballyhoo the great smokeout in the sky as a boon to passengers, is really concerned about "the cost of changing filters and cabin air outlets gummed up by tar and nicotine" (*Christian Science Monitor*, 23 March, [1988]). The name of the game is "Increasing Productivity Through On-Site Smoking Control," the title of an April 1985 article in *Health Care Strategic Management*, which among other things claims that "approximately 92 nonsmokers can accomplish the same workload as 100 smokers." *Occupational Health and Safety* (July/August 1984) reports that "The American Lung Association puts a price tag of $25 billion annually on lost productivity, lost wages and absenteeism." *Military Medicine* (August 1986) says smokers take 50 percent more sick leave, need more medical care, "waste 6 percent of [their] working hours to the smoking ritual," require expensive ventilation and exact "a high price in employee morale."

"More and more office workers are crammed into ever smaller workspaces in buildings with no windows and minimal outside air, and they blame smokers for fouling it up!"

Over and over, articles aimed at managers stress that by making workers quit smoking, anywhere from $300 to $1,000 per smoker per year can be added to the till. And, as a nice bonus, corporations get a made-to-order mechanism for all-out repression of the workforce. In true Big Brother fashion, USG Acoustical Products (a defendant in thousands of lawsuits brought by workers who got lung disease through working with asbestos and other fibers) has threatened to use urine tests to detect workers who

smoke, *even at home!* Business has never been overly concerned with job-related health risks to workers, from the now notorious asbestos industry to the horrible mutilation of packinghouse workers: it's "part of the job." But given a chance to control the private lives of the workforce, the ruling-class killers of tens of thousands of workers scream bloody murder about "liability" for "second-hand" smoke. *Profits*, not health, are the bottom line of the anti-smoking crusade.

Airlines

The airlines, for instance, are gleefully jumping on the anti-smoking bandwagon. Clean air for the passengers was never their strongest point anyway, but if it seems worse lately that's not because your seatmates are lighting up more often. *WV [Workers Vanguard]* spoke to the flight attendants union and several FAA officials who confirmed that the airlines are typically using only part of their air conditioning capacity, in the interests of "fuel efficiency." A Boeing 747 has three air conditioning packs, a 737 has two, but frequently they run on one: there are no FAA requirements for minimum ventilation standards. Extra air is routinely pumped to the cockpit to keep the pilot and copilot functioning efficiently and to cool the instruments: "I know that's been an issue for some time, why does the crew get ten times the air as the passengers, and so on," an FAA official told us. So instead of banning cigarettes, how about turning on all the air conditioning units with their filtering capacity?

It's completely within the power of modern technology to adequately ventilate airplanes, offices, wherever. Even in taxis where you have a really small enclosed space, it's easy enough to completely separate the driver from the passenger, like in the big London taxis, adding greatly to driver safety (as CB radios would also), privacy, and keeping smoke in the appropriate area. But proper ventilation isn't profitable. In new office and institutional construction, heating, ventilation and air conditioning (HVAC in the trade) is the second most expensive component in finishing a building; and since electrical wiring is pretty strictly regulated by codes, and insurance companies inspect closely (because of fire danger), HVAC is a prime target for cost-cutting. You get lousy air quality so the board of directors can breathe easy about their bonuses and stockholder dividends.

No Windows

In fact, ventilation has been getting *worse*, not because of smokers but because corporate owners decided after the mid-'70s increase in oil prices to become more "energy efficient." Their solution was to cut down—in fact, almost *eliminate*—the intake of fresh air in the ventilation systems of newer construction. This has created the phenomenon of the "sick building," where all the chemicals, molds, viruses and bacteria are simply recirculated through the building, with the result that office workers get sick a lot. In addition to clogged filters, contaminated air ducts, etc., a five-year study of 240 buildings found more than a third had their air intakes completely sealed off (*New York Times*, 8 May, 1988). Another found fungi levels "comparable to that in a chicken coop or a swine confinement facility" (*Heating/Piping/Air Conditioning*, February 1986). More and more office workers are crammed into ever smaller workspaces in buildings with *no* windows and minimal outside air, and they blame smokers for fouling it up!

The Medical Evidence

As Peter Berger, a Boston University sociologist, recently noted (*New York Times*, 24 April, [1988]), the furor over "passive smoking" is "not because of the weight of the evidence but because of the ideological usefulness of the idea. . . . What people believe comes from placing faith in a certain authority. People say, 'The Surgeon General said so'." Surgeon General C. Everett Koop gets on TV in his gold-braided admirals' uniform, and everyone is supposed to believe it is true. Koop has won respect for his relatively (by Reagan standards) decent position on AIDS, but people forget that he was put in office as an anti-abortion crusader. And the data this spokesman for the Reagan administration has marshaled to back up his drive against smoking falls far short of proving anything.

S. Colman queries our statement that medical evidence on the effects of "secondary smoke" is "inconclusive." So what is the "proof" cited by proponents of smoking bans? The 1986 U.S. Surgeon General's report on *The Health Consequences of Involuntary Smoking* makes three major assertions: 1) "Involuntary smoking is a cause of disease, including lung cancer, in healthy nonsmokers"; 2) "The children of parents who smoke, compared with the children of nonsmoking parents, have an increased frequency of respiratory infections . . . "; and 3) "Simple separation of smokers and nonsmokers within the same air space may reduce, but does not eliminate, exposure of nonsmokers to environmental tobacco smoke."

The Surgeon General's report cited 13 major studies, six of which he claims show some statistically significant correlation between "passive smoking" and lung disease, cancer in particular—and not a large correlation at that. Even taken at face value, you have to be wary of spurious correlations. As *Chest* (September 1985), a journal of thoracic medicine, pointed out, "associations may exist that have nothing to do with causation, such as the parallel decline in European birth rates and the stork population," or a recent international study which showed a higher correlation of lung cancer with beer

drinking than with cigarettes. Moreover, the studies cited are scientifically highly suspect. Seeking an aura of scientific respectability, the Surgeon General's report even acknowledges many of the criticisms, admitting for example that two studies were "not designed to study the long-term effects of involuntary smoking," or that "the findings of this study were questioned because the diagnosis of cancer was not pathologically confirmed in 35 percent of the cases." But having failed to refute many of these criticisms, the report accepts the validity of the studies!

"If 'sidestream smoke' were an important causal factor, smoking pipes would be a much higher risk than it is for lung cancer."

A 1987 article by West German biostatistician K. Überla in the *International Archives of Occupational and Environmental Health* reviews the available studies, noting: "None of the six case control studies yielding a positive relationship" produced "reasonable and sound evidence which cannot be explained by chance, bias, confounding or misclassification." Even the one study which may show a real correlation, of about 200,000 Japanese women, is tainted: who is or isn't a smoker was determined once, in 1965—if a subject forgot she had smoked previously, didn't report that she smoked or started smoking later and died of lung cancer, she was listed as a non-smoker. There was also no consideration of exposure to other substances in the workplace, outdoor and indoor air pollution, genetics, food, medical care. Überla also points out that if "sidestream smoke" were an important causal factor, smoking pipes would be a much higher risk than it is for lung cancer; non-smoking bartenders should also have a higher incidence, which hasn't been shown. The review concludes:

> The volume of accumulated data is conflicting and inconclusive. The observations on nonsmokers that have been made so far are compatible with either an increased risk from passive smoking or an absence of risk.

Children and Smoke

The Surgeon General's second assertion, over the effect on children, has the most emotional impact. Studies indicate it's probably true that infants under one year of age who live with parents who smoke are subject to an increased risk of respiratory infections. This would stand to reason with infants' smaller pulmonary passages and developing immune systems. However, even here, if you take into account parental respiratory symptoms—i.e., baby got bronchitis because mommy caught the bug first—the evidence of a connection is not so clear. And this tendency disappears altogether among older infants. A review of studies through 1985 reports, "A deleterious effect of passive smoking in older children is unproven" (*Chest*, September 1985). Factors which have been ignored in most studies include use of gas stoves for cooking, low birth weight, the number of siblings, poor nutrition, crowding in inadequately ventilated housing, and lack of medical care. *And these are all the more important as poor and working-class parents are far more likely to smoke.*

As for the Surgeon General's third "conclusion," that it is hard to segregate smokers' air from non-smokers', this is undoubtedly true. But there is something that can be done about it other than discriminating against smokers—namely, improved ventilation. All the report has to say on this, in one short paragraph out of *64 pages* of policy recommendations, is that it "can be prohibitively expensive." Studies have been done to figure the amount of ventilation required to create a comfortable environment; one calculated that two to four times the going rate of fresh air flow in a typical office would remove the irritants of cigarette smoke. However, the researcher noted, "increased ventilation as a measure to protect passive smokers is not recommendable from the energetical point of view" (*Tokai Journal of Experiments in Clinical Medicine* [1985]). For "energetical" read "profits."

"With all the yuppie yapping about health through clean living, what about the truly murderous respiratory diseases caused by polluted air at industrial job sites?"

The starting point for any consideration of the medical effects of "passive smoking" is that the volume of smoke inhaled is tiny compared to that of someone smoking a cigarette. One study shows that an airline stewardess working the smoking section on a 16-hour San Francisco-Tokyo round trip would inhale the amount of nicotine of one cigarette. Japanese researchers testing smoky pubs, cars, etc., found in all-day monitoring that the highest "dose" was equal to one-third of a cigarette. But it's yet to be proven that there is any correlation between such low levels of inhaled smoke and serious pulmonary disease. And there is hardly the evidence which would justify such drastic measures as banning smoking.

The vague conclusions of the Surgeon General's report rest on poor scientific foundations. There is

presently inadequate evidence to justify the bans and the social heat being put on smokers. What's called for is not a hysterical witchhunt against smoking but accurate and precise studies to determine the effects of environmental tobacco smoke on non-smokers, and to determine effective measures to ensure decent air quality. But you aren't going to get that from this government of Moral Majority crusaders, whose hypocritical "concern" for the health of "passive smokers" goes hand in hand with their callous disregard for AIDS victims, not to mention tens of thousands of psychiatric patients thrown onto the streets or millions disabled by industrial accidents.

Industrial Deathtraps

With all the yuppie yapping about health through clean living, what about the truly murderous respiratory diseases caused by polluted air at industrial job sites? Millions of workers spend upwards of 43 hours a week in atmospheres infinitely more poisonous than that in an air conditioned office where people light up cigarettes. In coal pits, the miners work in grimy, poorly ventilated shafts where swirling dust clogs the lungs. Company doctors used to claim that coal dust was actually beneficial to health. But miners knew that after years in the pits they were short of breath, wracked by coughing, spitting up blackened sputum. And after years of research, study and hard labor struggle, it was finally admitted that a disease exists. A 1972 pamphlet by the United Mine Workers of America (UMWA) estimated that 125,000 active and former miners suffer from coal workers pneumoconiosis, commonly called "black lung." A UMWA official estimated that 4,000 miners die from the disease yearly. . . .

And for black workers, concentrated in the most dangerous, dirtiest and lowest-paying jobs, the statistics are much worse. As compared to whites, black workers have a 37 percent greater chance of suffering an occupational illness, and are 1.5 times more likely to be severely disabled from job illnesses and injuries (Frank Goldsmith and Lorin Kerr, *Occupational Safety and Health* [1982]). The bosses, of course, blame all industrial respiratory diseases on smoking—the routine response from coal operators when faced with demands for black lung benefit payments. But the miners responded with class struggle. A three-week political wildcat strike by 30,000 West Virginia miners in 1969, culminating in a UMWA march on the state capitol, finally forced passage of a bill making black lung a compensable disease.

In 1986, 11,700 people died from work-related causes and 1.9 million were disabled by injuries at work. Industrial accident rates in high-risk occupations are soaring and many workplaces are deathtraps because of the bosses' "economy" drives;

safety inspections are all but nonexistent. According to the *San Francisco Chronicle* (7 September, 1987), a report based on data from the National Safety Council and the Bureau of Labor Statistics estimated that "nearly 6,000 workers in high-risk jobs who died in the first half of the 1980s would still be alive" but for the decline in enforcement of standards by the Occupational Safety and Health Administration. Out in "lotus land," California governor Deukmejian tried to get rid of CalOSHA, the state inspection agency, entirely! As profit margins fall, the bosses' attention turns to chopping safety measures, cutting the workforce and squeezing every last penny they can out of those who remain.

A Return to McCarthyism

On the heels of the Surgeon General's report, municipalities, states and companies began pushing anti-smoking laws and policies. Most were passed and went into effect with barely a whimper. Across the country, cowed smokers have retreated to stairwells, fire escapes or back alleys to enjoy a cigarette. Soon job applications will read: "Are you now or have you ever been a smoker?" The attempt to make smoking into an anti-social activity ominously recalls the days of McCarthyism and the '50s ditty, "if your mommy is a commie, turn her in." Indeed, there has been a rash of children turning their parents in for having drugs at home. To talk of "health fascism" here is not entirely facetious—the Nazis encouraged such junior finks (and Hitler, by the way, was a rabid anti-smoker).

> *"The attempt to make smoking into an anti-social activity ominously recalls the days of McCarthyism and the '50s ditty, 'if your mommy is a commie, turn her in.'"*

The argument about tobacco industry power is specious. Yes, cigarette ads used to claim that smoking was good for the lungs and stomach, and the companies poured a lot of money into finding "proof" to deny the very real risks of smoking. But all that proves is that the tobacco industry's "moral standards" are no better or worse than any other capitalist endeavor—which is to say they're for profit first, last and all the time. . . .

Regimented Behavior

Sociologist Barry Glassner ruefully notes that if the current trend of regulating and regimenting our behavior continues, "we'll have a homogenized population in which everybody will be within the recommended weight ranges, and nobody will smoke anymore and nobody will drink and everybody will work out" (*New York Times*, 7 May, 1988). In the end, all that clean living may do zilch for your health. But it will help regiment the population for greater productivity and profits, and make people into excellent cannon fodder for war. And when you're in the trenches, they'll probably start passing out cigarettes again like they did in WWII to keep soldiers alert.

Workers Vanguard is the biweekly newspaper of the Spartacist League, an organization that advocates a revolution of the working class to establish socialism in the US.

"'[The rage of] a nonsmoker forced to take in secondhand smoke' inevitably clashes with the rage of the smoker determined to enjoy firsthand smoke."

Restricting Cigarette Smoking: An Overview

Nancy R. Gibbs

Sirio Maccioni, owner of Manhattan's elegant Le Cirque, is in a state. A suave restaurateur who prides himself on his ability to solve any crisis with aplomb, Maccioni caters to high-profile customers who think nothing of dropping $100 for lunch. For him, no whim is too outrageous to be cosseted, no ego too blatant to be stroked. But Maccioni faced an uproar that rattled even his finesse. Some of his most faithful customers were annoyed. His reservation book was a jumble. Phone callers adopted a threatening tone. The problem: New York City's new Clean Indoor Air Act had come to Le Cirque, and for the restaurant's denizens, as for millions of other New Yorkers, life would never be the same again.

The new law requires that half the tables in restaurants with more than 50 seats be reserved for nonsmokers. Maccioni was already agonizing over the nightmares that lay ahead. "One of my regular customers comes in and says, 'Why can't I have my table? I have had that table for 15 years.' I reply that he and his guests are smokers and their table is now in the nonsmoking section." Or worse: "I give Donald Trump his table in the nonsmoking section, and one of his guests lights up. Those at the next table jump up and say, 'If you don't make him stop, I'll call the police.'"

The new legislation also restricts smoking in stores, theaters, hospitals, offices, museums, banks and virtually all other enclosed public places. It is a pitiless law, leaving many smokers few havens except for parking lots and the airless privacy of their own apartment. No sooner had it taken effect than reports began circulating of two commuters pummeling a recalcitrant smoker at a train station, of a business executive trying self-hypnosis to make it through the day at work, of mass defiance at the

city's smoke-filled Offtrack Betting offices. Yet, predicts New York Mayor Ed Koch, the city will scarcely have to enforce the ban; New Yorkers will take care of that themselves. "This is going to be one of the best self-enforced laws in the country," says Koch, who has not smoked since 1952. "There is no one more enraged than a nonsmoker forced to take in secondhand smoke." Unfortunately, that rage inevitably clashes with the rage of the smoker determined to enjoy firsthand smoke. All in all, the law promises to play further havoc in a city not known for the civility of its communal life.

New York thus becomes the latest battlefield in a war that has been raging in the U.S. for some time. All across the country, in large towns and small, in the skies, the offices, the courts, in every cranny of common space, Americans are fighting over where, when and whether a smoker may smoke. Even in their homes, where new laws do not apply, new attitudes do: children threaten to withhold good-night kisses from smoky parents, spouses are exiled to the garage. Fumes Ray Cahoon, 53, a computer specialist in Woodlawn, Md.: "It's gotten to the point where the smoker has no rights at all."

Some 26% of American adults now smoke, down from 38% thirty years ago. But if smokers are becoming a minority, they are an increasingly belligerent one. Even those who would like very much to quit want to do so in their own sweet time—not under a legal gun. They are sick of having glasses of water dumped on their ashtrays or ashtrays dumped on their beds. "The antismoking movement has to do with power lust," argues Paul Corkery, a New York free-lance journalist partial to cigars. "It is a movement that brings out the worst in the worst sort of people."

The worst sort of people in this case includes the U.S. Surgeon General, Congress, hundreds of municipalities, most of the nation's corporations and millions of newly militant nonsmokers who have joined in a campaign to clear the air. Forty-two states have passed laws restricting smoking in public places. Maine has removed cigarette-vending machines from sites where teenagers might have easy access. Utah forbids cigarette ads on billboards, while California has banned smoking on trains, buses and planes traveling within the state.

"Some workers welcome the added incentive to quit smoking and feel that employers are taking a reasoned and sympathetic approach."

The new rules are sparking explosive confrontations on all fronts. The most combustible atmosphere of all is the workplace, where smokers and nonsmokers have grated on each other for years. Signs on office walls that used to smile THANK YOU FOR NOT SMOKING now growl IF YOU SMOKE, DON'T EXHALE. As more and more firms impose tough regulations, millions of smokers are being forced to choose among quitting, hiding, and moving their desk to the rest room. More than half of America's companies have now restricted smoking at work. Some ban it altogether; others, such as Turner Broadcasting in Atlanta and Northern Life Insurance in Seattle, simply refuse to hire smokers. Most require that common areas—open office space, hallways, lounges, conference rooms and rest rooms—be smoke free.

Employees in the ceiling-products division of Chicago's USG Interiors have been told they may not smoke at home either. Such broad restraints strike some as intrusive: "If you want to regulate my life for 24 hours," observes Chicago Labor Lawyer Marvin Gittler, "pay me for the 24 hours or get the hell out of my life."

Some smokers must go to extremes to indulge their habit while keeping their job. At Methodist Hospital in suburban Minneapolis, a worker stepped out onto a second-floor balcony to smoke, despite the frigid temperature. When the door accidentally locked behind her, she jumped to the ground, broke a foot in two places and fractured a wrist. On that very day, the first of a smoking ban, the employees' union had filed a grievance against the hospital for not providing a smoking lounge for workers.

In many companies, the battle lines are drawn between the factory floor and the executive suite. Though workers in open areas must abide by the new rules, anyone with an office door to shut may puff away to his heart's content—though, ironically, relatively few high-ranking professionals do so. According to Donald Garner, an expert in liability law at Southern Illinois University, only 25% of white-collar workers smoke, compared with 50% of blue-collar workers. "This, in a sense, has put over on the nonsmokers' side an enormous reservoir of talent and social prestige that was not there 25 years ago," he says. "Now that the chairman and the CEO aren't smokers, they've become instigators of the nonsmoking workplace."

Company officials responsible for enforcing the restrictions do not relish the task. "Nobody thanks you for putting in a smoking ban," says John Bowyer, a personnel director in Charleston, W. Va. When Bowyer learned that smokers at his company were sneaking off into nearby offices, "I went over with a fire extinguisher and dropped a rather strong hint." If all else fails, employers may be forced to take stronger measures. Judy Caron, a social worker at the state welfare department office in Attleboro, Mass., was dismissed for insubordination after a five-year battle over her smoking, during which her legal fees were paid by the Tobacco Institute, an industry group. "I never smoked with clients," she insists, "and I could no longer enjoy a cigarette at my desk." She resented having to give up her private office and smoke in the company kitchen when the department ran out of space. Now at home in Easton, Mass., she has hired new lawyers to fight for reinstatement.

In many cases, of course, the response has been much less rancorous. Some workers welcome the added incentive to quit smoking and feel that employers are taking a reasoned and sympathetic approach to their plight. Many companies pay all or part of the costs of cessation programs, hypnosis therapy, special classes and self-help kits. Most of them have discovered that they have a lot to gain from helping employees kick the habit. "They will he healthier, their attendance will he better, and this will keep medical costs down," says Arthur Hilsinger, owner of a 100-worker optical-accessories company in Plainville, Mass. . . .

As for the countless other public battlegrounds— store lines clogged with puffing shoppers, taxicabs, hotel lobbies, hospitals and sports arenas—the friction level depends largely on how vigorously and graciously people go about policing their fellow citizens. Employers, after all, have far more leverage over their workers, and airlines over their passengers, than citizens do over one another. Who is really going to enforce the regulations, apart from those who have always been willing to pipe up and demand that a smoker crush out a cigarette? "Usually it's older women who are more aggressive," jokes South Dakota State Representative Gust Kundert, 74, who smokes a pack a day. "They get a little sarcastic with me. They figure I can't pop them one."

On the other hand, officials in some of the hundreds of cities that have passed antismoking ordinances of various descriptions have been surprised at the calmness of the citizen response. "I anticipated more argumentative confrontations among people in lines at banks and supermarket check-out counters, says City Manager Robert Healy of Cambridge, Mass., where smoking restrictions went into effect a year ago, "but so far we have had very little quarreling." And this without an official show of force. "We don't have police cruisers going around with water pistols trying to shoot out people's cigarettes." . . .

For two centuries, tobacco remained a staple of American life. Cigarettes' image of sophistication curled through popular culture, especially the movies, which taught viewers that they could look like Lana Turner or Marlene Dietrich or Humphrey Bogart by lighting up. Edward R. Murrow interviewed guests through a cloud; tycoons fueled deals with cigars. Without smoking, it seemed, great detectives could not detect, writers could not write, lovers could not languish, heroes were deflated and vamps declawed.

Consider how the image has changed. One of the last smoking TV heroes was Don Johnson's ice-cool cop, Sonny Crockett, on *Miami Vice*, and they—actor and character—have conspicuously quit. One of the latest movie sirens to light up was Glenn Close in *Fatal Attraction*: the cigarette seemed a beacon of her madness. "For a long time, we saw Bette Davis' sitting at the bar smoking a cigarette as sexy," observes Robert Rosner of the Smoking Policy Institute in Seattle. "But then, as a society, we got close enough to smell her breath, and we realized it wasn't sexy at all."

"I wish the antismokers would try to understand that there is a physical addiction here. They seem to think we smoke just to mess up their air or something."

For society to have changed its mind so extensively, so quickly, marks the triumph of a crusade that actually began generations ago. As long as there have been smokers, there have been those who would snuff out the habit. A cigar, said Editor Horace Greeley more than a century ago, is a "fire at one end and a fool at the other." Justice Oliver Wendell Holmes passed along some memorable ammunition to 19th century schoolchildren:

Tobacco is a filthy weed,
That from the devil does proceed;
It drains your purse, it burns your clothes,
And makes a chimney of your nose.

Concerns about health were always at the heart of the antismoking movement. Victorian women were warned that they would become sterile, grow a mustache or come down with tuberculosis if they dared to light up. Yet it was not until the Surgeon General's 1964 report linking cigarettes to cancer that health officials won their point. Warning labels appeared on packages after 1965, ads were pulled from television and radio in 1971, and four years later, Minnesota passed the first comprehensive clean-indoor-air law. Smoking continued to taper off throughout the 1970s. Even then, however, people were content to live and let smoke: the public spirit of laissez-faire survived every attempt by health officials to reclassify cigarettes as a hazard rather than a nuisance.

All that changed with Surgeon General C. Everett Koop's explosive report on the effects of passive, or involuntary, smoking, released in 1986. Koop's review, which coincided with a study by the National Academy of Sciences, reported that pregnant women who smoke are more likely to miscarry, while children of smokers suffer more bronchitis, pneumonia and other respiratory illnesses. The NAS study found that nonsmoking spouses of smokers face a 25% greater risk of contracting lung cancer than do spouses of nonsmokers. "It pulled together all that we had known for decades," says Mark Pertschuk of Americans for Nonsmokers' Rights, "and changed the question from Do we have enough evidence to take action? to Why aren't we doing more?"

Koop's report galvanized antismokers, who until then had limited their weaponry to burlesque winces and conspicuous coughs. "After having had smoke blown in their faces for years when smokers ruled," says Rosner, "the asthmatics are finally having their day." And not only asthmatics. Opera Singer Marjorie Kahn was married to a smoker and "hated it. I screamed all the time. I'm divorced from him now." Kahn's attitude toward smokers remains unyielding. "If they want to kill themselves, they should do it in private and not pull down someone else with them."

Smokers know, of course, that it is not quite that simple. "You can't blame people for not wanting to breathe smoke," says Kay Michael, a reporter for the Charleston (W. Va.) *Daily Mail*, "but I wish the antismokers would try to understand that there is a physical addiction here. They seem to think we smoke just to mess up their air or something." . . . Most experts now agree that cigarettes are every bit as addictive as drugs or alcohol. "Smoking a cigarette is like free-basing nicotine," says Dr. Joseph Frawley, chief of staff at Schick Shadel Hospital in Santa Barbara, Calif. "And for some people, it is virtually impossible to quit."

The new findings help explain behavior among smokers that would otherwise defy all reason. "If you tell cocaine users that if they don't stop, their leg will be cut off, most will stop," observes Dr. Jerome Jaffe, director of the Addiction Research

Center at the National Institute on Drug Abuse. "After smokers have a lung operation, bypass surgery or a heart attack, about half continue smoking." A. Burton Bradley, who runs a stop-smoking clinic in Atlanta, has seen his share of hard-core addicts. "You would be amazed at the people who have had their larynx removed," he says, "and who put cigarettes in the tracheotomy hole in the hospital."

CNN Talk-Show Host Larry King, 54, smoked two packs a day from the age of 18. In February 1987 he had what he calls his "lucky" heart attack. He smoked on the way to the hospital. But after three days in intensive care, he says, he made a pact. "I said to myself, 'If you survive, you will never smoke again.'" He too is amazed at others who react differently. "When Martin Sheen visited me, he was smoking again after his heart attack, and I asked why. He said, 'It is my friend it is always there and doesn't pass judgment.' I said, 'Your friend is going to kill you.'"

"The best short-term hope is that sanctimonious nonsmokers will learn sympathy, and adamant smokers will learn courtesy."

Since nearly all smokers have tried and failed to give up their habit, they are well aware of the pain of withdrawal. Quitting is estimated to be a $100 million-a-year industry, and yet very few smokers succeed on the first try, or even the second or third. The relapse rate is comparable to that of heroin; most do not last even a year. All across the country, as deadlines for still more laws approach, there are households full of people drinking lots of water, gnawing licorice, knitting feverishly, gripping pencils, breathing deeply, or gift-wrapping their cigarettes to make smoking as inconvenient as possible. . . .

Many would-be quitters discover that they cannot concentrate without their cigarettes; others get depressed, gain weight, or acquire a new addiction—such as nicotine gum. "I know a guy who started chewing Nicorettes," says Cartoonist Mell Lazarus, "and now he smokes *and* chews Nicorettes." Beatrice Burstein, a justice of the New York Supreme Court, was a three-pack-a-day smoker for 50 years. She quit three years ago, though now she is hooked on the gum. "I can't sit on the bench and chew, so I chew in my chambers," she says. "I'm ashamed of the habit, so I tell lawyers I must chew because I just quit smoking. I even swim laps with a Nicorette in my mouth."

In time, as the laws and the public pressure become overpowering, some holdout smokers may finally find the willpower to lay down their packs for good. How many remains to be seen. "There is one school of thought that says we are now down to the hard-core smokers—the mild smokers have dropped off," says Adele Paroni of the American Cancer Society. "But there is another school of thought that says the percentage will just continue to decline to nearly zero." In the meantime, the war goes on. And since even wars have rules, the best short-term hope is that sanctimonious nonsmokers will learn sympathy, and adamant smokers will learn courtesy, and an air of understanding will ease the discomfort on both sides.

Nancy R. Gibbs is a staff writer at Time *magazine.*

"Smoking on the job... is injurious to the health of employees, it leads to tensions and lowered employee morale, and it adds to the costs of doing business."

Restrictions Against Smoking Are Beneficial

Martin Dewey

Beginning with a startling series of medical findings in Britain and the United States in the 1960s, the world has been left in no doubt that active smoking is a cause of disease and early death. In Canada alone, government estimates indicate that more than 550 smokers die from smoking-related diseases every week.

More recently, however, international studies have found that it not just active smokers who are harmed. Health damage is suffered by all who share indoor space with smokers—and the greatest damage of all is suffered by nonsmoking fellow workers.

Surveys show that few nonsmokers are indifferent to second-hand smoke. In some, the reaction is mere annoyance. In others it produces physical irritation. In still others it produces disease and, yes, even death.

A U.S. survey found that more than 60 per cent of respondents—and they included smokers as well as nonsmokers—agreed with the statement: "It is annoying to be near a person who is smoking cigarettes."

A study of nonsmoking government workers in Baltimore, Md., found that more than half felt their productivity was impaired by second-hand smoke and 14 per cent found it difficult to produce work.

A survey covering more than 1,000 Canadians and published in the *Canadian Journal of Public Health* reported that 52.5% were annoyed by smoking in offices, with 26 per cent complaining of "major" annoyance and nearly half the sample were smokers.

The same Canadian Survey showed that more than eight out of 10 respondents experienced physical discomfort in the presence of second-hand smoke.

According to James Repace, a Scientist with the U.S. Environmental Protection Agency and a leading international authority on indoor air pollution: "Several studies have indicated that from one-half to three-fourths of nonsmoking adults experience symptomatic effects from ambient tobacco smoke exposure, including eye, nose, and throat irritation, headache and nausea, with much more severe effects reported in persons with cardiac or obstructive pulmonary disease."

Disease and Death

An electrifying report in the *British Medical Journal* found in Japan that nonsmoking wives of heavy smokers develop lung cancer at nearly twice the rate of those whose husbands are nonsmokers.

A smaller study of nonsmoking wives in Greece found that the lung cancer risk to those married to smokers is twice to three times the risk run by those married to nonsmokers.

A study of 1,338 lung cancer patients in Louisiana found that nonsmokers married to heavy smokers run an increased risk of cancer, and so do nonsmokers whose mothers smoked.

A U.S. study found that nonsmokers married to smokers had 60 per cent more cancers of all types than nonsmokers never married to smokers.

The U.S. Environmental Protection Agency estimates that second-hand smoke is to blame for up to 5,000 lung cancer deaths among nonsmoking Americans every year.

A 10-year study involving 2,100 San Diego office workers found a "significant" impairment of small airways function among nonsmokers who had worked 20 years or more in enclosed areas where smoking was permitted. **They were found to have the same level of impairment as people who smoke up to 10 cigarettes a day.**

A French study of 8,000 adults found that nonsmokers 40 years of age and older who were married to smokers had impaired lung function which could be explained only by exposure to

Martin Dewey, *Smoke in the Workplace—An Action Manual for Non-Smokers.* Toronto, Ontario: Non-Smokers' Rights Association, 1985. Reprinted with permission from the Non-Smokers' Rights Association, Suite 308, 344 Bloor Street West, Toronto, Ontario M5S 1W9 second-hand smoke in the home.

Other studies have found that children of smokers have higher-than-average rates of respiratory impairment and disease. It has also been shown that sudden infant death syndrome is more prevalent in smoking households.

A recent U.S. study calculates that 10,000 to 50,000 American nonsmokers actually die every year as a result of long-term exposure to relatively low levels of second-hand smoke. . . .

The Workplace as Smoke Trap

At first glance, the workplace is where nonsmokers would be least likely to suffer health damage from second-hand smoke. Unlike our homes, which usually rely on random ventilation, the places in which we work are frequently equipped with complex ventilation systems. Designers of modern buildings speak glowingly of "computerized climate control," of "filtered air" and of three, four and five "complete air changes" per hour. In addition, the lawbooks are heavy with regulations designed to ensure that employers provide safe and healthy working conditions. Where the workplace is concerned, it would seem that indoor man has truly made up for God's outdoor deficiencies.

The reality, however, is that one pollutant—tobacco smoke—has managed to beat the system. According to Repace: "The smoke pollution inhaled indirectly from cigarettes, pipes and cigars indoors is not only chemically related to the smoke from factory chimneys, but routinely occurs at far higher levels indoors than does factory smoke or automobile exhaust outdoors. . . . Substantial air pollution burdens are inflicted upon nonsmokers far in excess of those encountered in smoke-free indoor environments, outdoors, or in vehicles on busy commuter highways."

"A nonsmoker in an office with typical ventilation and a typical population of smokers inhales the equivalent of three low-tar cigarettes in an eight-hour day."

Repace and a co-researcher, Alfred Lowrey of the U.S. Naval Research Laboratory, have calculated average exposures to second-hand smoke in the home and at work. "Our estimates show," they write, "that the ratio of workplace dose to the exposure received at home is nearly four to one—indicating that, on average, the workplace is a more important source of exposure than the home environment." They conclude that a nonsmoker in an office with typical ventilation and a typical population of smokers inhales the equivalent of three low-tar cigarettes in an eight-hour day. But if

the office is poorly ventilated—which, as we will see, is more common than you may think—nonsmokers may inhale the equivalent of 10 cigarettes in their working day, and possibly more!

In other words the workplace, which **should** be a refuge from tobacco smoke, is the place of greatest exposure for nonsmokers. It also tends to be the place of **longest** exposure. Substances that have been shown to attack the respiratory systems of test animals after mere hours of exposure may be absorbed by the nonsmoker as a matter of daily routine throughout his or her working life. Worse, the workplace is where nonsmokers tend to have least control over their surroundings. We can choose whether to put up with second-hand smoke in many situations, but most of us have to go to work and accept the conditions we find there. The workplace is where the term "forced smoking" all too often has literal meaning; it is where the need to attack the second-hand smoke problem is most urgent, and where the potential gains for the nonsmoker are greatest.

The Ventilation Problem

To understand how tobacco smoke beats the system, we must take a closer look at its chemical composition. An exceedingly fine aerosol, it contains at least 3,800 identified compounds and occurs in two phases—gases and airborne particles. The gas phase contains such poisons and irritants as carbon monoxide, formaldehyde, acrolein, ammonia, nitrogen oxides, pyridine and hydrogen cyanide. It also contains 16 known or probable cancer-causing agents. One of these is N-nitrosodimethylamine—or NDMA—which, according to the International Agency for Research on Cancer, "produces cancer in all animal species in which it has been tested and does so by various exposure routes, including inhalation, and after single doses."

The particulate phase contains tars and nicotine (itself a powerful poison) as well as 38 known or probable carcinogens. Among them are 2-naphthylamine and 4-aminobiphenyl. According to guidelines published by the American Conference of Governmental Industrial Hygienists, there is no safe exposure level for these two substances: "No exposure or contact by any route—respiratory, skin or oral, as detected by the most sensitive methods—shall be permitted." . . .

Filters That Don't Filter

Although building engineers talk of air changes per hour, or ACH, the air is not changed so much as it is recycled. It is drawn out of an indoor space, passed through filters, and then returned. It's the same air as before, the only difference being that standard ventilation specifications call for adding 10 per cent new outdoor air to the flow.

Even this rudimentary recycling would help if the air were properly cleaned. Unfortunately, most buildings are equipped with low-efficiency mechanical filters that do little to control airborne contaminants. Although there are high-efficiency filters that remove many pollutants from the air, they are expensive to install and maintain, and tend to be used only in special circumstances where air purity is deemed to be of overriding importance.

"It's really a cost situation," says Herbert Maybank, a Toronto consulting engineer and filtration specialist. "Building designers won't make ventilation systems any better than they have to. When a construction project goes over budget, almost without exception it is filter quality that will be cut. The value of filters is generally not perceived." . . .

We've seen that even a conscientiously operated ventilation system provides only about 10 per cent fresh air, which means the dilution process is a very slow one. Repace has shown that in a work area ventilated at the rate of one air change an hour, it takes more than three hours to get rid of the smoke from a single cigarette. Even at three air changes an hour it takes an hour to get rid of most of the smoke. The catch is that the average smoker goes through 1.5 to two cigarettes an hour. With a single smoker in a room, smoke from Cigarette Two will be added to the atmosphere while the system is still laboring with the smoke from Cigarette One. Usually, of course, there will be more than one smoker in an indoor space—which means that the ventilation system will fall behind all the faster.

Writes Repace: "Under the practical range of ventilation conditions and building occupation densities, the respirable particle levels generated by smokers under typical conditions overwhelm the effects of ventilation even when applicable standards are observed." . . .

Counting the Costs

An employer who is nervous about upsetting smokers may feel that the most expedient thing to do is to leave matters alone in hopes of maintaining the status quo. But such an employer should realize that the status quo is not neutral. Smoking on the job exerts a negative effect on the workplace: It is injurious to the health of employees, it leads to tensions and lowered employee morale, and it adds to the costs of doing business. We will look at these added costs in this section; the numbers will amaze you.

Smoking is a more expensive pastime than most Canadians realize. The costs are borne not just by smokers as they dig into their pockets at the cigarette counter but by society as a whole. A study for the Laboratory Centre for Disease Control, Health and Welfare Canada, estimates that Canada's dollar loss in 1979 due to tobacco-related death,

disability and disease totalled $5.2 billion. An earlier study in California estimated one year's loss due to smoking-related illness, property damage and absenteeism to be $1 billion in that state alone.

Much of this continuing cost is shouldered directly by employers. According to Dr. Marvin Kristein, chief of the Health Economics Division, American Health Foundation, an average employee smoking a pack a day or more costs an employer about $624 a year (1980 U.S. dollars) in extra expenses due to higher insurance premiums of various kinds, lowered productivity (including that of nonsmoking co-workers), absenteeism, disability and premature death.

> "An average employee smoking a pack a day or more costs an employer about $624 a year (1980 U.S. dollars) in extra expenses."

Among the direct losses, he writes, are those resulting from "time lost due to smoking rituals; extra cleanup costs; extra damage to equipment, furniture and fixtures." Other costs result from "inefficiency and errors based on the established literature as to the effects of higher carbon monoxide levels in smokers, eye irritation, measured lowered attentiveness, cognitive and exercise capacity functioning."

Another authority puts the loss much higher. William Weis of Seattle University lists the **extra** costs to an employer of a smoker whose total payroll costs are $30,000 a year as follows:

absenteeism	$ 330
medical care	230
disability, early death	770
fire, industrial accidents	90
time spent on smoking rituals	2,710
property damage, depreciation	500
maintenance	500

To these costs he adds the losses created by the chronic exposure of nonsmoking employees to second-hand smoke, which he calculates to be $245 per nonsmoker. Since statistics indicate that each smoker in the workplace is likely to share space with two nonsmokers, each smoker thus becomes responsible for another $490 in costs to the employer.

Prof. Weis's conclusion: A smoker whose total payroll costs are $30,000 a year costs his or her employer an additional $5,620 [in 1981 U.S. dollars] compared with a nonsmoking employee earning the same.

After listing the studies on which he bases his findings, he says: "Trying to satisfy the sceptic that all these studies are accurate is a battle best left unengaged. One fact remains unchallenged: No matter how it is measured, smoking is a terrible drain on our economic resources."

The Message of the Balance Sheet

Even sceptics must pay heed to the experience of a company like Dow Chemical. Concerned about possible smoking-related operating costs, the company instructed its medical department to undertake an extensive 3 1/2-year study covering 1,400 employees at its Midland location in Texas. Here are some of the findings:

•Smokers were absent 5.5 days more per year than nonsmokers, costing Dow $657,146.73 annually in excess wage costs alone. This didn't include extra health care costs.

•Smokers registered 17.4 disability days per year, compared with 9.7 days for nonsmokers.

•Compared with nonsmokers, smokers had twice the circulatory disease problems, three times more pneumonia, 41% more bronchitis and emphysema, and 76% more respiratory diseases of all types.

•For every two nonsmokers who died during the study period, seven smokers died.

"There is only one way to protect the health of nonsmokers in the workplace. It is to ban smoking altogether."

A study of absenteeism at the United States Steel Corp. found, among other things, that "employees who smoke have more work-loss days than those who have never smoked. In every age group, as the number of cigarettes per day in confirmed smokers increases, so also does sick absence. Male smokers of more than two packs per day have nearly twice as much absence as their nonsmoking associates; the heaviest women smokers of more than two packs per day miss more than twice as much time as their counterparts who do not smoke."

The fire department in Alexandria, Virginia, began hiring nonsmokers exclusively after discovering that every firefighter who retired with smoking-related disabilities was costing the city an extra $140,000 in retirement benefits. "Why should the taxpayers subsidize it?" asked the fire chief.

Fighting Back

As employers become aware of the costs of smoking in the workplace, many are starting to do something about it. Seattle-based Radar Electric Inc. doesn't hire smokers. The company president, Warren McPherson, says he instituted the policy after a company survey showed smokers were less productive than nonsmokers.

Comments a report in the *Wall Street Journal*: "Employers who shun smokers usually echo Mr. McPherson's complaint. . . . They argue that people use cigarettes as a break from work. So smoking a pack of cigarettes on the job could mean 20 breaks a day. Smoking-related illness can also cause high absenteeism, says the National Centre for Health Statistics, which estimates that sick smokers cost [U.S.] businesses $25.8 billion in lost productivity in 1980."

One U.S. daily quotes the owner of a company employing 240 people as saying: "You'd have to be crazy to hire smokers. They have a 22% higher sick time than nonsmokers. We save a half-million dollars in health benefits each year." . . .

The 'Rights' Debate

It's been shown that there is only one way to protect the health of nonsmokers in the workplace. It is to ban smoking altogether—or, as a second-best solution, to restrict it to separately ventilated smoking lounges. But any attempt to curtail smoking inevitably runs into the cry: What about the rights of smokers? What about freedom of choice? . . .

Here, from a recent magazine advertisement, is a "message to nonsmokers" from the United States Tobacco Institute:

Smoking is "a small ritual that welcomes strangers, provides companionship in solitude, fills empty time, marks the significance of certain occasions and expresses personal style. For **some** people. And by personal choice, not for you. That's the way it ought to be. Whether your preference is carrot juice or bottled water, beach buggies or foreign cars, tobacco smoking or chewing gum or none of the above. Personal style."

Behind the chatty tone lie several messages. The industry wants the public to believe that:

•There is a right to smoke.
•Smoking is a personal matter.
•It's a matter of freedom of choice.
•It is a friendly, harmless pastime.

By hammering away at such themes in its advertising and publicity efforts, the tobacco industry has managed to persuade a lot of people that the debate over second-hand smoke is not about health at all, but about individual rights and freedoms. The notion is clearly nonsensical, but nonsmokers have to be able to show it to be so. Let's look at the tobacco industry's messages one by one.

A Right To Smoke?

When the tobacco industry or smokers themselves say there is a right to smoke, they are talking in code. They are not really asserting a right to **smoke**, for it's generally conceded that people have every right to do so—just as they have every right to drink pop, chew gum or beat themselves over the head with a board. What they are asserting is a right to smoke **at will**—that is, to smoke without regard for the consequences to others. They are claiming a right to pollute—and the long and the short of it is that there is no such right in society.

"I assert," writes Repace, "that smokers have the right to enjoy the risks and benefits [?] of smoking, just as they have the right to play Russian roulette. When they smoke indoors in the presence of others, however, they are playing Russian roulette with nonsmokers' health. This they do not have the right to do."

"Smoking is the most widespread and destructive drug addiction ever seen on the face of the earth."

Put another way, we have every right to walk down the street, but not to walk on our neighbor's flower bed. We can use a power mower all day long, but not at night when that same neighbor is trying to sleep. We can get drunk, but we can't endanger someone else's life by getting behind the wheel of a car. . . .

A Personal Matter?

"Personal style," says the Tobacco Institute ad. "Whether your preference is carrot juice or bottled water, beach buggies or foreign cars, tobacco smoking or chewing gum or none of the above."

Clearly, most of these choices are personal; whether one chooses carrot juice or bottled water bothers no one else and therefore concerns no one else. But how personal can smoking be when it is routinely carried out in the presence of others? When only a small fraction of the smoke produced by a cigarette is consumed directly by the smoker and the rest is discharged into the common air for others to breathe? When the health consequences are routinely visited on others?

If smokers want smoking to be regarded as a personal matter, they should make it so. In the meantime, sad to say, it remains very much a public matter.

The great and glaring irony of the tobacco industry's constant reference to freedom of choice is that, where its products are concerned, accustomed users have woefully little choice in the matter. Nicotine is one of the most fiercely addictive substances on earth. According to the American Psychiatric Association, in its Diagnostic and Statistical Manual of Mental Disorders, regular smokers suffer from "a dependence disorder"—a designation which places smoking in a family of dependence disorders that includes alcoholism and heroin addiction. "In fact, as measured by inability

to abstain," observes William Pollin, director of the U.S. National Institute on Drug Abuse, "**smoking is much more addictive than alcohol** [emphasis added]." Researchers have also found that it is more resistant to treatment than heroin addiction. . . .

A Destructive Addiction

"A small ritual," says the tobacco ad, "that welcomes strangers, provides companionship in solitude, fills empty time, marks the significance of certain occasions. . . .'

The ad certainly makes smoking seem harmless enough. And it's true that smokers don't begin to reel wildly about after a few puffs; they don't have to embark on a life of crime to support the practice; they still go to work and still function as ordinary members of society. Yet, while all of this is true, epidemiologists will confirm a single and inescapable fact: Smoking is the most widespread and destructive drug addiction ever seen on the face of the earth.

Author Martin Dewey wrote Smoke in the Workplace *for Non-Smokers' Rights Association, a national organization in Canada. Dewey won a National Newspaper Award for his editorial writing for* The Toronto Star *and he has been a writer and editor for the Canadian Broadcasting Corporation's television news program.*

"Thirty percent of adult Americans smoke. Restricting their rights is not the path to harmonious working conditions."

Restrictions Against Smoking Are Harmful

Jody Powell

As any manager knows, the biggest challenge in running a business is people—finding and keeping the right ones and ensuring their productivity and satisfaction on the job. As the chief executive officer of a growing Washington public affairs firm, I spend much of my time locating the paragons of virtue I need to run and staff our accounts. And while I'm searching for creative, experienced, detail-oriented, seventy-hour-a-week types, I don't want to worry about the personal habits of prospective and current employees that bear no relationship to the smooth functioning of my business.

To its credit, the American business community has learned to ignore differences that don't matter when dealing with personnel—class, race, gender, age, family situation, and what can only be called personal style. I'll hire an Albanian grandmother who rides to work on a Harley-Davidson if she can do the job. I am convinced that the evolution in corporate thinking toward policies that evaluate employees on only job-related factors brings greater fairness and productivity to the workplace. Managers who use their position to impose personal preferences on their subordinates ask for trouble. And the more intelligent and creative those subordinates are, the bigger the trouble will be.

Particularly ludicrous is the notion that I should ignore all extraneous considerations save one—whether or not my employees use tobacco products. . . .

I am neither a libertarian zealot nor a fanatic antismoker; I am a businessman trying to get the job done. I feel that the smoking issue has been blown far out of proportion by activists with little understanding and fewer facts on the controversy. I am convinced that workplace smoking can be handled by common sense, logic, and a good notion of a business's overall objectives.

The Legal Angles

Before making a decision about smoking policies in a business, it is important to understand what the law compels. The history of employee-initiated litigation on workplace smoking issues is complex, but for the most part it demonstrates a reasonable regard by the courts for employer latitude and common sense.

Although a meticulous interpretation of workplace smoking lawsuits should be left to the lawyers, here is a brief summary of the legal requirements placed on an employer:

Nonsmokers have no constitutional right to compel a smoke-free workplace. Although antismoking activists have searched for the right to a smoke-free environment as a concomitant of freedom of speech, due process, and the preservation of other unspecified "fundamental rights," federal courts have given short shrift to these arguments. In several cases in the 1970s, various district courts dismissed the notion of a right to smokeless air as nonsensical.

There is not much support in common law for attempts to compel a smoke-free working environment. One case, *Shimp versus New Jersey Bell*, granted a secretary the right to a smoke-free workstation; however, this case was never contested by the defendant, New Jersey Bell, in court. Attempts by antismoking activists to establish this case as a precedent have failed. The same state court that granted the *Shimp* ruling denied another complainant's request against the same employer several years later. Generally, courts have held that while employers are responsible for providing safe working environments, there is no correlation between "safe" and "smoke-free." Employees complaining of hypersensitivity to tobacco smoke are not guaranteed smokeless environments by reason of their own perceived needs or allergies.

Employees who smoke are entitled to consideration of their rights before smoking restrictions can be imposed. One court decision put this best by stating that "there is no warrant and no justification as a matter of civilized management to treat smokers as if they were moral lepers." For that matter, if there is a collective bargaining agreement with a group of employees, unilateral smoking restrictions *cannot* be imposed without risking litigation based on unfair labor practice. In other words, there may be as much potential legal liability from imposing a smokeless environment as in "neglecting" to provide one; a smart employer will look for compromise solutions.

That leaves the conscientious—or litigation-wary—manager with a feeling of some security from nuisance lawsuits. This does not mean that employers will not be sued by militant antismokers, only that demands for a smoke-free workplace based on federal or common law will probably not be upheld by the courts. There are, however, some exceptions where businesses can be held responsible for restricting workplace smoking, because of local ordinances or safety requirements specific to certain types of businesses.

The federal government, for example, has restricted smoking in government buildings since 1986. Most civil servants are permitted to smoke only in hallways and rest rooms; smokers who light up in their offices are liable to enforcement from the building's security officers. These restrictions are too new for any organized survey of the results to be available, but preliminary indications are that a great deal of tax-paid time is lost as a result of this prohibition against smoking and working at the same time.

Other businesses with a legalized antismoking policy include concerns where workers routinely handle food, flammable materials, chemicals, or sensitive equipment. In most of these situations, workers understand the smoking restrictions when they apply for employment and accept them as safe and necessary. No one objects to these restrictions in specified environments—just as no one objects to the wearing of protective clothing or the use of special procedures that are appropriate to certain types of businesses. . . .

The Shell Game of Smoking Economics

For years, certain economists and efficiency experts have claimed that smoking on the job contributes to a loss of productivity and higher insurance costs. These experts support bans on workplace smoking in the name of cost-effectiveness; an argument that, if true, should concern every manager in every business or industrial environment.

But the true costs of smoking and/or smoking restrictions are difficult to discern. One advocate of restrictions, William Weis, serenaded the business community for years with claims that a flat refusal to hire smokers could "shave personnel costs by 20 percent, insurance premiums by 30 percent, maintenance charges by 50 percent, furniture replacement by 50 percent, and disability payments by 75 percent." According to Mr. Weis, the total costs per smoker exceed $4,000 per year. That is a powerful bottom-line argument. But few executives acted on Weis's recommendations, and their skepticism appears to have been justified.

Weis admitted that "skeptics might argue that these numbers are as soft as the underside of a porcupine, and that may be true." A close look at those numbers bears that out. Consider the statistics on worker absenteeism. Data from the 1976 National Health Survey demonstrate that male smokers are absent less frequently than nonsmokers; that work loss for women is lowest among women who smoke the most; and that women who smoke fewer than twenty-four cigarettes a day miss less work than former smokers. Moreover, statistics on absenteeism that measure only the smoking habits of employees fail to take into account other determining factors— age, gender, family responsibilities, personal problems, type of employment, job satisfaction, and even the weather for commuting employees. One obvious correlation missed by restriction advocates is that blue-collar workers smoke more than white-collar workers and have higher rates of absenteeism. Is this because blue-collar workers smoke or because they enjoy their jobs less and feel less involved in them than do their white-collar counterparts?

"Male smokers are absent less frequently than nonsmokers; . . . work loss for women is lowest among women who smoke the most."

When considering increased insurance and medical costs, the correlation between smoking and higher premiums is shaky at best. Again, job category is the crucial factor. Blue-collar workers smoke more than white-collars; they also lift more, carry more, are exposed to dangerous industrial substances, and work with heavy and occasionally dangerous equipment. Premium rates for workers' compensation are determined not by employee smoking habits, but by occupational category, carrier experience with the business, and the statutory level for workers' compensation for the particular state. Marvin Kristein, an American Health Foundation economist who has claimed that the average smoker costs his or her employers between $336 and $601 a year, admits that "we lack meaningful 'case-controlled' company comparisons of experience with smoking employees versus nonsmoking employees versus ex-smokers and the impact on company costs."

Productivity

One issue that is not really quantifiable but about which exists informed opinion, is productivity. Despite allegations by antismoking groups that smokers accomplish less on the job than their nonsmoking counterparts, a survey of 1,900 supervisors has demonstrated that those who know their employees best do not concur. In that survey, conducted by Response Analysis Corporation, more than 90 percent of these first-line supervisors denied that employee smoking on work breaks affected their performance. Two-thirds of the supervisors denied any link between smoking *while working* and productivity; the one-third that did acknowledge a negative influence on performance are mostly in the manufacturing, transportation, communications, and utilities industries, where work is often manual.

Most of these supervisors were also negative toward smoking restrictions. Sixty-four percent had none in their businesses; those that did have formal policies cited safety, legal, and "aesthetic" (it might annoy the customers) reasons as motives for instituting the policy. But the overall attitude toward smoking employees was tolerant—only 6 percent of those queried agreed that a smoking ban in their workplace would allow them to accomplish the same amount of work with fewer employees. Only 3 percent believed that refusing to hire qualified applicants because they smoke was a sensible personnel policy.

When a manager evaluates the effect of restrictive smoking policies, it is not enough to deny a link between smoking and higher costs. Too little has been written about the negative effects on productivity, costs, and employee morale due to *smoking restrictions*, particularly in the white-collar environment.

A Costly Alternative

Antismoking policies come in all shapes and sizes. Some businesses limit smoking to designated areas. Others allow smoking only at designated times; some permit no smoking at all; and still others restrict smoking in the presence of clients or the public. Most (like my own) leave the issue up to the good manners and good sense of employees and negotiate any conflict between smokers and nonsmokers.

If a manager does institute some type of formal restriction, it is important to note the economic penalties involved. Telling employees that they may smoke only in the rest rooms, cafeteria, or hallways practically ensures that they will not be at their workstations as often as if they were permitted to smoke there. In an office environment, where there is no foreman or assembly line to compel attendance at a certain physical location, this means unanswered phones, untyped letters, unwritten proposals—undone work.

If smoking is limited by time, someone must devise a schedule of smoking breaks that staggers the workload done by professional and clerical staff. In my business, which usually demands ten-hour days, it would be impossible to create a schedule that recognized the clients' need for fast turn-around. Any business with time constraints will find that half its secretaries are on break when the final copy is due, or one-quarter of its account personnel is in the lunchroom when an emergency brainstorming meeting is called. I certainly don't want to send out bloodhounds for my supervisors when a late-breaking story affecting a client's interest comes over the wire.

"If a manager does institute some type of formal restriction, it is important to note the economic penalties involved."

Then there's the alternative that often works, but must be well loved by those in the building-remodeling business—physically separating smokers and nonsmokers. This policy is useful when flexibly implemented, but too rigid a set of restrictions can hamstring efficient operations. For example, every account group in my office has both smokers and nonsmokers. These people are in and out of each others' offices dozens of times a day; they share support staff, files, data-processing equipment, reference books, and sometimes, it seems, each others' brain stems. Like many managers paying high rent in urban locations, I have found that the only cost-effective and sensible way to arrange these groups is to have support staff share clerical bays, junior professionals share offices, and the whole account group share a corridor and meeting room.

Separating account groups by their smoking habits—at least on the basis of a formal, square-foot-specified policy—would lead to a nightmare of lost productivity. Obviously, if we have two junior account executives who smoke and work on the same accounts, putting them in the same office is a great solution. But smoking cannot be the determining factor in our physical layout, not without sacrificing the efficiency and quality of the work we do for our clients. This is not to say that we ignore nonsmokers' requests concerning sidestream smoke; we accommodate them as best we can. Investing in fans, portable air cleaners, and smokeless ashtrays often solves the problem of proximity between smokers and nonsmokers.

Any white-collar manager facing a space shortage, high rents, and the need to station employees by function has to reject rigid smoking restrictions for cost reasons alone. But the implications of antismoking policies go beyond the dictates of bean counting; the entire morale and esprit de corps of an enterprise can be compromised by directives that traduce employees' personal rights.

How To Offend Your Employees

Tell your employees what to do, what to think, and how to behave in areas that do not affect job performance. For example, one of my employees thinks it's barbaric to hunt ducks and turkeys—one of my favorite pursuits. In my view, she's not just soft-hearted but soft-headed on this issue, and I suppose that in hers I'm a practitioner of avian genocide. Does this affect her salary, promotions, job performance, or willingness to keep working here? Obviously, it does not.

I put the smoking habits of my employees—and for that matter, myself—in the same category. It is a traditional if unspoken American notion that the less we interfere with one another, the better off we all are. Rights in this country focus on the individual, not the government, the employer, or the opinions of other people. A country whose legal and moral dictates do not permit employers to discriminate on the basis of age, gender, handicap, and so forth should think long and hard before legislating or dictating personal habits to adults.

"Smoking is the least of a manager's problems in providing a safe and healthy indoor environment for workers."

Beyond the philosophical issues associated with any form of institutionalized smoking policy lies the practical problem of enforcement. If my business were located in a jurisdiction that demanded some type of smoking policy, presumably I would be responsible for calling in the cops if any employee continually broke the rules. Even a policy that was set up at my own discretion would require enforcement by me, another member of senior management, or the office manager. I shudder at the idea of disciplining adults—particularly talented, egotistical, creative adults—about a personal habit. Just trying to figure out an appropriate "punishment" for the "crime" of smoking demonstrates the ludicrous nature of the whole enterprise.

In the Response Analysis survey cited earlier, more than 63 percent of the supervisors queried believed that imposing any type of smoking regulations would worsen employee morale. Many sensible people concur but still worry about the charges hurled by antismoking activists from Surgeon General C. Everett Koop on down—that environmental tobacco smoke endangers the health of nonsmokers. But in looking carefully at the scientific data on sidestream smoke, I can only conclude that smoking is the least of a manager's problems in providing a safe and healthy indoor environment for workers.

Sick Buildings

Three recent scientific workshops on tobacco smoke in the air concluded that the evidence on negative health effects on nonsmokers is, at best, inconclusive. Without delving into the scientific jargon, it's best to quote one of these reports: "Should lawmakers wish to take legislative measures with regard to passive smoking, they will, for the present, not be able to base their efforts on a demonstrated health hazard from passive smoking."

This conclusion, from an international workshop held in cooperation with the World Health Organization in Vienna in 1984, sums up the current state-of-the-art evaluation of the effects of tobacco smoke in general. But an even more important source of specific data is available. Two researchers from the Harvard School of Public Health, who examined various indoor environments for the presence of carbon dioxide and nicotine, discovered insufficient amounts of either to affect the health of nonsmokers. The amounts of carbon dioxide ranged from one-tenth to one-fifth of the levels permitted by the Occupational Safety and Health Administration; the amounts of nicotine were so small that a nonsmoker would have to spend 100 straight hours in the smokiest bar to inhale the equivalent of one filtered cigarette. . . .

Most important, managers have as allies the common sense and courtesy of their staffs, who should be encouraged to negotiate about smoking issues the way they must about other shared concerns. Thirty percent of adult Americans smoke. Restricting their rights is not the path to harmonious working conditions. Dictating standards of personal behavior that do not affect job performance to employers and employees alike has far-reaching consequences, none of which are in the interest of American business or American workers.

Jody Powell was former President Jimmy Carter's press secretary from 1976 to 1980. He has also been a news analyst and columnist. Powell is currently the chief executive officer of Ogilvy and Master Public Affairs in Washington, DC.

"In addition to the important health reasons for controlling workplace smoking there is a sound business reason: smoking is an unnecessary business expenditure."

Employers Should Restrict Smoking

American Nonsmokers' Rights Foundation

The hazards of smoking are not a matter of controversy. There is no longer any disagreement among scientists that smoking tobacco, particularly cigarettes, is extremely hazardous. Every U.S. Surgeon General since 1964 has emphasized the uniquely dangerous qualities of cigarettes. In 1982, Surgeon General C. Everett Koop wrote in his report to the Congress, "Cigarette smoking . . . is the chief single avoidable cause of death in our society and the most important public health issue of our time." Over 350,000 Americans die each year of smoking-related diseases—lung cancer, heart attacks, emphysema and other diseases.

Cigarette smoke can harm nonsmokers too. Involuntary smoking, the exposure of nonsmokers to others' smoke, is now considered a serious health hazard. Indeed, cigarette smoke is now widely recognized as the most serious indoor air pollutant— a leading cause of exposure to toxic chemicals for most workers.

Smoking is an addiction. Although the percentage of Americans who smoke declines each year, there are still almost 50 million who smoke. The reason is that smoking is an addiction—90% of smokers say they want to quit and can't. The federal government's National Institute of Drug Abuse, the World Health Organization, and the American Psychiatric Association all classify smoking as a drug dependency, like alcoholism or heroin addiction. In addition to the physical addiction caused by nicotine, there is an important behavioral component. Many experts feel that the principal reason smokers find it so hard to quit is that smoking is socially acceptable. *Restricting opportunities to smoke helps smokers kick a deadly habit.*

Most Americans are nonsmokers. The U.S. government has determined that over two-thirds of adult Americans are nonsmokers. Probably as a result of this, the social climate that once tolerated and even encouraged smoking is gone. A Gallup poll in April 1983 found that 82% of nonsmokers and 55% of smokers believed that smokers should refrain in the presence of nonsmokers.

Smoking costs America billions. It has been reliably estimated that smoking costs the country over $42 billion per year in health care costs and decreased productivity due to absenteeism, sickness, disability and premature death, property damage, and a host of related effects. Business and industry bear a large part of this economic burden. . . .

Smoking and the Law

Government is getting into the workplace more and more—especially when it comes to protecting the health of nonsmokers. Legislators, judges, and administrative officials have been making decisions that employers must understand and to which they must respond.

Since 1980 many cities and counties have passed laws restricting smoking in the workplace. Most require the employer to establish a nonsmoking policy of some sort. While there is usually a significant degree of flexibility, these laws require the needs of nonsmokers for clean air be given priority over the desire of some employees to smoke. Compliance with local ordinances will be much more likely if the employer adopts the attitude that *nonsmoking is the norm. Smoking is allowed, if at all, only in designated areas.* . . .

Nonsmokers have successfully used administrative agencies and courts both to enforce the right to clean air at work as well as to recover benefits as a result of being exposed to smoke in the workplace. Although these cases have until now been fairly uncommon, we can expect to see more and more of them in the future as the scientific evidence mounts regarding the hazards of involuntary smoking.

A Smokefree Workplace: An Employer's Guide to Nonsmoking Policies, published in 1985 by the American Nonsmokers' Rights Foundation. Reprinted with permission.

Indeed, employers who allow nonsmokers to be exposed to cigarette smoke may in the future become liable in ways we cannot now determine.

Recent cases on both the federal and state levels have held that nonsmokers who are sensitive to cigarette smoke may be considered "handicapped" for purposes of nondiscrimination laws. In October of 1984 the California Fair Employment and Housing Commission ruled in a precedent-setting settlement that an employee was entitled to $27,000 in back pay plus $10,000 in damages for emotional distress because her employer refused to accommodate her need for a smokefree workplace. The federal Rehabilitation Act of 1973 requires employers to make "reasonable accommodation" for handicapped employees, among whom are those who are extremely sensitive to tobacco smoke. Discrimination suits against employers may be brought directly with the Equal Employment Opportunity Commission of a state or the federal government or a lawsuit may be brought directly to the courts.

Workers' Compensation Benefits

In addition to the potential for increased workers' compensation premiums resulting from the claims of smokers for other job-related illnesses and injuries, recent cases indicate that employers may be liable for allowing an employee to smoke at work and thus endanger his own health. In another case, a stewardess was awarded workers' compensation benefits because of an allergic reaction to the smoky air inside an airplane cabin. The EPA's study showing that one-third of all lung cancers in nonsmokers are caused by involuntary smoking could result in workers' compensation death cases being brought by next of kin of nonsmoking employees exposed to heavy tobacco smoke at work.

"Up to one-third of all lung cancers in nonsmokers are caused by secondhand exposure to tobacco smoke."

Several cases in California have held that nonsmokers who are very sensitive to cigarette smoke may be considered to have quit for "good cause" and thus be eligible for unemployment benefits if their employer did not offer them an equivalent job in a smokefree environment (Alexander v. The California Unemployment Insurance Appeals Board, 1980, also Gibson v. Starkist, 1983).

Cases in New Jersey (Shimp v. New Jersey Bell Telephone Company, 1976) and Missouri (Smith v. Western Electric, 1982) have held that employers have a common law duty to provide a safe workplace, and that this duty required the employer to protect nonsmokers from the hazards of secondhand smoke. In both of these cases the plaintiffs demonstrated that secondhand smoke was a hazard to all employees exposed to it and in both cases the court ruled that an injunction against the employer was the proper legal remedy.

Cases of this sort are being litigated in California as well as other states.

Another potential source of liability for the employer is a suit for wrongful discharge and retaliation by the employer because of an employee's protest against workplace smoking. One Court of Appeals in California has ruled that an employee cannot be discharged or discriminated against for complaining in good faith about workplace conditions felt to be unsafe.

Federal employees may be eligible for disability benefits or even retirement if they are extremely sensitive to cigarette smoke and their employer does not provide them with a smokefree environment. The Ninth Circuit Court of Appeals held in the case of Parodi v. Merit System Protection Board (1982) that suitable employment should be provided if available, and if it is not available or not offered, the employee may be eligible for disability retirement benefits.

The Risks of Smoking

Most Americans have a vague understanding that smoking is hazardous. Few know just how dangerous smoking really is. 80% of lung cancer in men is caused by smoking, while lung cancer caused by smoking is fast replacing breast cancer as the number one cancer killer of women. But lung cancer, almost invariably fatal, is not the largest cigarette-related cause of death. Over 150,000 Americans die of smoking-related heart attacks each year. Millions of Americans suffer from the ravages of smoking-caused emphysema. . . .

The only good news about smoking is that most of its effects are reversible. One very large study found that ten years after quitting the risk of dying among ex-smokers approached the same risk as among people who had never smoked. Quitting, although difficult for some, has immediate results for the ex-smoker. Greatly improved taste and smell are experienced within days or weeks of quitting.

Exposure to others' cigarette smoke is not just unpleasant. It can be a significant health hazard. Tobacco smoke, which is the principal source of indoor air pollution, contains over 2000 compounds many of which are known carcinogens and irritants. Since most people spend between 75% and 90% of a 24-hour day indoors it is evident that exposure to tobacco smoke can become a serious hazard.

An important 1980 study showed that nonsmoking employees chronically exposed to secondhand smoke in the workplace experienced the same degree of lung damage as light smokers. Several newer studies have pointed toward the possibility that secondhand smoke increases the risk of lung cancer and other cancers in nonsmoking spouses. A recent Japanese study shows that involuntary smoke exposure at work is at least as serious as exposure at home.

Staff of the U.S. Environmental Protection Agency have prepared a report which says that up to one-third of all lung cancers in nonsmokers are caused by secondhand exposure to tobacco smoke. At the minimum 500 people per year die of lung cancer from breathing others' smoke, while the maximum is about 5000. This contrasts with the next most serious airborne toxic exposure at work, coke oven emissions in steel mills. One hundred and fifty people per year are estimated to die of cancer from exposure to this pollutant.

"Repeated studies have shown a 33% to 45% higher absenteeism rate among smokers than nonsmokers."

While even completely healthy adults may be adversely affected by cigarette smoke, those with preexisting health conditions may experience much more severe reactions to secondhand smoke. Conditions such as asthma, bronchitis, cardiovascular disease, rhinitis, colds and allergies are often particularly hard hit by secondhand smoke. Also, millions of people are sensitive to tobacco smoke. While apparently not technically an allergen, tobacco smoke's irritant qualities resemble those that characterize an allergic response. Concentrations of secondhand smoke that would not affect a healthy person appear to present an increased risk to those with preexisting health conditions.

Certain effects of tobacco smoke occur in both healthy and impaired people. Researchers experimentally investigated the effect of side stream smoke (smoke from the burning end of the cigarette) on cardiovascular health in both smokers and nonsmokers. They found that side stream smoke increased heart rate, blood pressure and oxygen consumption. These responses were more prominent in nonsmokers than in smokers. Further, these researchers noted a decrease in work capacity in most groups.

It's not too surprising that passive smoking can have such significant effects. Tobacco smoke contains a veritable witches' brew of hazardous substances, among which are tar, nicotine, carbon monoxide, cadmium, nitrogen dioxide, nitrosamines, benzene, formaldehyde, hydrogen sulfide, and hydrogen cyanide. Side stream smoke contains more of these compounds than are found in mainstream smoke inhaled by the smoker.

Employers must bear a very large part of the cost of smoking. In 1982, the Surgeon General said that smoking was responsible for up to $13 billion in lost productivity. Other experts insist that the losses due to smoking are much higher—as high as $47 billion per year. Employer costs are incurred in the following areas:

Insurance

Specific insurance costs attributable to smoking depend on the type of insurance coverage a company offers its employees. Naturally, the more extensive the coverage the more cost saving can be expected by restricting smoking at work.

Health insurance is the most obvious type of insurance which has increased costs associated with smoking. Because it is estimated that 30% of all cancers (Richard Doll and Richard Peto 1980), 25% of all cardiovascular disease (M.M. Kristein, C.B. Arnold and E.L. Wynder, 1977), and 80% of all deaths from respiratory disease (U.S. Surgeon General's Report 1984) are related to smoking, it is not difficult to understand why health insurance costs are increased by smoking. Using the Surgeon General's data and estimating that smokers use 50% more health care services than nonsmokers, it is estimated that business pays an additional $75 to $150 per year in health insurance for each smoker on the payroll.

Life insurance costs are increased by employee smoking, because of the increased mortality rates between smokers and nonsmokers. Each smoking employee adds between $20 and $33 per year to the annual life insurance bill.

Fire insurance costs are also increased because of smoking. $5 per smoker per year is a conservative estimate of the additional fire insurance costs to businesses having employees who smoke (Kristein, 1983).

Absenteeism and Sickness Benefits

The effects of smoking upon absenteeism are well documented. Repeated studies have shown a 33% to 45% higher absenteeism rate among smokers than nonsmokers (Kristein, 1983). In 1979, the Surgeon General reported that 81 million work days are lost per year due to smoking. It has been estimated that smokers are absent about two days more per year than nonsmokers. While this represents a staggering cost to society it also can have a large impact on your specific business.

Reduced Productivity

Smokers spend some of their work time smoking instead of working. Researchers vary in their estimates of the work time lost to the smoking ritual, clean-up costs, and damage to furniture and equipment, but even the most conservative estimate (Kristein) is that the average smoker costs the average business $166 per year in lost productivity, based on an estimate of a loss of one minute per hour to smoking. Another researcher (William L.

Weis, 1981) believes that the average annual on-the-job time loss attributable to smoking is over $1800 per year. In addition to this, Weis estimates the cost of smoking-related repairs at an annual cost of $1000.

Smoking and exposure to some hazards at work act in a synergistic manner to greatly increase the likelihood that an employee will develop an occupational disease. Entitlement to workers' compensation may occur for cases of lung cancer, chronic obstructive pulmonary disease, and heart attack when there is a job-related cause even though the condition might not have occurred if the employee had not smoked. Furthermore, corporations may have an obligation under OSHA [Occupational Safety and Health Administration] regulations to control workplace smoking in the presence of certain occupational hazards such as asbestos, coal dust, and radiation.

"The health reasons show why a non-smoking policy is for the benefit of employees."

Researchers have shown that the costs of smoking in the workplace are significant. This confirms what many employers already suspect. Thus in addition to the important health reasons for controlling workplace smoking there is a sound business reason: smoking is an unnecessary business expenditure.

A successful nonsmoking policy is usually one which has been developed by an employer who has taken the time to explain to his or her employees some of the reasons behind its development and implementation. The health reasons show why a nonsmoking policy is for the benefit of employees; the legal and economic reasons demonstrate that a nonsmoking policy is a matter of sound business judgment.

The American Nonsmokers' Rights Foundation has been a leader in advocating restrictions on smoking in public places throughout the country.

"There is evidence that some smoking restrictions may actually increase business costs."

Employers Should Not Restrict Smoking

The Tobacco Institute

Today, management and workers alike are faced with an increasing barrage of information and misinformation regarding workplace smoking issues.

Smokers and nonsmokers have lived and worked together in harmony for generations. Occasional disputes about when and where to light up have been settled individually, with common sense and courtesy. Now, there are some who would substitute laws and fines.

In many cases, proponents of workplace smoking restrictions are simply trying to enforce their own lifestyles on others. Unsuccessful in attempts to persuade many adults to quit smoking, those calling for broad restrictions are trying to keep people from smoking by segregating or otherwise punishing them for exercising their right of free choice.

Some smoking restriction advocates claim that cigarette smoke is a health hazard to nonsmokers; others say smokers are more costly to their employers than nonsmokers. Still others claim a legal right to a smoke-free environment.

Health Hazard Not Proven

A detailed review of the scientific literature on environmental tobacco smoke (ETS) yields two basic conclusions:

• First, that ETS has not been shown scientifically to pose a health hazard to nonsmokers.

• Second, as a National Academy of Sciences panel noted recently, more and better research needs to be done.

Three major scientific conferences since 1982 have concluded that there is no persuasive evidence that ETS poses any significant risk to the health of nonsmokers.

The first workshop, in March 1983, which drew medical researchers from nine countries to the

University of Geneva, concluded: "An overall evaluation based upon available scientific data leads to the conclusion that an increased risk [in lung cancer] for nonsmokers from [ETS] exposure has not been established."

Another, convened in 1983 by the National Institutes of Health, U.S. Department of Health and Human Services, determined that the possible effect of ETS on the respiratory system "varies from negligible to quite small."

And in April 1984, Ernst Wynder of the American Health Foundation and H. Valentin of the Bavarian Academy for Occupational and Social Medicine, organized a workshop in cooperation with the International Green Cross. That workshop, in Vienna, Austria, concluded:

> Should lawmakers wish to take legislative measures with regard to passive smoking, they will, for the present, not be able to base their efforts on a demonstrated health hazard from passive smoking. . . .

Indoor air pollution is becoming a major work issue in some office buildings. The universal use of air conditioning and increased reliance on controlled environments in modern office buildings has focused attention on "sick building syndrome."

Employee complaints of sore and watery eyes, abnormally high absentee rates and visible signs of poor ventilation, such as dust around ventilation ducts, all are potential signs of "sick building syndrome." And although visible cigarette smoke often is targeted as a cause of the problem, we know now that in almost all cases, it is a symptom, not a cause.

In fact, when it comes to poor indoor air quality, tobacco smoke appears to be among the least of our worries. Reports by federal and private experts show that environmental tobacco smoke is a cause of discomfort by building occupants in just two to four percent of all cases. And even those cases, findings

Smoking in the Workplace: Some Considerations, published in 1987 by The Tobacco Institute. Reprinted with permission.

show, can be solved by improved ventilation.

That means lawmakers and business managers will accomplish little or nothing even if they succeed in removing every last wisp of tobacco smoke from the workplace. Complaints of health problems and irritations will persist.

The government's National Institute for Occupational Safety and Health (NIOSH) reports that of the 203 buildings it examined recently following occupant complaints, just four cases—or two percent—were attributable to cigarette smoke. An independent analysis of more than 125 major private and public buildings by ACVA Atlantic, Inc., an indoor air quality analysis firm, identified tobacco smoke as a major contributing factor to air quality complaints in only four percent—five buildings.

While NIOSH identified ETS as the problem in a tiny handful of cases, inadequate ventilation was blamed in 50 percent. ACVA investigations show improper attention to indoor air circulation was responsible in the majority of cases for the spread and breeding of infectious germs and allergenic dusts and spores—not to mention fiberglass particles, asbestos, chemical fumes and a host of other hazardous airborne particles undetectable to the eye and nose.

Under normal conditions with ventilation that is operating according to established building codes, tobacco smoke very quickly dissipates. In fact, this disappearing act confirms that the ventilation system in an indoor area is working properly. In those few cases where visible ETS persists, the ventilation must be suspect immediately.

Problems with cigarette smoke should be viewed as a "tip off" to the much more serious underlying problem of inadequate or improper ventilation. The good news is that once the underlying problem of poor air circulation is corrected, so too is any problem with ETS.

Costs to Employers?

Eighty-two percent of the respondents to a 1986 survey of employers by the Bureau of National Affairs (BNA) for the American Society for Personnel Administration (ASPA) either noted no reduced costs, or did not know whether adoption of a smoking policy resulted in a drop in company costs. Only three percent said a smoking policy had reduced costs in some way.

Still, many proponents of workplace smoking restrictions cite studies that claim to show smokers are absent more frequently and incur higher insurance costs than nonsmokers.

But according to Marvin Kristein, an American Health Foundation economist who promotes economic arguments for workplace smoking restrictions, "we lack meaningful 'case-controlled' company comparisons of experience with smoking employees vs. nonsmoking employees vs. ex-smokers

and the impact on company cost." To achieve a scientific basis for such cost claims, Kristein admits, "would require studies and data we do not now—and most likely will never—possess."

In fact, there is evidence that some smoking restrictions may actually increase business costs. For example, Dr. Robert Tollison, chairman of the Center for the Study of Public Choice at George Mason University, estimates that proposed legislation severely restricting smoking in federal buildings could cost $309.5 million per year—$867 per employee. . . .

Morale? Productivity?

Are smokers less productive than nonsmokers? The evidence says no.

Ninety-two percent of respondents to the 1986 BNA survey for ASPA said either that imposition of smoking restrictions had not increased worker productivity, or that they did not know whether an increase in productivity had occurred. Only four percent believed restrictions had in fact increased worker productivity. And one 1984 study released by University of Minnesota researchers found that people who smoke tended to be *more productive* than those who do not.

"Decisions involving smoking in the workplace are more appropriately committed to the good sense and common courtesy of smoking and nonsmoking employees."

A recent survey of union representatives and managers in business, industry and government by Response Analysis Corporation of Princeton, N.J., found that among almost 2,000 local union officials and first-level supervisors:

• Two-thirds of survey respondents said employee smoking either has a positive effect or no effect on productivity.

• Seventy-eight percent said a smoking ban would not enable their organization to accomplish the same work with fewer employees.

• Only three percent of respondents agreed that "not hiring people simply because they smoke makes sense."

• Of the respondents who said their organizations restrict smoking, less than three percent said they did so because smoking interferes with job performance.

No Legal 'Right'

Relevant case law provides virtually no support for the efforts of some anti-smokers to impose their views on employers and fellow workers. The courts have uniformly rejected arguments that a tobacco smoke-free environment is guaranteed by provisions of the U.S. Constitution.

In cases where employees have tried to use common law to impose smoking restrictions, the courts generally have sided with the employer, most recently in a 1985 decision in *Smith v. AT&T Technologies, Inc.* There, the court noted that it "specifically does not believe or find from the evidence that the tobacco smoke at plaintiff's former workplace was harmful or hazardous to his health" or to the health "of the other employees in that area."

Accordingly, the court held that the employer had not breached any duty to its employees by refusing to segregate smokers from nonsmokers and to limit smoking to non-work areas of the building.

In Washington, D.C., in 1983, Judge William Pryor ruled that "Common law does not impose upon an employer the duty or burden to conform his workplace to the particular needs or sensitivities of an individual employee." . . .

The 1976 *Shimp* case is the only [decision] that has actually prohibited smoking in the workplace based on the theory that general common law can be used to compel smoking restrictions. A key determinant in *Shimp*, however, was the lack of any active defense by New Jersey Bell, which filed no answer to the complaint and submitted no affidavit in opposition to Shimp's request for a court order.

That the case has little precedential value is suggested by the court's dismissal of an identical complaint subsequently filed by Shimp's attorney before the same judge on behalf of another New Jersey Bell employee. In the second case, New Jersey Bell elected to defend itself. . . .

Legal questions aside, however, who would want to discriminate against smokers if the primary motive in hiring is to employ the best individual for the job?

Courtesy and Common Sense

Decisions involving smoking in the workplace are more appropriately committed to the good sense and common courtesy of smoking and nonsmoking employees. The question of when and how workers may smoke in the office is best settled by employer and employee consensus rather than by city council or state legislature.

The Tobacco Institute is an influential Washington-based group whose members include tobacco manufacturers and growers.

Cigarette Advertising Should Be Banned

Consumer Reports

Americans have historically shown forbearance toward the practice of advertising. That tolerance may be based in part on amusement at the huckster's ingenuity. Beneath that, however, lies the quintessentially American regard for the right of anyone—hucksters included—to speak and write freely. Indeed, it is widely believed that advertising, like other forms of communication, is protected under the First Amendment to the Constitution. For that reason, many questionable advertising practices have been tolerated as natural and necessary penalties attending a fundamental American privilege.

Now, however, a growing number of thoughtful people—civil libertarians among them—are beginning to question whether the Constitution indeed protects advertising of an inherently hazardous substance like tobacco.

If the constitutional issue is in doubt, the medical issue is not. Countless studies support the almost universal certainty of health professionals that smoking is an extremely serious health hazard. The U.S. Public Health Service puts cigarette-induced premature deaths in this country at 350,000 a year. That's 50 percent more than the combined total of Americans killed yearly by auto, fire, and other accidents, by alcohol-related causes, by murder and suicide, and by AIDS, cocaine, and heroin. The medical bills resulting from smoking-related illnesses are estimated at $22-billion a year. The total social costs appear beyond reckoning.

If smoking is disastrous to smokers, it's hardly innocuous to nonsmokers, particularly those with allergies or asthma. Beyond the discomfort many nonsmokers experience—eye and nasal irritation, headache, cough, and the like—exposure to tobacco smoke can increase the risk of adverse health effects for both children and nonsmoking adults. Bronchitis and pneumonia occur up to twice as often among infants of smokers as among those of nonsmokers. Pregnant women who smoke expose the fetus to an increased risk of miscarriage and stillbirth. And the National Research Council reports that nonsmokers heavily exposed to tobacco smoke, such as the spouses of smokers, run a higher risk of lung cancer than do those without such exposure.

Yet despite what one Government spokesman has described as "the most devastating epidemic of disease and premature death this country has ever experienced," smoking and nicotine dependency have never evoked a crisis atmosphere. Perhaps that's because cigarettes are both legal and commonplace. In many other ways, though, nicotine bears striking similarities to other drugs of abuse.

The Crisis of Addiction

CU [Consumers Union] reported at length on nicotine addiction in our 1972 book, "Licit and Illicit Drugs." [In 1986] the Harvard School of Public Health reported on what it called a "stunning" parallel between heroin and nicotine addiction. Both substances, the report noted, cause changes in mood and feeling; both produce withdrawal symptoms that generally begin within 24 hours of cessation; and both cause one's body to demand a steadily increasing dose over a period of time, until finally a dosage level is established that satisfies the persistent craving. In the language of the report's conclusion, "nicotine has a profile of behavioral and physiologic effects typical of other drugs of abuse and, like heroin derived from opium, meets rigorous experimental criteria as a drug with considerable potential to cause dependence." As it happens, the relapse rates reported for cigarette smokers and for heroin users are virtually identical: About 75 percent of those who have tried to kick either habit return to their addiction within a year.

An overwhelming percentage of smokers get hooked on nicotine when they're teenagers. According to the Office on Smoking and Health, a division of the U.S. Public Health Service, about three-quarters of all smokers start the habit by age 19. A survey of high-school seniors revealed that half who smoked regularly began smoking in the ninth grade or earlier, and more than half of the regular smokers had already tried—and failed—to give it up. In a British study along the same lines, it was found that only 15 percent of those young people who smoked more than a single cigarette managed to avoid becoming regular smokers.

"One may wonder at the business judgment of an industry willing to spend $2-billion a year in advertising with no expectation of creating new customers."

Each year, Lloyd Johnston, program director for the Institute for Social Research at the University of Michigan, conducts a survey of high-school seniors. [In 1986] he reported that 53 percent of those seniors who smoke at least a pack a day say that they have already tried to quit smoking and found that they couldn't. Moreover, he projects from follow-up reports of earlier classes that nearly three-quarters of those young smokers will still be daily smokers eight years after high school.

CU believes that the addictive properties of tobacco must be considered in weighing a proposal to ban all tobacco advertising and promotion. The toll of death and disease recorded from smoking does not result from a lifetime of voluntary behavior but from a lifetime of addiction—an addiction usually begun before adulthood.

Appeal to Youth

The tobacco industry is sensitive about allegations that some of its advertising and promotional efforts appear to be directed at teenagers. At the mention of that subject, the industry is apt to duck behind its voluntary code. . . . It's supposed to keep cigarette advertising from influencing young people until they attain their majority.

"We feel very strongly about the code," a spokeswoman for the Tobacco Institute told CU. "It's one of the ways we insure our advertising is responsible and meets the standards we set out."

Alas, despite the industry code some cigarette advertising does manage to sneak by the standard-holders to reach the nation's youth directly or indirectly. In 1986, tobacco interests placed $33-million in ads in TV Guide, which receives more cigarette-advertising revenue than any other magazine. TV Guide makes a point of telling its

advertisers that each new issue reaches, among others, 6.1 million children between the ages of 12 and 17.

In other respects, too, the tobacco industry has displayed itself as less than fastidious about policing its code. Its manipulations involving movies—that ideal medium for reaching young people—constitute interesting examples. Sometimes, as when ABC news revealed that an ad for *Kool* cigarettes was being shown in a Massachusetts theater just before the movie "Snow White," the code violation is absurdly obvious. On other occasions, plugs for one cigarette or another become imbedded in the movies themselves.

In "Beverly Hills Cop," for example, Eddie Murphy, after stealing a truckload of *Pall Malls* and *Lucky Strikes*, opens a case of *Luckies* and remarks, "These are very popular cigarettes with the children." But, he admits, "I don't smoke *Lucky Strikes*. I smoke king-size *Kents*." In Walt Disney's "Baby," about two explorers who find a baby dinosaur in Africa, ingenious excuses are found for *Marlboro* to make cameo appearances throughout the movie.

Lois Lane's Lungs

But it's in "Superman II" that *Marlboro* really stars. Lois Lane smokes them constantly, and at one point Superman is hurled into the side of a truck with the bright red and white *Marlboro* logo painted on the side. Those plugs earned the movie a review by the New York State Journal of Medicine, which published an article titled "Superman and the Marlboro Woman: The Lungs of Lois Lane." The article charged that "for an undisclosed consideration, the moviemakers permitted repeated juxtaposition of a children's hero with a brand of cigarettes." . . .

What Do Big Bucks Buy?

In 1970, tobacco companies spent $361-million on advertising and promotion. More than half of that amount went to TV. By 1984, without a penny going for TV ads (which had long since come off the air), total spending on tobacco advertising and promotion had risen to $2.1-billion.

Some $619-million of the 1984 total went for newspaper and magazine ads, compared with just $64-million spent on the same media in 1970. Advertising on billboards jumped from $7-million in 1970 to $284-million in 1984. The cost of dispensing free cigarette samples increased twelvefold, to $148-million. And spending by tobacco interests on "public entertainment," mainly sports and cultural events, soared from $544,000 to $60-million.

One may wonder at the business judgment of an industry willing to spend $2-billion a year in advertising with no expectation of creating new customers. But perhaps the industry's agenda is a little more ambitious than that.

In 1985, the Washington Post surveyed the editorial content of three big magazines that reject tobacco advertising: Reader's Digest, Good Housekeeping, and the Saturday Evening Post. Over a 10-year period, the three had published an average of 15 articles apiece on the health aspects of smoking.

"Of 10 other major magazines surveyed that do accept cigarette advertising," the Washington Post reported, "none published more than four stories on smoking, and five published no articles on the subject during the same 10 years." By way of a conclusion, the newspaper quoted Helen Gurley Brown, the editor of Cosmopolitan: "Who needs somebody you're paying millions of dollars a year, to come back and bite you on the ankle?"

"There are well-established differences in U.S. constitutional law between the right of free citizens to express themselves and the right of a corporation to advertise what it pleases to whom it pleases."

In a similar study, the American Council on Science and Health found expressions of much the same attitude. From 1982 through 1985, for example, the council discovered that Redbook magazine "had not a single article of any kind about smoking, while it carried 11 about food and disease, 10 about stress, and 7 about skin care." In the same period, the council also noted, U.S. News and World Report carried 18 articles about cancer, but none of them mentioned smoking.

None of those findings can be passed off as coincidental, says Cory Ser Vaas, editor and president of the Saturday Evening Post. She told CU that her magazine experienced a "drastic decline" in cigarette advertising during the 1970s, as it repeatedly featured articles about the hazards of smoking. "The tobacco companies told the ad representatives that they wouldn't continue to advertise," she said. "They wouldn't renew the contracts." Finally, for what little it was worth by then, the magazine stopped accepting cigarette advertisements in 1982.

If a substance as hazardous and addictive as tobacco were to be introduced today, it would undoubtedly be quickly banned with scarcely any opposition. But tobacco, like alcohol, was in common use for centuries before its dangers were fully understood. There's little reason to suppose that banning tobacco outright would be greeted with any more popular respect for law than was the ill-fated

prohibition of alcohol by the Eighteenth Amendment.

Indeed, a less-celebrated historical incident suggests that attempts to curtail the use of tobacco among the already addicted would prove even less successful than did the prohibition of alcohol. Following World War II, when the German cigarette rations in occupied zones were cut drastically, an overseas researcher reported in the American Journal of Psychology: "Up to a point, the majority of the habitual smokers preferred to do without food, even under extreme conditions of nutrition, rather than to forego tobacco. Thus, when food rations in prisoner-of-war camps were down to 900-1000 calories, smokers were still willing to barter their food rations for tobacco."

Discourage Smoking

More sensible than a ban, in our judgment, are measures that attempt to discourage interest among nonsmokers rather than prohibit tobacco use by habitués. Two proposals represent significant steps in that direction. One would double the excise tax on cigarettes, which currently stands at 16 cents a pack. The other, introduced by Representative Mike Synar (D., Okla.) acting on a proposal by the American Medical Association, calls for banning all advertising and promotional activities of tobacco firms.

Of the two, the proposed excise-tax increase is considerably less controversial. Even the Reagan Administration has indicated that, although it generally opposes tax increases, it might accept a cigarette-tax hike as a revenue-raising device.

Kenneth Warner, chairman of the Department of Public Health Policy at the University of Michigan, estimates that a doubling of the cigarette excise tax, to 32 cents, would deter 800,000 teenagers from taking up the habit or continuing it.

There's no way to quantify the anticipated effect of a ban on cigarette promotion. (At least CU could locate no authority willing to hazard such a prediction.) The effect of pulling cigarette ads off television in 1971 is impossible to gauge because, as we've observed, the tobacco companies responded by increasing their advertising and promotion activities enormously in other media.

Free Speech

Given the hazards of tobacco, the addictive nature of nicotine, which makes tobacco use less than voluntary, the sophisticated manipulation of cigarette advertising, the violations of the spirit (if not the letter) of the tobacco industry's own code of advertising conduct, the indications of an inverse relationship between cigarette advertising and media discussion of smoking hazards, the reinforcement of smoking by advertising that portrays cigarettes as not only socially acceptable but desirable—given all these, Congressional action to ban cigarette advertising and promotion is fully justified, in CU's judgment. . . .

One negative argument that CU regards with great respect holds that such a ban would constitute an infringement on the First Amendment right of free speech.

Supreme Court Rulings

We believe that that argument merits special scrutiny. There are well-established differences in U.S. constitutional law between the right of free citizens to express themselves and the right of a corporation to advertise what it pleases to whom it pleases. The Supreme Court has repeatedly distinguished between the protections afforded commercial speech and the protections afforded the kind of speech that the First Amendment has traditionally protected.

In 1980, in a case known in judicial shorthand as Central Hudson, the Court laid out a specific approach for determining whether advertising can be banned.

"Because government has the power to prohibit something, it is 'permissible for the government to take the less intrusive step of allowing the conduct, but reducing the demand through restrictions on advertising.'"

What it comes down to is this: Commercial speech on behalf of a legal activity loses First Amendment protection if it is shown to be misleading. Failing that, commercial speech can still be restricted or regulated if three other conditions are met: If it affects a "substantial" government interest, if its "regulation directly advances the government interest asserted," and if such regulation "is not more extensive than is necessary to serve that interest."

There seems to be a lot of room for argument in legal precedent for what precisely constitutes misleading advertising. The American Medical Association sums up its argument this way: "A powerful, and to our minds convincing, case can be made that the [tobacco] industry's current advertising is inherently deceptive and misleading: this advertising fails to disclose adequately the lethal and addictive qualities of the product; indeed, whether or not by conscious design, its effect is to allay any such fears, particularly among poorly informed and highly vulnerable young adolescents. Thus not only are the conditions for rational and informed choice lacking, they have been completely subverted." The AMA does, however, guard its opinion with the alternative conclusion that "even

were this promotional advertising to escape condemnation as deceptive and misleading, it is subject to prohibition."

That prohibition of advertising would presumably be held constitutionally valid if the other three conditions of the Central Hudson decision were met. And it's here that other proponents of a ban of cigarette advertising feel on surer ground.

A Clear Government Interest

Given that the medical, financial, and social costs of smoking are plentifully documented, the government interest is easily shown. Whether or not a ban would advance that interest directly might be a trickier proposition to demonstrate. No one is in a position to supply conclusive evidence that U.S. cigarette advertising promotes smoking, if only because the absence of U.S. cigarette advertising has never been tested.

Finally, with respect to the condition of whether the government interest could be served by less restrictive measures, tobacco companies may argue that it already is—that the ban on TV advertising and the required warning labels should represent sufficient public protection. Yet it is precisely because such measures have been attempted and have proven ineffective that a stronger measure seems warranted.

Those in search of some effective measure short of a ban on cigarette advertising point to counteradvertising as an alternative. An effective program of counteradvertising might be patterned after the antismoking advertising campaigns aired from 1967 to 1970. They were distributed by the American Cancer Society and broadcast on television during time periods donated by the networks under mandate of the "fairness doctrine." So successful were those ads in reducing cigarette sales that cigarette makers "volunteered" to remove their commercials from the air even before Congress banned them. But when cigarette commercials left the air, the networks' obligation to provide time for counteradvertising also came to an end.

A number of members of Congress have introduced a resolution that would "direct" the President to "call upon" broadcasters to educate the public about the dangers of cigarette smoking. (A more effective plan would require that tobacco advertisers contribute a small percentage of their total promotional budget to a fund that pays for counter-ads.)

In the judgment of CU's legal analysts, the constitutionality of a cigarette promotion ban was strengthened when the Supreme Court upheld a Puerto Rican ban against casino advertising. The Court said that because government has the power to prohibit something, it is "permissible for the government to take the less intrusive step of allowing the conduct, but reducing the demand through restrictions on advertising." The Supreme Court noted that harmful products, including cigarettes, have been the subject of restrictions from "outright prohibition" to "restrictions on stimulation of its demand." To rule out the latter, the Court said "would require more than we find in the First Amendment."

Civil Libertarians and Ad Bans

To some civil libertarians, the issue goes beyond a question of whether a ban would pass muster with the Supreme Court. Writing in The Nation magazine, Ira Glasser, executive director of the American Civil Liberties Union, warned that "we do not want courts deciding what speech is too dangerous for us to hear. . . . When they come after abortion clinic ads, using as precedent the liberal arguments in favor of banning cigarette ads, it will be too late to invoke the protection of the First Amendment."

Not all civil libertarians, however, agree with that position. Melvin L. Wulf, legal director of the ACLU from 1962 to 1977, contends that corporations are "artificial creatures of the state," and as such can be treated differently from the "natural persons" that the First Amendment is intended to protect. In an article in Commonweal magazine, Wulf contended that corporations "acquire a disproportionate power because of their financial resources, which can be and has been used to dominate portions of public life. These special aspects of the nature of corporations make them subject to broad regulation and control."

Wulf went on to indicate his disappointment with a central argument voiced by the ACLU in Congressional hearings: "The evidence to date that tobacco advertising in fact is a substantial reason why persons begin to smoke, or continue to smoke once they start, is largely unpersuasive," the ACLU testified.

Wulf's comment: "That must surely have amused the marketing geniuses on Madison Avenue, who seduce us with promises of romance and cattle round-ups, and then abandon us to addiction. You bet advertising works."

Consumer Reports *is the monthly magazine of Consumers Union, a national consumer advocate organization.*

"Banning or restricting commercial speech about tobacco products ignores basic rights and liberties."

Cigarette Advertising Should Not Be Banned

Douglas J. Den Uyl and Tibor R. Machan

The American Medical Association has called for a ban on the advertising and promotion of all tobacco products. A new wave of debate on Constitutional questions and on the nature of advertising is sure to follow and, indeed, has already begun. We intend to sidestep the "public policy" approach and focus instead on what is less discussed: basic moral and political values.

We consider the main values embodied by our Constitution to be basic moral values as well. Central among these values are liberty, limited government, and natural or human rights. We also take it that these values are not subject to majority rule. This point was clearly expressed by the U.S. Supreme Court when it stated in *West Virginia State Board of Education v. Barnette* (1943) that

> The very purpose of the Bill of Rights was to withdraw certain subjects from the vicissitudes of political controversy, to place them beyond the reach of majorities and officials, and to establish them as legal principles to be applied by the Courts. One's right to life, liberty and property, to free speech, a free press, freedom of worship and assembly and other fundamental rights may not be submitted to a vote; they depend on the outcome of no elections.

Our particular issue is commercial speech and its deserved protection under the First Amendment. Tobacco advertising is a clear though controversial example of the principles we wish to address.

The Right To Do Wrong

Virtually all attacks on liberty, including the liberty to express various viewpoints, ideas, theories, beliefs, appeals, requests, and so forth rest upon a basic moral error. This is the error of confusing basic rights with what is morally or ethically right.

The recent attempt to ban commercial speech about tobacco products is one of the purer examples

Douglas J. Den Uyl and Tibor R. Machan, "Should Cigarette Advertising Be Banned?" *The Freeman*, December 1987.

of this error. If we assume, for the sake of argument only, that it would be right for people to stop smoking, we have, as yet, said absolutely nothing about the rights of the case. It may turn out that forcing people to quit smoking, restricting their access to tobacco products or information about such products, violates their rights. The paradox here is that in the pursuit of what is right, one may do what is morally wrong!

The reason for the paradox is that the particular way in which the "good" (or right thing) in question is pursued may conflict with another good that takes priority. All social moral principles are not created equal. Some are more fundamental than others. What is characteristic of rights is that, almost by definition, they are foundational or basic. Other social values must give way to them in cases of conflict. We can see this in everyday speech. It makes perfect sense to say, "It may not be right for someone to do (or believe) this, but he or she has every right to do so."

But what rights do we have? Some rights seem to be dictated by common sense. The "right" not to be harmed seems to be one of these rights. If this is a right, shouldn't tobacco products or information about such products be restricted or banned?

Voluntary Risk

Unfortunately, common sense is not always accurate. There is in fact no basic "right not to be harmed." The reason for this is twofold: People can voluntarily undertake risks, and people can have their rights violated without being harmed. In the first case, people voluntarily pursue dangerous activities all the time. They take on dangerous jobs, pursue dangerous sports, drive cars, and so on. What we expect in such situations is that the people involved have some conception of the risks they are undertaking—not that they be free from harm. In the second case, if the government restricts my freedom to speak on behalf of a cause I do not believe in, I have not been harmed, but my rights have been violated. In the end, then, rights and harms are not necessarily connected.

In a similar vein, rights and government have no necessary connection with each other. Some people mistakenly believe that rights are what the government allows us to do. But if this were true, it would make no sense to say that governments can violate people's rights, something they in fact do quite often. Since, as the Declaration of Independence so clearly notes, we are "endowed . . . with certain unalienable rights," we can possess rights that were not given to us by government and which government cannot legitimately take away. The first ten Amendments were designed to protect us from government infringement of rights we were said to possess "by nature."

"We should abandon the distinction between private and public speech and accord commercial speech the same full First Amendment protection given to all speech."

The Amendment that concerns us here is the First; but the principle behind all of them is the same: People have basic rights independent of governments. This principle further enforces our claim that a fundamental error occurs when one confuses rights with what is right. For what one discovers about basic rights is that they represent liberties, and liberty implies the possibility of *choosing* a "wrong" course of action as much as a "right" one. This point is clearly evident in freedom of speech cases where many wrongheaded causes and ideas are allowed to have their say with the same degree of legitimacy as those that are closer to the truth. Our basic rights, therefore, must be understood as essentially liberties; and these liberties are given political expression through Constitutional guarantees against government interference.

The main remaining issue here is whether people can have their liberties restricted in the name of "paternalism"—using the power of government to protect us from ourselves. But in a free society, if paternalism has a place at all, it would arise only in cases where information about alternatives was lacking. But clearly such is not the case with tobacco products and their use.

Is Smoking a Wrong?

Of course, we are not arguing or conceding that smoking is the "wrong" that must be protected by our distinction. Whether someone's smoking

qualifies as wrong conduct is certainly not a simple matter to decide. Even if in some cases it is clearly wrong to smoke, there can be many others when it is not. Yet some certainly regard smoking in this way; and it is useful to recognize that even if one concedes the point about the "wrongfulness" of smoking, no foundation has yet been laid for waiving basic rights or Constitutional protections.

In a recent case, the Federal Trade Commission (FTC) charged the R. J. Reynolds Tobacco Company with running a false and misleading advertisement ("Of Cigarettes and Science") on the health effects of cigarette smoking. The FTC believed the advertisement to be deceptive because R. J. Reynolds had interpreted a government study on the causes of heart disease in a way that was not detrimental to smoking. The FTC lost the case because the judge ruled that the advertisement qualified as noncommercial speech, since no prices, brands, or products were mentioned. Had prices, brands, or products been mentioned, the FTC would have had the power to regulate the advertisement under the limited First Amendment protections granted to commercial speech.

The question arises, however, as to why R. J. Reynolds would not enjoy full First Amendment protection even if it had mentioned its own products?

Assaults on Commercial Speech

In the last few years, the courts have given commercial speech secondary status with respect to First Amendment protection. Although the courts clearly protect the right to advertise, they nevertheless subject advertisers and producers to the myriad of government regulations.

The secondary status of commercial speech is the inevitable result of trying to reconcile free speech with a regulated economy. But this reconciliation is conceptually unstable. It assumes, on the one hand, that economic activities can be divorced from communication and information about such activities. Since these two cannot be separated, the right to free speech is compromised in an attempt to retain the government's power to regulate voluntary economic transactions. On the other hand, the reconciliation assumes that the right of free speech applies to some categories of speech and not others. Commercial speech needs to be wrenched from other forms of speech to make this argument fly, yet no logical and legal ground can be found for this in the U.S. Constitution.

The main way of trying to separate commercial from noncommercial speech is to argue that the latter is "public" speech while the former is "private" because it serves some private interest. This distinction is used to argue that the court has gone too far in allowing First Amendment protection of commercial speech. The First Amendment, these critics claim, was meant to cover cases of public speech, not private. They would agree with us that it is incoherent to grant commercial speech only partial protection; but their solution is to afford commercial speech no First Amendment protection at all!

The distinction between public and private speech is simply not viable. In the first place, it is typical for those who object to First Amendment protection of commercial speech also to fail to object to government regulation of the economy. But if economic matters were purely private, the government could have no "public" interest in regulation, and it is the supposed public interest of government in economic regulation that refutes the claim that commercial speech is a purely private affair.

In addition, those who speak are seldom, if ever, as disinterested as the concept of "public" speech would lead us to believe. Groups which have causes to advance in the name of the "public interest" have at stake precisely the same things as corporations do in their advertisements: organizational growth, jobs, visibility, competitive advantage (relative to other groups with a cause), and the like. Individuals, too, seldom make disinterested public pronouncements, especially on controversial issues of public policy (e.g., taxes and zoning changes). If the First Amendment is not designed to protect self-interested speech, there is precious little that it does protect.

All Speech Is Public

Finally, speech, by its very nature, is public, since it is communication. And advertising is most certainly public, because it is addressed not to particular individuals, but to unknown members of the public. We should abandon the distinction between private and public speech and accord commercial speech the same full First Amendment protection given to all speech.

"There is nothing wrong with presenting something in its most attractive light."

Does it now follow that advertisers can make any false or fraudulent claim they wish about their products? The answer here is no, because there is a significant moral difference between making a promise and expressing a belief. The informational components of advertisements can plausibly be construed as an initial statement of terms between seller and buyer. This is why it is legitimate to hold advertisers accountable to some degree for the truth of their ads. Expressions of belief, on the other hand, do not function like promises, because no one is called upon to deliver a good according to stated terms. No one has the right to defraud another. But

to say that hardly justifies intrusive governmental regulation of commercial speech.

If the R. J. Reynolds advertisement had included accurate product information, the ad could not be held morally and legally culpable. The court should have ruled in Reynolds' favor, even if they had included product information as part of the advertisement. The court's attempt to dodge the issue by calling the Reynolds advertisement "noncommercial" may have been convenient, but it leaves commercial speech vulnerable to attack by foes of liberty.

A Poor Court Ruling

In this respect, the court has strayed even wider of the mark in its ruling in *Posadas*, a case that arose in Puerto Rico in which once again the court distinguished between commercial and other types of speech, a distinction that is inexcusable despite the specious claim that the "original intent" of the First Amendment was to cover only political speech. In fact, however, the precise *meaning* of the First Amendment concerns any kind of speech whatever, and a law must be interpreted to mean what it says—legislative intentions are too diffuse and varied for us to be guided by them.

It is true that the First Amendment does not unequivocally grant protection to commercial speech, but that is irrelevant—it certainly does not bar such protection either, just as it does not bar protection for religious, philosophical, ideological, poetical, or any other special kind of speech.

If this is not sufficient, as it should be, we should also recall here the Ninth Amendment which says that "The enumeration in the Constitution, of certain rights, shall not be construed to deny or disparage others retained by the people." This Constitutional provision can only be understood as wisely extending protection to many matters not explicitly mentioned or foreseen by the Founders. So when the First Amendment is coupled with the Ninth, one must assume that commercial speech is still speech and hence Constitutionally protected. When we also add to all this that the Fourteenth Amendment requires that "No State shall . . . deny to any person within its jurisdiction the equal protection of the laws," it becomes clear that a ban on any kind of honest advertising would constitute a form of discrimination against people in business vis-à-vis other professions, activities, and forms of speech. In short, the principles embedded in the Constitution clearly favor the argument for full Constitutional protection of commercial speech.

Is Advertising Deceptive?

Nevertheless, the argument persists and is a simple one: Cigarettes are "lethal" products while the images conveyed by cigarette ads in no way convey this danger—indeed the opposite message is conveyed. The consumer is therefore deceived into believing that cigarette smoking is acceptable, attractive, or without risks and hazards. This argument, however, is nothing but a version of the old shibboleth that advertising itself is inherently deceptive.

Advertisements are said to be inherently deceptive because they "selectively emphasize" certain features of a product to make the product appear more attractive. Since this technique ignores or de-emphasizes other features, the consumer is deceived. The moral conclusion many draw is that since advertising is deceptive, and deception is morally wrong, advertising is morally wrong.

But the case for "generic deception" depends upon there being something wrong with presenting something in a positive light and upon the likelihood that people are unaware of the type of message being delivered. Neither condition can be satisfied.

There is nothing wrong with presenting something in its most attractive light. We do this all the time. On our resumés we do not list the jobs we lost or the failures we had. In our personal grooming we take care to look attractive and hide our "flaws." As to the nature of the message, what is generic to advertising is precisely the effort to present something in its most attractive light. Since attractive presentation of information is virtually what we mean by an advertisement, it is nonsensical to claim generic deception when one confronts an advertisement. Selective emphasis does not violate the canon of truthfulness *per se*, because the basic truth conveyed by advertising is that when you see it you expect to see the item portrayed in its best light. And surely there are (some) attractive people who use tobacco products.

"*Despite continual subjection to claims about the evils of tobacco, we are being told that we are too incompetent to make up our own minds about these products.*"

After examining basic moral and Constitutional values, one is forced to conclude that the tobacco industry is on the side of principle in its opposition to the AMA. It is obvious that banning or restricting commercial speech about tobacco products ignores basic rights and liberties and opens the door to further coercive control of speech.

A World of Fools

What is perhaps less obvious is the damage already done. That Congress and the media could take a proposal like the AMA's seriously, and indeed that well-educated medical professionals could be so completely ignorant of the meaning of liberty, signifies a national crisis of understanding of our own heritage of political liberty. Furthermore, the *ad hoc* attitudes of the present Court concerning commercial speech offer little hope that this crisis will be remedied from this quarter.

Yet in the end, what disturbs us most is how insulting all this is. Despite continual subjection to claims about the evils of tobacco, we are being told that we are too incompetent to make up our own minds about these products. The damage that has already been done is reflected in the fact that we take such insults on a daily basis. Let us reverse the trend and identify the insult as just that. It is a first, but necessary, step in preventing the world from filling up with fools.

Douglas J. Den Uyl is an associate professor of philosophy at Bellarmine College in Louisville, Kentucky. Tibor R. Machan is a professor of philosophy at Auburn University in Alabama.

Banning Cigarette Advertising Is Constitutional

John F. Banzhaf III

Editor's note: The following viewpoint is testimony John F. Banzhaf III presented before Congress.

I appear before you in several different but obviously related capacities:

as the Executive Director of Action on Smoking and Health (ASH), the only national organization devoted solely to the problems of smoking, and the organization which serves as the legal-action arm of the antismoking movement;

as a law professor with considerable experience concerning constitutional interpretation, who was recently asked twice by Members of Congress to testify as an expert witness on constitutional issues, including proposed ad bans;

as a public interest lawyer who successfully defended the constitutionality of applying the "Fairness Doctrine" to cigarette commercials, and the statutory ban on cigarette commercials which resulted from that decision;

and as the litigator who first argued the theory that the governmental power to ban a product includes the less-intrusive power to restrict its advertising, which has just been adopted by the U.S. Supreme Court in the casino advertising case.

The Casino Case

Hereinafter cited as the "casino case," *Posadas de Puerto Rico Assoc. v. Tourism Company of Puerto Rico* was decided July 1, 1986. In that opinion, Chief Justice designate William Rehnquist, writing for a majority of the Court, held that

"In our view, the greater power to completely ban casino gambling necessarily includes the lesser power to ban advertising of casino gambling . . ."

"It is precisely *because* the government could have enacted a wholesale prohibition of the underlying conduct that it is permissible for the government to take the less intrusive step of allowing the conduct,

John F. Banzhaf III, "Cigarette Ads: A Ban or Other Restrictions Are Constitutional," testimony before the US House of Representatives Subcommittee on Health and the Environment on August 1, 1986.

but reducing the demand through restrictions on advertising."

"It would just as surely be a strange constitutional doctrine which would concede to the legislature the authority to totally ban a product or activity, but deny to the legislature the authority to forbid the stimulation of demand for the product or activity through advertising on behalf of those who would profit from such increased demand."

In summary, I conclude—as did a former top A.C.L.U. [American Civil Liberties Union] official who fortunately did not wind up [like one of his colleagues] in the pay of the tobacco industry—that it would clearly be constitutional for Congress to ban all cigarette advertising for several reasons:

(1) The Supreme Court's casino decision, which upholds a form of prior restraint imposed by a non-governmental body on ads designed to protect against conjectural harms with no history of the government trying less extreme measures;

In contrast, with regard to cigarette smoking, there is a considerable history of trying to use other means to deal with the problem, including: governmental health warning messages and educational campaigns, application of the "Fairness Doctrine" to cigarette commercials, a variety of different health warnings initially on cigarette packs and ultimately in print and other advertising, required disclosure of tar and nicotine content, increased taxes, etc. If, having seen that the evils persist despite these efforts, and that millions of children are still seduced into taking up an addictive and often fatal habit, the Congress determines that a total advertising ban is necessary, there is—in contrast to the casino case—a very considerable factual basis for that determination. Surely the Supreme Court will not require the Congress to experiment with every possible permutation and combination of restrictions to prove that a total ban is necessary—not when cigarette smoking among young girls is rising dangerously!

(2) A detailed analysis, prepared by the impartial and respected Congressional Research Service of the Library of Congress, concluding even prior to the Supreme Court's casino decision that a cigarette ban would be constitutional;

Johnny H. Killian, Senior Specialist on American Constitutional Law, Congressional Research Service of the Library of Congress, prepared a very detailed, thoughtful, and impartial analysis of this very issue some time ago. He concluded that: a ''ban or a substantial restriction [on tobacco advertising] would likely be sustained if Congress in the course of consideration of legislation established the appropriate foundation for it.''

(3) Many Supreme Court and other decisions upholding restrictions on truthful commercial advertising where the ''evil'' addressed was far less serious and the connection with the ads less clear;

(4) The inherently deceptive nature of cigarette advertising—which affects children who are too young to read or appreciate a written health warning, but who can understand the glamor of smoking the ad attempts to convey—and which therefore provides an additional basis for governmental restrictions.

''By placing ads the tobacco industry . . . is able to get its message across without the risk of opposing views.''

The Federal Trade Commission [FTC] and its staff have frequently concluded that cigarette ads tend to be deceptive, even if they contain a health warning. This is so for many reasons, only two of which can be very briefly summarized here.

The Commission has found evidence, in the form of documents obtained by subpoena and otherwise, that the tobacco industry deliberately attempts to persuade children and others who view their ads to overlook or give less credence to the health warnings. Common techniques include showing smokers engaged in vigorous healthy outdoor activities, showing smokers next to sports equipment suggesting good health, sponsoring sporting events and otherwise associating the product with sports, etc.

It would also appear that any ad showing a person smoking will be deceptive to the millions of children who view the ads—often despite the best efforts of their parents—on billboards (where they are the most widely advertised product), point-of-purchase display ads, panel ads in or on the side of buses and trains, on the back covers of magazines (where they always seem to appear), etc. This is because children below a certain age cannot read a written health warning, and even older children cannot understand and appreciate the warning. Thus, short of a ''skull and crossbones'' or ''Mr. YUK'' symbol prominently displayed on such ads, they will be deceptive with regard to children who, deliberately or otherwise, make up a very substantial portion of the audience.

All of the commercial advertising cases have made it clear that any ad which tends to be deceptive or misleading may be regulated or prohibited on that ground alone, notwithstanding any other conditions or factors. Indeed the very basis of the regulation of advertising of products generally by the FTC, or drugs by the FDA [Food and Drug Administration], of financial ads by the SEC [Securities and Exchange Commission], of ads by banks, other financial institutions, insurance companies, etc. by various agencies is that misleading ads may constitutionally be regulated.

Thus, if Congress finds, as it easily may upon the evidence which already exists, that cigarette ads tend to be misleading and deceptive, this finding would provide an alternative basis and foundation for their prohibition.

Options to an Ad Ban

In addition to a total ban on all cigarette advertising which Action on Smoking and Health strongly supports, ASH also urges the Congress to consider, as possible but obviously less effective alternatives, several measures which ASH proposed more than 10 years ago, and which have subsequently been recommended by other major national health organizations like the American Cancer Society. These include:

A. Restricting cigarette ads to the same ''tombstone'' format now required for many ads for stocks and bonds—i.e., providing no less protection to children and unsophisticated adults than we have long provided to sophisticated financial investors, even though the harm investors face is only financial;

In many cases ads have been regulated or in some cases even prohibited even though they may pertain to products or services as to which the consumer may easily judge the merits of the claims (e.g., the taste of hamburgers or other foods); as to which there are many competing ads which serve as sources of alternative and corrective information (e.g., various pills); and/or where the only harm is a small financial loss. In contrast, cigarettes are a product as to which the consumer is completely incapable of determining for himself the correctness of various assertions as to the health risks; as to which there are virtually no competing ads which can help to correct misrepresentations; and where the clearly foreseeable harm is addiction, illness, disability, and death. Thus, the government's interest, and therefore its legal basis, for regulating such ads is much stronger.

B. Requiring that cigarette ads consist only of text with no pictures whatsoever, or restricting any pictures which appear in cigarette ads to the product itself—e.g., the cigarette, the pack, the filter, etc.

Congress and other legislative bodies have long recognized the potential dangers posed by many products and services, and the resulting need to regulate or in some cases even to prohibit their advertising. And, more importantly, the U.S. Supreme Court and other courts have continued to uphold such enactments, even with regard to truthful commercial advertising, and long after the Supreme Court adopted a doctrine of providing limited protection to truthful commercial speech.

The Most Dangerous Consumer Product

Cigarettes are, by a very wide margin, the most dangerous of all consumer products—

—the only one universally acknowledged to be dangerous even when not abused and when used in moderation;

—one of the few found to be so addictive that many who start as kids soon find themselves unable to stop;

—one whose use costs the American public over $100 billion each year paid largely by nonsmokers;

—and where most experts believe as ASH does that advertising is a major factor in persuading kids to try that first puff.

The tobacco industry frequently tries to argue that it is peer pressure, rather than advertising, which is the primary factor in persuading kids to take up smoking. But most experts agree that several factors—e.g., parental smoking habits, peer pressure, and cigarette ads—all play a role.

In any event, blaming peer pressure is only to pass the buck, since logically we must then ask where that peer pressure comes from, and why many kids think it's "cool" and grown up to smoke cigarettes rather than to engage in other activities. Certainly one factor behind peer pressure is the image of smoking which children, and even their parents, receive of smoking from the hundreds of millions of dollars of ads they see every year.

For all of these reasons ASH believes that the Congress must take more effective action against advertising which has repeatedly been found to be deceptive, and which—for children—is inherently so despite health warnings, and which still exacts such a deadly toll each year.

Protecting First Amendment Rights

Even with a total ban on cigarette advertising, the tobacco industry would retain its First Amendment rights to present its point of view through press releases, press conferences, appearances on talk shows, and the other means which now must be relied upon by antismoking organizations. What they would lose is only the power to avoid the scrutiny and debate which should characterize free speech, the ability to overwhelm people through the non-electronic media with their messages, and to stifle in that media—so dependent on cigarette advertising—a fair presentation of the opposing point of view.

"Cigarettes are, by a very wide margin, the most dangerous of all consumer products."

When tobacco industry representatives express views about the desirability of smoking and/or of the risks allegedly associated therewith by holding press conferences, appearing on talk shows, granting interviews, etc., it is common practice for representatives of the media to seek to expose misleading statements by asking pointed questions, and by presenting opposing views from knowledgeable persons. By placing ads the tobacco industry avoids this, and is able to get its message across without the risk of opposing views. But this is clearly not required or protected by the First Amendment; indeed, it is antithetical to the First Amendment which is based upon spirited, open, and robust debate.

It is undeniable that the average reader of most popular magazines—e.g., women's magazines, men's magazines, news magazines, etc.—is dozens of times more likely to encounter an ad portraying cigarette smoking in a favorable light and in a way designed to undercut or distract attention away from the health hazards than he or she is to find a news item, an editorial, an ad, or any other countervailing communication which presents an opposing point of view. The ability to overwhelm the other side by the sheer weight of the advertising dollar is not essential to the protection of true First Amendment rights.

This is NOT constitutionally-protected speech!

John F. Banzhaf III has been a leader in the fight against smoking. He teaches law at the National Law Center of George Washington University in Washington, DC and is the executive director of Action on Smoking and Health (ASH), a national anti-smoking organization.

viewpoint **43**

Banning Cigarette Advertising Is Unconstitutional

Richard E. Wiley

In 1970, when I was serving as General Counsel of the FCC, I encountered a regulatory problem which, sad to say, is directly relevant to a serious challenge facing the advertising community today. As is well known, the Commission's Fairness Doctrine requires broadcasters to cover controversial issues of public importance and, in doing so, to provide an opportunity for contrasting views somewhere in their overall programming. Prior to my joining the Commission, the FCC had decided (in a considerable departure from its established Fairness Doctrine procedures) to require counter-advertisements to balance cigarette ads (which *implicitly* argued one side of the public health issue involved). In doing so, the agency stated that cigarettes presented a unique health hazard and, thus, were the only product to which the ad/counter-ad treatment would apply.

Within a year, I found myself in the court of appeals arguing that this "unusual" procedure should not apply to high octane gasoline and air-polluting automobile commercials; and I also found my argument to be a loser. The court of appeals ruled that the public health issues raised by ads for cigarettes and those other products were indistinguishable. To put it succinctly, the court found that cigarettes simply were not unique.

Happily, the end of the story came in 1974. By that time, I was Chairman of the FCC and was able to convince the Commission to change the Fairness Doctrine's entire application to advertising. We ruled that only if commercials made an obvious and meaningful argument on a controversial issue would fairness even come into play. In other words, there would be no application of the doctrine to implicit claims, for example, an automobile advertisement showing healthy people simply enjoying the product.

I thought this was the end of the story until the American Bar Association began debating whether to support the American Medical Association's call for a ban on all advertising of tobacco products. And why such a ban? Once again, the clarion call was sounded: cigarettes allegedly presented a *unique* health danger justifying this action.

It all sounded very familiar and, to me, very disturbing. Accordingly, I became involved with the American Advertising Federation and other advertising-based entities in opposing this action. Fortunately, the ABA rejected a resolution calling for it to join in AMA's ad ban campaign.

This debate is highly important. What is at stake is *not* just an argument over a product's uniqueness. Instead, it is a challenge to the whole question of freedom of expression and freedom of advertising in a free society.

Superficially Attractive

The themes being voiced in support of the current advertising ban movement are superficially attractive: good health, the welfare of our youth, a public-spirited cause supported by the medical profession, etc. But these seductive messages cannot be allowed to conceal what is really involved in the proposed tobacco advertising ban. It is nothing less than a program of censorship, one which is contrary to the values which are central to our American way of life. As the Supreme Court has phrased it, the dissemination of truthful information "is not in itself harmful . . . our citizens will perceive their own best interests if they are well enough informed, and . . . the best means to this end is to open channels of communications rather than close them."

Of course, the ban proponents assert that commercial speech is somehow different, that while it would be unthinkable to use thought-control techniques in the area of political or aesthetic

Richard E. Wiley, "The Movement to Ban Tobacco Ads: Opening the Door to Censorship?" Washington Legal Foundation *Legal Backgrounder*, June 12, 1987. Reprinted with permission.

speech, no serious threat to our freedoms would be posed by censoring commercially-oriented expression.

In my judgment, this view seriously undervalues the free flow of information about goods and services in our country. Unlike societies that have opted for state-managed economics, this country is committed to a system in which individual citizens have personal autonomy in their consumer choices. Moreover, I believe that censorship is contagious. If you sanction it in order to deal with one perceived social evil, it will only be a matter of time until that precedent will be used in other areas, to the detriment of our free society. In my opinion, this is a lesson that a lot of good people are forgetting in their concern over tobacco products. Once you go down the censorship road, there is simply no turning back.

The Puerto Rico Case

Finally, a long line of Supreme Court cases has recognized that, in fact, the First Amendment does apply to the truthful advertising of lawful products. Now, the would-be censors would be quick to cite the Supreme Court's 1986 decision in a case upholding a ban on casino advertising in Puerto Rico, *Posadas de Puerto Rico v. Tourism Company of Puerto Rico.* But the set of facts considered there were extremely unusual. Significantly, the "prohibition" in that case did not extend to ads directed at tourists, but only to local residents.

I do not believe that this one, aberrational case has overruled the entire body of commercial speech precedent developed by the Supreme Court over two decades. However, even if the current Supreme Court could be persuaded that a tobacco advertising ban could pass constitutional muster, this would be very poor and, indeed, dangerous public policy for a number of reasons.

The Dangers of a Ban

First, as indicated, the ban simply could not be limited to cigarettes. It quickly would spread to other products—indeed, any product which might be deemed hazardous by someone. And, without question, this would seriously damage our system of commercial advertising and, in the process, our entire economy.

Second, the ban advocates assert that tobacco advertising is *not* truthful (and, thus, deserves no constitutional protection). They do so on the theory that such advertising does not tell "the whole story." But under such a standard, all advertising would be subject to attack.

Third, the Supreme Court has indicated that any limitation on commercial speech must represent the least restrictive means necessary to accomplish the goal intended. However, clearly that would not be the case here, given the possible alternatives that could be considered (if deemed necessary), including requiring *more* information about any harmful qualities of the product.

Finally, there exists no solid evidence that a ban would affect consumption of the product. Tobacco advertising has already been prohibited in a number of other countries (many of which don't enjoy our constitutional freedoms) and there is little to demonstrate that cigarette use has declined in those areas. In fact, in some cases, usage actually may have increased where advertising has been prohibited. In all, what the data drawn from other countries seem to show is that other factors (such as market structure, product availability and price, societal norms, and health issue publicity) are the underlying determinants of demand and *not* a prohibition on advertising.

The Benefits of Advertising

The ban-the-ad crowd then would argue: if it's true that commercials don't affect usage then why would anyone advertise in the first place? The answer lies in the opportunity to introduce new products and to tout the asserted advantage of existing products. In other words, tobacco advertising is primarily designed to affect brand loyalty. There is absolutely nothing wrong with this. Indeed, I think the public is greatly benefited in terms of enhanced consumer choice. . . .

"Tobacco advertising is primarily designed to affect brand loyalty. . . . The public is greatly benefitted in terms of enhanced consumer choice."

According to the Department of Justice: "A federal ban on advertising of a lawful product raises serious questions in light of our constitutional structure and the free expression guaranteed by the First Amendment." And FTC Chairman Daniel Oliver recently observed: "I believe that a ban on tobacco advertising would be more likely to harm consumers than to help them."

The principle being defended can be simply stated: the right to advertise truthfully a lawful product. And the challenge to this principle is also abundantly clear: it is a proposed program of censorship which is alien to our traditions and our cherished freedoms.

Richard E. Wiley is a partner in the Washington, DC, law firm of Wiley, Rein & Fielding. He was formerly the general counsel, the commissioner, and the chairman of the Federal Communications Commission.

Legalizing Drugs: An Overview

George J. Church

Neat little packets of marijuana, coke and even heroin nestling against the vitamins at the neighborhood drugstore? And selling at a low Government-set price with a guarantee of purity? It sounds like a black comedy or perhaps a gaudy hallucination. In fact, it is the extreme version of a new policy course being advocated in dead seriousness by a growing number of those frustrated by the futility of the drug war. The 74 years of federal prohibition that have passed since the Harrison Narcotics Act of 1914 have been a costly and abject failure, they say, and the effort is doomed. It has mainly served to create huge profits for drug dealers, overcrowded jails, a distorted foreign policy and urban areas terrorized by bloodthirsty gangs. So why not end all these problems in a way that would save money, perhaps even raise it, and free more resources to treat addiction and abuse? Why not just make drugs legal?

Those who have begun to take this question seriously do not in the least want to condone, let alone encourage, drug use. The swelling chorus includes conservative scholars, police officers and city officials who would love to see a dope-free nation. But they feel that the best way to curtail drugs is to treat them as a public health problem rather than a criminal one. In the process, the Government could take the drug market out of the hands of the gangs that have turned large sections of major cities into shooting galleries, in more ways than one.

Such talk horrifies many critics equally bedeviled by the drug dilemma. To them legalization is an immoral and dangerous policy that would vastly increase the number of addicts and turn the U.S. into a "society of zombies," in the words of New York Republican Senator Alfonse D'Amato. If drugs were freely available, what is now a nagging but contained problem could end up tearing apart the nation's social fabric.

Whether it is inspired or insane, drug legalization has become the idea of the moment. That in itself shows the intensity of the national frenzy that has erupted once again to do something—anything—about drugs and related crime. . . .

The case begins with a simple proposition: all wars on drugs are doomed to fail, no matter how many Viet Nam-style escalations the authorities order. It is a simple matter of supply and demand: as long as demand exists on the scale of the U.S. craving for, say, cocaine, someone is going to supply it, legally or illegally. Significantly, this line is voiced by a growing number of public officials who were once enthusiastic soldiers in the war on drugs but have been bitterly disillusioned.

Baltimore Mayor Kurt Schmoke claims to have "won thousands of convictions for drug-related crimes" during his seven-year career as a prosecutor. But it was he who started much of the furor over legalization by calling for a national debate on the issue in an April [1988] speech to the U.S. Conference of Mayors. For drug dealers, says Schmoke, "going to jail is just part of the cost of doing business. It's a nuisance, not a deterrent."

Joseph McNamara, police chief in San Jose, in the drug-ridden Silicon Valley, estimates that his department spends 80% of its time trying to enforce the drug laws. "The fight against drugs for the past 70 years has been one long glorious failure," he says. "The courts are overflowing, there is violence on the streets, and the problem seems to be getting worse."

Indeed, say most proponents of legalization, the antinarcotics laws create an evil worse than the drugs themselves: violent crime. Laws to stop the supply do not prevent anyone who really wants cocaine or heroin from getting it. But they do permit the sellers to charge sky-high prices as a kind of risk premium. The high prices, in turn, produce enormous profits that irresistibly lure vicious gangs, who are taking over large areas of cities. The gangs employ armies of pushers who spread the very plague the drug laws are supposed to combat. Says Milton Friedman, guru of free-market economists and a Nobel prizewinner: "The harm that is done by drugs is predominantly caused by the fact that they are illegal. You would not have had the crack epidemic if it was legal." Finally, addicts too are irresistibly driven to crime—prostitution, mugging, burglary—to finance their habits.

The great promise of legalization, say its advocates, is that it would rip this cancer out of the cities. If drugs were legal, the Government could regulate their sale and set a low price. Addicts could get a fix without stealing, and a lack of profit would dismantle the booming criminal industry that now supplies them. Drug gangs would disappear as bootleggers did after the repeal of Prohibition; with them would go the current, pervasive corruption of police officers, lawyers, judges and politicians bribed by drug money. Drug dealing would no longer seem to be the only way out of the ghetto for underclass youths. Says Mayor Schmoke: "If you take the profit out of drug trafficking, you won't have young children hiding drugs [on behalf of pushers] for $100 a night or wearing beepers to school because it makes more sense to run drugs for someone than to take some of the jobs that are available. I don't know of any kid who is making money by running booze." The bottom line for those favoring legalization: drug-related crime damages society far more than drug usage itself.

"The bottom line for those favoring legalization: drug-related crime damages society far more than drug usage itself."

But many see benefits from legalization that go beyond easing the crime problem. Princeton Professor Ethan Nadelmann estimates that federal, state and local governments are spending around $8 billion a year on direct drug-enforcement activities and billions more for such indirect costs as care and feeding of imprisoned drug dealers (people convicted of drug-related crimes constitute more than one-third of all federal prisoners). Legalization not only would save these enormous expenditures but also could bring in billions more in new revenues if governments chose to tax the sale of newly legal drugs (as they surely would). Nadelmann and others suggest that the money be used to fund an antidrug program that might actually work: a long, persistent educational effort of the sort that has reduced

cigarette smoking, plus expanded treatment programs for drug abusers.

One of the most shocking deficiencies in the fight against drugs is that addicts who want to kick their habits often must wait months before being admitted to a rehabilitation center, if they can find one at all. Legalization, say advocates, might at last give governments the revenue to fund rehabilitation and treatment adequately.

Other arguments for legalization differ widely depending on the speaker. That is hardly surprising, since the trend cannot properly be called a "movement." It is a very unorganized current of thought with adherents from every part of the political spectrum. Some extreme libertarians contend that the Government has no business telling citizens what they may or may not put into their bodies. A much larger group contends that it is hypocritical to ban narcotics while allowing the sale of alcohol and tobacco, two substances that, this group insists, kill far more people by undermining their health and, in the case of alcohol, lead to innumerable auto crashes, barroom brawls and savage family fights. "We've already decriminalized two drugs, alcohol and tobacco," says Harvard Law School Professor Alan Dershowitz. "Now it's time to decriminalize a third, heroin."

Some advocates contend that legalization will also help U.S. foreign policy. They assert, with some justification, that the futile effort to stop drug smuggling is poisoning American relations with such important and otherwise friendly Latin nations as Colombia and Mexico that have been unable or unwilling to crack down on the drug trade. Finally, on the left, some advocates contend that legalization would remove a severe threat to individual freedom that is posed by widespread drug searches, demands for wholesale testing and the pending use of the military to enforce drug laws. If the sale of narcotics is permitted, says Harvard Psychiatrist Lester Grinspoon, "there won't be the tremendous encroachment on our civil liberties. Are we willing to sacrifice our freedom for the small increase in the number of people who may use the drugs under a legalized system?"

Advocates of legalization are still more disunited when it comes to spelling out a practical program, which hardly anyone has ventured to do. Democratic Congressman Charles Rangel, who represents a drug-riddled district in New York City's Harlem, poses a long string of questions for those who would legalize drugs. Among them: Which drugs should be permitted, just marijuana or the more damaging heroin, cocaine and angel dust? How would they be sold, by prescription through hospitals and clinics or in "drugstores," tobacco shops, even supermarkets? Would there be an age limit, and how would it be enforced? Would users be permitted to buy as much as they wanted, even if their demands became insatiable as their addictions deepened? Or would there be some kind of so-many-grams-per-customer limit? If so, again, how would it be enforced? As long as these questions cannot be satisfactorily answered, says Rangel sarcastically, legalization will remain "idle chitchat as cocktail glasses knock together at social events."

Attempts to answer such questions scatter all over the lot. A common proposal is to handle the sale of narcotics in a manner similar to the sale of alcohol. The substances could be sold only by licensed dealers, who would be taxed and heavily regulated; for example, they would be forbidden to sell to anyone under 21 years old. But there are many variations. Some supporters would permit the legal sale of marijuana only; Washington Mayor Marion Barry might add cocaine but is dead set against legalizing PCP (angel dust). Economist Friedman would permit the sale of every imaginable brand of upper and downer at the local drugstore. Dershowitz would go so far as to distribute heroin free from mobile vans in inner cities to "medically certified addicts."

A good many people would stop short of full-scale legalization and opt for a rather vague concept known as decriminalization. It is generally taken to mean reducing or eliminating criminal penalties for the use and perhaps sale of drugs, while retaining some form of legal disapproval. Such a halfway solution might accelerate the problems that would come from legalization without solving most of those that arise from the current tough drug laws. Author Claude Brown (*Man-child in the Promised Land*), himself a reformed drug dealer, suggests decriminalizing the sale of drugs by hospitals and clinics in order to "deglamorize [narcotics use] and associate it with being sick. That would turn the kids off."

"One peculiar aspect of modern American society is that little distinction is made between what is legal and what is socially condoned."

Intuitively and emotionally, the case for legalization may be hard to accept. Opponents insist that on a pragmatic and logical level it is also a dangerous and harebrained folly.

However loudly Washington might proclaim that it was not condoning narcotics abuse, the message that would come through on the streets would be "the Government says it's O.K.," and that message would overpower any stepped-up educational efforts about the dangers of drugs. One peculiar aspect of modern American society is that little distinction is made between what is legal and what is socially condoned.

With the legal stigma gone, even law-abiding citizens would be tempted to experiment with narcotics. For one thing, it is much easier to resist the urge to try drugs when the purchase involves a drive into a dark and crime-ridden part of town to make a furtive connection in a garbage-strewn alley, much more difficult when the buy requires nothing more dangerous than walking into a pharmacy. And a large number of those who experimented would get hooked.

So, opponents predict, the result of legalization would be an enormous increase in drug abuse, with all of its penalties of shattered health, families and lives. This belief, significantly, is particularly strong among many people who work with addicts. "To legalize drugs would give us a vast army of people who would be out of control," says Mitchell Rosenthal, president of Phoenix House, a New York City-based drug-rehabilitation program. "People say only 10% of those who drink are problem drinkers, so they assume that only 10% of the people who take drugs will become addicts. But there is no reason to believe that if we made crack available in little crack shops that only 10% would be addicted; the number would probably be more like 75%."

To risk such a debacle, in the view of many, is not just mistaken policy but morally wrong. Legalization, says Harvard Psychiatrist Robert Coles, would be a "moral surrender of far-reaching implications about the way we treat each other." Coles specializes in working with children and says they "need the societal order to say we stand for something." He fears that legalization would instead send a message of unrestricted hedonism. "I'm not prepared as a parent, as a citizen or as a doctor to say that," Coles asserts.

Opponents of legalization also turn the comparison with alcohol around. Sure, alcohol may be as dangerous as some illegal drugs, but the very fact that it is so harmful to society is all the more reason not to add to the number of dangerous substances that can be abused. "We're just finally beginning to recognize what it means to use cigarettes," says Coles, "and to turn around and say it's all right to use heroin and marijuana is wrong."

John Lawn, head of the Drug Enforcement Administration, summarizes pithily: "Drugs are not bad because they're illegal. They're illegal because they're bad." The legal production and sale of drugs would threaten all of society. But there is, some say, an insidious racist aspect. Notes Lawn: "Anyone who talks in terms of legalizing drugs is willing to write the death warrants for people in the lower socioeconomic classes."

At least one person with still greater firsthand experience with drugs agrees. "Paul," a Los Angeles musician, has been using cocaine for three years and spends about $300 a weekend on the drug. He readily admits that it is rapidly destroying both his marriage and his life. "I'm trying to gear myself up for seeking treatment," he says. But what would he do if the drug were legally available at lower prices? "I'd be dead right now," he says. "I'd just sit down with a big pile of the stuff and snort it until I dropped. Only a real cocaine connoisseur can appreciate what I mean."

Some advocates of legalization, like Professor Nadelmann, insist that there is a natural limit to addiction that will hold down any increase; those who do not have addictive personalities will not be tempted whether drugs are legal or illegal. But others fear the opposition just might be right. "I have a horrible feeling that addiction definitely will increase," says Conservative Columnist William F. Buckley, who nonetheless advocates legalization because of the prospective drop in crime.

Yet some opposed to legalization doubt that it would really wipe out drug crime, at least to the extent that the supporters claim. The contention of those opposed: unless the Government allows users to purchase unlimited quantities of drugs anonymously—an idea that makes most legalizers squirm—there will always be a black market. The market might be broadened if, as many legalizers advocate, the Government taxed legal sales of narcotics. In addition, drug abuse even at legal prices would require money; few addicts could hold regular jobs; and many would thus continue to steal or prostitute themselves for drug money.

Another kind of crime might actually increase with the number of addicts: crimes committed by those whose minds are fuddled and emotions inflamed by drugs. Says President Reagan's drug adviser Donald Macdonald: "These drugs cause crime. PCP makes people crazy. Cocaine makes people paranoid. The airplane flying into the mountain in Durango with the pilot on cocaine, that will increase. Highway accidents, family violence, spouse abuse, child abuse, incest will all increase."

Opponents are particularly upset that the cry for legalization is rising just as some signs—faint and ambiguous, to be sure—indicate that the war on drugs might be gaining ground. In the University of Michigan's annual survey, the number of high school seniors who admitted to having tried cocaine dropped from 12.7% in 1986 to 10.3% [in 1987]; among college students, the proportion fell from 17% to 14%. Perhaps more significant, 48% of high school seniors surveyed [in 1987] viewed cocaine as a "great risk," vs. only 34% in 1986.

The figures are not conclusive; they do not include dropouts, who would be much more likely to abuse drugs than youths who stay in school. Nonetheless, says Rudolph Giuliani, U.S. Attorney in New York and a celebrated prosecutor of drug cases, "it's a particularly strange time to raise the specter of legalization because we are finally beginning to change the drug culture of the 1960s and '70s."

Legalization, he fears, would wipe out all the progress. "You can't say drugs are bad at the same time that you are making them legal. Law is a teaching instrument, among other things."

The legalization debate, to some extent, pits proponents, who would accept more drug abuse as the terrible price of reducing crime, against opponents, who would accept a continued high level of crime as the equally dreadful price of holding down addiction. In fact, neither side can be sure to what extent legalization would reduce crime and increase addiction, unless it is tried. But the idea is risky, exceedingly risky.

"The debate is over the role of law in upholding the nation's moral fabric."

More fundamentally, the debate is over the role of law in upholding the nation's moral fabric. One function of the law is to express society's moral disapproval of or repugnance to an activity. Although that may sometimes conflict with personal freedom or even pragmatic considerations, it is still a principle that helps order American society, as it does every civilization.

The emergence of a strong and cogent case for drug legalization, even if it is a misguided approach, has pointed out a real and serious fault in current policy. It is heavily unbalanced in favor of ineffective attempts to cut the supply through police action, while neglecting potentially more effective efforts to reduce demand through education and treatment. Says Minneapolis Mayor Donald Fraser: "Personally, I'm not willing to say drugs should be decriminalized. But investing large amounts of money to interdict supply obviously is not working. . . ."

So even though corner drug shops are not going to pop up anytime soon, nor should they, the hot new debate over legalization is a significant one. It reflects the widespread and understandable dismay over antidrug efforts that have gone to such discomforting lengths as to call in the military without noticeably making a dent in the crime and abuse problems. And it could turn attention to the need for more effective treatment and education efforts.

George J. Church is a reporter for Time, *a weekly newsmagazine.*

"Legalization may well be the optimal strategy for tackling the drug problem."

Drugs Should Be Legalized

Ethan A. Nadelmann

What can be done about the "drug problem"? Despite frequent proclamations of war and dramatic increases in government funding and resources in recent years, there are many indications that the problem is not going away and may even be growing worse. During 1987 alone, more than thirty million Americans violated the drug laws on literally billions of occasions. Drug-treatment programs in many cities are turning people away for lack of space and funding. In Washington, D.C., drug-related killings, largely of one drug dealer by another, are held responsible for a doubling in the homicide rate. In New York and elsewhere, courts and prisons are clogged with a virtually limitless supply of drug-law violators. In large cities and small towns alike, corruption of policemen and other criminal-justice officials by drug traffickers is rampant. . . .

The Legalization Option

If there were a serious public debate on this issue, far more attention would be given to one policy option that has just begun to be seriously considered, but which may well prove more successful than anything currently being implemented or proposed: legalization. Politicians and public officials remain hesitant even to mention the word, except to dismiss it contemptuously as a capitulation to the drug traffickers. Most Americans perceive drug legalization as an invitation to drug-infested anarchy. Even the civil-liberties groups shy away from this issue, limiting their input primarily to the drug-testing debate. The minority communities in the ghetto, for whom repealing the drug laws would promise the greatest benefits, fail to recognize the costs of our drug-prohibition policies. And the typical middle-class American, who hopes only that his children will not succumb to drug

Ethan A. Nadelmann, "The Case for Legalization," *The Public Interest*, Summer 1988. Reprinted with the author's permission.

abuse, tends to favor any measures that he believes will make illegal drugs less accessible to them. Yet when one seriously compares the advantages and disadvantages of the legalization strategy with those of current and planned policies, abundant evidence suggests that legalization may well be the optimal strategy for tackling the drug problem. . . .

There is, of course, no single legalization strategy. At one extreme is the libertarian vision of virtually no government restraints on the production and sale of drugs or any psychoactive substances, except perhaps around the fringes, such as prohibiting sales to children. At the other extreme is total government control over the production and sale of these goods. In between lies a strategy that may prove more successful than anything yet tried in stemming the problems of drug abuse and drug-related violence, corruption, sickness, and suffering. It is one in which government makes most of the substances that are now banned legally available to competent adults, exercises strong regulatory powers over all large-scale production and sale of drugs, makes drug-treatment programs available to all who need them, and offers honest drug-education programs to children. This strategy, it is worth noting, would also result in a net benefit to public treasuries of at least ten billion dollars a year, and perhaps much more.

There are three reasons why it is important to think about legalization scenarios, even though most Americans remain hostile to the idea. First, current drug-control policies have failed, are failing, and will continue to fail, in good part because they are fundamentally flawed. Second, many drug-control efforts are not only failing, but also proving highly costly and counter-productive; indeed, many of the drug-related evils that Americans identify as part and parcel of the "drug problem" are in fact caused by our drug-prohibition policies. Third, there is good reason to believe that repealing many of the drug laws would not lead, as many people fear, to a dramatic rise in drug abuse. In this essay I expand on each of these reasons for considering the legalization option. Government efforts to deal with the drug problem will succeed only if the rhetoric and crusading mentality that now dominate drug policy are replaced by reasoned and logical analysis. . . .

Why Current Drug Policies Fail

By most accounts, the dramatic increase in drug-enforcement efforts over the past few years has had little effect on the illicit drug market in the United States. The mere existence of drug-prohibition laws, combined with a minimal level of law-enforcement resources, is sufficient to maintain the price of illicit drugs at a level significantly higher than it would be if there were no such laws. Drug laws and enforcement also reduce the availability of illicit drugs, most notably in parts of the United States where demand is relatively limited to begin with. Theoretically, increases in drug-enforcement efforts should result in reduced availability, higher prices, and lower purity of illegal drugs. That is, in fact, what has happened to the domestic marijuana market (in at least the first two respects). But in general the illegal drug market has not responded as intended to the substantial increases in federal, state, and local drug-enforcement efforts.

"The dramatic increase in drug-enforcement efforts over the past few years has had little effect on the illicit drug market in the United States."

Cocaine has sold for about a hundred dollars a gram at the retail level since the beginning of the 1980s. The average purity of that gram, however, has increased from 12 to 60 percent. Moreover, a growing number of users are turning to "crack," a potent derivative of cocaine that can be smoked; it is widely sold in ghetto neighborhoods now for five to ten dollars per vial. Needless to say, both crack and the 60 percent pure cocaine pose much greater threats to users than did the relatively benign powder available eight years ago. Similarly, the retail price of heroin has remained relatively constant even as the average purity has risen from 3.9 percent in 1983 to 6.1 percent in 1986. Throughout the southwestern part of the United States, a particularly potent form of heroin known as "black tar" has become increasingly prevalent. And in many cities, a powerful synthetic opiate, Dilaudid, is beginning to compete with heroin as the preferred opiate. The growing number of heroin-related hospital emergencies and deaths is directly related to these developments.

All of these trends suggest that drug-enforcement efforts are not succeeding and may even be backfiring. . . .

The Costs of Prohibition

The fact that drug-prohibition laws and policies cannot eradicate or even significantly reduce drug abuse is not necessarily a reason to repeal them. They do, after all, succeed in deterring many people from trying drugs, and they clearly reduce the availability and significantly increase the price of illegal drugs. These accomplishments alone might warrant retaining the drug laws, were it not for the fact that these same laws are also responsible for much of what Americans identify as the "drug problem." Here the analogies to alcohol and tobacco are worth noting. There is little question that we could reduce the health costs associated with use and abuse of alcohol and tobacco if we were to criminalize their production, sale, and possession. But no one believes that we could eliminate their use and abuse, that we could create an "alcohol-free" or "tobacco-free" country. Nor do most Americans believe that criminalizing the alcohol and tobacco markets would be a good idea. Their opposition stems largely from two beliefs: that adult Americans have the right to choose what substances they will consume and what risks they will take; and that the costs of trying to coerce so many Americans to abstain from those substances would be enormous. It was the strength of these two beliefs that ultimately led to the repeal of Prohibition, and it is partly due to memories of that experience that criminalizing either alcohol or tobacco has little support today.

A Tobacco Prohibition Scenario

Consider the potential consequences of criminalizing the production, sale, and possession of all tobacco products. On the positive side, the number of people smoking tobacco would almost certainly decline, as would the health costs associated with tobacco consumption. Although the "forbidden fruit" syndrome would attract some people to cigarette smoking who would not otherwise have smoked, many more would likely be deterred by the criminal sanction, the moral standing of the law, the higher cost and unreliable quality of the illicit tobacco, and the difficulties involved in acquiring it. Non-smokers would rarely if ever be bothered by the irritating habits of their fellow citizens. The anti-tobacco laws would discourage some people from ever starting to smoke, and would induce others to quit.

On the negative side, however, millions of Americans, including both tobacco addicts and recreational users, would no doubt defy the law, generating a massive underground market and billions in profits for organized criminals. Although some tobacco farmers would find other work, thousands more would become outlaws and continue to produce their crops covertly. Throughout Latin America, farmers and gangsters would rejoice at the opportunity to earn untold sums of gringo greenbacks, even as U.S. diplomats pressured foreign governments to cooperate with U.S. laws. Within the United States, government helicopters would spray herbicides on illicit tobacco fields; people would be rewarded by the government for informing on their tobacco-growing, -selling, and -smoking neighbors; urine tests would be employed to identify violators of the anti-tobacco laws; and a Tobacco Enforcement Administration (the T.E.A.) would employ undercover agents, informants, and wire-taps to uncover tobacco-law violators. Municipal, state, and federal judicial systems would be clogged with tobacco traffickers and "abusers." "Tobacco-related murders" would increase dramatically as criminal organizations competed with one another for turf and markets. Smoking would become an act of youthful rebellion, and no doubt some users would begin to experiment with more concentrated, potent, and dangerous forms of tobacco. Tobacco-related corruption would infect all levels of government, and respect for the law would decline noticeably. Government expenditures on tobacco-law enforcement would climb rapidly into the billions of dollars, even as budget balancers longingly recalled the almost ten billion dollars per year in tobacco taxes earned by the federal and state governments prior to prohibition. Finally, the State of North Carolina might even secede again from the Union.

"In many ways, our predicament resembles what actually happened during Prohibition."

This seemingly far-fetched tobacco-prohibition scenario is little more than an extrapolation based on the current situation with respect to marijuana, cocaine, and heroin. In many ways, our predicament resembles what actually happened during Prohibition. Prior to Prohibition, most Americans hoped that alcohol could be effectively banned by passing laws against its production and supply. During the early years of Prohibition, when drinking declined but millions of Americans nonetheless continued to drink, Prohibition's supporters placed their faith in tougher laws and more police and jails. After a few more years, however, increasing numbers of Americans began to realize that laws and policemen were unable to eliminate the smugglers, bootleggers, and illicit producers, as long as tens of millions of Americans continued to want

to buy alcohol. At the same time, they saw that more laws and policemen seemed to generate more violence and corruption, more crowded courts and jails, wider disrespect for government and the law, and more power and profits for the gangsters. Repeal of Prohibition came to be seen not as a capitulation to Al Capone and his ilk, but as a means of both putting the bootleggers out of business and eliminating most of the costs associated with the prohibition laws. . . .

Physical Costs

Perhaps the most paradoxical consequence of the drug laws is the tremendous harm they cause to the millions of drug users who have not been deterred from using illicit drugs in the first place. Nothing resembling an underground Food and Drug Administration has arisen to impose quality control on the illegal-drug market and provide users with accurate information on the drugs they consume. Imagine that Americans could not tell whether a bottle of wine contained 6 percent, 30 percent, or 90 percent alcohol, or whether an aspirin tablet contained 5 or 500 grams of aspirin. Imagine, too, that no controls existed to prevent winemakers from diluting their product with methanol and other dangerous impurities, and that vineyards and tobacco fields were fertilized with harmful substances by ignorant growers and sprayed with poisonous herbicides by government agents. Fewer people would use such substances, but more of those who did would get sick. Some would die.

The above scenario describes, of course, the current state of the illicit drug market. Many marijuana smokers are worse off for having smoked cannabis that was grown with dangerous fertilizers, sprayed with the herbicide paraquat, or mixed with more dangerous substances. Consumers of heroin and the various synthetic substances sold on the street face even severer consequences, including fatal overdoses and poisonings from unexpectedly potent or impure drug supplies. More often than not, the quality of a drug addict's life depends greatly upon his or her access to reliable supplies. Drug-enforcement operations that succeed in temporarily disrupting supply networks are thus a double-edged sword: they encourage some addicts to seek admission into drug-treatment programs, but they oblige others to seek out new and hence less reliable suppliers; the result is that more, not fewer, drug-related emergencies and deaths occur. . . .

A Moral Issue?

Most Americans perceive the drug problem as a moral issue and draw a moral distinction between use of the illicit drugs and use of alcohol and tobacco. Yet when one subjects this distinction to reasoned analysis, it quickly disintegrates. The most consistent moral perspective of those who favor drug laws is that of the Mormons and the Puritans, who regard as immoral any intake of substances to alter one's state of consciousness or otherwise cause pleasure: they forbid not only the illicit drugs and alcohol, but also tobacco, caffeine, and even chocolate. The vast majority of Americans are hardly so consistent with respect to the propriety of their pleasures. Yet once one acknowledges that there is nothing immoral about drinking alcohol or smoking tobacco for non-medicinal purposes, it becomes difficult to condemn the consumption of marijuana, cocaine, and other substances on moral grounds. The "moral" condemnation of some substances and not others proves to be little more than a prejudice in favor of some drugs and against others. . . .

The Benefits of Legalization

Repealing the drug-prohibition laws promises tremendous advantages. Between reduced government expenditures on enforcing drug laws and new tax revenue from legal drug production and sales, public treasuries would enjoy a net benefit of at least ten billion dollars a year, and possibly much more. The quality of urban life would rise significantly. Homicide rates would decline. So would robbery and burglary rates. Organized criminal groups, particularly the newer ones that have yet to diversify out of drugs, would be dealt a devastating setback. The police, prosecutors, and courts would focus their resources on combatting the types of crimes that people cannot walk away from. More ghetto residents would turn their backs on criminal careers and seek out legitimate opportunities instead. And the health and quality of life of many drug users—and even drug abusers— would improve significantly.

"Repealing the drug-prohibition laws promises tremendous advantages."

All the benefits of legalization would be for naught, however, if millions more Americans were to become drug abusers. Our experience with alcohol and tobacco provides ample warnings. Today, alcohol is consumed by 140 million Americans and tobacco by 50 million. All of the health costs associated with abuse of the illicit drugs pale in comparison with those resulting from tobacco and alcohol abuse. . . .

Use and Abuse

Most Americans are just beginning to recognize the extensive costs of alcohol and tobacco abuse. At the same time, they seem to believe that there is something fundamentally different about alcohol and tobacco that supports the legal distinction between those two substances, on the one hand, and the

illicit ones, on the other. The most common distinction is based on the assumption that the illicit drugs are more dangerous than the licit ones. Cocaine, heroin, the various hallucinogens, and (to a lesser extent) marijuana are widely perceived as, in the words of the President's Commission on Organized Crime, "inherently destructive to mind and body." They are also believed to be more addictive and more likely to cause dangerous and violent behavior than alcohol and tobacco. All use of illicit drugs is therefore thought to be abusive; in other words, the distinction between use and abuse of psychoactive substances that most people recognize with respect to alcohol is not acknowledged with respect to the illicit substances.

"The dangers associated with . . . illicit substances are . . . not nearly so great as many people seem to think."

Most Americans make the fallacious assumption that the government would not criminalize certain psychoactive substances if they were not in fact dangerous. They then jump to the conclusion that any use of those substances is a form of abuse. The government, in its effort to discourage people from using illicit drugs, has encouraged and perpetuated these misconceptions—not only in its rhetoric but also in its purportedly educational materials. Only by reading between the lines can one discern the fact that the vast majority of Americans who have used illicit drugs have done so in moderation, that relatively few have suffered negative short-term consequences, and that few are likely to suffer long-term harm.

Marijuana

The evidence is most persuasive with respect to marijuana. U.S. drug-enforcement and health agencies do not even report figures on marijuana-related deaths, apparently because so few occur. Although there are good health reasons for children, pregnant women, and some others not to smoke marijuana, there still appears to be little evidence that occasional marijuana consumption does much harm. . . .

Nor is marijuana strongly identified as a dependence-causing substance. A 1982 survey of marijuana use by young adults (eighteen to twenty-five years old) found that 64 percent had tried marijuana at least once, that 42 percent had used it at least ten times, and that 27 percent had smoked in the last month. It also found that 21 percent had passed through a period during which they smoked "daily" (defined as twenty or more days per month), but that only one-third of those currently smoked "daily" and only one-fifth (about 4 percent of all young adults) could be described as heavy daily users (averaging two or more joints per day). This suggests that daily marijuana use is typically a phase through which people pass, after which their use becomes more moderate. . . .

Other Drugs

The dangers associated with cocaine, heroin, the hallucinogens, and other illicit substances are greater than those posed by marijuana, but not nearly so great as many people seem to think. Consider the case of cocaine. In 1986 NIDA reported that over 20 million Americans had tried cocaine, that 12.2 million had consumed it at least once during 1985, and that nearly 5.8 million had used it within the past month. Among those between the ages of eighteen and twenty-five, 8.2 million had tried cocaine, 5.3 million had used it within the past year, 2.5 million had used it within the past month, and 250,000 had used it weekly. Extrapolation might suggest that a quarter of a million young Americans are potential problem users. But one could also conclude that only 3 percent of those between the ages of eighteen and twenty-five who had ever tried the drug fell into that category, and that only 10 percent of those who had used cocaine monthly were at risk. (The NIDA survey did not, it should be noted, include people residing in military or student dormitories, prison inmates, or the homeless.)

All of this is not to deny that cocaine is a potentially dangerous drug, especially when it is injected, smoked in the form of crack, or consumed in tandem with other powerful substances. Clearly, tens of thousands of Americans have suffered severely from their abuse of cocaine, and a tiny fraction have died. But there is also overwhelming evidence that most users of cocaine do not get into trouble with the drug. So much of the media attention has focused on the small percentage of cocaine users who become addicted that the popular perception of how most people use cocaine has become badly distorted. In one survey of high school seniors' drug use, the researchers questioned recent cocaine users, asking whether they had ever tried to stop using cocaine and found that they couldn't. Only 3.8 percent responded affirmatively, in contrast to the almost 7 percent of marijuana smokers who said they had tried to stop and found they couldn't, and the 18 percent of cigarette smokers who answered similarly. Although a similar survey of adult users would probably reveal a higher proportion of cocaine addicts, evidence such as this suggests that only a small percentage of people who use cocaine end up having a problem with it. In this respect, most people differ from monkeys, who have demonstrated in experiments that they will starve themselves to death if provided with unlimited cocaine.

With respect to the hallucinogens such as LSD and psilocybic mushrooms, their potential for addiction is virtually nil. The dangers arise primarily from using them irresponsibly on individual occasions. Although many of those who have used one or another of the hallucinogens have experienced "bad trips," others have reported positive experiences, and very few have suffered any long-term harm.

Opiates and Legal Drugs

Perhaps no drugs are regarded with as much horror as the opiates, and in particular heroin, which is a concentrated form of morphine. As with most drugs, heroin can be eaten, snorted, smoked, or injected. Most Americans, unfortunately, prefer injection. There is no question that heroin is potentially highly addictive, perhaps as addictive as nicotine. But despite the popular association of heroin use with the most down-and-out inhabitants of urban ghettos, heroin causes relatively little physical harm to the human body. Consumed on an occasional or regular basis under sanitary conditions, its worst side effect, apart from addiction itself, is constipation. That is one reason why many doctors in early twentieth-century America saw opiate addiction as preferable to alcoholism, and prescribed the former as treatment for the latter when abstinence did not seem a realistic option.

"An additional advantage of the illicit drugs is that none of them appears to be as insidious as either alcohol or tobacco."

It is important to think about the illicit drugs in the same way we think about alcohol and tobacco. Like tobacco, many of the illicit substances are highly addictive, but can be consumed on a regular basis for decades without any demonstrable harm. Like alcohol, most of the substances can be, and are, used by most consumers in moderation, with little in the way of harmful effects; but like alcohol, they also lend themselves to abuse by a minority of users who become addicted or otherwise harm themselves or others as a consequence. And as is the case with both the legal substances, the psychoactive effects of the various illegal drugs vary greatly from one person to another. To be sure, the pharmacology of the substance is important, as is its purity and the manner in which it is consumed. But much also depends upon not only the physiology and psychology of the consumer, but also his expectations regarding the drug, his social milieu, and the broader cultural environment—what Harvard University psychiatrist Norman Zinberg has called the "set and setting" of the drug. It is factors such as these that might change dramatically, albeit in indeterminate ways, were the illicit drugs made legally available.

Can Legalization Work?

It is thus impossible to predict whether legalization would lead to much greater levels of drug abuse, and exact costs comparable to those of alcohol and tobacco abuse. . . .

There are, however, reasons to believe that none of the currently illicit substances would become as popular as alcohol or tobacco, even if they were legalized. Alcohol has long been the principal intoxicant in most societies, including many in which other substances have been legally available. Presumably, its diverse properties account for its popularity—it quenches thirst, goes well with food, and promotes appetite as well as sociability. The popularity of tobacco probably stems not just from its powerful addictive qualities, but from the fact that its psychoactive effects are sufficiently subtle that cigarettes can be integrated with most other human activities. The illicit substances do not share these qualities to the same extent, nor is it likely that they would acquire them if they were legalized. Moreover, none of the illicit substances can compete with alcohol's special place in American culture and history.

An additional advantage of the illicit drugs is that none of them appears to be as insidious as either alcohol or tobacco. Consumed in their more benign forms, few of the illicit substances are as damaging to the human body over the long term as alcohol and tobacco, and none is as strongly linked with violent behavior as alcohol. On the other hand, much of the damage caused today by illegal drugs stems from their consumption in particularly dangerous ways. There is good reason to doubt that many Americans would inject cocaine or heroin into their veins even if given the chance to do so legally. And just as the dramatic growth in the heroin-consuming population during the 1960s leveled off for reasons apparently having little to do with law enforcement, so we can expect a levelling-off—which may already have begun—in the number of people smoking crack. The logic of legalization thus depends upon two assumptions: that most illegal drugs are not so dangerous as is commonly believed; and that the drugs and methods of consumption that are most risky are unlikely to prove appealing to many people, precisely because they are so obviously dangerous. . . .

What Legalization Is Not

It is important to stress what legalization is not. It is not a capitulation to the drug dealers—but rather a means to put them out of business. It is not an endorsement of drug use—but rather a recognition of the rights of adult Americans to make their own choices free of the fear of criminal sanctions. It is not a repudiation of the ''just say no'' approach—but rather an appeal to government to provide assistance and positive inducements, not criminal penalties and more repressive measures, in support of that approach. It is not even a call for the elimination of the criminal-justice system from drug regulation—but rather a proposal for the redirection of its efforts and attention.

''[Legalization] is not a capitulation to the drug dealers—but rather a means to put them out of business.''

There is no question that legalization is a risky policy, since it may lead to an increase in the number of people who abuse drugs. But that is a risk—not a certainty. At the same time, current drug-control policies are failing, and new proposals promise only to be more costly and more repressive. We know that repealing the drug-prohibition laws would eliminate or greatly reduce many of the ills that people commonly identify as part and parcel of the ''drug problem.'' Yet legalization is repeatedly and vociferously dismissed, without any attempt to evaluate it openly and objectively. The past twenty years have demonstrated that a drug policy shaped by exaggerated rhetoric designed to arouse fear has only led to our current disaster. Unless we are willing to honestly evaluate our options, including various legalization strategies, we will run a still greater risk: we may never find the best solution for our drug problems.

Ethan A. Nadelmann is a professor at the Woodrow Wilson School of Public and International Affairs at Princeton University.

Drugs Should Not Be Legalized

Morton M. Kondracke and Charles B. Rangel

Editor's note: The following viewpoint is in two parts. Part I is by Morton M. Kondracke. Part II is by Charles B. Rangel.

I

The next time you hear that a drunk driver has slammed into a school bus full of children or that a stoned railroad engineer has killed 16 people in a train wreck, think about this: if the advocates of legalized drugs have their way, there will be more of this, a lot more. There will also be more unpublicized fatal and maiming crashes, more job accidents, more child neglect, more of almost everything associated with substance abuse: babies born addicted or retarded, teenagers zonked out of their chance for an education, careers destroyed, families wrecked, and people dead of overdoses.

The proponents of drug legalization are right to say that some things will get better. Organized crime will be driven out of the drug business, and there will be a sharp drop in the amount of money (currently about $10 billion per year) that society spends to enforce the drug laws. There will be some reduction in the cost in theft and injury (now about $20 billion) by addicts to get the money to buy prohibited drugs. Internationally, Latin American governments presumably will stop being menaced by drug cartels and will peaceably export cocaine as they now do coffee.

However, this is virtually the limit of the social benefits to be derived from legalization, and they are far outweighed by the costs, which are always underplayed by legalization advocates such as the *Economist*, Princeton scholar Ethan A. Nadelmann, economist Milton Friedman and other libertarians,

columnists William F. Buckley and Richard Cohen, and Mayors Kurt Schmoke of Baltimore and Marion Barry of Washington, D.C. In lives, money, and human woe, the costs are so high, in fact, that society has no alternative but to conduct a real war on the drug trade, although perhaps a smarter one than is currently being waged.

Prohibition

Advocates of legalization love to draw parallels between the drug war and Prohibition. Their point, of course, is that this crusade is as doomed to failure as the last one was, and that we ought to surrender now to the inevitable and stop wasting resources. But there are some important differences between drugs and alcohol. Alcohol has been part of Western culture for thousands of years; drugs have been the rage in America only since about 1962. Of the 115 million Americans who consume alcohol, 85 percent rarely become intoxicated; with drugs, intoxication is the whole idea. Alcohol is consistent chemically, even though it's dispensed in different strengths and forms as beer, wine, and "hard" liquor; with drugs there's no limit to the variations. Do we legalize crack along with snortable cocaine, PCPs as well as marijuana, and LSD and "Ecstasy" as well as heroin? If we don't—and almost certainly we won't—we have a black market, and some continued crime.

But Prohibition is a useful historical parallel for measuring the costs of legalization. Almost certainly doctors are not going to want to write prescriptions for recreational use of harmful substances, so if drugs ever are legalized they will be dispensed as alcohol now is—in government-regulated stores with restrictions on the age of buyers, warnings against abuse (and, probably, with added restrictions on amounts, though this also will create a black market).

In the decade before Prohibition went into effect in 1920, alcohol consumption in the United States averaged 2.6 gallons per person per year. It fell to 0.73 gallons during the Prohibition decade, then doubled to 1.5 gallons in the decade after repeal, and is now back to 2.6 gallons. So illegality suppressed usage to a third or a fourth of its former level. At the same time, incidence of cirrhosis of the liver fell by half.

Drug Use Will Increase

So it seems fair to estimate that use of drugs will at least double, and possibly triple, if the price is cut, supplies are readily available, and society's sanction is lifted. It's widely accepted that there are now 16 million regular users of marijuana, six million of cocaine, a half million of heroin, and another half million of other drugs, totaling 23 million. Dr. Robert DuPont, former director of the National Institute of Drug Abuse and an anti-legalization crusader, says that the instant pleasure afforded by drugs—superior to that available with alcohol—will increase the number of regular users of marijuana and cocaine to about 50 or 60 million and heroin users to ten million.

Between ten percent and 15 percent of all drinkers turn into alcoholics (ten million to 17 million), and these drinkers cost the economy an estimated $117 billion in 1983 ($15 billion for treatment, $89 billion in lost productivity, and $13 billion in accident-related costs). About 200,000 people died last year as a result of alcohol abuse, about 25,000 in auto accidents. How many drug users will turn into addicts, and what will this cost? According to President Reagan's drug abuse policy adviser, Dr. Donald I. McDonald, studies indicate that marijuana is about as habit-forming as alcohol, but for cocaine, 70 percent of users become addicted, as many as with nicotine.

So it seems reasonable to conclude that at least four to six million people will become potheads if marijuana is legal, and that coke addicts will number somewhere between 8.5 million (if regular usage doubles and 70 percent become addicted) and 42 million (if DuPont's high estimate of use is correct). An optimist would have to conclude that the number of people abusing legalized drugs will come close to those hooked on alcohol. A pessimist would figure the human damage as much greater.

Another way of figuring costs is this: the same study (by the Research Triangle Institute of North Carolina) that put the price of alcoholism at $117 billion in 1983 figured the cost of drug abuse then at $60 billion—$15 billion for law enforcement and crime, and $45 billion in lost productivity, damaged health, and other costs. The updated estimate for 1988 drug abuse is $100 billion. If legalizing drugs would save $30 billion now being spent on law enforcement and crime, a doubling of use and abuse means that other costs will rise to $140 billion or $210 billion. This is no bargain for society.

If 200,000 people die every year from alcohol abuse and 320,000 from tobacco smoking, how many will die from legal drugs? Government estimates are that 4,000 to 5,000 people a year are killed in drug-related auto crashes, but this is surely low because accident victims are not as routinely blood-tested for drugs as for alcohol. Legalization advocates frequently cite figures of 3,600 or 4,100 as the number of drug deaths each year reported by hospitals, but this number too is certainly an understatement, based on reports from only 75 big hospitals in 27 metropolitan areas.

"It's clear that legalization of drugs will not benefit human life."

If legalization pushed the total number of drug addicts to only half the number of alcoholics, 100,000 people a year would die. That's the figure cited by McDonald. DuPont guesses that, given the potency of drugs, the debilitating effects of cocaine, the carcinogenic effects of marijuana, and the AIDS potential of injecting legalized heroin, the number of deaths actually could go as high as 500,000 a year. That's a wide range, but it's clear that legalization of drugs will not benefit human life.

All studies show that those most likely to try drugs, get hooked, and die—as opposed to those who suffer from cirrhosis and lung cancer—are young people, who are susceptible to the lure of quick thrills and are terribly adaptable to messages provided by adult society. Under pressure of the current prohibition, the number of kids who use illegal drugs at least once a month has fallen from 39 percent in the late 1970s to 25 percent in 1987, according to the annual survey of high school seniors conducted by the University of Michigan. The same survey shows that attitudes toward drug use have turned sharply negative. But use of legal drugs is still strong. Thirty-eight percent of high school seniors reported getting drunk within the past two weeks, and 27 percent said they smoke cigarettes every day. Drug prohibition is working with kids; legalization would do them harm.

And, even though legalization would lower direct costs for drug law enforcement, it's unlikely that organized crime would disappear. It might well shift to other fields—prostitution, pornography, gambling or burglaries, extortion, and murders-for-hire—much as it did in the period between the end of Prohibition and the beginning of the drug era. As DuPont puts it, "Organized crime is in the business of giving people the things that society decides in its own interest to prohibit. The only way to get rid of organized crime is to make everything legal." Even legalization advocates such as Ethan Nadelmann admit that some street crimes will continue to occur as a result of drug abuse—especially cocaine paranoia, PCP insanity, and the need of unemployable addicts to get money for drugs. Domestic crime, child abuse and neglect surely would increase.

Some legalization advocates suggest merely decriminalizing marijuana and retaining sanctions against other drugs. This would certainly be less costly than total legalization, but it would still be no favor to young people, would increase traffic accidents and productivity losses—and would do nothing to curtail the major drug cartels, which make most of their money trafficking in cocaine.

Legalizers also argue that the government could tax legal drug sales and use the money to pay for anti-drug education programs and treatment centers. But total taxes collected right now from alcohol sales at the local, state, and federal levels come to only $13.1 billion per year—which is a pittance compared with the damage done to society as a result of alcohol abuse. The same would have to be true for drugs—and any tax that resulted in an official drug price that was higher than the street price would open the way once again for black markets and organized crime.

So, in the name of health, economics, and morality, there seems no alternative but to keep drugs illegal and to fight the criminals who traffic in them. . . .

There is, though, room to debate how best to wage this war. . . .

DuPont and others, including Jeffrey Eisenach of the Heritage Foundation, make a strong case that primary emphasis ought to be put on the demand side. . . .

They say that prohibition policy should emphasize routine random urine testing in schools and places of employment, arrests for possession of drugs, and "coercive" treatment programs that compel continued enrollment as a condition of probation and employment. DuPont thinks that corporations have a right to demand that their employees be drug-free because users cause accidents and reduce productivity. He contends that urine testing is no more invasive than the use of metal detectors at airports.

"Liberals have a terrible time with this," says DuPont. "They want to solve every problem by giving people things. They want to love people out of their problems, while conservatives want to punish it out of them. What we want to do is take the profits out of drugs by drying up demand. You do that by raising the social cost of using them to the point where people say, 'I don't want to do this.' This isn't conservative. It's a way to save lives.'"

It is, and it's directly parallel to the way society is dealing with drunk driving and cigarette smoking—not merely through advertising campaigns and surgeon general's warnings, but through increased penalties, social strictures—and prohibitions. Random testing for every employee in America may be going too far, but testing those holding sensitive jobs or workers involved in accidents surely isn't, nor is arresting users, lifting driver's licenses, and requiring treatment. These are not nosy, moralistic intrusions on people's individual rights, but attempts by society to protect itself from danger.

"Were drugs to be legalized now, we would be establishing a new vice—one that, over time, would end or ruin millions of lives."

In the end, they are also humane and moral. There is a chance, with the public and policy-makers aroused to action, that ten years from now drug abuse might be reduced to its pre-1960s levels. Were drugs to be legalized now, we would be establishing a new vice—one that, over time, would end or ruin millions of lives. Worse yet, we would be establishing a pattern of doing the easy thing, surrendering, whenever confronted with a difficult challenge.

II

The escalating drug crisis is beginning to take its toll on many Americans. And now growing numbers of well-intentioned officials and other opinion leaders are saying that the best way to fight drugs is to legalize them. But what they're really admitting is that they're willing to abandon a war that we have not even begun to fight.

For example, the newly elected and promising Mayor of Baltimore, Kurt Schmoke, at a meeting of the United States Conference of Mayors, called for a full-scale study of the feasibility of legalization. His comments could not have come at a worse time, for we are in the throes of the worst drug epidemic in our history.

No National Strategy

Here we are talking about legalization and we have yet to come up with any formal national strategy or any commitment from the Administration on fighting drugs beyond mere words. We have never fought the war on drugs like we have fought other legitimate wars—with all the forces at our command.

Just the thought of legalization brings up more problems and concerns than already exist.

Advocates of legalization should be reminded, for example, that it's not as simple as opening up a chain of friendly neighborhood pharmacies. Press them about some of the issues and questions surrounding this proposed legalization, and they never seem to have any answers. At least not any logical, well thought out ones.

Those who tout legalization remind me of fans sitting in the cheap seats at the ballpark. They may have played the game, and they may think they know all the rules, but from where they're sitting they can't judge the action.

Questions

Has anybody ever considered which narcotic and psychotropic drugs would be legalized?

Would we allow all drugs to become legally sold and used, or would we select the most abused few, such as cocaine, heroin and marijuana?

Who would administer the dosages—the state or the individual?

What quantity of drugs would each individual be allowed to get?

What about addicts: Would we not have to give them more in order to satisfy their craving, or would we give them enough to just whet their appetites?

What do we do about those who are experimenting? Do we sell them the drugs, too, and encourage them to pick up the habit?

Furthermore, will the Government establish tax-supported facilities to sell these drugs?

Would we get the supply from the same foreign countries that support our habit now, or would we create our own internal sources and "dope factories," paying people the minimum wage to churn out mounds of cocaine and bales of marijuana?

Would there be an age limit on who can purchase drugs, as exists with alcohol? What would the market price be and who would set it? Would private industry be allowed to have a stake in any of this?

What are we going to do about underage youngsters—the age group hardest hit by the crack crisis? Are we going to give them identification cards? How can we prevent adults from purchasing drugs for them?

How many people are projected to become addicts as a result of the introduction of cheaper, more available drugs sanctioned by government?

Since marijuana remains in a person's system for weeks, what would we do about pilots, railroad engineers, surgeons, police, cross-country truckers and nuclear plant employees who want to use it during off-duty hours? And what would be the effect on the health insurance industry?

Many of the problems associated with drug abuse will not go away just because of legalization. For too long we have ignored the root cause, failing to see the connection between drugs and hopelessness, helplessness and despair.

We often hear that legalization would bring an end to the bloodshed and violence that has often been associated with the illegal narcotics trade. The profit will be taken out of it, so to speak, as will be the urge to commit crime to get money to buy drugs. But what gives anybody the impression that legalization would deter many jobless and economically deprived people from resorting to crime to pay for their habits?

"Many of the problems associated with drug abuse will not go away just because of legalization."

Even in a decriminalized atmosphere, money would still be needed to support habits. Because drugs would be cheaper and more available, people would want more and would commit more crime. Does anybody really think the black market would disappear? There would always be opportunities for those who saw profit in peddling larger quantities, or improved versions, of products that are forbidden or restricted.

Undermines Education

Legalization would completely undermine any educational effort we undertake to persuade kids about the harmful effects of drugs. Today's kids have not yet been totally lost to the drug menace, but if we legalize these substances they'll surely get the message that drugs are O.K.

Not only would our young people realize that the threat of jail and punishment no longer exists. They would pick up the far more damaging message that the use of illegal narcotics does not pose a significant enough health threat for the Government to ban its use.

If we really want to do something about drug abuse, let's end this nonsensical talk about legalization right now.

Morton M. Kondracke is an editor for The New Republic. *Democratic congressman Charles B. Rangel is chairman of the House Select Committee on Narcotics Abuse and Control.*

viewpoint 47

Legalizing Drugs Would Be Beneficial

Randy E. Barnett

Some drugs make people feel good. That is why some people use them. Some of these drugs are alleged to have side effects so destructive that many advise against their use. The same may be said about statutes that attempt to prohibit the manufacture, sale, and use of drugs. Using statutes in this way makes some people feel good because they think they are "doing something" about what they believe to be a serious social problem. Others who support these laws are not so altruistically motivated. Employees of law enforcement bureaus and academics who receive government grants to study drug use, for example, may gain financially from drug prohibition. But as with using drugs, using drug laws can have moral and practical side-effects so destructive that they argue against ever using legal institutions in this manner.

Addicted to Drug Laws

One might even say—and not altogether metaphorically—that some people become psychologically or economically *addicted* to drug laws. That is, some people continue to support these statutes despite the massive and unavoidable ill-effects that result. . . .

Yet in a free society governed by democratic principles, these addicts cannot be compelled to give up their desire to control the consumption patterns of others. Nor can they be forced to support legalization in spite of their desires. In a democratic system, they may voice and vote their opinions about such matters no matter how destructive the consequences of their desires are to themselves, or—more importantly—to others. Only rational persuasion may be employed to wean them from this habit. As part of this process of persuasion, drug-law addicts must be exposed to the destruction

their addiction wreaks on drug users, law enforcement, and on the general public. They must be made to understand the inherent limits of using law to accomplish social objectives. . . .

The Effects on Drug Users

At least part of the motivation for drug prohibition is that drug use is thought to harm those who engage in this activity. A perceived benefit of drug prohibition is that fewer people will engage in self-harming conduct than would in the absence of prohibition. While this contention will not be disputed here, there is another dimension of the issue of harm to drug users that may seem obvious to most when pointed out, but nonetheless is generally ignored in policy discussions of drug prohibition. To what degree are the harms of drug use caused not by intoxicating drugs, but by the fact that such drugs are illegal?

The most obvious harm to drug users caused by drug laws is the legal and physical jeopardy in which they are placed. Imprisonment must generally be considered a harm to the person imprisoned or it would hardly be an effective deterrent. To deter certain conduct it is advocated that we punish—in the sense of forcibly inflict unpleasantness upon—those who engage in this conduct. In so doing it is hoped that people will be discouraged from engaging in the prohibited conduct.

But what about those who are not discouraged and who engage in such conduct anyway? Does the practice of punishing these persons make life better or worse for them? The answer is clear. As harmful as using drugs may be to someone, being imprisoned makes matters much worse. . . .

Illegalization makes the prices of drugs rise. By increasing scarcity, the confiscation and destruction of drugs causes the price of the prohibited good to rise. And by increasing the risk to those who manufacture and sell, drug laws raise the cost of production and distribution, necessitating higher prices that reflect a "risk premium." (Price increases will not incur indefinitely, however, because at some level higher prices will induce more production.) Like the threat of punishment, higher prices may very well discourage some from using drugs who would otherwise do so. This is, in fact, the principal rationale for interdiction policies. But higher prices take their toll on those who are not deterred, and these adverse effects are rarely emphasized in discussions of drug laws.

Higher prices require higher income by users. If users cannot earn enough by legal means to pay higher prices, then they may be induced to engage in illegal conduct—theft, burglary, robbery—that they would not otherwise engage in. The increased harm caused to the victims of these crimes will be discussed below as a cost inflicted by drug laws on the general public. Of relevance here is the adverse effects that drug laws have on the life of drug users. By raising the costs of drugs, drug laws breed criminality. They induce some drug users who would not otherwise have contemplated criminal conduct to develop into the kind of people who are willing to commit crimes against others. . . .

Drug laws attempt to prohibit the use of substances that some people wish to consume. Thus because the legal sale of drugs is prohibited, people who still wish to use drugs are forced to do business with the kind of people who are willing to make and sell drugs in spite of the risk of punishment. Their dealings must be done away from the police. This puts users in great danger of physical harm in two ways.

First, they are likely to be the victims of crime. I would estimate that approximately half the murder cases I prosecuted were "drug related" in the sense that the victim was killed because it was thought he had either drugs or money from the sale of drugs. Crimes are also committed against persons who seek out criminals from whom to purchase prohibited drugs. These kinds of cases are brought to the attention of the authorities when the victim's body is found. A robbery of a drug user or dealer is hardly likely to be reported to the police.

Second, users are forced to rely upon criminals to regulate the quality and strength of the drugs they buy. No matter how carefully they measure their dosages, an unexpectedly potent supply may result in an overdose. And if the drug user is suspected to be a police informant, the dosage may deliberately be made potent by the supplier. . . .

Drug Laws Criminalize Users

Prohibition automatically makes drug users into "criminals." While this point would seem too obvious to merit discussion, the effects of criminalization can be subtle and hidden.

Criminalized drug users may not be able to obtain legitimate employment. This increases still further the likelihood that the artificially high prices of illicit drugs will lead drug users to engage in criminal conduct to obtain income. It is difficult to overestimate the harm caused by forcing drug users into a life of crime. Once this threshold is crossed, there is often no return. Such a choice would not be nearly so compelling if prohibited substances were legal.

Further, criminalization increases the hold that law enforcement agents have on drug users. This hold permits law enforcment agents to extort illegal payments from users or to coerce them into serving as informants who must necessarily engage in risky activity against others. Thus illegalization both motivates and enables the police to inflict harm on drug users in ways that would be impossible in the absence of the leverage provided by drug laws.

"Drug laws harm users of drugs well beyond any harm caused by drug use itself."

In sum, drug laws harm users of drugs well beyond any harm caused by drug use itself, and this extra harm is an unavoidable consequence of using legal means to prevent people from engaging in activity they deem desirable. While law enforcement efforts typically cause harm to criminals who victimize others, such effects are far more problematic with laws whose stated goals include helping the very people that the legal means succeed in harming. Support for drug laws in the face of these harms is akin to saying that we have to punish, criminalize, poison, rob, and murder drug users to save them from the harmful consequences of using intoxicating drugs.

To avoid these consequences, some have proposed abolishing laws against personal use of certain drugs, while continuing to ban the manufacture and sale of these substances. However only the first and last of the five adverse consequences of drug prohibition just discussed result directly from punishing and criminalizing users. The other three harms to the user result indirectly from punishing those who manufacture and sell drugs. Decriminalizing the use of drugs would undoubtedly be an improvement over the status quo, but the remaining restrictions on manufacturing and sale would continue to cause serious problems for drug users beyond the problems caused by drug use itself.

As long as force is used to minimize drug use, these harms are unavoidable. They are caused by (1) the use of force (the legal means) to inflict pain on users, thereby directly harming them; and (2) the dangerous and criminalizing black market in drugs that results from efforts to stop some from making and selling a product others wish to consume. There is nothing that more enlightened law enforcement personnel or a more efficient administrative apparatus can do to prevent these effects from occurring. . . .

The Effects on the Public

The harmful side effects of drug laws are not limited to drug users. This section highlights the various harms that drug laws inflict on the general public. There is an old saying in the criminal courts that is particularly apt here: "What goes around, comes around." In an effort to inflict pain on drug users, drug laws inflict considerable costs on nonusers as well.

The most obvious cost of drug prohibition is the expenditure of scarce resources to enforce drug laws—resources that can thus not be used to enforce other laws or be allocated to other productive activities outside of law enforcement.

Every dollar spent to punish a drug user or seller is a dollar that cannot be spent collecting restitution from a robber. Every hour spent investigating a drug user or seller is an hour that could have been used to find a missing child. Every trial held to prosecute a drug user or seller is court time that could be used to prosecute a rapist in a case that might otherwise have been plea bargained. These and countless other expenditures are the "opportunity costs" of drug prohibition.

"Every hour spent investigating a drug user or seller is an hour that could have been used to find a missing child."

By artificially raising the price of illicit drugs and thereby forcing drug users to obtain large sums of money, drug laws create powerful incentives to commit property and other profitable crimes. And the interaction between drug users and criminally inclined drug sellers presents users with many opportunities to become involved in all types of illegal conduct.

Finally, usually neglected in discussions of drugs and crime are the numerous "drug-related" robberies and murders (sometimes of innocent parties wrongly thought to have drugs) that the constant interaction between users and criminal sellers creates. Drug dealers and buyers are known to carry significant quantities of either cash or valuable substances. They must deliberately operate outside the vision of the police. They can rely only on self-help for personal protection. . . .

Drug Laws and Invasion of Privacy

The fact that drug use takes place in private, and that drug users and sellers conspire to keep their activities away from the prying eyes of the police, means that surveillance must be extremely intrusive to be effective. It must involve gaining access to private areas to watch for this activity.

One way to accomplish this is for a police officer, or more likely an informant, to pose as a buyer or seller. This means that the police must initiate the illegal activity and run the risk that the crime being prosecuted was one that would not have occurred but for the police instigation. And, since possession alone is also illegal, searches of persons without probable cause might also be necessary to find contraband.

Such illegal conduct by police is to be expected when one seeks to prohibit activity that is deliberately kept away from *normal* police scrutiny by the efforts of both parties to the transaction. This means that the police must intrude into private areas if they are to detect these acts. The police would be overwhelmed if they actually obtained evidence establishing probable cause for every search for illicit drugs, no matter how small the quantity. But if no constitutional grounds exist for such an intrusion, then a police department and its officers are forced to decide which is more important: the protection of constitutional rights or the failure to get results that will be prominently reported by the local media.

The Weakening of Constitutional Rights

The fact that such privacy-invading conduct by police may be unconstitutional and therefore illegal does not prevent it from occurring. Some of those who are most concerned about the harm caused by drug laws are lawyers who have confronted the massive violations of constitutional rights that drug laws have engendered. Such unconstitutional behavior is particularly likely, given our bizarre approach to policing the police.

At present we attempt to rectify police misconduct mainly by preventing the prosecution from using any illegally seized evidence at trial. While this would generally be enough to scuttle a drug law prosecution, it will not prevent the police from achieving at least some of their objectives. They may be more concerned with successfully making an arrest and confiscating contraband than they are with obtaining a conviction. This is especially true when they would have neither confiscation nor conviction without an unconstitutional search.

In most instances, the success of a suppression motion depends on whether the police tell the truth about their constitutional mistake in their report and at trial. They may not do so if they think that their conduct is illegal. "There is substantial evidence to suggest that police often lie in order to bring their conduct within the limits of the practices sanctioned by judicial decisions." The only person who can usually contradict the police version of the incident is the defendant, and the credibility of defendants does not generally compare favorably with that of police officers.

Those who have committed no crime—who possess no contraband—will have no effective recourse at all. Because no evidence was seized, there is no evidence to exclude from a trial. As a practical matter, then, the police only have to worry about unconstitutional searches if something illicit turns up; but if something turns up and they can confiscate it and make an arrest, they may be better off than if they respect constitutional rights and do nothing at all. Moreover, by encouraging such frequent constitutional violations, the enforcement of drug laws desensitizes the police to constitutional safeguards in other areas as well.

The constitutional rights of the general public are therefore threatened in at least two ways. First, the burden placed on law enforcement officials to enforce possessory laws without victims virtually compels them to engage in wholesale violations of constitutional prohibitions against unreasonable searches and seizures. For every search that produces contraband there are untold scores of searches that do not. And given our present method of deterring police misconduct by excluding evidence of guilt, there is little effective recourse against the police available to those who are innocent of any crime.

"By demanding that the police do a job that cannot be done effectively without violating constitutional rights, drug-law users ensure that more constitutional rights will be violated."

Second, the widespread efforts of police and prosecutors to stretch the outer boundaries of legal searches can be expected, over time, to contribute to the eventual loosening up of the rules by the courts. The more cases that police bring against obviously guilty defendants (in drug prosecutions, the evidence being suppressed strongly supports the conclusion that the defendants are guilty), the more opportunities and incentives the appellate courts will have to find a small exception here, a slight expansion there. And instead of prosecuting the police for their illegal conduct, the prosecutor's office becomes an insidious and publicly financed source of political and legal agitation in defense of such illegal conduct.

One point should be made clear. The police are not the heavies in this tale. They are only doing what drug-law users have asked them to do in the only way that such a task may effectively be accomplished. It is the drug-law users who must bear the responsibility for the grave social problems caused by the policies they advocate. By demanding that the police do a job that cannot be done effectively without violating constitutional rights, drug-law users ensure that more constitutional rights will be violated and that the respect of law enforcement personnel for these rights will be weakened. . . .

The actions of drug law enforcement create an artificial scarcity of a desired product. As a result sellers receive a *higher* price than they would without such laws. While it is true that drug prohibition makes it more costly to engage in the activity, this cost is partially or wholly offset by an increased return (higher prices) and by attracting individuals to the activity who are less risk-averse (criminals)—that is, individuals who are less likely to discount their realized cash receipts by their risk of being caught. For such persons, the subjective costs of providing illicit drugs are actually less than they are for more honest persons.

Social Consequences

The social consequences of the wholesale corruption of our legal system by the large amounts of black-market money to be made in the drug trade have never been adequately appreciated. The extremely lucrative nature of the illicit drug trade makes the increased corruption of police, prosecutors, and judges all but inevitable. And this corruption extends far beyond the enforcement of drug laws.

Since the prohibition of alcohol we have witnessed the creation of a multibillion dollar industry to supply various prohibited goods and services. The members of this industry are ruthless profit-maximizers whose comparative market advantage is their ability and willingness to rely on violence and corruption to maintain their market share and to enforce their agreements.

The prohibition of alcohol and other drugs has created a criminal subculture that makes little of the distinction between crimes with victims and those without. To make matters worse, to hide the source of their income from tax and other authorities requires these criminals to become heavily involved in "legitimate" or legal businesses so that they may launder their illegally obtained income. They bring to these businesses their brutal tactics, which they employ to drive out the honest entrepreneur.

The fact that law enforcement personnel are corrupted by drug laws should be no more surprising than the fact that many people decide to get high by ingesting certain chemicals. The tragic irony of drug laws is that by attempting to prevent the latter, they make the former far more prevalent. Drug-law users must confront the question of whether the increased systemic corruption that their favored policies unavoidably cause is too high a price to pay for whatever reduction in the numbers of drug users is achieved. . . .

Legal institutions are not capable of correcting every ill in the world. On this point most would agree. Serious harm results when legal means are employed to correct harms that are not amenable to legal regulation. . . .

Curing the Drug-Law Addiction

An addiction to drug laws is caused by an inadequate understanding of individual rights and the vital role such rights play in deciding matters of legality. As a result, policies are implemented that cause serious harm to the very individuals whom these policies were devised to help and to the general public.

"An addiction to drug laws is caused by an inadequate understanding of individual rights and the vital role such rights play in deciding matters of legality."

If the rights of individuals to choose how to use their person and possessions are fully respected, there is no guaranty that they will exercise their rights wisely. Some may mistakenly choose the path of finding happiness in a bottle or in a vial. Others may wish to help these people by persuading them of their folly. But we must not give in to the powerful temptation to grant some the power to impose their consumptive preferences on others by force. This power—the "essence" of drug laws—is not only "addictive" once it is tasted, it carries with it one of the few guaranties in life: the guaranty of untold corruption and human misery.

Author Randy E. Barnett is associate law professor at the Illinois Institute of Technology at the Chicago-Kent College of Law.

"We need to send a simple and unambiguous message through the narcotics underworld: If you deal drugs, you're going to do time."

Legalizing Drugs Would Be Harmful

George Bush

Editor's note: The following viewpoint is an excerpt from George Bush's speech to the Fraternal Order of Police in Columbus, Ohio.

To win the war on drugs, we must go forward on four fronts at once—prevention, interdiction, law enforcement, and treatment:

—First and most important, we must try to stop drug use before it starts, with education programs like DARE, Drug Abuse Resistance Education, early in life, when they are most effective, and on into the work place.

—Second, we must curtail the narcotics supply with bold and determined action to destroy crops and labs, both at home and abroad, and by patrolling our borders vigorously. You have been part of this effort, working with federal agents to intercept drug shipments in record amounts. But we must do more.

—Third, we must increase the certainty and the severity of punishment, for dealers and users alike—and I'll talk more about this.

—And fourth, we must help those who are trying to escape the quicksand of addiction with programs of rehabilitation, evaluated and funded on the basis of their success rate.

There are those who simply look for the easy, comfortable answers—blame foreigners for growing the crops, tell the cops to catch the dealers—but that, my friends, is demagoguery.

Fundamentally, the drug problem in America is not one of supply, but of demand. As long as there is a demand for drugs, there will always be a supply.

Enlisted in the War on Drugs

The single greatest victory we've had in this war on drugs is the fact that America has enlisted. Since we took office, there has been a dramatic shift in the public's attitude toward drugs, from tolerance to intolerance, and where attitudes change, behavior follows.

The climate is now there, as it was never before, to cut drug use by making the users pay a price.

Testing for drug use should be required of anyone responsible for the public safety—airline pilots, for example, or prison guards. Indeed, testing should be required of anyone whose actions at work could put others at risk.

There are those who say that drug testing is an invasion of individual rights. But the use of drugs is not just a personal matter, like buying a coat or a car . . . it's a matter that affects the health and safety of others. We've run out of patience, and we've run out of pity. And it's time to say: We've had enough.

Some say drug use is just a health problem; I say it's a criminal problem. More than 70 percent of the men arrested for serious crimes test positive for drugs. Half of all the murders in the country are drug-related.

There's no such thing as "casual" drug use when it's financing the drug traffic that's tearing our cities apart. And that money is just as likely to come from the suburbs as it is from downtown.

States that have decriminalized possession should *re*criminalize it. And to those who say drugs should be legalized, I say this—legalization is just another word for surrender—and surrender is not in America's vocabulary.

While we should be concerned about rehabilitation and saving the life of a kid, drug users and possessors should know that they may end up in prison if they don't straighten out. We should deny bail or parole to those who fail to stay drug-free after arrest and release, with periodic drug testing.

The new "zero tolerance" policy—the one that's led to the seizure of cars and planes and yachts—is important not because it will stop the flow of drugs into this country, but because it sends the right

George Bush, a speech delivered to the Fraternal Order of Police in Columbus, Ohio on June 26, 1988.

message: No amount of drug use is acceptable.

I don't mind inconveniencing a yacht owner or a car driver if it saves the life of a kid. If people can lose their cars for parking violations, surely they should lose them for carrying drugs. ''Zero tolerance'' should be the policy of every state in the country.

Asset seizures work. The mayor of Newark told me of one offender who didn't agree—at first. The mayor said, ''We took away his Mercedes. He said, 'I'll get another one.' We took away that one,'' the mayor said, ''and now he's riding a bicycle.''

In the Washington, D.C. suburbs, asset seizures have paid for the tools police sought to use against drug dealers—new Berettas, high-powered binoculars and surveillance cameras, and the cash needed for drug buys.

Fund Law Enforcement

At the federal level, we must provide the resources to fight this war. Congress is full of rhetorical heroes on the issue of drugs, but when it comes to law enforcement, they all go AWOL.

They cut our budget request for the Coast Guard in 1987 by $72 million—to provide more money for mass transit and Amtrak. Over the last 4 years, they also cut the DEA [Drug Enforcement Administration] by $28 million; the FBI by $10 million; the U.S. Marshals Service by $11 million; and the U.S. Attorneys by $22 million.
Attorneys by $22 million.

One sickening result: Federal drug task forces are turning down important cases—simply because there aren't enough prosecutors.

''Federal drug task forces are turning down important cases—simply because there aren't enough prosecutors.''

With cuts like these, we can't even eradicate the drugs being grown on our own public lands.

And when we've asked for new prison funds, Congress has ''just said no.'' That's not good enough.

The single most important thing Congress could do in the war on drugs is alleviate the shortage of state prison space, responsible for the premature release of countless criminals.

According to some studies, we are spending anywhere from $2 billion to $5 billion a year on domestic military bases that we don't need any more. A priority of mine will be to work with Congress to eliminate such bases. Where needed, we should convert them to minimum-security prisons for use by the states.

Congress also should recodify the federal death penalty statutes to meet constitutional standards set

in a 1972 Supreme Court decision. But instead, it has been going in the wrong direction. The liberals in the Senate singlehandedly derailed the sentencing guidelines needed to implement a federal death penalty.

We've heard a lot of tough political talk about drugs, but when are we going to see some tough action? In my view, some crimes are so heinous, so outrageous, so brutal that the death penalty is warranted. And furthermore, I believe the death penalty in these circumstances would be a deterrent.

For those who commit drug-related murders, for the drug kingpins who are poisoning our kids, the penalty should be death. If this is war—then let's treat it as such. Let's get these killers off the street.

And for anyone who kills a law enforcement officer, no penalty is too tough.

In Connecticut, a patrolman was shot and killed during a routine traffic check, by a guy with a history of shooting at, and assaulting, police officers. But because the killer said he was high on cocaine, he avoided the death penalty under Connecticut law. It seems that being on cocaine is a (quote) ''extenuating circumstance.''

That's not justice. The patrolman's fiancee put it exactly right when she said of the killer, ''He will be allowed visits with his family; we will visit the cemetery.''

Our Administration, I'm proud to say, has appointed tougher judges and tougher prosecutors, and they're getting results—two and a half times as many drug offenders charged, convicted, and sent to prison in 1987, compared to 1980. We've increased our conviction rate from 75 percent to 84 percent, and the sentences are one-third longer than they were.

But our work is far from over. We need to unlock the law enforcement handcuffs designed by politicians and judges who worry more about the rights of criminals and the views of the ACLU [American Civil Liberties Union] than they do about keeping the rest of us safe in our homes and communities.

No Deals, No Mercy

Drug dealers are domestic terrorists, killing cops and kids, and should be treated as such: No deals and no mercy.

Certainty of sentencing is the key to deterrence. We need to send a simple and unambiguous message through the narcotics underworld: If you deal drugs, you're going to do time.

We can start by implementing the new federal sentencing guidelines that mandate consistent, tougher sentences for drug offenders, guidelines developed by the U.S. Sentencing Commission. If judges won't adopt these guidelines, we should enact them into law.

And the states should do the same. Case in point: A woman in New York was arrested recently for the attempted sale of 174 vials of crack. It is bad enough that the penalty for this felony is only one year in prison. But after a plea bargain, the woman walked off with probation. She won't spend a day in prison for her crime.

Only 14 percent of the drug felons convicted in New York City in 1987 were sentenced to as much as a year with no probation.

One official of the New York Police Department said, "It is not unusual to arrest the same person 30 to 40 times for selling drugs on the street," and he said one drug dealer had been arrested 68 times.

The view that all convicts can be rehabilitated is not just naive, it's dead wrong. Career criminals commit 70 percent of the violent crimes in this country.

The idea that first-degree murderers sentenced to life without parole should get unsupervised weekend furloughs and commuted sentences is not just naive, it's dangerous. If a judge says "life without parole," it should mean just that.

The 1984 Armed Career Criminal Act makes it a federal offense for a criminal convicted of 3 major felonies to be found with a gun. The sentence is a mandatory 15 years to life. That's a step in the right direction.

"We are all the victims of these drug lords, these predators on our society."

To encourage states to use *their* habitual offender statutes, we should provide federal jail space for them where needed.

We also need to change the legal technicalities that set criminals free. There's something wrong with the system when the modern-day version of a prison break is crawling through a loophole. . . .

Finally, let me say to those of you in the front lines of this war: We owe you more than just gratitude. We owe you our support for measures to improve your physical safety. Those include:

—Tough mandatory penalties for any violent crime against a law enforcement officer;

—Clarifying the FBI's authority, upon the request of the appropriate law enforcement agency, to institute a full field investigation of the murder or serious attack of any law enforcement officer; and

—Ensuring that every law enforcement officer in the nation who wants body armor has access to it.

The war on drugs wasn't started by a foreign power or declared by Congress. It is a spontaneous uprising of the American people. And to win it, we need to be as tough and resourceful now as we had to be when we went to war 40 years ago.

We are all the victims of these drug lords, these predators on our society—our families and our communities, peaceful, orderly places that are all too often now just a memory—places where doors weren't always locked, and parents didn't worry about their children when they went out to play, and schools where the corridors were safe, and teachers didn't worry about getting knifed or assaulted in the classroom.

To recapture America, we've got to do, in the words of Los Angeles Police Chief Daryl Gates, "whatever it takes, for as long as it takes."

After serving as Vice President for eight years under Ronald Reagan, George Bush was elected US President in November 1988.

"Only one policy offers any hope of improvement: To stop treating people who use or sell illicit drugs as criminals."

Drug Laws Increase Crime

Stephen Chapman and Lawrence Wade

Editor's note: The following viewpoint is in two parts. Part I is by Stephen Chapman. Part II is by Lawrence Wade.

I

"The casual user may think when he takes a line of cocaine or smokes a joint in the privacy of his nice condo, listening to his expensive stereo, that he's somehow not bothering anyone. But there is a trail of death and destruction that leads directly to his door. I'm saying that if you're a casual drug user, you are an accomplice to murder."

That was Nancy Reagan's broadcast against drug use. It was certainly timely. A few days earlier, a New York City policeman, assigned to guard a man who had been threatened by drug dealers, was shot to death in his patrol car. The nation's capital is being terrorized by a wave of drug-related killings. The attorney general of Colombia was murdered, apparently in revenge for his campaign against the nation's cocaine cartel.

But neither the first lady nor anyone else in the government appears ready for a remedy that might actually put a stop to incidents like these. Despite the apparent urgency of the problem, and despite the fierce rhetoric, the only proposal is more of the same.

The Prohibition Precedent

A 20-year war on drugs, which has been escalated by the administration, has done nothing to make us safer. Only one policy offers any hope of improvement: To stop treating people who use or sell illicit drugs as criminals.

Americans forget that there is a precedent for the crisis. During the 1920s, cities like Chicago served as battlefields for a grim war between criminals and police. In one three-year stretch, the violence in Chicago claimed the lives of more than 400 criminals and policemen. Between 1920 and 1933, New York City had more than 1,000 gangland murders.

The cause of all this was a war on another drug—alcohol. The roots of the violence lay not in the inherent qualities of alcohol, but in its prohibition. Likewise, what spurs the bloodshed in the drug trade is not the drugs but the attempt to suppress them. What ended the Prohibition-era violence was the legalization of alcohol. Today, distillers and liquor store owners don't fight for market share with machine guns.

A Crime Epidemic

In some places, especially Washington, D.C., drug-related crime is an epidemic. In 1985, the capital had 25 drug-related murders. In 1987, there were 130. In the first two months of 1988, at least 42 people died in such episodes, double the rate [in 1987]. Other crimes in the capital show the same trend. The number of indictments on drug-related felonies has risen sevenfold since 1982.

These developments happened even as the administration was mounting its anti-drug offensive, which has accomplished little in slowing the flow. *The Washington Post* reports that cocaine use "is up, inventories are high, prices are down and the cocaine sold on the street has never been higher." When New York Democrat Charles Rangel, chairman of the House committee on narcotics abuse, was asked about advances in halting drug traffic, he replied, "We haven't made any."

While drug use persists, the illegal commerce in drugs has gotten more violent. Execution-style slayings now dominate the news in Washington, where the crime wave springs from an attempt by Jamaican drug gangs to seize a share of the business, something resisted by established dealers.

Stephen Chapman, "Real Villians of Drug War in Our Backyard," *Conservative Chronicle*, March 16, 1988. Reprinted by permission of Creators Syndicate Inc.
Lawrence Wade, "Do Our Drug Laws Make Things Worse?" *The Washington Times*, March 9, 1988. Reprinted with the author's permission.

A police spokesman in suburban Prince George's County, Maryland, explained it: "When you're an outsider, you have to cut yourself a piece of the territory that's already owned by someone else. How do you do it? You start shooting."

The pathology exactly matches that of Prohibition. By making drugs illegal, the government raises their price. That makes them more profitable. The more profitable they are, the more attractive to those suppliers who are willing to use illegal and even violent methods to sell them.

Raising the price also incites crime of another sort. Addicts who need hundreds of dollars a day to finance their addictions have few options but to steal. So it's not surprising to discover, as a Justice Department study did, that some 70 percent of the people arrested for serious crimes are drug users. The lesson is not that drug use itself causes larceny and violence, but that the illegality of these drugs pushes users into other, more serious types of crime.

"To a growing number, it is becoming obvious: The enemy may be our drug laws."

Legalizing the illicit drugs that have been the object of so much hysteria may sound like a drastic step. Nothing else, though, holds any prospect of restoring a measure of security to our cities.

Nancy Reagan and the other crusaders against drugs may continue to preach that still tougher measures are needed. But no one should imagine they will succeed at anything but perpetuating the bloody status quo. And no one should have any doubt who are the real accomplices to murder.

II

New York Mayor Ed Koch doesn't come to mind when you think of compassion.

But in a full-page New York Times ad aimed at President Reagan, Mr. Koch showed heart-rending concern about the failing war on drugs.

Atop the ad was a grainy photo of young Edward Byrne, a New York policeman gunned down—Mr. Koch suspects—by a drug kingpin.

"Let's make certain he didn't die for nothing," the mayor wrote to Mr. Reagan. He called on the president to cut foreign aid to countries such as Panama and Mexico that export illegal drugs.

"We must band together as one race with one voice," the mayor wrote. "For once, we must fight our common enemy instead of fighting each other."

Mayor Koch is right. We cannot afford to squabble, while drugs like cocaine and heroin cause more than $60 billion in social devastation.

But to a growing number, it is becoming obvious: The enemy may be our drug laws.

Until recently the very idea of legalizing drugs was thought to be so radical that it was dismissed upon mention. This was before we spent $21.54 billion—*in just seven years*—fighting the war on drugs.

Critics like Mr. Koch say, "Take better aim." And he correctly fingers Panama and Mexico.

And Education Secretary William J. Bennett, speaking before the White House Conference for a Drug Free America, suggested that to cut off drugs we should send in the Marines.

Making Things Worse

But even a grad of Sesame Street economics knows that cutting the drug supply would only worsen crime and social unrest related to illegal drugs.

With an estimated 23-41 million regular users, what would happen if we cut back cocaine, marijuana and heroin? The users would gladly pay even higher prices for the highs their drugs give them. And this inflation would escalate related crime.

The Justice Department studied 12 cities—Los Angeles, Phoenix, Washington and Detroit among them—and found that a shocking 53-79 percent of men arrested used drugs.

David Boaz of the Cato Institute, a Washington think tank, writes that addicts here each steal an estimated $600 worth of goods daily to feed $100-a-day habits.

Much drug-related crime happens in cities. But where would users turn if drug prices were inflated by interdiction? They would turn to the wealthy suburbs, many of which already see increasing rates of crime.

The Rambo Solution

And how would we cut the supply? What weapons could we muster that we've not used already?

Like Education's Mr. Bennett, some folk are so frustrated that they're suggesting weaponry that would pillage our budget and rape our freedoms and rights.

"Call out the National Guard!"

"Use more of the Coast Guard!"

"We need a drug czar," says New York Democratic Rep. Charles B. Rangel.

What makes these Rambos think federal forces would help? Sure, we'd cut many types of crimes by placing gunners on every corner. But at what price?

Would Mr. Bennett sacrifice his proposed $20.3 billion budget?

Would AIDS sufferers give up $1.3 billion in research and education to help us beat drugs?

America is broke. We already borrow billions to pay for services we demand of government.

We could barely afford the $22 billion spent on drug battles. Can we afford to sacrifice freedom in a losing war against drugs?

Suppliers of illegal drugs are immoral and despicable. But these suppliers aren't the big enemy. Mayor Koch's intentions are good. But his aim is faulty. Taking potshots at the Manuel Noriegas won't win the war on drugs.

Nations that export drugs aren't the big enemy, and neither are drug users. As First Lady Nancy Reagan says, users are "accomplices to murder." But with all respect for Mrs. Reagan's successes, "just say no" cannot win the big war on drugs.

Saying no won't win, because drug users are addicted. If millions of us can't give up legal drugs like alcohol and cigarettes, how can we expect 40 million hard-core users to kiss off marijuana, heroin and cocaine?

Perhaps you've seen the movie of H.G. Wells' classic, "The War of the Worlds." There's a scene where the military nukes the alien invaders. The mushroom cloud rises. But from within the swirling dust, the aliens' deadly spaceships emerge—unscathed.

"Guns, tanks, bombs! They're like toys against them!" shouts a frustrated officer.

Earlier, a scientist had warned them, "This kind of defense is useless against that kind of power."

What's going on in America isn't science fiction. It's a real war against a real enemy. But we've been fighting a force as invincible as Wells' aliens: the mighty force of supply and demand.

How *can* we win?

"Saying no won't win, because drug users are addicted."

What makes supplying drugs worth the risk is that drugs are made cheaply, then sold at astronomical prices. Our drug laws support these prices. It is as frightening—and as simple—as that.

And this is why Mr. Koch's ad would do little good, even if Mr. Reagan were to end aid to drug exporting countries. California's annual crop of marijuana is massive. Soon, botanists would devise ways to grow other illegal drugs domestically.

Not Advocating Drugs

Don't get me wrong.

I'm not advocating cocaine, heroin or marijuana. I am not a user. Misuse of just one legal drug—alcohol—cost an estimated 24,000 motor vehicle deaths in 1986.

My father's brother was an alcoholic. He died so young, I barely knew him.

I've known big-hearted folk whose lives were blown senseless by legal and illegal drugs.

A drug addict can get cocaine or heroin as easily as a bottle of Jack Daniels. Because his habit is illegal, however, he can't get the help needed to get off drugs.

I agree with Mayor Koch: While we're defeating each other, the fat and filthy drug barons are winning.

But it could be we're hitting the wrong targets. The real enemy may be our drug laws.

Stephen Chapman and Lawrence Wade are nationally syndicated columnists.

Drug Use Increases Crime

Nancy Reagan

Editor's note: The following viewpoint is taken from a speech by Nancy Reagan given at the March 1988 White House Conference for a Drug Free America.

Over the past nearly eight years I've focused mainly on education, on prevention, and on the need to change attitudes. Although we're making progress, still many ignorant ideas persist. And one of the worst is the casual user's justification that drug use is a victimless crime, that drugs don't hurt anyone except the person who's using them. Yet there are consequences to drug use beyond an individual's personal and selfish high. And that's what I'd like to talk to you about this morning.

The drug cartel murdered Colombia's attorney general, Carlos Mauro Hoyos, who was active in trying to halt cocaine traffic to the United States. Half-a-dozen men in three jeeps ran his car into a curb, sprayed it with machine gun fire and killed his two body guards. Mr. Hoyos was later found, blindfolded and handcuffed, his skull shattered by bullets.

And, ladies and gentlemen, the people who casually use cocaine are responsible, because their money bought those bullets.

They provided the high stakes that murdered those men, plus hundreds of others in Colombia, including Supreme Court justices, 21 judges handling drug cases and scores of policemen and soldiers.

Drug Use and Murder

The notion that the mellow marijuana user doesn't hurt anyone is just as phony. As a result of an intensive effort by the Drug Enforcement Administration in Guadalajara, Mexico, and particularly Special Agent Enrique Camarena, over 10,000 acres of marijuana that were ready for

harvest and eventual sale in the United States were destroyed. And this caused a major financial loss for a notorious trafficking group.

On Feb. 7, 1985, less than three months after the destruction of the 10,000-acre plantation, Special Agent Camarena was kidnapped by the traffickers. He was tortured and beaten to death. And this country's casual marijuana users cannot escape responsibility for their fellow American's death, because they, in effect, bought the tools for his torture.

As you know, many others have had their lives taken to protect our society from the corruption of drugs. Two DEA agents in California were killed on February 5, 1988. On February 26, while guarding the home of a witness in a drug crime, a rookie policeman in New York was assassinated in a patrol car. The traffickers and dealers will murder anyone who stands in their way. Recently, an innocent young girl in Los Angeles was shot to death in the cross-fire between two rival drug gangs. And who will tell the grief-stricken families that drug use is a victimless crime?

The casual user may think when he takes a line of cocaine or smokes a joint in the privacy of his nice condo, listening to his expensive stereo, that he's somehow not bothering anyone. But there is a trail of death and destruction that leads directly to his door. The casual user cannot morally escape responsibility for the action of drug traffickers and dealers. I'm saying that if you're a casual drug user, you're an accomplice to murder.

Facing Responsibility

The casual user also cannot morally escape association with those who use drugs and then endanger the public safety. The message from casual use is that drugs are acceptable, that they can be handled, that somehow it's simply a matter of

Nancy Reagan, "Casual Drug Users Accomplice to Murder," *Human Events*, March 12, 1988.

dosage. Casual use sets the tone for tolerance and that tolerance has killed.

Anne and Arthur Johnson are from Potomac, Md. On Jan. 4, 1987, the Johnson's daughter—20-year-old Christy—was taking the train to New York to visit her sister before heading back to classes at Stanford University. The Sunday afternoon Amtrak train was crowded with students returning to school and families returning home from Christmas and New Year's holidays.

Unknown to the passengers, a Conrail locomotive passed several warning signals and crossed into the path of the Amtrak train. The crash killed 16 innocent people and injured 175 others. Christy never made it to her sister's; she was killed in the crash.

> "Society's attitude has enabled the casual drug user to avoid facing his role in the murder and brutality behind drugs."

The investigation determined that the engineer and brakeman on the Conrail train were smoking marijuana prior to the crash—16 people killed because of an engineer's personal indulgence in a joint of marijuana. Now don't tell the Johnsons that casual drug use is a victimless crime. And don't try to tell the Johnsons that drugs hurt no one but the user. . . .

Ladies and gentlemen, I want to make it impossible for casual users to escape responsibility for any innocent death due to drugs. I want to make them fully face the brutality of drug use.

Real Stories

I don't mind admitting that I have reservations about telling the following two stories, because they're real stories of anguish and inhuman brutality. Yet, Betty Jean Spencer, and Vince and Roberta Roper can't ignore the brutality of drugs; they live with it every day. They're with us today, and if they can't forget, neither should we.

First, let me tell you about Betty Jean Spencer. Mrs. Spencer was at home in her rural farm house in Indiana with her four sons. They were 14, 16, 18 and 22 years old. Four men barged into the house, men out on bail on drug trafficking. The men didn't know her. They didn't know her sons. Mrs. Spencer says they were obviously high on something; they were laughing about the other people they were going to kill when they finished there.

They ordered Mrs. Spencer and her four sons to line up face down on the floor, and then the men began shooting them at point blank range with a shotgun. Mrs. Spencer miraculously survived two shotgun blasts to the back of her head. But her sons were murdered. And the men are in prison.

That's a brutal, brutal story. And it makes me angry. And no one—absolutely no one—should be allowed to say that drug use is a victimless crime. No one should be able to get away with the argument that drugs are a harmless, private indulgence.

Finally, let me tell you about the nightmare that Vince and Roberta Roper must endure. Their daughter, Stephanie, a 22-year-old student, was returning to school in Maryland when her car broke down. Two men offered assistance. They drove her a short distance in their car, pulled a gun on her and each raped her. They drove to another location and raped her again.

They then decided to kill her. I don't want to repeat what they did to her, but we can't ignore the brutality of drugs—one of the men whipped Stephanie on the head with a chain. And as she tried to run away, he shot her. He then poured gasoline on her and set fire to her. Both men were users of PCP, LSD, amphetamines, barbiturates—virtually any drug they could obtain.

Now, who would dare stand before the Ropers and tell them that drug use is a victimless crime? What apologist for casual drug use will look the Ropers in the eye and say it's all a matter of moderation? Who could be so brazen? . . .

Stop Enabling Drug Use

You know, in the field of drug and alcohol abuse there's something called the enabling concept—if I don't do something about your behavior, then I enable it to happen. Society's attitude has enabled the casual drug user to avoid facing his role in the murder and brutality behind drugs. We can no longer let the casual user continue without paying the moral penalty.

We must be absolutely unyielding and inflexible in our opposition to drug use. There's no middle ground. We must be as adamant about the casual user as we are about the addict. And whereas the addict deserves our help, the casual user deserves our condemnation. Because he could easily stop and yet he chooses not to do so. He must be made to feel the burden of brutality and corruption for which he's ultimately responsible. We must get the message out—we will not stand for illicit drug use of any kind, period.

During her eight years as US First Lady, Nancy Reagan has spoken extensively on drug abuse.

"The more law-enforcement apparatus there is applied to drugs, the greater the likelihood of interference with our personal well-being."

Legalization Would Improve Law Enforcement

Michael Kennedy, interviewed by John Holmstrom

High Times: How would you describe who you are and what you do? In 1977, you were described as a "radical dope lawyer."

Michael Kennedy: That was the description, but I've never considered myself a radical. I consider people like Reagan a radical. I'm actually the middle-of-the-road. I think the best way to describe me would be as a trial lawyer specializing in Constitutional defenses.

HT: Current drug laws, such as the forfeiture laws, seem to be targeting the Constitution as well as pot smokers. Have you defended any pot growers in the last few years?

MK: Yes.

HT: Have you dealt with any cases that involve the forfeiture laws?

MK: No, because the forfeiture laws are a rather recent innovation. Most of those cases are now in Northern California and Oregon. But that's precisely the direction in which the law seems to be going. And that's mostly because pot's a target of easy opportunity. It's a whole lot easier to try to go after a pot grower or a pot smoker than some ex-Cuban or Colombian killer cocaine dealer, who, if you run him up against a wall, is apt to blow you away. The narcs know it's a whole lot safer to go after the pot.

HT: That's one of the reasons. I suspect another reason is that some of the people dealing in hard drugs might be in the employ of the people who are behind the arrests of pot growers.

MK: As you know, our government has a great tradition of involving itself in drugs. I'm defending a book written by Leslie and Andrew Cockburn, called *Out of Control*, where they trace Air America running drugs, including morphine bases, out of Laos to processing plants during the '60s, ultimately for introduction into the United States. So, we

financed the war in Laos with drugs. We're financing the Contras in Nicaragua with drugs. The "War on Drugs" is really nothing more than a sham, nothing more than a hypocritical way of hiding our government's drug dealing.

Legalization Is Inevitable

HT: The House Select Committee on Narcotics and Drug Abuse has scheduled hearings on drug legalization for September 29th, 1988. Could this be the first step toward legalization, or just another step ahead in the fight to keep drugs illegal?

MK: Legalization is inevitable. But actually, the hearings could be both. The government has the population really confused about it. The reason legalization is inevitable is because there is no way, given the taxing of our resources, and given how little money we have to solve so many of the social problems we have, that we can continue spending and wasting so much money on narcs. We've established a police apparatus so huge that if we don't dismantle it, it will dismantle *us*. Increasingly, people will realize, as I think they did during liquor prohibition, that you can't legislate what people are going to do to themselves or to their own bodies. I think all drugs should be legalized.

HT: Including crack?

MK: Including crack. Every drug should be legalized, because the real menace is not drugs; the menace is the money that is made from drugs. I think crack is deplorable. I think heroin is deplorable. But the only way to stop it is to take the money out.

The popular conception of politicians is that everyone is anti-drug. The fact of the matter is, everybody is anti-problem: We want that problem to go away. We don't make that problem go away by passing draconian laws such as the Rockefeller laws in New York. We proved that. All we did was fill up our prisons, cause our prisons to be overcrowded,

Michael Kennedy interviewed by John Holmstrom, "Legalization Is Inevitable," *High Times*, November 1988. Reprinted with permission.

and cause a criminalization of another class of people who are basically nonviolent. I'm thinking particularly of marijuana growers and small marijuana dealers.

The Chief of Staff of the United States Army had just admitted that even if we put all our military resources into trying to intercept drugs at our borders, we still couldn't stop it. So we can't stop it. What we have to do is learn to try and control it, maybe regulate it a little bit.

I don't think it's a war on drugs. I think it's a war on law. The attack of the Reagan administration and Meese is really an attack on law, and an attack on the Constitution—an attack on the right to privacy of citizens and an attack on our citizens. They're not attacking drugs. They're attacking us.

Crowded Jails

HT: How seriously have the drug laws broken down our justice system?

MK: The jails are so crowded, we can't put people in. We can't keep them in. We can't warehouse them. We don't have enough room. Governor Mario Cuomo has actually built more prisons and prison cells than any governor in New York State history, and he has not even been able to keep up with the demand. Mayor Edward Koch can't keep up with the demand. These are people who really want to build prisons. They can't find the space, and they can't get the legislature to give them the money.

Have you heard of the NIMBYs? It's an acronym for Not In My Backyard. NIMBYs are releasing more people from prison than any of us lawyers because they're saying, ''You can't build a prison here.'' In Oregon, for example, the legislature couldn't find a place to build another prison. As a result of that, they had to release an entire tier of low-level, nonviolent people who didn't belong in jail in the first place. Hundreds of people were released because they had no more room.

That same kind of pressure is going to come here, but the real attack of the so-called war on drugs, which is a war on law, comes in the courts. When you come up to a judge now, representing some drug dealer, and you start to argue that he was illegally arrested—he wasn't given his Constitutional rights, they illegally searched his apartment, they illegally stopped his car, they illegally went into his glove compartment and into his hood, or into his trunk and searched the car, they illegally arrested and detained his wife and children, used them against him, all of these things that are lawless activities— the judge will sweep it under the rug and say, ''I don't care because this is a drug case. So I'm throwing the rules out the window.'' If they throw the rules out in a drug case, they can throw the rules out in any case.

HT: Why aren't more pot smokers and drug users becoming politically motivated? It seems like there's more of a motivation now than ever for people to go back to the tactics of the '60s and early '70s and protest, or demonstrate. People have to be angry about what's going on.

MK: I agree with you. It's important to note the distinction between cocaine and marijuana, though. Marijuana has always been an adjunct of rebels in our society. It was an adjunct of jazz musicians in the '40s and early '50s. In the '60s, almost all of us who were politically active also were social users of marijuana. But the difference between those of us who were using marijuana, and those who used cocaine and heroin, is a very significant difference. The cocaine dealers are so greedy they're not about to change the laws. They're not about to get political. Also, they're probably so psychotic, because I think cocaine causes psychosis, that they couldn't become political anyway. So we can't expect any kind of radical political activity to come from cocaine or heroin dealers.

The individuals who are now growing marijuana in the United States, and are able to avoid Meese, the paraquat squads and what have you, tend to be highly political people. They're not in it for profit as much as personal use and social enjoyment, and they want to be left alone. And the awareness they get being on a fringe, outlaw element of society causes them to be highly radical. That radicalization is extremely good because it directs their energies against government, against these arcane drug laws.

HT: Speaking of growers, do you have any free legal advice?

MK: Well, I think the most intelligent thing for a marijuana grower to do is keep it simple, keep it small, and keep it highly personal. The larger the crop, and the more sophisticated the growing apparatus used, the more likely they are to be detected—either by aerial surveillance, by some competitor turning them in, or by some Smokey the Bear-type ranger wandering through the forest and finding them.

''We can't be using our courts for small growers. There's no room. We've got to get the child molesters in jail. We've got to get people like that . . . some justice.''

Also, the best defense in a growing case is, ''Listen, judge, this smoke is for me and my immediate family. To be sure, it's not a nuclear family, you know, and we're not all related by blood the way you might want us to be, but this is really our family. We're growing it for ourselves and we're not hurting anybody.''

That kind of argument is very compelling because I don't care how anti-marijuana you are, you know we can't be using our courts for small growers. There's no room. We've got to get the child molesters in jail. We've got to get people like that who are really hurting people into our courtrooms, get them some justice, and if they're convicted, get their ass in jail. So if you stay small, the likelihood of you being busted is substantially reduced.

HT: How small is small?

MK: There isn't any arbitrary limit. I think small is probably a few plants.

HT: In the '60s, people would wear pink underwear, invent foot problems, or try anything to avoid the draft. Is there a medical problem, like headaches or glaucoma, that someone could invent so if they go to trial they can claim a medical defense?

MK: I don't know. I have made the argument in cases where individuals have been growing marijuana for their own use, involving a few plants and for the most part, I've been able to persuade prosecutors not to bring the case. Occasionally, we've even been able to persuade judges that there's a right to privacy and to a commitment to growing marijuana for personal use, and there's no overriding state interest that should overcome it. So if an individual is growing a small amount of marijuana and he says, "This is for my personal use," I think that is a very legitimate defense. If he says, I'm growing it because a friend of mine has to take chemotherapy, because he's got AIDS, or he's dying of cancer" or whatever, I think that's the very kind of genuine, human comfort that most judges in this day and age would be able to acknowledge.

Frankly, for years I have gotten marijuana to friends of mine who have been taking chemotherapy who couldn't overcome the nausea in any other way. And I've seen it work.

I remember one time we were defending a guy who had glaucoma. The trouble was, he had enough marijuana to treat 40 or 50 people with glaucoma. So we called that the "Cyclops Glaucoma Defense." The Cyclops was the Greek one-eyed monster who's eye was so big it would take 40 lbs. of pot to cure his glaucoma.

HT: What is the current state of dope laws? Does someone have a better or worse chance of getting sent up in 1988 than in 1978, or 1968?

MK: With cocaine and heroin and crack, there is no question. There's a greater chance of going to jail. The only thing that mitigates against going to jail is that we don't have enough jail space. In marijuana cases here in New York City, the prosecutors and the police look the other way.

HT: What about LSD?

MK: There are so few LSD cases anymore, because there's so little LSD around. I haven't seen an LSD case in a couple of years.

HT: That's interesting, because there's such a resurgence of interest in psychedelics nowadays.

MK: There's no question about it. And with the resurgence of interest in hallucinogenics, there's going to be a resurgence of police interest in hallucinogenics. . . .

HT: You have to wonder how they can legislate against marijuana, which was used for so many years as rope and medicine. It's crazy.

MK: It is crazy. And to be sure, there probably will be some right-wing, Baptist legislators who want to outlaw Synchro-Energizer devices, isolation tanks, and things of that sort. But I can't conceive of them getting very much help from society generally.

Keeping Government Out

HT: Do you find it amusing that the legalization of drugs is now being proposed by right-wing types such as William F. Buckley, when for so many years legalization has been a radical left-wing cause?

MK: Yes, I think it's ironic. I happen to think they're absolutely right and I think they're doing it for the right reasons. He's not stupid. He knows that criminalization hasn't solved the problem. And the right-wing comes to it from the standpoint of a libertarian view, that is: Government, stay out of our lives. Because they know that the more law-enforcement apparatus there is applied to drugs, the greater the likelihood of interference with our personal well-being. I mean, because of the police apparatus in existence today, the likelihood of you and I being shot in a crossfire between cops and drug dealers, or undercover cops just shooting one another, not knowing the other is a narc, is greater. . . .

"Because of the police apparatus in existence today, the likelihood of you and I being shot in a crossfire between cops and drug dealers . . . is greater."

We've got to use social and government forces to develop some kind of economic parity among people. In law enforcement, there is no need to be spending this kind of money. Instead of giving all this money to cops, let's start paying our teachers more.

A member of the California and New York Bar Associations, Michael Kennedy is a trial lawyer who specializes in criminal defense and libel cases. Kennedy's clients have included 1960s activist Timothy Leary. John Holmstrom is the executive editor of High Times *magazine, a monthly periodical that supports legalizing drugs.*

"Police face the devastating effects of drugs in our communities on a daily basis and cannot condone their greater availability."

Legalization Would Harm Law Enforcement

Police Executive Research Forum

The members of the Police Executive Research Forum, an organization of law enforcement chief executives from the nation's largest jurisdictions dedicated to public debate of significant criminal justice issues, have long been involved in addressing the problems of drug abuse. As police executives they are in a unique position to see the devastating effects of this national tragedy. At its annual meeting in May of 1988, members of the Forum joined the debate initiated by Baltimore, Maryland Mayor Kurt Schmoke regarding the legalization of drugs as a response to the perceived failure of the country's efforts to control drugs. No issue is more important at the current time, and no group feels a greater sense of frustration about the drug issue than the police. In spite of this sense of frustration, Forum members believe the current level of knowledge about the effects of legalization does not support such a significant change in policy. Therefore, the Forum enters the debate on the side of developing new solutions to drug abuse.

This debate is limited in its effectiveness, however, by the paucity of research that exists and the lack of hard evidence on where new proposals might lead us. Over the years we have seen other policy changes implemented without regard to the resulting difficulties experienced by law enforcement. To this day, police continue to deal with the results of such policies as the deinstitutionalization of the mentally ill. Housing policies, too, have contributed to the legions of homeless. And, even strict drug enforcement policies have left the police with the burden of explaining to citizens why it takes so long for a case to come to trial and why the jails are full.

While law enforcement shares society's sense of frustration in dealing with this problem, we do not subscribe to the notion that the police have failed in this arena. We are arresting more drug dealers and drug abusers than ever before. We are recovering and destroying more illegal drugs than ever before. The mission of law enforcement as currently defined *is* being fulfilled, sometimes at the cost of our lives.

What has failed is society's ability to reduce the demand for narcotics. Drug use is pervasive, not only among the criminal element, but among otherwise law-abiding citizens as well. It is estimated that billions of dollars each year are lost to absenteeism, injuries, and poor productivity in the workplace and schools.

Unmitigated Demand

Because of this unmitigated societal demand for drugs, law enforcement at all levels of government has expanded its mission to include education, training, and assistance. Police are responsible for developing many of the more successful drug educational efforts in our nation's schools. Police have joined the business community to fight drugs in the workplace while supporting programs that help addicts kick the drug habit. There hasn't been enough time or resources to measure the effectiveness of these new law enforcement initiatives.

However, questions raised in the national press and political forums challenge these efforts and suggest legalization as an answer. While this idea is repugnant to many law enforcement leaders based on current knowledge, a national debate on the wider issue of drugs in America makes sense. Discussion and research may uncover approaches never before considered and serve to heighten public awareness of the problem. Communities might adopt broader drug testing for schools and workplaces, and enforce strict mandatory prison sentences for drug smugglers or otherwise reduce the demand for drugs. An educated and mobilized citizenry is the strongest weapon in our attempt to control drug abuse.

"The Legalization of Drugs," a policy paper published by the Police Executive Research Forum. Reprinted with permission.

While proponents of drug legalization claim that law enforcement will be spared great expense because they will be freed from policing drug trafficking, the Forum believes that these savings are illusory. The burden to police and society will only be intensified. Police face the devastating effects of drugs in our communities on a daily basis and cannot condone their greater availability. Legalization would bring with it new and more damaging problems. In addition to the moral issues expressed by Forum members, there are a number of practical premises for rejecting the legalization of drugs, including:

• Given the well-known deleterious effects of drugs, it seems unreasonable for government to expose greater numbers of people to them. Unlike cigarette smoking, or other so called "vices," drug use has been shown to contribute to violent criminal behavior. Its influence drives victims to behave in ways that are unacceptable and dangerous.

> "Proponents of drug legalization claim that law enforcement will be spared great expense . . . , these savings are illusory. The burden to police and society will only be intensified."

• The legalization of drugs would send a mixed message to the children of this nation. At a time when we have urged them to "just say no" to drugs, legalization would suggest that they only say no until they are older. Children anxious to "feel adult" would no longer stop at smoking cigarettes, but would bend to the certain peer pressure to try drugs. Children might also wonder how bad drugs can be if they are made more available to those just a few years older. And the greater availability of drugs to adults will surely open the way for easier access to our elementary schools and playgrounds.

• Law enforcement may not be required to dedicate as many resources to drug enforcement if drugs are legalized. (Though, this result is by no means certain.) Yet, the consequences will be so costly that the initial savings would create a loss of a much greater magnitude. Society bears the costs of those who can't care for themselves. Through legalization we open the door to citizens who never had the opportunity to buy drugs inexpensively and without fear of criminal sanctions, to get substances that may well debilitate them and those that depend on them.

• There is no definitive research indicating that legalization of drugs would reduce the number of addicts or the crimes they commit. Police experience suggests just the opposite—drugs would be purer, less expensive, more easily available, and perhaps less stigmatized. Without reliable data to indicate otherwise, drug legalization most likely would foster the growth of an unproductive and dangerous generation. Experience has shown that just because prices are lowered, drug-related crime does not necessarily diminish. Greater availability would mean that many more people might gain access to drugs. There would be fewer obstacles to purchasing and some individuals might spend their entire savings and earnings on drugs, leaving police to cope with crimes that would support the drug habits of a large segment of the population.

• Supporters of legalization claim that we can shut down the unregulated flow of drugs into our communities by denying drug dealers their profits. While legalization may make drug trafficking "bad business," it would not solve the problem of drugs in our schools and cities. It would only shift the profit and make marginal improvements in quality and control. Certainly drugs such as PCP and LSD would not be legalized given their propensity to cause violent and bizarre behavior. As a result, the black market would continue to function by dispensing these dangerous drugs.

At a time when AIDS and other infectious diseases are being spread through the use of drugs, abstinence would seem to be our best defense. While addicts may be unable to refrain, it would seem contrary to public health and safety to condone drug use among those previously deterred by high prices, inaccessibility and the threat of arrest.

Lessons from the Past

Our only hint at the ramifications of legalization are our experiences with the prohibition of alcohol and the policies of other countries on drugs.

Prohibition of alcohol is not like prohibition of heroin, cocaine and other similar classes of drugs in a number of ways, making comparisons questionable at best. Yet, if there is a lesson to be learned from the legalization of alcohol, it might be that greater availability equals greater addiction. Following the legalization of alcohol, alcohol-related deaths and driving accidents rose. Children had greater access to alcohol with tragic results. And easier access and loosening of regulations did not temper the demand for alcohol; likewise, there is no reason to believe that legalizing drugs would curb the public's appetite for these substances. The decision to legalize alcohol was a moral, social decision—one that society may not be ready to make regarding drugs known to be harmful.

Also, at the turn of the century in America, heroin and cocaine use were legal. The number of addicts was at its peak during that period—higher than any other time in our history. As a result, the Harrison Act was passed in 1914 to restrict the public's access to these narcotics. In the years that followed, reports of addiction to this drug fell significantly.

In other countries where heroin is available, the addiction rate is 10% higher than in the U.S. (Kaplan 1983). The British instituted a system whereby heroin was legally available to addicts at a very low cost while sale of the drug to others was prohibited. But it was difficult to identify "addicts" and their maintenance programs became very expensive. The old black market did not disappear and soon the program became ineffective. Holland also currently allows some drugs to be legally available, but cultural differences regarding the stigma of drug use may make comparisons with the U.S. meaningless.

Examine US Policy More Closely

The simple truth is that we do not have enough information to justify a change in policy and practice regarding drug abuse. Insufficient research on current drug legalization experiments hampers efforts to determine the impact of the policies. A clear need exists to expand and intensify the inquiry into both the medical aspects of drug abuse and the efficacy of current policy. There is a perception that our drug problems are worsening. Yet we do not know where and why, or what effect certain activities will have on drug trafficking. A vigorous discussion of all alternatives is the first step in identifying the factors that must be analyzed before a plan of action is embarked upon. Some of the questions that must be answered include:

Is our drug problem getting worse? Are there more addicts now than in previous years? Is crime related to drug trafficking and supporting a habit on the rise? If there are no significant increases in the number of addicts and crime, is there a need to dramatically change our approach to drug enforcement, prevention and treatment?

"Current knowledge makes legalization out of the question for the majority of police executives."

Can we talk about legalization of "drugs," when that umbrella term includes drugs of varying potency and danger? What drugs would be legalized? How would that determination be made? If some drugs were not legalized, how would that affect the black market and related crime? Who are "addicts," and what would be a reasonable level of habit maintenance? Who would pay for the resulting health care costs for those suffering the effects of these drugs? How will we ensure that the drugs are not resold on the black market to children, by eligible recipients?

What would legalization mean to occupational drug testing? Would drugs be O.K. in the workplace if legalized? Would police and others in sensitive positions be allowed to use certain types of drugs? How would legalization affect productivity, the economy and social welfare?

The questions are endless, but the very act of raising them helps to clarify our priorities and moral boundaries. The debate is welcomed for its role in shaping a meaningful national drug policy. While current knowledge makes legalization out of the question for the majority of police executives, its emergence as an issue for national debate may shift attention to an old problem in need of fresh perspectives and new ideas.

Founded in 1975, the Police Executive Research Forum works to increase public interest in and understanding of issues facing the criminal justice system. The Forum's members are executives from police forces across the country.

viewpoint **53**

The Harmful Effects of Marijuana Are Undeniable

George Biernson and Otto Moulton

Marijuana, known scientifically as cannabis sativa and popularly as pot, contains 61 chemicals, called cannabinoids, which are found nowhere else. Its primary psychoactive ingredient is delta-9-tetrahydrocannabinol or delta-9-THC. Three other cannabinoids are known to be psychoactive, but occur in much lower concentration. . . . However, the evidence against delta-9-THC is sufficient to brand it, by itself, an extremely dangerous drug. Often delta-9-THC is shortened to THC.

Storage of THC in the Body

THC is strongly fat soluble, and so is stored in the fatty tissues of the body for months. The fatty tissues act like time-release capsules, which steadily release THC into the blood, keeping the regular marijuana smoker in continual sedation. The THC molecules are very sticky, and so THC is very difficult to measure quantitatively; it sticks to the sides of test tubes and other equipment. . . .

THC is called lipophilic, meaning "fat-loving." Its fat-storage properties are quite similar to those of the banned insecticide DDT. That lipophilic insecticide was thought to be harmless to vertebrates, until we discovered, to our dismay, that it was accumulating in the bodies of animals, and so was destroying our environment.

The brain is isolated from the main blood supply by the blood-brain barrier, which is a protective sieve of capillary walls and membranes that shields the brain against toxic substances. Lipophilic THC molecules stick to this sieve, and so the flow of THC to the brain is slow.

As THC is absorbed into the blood, most of it leaves very rapidly, to be stored in different physiological processes, which later feed THC back into the blood. As blood passes through the liver,

part of the THC is metabolized to form other chemicals called metabolites, which are eventually excreted from the body. Unmetabolized THC is not excreted.

Because of these storage processes, the concentration of THC in the blood drops to a few percent of the initial level by the time the THC molecules have worked their way through the blood-brain barrier. Hence, only a small amount of the THC entering the body contributes to the "high" sensation. In a light marijuana smoker, the concentration of THC in the brain blood that produces a strong "high" is about 10 micrograms (10 millionths of a gram) distributed throughout the total blood supply of the body.

Thus, THC is an extremely potent drug. It appears to be mild because its high fat solubility makes it slow acting. With this slow action, serious physical trauma from marijuana overdose is rare. On the other hand, being lipophilic makes marijuana very dangerous and insidious when used regularly.

There are four different types of THC storage processes in the body, which feed THC back into the blood at different rates: (1) fast storage, predominating in the first 10 minutes, (2) medium storage, predominating in the first hour, (3) slow storage, predominating in the first 12 hours, and (4) very slow storage, which controls THC blood concentration after one day. Very slow storage is caused by THC absorbed into fatty tissues. About 1/3 of the THC entering the body is absorbed into the fat tissues, which release it with a half life of approximately one week. Hence, it takes one week after marijuana smoking has ceased for THC stored in the fat to drop to 1/2, 2 weeks to drop to 1/4, 3 weeks to drop to 1/8, etc.

All of the marijuana joints smoked over the past month contribute significantly to the THC in the fatty tissues, which is steadily released into the blood. The THC blood concentration from this

George Biernson and Otto Moulton, "Summary of the Biological Effects of Marijuana," *Drug Awareness Information Newsletter*, January 1988. Reprinted with permission.

steady release is low. Nevertheless, for a regular marijuana smoker, it is sufficient to cause sedation, because (1) THC is released so slowly it passes unimpeded through the blood-brain barrier, and (2) THC is extremely potent.

One-third of the brain is fat tissue, and so an appreciable amount of THC is stored directly in the brain. Although the blood-brain barrier reduces THC flow to the brain, about half of the THC stored in the fat arrives so slowly it passes unimpeded through the blood-brain barrier. Hence, THC concentration in brain fat tissue should be about half of that in general body fat. (This slowly arriving THC comes partly from THC originally stored in the fat, which is recycled back into the fat, and partly from the slow storage process, described earlier.)

Effect of THC on the Brain

What is the effect of THC stored in brain cells? Dr. Robert Gilkeson explains that the membranes of nerve cells are fat (or "lipid") tissue, and so are sites for storing THC molecules. The nerve cell membrane is crucially important because: (1) nutrients and waste products for the cell must pass across the cell membrane, and (2) this membrane is the primary source of neural electrical activity. When sticky THC molecules are stored in the nerve cell membrane, they degrade cell nutrition, and suppress electrical activity.

Hence, one would expect that long-term use of marijuana should cause serious brain damage. That this is so was demonstrated by experiments performed on the monkey by Dr. Robert Heath of Tulane Medical School, who is world renowned for his research on the brain. . . .

"The misinformation presented in most drug education programs is atrocious."

The following experiment was performed several times. For 6 months a monkey smoked the equivalent of 2 joints of marijuana per day, 5 days per week, using monkey-sized joints. After recovering for 6 months, the monkey was sacrificed and its brain cells examined under the electron microscope. EEG brain waves were measured from electrodes imbedded in the brain. The EEG waves became severely distorted after 2 months of smoking, and remained severely distorted 6 months after smoking had stopped.

The brain cells showed serious damage, particularly those in a deep part of the brain called the limbic system, which is the center of motivation. For example, over 30% of the limbic brain-cell nuclei had inclusion bodies, which are clots in the nuclei. In normal brains, less than 0.5% of brain-cell nuclei have inclusion bodies. The incidence is much higher

in old brains, particularly those of senile patients, but even then is much less than was observed in the brains of these young monkeys. When the researchers first observed the enormous brain-cell damage, they were shocked at what they saw.

Defending Heath's Experiment

This research by Heath is often dismissed with the argument that the monkeys were "chain-smoking" marijuana, using huge doses. This is not true. Early in this experiment the smoking apparatus was very inefficient, and little of the THC was absorbed into the monkey's body. This problem was corrected by developing a respirator that forced the monkeys to smoke in a human-like pattern.

With this respirator, a monkey weighing 11 pounds smoked a 0.25-gram joint of marijuana, containing 2.5-3% THC. (A normal marijuana joint is 1 gram, and good street pot today is usually 3.5-4% THC.) This dosage produces the same THC blood concentration, 10 minutes after smoking, as a human smoking a 1-gram joint.

If we scale the monkey's dose by weight, 0.25-gram of marijuana for an 11-pound monkey would be equivalent to 3 grams (or 3 joints) for a 132-pound teenager. However, equivalent drug dosages for different species are not scaled by weight. Extensive studies of drug equivalency have been made for cancer chemotherapy. For the many drugs evaluated, the maximum tolerable dose for man, per pound of body weight, is approximately 1/3 of that for the monkey. When this factor 1/3 is included, the 0.25-gram monkey-sized joint is equivalent to a 1-gram joint for the 132-pound teenager.

To bury this dosage argument completely, let us ignore this 1/3 factor and assume, very optimistically, that dosage is scaled directly with body weight. Since the monkey smoked 10 times per week, this very optimistic assumption would yield 30 joints per week for the teenager, or 4.3 joints per day. In 1979 the National High-School Senior Survey showed that 10% of U.S. high-school seniors smoked marijuana daily, and the average consumption for the daily marijuana smokers was 3.5 joints per day. This average is very close to the very optimistic 4.3 joints per day corresponding to the monkey experiment, a smoking level that produced serious brain damage after 6 months of smoking.

Clearly, this experiment by Heath is crucially important to our youngsters. Yet, very few have received a reliable account of it in their drug education classes, even though its results were published in 1979. As Peggy Mann reported in the Nov. 1987 *Reader's Digest*, "We are teaching our kids to use drugs" in drug education. The misinformation presented in most drug education programs is atrocious.

In 1981 the National Institute on Drug Abuse (NIDA) discontinued funding of this research by Dr. Heath, which is by far the most important research on marijuana ever performed anywhere in the world. This action was preceded in 1980 with the following derogatory evaluation by NIDA of Heath's work:

> A researcher who used electrodes implanted deep within the brains of monkeys, instead of the more conventional scalp recording techniques, has found persistent changes related to chronic use. This same investigator has reported that rhesus monkeys administered marijuana smoke from one joint daily for five days per week for six months show persistent microscopic changes in brain cellular structure following this treatment. While these experiments demonstrate the possibility that more subtle changes in brain functioning or structure may occur as a result of marijuana smoking in animals, the implications of these changes for subsequent human or animal behavior is at present unknown. Other studies, using more conventional EEG techniques to measure brain electrical activity, have found changes temporarily associated with acute use, but no evidence of persistently abnormal EEG findings related to chronic cannabis use.

In EEG (electroencephalogram) tests on man, the electrodes are almost always placed on the scalp, because it is dangerous to insert them into the brain. Only under extreme conditions, associated with brain surgery, has it been possible to place EEG electrodes inside the human brain. It is well known that EEG scalp records give an extremely limited measure of brain electrical activity. Doctors use the scalp EEG because it is the best that they can get, *not because it is "conventional".*

With NIDA's unscientific approach to research, is it any wonder that we have a drug epidemic?

Studies on Humans

The strong brain-wave distortions found by Heath on monkeys were detected only from electrodes implanted within the brain, and were not observed from those placed on the scalp. Hence one would not expect EEG scalp recordings of humans to show strong brain-wave distortion

On the other hand, psychiatrist Dr. Robert Gilkeson has observed more subtle brain-wave changes from the scalp EEG. Gilkeson has developed EEG techniques to pinpoint learning disabilities, which he applied to 50 youngsters, ages 13-18, who had used pot at least twice a week for 4 months. They abstained from pot for 2 days preceding the test.

Gilkeson found that all of these EEG records were "markedly immature for age", and had an abnormal amount of slow theta rhythms, "sufficient to be diagnostic of diffuse brain impairment. In the EEG section of academic tasks, none of these youngsters could speed up when challenged. Their brain waves failed to respond to these stimuli in the usual way."

These subtle distortions of scalp EEG signals disappeared after the youngsters abstained from pot for 3 months. On the other hand, the severe distortions observed by Heath from deep-brain recordings persisted after 6 months of abstinence.

"The damage to chromosomes caused by marijuana can produce serious birth defects."

In 1973, Dr. Akira Morishima of Columbia University examined, from healthy pot-smoking young men, the chromosomes of T-lymphocytes, which are important cells of the immune system. The men had smoked marijuana for an average of 4 years, and did not take other illegal drugs. For those smoking 2 joints per week, about 1/3 of the T-lymphocyte cells had about half the normal number of chromosomes (46). For the daily marijuana smokers, cell damage was greater, with some cells containing only 5 to 10 chromosomes. This study has been verified by many other researchers. . . .

Effect on Reproduction and the Lungs

The damage to chromosomes caused by marijuana can produce serious birth defects, which are transmitted through many generations. In experiments by Dr. Susan Dalterio, male mice were given a human equivalency dose of 1 to 3 joints of THC, 3 times per week, for 5 weeks. These mice were mated for a month with normal females. Twenty percent of the females either did not conceive, or had babies that were born dead or died soon after birth.

The resultant sons that matured were not exposed to any drugs and were mated with normal females. About 25% of these female mice did not achieve a normal pregnancy. The resultant grandsons of the THC-dosed mice that matured were not exposed to drugs and were mated with normal females. Many of their offspring showed severe abnormalities, including intestines outside the bodies, and exposed brains and spinal cords. Many of the sons and grandsons showed severe chromosome defects.

When mice or monkeys are exposed to marijuana, they have little sex drive: it is difficult to get them to mate. Similar results are observed in humans. A high incidence of impotence has been reported among men in Jamaica who smoked marijuana for 5 years. Dr. Ingrid Lantner, who has discussed marijuana on many radio call-in shows, reports: "Chronic pot smokers often tell me they are impotent, but this doesn't bother them—since they no longer feel sexual desires."

Marijuana causes serious lung damage, particularly when cigarettes are also smoked. In 1971, studies were performed by Dr. Forrest Tennant on U.S. soldiers in Germany who smoked hashish daily, equivalent to 1-5 joints of marijuana. He found that 1/3 of the cigarette smokers had squamous metaphlasia, a dangerous precancerous condition of the lungs; while 91% of those using hashish plus cigarettes had it. . . .

Addiction and Drug Dependence

Marijuana is often claimed to be physically non-addictive because the user does not experience strong physical withdrawal symptoms when he stops smoking it. However, the reason for this is that THC cannot be withdrawn rapidly; the body has its own supply. It takes one week for the THC stored in the fat to drop to 50%, and one month to drop to 5%.

Actually, marijuana probably produces stronger physical drug dependence than any other drug. It generates a ''pot personality'' and often leads to escalated use of many drugs, because:

(1) As marijuana builds up in the body, it gradually drags the smoker into continual sedation, separating him from reality and forcing him into a dream world of drugs.

(2) As demonstrated by Heath's experiments on the monkey, marijuana weakens the center of motivation of the brain, and in time permanently damages it. Clinical experience has shown that prolonged marijuana smoking destroys normal motivational reflexes, so that the smoker experiences great difficulty living a drug-free existence.

"Marijuana's dangers are deceptive because its main action is slow and delayed, and so it is difficult for the user to relate cause and effect."

---

(3) Since marijuana is present in the body all the time, the body rapidly builds up tolerance to it, and the smoker must steadily escalate its use to achieve the same ''high''. Eventually, the kick from marijuana is not satisfying, and so he reaches for other drugs.

(4) Since marijuana inhibits nausea, people with marijuana stored in their bodies can drink alcohol very heavily without getting sick. Consequently, marijuana has caused an epidemic of alcohol abuse, drunk driving, and death from alcohol overdose. Teenage death from alcohol overdose used to be very rare; without marijuana in the system, the body protects itself by vomiting.

A Gateway Drug

Marijuana is often called a ''stepping stone'' or ''gateway drug'' because it leads to drugs giving a stronger kick. However, these terms are misleading:

they imply that the primary damage of marijuana comes from drugs evolving from its use. Marijuana's dangers are deceptive because its main action is slow and delayed, and so it is difficult for the user to relate cause and effect.

Remember that THC is extremely potent and is stored for months in the body, causing serious damage to the brain, to chromosomes, and to the immune system. THC appears to be mild because it acts slowly. Hence, marijuana is at least as harmful as cocaine and heroin, but is really more dangerous because it is so insidious. In societies where marijuana is readily available, and heroin and cocaine are not, the smoker usually sticks to marijuana, until it destroys him. For example, in Morocco and Jamaica, marijuana-induced insanity is common.

Survey after survey have shown that essentially all users of other illegal drugs started with marijuana, and most continue to use marijuana along with the other drugs. The great reluctance of a heroin addict to stop may be due more to the marijuana he has taken than the heroin. . . .

These studies were glibly dismissed as being irrelevant. They were buried by using the fallacious argument: ''Since marijuana is not addictive, it cannot by itself lead to other drugs; hence these correlations cannot be the result of cause-and-effect relationships.''

We hear of statistical studies everywhere we turn. Elections are predicted with remarkable accuracy from them. Our knowledge of the dangers of tobacco is largely the result of statistical evidence. Most of the decisions in modern medicine concerning medical procedures are based strongly on statistical data. Yet, strangely, statistical studies relating marijuana to other drugs, or to crime, suicide, and insanity, are considered to be irrelevant. . . .

Conclusion

The scientific evidence is more than sufficient to brand marijuana an extremely dangerous drug, yet few youngsters are aware of this. They smoke marijuana because it is there, and they believe it is no more harmful than alcohol. The only way they learn otherwise is to see their classmates being destroyed by it. However, for this mechanism to operate, many young lives must be sacrificed. It is about time that science provided a better learning mechanism.

George Biernson is an electrical engineer and a regular contributor to the Drug Awareness Information Newsletter, *a newsletter published by the Committees of Correspondence, a non-profit agency that disseminates information on drugs. Otto Moulton edits the newsletter.*

The Harmful Effects of Marijuana Are Uncertain

Peter Gorman

Although cannabis has been subjected to endless study and clinical analysis, very little can be stated categorically as to its effect on health. The scientific literature is confusing and contradictory, and the marijuana issue polarizes emotions, making moralists of scientists. Since every researcher is aware that his or her work is going to be used somehow by someone in the case for legalizing or not legalizing public consumption, personal and political bias seems to filter through the work.

Marijuana and its compounds are not simple drugs. What shows up theoretically doesn't always appear in the lab; what appears in the lab doesn't always appear in clinical practice. Being a psychotropic, its effects can vary widely from user to user. Perhaps it confounds science because it is a psychotropic. Spiritual aids are rarely classifiable. . . .

Of the 420 known components of cannabis, the major if not the only, active component is Tetrahydrocannabinol, commonly called THC. This is a group of cannabinoids, sixty-one of which have been identified, many of which produce some biological activity. Delta 9 THC, the principal active component in natural cannabis, produces almost all of the characteristic effects of grass. It is by far the most often studied of the active isomers found in pot.

The natural cannabinoids are relatively insoluble in water but dissolve in fats and fat solvents and are called lipid-soluble. When smoked, the THC is rapidly absorbed by the blood in the lung; high concentrations of THC there begin to fall rapidly within 30 minutes of smoking. From that point on elimination slows considerably. Roughly 25 percent of the initial THC and its metabolites remain in the body after a week, and traces from a single dose can be found for up to thirty days. In the body, the THC binds to fatty acids where it remains, unchanged, until it passes back into the blood stream for elimination.

Is Accumulation Harmful?

Generally, lipid-soluble compounds are completely neutralized when bound to fatty acids, but some controversy exists over whether this rule holds true for the psychoactive ingredients of marijuana. There is no medical question about its distribution area— the fat cells of the entire body from the toes to the brain—or that it remains unchanged while bound there. The questions are what effect the THC has on the user while it waits for elimination, and whether the repeated administration of even small doses may lead to an accumulation of drug which is potentially higher than levels reached at any time after a single dose.

On one side of the argument, many researchers feel that general toxicity studies have shown marijuana to be one of the safest drugs ever studied for cumulative effects. Another group feels that since so much is not understood about how the THC acts on the brain, it is possible that minute doses of active THC released back into the system may have a continued toxic effect. Reese T. Jones of the University of California at San Francisco said in recent correspondence that "When you say active, right now, that's an unanswerable question . . . it's in the brain, there's no question of that, but the activity issue, that depends on whom you talk to."

The problem encountered with the issue of accumulation is typical of issues involving marijuana. There is continued debate over long-term effects to both the chronic and casual user. Obviously, in areas of concern, researchers find the chronic user at more risk. Few studies have shown serious concern regarding long-term effects for the light smokers, even among antagonists to the drug.

Little controversy exists in discussion of the short-

Peter Gorman, "Marijuana and Health: An Update of Research Results," *High Times*, November 1987. Copyright 1987 by Peter Gorman. Reprinted with the author's permission.

term or acute effects of smoking marijuana or hashish. These occur while high levels of THC are still in the metabolism. These short-term effects can include an increased pulse rate, giddiness, euphoria, hallucinations, reddening of the eyes, dryness of the mouth, sudden hunger, heightened sensory perception, sedation and conceptual changes. A number of these—in combination—are what is called "getting high."

Along with these generally pleasant changes, the user may also experience nausea, anxiety, paranoia, changes in blood pressure and body temperature, disorientation, confused states, short-term memory loss, temporary alteration of motor skills, changes in depth perception, poor attention span and depression. Some researchers have found that smoking grass inhibits verbal and analytical skills in users while facilitating nonverbal tasks.

Additionally, marijuana, when coupled with other substances, can have an addictive effect. Alcohol and marijuana in combination can render the user dysfunctional; marijuana used in combination with barbiturates can prolong the effect of the barbiturate, and, in extreme cases (at least theoretically), cause nonlethal doses of barbiturate to become lethal doses.

In general, researchers agree that these effects, both pleasant and unpleasant, are temporary. Even acute anxiety or paranoid reactions can be managed with verbal reassurance. A study of 700,000 hospital admissions in the United States in 1971 revealed that only ten of those were for acute cannabis reaction.

Certain tasks requiring fine motor skills—driving a vehicle or operating certain types of machinery and equipment—should not be undertaken while under the influence of marijuana. How long the driver will be impaired remains under debate, but even the most liberal thinkers acknowledge that driving should not be undertaken for three to four hours after smoking. The other end of the spectrum puts it at more like sixteen hours—depending on the individual, the quantity and quality of cannabis smoked and other factors.

"As yet there has not been a single instance of human lung cancer attributable solely to marijuana use."

In certain circumstances—people taking medication which cannabis might interfere with—individuals may have a short-term reaction deleterious to their health, and judgment should be exercised in the use of cannabis.

The effects mentioned above are considered to be of short duration and depend on the potency of the cannabis, the setting, and the user's orientation and state of mind at time of use. Generally, some of the negative—and, sorry to say, the positive as well—effects are expected to be more pronounced in the newer user rather than in the more experienced individual.

Pulmonary Effects

The lungs are the natural target for the harmful effects of smoked material, and among chronic smokers, chronic bronchitis and mild airway constriction occur regularly. There are several known carcinogens in marijuana smoke and certainly more tar—though no nicotine—and incidental particulates than in tobacco smoke. But as yet there has not been a single instance of human lung cancer attributable solely to marijuana use.

The bronchial problems mentioned are somewhat more related to the act of smoking than they are to the active ingredients in grass, and the use of a water pipe can eliminate most of them.

Theoretical problems with fungi found in marijuana—Aspergillus, among others—are repeatedly mentioned in the literature. However, there has only been one official case of actual Aspergillus poisoning, and that was in a man whose immune function was depressed as a result of intensive chemotherapy treatments. Fungi can be killed by cooking the marijuana before use (100°C for 30 minutes), though in most healthy people this has not shown itself to be a problem. Marijuana smoke has been shown to inhibit pulmonary antibacterial defense systems, but the toxin involved is reportedly related to the smoke itself and not to any psychoactive component in the drug.

I spoke with Dr. Tashkin of UCLA, one of the leading pulmonary specialists in the country, and asked him what the real risks—long-term—to the smoker were. "We've found changes in the airways of marijuana smokers which are also found in the airways of cigarette smokers who go on to develop cancer . . . it doesn't mean they will develop cancer. That hasn't been shown to have happened yet, it's just a marker of increased risk we've found in smokers using two or more joints a day for more than five years. The smoking of marijuana can lead to pulmonary complications, and that really is the bottom line. Of course, to find out the real risk we're going to have to rely on doctors asking their patients as to whether or not they smoke. We'll have to record that information, and that information will have to be made available to pathologists, and they will have to study the results."

Heart and Hormonal Effects

Smoking marijuana clearly changes heart function. The most common and important of which is through tachycardia—a speeding up of the heart rate that is sometimes accompanied by temporary changes in blood pressure—and, occasionally, by ventricular fibulation—a condition where ventricle contractions become uncoordinated.

These effects have been shown to be temporary and reversible and not problematic in healthy individuals. In certain circumstances, however, they could lead to serious complications—specifically in people with heart problems or angina pectoris. Those taking medication for the heart are recommended to avoid smoking cannabis, since the THC may interfere with those medications.

The side effects of the speeding up of the heart rate (which also occur with tobacco smoking, though not to as great a degree) can include a temporary change in body temperature, dizziness on standing and a diminished capacity for exercise.

There is as yet no evidence of heart disease caused by marijuana or any evidence of permanent effects to the hearts of healthy individuals, though Reese T. Jones cautions that, "The lessons learned from chronic tobacco use are worth considering [since] THC seems to have a far more profound effect on the cardiovascular system than does nicotine."

Effects from both acute and chronic exposure to cannabis have been shown in laboratory animals. In male animals, the primary effects have been a lower sperm production and changes in the serum testosterone levels in the blood. In female animals, changes include disrupted menstrual cycles and a decrease in the production of prolactin, a hormone which aids in the production of breast milk.

In humans, there appears to be a modest reversible suppressive effect on sperm production, which some studies debate, noting that tolerance quickly develops and sperm production rises again (even during smoking) with no evidence that this has a deleterious effect on male fertility. Female hormonal study, at best, indicates a slight disruption of menstrual cycles. Some researchers are quick to point out that this disruption would have an obvious effect on those trying to conceive on particular days, while others don't feel this is a particularly negative effect.

Some scientists feel that for men with marginal procreative or sexual functions, even a slight lowering of their testosterone levels might cause problems—though studies have failed to show this clinically.

Scientists across the board are concerned with the possible problems connected with prepubescent, chronic smokers and what effect even minor and reversible hormonal changes would have on their development. As yet there is little evidence to suggest any great problems in this area, but there is general agreement that this situation requires further study.

Cells and the Immune System

The numbers and kinds of chromosomes—structures in a cell nucleus which contain and transmit genetic information carried by DNA—are characteristic for a given species. Structural variation and changes in the numbers of chromosomes may be evidence of genetic damage due to drugs or other chemical agents. While there have been studies which indicate that tar found in marijuana smoke can inhibit cell division in certain types of cells, there have been fairly conclusive studies made which indicate that marijuana does not break chromosomes.

Studies that do indicate chromosomes have either been conducted on lab animals—using doses of THC which were larger than humans could conceivably take—or on multiple drug abusers, and those results "may be due to other factors associated with a life of heavy drug use."

"There have been fairly conclusive studies made which indicate that marijuana does not break chromosomes."

The Relman Report—a government-sponsored study of marijuana and health conducted in 1980 to 1981 to review all then-existing marijuana research—concludes that "the weight of evidence from human studies indicates that neither marijuana nor THC causes chromosome damage."

The immune system functions in protecting the body against viruses, bacteria, poisons and other infections. It also plays a major role in preventing the growth and dissemination of cancerous cells. The primary components in the system are two active white blood cells (T-cell and B-cell) and macrophages. B-cells identify specific body enemies and produce antibodies to chemically disarm them. T-cells consume viruses, poisons and cancerous cells. The primary job of macrophages is to stop anything breathed in that could cause disease by absorbing it. Both the T-cell and macrophages grow as they consume, and they divide when they have reached their size limit, creating more of themselves.

Any inhibition of these functions, either in identification, consumption or creation of antibodies to fight off the invading agents, is called an immunosuppressive effect. The body simply isn't handling the problem.

Some early studies in this area indicated that the T-cell's ability to divide was inhibited by THC, though these studies were conducted only in the laboratory. Later studies have shown a weak immunosuppressive effect in macrophages, though these effects varied from subject to subject and were regarded as transitory. That is, shortly after smoking, while there was a high concentration of THC in the body, there was a measurable change; the response returned to normal as THC levels dropped.

More recent studies, conducted by Munson and Fehr, conclude that marijuana reduces resistance to infection but acknowledged that this change would vary from person to person and would most often be minor: "It is likely that we would now be aware of profound changes in the resistance of humans if they occurred frequently. But even minor effects would be significant among those with immune disorders or with immunity otherwise suppressed."

On this last count, there is some concern from several quarters. Even minor changes in immune response have to be looked at critically in the light of the current AIDS epidemic, *not as a cause by any stretch of the imagination*, but simply because it is an area which has not yet been researched.

This is not a cause of concern for the user. It is only mentioned because a number of scientists feel that *any* drug which relates, even mildly, to the immunosuppressive response cries out for research in view of this new problem.

Pregnancy and Offspring

Early reports which tied cannabis use to birth defects in humans on the grand scale—webbed feet, retardation, and so on—have been discounted by even the most anti-cannabis scientists. Those studies that reported these findings generally dealt with lower-economic groups who practiced poor nutrition, drank heavily and were often multiple drug abusers. Even then, such major birth defects showed up with such rarity that few people took them seriously.

The reality is that while there are some effects to the offspring of both humans and animals from cannabis use—generally from pure THC—the changes are not very dramatic. Saraseth, Carol Grace Smith, Susan Dalterio and Peter Fried, among others, have found unhealthy changes in offspring of lab animals exposed to THC, but most of these involved short-term nervous disorders, aberrant visual attention spans, lighter birth weights and shorter gestation periods. Radical doses of THC have had greater effects, but only in lab animals and these did not correspond with human test results. Of the above mentioned researchers, all but Dalterio agreed that offspring whose mothers were exposed to cannabis or THC caught up with nonexposed offspring within thirty days after birth. Dalterio's work deals with second generation mice, and her early result—roundly disputed—suggests that fertility and hormonal production can be affected in those second generational lab mice.

Dr. Peter Fried, a leading researcher in the field who works with human offspring, says, "There are no major effects to offspring when marijuana is used in conjunction with good nutrition during pregnancy. Marijuana has been used by middle-class women very comfortably during pregeancy since the '60s. If there were any major effects they would have been noticed by now. But that doesn't mean that there aren't subtle effects that might be important." Those effects include "a significant increase in symptoms associated with nervous symptom abnormalities which might indicate a mild form of withdrawal . . . the optimum condition is for a pregnant woman not to use any exogenous agents at all."

Because THC is known to cross the placenta and to be found in breast milk, and because the effects—even minor effects—are not fully understood, this sentiment is generally echoed in the scientific community; use of cannabis by pregnant women is not recommended.

The Brain

Despite two outlandish studies published in the 1970s which concluded that marijuana caused brain atrophy, researchers universally agree that there is no evidence that cannabis causes structural changes in the brain. On the other hand, several teams of researchers have found changes in the brain's electrical activity in human beings during the most active periods of THC action. These changes diminish as the effects of the "high" wear off.

More to the point are the chemical changes marijuana causes, since these changes are what produce the "high," and the issue of accumulation. Most researchers agree that while THC in minute doses remains in the brain for some time after smoking, it is neutralized. New studies have found traces of subcortical activity, presumably related to marijuana use and isolated to that use, long after the "high" has worn off.

"Researchers universally agree that there is no evidence that cannabis causes structural changes in the brain."

Reese T. Jones had written in 1980, after much study, that "the weight of evidence [indicates] that lasting neurophysiological impairments are possibly, but not inevitably, associated with some undetermined level of heavy, prolonged marijuana use." Dr. Jones was one of the members of the Relman Committee, and when I spoke with him about his 1980 findings he said, "The conclusion of the National Academy of Science group—the Relman Report—was that not all the answers were known but that one should not be complacent and assume you're gonna get away scot-free. They were a very good group of researchers, most of whom had no axe to grind about marijuana. It's a very complicated drug, or series of drugs and there's so much we don't know."

Several other scientists I spoke with felt the same way. The brain is very complicated, and the effect of cannabis on it is not fully understood. Subtle changes invisible to testing methods may occur. Gilekson, making a humorous report to a Senate subcommittee in 1980, concluded, "Marijuana may not lead to death, but it might reduce the chronic smoker to mediocrity."

Still others are not convinced that there is any evidence to support the idea of accumulated toxicity or any other effects which are not entirely reversible once smoking stops. But even they would like to see more research money spent to study long-term effects to chronic, heavy smokers, and almost no one is willing to commit themselves to saying there are absolutely *no* lasting effects, because so much remains to be understood about how the brain really works.

No scientist of repute suggested any real hazards in this regard for the casual user.

Behavioral Syndromes

Although there is no evidence to suggest that a specific cannabis psychosis exists, there has been enough clinical evidence of negative behavioral patterns among chronic cannabis users for researchers to recognize the interaction of the drug with previously existing problems. In other words, psychological problems and psychiatric illnesses, while not necessarily caused by chronic smoking, can certainly be worsened by it, according to Rick Seymour, of the Haight-Ashbury Drug Abuse Clinic. These "long-term problems or situations—where marijuana is being used to self-medicate underlying psychological problems—call for appropriate counseling by health professionals."

Frequently discussed behavioral patterns among chronic smokers include:

• Antimotivational Syndrome: Characterized by apathy, loss of ambition, loss of effectiveness, diminished ability to carry out long-term plans, difficulty in concentrating and a decline in school and work performance. This syndrome may be seen in nonsmokers of marijuana, and even chronic use is not always associated with loss of motivation, but people experiencing these symptoms will, again according to Seymour, "Probably worsen the situation by taking any sedating drug." Biologically, this syndrome does not exist, but, as Hollister, a reputable researcher notes: "One cannot help being impressed by the fact that many promising youngsters change their goals in life drastically after entering the illicit drug culture, usually by way of cannabis. With cannabis, as with most other pleasures, moderation is the key word." The problem, for the user, is to determine the difference between use and abuse.

• Toxic Delerium: Also known as acute brain syndrome, it is characterized by a clouding of

consciousness manifested by impairment of ability to sustain attention to a goal or stimuli, changes in sleep patterns and sustained disorientation. These symptoms are found only occasionally, and then usually in long-term heavy users. Reese T. Jones has said, "Almost anyone given the right dose in the right setting can be made to exhibit a set of schizophrenic-like symptoms." Symptoms disappear with abstinence, provided there is no additional psychological or physiological problem.

• Effects on Pre-existing Mental Illness: Clinical, not biological, evidence suggests that some cases— particularly patients with mood disorders and schizophrenia—may be negatively affected by smoking grass.

"The adverse effects [of marijuana] appear fully reversible through abstinence."

• Flashback Syndrome: While there is no biological evidence yet of a flashback syndrome, many researchers feel that there is a kind of *deja vu*—often relating to acute anxiety—that many marijuana users encounter. Mike Wizner of the Beverly Hills Detox Center, says he regularly treats people for these negative feelings, which in some cases can be quite severe whether chemically induced or not.

• Effects on Aggression: With the exception of the occasional rare individual with some special disposition to violence, every experiment conducted with cannabis has shown a decrease in aggression in the user.

Addiction

Most researchers agree that addiction, literal and physiological, to cannabis can occur after an unspecified, long-term, heavy exposure to the drug. But withdrawal symptoms are very mild—slight depression, anxiety, possible nausea—and of very short duration—several days or less. Fear of withdrawal is not seen as a reason for continuing use. On the other hand, "You have the same sort of psychological syndromes you do with any other addiction," according to Dr. Norman Zinberg of Harvard Medical School's Department of Psychiatry.

Quantities of cannabis needed to attain addiction are nonspecific (varying from person to person) but because they are known to be high, the casual user does not run the risk of physical addiction.

Marijuana and Drug Abuse

Marijuana use does not physically lead to the use of, or experimentation with, any other substances. Moreover, government studies indicate that changes in an individual's behavior start before drug use. On the other hand, clinical studies indicate that experimentation with one drug seems to open a gate for experimentation with others. According to the National Institute for Drug Abuse, those people who are going to have drug problems generally begin by drinking alcohol and smoking cigarettes, becoming addicted to one or the other of these substances, and then experiment with speed or cocaine.

Rick Seymour has been working for years with people who have drug related problems and has written extensively for a number of journals and magazines, including HIGH TIMES. When asked whether marijuana is harmful to addicts trying to stay clean, he says, ''People who are getting off alcohol or other drugs are in a position of having to deal very carefully with what they are doing with their lives, from their diet to their behavior and so on. What happens when they smoke is that grass creates a sense of euphoria that reminds them of how nice it was to be loaded and there it goes. It's as simple as that. There could even be a physiological factor we don't know about . . . [smoking] does seem to contribute to relapses among addicted people.''

Obstacles to Marijuana Research

1. There is a problem of relating animal research to human experience. In many areas the crossover is not accepted as accurate.

2. Problems are encountered in regulating the dose. In research it is easier to use isolated Delta 9-THC, though this is rarely used by itself in the individual, and the isolated component doesn't necessarily act the same way when it is found as part of the whole plant.

3. Since researchers are not permitted to take nonsmokers and make them smokers—grass being illegal—they must study subjects who already smoke. Since smokers are often multidrug users, assessing what part of a health issue is directly associated with grass is often a difficult and, certainly, a manipulable factor.

4. In studies of cross-cultural smokers, ganja smokers in Jamaica for example, critics of these studies point out that the accurate histories of the subjects contain variables that researchers cannot control. Proponents of these cross-cultural studies point out that these populations have a generational history of smoking. Critics point out that in cultures where cannabis is acceptable, it is acceptable only among laborers, not intelligentsia, and so results are not applicable to our society.

5. Not every researcher is scrupulous, and the lure of a research buck or continuing research bucks for information the funding organizations want to hear cannot be overlooked.

Summary

Enough is known about the effects of marijuana to keep most researchers from saying that the heavy, chronic smoker will get a completely free ride. There have been demonstrable negative effects to the lungs and unanswered questions regarding several other bodily functions. It's questionable whether these represent a serious danger to the user: The answer you get depends on the researcher you speak with. At this time, the adverse effects appear fully reversible through abstinence, though a good deal more research is hoped for in several areas to clarify the issue.

Peter Gorman is a contributing editor of High Times, *a magazine which advocates legalizing marijuana.*

"The use of marijuana can become a stepping-stone to other drugs."

Marijuana Encourages More Serious Drug Use

Helen C. Jones and Paul W. Lovinger

"One of the public's greatest fears about marihuana is that its use will lead to the use of other drugs (the 'stepping-stone' theory). This appears to be a myth." A sociology textbook made that statement (1973) without offering any documentation.

Once prevalent, the stepping-stone theory fell out of favor with academics amid America's big drug boom. They paid little heed to studies showing relationships between marijuana and other drugs. . . .

Three Surveys

Professor Hardin B. Jones, of the University of California at Berkeley, made three surveys of multiple drug use, two of them among male students there and one in the military.

- The first (1971) covered 400 students, of whom 280 regularly smoked marijuana. Two-fifths of those smokers, 118, had taken heroin or another opiate one or more times. Of the 120 who never had used marijuana, not one ever had tried an opiate.
- Next, of 367 heroin addicts studied in the U.S. armed forces at different world stations (1971-73), 363 had used marijuana before starting heroin. Only four began heroin without having first tried marijuana.
- In the final survey, of 150 marijuana smokers and 48 nonsmokers (1975-76), only those who had smoked marijuana went to other illegal drugs—about a quarter of them to opiates, nearly half to cocaine, and more than half to LSD. In addition, substantially larger percentages of marijuana users than nonusers smoked tobacco and drank coffee, alcohol, and even tea. . . .

In 1976 the report on the nationwide survey of 2,510 young men and drugs had come out. It presented facts like these:

- Of all those surveyed, 148 took heroin. All of the heroin takers except two also used marijuana. Put another way, 11 percent of the 1,382 marijuana users also took heroin while less than two-tenths of one percent of the nonusers of marijuana did.
- Nine out of every ten of those dual drug takers had consumed marijuana first; 7 percent tried heroin first; and for the remaining 3 percent, the order could not be determined.
- One-quarter of marijuana users and almost no nonusers took cocaine; 96 percent of the dual users had started marijuana before starting cocaine.
- One-third of marijuana users and 4 percent of nonusers also took opiates (besides heroin); marijuana came first in 77 percent of the dual-use cases.
- Two-fifths of marijuana users and almost no nonusers consumed psychedelics; 80 percent of the psychedelic users had first smoked marijuana.

Six Years Later

Two of those who carried out the survey continued to analyze the data and reached a conclusion six years later on the relation of cannabis use and heroin use. Reviving the stepping-stone theory, Kentucky sociology professors O'Donnell and Clayton argued that "marijuana use is a cause of heroin use in the U.S. . . ." They marshaled additional statistics, derived from the survey:

- The more times a young man had smoked marijuana, the more likely he was to have taken heroin. One-third of the 1,000-time smokers consumed heroin. Of those who had used marijuana 1 to 9 times, only 1 percent also had used heroin; 10 to 99 times, 4 percent; 100 to 999 times, 12 percent; and finally, 1,000 times or more, 33 percent. Three-fifths of the heroin takers had smoked marijuana 1,000 or more times.
- The top heroin addicts were also in the top marijuana category. Of eighteen men who had taken

heroin 1,000 or more times, fifteen also had taken marijuana 1,000 or more times (two, 100 to 999 times; and one, 10 to 99 times).

• Cocaine followed the same pattern: the greater the use of marijuana, the greater the likelihood of cocaine too being used. Only one cocaine user had not tried marijuana. Among those who had smoked marijuana 1,000 times or more, three-quarters had used cocaine too.

Marijuana and Heroin

That a "new government-funded study" linked marijuana with "harder stuff" received conspicuous albeit sketchy press coverage (via testimony of Dr. William Pollin, director of the National Institute on Drug Abuse, before a Senate committee, 1981).

O'Donnell (now deceased) and Clayton summarized their case as follows. Marijuana use is a cause of heroin use because:

"1. Marijuana use and heroin use are statistically associated.

"2. Marijuana use precedes heroin use, not invariably, but in the vast majority of cases; and

"3. The association has not been shown to be spurious."

They rebutted the argument that drinking of alcohol or smoking of tobacco is the real culprit, not marijuana. Marijuana is a better predictor of other-drug use; the statistical associations are stronger, whether number of users or extent of use is considered, they said. The sample of young men had many who avoided marijuana but few who shunned tobacco and fewer nondrinkers.

"Marijuana is a better predictor of other-drug use [than alcohol or tobacco]; the statistical associations are stronger."

Illustrating how overwhelming was the rejection of the stepping-stone theory in the social-scientific community, they cited nine sociology textbooks, 1971-75. Each treated lack of causal relation as almost a self-evident fact, needing no documentation.

According to some writers, to say that the use of one drug "causes" the use of another, you must demonstrate that nearly every user of drug A proceeds to drug B. Obviously, this did not happen to most of the young men. Only one marijuana user in four proceeded to cocaine and only one in ten went on to heroin. By the above standard, marijuana use did not cause heroin use.

O'Donnell and Clayton wondered if such writers denied "that cigarette smoking is a cause of lung cancer, on the grounds that only a minority of smokers develop the disease?"

They suspected that the denial of causality expressed a political rather than a scientific viewpoint of social scientists: possibly the sociologists (at least those active in the drug field) had reacted against the arguments of law enforcement officials that the progression from marijuana required severe penalties for marijuana possession. . . .

Certainly a multiplicity of illegal drugs are available in the drug subculture. Although signs indicate a modest decrease in heroin usage as the law has grown softer on marijuana users, the use of cocaine has soared. (For example, it tripled in ten years through 1982 in polls of young adults—more than one out of four having used it.) If marijuana were completely legalized, we would expect a significant percentage of the new, legal users eventually to seek out "better highs." . . .

A Stepping-Stone

"The use of marijuana can become a stepping-stone to other drugs for rather simple reasons," said Dr. Robert G. Heath, the Tulane University brain researcher (1978). "Use of pleasure-inducing agents tends to lead to increased desire for the pleasure derived. This leads to increased use and, often, increased dosages.

"Marijuana doesn't supply the brain with the fundamental chemicals that produce pleasure, but it stimulates other chemicals in the brain that do so in turn. And with protracted stimulation, these other chemicals are used up or lose their strength. So, to maintain the pleasure feeling, the system needs to be stimulated more strongly. This can lead to the selection of something stronger to do the job."

One social researcher who has rejected the stepping-stone theory—"too simplistic and based on faulty logic"—is Denise Kandel (Columbia University and New York State Psychiatric Institute). She has denied that one drug "causes" the use of another, although her research demonstrated that one type of drug usually would follow another in a definite sequence, marijuana preceding the so-called "harder" drugs. . . .

The trouble with the stepping-stone theory, in her opinion, is this: "The fact that 100% of heroin users have had experience with marijuana does not mean that the reverse is true and that 100% of the marijuana users will end up using heroin" (1979).

We don't know of anyone who says the reverse is true. Plainly it is not. But this fact should not invalidate the theory.

Let us imagine a series of five stepping-stones leading to a little island in the middle of a stream. Everyone visiting the island steps on the five stones. But not everyone stepping on stones visits the island; some step upon only one or two or three stones, enjoy the view, and turn back. All five stones are necessary, however, for those going all the way.

Alcohol and cigarettes could be two such stepping-stones. (We do not dispute those who emphasize their dangers.) Marijuana could be another.

Personal Accounts

Senators at two hearings listened to personal accounts of childhood drug abuse from rehabilitated addicts. Ron was fifteen when he testified in 1983 before a Senate appropriations subcommittee: "When I was eleven, everyone in school was getting high. I didn't know anybody that didn't do it. I was stealing, failing in school [parochial school in New York City] and getting in trouble all over the place. I stole from anybody I could." Ron had begun smoking marijuana at the age of seven. He graduated to alcohol, cocaine, and peyote.

Jeff, aged twenty-five, of southern California, had testified in 1980 that "I started smoking pot when I was nine in New York. I said I would never ever do any other drugs." By the age of twelve he had taken LSD, cocaine, and nearly everything else the "drug culture" offered. The taking of marijuana and other drugs was rebellious, but at the same time it had "a lot of acceptance and peer pressure" behind it. Leaving bad company and moving to a wealthier environment in California did not help; things were worse. "I have shot heroin. . . . In 1979 I spent $30,000 on cocaine. . . . I have taken pills day in and day out." He said decriminalizing marijuana put an official OK on it, inevitably meaning that "drug abuse of other kinds will follow. This is not only from my own experience. I am a very average case of drug abuse in schools."

His brother and two sisters also suffered addiction to other drugs after starting with marijuana. Treatment rehabilitated the four.

In a letter to the presiding senator, Jeff wrote that a decade earlier his best friend "was smoking pot that wasn't satisfying enough anymore. He decided to shoot (mainline) heroin, which he had tried a few times prior to this. He took too much, the result was death. . . . I could write of many examples resulting in death. . . . The truth in this matter of smoking pot is that out of literally hundreds of adolescents and adults I have encountered personally, I have not met one person involved that has not gone on to try at least some other kind of drug whether it be uppers, downers, heroin, angel dust, and most of all cocaine and Quaaludes."

The Phillips' Story

A grim picture of drug addiction emerged from a three-show series on Dick Cavett's television program featuring popular musician John Phillips and his actress daughter Mackenzie Phillips (together with psychiatrist Mark S. Gold, who was treating them at a New Jersey hospital). Father and daughter were recovering drug addicts. Independently, he had become hooked on heroin, she on cocaine. The family blew "millions" on drugs. Aside from shooting the drugs into their bodies, nothing in the world mattered to them—not love, not food, not even survival. She married because her husband could get cocaine for her. Seeing themselves deteriorate and people they knew die from drugs made no difference.

Portions of the TV conversation follow.
CAVETT: Legalization of marijuana?
MACKENZIE: No.
CAVETT: For a time the idea was very fashionable.
JOHN: I believed in it.
MACKENZIE: I did too. I disagree now. . . . I started with marijuana. He started with marijuana.
JOHN: There are lots of people who smoke marijuana . . . and they go no further, and they can handle it. There are lots of other people who start with marijuana [and] end up being drug addicts.

"The truth in this matter of smoking pot is that . . . I have not met one person involved that has not gone on to try at least some other kind of drug."

It was in the early sixties I started smoking marijuana, then hallucinogens in the sixties . . . then cocaine in part of the seventies. And then around 'seventy-six it [heroin] also caught up with me. I'm living proof that the domino theory works. You know: one drug to the next, to the next, to the next, to the next. . . .

If I smoked marijuana, I wouldn't really be satisfied. I'd have to smoke something else. It would just be the whole circle over again . . . in record time.

Helen C. Jones is a drug researcher, writer, and lecturer. Paul W. Lovinger is a free-lance writer and former newspaper reporter.

"Pot smoking usually leads only to more pot smoking."

Marijuana Does Not Encourage More Serious Drug Use

Arnold S. Trebach

"After pot parties at night, kids would go to the manhole and shine a flashlight down on the decomposing corpse . . . for kicks." So wrote Peggy Mann in a highly influential article, "The Parent War Against Pot," in 1980. The popular writer was describing a situation in which a 15-year-old Cleveland-area boy had been murdered and his body stuffed down a manhole; it remained there known to perhaps 100 teenagers but not the police for six months. While admitting that this was "hardly a typical story," Ms. Mann felt it important enough to report and to connect with today's youth and marijuana in the public mind. She quoted the boy who revealed this story as saying to a doctor that he had to get into a "drug removal center" because "I suddenly realized how pot can make you do crazy things." . . .

Both reason and the evidence are securely upside down when it comes to marijuana. Marijuana is increasingly proclaimed as the major cause of the downfall of our youth. In her foreword to Peggy Mann's *Marijuana Alert* in 1985, the First Lady (Nancy Reagan) went even further when she declared that the book was "a true story about a drug that is taking America captive." Not only our youth, but the whole country. That book is one of the latest and most sophisticated examples of marijuana-scare literature. By mentioning only the research that tends to show marijuana's unique harmfulness, Ms. Mann implies that science has documented that the drug has spread over the country almost like a new nerve gas, paralyzing its people, especially youth. . . .

A balanced review of all the authoritative research during the past century documents no distinctive harm from marijuana. Its addictive threat comes from the fact that it is an intoxicant, but any intoxicant taken compulsively presents possible dangers to young people. Its threat to physical health comes from the fact that it is absorbed in the form of smoke, but any smoke, even from corn silk or chopped parsley, taken regularly into the body could eventually cause serious harm to some people. . . .

Is Marijuana a Gateway Drug?

My greatest objection to marijuana is that it involves smoking. My personal fear is that if I ever used it, the habit of smoking might lead me back to tobacco and not on to heroin or cocaine, as the gateway-drug theorists claim. That theory is also sometimes described as the escalation theory. However it is labeled, it does not make much sense in reality. Just about as much sense, in fact, as the statement by the heavy drinker who said he was going to quit drinking water since he found that he got in trouble when he took bourbon and water, Scotch and water, and gin and water; water was the only common factor. So water was clearly his real problem.

Nevertheless, there are few ideas so commonly accepted by all of the drug-war and marijuana-scare proponents as the escalation or gateway theory. Since he became attorney general in 1985, Edwin Meese keeps repeating the theory, almost as a testament to his faith. In its 1986 report, the President's Commission on Organized Crime declared flatly, "While many beliefs about marijuana have been proven wrong by subsequent research, this concept has been affirmed." The warrior medical experts seem to imply that there is something in the chemical structure of the drug that sucks many young occasional users through that gate and on to harder drugs and into the whole drug culture. Thus if that gate is kept closed to our youth, then that illegal culture is never entered. However, except in the imaginations of a few people, there is no identifiable element that makes the illegal drugs, on the whole, significantly worse than the legal ones.

In fact, many of those unfortunate people who feel impelled to use and then to abuse mind-altering drugs often do not distinguish between legal and illegal substances. Certain drug addicts may specialize in taking heroin and to that extent they are involved in a criminal subculture. When heroin runs dry, however, they will turn to alcohol or prescribed methadone or Valium, all legal. Many of these addicts tried marijuana before they tried heroin but pot did not impel them to heroin. Their drive to alter consciousness with chemicals led them to both and they chose the former because pot is often the easiest drug to find, even more available to many young people than beer. Repeated studies have documented, though, that the first mind-altering chemical most young people use is alcohol. On the basis of such irrefutable evidence, we could postulate that the major gateway drug for millions of our kids is not pot, but alcohol, that alcohol leads to all drugs, and that therefore we should have a war on alcohol, starting with a new prohibition law. Other research suggests a similar role for tobacco, thus raising the possibility of another prohibition law based upon a different gateway drug.

Looking at the Evidence

I find little support for the gateway theory as applied to pot in any of the data issued by the government, including the massive surveys of residents of households put out periodically by NIDA. To me, they prove conclusively that (1) pot smoking usually leads only to more pot smoking; (2) many young people smoke pot a great deal, then get bored with it, and cut down or stop totally; (3) a minority of pot smokers move on to harder drugs or continue to smoke pot along with those more potent chemicals. I can find no evidence of a causal link between, say, pot smoking and heroin injection or cocaine sniffing in these surveys.

"I can find no evidence of a causal link between . . . pot smoking and heroin injection or cocaine sniffing."

I searched for clues on the gateway theory in *The National Survey on Drug Abuse: 1982*, based upon detailed personal interviews with a scientific sample of over 5,000 people, which concluded that the great majority of marijuana users smoke it only occasionally as children (12-17 years) and also as young adults (18-25). What about the young kids who seem preoccupied with pot during some phases of their adolescence? While this can lead to terrible problems for a small percentage of children, the

report saw even this kind of use as not harmful to the great majority. "A particularly intensive level of marijuana use often represents a passing phase in the marijuana use career," according to *The National Survey*, which then explained that many "'occasional' users quit entirely" and that "many 'intensive' users drop back to moderate levels of consumption."

If the escalation theory worked for large numbers, then the percentage of users would be higher for other drugs, especially the illegal ones and especially for older users. The opposite was true.

Results of the larger 1985 household survey of drug use were similar in respect to the gateway theory, in my opinion. Projections were made of the total number of people in the United States who had ever used an illegal drug and of those who were current users (who had used it at least once in the 30 days prior to the survey). It was estimated that 61,940,000 people had used pot and that 18,190,000 were current users. Yet there were only 5,750,000 current users of cocaine and the number of current heroin users was so small (less than .5 percent of the sample) that estimates were impossible. I do not mean to downplay the problem of heroin and cocaine—only to point out humbly that if the marijuana gateway theory made any sense, then many more of those 61 million who had smoked pot would have gone on to those harder drugs.

These comprehensive federal studies document the continued existence in America of the responsible, controlled use of marijuana. Millions of our children and young adults are sufficiently in control of their minds and bodies to use marijuana for months and years—and then to make significant changes in their patterns of use as a matter of personal choice. Those changes rarely entail moving on to harder drugs.

Marijuana a Filter

It could be that for many of these young people marijuana may well work more as a filter than a gateway. Dr. Dale Beckett of Surrey, just south of London, has spent over two decades in the medical front lines treating heroin addicts and other people with drug problems. He found that as many adolescents struggle with the agonies of that stressful period they reach for some form of a chemical crutch. The physician believes that many potential addicts are able to calm their anxieties with minor drugs such as marijuana in moderate doses. "However, if personality defects are so great that minor drugs do not help him enough then it is possible he will try heroin," Dr. Beckett wrote. "It seems that the presence of minor drugs may actually filter off some adolescents who, if they were not available, would be likely to use narcotics from the start." Viewed in this novel light, the wide availability of marijuana may well be a positive force for society. The Beckett theory stands the escalation theory neatly on its head.

Whether it is a gateway or a filter, marijuana is smoked mainly by adults. Only about one in seven of current American marijuana smokers is a child, according to that NIDA household survey in 1985. Smokers between the ages of 12 and 17 accounted for 14.6 percent of the total of current users.

One of the few facts put forth by the drug alarmists that I found to be absolutely true is that illegal drug use has indeed risen since the early Sixties. Back then, approximately 2 percent of youth had ever used an illegal drug; that figure peaked at 68 percent in 1979. The rise is conventionally trumpeted as an epidemic of crisis proportions. And yet we have seen that our children are not dying in huge numbers from these drugs and also that their death rates are at a historical low and life expectancy at a historical high. There is reason to believe that this generation of our youth, along with the rest of the population, are using great quantities of illicit drugs but that their physical and mental health, on the whole, are not being seriously harmed by those drugs. At the same time, too many of our young people are tormented by the disease of drug addiction and deserve all of the help that society can muster. Those young people in need of treatment will not be helped, however, by wild claims that the entire generation is being destroyed by illegal chemicals.

Arnold S. Trebach founded the Institute on Drugs, Crime, and Justice of Washington and London, and has written many articles on drugs.

viewpoint 57

Marijuana Should Be Legalized

Alfred C. Villaume

The medical profession has a maxim, *nihil nocere*, which means in essence that physicians must take precautions against doing more harm than good, that they must make certain that whatever treatments they prescribe for patients with ailments or injuries are less devastating to the patients than the ailments or injuries would be if left untreated.

A similar maxim is sorely needed to circumscribe the actions of those who create and enforce our laws as well as the nature and scope of the laws themselves. Inasmuch as the purpose of society's laws is to regulate the behavior of the members of society for the common good, a rule or maxim should exist to the effect that any law that does more social harm than would the behavior it regulates were it left unregulated is a bad law and must be rescinded.

Such a rule or maxim would be no more than logical. A physician who routinely chose to amputate fingers as a treatment for hangnails would quickly be branded as a butcher and a quack and drummed out of the medical profession. Similarly, a law that harms or destroys society's members in order to save them or society from the relatively minor consequences of their own predilections and pecadillos should be recognized as being illogical and counterproductive and stricken from the books.

Unfortunately, we here in the United States are protected by no such logical maxim or rule of law. There are many laws in our complicated and overlapping array of legal codes that are without question more harmful to the public than the behavior they are intended to control would be if it were left completely unregulated. Such laws are not only on the books, but they are also too often zealously enforced by one governmental agency or another, frequently because continued agency funding or existence depends on perpetuation of these laws.

Drug Laws

Of such laws, the so-called drug laws are the most glaring examples. These laws, which proscribe the preparation, distribution, possession, or use of certain substances that some members of our society previously decided were "dangerous drugs," are a disgrace and are antithetical to our avowed concept of "liberty and justice for all." This is especially true because many other substances that are equally or more harmful to individuals than those proscribed by the drug laws are not defined as drugs and are dispensed and used more or less freely.

While all of the drug laws contain certain inherent fallacies and contradictions and are at best misguided attempts by one group of people to legislate the morality of other groups, the laws against marijuana are by far the most illogical, ill-founded, and socially destructive. It is the purpose of this paper to focus briefly on the historical uses of marijuana, the origins of the marijuana laws here in the United States, and the status and effects of these laws as they exist today, and to then present a few facts regarding marijuana and marijuana users. By so doing, it is intended to demonstrate that the marijuana laws were predicated on deceit, media manipulation, half-truths, and outright fabrications; that today's marijuana laws are perpetuated through those same ignoble methods; and that the marijuana laws themselves are far more harmful and socially destructive than any degree of widespread and unregulated marijuana use could ever be. It is hoped that this will lead the reader to share the author's conclusion that the marijuana laws are bad laws and to join him in advocating their immediate abolition.

Historically, the medicinal, religious, and recreational uses of marijuana are inextricably

Alfred C. Villaume, "Law Without Order: The Marijuana Laws," *ACJS Today*, September 1986. Reprinted with permission.

intertwined. It is quite definite, however, that marijuana and its uses were known well by the ancients at least as far back as the second millenium B.C. Interestingly enough, except for a relatively few isolated instances, marijuana usage was confined to cultures other than those from which we can trace our socio-cultural descent.

Here in the United States, we generally trace our cultural antecedents back to Attic Greece by way of Western Europe and Imperial Rome. The Greeks, Romans, and Europeans were all enthusiastic imbibers of ethyl alcohol in their recreational pursuits. And while all had frequent and well-documented contact with civilizations that preferred instead to use marijuana for recreational purposes, that preference for some reason never caught on with our ancestors. Hence, until very recent times marijuana usage remained something that was indulged in predominantly by others—by nonwhite, non-Christian, non-European peoples.

Our good, white, Christian forefathers shunned such heathen practices, preferring instead to pickle their brains and livers in ethyl alcohol in its various concoctions. And so things remained for nearly four millenia.

"Historically, the medicinal, religious, and recreational uses of marijuana are inextricably intertwined."

It is quite possible, perhaps even probable, that the fact that marijuana use was largely confined to people of non-European descent is what made it relatively easy for the first marijuana laws here in the United States to be passed some 50 years ago. At the time these laws were passed, aside from a modest few medicinal preparations containing marijuana that were readily available from either apothecaries or physicians, most marijuana being used here in the United States was being used by a few jazz musicians and itinerant agricultural workers, by nonwhites who were either on the far fringes of society or actually beyond the pale. And, it is easy and painless for a society to prohibit the use of a substance that very few of its members use in any case.

Harry Anslinger and Marijuana Laws

On January 1, 1932, a dour former Assistant Prohibition Commissioner took office as the head of the newly established Federal Bureau of Narcotics, a subunit of the U.S. Treasury Department. It is impossible to discuss the marijuana laws here in the United States without referring to Harry Anslinger, as the former are almost exclusively the creation of the latter.

Commissioner Anslinger, whose initial mandate

had nothing to do with marijuana in any way, shape, or form, soon embarked on a lifelong crusade to first outlaw marijuana and then savagely prosecute any and all of those who used it. Exactly why Harry Anslinger developed his almost psychopathic hatred for marijuana and its users is not known.

What is known is that Harry Anslinger, through media manipulation, exaggeration, and gross misinformation, cajoled most of the states into passing laws against marijuana; that he tricked the Congress of the United States into passing harsh laws prohibiting the cultivation, importation, sale, or possession of marijuana, and into making these laws increasingly harsher as the years went by; that he coerced the Committee of Revision of The United States Pharmacopoeia (U.S.P.) to delete marijuana from the publication, which had previously listed it as having valuable medical properties; and that directly and indirectly over the past 50 years he has destroyed more young American lives than polio, rheumatic fever, and cancer combined. Harsh words? Perhaps. But then Harry Anslinger left a harsh legacy, the cost of which is still escalating after the passage of half a century.

The evidence that Harry Anslinger and his colleagues supplied bogus or exaggerated information to the media and manipulated state and federal lawmakers in their campaign to outlaw marijuana is too widespread to be ignored. And, that campaign was definitely successful. By the time the federal government outlawed marijuana in 1937, most of the states had already passed such legislation. The rest soon followed. And, as there were few mainstream Anglo-American marijuana users in the United States at that time, aside from periodic Anslinger-inspired horror stories detailing the evils of the "killer weed" that were used as rationalizations for further tightening of the marijuana laws, little was heard about marijuana and its users for the next 30 years.

Racial Prejudice

This is not to suggest that the marijuana laws were not used. They were, and savagely. But, they were used almost exclusively against nonwhites, who were arrested, found guilty, and shuffled off to prison with scant attention from the media or the public. As noted, the marijuana laws were also toughened periodically by the various states and by the United States Congress in 1951, again, primarily through the efforts of Harry Anslinger and his cohorts. But, the victims of the marijuana laws, and victims they most certainly were, were for the most part nonwhites who lived and worked and got high in ways that were different from those that were practiced by mainstream America. It was those others who suffered first and most.

By the midsixties, however, despite the horror stories and harsh penalties, the situation had changed markedly; the children of the white middle-class had begun to use a variety of drugs, the most pervasive of which was marijuana. By 1969, there were an estimated 4 million regular marijuana users in the United States, a figure that was, if anything, a gross underestimate. Moreover, the falsehoods and exaggerations on which the marijuana laws were predicated were for the first time being confronted by the reality of widespread, relatively open marijuana use by young middle-class whites. Not black musicians, not itinerant Hispanic laborers, but our own children were using marijuana. And, it was not causing them any noticeable physical or psychological harm. Suddenly the laws had to change.

> "After 50 years of prohibition, . . . how successful have been the attempts to stamp out marijuana use? Not very."

During the ensuing decade, the marijuana laws throughout the country were relaxed greatly. The federal government reclassified marijuana (as a non-narcotic) in 1970, and markedly decreased the penalties for violations of the marijuana laws. Various states went even further, several reducing simple possession of marijuana to a petty misdemeanor punishable only by a small fine. But, marijuana was never decriminalized, far less actually legalized. Although it was suggested and widely discussed by one legislature and another in various parts of the country, no legislative body was ever able to take the step of ending the prohibition against marijuana completely.

A New Era of Repression

In 1980, Ronald Reagan took office as President of the United States and a new era of repression began. In the ensuing years most of the liberalization of the previous decade has been eroded. The penalties for violations of drug laws, including the marijuana laws, have been increased and the harshened laws are being enforced with a zealousness unmatched since the repeal of the Volstead Act in 1932 to end the prohibition of alcohol.

How did this happen? For one thing, soon after taking office as President, Ronald Reagan appointed as his Special Assistant for Drug Abuse Policy a man by the name of Carlton E. Turner, a onetime chemist who is cast in the mold of his philosophical predecessor, Harry Anslinger. . . .

Like Harry Anslinger before him, Carlton Turner manipulates the media by overtly supplying misleading or exaggerated horror stories, by leaking the results of poorly done and scientifically unsound clinical studies, and by generally attempting to whip up public hysteria against drugs in general and marijuana in particular. While this antidrug campaign has not been notably successful in curbing drug use, it has resulted in a reversal of the liberal drug law reforms of the previous decade, in a slowing of the movement to legalize marijuana, and in a return to aggressive, harsh enforcement of the existing marijuana laws. Unfortunately, the public is still ambivalent about marijuana. And, the antidrug forces in the Reagan Administration are taking full advantage of this public apathy.

Marijuana Use in the United States

After 50 years of prohibition and in an increasingly repressive antidrug climate, how successful have been the attempts to stamp out marijuana use? Not very. Recent figures indicate that marijuana is one of the four major cash crops grown in the United States. . . .

Quite probably, an even larger quantity of marijuana is grown abroad, in Mexico, Colombia, Panama, Jamaica, and many other third-world countries. This huge quantity of marijuana is then smuggled into the United States by planes, boats, cars, mules, and individuals who sneak across the international borders on foot, to be added to the multibillion-dollar crop grown domestically. This massive amount of marijuana is not grown and imported just to give the Administration's drug agents something to do. By their own admission, the amount of marijuana seized in the United States by all law-enforcement agencies combined is only a minuscule fraction of what escapes detection and seizure on its way to its final destination. Someone is paying billions of dollars annually for the marijuana that gets through. And, that someone is the American public.

Other recent figures indicate that marijuana is one of the four most commonly used recreational drugs in the United States today, along with ethyl alcohol (beer, wine, and liquor), nicotine (cigarettes, cigars, snuff, and other tobacco products), and caffeine (coffee, tea, and cola-based soft drinks). Of course, most Americans don't think of their booze or their cigarettes or their coffee as being drugs. But, they are wrong. All three, along with marijuana, the opiates; cocaine and many other compounds are psychotropic (mood-altering) in their effects and must be considered drugs by any rational definition. The main difference between marijuana and the three other major recreational drugs used here in the United States today is that, unlike them, marijuana has been legally defined as a drug and is prohibited by statute.

The Effects of Marijuana

Is marijuana more harmful than alcohol or nicotine or caffeine and, thus, perhaps justifiably prohibited by law while the others are more or less dispensed and used freely? Emphatically not. Is marijuana harmful at all? Probably. Although it has never been demonstrated conclusively despite frenetic governmental efforts to do so, it is quite probable that excessive use of marijuana will eventually cause some sort of physiological or psychological damage if continued long enough. Such is also true, however, of nearly every other substance people use, and certainly of all substances used for recreational purposes, and is thus hardly a rational basis for prohibition. Marijuana is certainly less harmful to the human mind and body than ethyl alcohol, which causes thousands of deaths annually through liver necrosis, *delerium tremens*, and a variety of other diseases. Marijuana is much less harmful than nicotine, which has been linked to lung cancer and heart disease and which reportedly causes hundreds of thousands of deaths each year. And, marijuana is at least arguably less harmful than caffeine, which heightens stress, causes ulcers, and may trigger cardiac arrhythmias. In fact, compared to the other three major recreational drugs in common use here in the United States today, marijuana is a relatively innocuous and harmless substance. No one has ever been shown to have died from an overdose of marijuana, nor even to have suffered any long-lasting ill effects. Too bad the same cannot be said of the major legal recreational drugs. The fact is that the major potential for harm connected with the use of marijuana is the likelihood that the user will be arrested and traumatized by the criminal justice system for violating the marijuana laws.

Thus, as was suggested at the beginning of this paper, the marijuana laws in and of themselves cause more social damage than the behavior they are intended to control. What makes this situation even worse is that the marijuana laws also fail utterly, as we have seen, to control or in any appreciable way curtail the use of marijuana.

Destructive Aspects

This is not to say that the marijuana laws have no impact. They do. While they fail to act as a general or even as a specific deterrent to marijuana use, the marijuana laws are applied, and savagely, against those relatively few individuals who are apprehended for their violation. Tens of thousands of individuals have been arrested and imprisoned since the Reagan Administration launched its frenzied "war on drugs" a few short years ago, many of them for violations of the marijuana laws. Many thousands more have been arrested, prosecuted, heavily fined, placed on probation, and forced to undergo treatment and counseling for "drug abuse."

Any arrest and conviction for violation of the marijuana laws has a potentially destructive social consequence. Persons so arrested and convicted are branded as drug abusers and criminals and are stripped of some or all of their rights as citizens. Such violent and destructive governmental intrusion into the private lives of the citizenry would scarcely be tolerable under any circumstances; its occurrence as part of an overwhelmingly unsuccessful but still vitriolic campaign to curb the use of so comparatively harmless and innocuous a substance as marijuana is ludicrous, discriminatory, and far more destructively "criminal" in terms of social consequences than any possible use of marijuana could ever be.

> "Any arrest and conviction for violation of the marijuana laws has a potentially destructive social consequence."

An ancillary destructive consequence of the drug laws in general and the marijuana laws in particular is the disrespect for the law itself that such ill-founded and illogical statutes promote throughout the citizenry. One bad law that can be identified easily as such by the public erodes our entire system of laws; a number of bad laws breed disregard for laws in general and, thus, foster chaos and the breakdown of the social order. Moreover, law enforcement personnel are not immune to the pervasive influence of bad laws. Humane police officers may be persuaded to overlook violations of bad laws, at least on an occasional basis. But, the step from that rather understandable point to outright corruption is a minor one. With a substantial percentage of the public openly and regularly flouting the law, as is the case with the marijuana laws, it is small wonder that we see increasing numbers of police officers and perhaps whole departments corrupted and caught up in the very laws they are sworn to uphold. The problem is not, as has been suggested, that drugs themselves are the cause of such corruption, but rather that the drug laws are bad laws and facilitate such unfortunate events. While this is true of all of the drug laws, it is especially true of the marijuana laws, for which no logical, medical, or moral justification exists.

The very extent of marijuana use in the United States today, coupled with the fact that there is really no rational basis for the prohibitions against marijuana, suggest that an end to prohibition is the only viable solution to the problem.

Alfred C. Villaume is a multiple convicted drug dealer, long-term prison inmate, and "jailhouse lawyer." He holds academic degrees in sociology and chemistry, and has had a wide range of experience in the practicalities of drug laws and their effects.

"Legalizing marijuana... would bring a disastrous increase not only in medical damage and monetary costs, but in psychological and psychiatric damage and costs as well."

Marijuana Should Not Be Legalized

Peggy Mann

Decriminalization is a legal term that applies only to marijuana. Indeed, it is a term made up *for* the marijuana situation by leaders of the organization with a purposefully contrived acronym—NORML [National Organization for the Reform of Marijuana Laws]. Founded in 1971, the organization attracted not only a fervent following of pot-smokers, but also a number of highly respected organizations that, at the time, favored the concept of decriminalization of marijuana.

Decriminalization—in the minds of many—did not mean that marijuana use would become legal, merely that possession of small amounts of marijuana for personal use would not be treated as a criminal offense with a possible jail sentence. It would, instead, be legally categorized as a civil offense, the penalty being a small fine and no criminal record. This seemed perfectly reasonable to many people. And if there had been no other agendas, and if NORML had reported fully on the marijuana health-hazard story as it unfolded from the scientific community, the organization might have served a useful function, as far as meaningful laws were concerned.

However, from statements made by NORML board members, it seems that the term "decrim" was a first step toward NORML's true goal—the legalization of marijuana. For example, at NORML's 1978 annual conference, Keith Stroup, then executive director of the organization, said, "It's time we finally took the honest step to declare to the world: We want legal marijuana." . . .

Decriminalization laws were passed in eleven states, the first being Oregon in 1973, the last, Nebraska, in 1978.

When decrim was passed in Oregon, Major H. D. Watson was head of the state police narcotics

division. "Within a matter of months," he recalls, "we saw a drastic change in people's attitudes about the use of marijuana. Many even thought it was legal and that they could smoke it on the street."

In California, one simple statistic indicates the immediate increase in problems that arose after decriminalization in 1976: In the first six months following decrim, arrests for driving under the influence of drugs increased 46.2 percent in the case of adults, and 71.4 percent in the case of juveniles, when compared to the same six months of the previous year.

NORML and other pro-pot forces continually quoted statistics such as these: "450,000 marijuana arrests were made last year." Invariably, the figure was followed up with a statement like this: "The trauma of an arrest and a child's being thrown into jail is far more harmful than the drug itself." Some pot proponents go much further, claiming this is the only really harmful thing about the drug.

What is *not* made clear is the fact that for simple possession, arrests are not followed by jail sentences. Indeed, according to Norman Darwick, executive director of the International Chiefs of Police, "Since 1976, most of those charged with 'simple possession' of an ounce or less of marijuana have really been arrested for some other violation of the law. Then, because marijuana was found on them, they were also charged with possession of marijuana."

No Decriminalization

For a time, when Dr. Robert DuPont was director of NIDA [National Institute on Drug Abuse], he favored decriminalization. But he is just one of a number of leading experts who have completely changed their minds on the issue. In June 1979 he said:

> I have learned that it is impossible to be pro-decrim and anti-pot because no matter how you try to explain it to them, young people interpret decrim as meaning

Peggy Mann, *Marijuana Alert.* New York: McGraw-Hill Book Company, 1985. Reproduced with permission.

that pot must be okay because the government has legally sanctioned it. Furthermore, while we do continue to arrest people for possession of marijuana each year, virtually none of those people go to jail for even one day. We therefore have *de facto* decriminalization in every state in the union.

In June 1984 DuPont pointed out:

Throughout this period a majority of Americans—young and old alike—have favored maintaining tough anti-pot laws. The brief romance with decriminalization was trendy in the early 70's, but never caught on with the American public. For example, in a March 1981 national Roper survey, when asked "How important to society do you feel it is that the laws related to the use of marijuana be enforced?" 58 percent answered that "Strict enforcement of the law is very important"; 20 percent said, "Fairly important"; 14 percent "Not very important"; 7 percent "Not at all important", and 2 percent "Don't know".

Since the National High School Senior Survey began in 1975, a consistent finding among seniors—the *least* anti-pot segment of our society—has been that a majority never favored legalization. For example, in the 1983 survey, 37 percent felt that marijuana use should be a crime, while only 19 percent felt that using pot should be legal. . . .

"Legalization of marijuana is . . . not the answer. It is the opposite of the answer."

At its 1982 annual conference, NORML introduced another route toward legalization. It sounded sensible to many people: Forget decrim, forget legalization, let's talk about regulation and taxation of marijuana. Some of the funds can then be earmarked for drug prevention, drug treatment, and . . . wiping out the national debt. An intriguing argument indeed—until we look at the alcohol model, where few if any designated funds from taxing alcohol have been authorized for treatment or prevention. An intriguing argument—until we look at the statistics engendered by our two legal drugs, alcohol and tobacco, statistics that show their toll in health care, sickness, and death, costs to our society that far outswell any monies derived from taxation of liquor and tobacco. It seems clear that legalizing marijuana, with its concurrent burgeoning increase in use, would bring a disastrous increase not only in medical damage and monetary costs, but in psychological and psychiatric damage and costs as well. Legalization of marijuana is thus not the answer. It is the opposite of the answer. . . .

The Present Crisis

Dr. Robert DuPont served for five years as founding director of the federal National Institute on Drug Abuse (NIDA). He also was chairman of the Drug and Alcohol Dependency Section of the World Psychiatric Association until 1979, and since 1980 has been president of the American Council on Drug Education. As a psychiatrist in private practice, he specializes in the treatment of drug-users, and among professionals he is recognized as one of the most experienced in the physical, psychological, and social ramifications of marijuana in our society.

DuPont sums up the present crisis in these words:

During the sixties and seventies there was a tumultuous change in values in the United States, particularly for young people. The emphasis was on the present tense and not the future, and also on the individual's personal pleasure and not on responsibilities to others in his or her life, or in society. This was something new and entirely out of character in terms of the previous history of our country. *The leading edge of this cultural change was marijuana use.*

Marijuana smoke promised this generation a harmless high; it seemed to be a way to have personal pleasure now, without paying a price later. We are now seeing not only the awful consequences of this shift in values for the individuals involved and for our society, but the dire reality of the marijuana epidemic. Many people caught up in this shift of values refused to look at the negative health effects of marijuana smoking, but with more than twenty million pot-smokers these effects can no longer be ignored—even by the pot apologists. The people who have covered up the evidence of marijuana's negative physical, psychological, and cultural effects will make the apologists for the cigarette industry look like sincere humanitarians. Their message that marijuana use is okay, which appeared so trendy in the 1970s, looks deadly in the 1980s.

In my personal experience, the most tragic result of our marijuana epidemic—visible wherever you look in our country today—is the fact that millions of young people are living as shadows of themselves, empty shells of what they could have been and would have been without pot.

There is a slowly growing awareness among some Americans, even young people, that the consequences of this tragic national search for a safe chemical high are already horrendous. I find it chilling, however, that young people accept the loss of 20 percent or more of their peer group to drugs and alcohol as the natural order of things. Instead of being angry about it and saying, "We've got to get organized and stop this!" kids tend to shrug it off and say, "Well, that's the way it is!"

If Americans of all ages do not create an active commitment to eliminating marijuana from the lives of our youth, this epidemic will pervade not only youth but all segments of our society—as has occurred with alcohol—vastly escalating the current damage being done by marijuana.

When Dr. DuPont left the directorship of NIDA in 1979, his successor was Dr. William Pollin, who had been director of NIDA's Division of Research since 1974. Pollin points out that marijuana is of particular concern for several major reasons:

It is used by four times as many people as any other illicit drug. Its use begins very often at a young and particularly vulnerable age—in junior high school, or even younger. It is the gateway drug par excellence, containing over four hundred different components. And the effects of many of these chemicals are only now beginning to be studied.

Peter Bensinger comes at the problem from another perspective. For five and a half years Bensinger was head of the Drug Enforcement Administration (DEA), and thus the principal law enforcement official with responsibility for illegal drugs in the United States. He served under presidents Ford, Carter, and, for seven months, under Reagan.

In 1981 Bensinger became president of one of the nation's principal consulting firms to private industry on the subject of drug abuse in the workplace. He therefore has a unique dual perspective on the matter of marijuana, and has this to say about it:

Marijuana is far and away the country's biggest drug problem. The statistics are overwhelming. Furthermore, there is not a state in the country where marijuana is not grown illegally. And I'm not talking about growing pot in windowboxes. In 1980, the DEA made a thorough countrywide survey and we found hundreds of acres of marijuana growing in every state. We found high-potency sinsemilla in well over a dozen states. And we found large trafficking organizations built and developed on the basis of marijuana, in as many as eighteen states. . . .

I do not want to dignify marijuana by comparing it to legitimate businesses, but it ranks only slightly lower in profits than AT&T and Exxon.

In Florida, for example, Colombian and Cuban drug trafficking organizations literally took over banks. In Miami alone a total of four banks were owned by U.S., Cuban, and Colombian traffickers, and they were laundering money in daily amounts that were regularly in excess of half a million dollars, and frequently in excess of a million dollars per banking day. In 1980, the Atlanta Federal Reserve Bank, which is in charge of the Florida area, reported an increase of over two billion dollars in circulating cash for that year, which law enforcement believes is principally fueled by illegal marijuana and cocaine traffic.

The illegal cash profits of the pot industry are threatening legitimate industries in the United States and abroad: several agricultural markets and timber-growing areas in California, for example; the fishing industry in Colombia; coffee and fruit products in Hawaii; coffee and sugar cane plantations in Jamaica. The damage of the illegal money flow is not only found in disrupted land values on the Florida coast, for example, but in offshore banking havens in the Caribbean. In Colombia, the U.S. dollar buys less on the black market than it does at the official rate of exchange because there is such a large amount of unauthorized U.S. currency. And, of course, violence goes hand-in-hand with the drug traffic, as the homicide rate in Miami clearly shows (the highest per capita in the country).

Another destructive area concerning the economics of marijuana is that it generates illegal business enterprises, which attract a wide spectrum of supposedly "respectable" Americans: Hollywood stars, sports stars, bank presidents, airline pilots, and public officials—to mention just a few categories. These are not white-collar criminals who deserve lenient treatment but, rather, the reverse. They are infiltrating and corrupting legitimate businesses and government while compromising health and safety in schools and colleges, on the highways, in the workplace, and in our armed forces. And all for their personal illegal pot profits. . . .

The many millions of people who now use marijuana in the United States do so because they haven't been discouraged from using it. This is what we now must do. We must cut both the supply and the demand. There needs to be enforcement of the laws that we have, a dedicated and concerted international effort to reduce availability, and a massive educational program to provide users, parents, teachers, and communities with accurate facts about the health hazards concerning this drug.

Some action is finally being taken on many fronts. But the front lines are still pitifully underfinanced and overextended. We must wake up to the full realities of what the marijuana epidemic has been doing to our country. We have not yet reached the point of no return. But time is running out.

"Marijuana is far and away the country's biggest drug problem."

Dr. Carlton Turner, who in 1983 was appointed special assistant to the president for drug abuse policy, put it this way:

The inescapable fact is that unless our current pot-smoking habits are reversed sharply, marijuana will have . . . destructive long-term effects that no laboratory experiments can anticipate. These effects are already clearly stamped in our workplace, in our armed forces, in our schools, on our highways. Furthermore, our escalating increase in such social ills as venereal disease and unwanted pregnancies are all patterns found in disproportionate numbers among chronic pot-users in our society. Chronic use is highest in the fifteen- to twenty-four-year-old age bracket. Within the past decade in America the death rate of *all* other age brackets has decreased. But—for the first time—the death rate among fifteen- to twenty-four-year-olds has *increased*. The primary contributor to the death-rate increase among our young people is alcohol and drug abuse. And our primary illegal drug is marijuana.

We must realize that there will be no free ride for marijuana users. Unless we come to grips with this problem, they may take our nation with them on their downhill course, one which we never traveled before. . . .

Cannot Eliminate Illegal Pot

There are many non-pot-smokers who favor legalizing marijuana for the perfectly sound-sounding reason that "then we could tax it, and use the money for drug education and so forth"—money that otherwise goes to pushers, drug traffickers, criminals. Furthermore, as they see it, the drug sold would then be pure, clean, a "reliable product."

However, the characteristics of cannabis almost ensure that even if pot were legalized, there would always be illegal marijuana—because of the development of *tolerance.*

After a while, the chronic user becomes tolerant to the effects of the drug. For example, a joint of 2 percent THC potency may no longer produce a high.

The user must therefore smoke more and/or more potent joints. Tolerance accounts for the fact that illegal growers continually aim to produce an ever more potent product. (The more potent, the higher price they can charge.) Consequently, even if the THC potency of "legal pot" *could* be standardized at, say, 2 percent (which itself is nearly impossible), many chronic users would eventually search out the illegal, more potent product. Since the aim is to get high, there would be no reason to pay for a product that "did nothing" for them.

"Even if pot were legalized, there would always be illegal marijuana."

The main reason, however, for not legalizing marijuana lies not in what the drug does *for* the user, but in what it does *to* the user. . . .

A staggering amount of research has been done proving that cannabis is harmful in a wide spectrum of ways, with impairing effects on the lungs, the heart, the sex organs, the reproductive system, the brain, the immune system, as well as on the babies born to animals and humans exposed to pot smoke or THC. Studies show that the damage done by this drug reaches from the molecular matter that is the cornerstone of life to the highest levels of human life—the mind and the personality.

Peggy Mann has written extensively on drug abuse for Reader's Digest *and other publications. This viewpoint was excerpted from her book* Marijuana Alert.

Legalizing Marijuana Would Reduce Drug Abuse

Andrew Kupfer

Drugs are dangerous. Even users agree on that. Yet the U.S. seems to be getting nowhere in its war against them. In frustration, large numbers of Americans, including academics, members of Congress, and some big city mayors, are talking about waving a white flag. Legalize the stuff, some of them say, and be done with it. Let multinational companies take the business—and the profits—away from criminals. Stop the gunfights, the car bombs, the street crime, the bribes. Drug barons can sell their fleets of airplanes and go back to stealing cars, or whatever they were doing when all this started.

The idea is tantalizing, but simplistic. It addresses only one aspect of drug use—the prevailing criminality—without raising the question of how people can be persuaded not to use drugs in the first place. Moreover, legalization would have different effects on the markets for different drugs. At best it is not a solution but a trade-off: lower crime, perhaps, in return for the risk of greater drug use, addiction, and health costs.

Still, as Ronald Reagan used to say about the economy when he was running for President in 1980, what we're doing now isn't working. America needs a radical rethinking of its stance toward drugs. There might even be a place for legalization as part—but only part—of a carefully crafted policy that seeks to create a legal market for marijuana separate from that for heroin, cocaine, and its cheaper derivative crack. The money and police time freed up by legalizing pot could help pay for a more effective crackdown on hard drugs plus more programs for rehabilitation of addicts.

A Half-Hearted War

Legalization of all drugs is a last-stand position based not on the notion that hard drugs are good for people, but on the widespread perception that the government has thrown all its resources into the struggle and failed. That perception is flawed. Despite the tough rhetoric, the war on drugs has been less than total. The Administration's most recent policy is Zero Tolerance, which is supposed to mean just that. The smallest pinch of drugs found in a million-dollar yacht would be enough to justify seizure. No holds barred, nobody gets off. The reality is different. Yachts were seized, then given back. Punishment of offenders is wildly inconsistent. A Florida court in May [1988] convicted Carlos Lehder, a handsome pilot who looks as if he stepped out of a television thriller. He faces a prison sentence of life plus 150 years for smuggling cocaine into the U.S. About the same time, a judge in Manhattan put on probation a woman convicted of attempting to sell 174 vials of crack. As long as street sellers go free, Carlos Lehder's colleagues in the Colombian cartel can keep on producing and shipping cocaine to the U.S.

Nor can it be said that society is uniformly tough on drug users. When traces of drugs were found in the body of a railroad engineer, killed when he rammed into the rear of a standing train in New York, his union resisted the understandable call for mandatory drug testing. Job seekers in other kinds of work aren't so keen on testing either.

Probably Americans have no stomach for pushing drug law enforcement anywhere near the max. In Malaysia, after all, drug trafficking is punished by hanging. The task is to develop a policy in line with American concepts of civil liberties and within the limits of U.S. resources.

A first step is to decide that a drug-free society should not be the goal of policy. The thinking behind Zero Tolerance, says Dr. David F. Musto, professor of psychiatry at Yale, "is part of a typically American ideal about the perfectability of man." Total success is unattainable and policymakers who try to achieve it will overlook intermediate measures that may do a better job of helping people kick the habit or keep from developing one in the first place.

Legalizing Marijuana

One of those steps could be the unthinkable: legalization of marijuana. Since the early 1970s aging flower children have pushed for legal pot on grounds of—as they would put it—common sense. They argue that the drug is nonaddictive, widely used, and probably no worse a health hazard than alcohol. This "Why not?" approach never got anywhere, because it was easily countered with "Why?" Who needed another social problem no worse than alcohol? Now some surprising data from the Netherlands suggest that there might be a more compelling reason to legalize marijuana.

Pot has already been decriminalized in some U.S. states, though not completely legalized. Possessing small amounts of marijuana is punishable only by a small fine in New York, Ohio, California, Oregon, and seven other states; it could result in prison elsewhere. In places where the harsher laws remain on the books, police often put a low priority on making arrests for small transactions involving marijuana and hashish, because of limits on the number of cops, courtrooms, and jail cells. The result is de facto decriminalization in much of the country at the local level. Still, the Drug Enforcement Administration (DEA) continues to watch out for marijuana use and U.S. Customs officers might confiscate your car if they catch you bringing in some joints from Mexico. Drug enforcement agents still spend a lot of time and money chasing down foreign suppliers.

The importance of a legal market for marijuana is that it could help steer young people away from hard drugs by breaking the connection between marijuana smokers and drug pushers. The chief agent in the descent of people into hard drugs is the pusher. In the inner cities especially, pushers are walking drugstores, selling marijuana and hashish, barbiturates, stimulants, cocaine, and heroin. The first sample is usually free. Data from the National Institute of Drug Abuse show that, aside from alcohol, marijuana is the first drug most young people try. If they are buying pot on the street, as most of them must, then they will be exposed to the rest of the pharmacopeia.

The Netherlands Example

The Netherlands provides a fascinating example of how creating a separate market for marijuana and hashish can help cut heroin use. As hard drugs washed across the world in the late 1960s and early 1970s, many young people in the Netherlands became addicted. A dozen years ago, in an attempt to reverse the trend, the government tripled the jail term for trafficking in hard drugs. At the same time

officials declared that they would not prosecute anyone found with less than 30 grams of marijuana and hashish, though laws against the drugs remained on the books.

Since then small amounts have been sold openly by operators of coffeehouses in Amsterdam, usually under the watchful eye of the police. "Because we want separation of markets," says ministry of justice drug policy adviser M.A.A. van Capelle, "we're interested in keeping a small market in soft drugs so people will know where to get it." Police don't look too closely into where the coffeehouses get their supplies, but if proprietors start mixing in hard drugs or sell amounts of pot deemed excessive, the place is shut down. The result is that a youngster curious about pot can buy it and use it in a safe place. He won't be arrested and he won't be exposed to pushers of hard drugs.

"The Netherlands provides a fascinating example of how creating a separate market for marijuana and hashish can help cut heroin use."

The Dutch worried at first that their new policy would cause a surge in marijuana use. In fact, according to the government, consumption has fallen. This decline may reflect the growing disaffection with drugs characteristic of the post-Flower Power era, but it is no less noteworthy that it occurred in a period of more open availability. The real payoff, though, is that use of heroin, the hard drug of choice in the Netherlands, has fallen too, particularly among young people. In 1981, 14% of heroin addicts were under 22; today the figure is 4.8%.

How Legalization Could Work

Critics of legalization will argue that the United States is not the Netherlands. Indeed not. The U.S. is a more heterogeneous society, with no institution quite comparable to the friendly Dutch coffeehouse. Americans might not be as comfortable relying on the discretion of local cops in the enforcement of—or in winking at—marijuana laws. Another approach here could be to legalize marijuana outright and make liquor stores the point of sale. The age restriction could be the same as for alcohol. The government could tax pot, with the revenue used to finance hard-drug treatment programs. If pot were taxed like cigarettes, it would generate an estimated $11 billion a year. Some $1.2 billion in state and federal money is now spent annually on drug treatment.

Legal pot would likely be a home-grown U.S. industry, removing it still further from the criminal elements in the international drug trade. American-grown marijuana now satisfies 25% of domestic demand, up from 9% when Reagan took office. The U.S. Drug Enforcement Administration believes that the U.S. will be the world's largest producer by the early 1990s, and soon after that a net exporter. Marijuana is already the largest cash crop in California.

Doctors still differ about the damage marijuana smoking inflicts, though they are beginning to agree that prolonged regular use may be risky, particularly to short-term memory and the lungs (marijuana contains tar, like cigarettes). As does alcohol, marijuana impairs perception, coordination, and memory. Long-term effects on the brain and the lungs are not yet known. The heart works harder, increasing blood pressure, a risk to people with hypertension. THC, the active ingredient, lowers the concentration of reproductive hormones in the bloodstream. But occasional use is unlikely to cause lasting health problems, and most people tend to use marijuana for only a short period of their lives.

A larger concern is whether more people would use marijuana if sanctions were removed. No one knows for sure. The ranks of drinkers grew by only about 10% after Prohibition ended. A survey of high school seniors across the nation by the University of Michigan shows that while fewer are smoking marijuana, the vast majority (85%) find it readily available. Those who don't probably haven't been looking.

Hard Drugs

The case against legalizing hard drugs is twofold. First and foremost, the possibility of an explosion of addiction is too grave a risk regardless of any supposed benefits. Second, many of those benefits are illusory. One of the arguments for legalization is that the price would drop dramatically with the elimination of the huge criminal-risk premium, and addicts would no longer have to steal to support their habits. Dr. Mitchell S. Rosenthal, president of Phoenix House, a New York-based drug rehabilitation center, disputes that. For many addicts, he points out, crime is the way they earn money for all their needs, not just for drugs; because they are addicts they are unsuited to ordinary occupations. "If you give somebody free drugs you don't turn him into a responsible employee, husband, or father," says Rosenthal. "A large number of drug addicts have serious underlying problems."

Some advocates of legalization point to the British system of the 1950s, when heroin was available to addicts by prescription. The number of addicts remained stable for many years, and almost all were known to doctors. The aim was to wean addicts from the drug, but if doctors could not, they gave small doses that prevented withdrawal without producing a high. That ended with the worldwide

drug boom of the 1970s. With drugs flooding into the country illegally, doctors could no longer control an addict's habit. Addicts will go for a kick if they can find one. Unable to get enough heroin from doctors, they turned to the illegal market. The prescription system died out.

"A survey of high school seniors across the nation ... shows that while fewer are smoking marijuana, the vast majority (85%) find it readily available."

Even if a separate, legal market for marijuana were successful in slowing the growth of hard-drug users, the U.S. would still have to contend with those already hooked. That means continued, even increased, pressure on heroin and cocaine dealers, but with a more balanced effort than the U.S. has been pursuing. The emphasis has been on stopping drugs in the source countries. The huge profits of drug producers have worked against that approach. The drug barons are so rich they have managed to bribe high officials and sometimes whole governments. "In the long run the real answer to the drug problem is not interdiction," says Robert Stutman, special agent in charge of the Drug Enforcement Administration office in New York. "Even using the military won't make a major difference." Peter Reuter, a senior economist at the Rand Corp., points out that since prices are so high, a drug dealer can still make big money even if lawmen seize most of a shipment.

What Can Be Done

But there are some steps the U.S. can take. International cooperation may be the most promising. Countries where drugs are produced once took the view that drug use was an American problem. Now that they are discovering that the number of addicts within their borders is growing, they have become more willing to explore joint action against drug producers and dealers.

At home, the U.S. needs a unified, coordinated policy that extends from federal drug enforcement officers down to local judges and cops. Agents from the DEA and the FBI conducted separate undercover investigations into laundering of Colombian drug money. Both operations hit pay dirt, but did there have to be two?

More enforcement dollars should be pushed down to the street. New York City officials claim to have had great luck with Operation Pressure Point, which focused police manpower on the streets of the Lower East Side. Says Sterling Johnson Jr., special narcotics prosecutor for the city: "Pressure Point was a tremendous success in taking the community back, literally, from the drug dealers." Mark Kleiman, a lecturer on criminal justice at Harvard University's Kennedy School of Government, says that if police are active in the streets, they can increase the time a drug user must spend to find dope. "If you are a heavy user and the probability of not connecting is great," says Kleiman, "that becomes a strong argument for getting into a treatment program."

If an addict looks for a program, however, he had better be able to get in. In New York City, New Haven, and Portland, Oregon, the waiting list for treatment can be several months long. Not every addict would avail himself of help even with limitless facilities, but it is unconscionable that people must be turned away when billions are being spent on interdiction that at most raises the street price of drugs by a few dollars. When a drug user is ready to go for help, he should be able to do so without a long wait. "One of the differences between drug users and us is time scale," says David Turner, director of the Standing Conference on Drug Abuse, based in London. "We want things immediately, but we can cope with delay. An addict is used to taking heroin and getting immediate relief. It's not surprising that if he is told he can have an appointment in four weeks, he will probably forget about it."

"A policy of compromise could give an outlet to people who wish to experiment with soft drugs . . ., deglamorizing those drugs while vilifying those that are deadly."

The best solution to the drug problem is societal change. That takes a long time. A good start is instilling an understanding of the potential hazards of drug use at an early age. Signs are that the numerous school programs across the country are beginning to work. The University of Michigan survey shows drug use among high school seniors down 13.6% since 1982. (The survey excludes teenagers who have dropped out, however, the biggest group of crack users.)

The role that education can play is apparent in Massachusetts, which has developed a range of curricula for kindergarten to the 12th grade. "The program is really one part hard facts about drug education and three parts comprehensive health education," says Marianne Lee, deputy director of the Massachusetts Governor's Alliance Against Drugs. "A fourth of all children live in a home where there is a substance-abuse problem. We teach kids how to deal with that, and how to keep their self-esteem intact." Since 1984 the number of high school students who have tried illicit drugs has dropped 11%, vs. a national decline of 7%. The downside is that alcohol use remains high in Massachusetts; 61% of students said they had used it at least once in the 30 days before the survey.

Just Say No?

Is the Just Say No campaign helping? "It's not enough to tell kids to say no," says Lee. "We have to give them a reason to say no." Perhaps the phrase has had to bear more weight than it was meant to. Originally coined as a slogan for very young children, it was latched onto as a motto by drug treatment programs of all types. More sophisticated kids are not impressed by it.

Some educators worry that legalizing marijuana while continuing a tough stance toward hard drugs might send a confusing message. But American society transmits many conflicting signals about addictive substances. For example, while the Surgeon General rails against smoking, Congress continues to subsidize tobacco growing. A policy of compromise could give an outlet to people who wish to experiment with soft drugs and their small intoxications, deglamorizing those drugs while vilifying those that are deadly. That just might help break the spiral of criminality and violence without throwing open the doors of chemical invention to those who may not be able to resist.

Andrew Kupfer is an associate editor of Fortune, *a business newsmagazine.*

"The benign image of marijuana and its use as painted for us by the experts 10 years ago is outdated and irrelevant to today's marijuana problem."

viewpoint **60**

Legalizing Marijuana Would Increase Drug Abuse

Robert L. DuPont Jr.

For most Americans over the age of 35—that is, those who passed through their drug-vulnerable teenage years before the drug epidemic of the late 1960s and 1970s—drugs like tobacco and alcohol are so familiar they are hardly considered to be "drugs." The "new" drugs, introduced for the first time to the majority of American youth only in the last two decades, are not new in any sense other than that they were not previously familiar to most Americans. Cocaine is now enjoying its third run as a drug of mass use and dependence (the earlier cocaine infatuations occurred in the 1880s and the 1920s). Marijuana has been around, and generally viewed quite negatively, in other cultures for thousands of years. Opiates, such as heroin, as well as many stimulants, depressants, and hallucinogens are also not new. Only our mass exposure is new. Here the simple, tragic fact is that American youth, in the last 20 years, have made themselves guinea pigs in a national "experiment" of unprecedented proportions. Never before in world history has so large a segment of a national population used such a large number of dependence-producing drugs—and become so hooked on them. When the full impact of this "experiment" is assessed, it will, I am convinced, be seen as a national tragedy of immense proportions.

Safe-Seeming Drugs Uniquely Dangerous

Another key to understanding which drugs emerged as major drug problems during the last two decades is the *image* each drug had. Drugs that were perceived as "safe" and "fun" shot ahead of drugs considered "dangerous." Thus, marijuana, cocaine, and—to a lesser extent—Quaaludes and stimulants like amphetamines shot far ahead of scarier drugs such as heroin, LSD, PCP, and even barbiturates.

These safe-seeming drugs I have called GATEWAY DRUGS, because they are the drugs most Americans now use to enter the world of drug dependence. The "gate" is attractive to millions of American youths precisely because these drugs are seen as harmless.

During the past two decades, young people doubted their elders on everything, but on nothing so profoundly as on drugs. Often the attitude was, "What do *they* have to teach *me*?" The fact that adults had little personal experience with these new drugs added to this conviction of the unique wisdom of young people. There was a widespread sense among youth that "you must find out for yourself," and that meant experimenting with drugs—lots of them. For many American youths during the last two decades, the outcome of all that experimenting was that they liked the drugs. They continued to use them, and they encouraged their friends to do the same.

In this vacuum of adult authority, many hoped the scientific community could be relied on to provide persuasive reasons for youth not to use drugs, including alcohol and tobacco as well as marijuana and other illegal drugs. There was no strong voice committed to helping adolescents avoid drug use. In fact, the scientists' repeated assertions that "We don't know yet" or the apparent conflict of experts' opinions in many ways fed the drug epidemic. Tens of millions of young people, as a result, concluded that in this, too, adults had little to teach them. Adult use of alcohol and tobacco often was seen by teenagers as revealing the hypocrisy of adult authority when it came to drug abuse prevention: "Pot's no worse than booze!" . . .

A Harmless Drug?

Marijuana plays a special role in the drug dependence process. It is almost universally the first illegal drug a youngster uses. The adolescent who avoids marijuana use is unlikely ever to use any

Robert L. DuPont Jr., *Getting Tough on Gateway Drugs*. Washington, DC: American Psychiatric Press, 1984. Reprinted with permission.

other illegal drug, including cocaine or heroin. In contrast, if young people use pot, they run a substantially increased risk of using other dangerous and illegal drugs. Up to 50 percent of regular users of marijuana also use heroin, for example. Marijuana use has become the GATEWAY to all illicit drug use in America. Recent studies also have shown that fully one-third of all Americans who try marijuana even once progress on to a period of daily use of marijuana.

One of the disastrous drug myths is that marijuana is a "soft" and therefore unimportant drug. Largely because of this myth, during the last two decades marijuana has been added to the use of alcohol and tobacco as one of the leading threats to the health of our nation. It poses, in my view, the single biggest *new* threat to our national health. Making this threat even more ominous is the fact that the contemporary marijuana epidemic has occurred in a nation pathetically unprepared to deal with it.

"One of the disastrous drug myths is that marijuana is a 'soft' and therefore unimportant drug."

For two decades many Americans have been saying that marijuana is a relatively harmless drug. During the last decade in particular, many experts have been advising parents and children that marijuana use has become a normal part of adolescence. One teenager succinctly summed up this prevalent "marijuana is harmless" fallacy when she added: "Parents and teachers should stop being so uptight about marijuana. It's no big problem for kids. Using pot is just a normal phase for kids who need to find out about it for themselves." Another teenager told me, "Marijuana is not a drug. It's like blue jeans—just part of life." Even more disturbing, the Presidential Commission on Marijuana and Other Drugs issued its first report in 1971 under the unfortunate title *Marijuana: A Signal of Misunderstanding.* The clear implication was that the marijuana problem was merely a difference of opinion between parents and their teenage offspring—a generational "misunderstanding"—rather than the rapidly escalating drug epidemic with far-reaching destructive consequences. These twin ideas—that marijuana is harmless and that its use is a normal part of adolescence—are among the most dangerous pieces of misinformation in our society.

A Past Mistake

I share some responsibility for this dismal state of affairs because 10 years ago I supported decriminalization for marijuana possession. I supported it under the mistaken assumption that marijuana use was not a big problem and that we did not have to employ the legal threat of prison to oppose marijuana use.

In 1974, while serving as the White House Drug Abuse Advisor, I spoke at the annual convention of the National Organization for the Reform of Marijuana Laws (NORML). After a lengthy (and hostilely received) discussion of the health hazards of marijuana use, I outlined a then popular concept called "decriminalization": remove criminal penalties for marijuana possession while keeping its sale illegal, thereby sparing the innocent, marijuana-using youth the trauma of arrest and criminal records. It was, I then argued, possible to discourage marijuana use by nonlegal means such as health education. This public support for decriminalization, delivered at the meeting of the nation's principal pro-marijuana lobby, made headlines in virtually every paper in the nation and was carried on all the television network news programs. To my embarrassment, the fact that I had spent most of the speech describing the health dangers of marijuana use was ignored. My plea for discouragement of marijuana use was also judged to be not news. All that came across was "White House Drug Chief Supports Decriminalizing Pot." That was my first painful lesson about the symbolic importance of anti-marijuana laws. If you favored removing criminal penalties, then—in the public view, at least—you favored pot. I now *reject* decriminalization as a dangerous concept. After 13 years of government service, the single biggest regret I carry is my naive support for decriminalization of marijuana. As I watched the marijuana-use figures double between 1974 and 1978, I felt the pain of regret with ever greater force. Of course, I was not alone in those days. Many people in public and private life shared this concept—and this responsibility. Many of us have also had some responsibility for similar errors of the past decade, errors which have fostered the unwise, unexpected, and unwanted increase in marijuana use.

The Scope of Marijuana Use

How big, specifically, is the problem of marijuana use? By 1982, 57 million Americans had used marijuana at least once, and more than 20 million were regular users of the drug. Of these 20 million, 2.6 million were 17 years of age and under. Among Americans 12 to 17 years of age, 2.8 million smoked tobacco cigarettes in 1982, barely more than those who smoked marijuana.

Numerous health indicators for adolescents— suicide, accidents, sexually transmitted disease, and premature pregnancy, for example—have shown a deterioration ranging, roughly, between 50 percent and 200 percent since 1960. In trying to assess the accelerating rate of the use of marijuana, we find that in 1962 only one percent of Americans aged 12 to 17 had ever smoked marijuana; by 1982 the figure was 27 percent—more than a 30-fold increase in a 20-year period. Among the 18- to 25-year-olds, only four percent had used marijuana in 1962; but by 1982, 64 percent had used it.

Many people are justifiably concerned about the age at which the young begin to use marijuana. Recent surveys make it clear that the peak ages for first-time use or incidence of marijuana use is 14 to 16 years—that's eighth grade to tenth grade. Thirty-five percent of high school seniors who have ever used marijuana first used it in the eighth grade or earlier. To pinpoint the age level where the biggest change is occurring, we must focus our attention on students in grades six through ten.

• Among American sixth and seventh graders, eight percent have already used marijuana, and four percent are regular users by the time they complete the seventh grade.

• Among American eighth and ninth graders, 32 percent have used marijuana, and 17 percent are regular users.

• Among tenth and eleventh graders, 51 percent have used the drug at least once, and 28 percent are regular users.

• Among 18- to 21-year-olds, 69 percent have used it, and 40 percent are regular users.

• As age increases beyond those years, the rates of marijuana use go down until, beyond the age of 35, only 10 percent of the American population as a whole have ever used the drug during their lives, and only two percent are continuing to use it.

"Marijuana use has been the leading edge of an intertwined, unprecedented rise in the use of dozens of other illegal drugs ranging from LSD and cocaine to PCP and heroin."

When we look at just the *daily use* of marijuana in 1983, we find the most disturbing statistic of all: among high school seniors in the United States, 5.5 percent smoked marijuana every day of their senior year. Fully 20 percent of high school seniors report smoking marijuana daily for at least a month at some time during high school. For purposes of comparison, an identical 5.5 percent of high school seniors drank alcohol every day, and 21 percent smoked tobacco cigarettes every day.

A few years ago, people said, "Well, marijuana users just use it *occasionally*." Or they tried to dismiss marijuana use, saying, "It is used only by healthy young adults." This relatively comforting picture, if indeed it ever was true, is *not* true today. We are now witnessing a strong movement among marijuana users toward very frequent use: *Over five percent of all high school seniors smoke an average of three and one-half marijuana joints per day.* We also know that dropouts (about 20 percent of the high school age group have already dropped out before the end of their senior year) are even heavier users of marijuana and other drugs.

What all this adds up to is that two very unhealthy facts about marijuana use are now inescapably evident: (1) *marijuana use on a large scale has grown rapidly since 1960,* and (2) *marijuana is smoked frequently by millions of Americans, especially by many of the young.*

Marijuana use has been the leading edge of an intertwined, unprecedented rise in the use of dozens of other illegal drugs ranging from LSD and cocaine to PCP and heroin. . . .

Marijuana Dangers

"But," you might ask, "just what is this stuff called marijuana? Is smoking a few joints of marijuana really so bad?" To answer these questions, you must first know that marijuana is not a chemical in the sense that alcohol is—alcohol being a relatively simple chemical, albeit one with complex effects on the human body. The marijuana that is smoked in the United States consists of the dried top leaves and flowers of a plant called *Cannabis sativa.* And, like every plant, the marijuana plant is a chemical factory. Marijuana, in its unburned state, contains over 400 separate chemicals, 60 of which are unique to the marijuana plant. These special chemicals are called cannabinoids. As the dried plant is burned to make smoke, it produces more than 2,000 chemicals which, with every puff, are brought into the smoker's body and distributed to every cell.

Pause and think for a moment about what 2,000 uniquely different chemicals may possibly do to the human body. Imagine, if you can, the prodigious research task required to identify and understand the far-reaching effects of such an intake. Think especially about the problem of understanding the *long-term* effects of prolonged use of this multichemical drug. Weigh also the challenge of understanding the combined effects of multiple drug use, since most marijuana users also use other drugs in combination with cannabis.

Any thinking we may do about the hazardous effects of marijuana on humans is complicated by another worrisome fact: Over the last decade we have had tremendous increases in the potency of marijuana. The major ingredient causing the "high" for marijuana smokers is delta-9-THC or, as more commonly called and more easily remembered, THC. Ten years ago the average or typical marijuana drug had a THC content of about 0.2 of one percent. Today, the content averages about five percent: a 25-fold increase in the potency of marijuana in the last 10 years.

In sum, the frequency of marijuana use is up, the age of first use is down, and the potency of the drug is up—well up. Taken together, these significant trends spell out a message that is loud and clear: The benign image of marijuana and its use as painted for us by the experts 10 years ago is outdated and irrelevant to today's marijuana problem. Old data and old attitudes are not only wrong; they are dangerous. . . .

The Risk of Experimentation

Because marijuana use, and use of other drugs as well, usually starts between the ages of 12 and 20, any delay in drug experimentation reduces the likelihood that the young person will ever start drug use. Research has also shown that the later the person starts using any drug, the less likely that person is to become dependent on it. Although most young people will now concede that frequent use of marijuana *is* hazardous, they often ask me, "Is it so bad, really, to smoke pot just *once*?" Large numbers of America's youth obviously are fascinated by the possibilities of experimentation. "Come on," they insist, "what is wrong with just *trying* it?"

These are seductive questions. I answer by saying that *nobody starts out intending to become dependent on any drug*. I have never known anybody who started using heroin for the purpose of becoming a heroin addict. I have never known anybody who started drinking in order to become an alcoholic. People do not start using drugs to become dependent on them. They start out using a drug, especially marijuana, in a casual way, seeking pleasure and relaxation, usually with peer encouragement and support. One of the great dangers of the casual acceptance of drug experimentation, however, is that a high percentage of the people who begin experimenting will move on to dependence. Neither they nor anyone else can predict with accuracy who will stop use of the drug, who will use it only occasionally for long periods, and who will become dependent.

"When somebody asks, 'Is there anything wrong with smoking a couple of joints of marijuana?' the answer must be an emphatic 'YES!'"

Only one thing is certain: *chronic dependence is a risk that all experimenters run*. One of the most shocking statistics is this: Half of the people in America who have ever at some time in their lives smoked a pack of cigarettes are currently addicted to smoking cigarettes. As a related statistic, I cite this one: One in three Americans who try one marijuana cigarette go on to daily marijuana use. You talk about *risks*! When somebody asks, "Is there anything

wrong with smoking a couple of joints of marijuana?" the answer must be an emphatic "YES!" If we are serious about trying to prevent drug abuse and reduce drug problems, in general we are going to have to be much tougher about experimentation—especially with marijuana—than we have been in the past.

Robert L. DuPont Jr. served as director of the National Institute on Drug Abuse from 1973 to 1978. He currently is a psychiatrist, professor, and writer, and continues to work against the problem of drug abuse.

The War on Drugs Is Succeeding

David Martin

That the United States is caught up in the most massive and pervasive drug epidemic in history is a fact beyond dispute. No one knows for sure just how many Americans use drugs, but it is estimated that Americans consume approximately 60 per cent of the entire world production of illegal drugs.

It is also estimated that one out of every four Americans has at one time or another tried marijuana and that some 10 to 20 million use it on a regular basis; that there are four to eight million regular users of cocaine; and that the heroin epidemic, which involves an estimated 500,000 to 600,000 addicts, remains more or less constant. All this, on top of an estimated population of some 10 million alcoholics.

'Crack': Most Addictive of Drugs?

The current epidemic of cocaine use in the form of "crack" is particularly worrisome, because it may very well be the most addictive of all drugs that has yet come to the market. It is reported that the national cocaine hotline (800-COC-AINE) has been receiving over 2,200 calls a day. . . .

The Drug Enforcement Administration, the Customs Service and the other government agencies concerned with drug control have worked very hard, and judged by any standard, their performance is impressive. Their intelligence has improved enormously, they are making far more arrests, and they have seized staggering quantities of drugs—according to President Reagan, drug seizures are up tenfold over what they were just a number of years ago. But despite their best efforts, the flood of drugs entering the country appears to increase in quantity.

Confronted with this situation, a number of prominent and responsible citizens, including the nationally respected lawyer Louis Nizer and my good friend William Buckley, have toyed around with the idea of legalizing drugs. As Bill Buckley put the matter, "The accumulated evidence draws me away from my own opposition, on the purely empirical grounds that what we have now is a drug problem plus a crime problem plus a problem of a huge export of capital to the dope-producing countries."

Although the war against drugs has thus far not been a sweeping success, I take very strong exception to the statement that it has been a complete failure.

Some Successes

For example, daily use of marijuana by high school seniors has fallen, year by year, from 10.7 per cent in 1978 to 3.2 per cent in 1985. Equally spectacular progress has been recorded by the Armed Forces. A 1981 survey showed that approximately 40-50 per cent of all enlisted men in the Navy, the Army, and the Marine Corps were using drugs on a current basis. In 1982 the Armed Forces embarked more or less simultaneously on a concerted campaign against drug abuse. By 1985, current drug use had been cut to 9 per cent or less.

There is also reason to believe that the American crop eradication and interdiction programs, backed up by a rigorous diplomatic effort, are beginning to bear fruit. There has been news about the use of American helicopters in the war against cocaine in Bolivia, about U.S.-Mexican plans for a joint border interdiction program that will cost $266 million, about the increasingly effective efforts of the Peruvian government, including the use of a squadron of jet fighters to bomb airstrips built by cocaine traffickers, and about the emergence of a cooperative anti-drug trafficking program involving Peru, Colombia and Ecuador.

According to an item which appeared in the Washington *Times* on August 13, [1986] ("Marijuana Drought Drives Price Sky-High"), the pro-drug

David Martin, "We Can Win the War on Drugs," *Human Events*, August 30, 1986. Reprinted with permission.

magazine *High Times* referred to the current marijuana drought as the worst in two decades, while Kevin Zeese, national director of the National Organization for the Reform of Marijuana Laws (NORML) lamented the fact that American and Colombian eradication efforts had killed almost 85 per cent of Colombia's marijuana crop.

But despite dramatic successes in these areas, the epidemic is still with us, and we have a long way to go before we are free of it.

As the National Institute on Drug Abuse said in a report: "Clearly, this nation's high school students and other young adults still show a level of involvement with illicit drugs greater than can be found in any other industrialized nation in the world." . . .

The High Schools

I have already spoken about the remarkable progress we have made in reducing the use of marijuana at senior high school level and in cleaning up the awesome drug situation in the Armed Forces.

Numerous independent surveys all confirm that over the past six or seven years there has been a dramatic shift in student attitude toward drugs since the epidemic erupted on the college and high school campuses as a result of the 1965 Berkeley uprising.

In addition to the marked decline in marijuana use, according to the authoritative survey conducted annually by the University of Michigan, barbiturate use among high school seniors during the same period had fallen by approximately 50 per cent over the period 1978 to 1985; the use of amphetamines and other stimulants was down from 21 per cent to 12 per cent; of LSD from 6.3 per cent to 2.2 per cent; of Quaaludes from 7.3 per cent to 6.3 per cent. Use of heroin (.2 per cent) and of cocaine (17.3 per cent) have remained virtually unchanged for a number of years. (Those statistics do not include the high school dropouts, among whom drug abuse is the general rule.)

Among the brightest of the high school seniors, the progress reported was even more spectacular. A survey of high achievers based on the high school "Who's Who," showed that only 4 per cent were using marijuana in 1983, compared with 21 per cent in 1971—while more than 90 per cent of the students queried said that they had never tried cocaine, PCP, hallucinogens, speed, or barbiturates.

Needless to say, these statistics reflect a fundamental shift in student attitudes toward marijuana and other drugs.

For example, in 1978 only 35 per cent of high school seniors expressed the belief that marijuana smokers risked physical harm. By 1983, the figure had grown to 65 per cent and 35 per cent of the student population considered drug abuse the biggest single problem facing their generation. Nationally, 70 per cent of the students queried were in favor of treating the possession of small amounts of marijuana as a criminal offense.

There is every reason to hope that the next generation of high school students will be even more resistant than the present generation because the thousands of parents' organizations which have proliferated around the country have paid a lot of attention to educational programs directed to grade school kids and to their parents.

"There is every reason to hope that the next generation of high school students will be even more resistant [to drug abuse] than the present generation."

In Atlanta, in Los Angeles, in Washington, D.C., and in other cities, there have been parades of tens of thousands of grade school children chanting the slogan, "We're strong enough to say no" or, more simply, "Just say no."

(It is really surprising how much some of the grade school kids know about the effects of drugs on human personality and mental abilities.)

[In 1986] the White House put on display two high school principals who have managed to impose rules which have effectively reduced the incidence of drug use in their respective schools.

One of them, Bill Rudolph of Northside High School in Atlanta, Ga., found himself saddled at the point of taking charge of his school with a typical drug-abusing student population, low in achievement and high on unexplained school absences and petty criminality.

Under the regime he introduced, students were notified that there would be no second chance for drug offenders—that the first time they were caught they would be turned over to the police and expelled from school. This rule was applied impartially; there was no special treatment for the sons and daughters of prominent citizens. The result is that there are today very few instances of drug abuse in Northside High School and the school itself has an enviable record of achievement and achievers.

The Colleges

In the colleges, the picture is admittedly not as bright. Dr. Lloyd Johnston, who directs the annual national survey on high school drug use conducted by the University of Michigan, recently told a colleague that "drug and alcohol use of college students represents a hole in our knowledge about the epidemiology of drug dependence." Even in the absence of a detailed study, however, there is no question that drug use increases dramatically among college students.

In part, this is due to the fact that drug use of all kinds tends to peak during the ages of 18 to 25. In part it is due to the sudden divorce from the influence of home and parents, plus the psychological stresses that generally attend the rites of passage from adolescence to adulthood.

In large measure, however, it is due to the indifferent attitude of college presidents and faculty members. Dr. Robert DuPont, former director of the National Institute on Drug Abuse (NIDA), recently had occasion to discuss the matter with a former dean of the law school of an American university. He asked if the police from the surrounding community had access to enforce the drug laws on the campus. The answer was "no." The former dean of the law school wound up by shouting at Dr. DuPont that his children would be much happier at Bob Jones University. In a recent talk before the Taylor Manor Hospital, Dr. DuPont excoriated the insouciant attitude of most university officials.

> "As a result of its random urinalysis program and the tough discipline . . . the Navy in 18 months was able to cut drug use from 48 to 17 per cent."

"How responsible," he asked, "are the university officials—from the president to the head of the Health Service, to the people responsible in the dorms, to the Board of Trustees, to the teachers, to the Dean of Students—to the parents?" Dr. DuPont said that "colleges have to assume responsibility for the drug and alcohol use of their students."

Dr. DuPont's presentation, incidentally, was entitled "Alcohol and Substance Abuse in College-Age Students: No Longer an Adolescent, Not Quite an Adult."

It is appropriate to recall that U.S. Education Secretary William Bennett took a very hard line against college drug use. He suggested that college presidents write a letter to students, incorporating the words, "Welcome back to your studies in September, but no drugs on campus. None. Period." One of the first major breakthroughs on the nation's campuses came on July 15, [1986], when President Robert M. O'Neil of the University of Virginia announced that illegal drug use would not be tolerated at the university. There is reason to hope that O'Neil's example will shortly be followed by other college presidents.

The US Armed Forces

Because the U.S. Navy was the first of the services to embark on a concerted anti-drug campaign, I take the Navy as an example of what has happened in the Armed Forces.

At the time it introduced its random urinalysis program in 1982, the U.S. Navy had discovered to its horror that 48 per cent of its men used drugs. A follow-up survey based on urinalysis conducted at major base areas came up with a result that was only one percentage point removed from this finding. Reacting to this confirmation, Chief of Naval Operations Adm. Thomas C. Hayward swore that he was going to take iron measures to get rid of "these druggers." The policy he promulgated was summed up in the two words: "Zero Tolerance."

As a result of its random urinalysis program and the tough discipline imposed on those who came up with positive test results, the Navy in 18 months was able to cut drug use from 48 to 17 per cent. According to [a] survey, which was made public in early August 1986, the figure is down to 10.2 per cent. For chief petty officers and officers, current use and annual use rated almost consistently zero for all types of drugs except alcohol. Even here, there had been a significant drop in use.

The other services have done approximately as well.

The Lost Generation

If the surveys on high school students and the Armed Forces are correct, where do the millions of people who are using record quantities of drugs come from?

A substantial part of the answer can be found in those students who graduated from high school or college from the time of the Berkeley uprising in 1965 until roughly 1979, and who had the misfortune to be part of a generation who grew up in a culture that condoned and even encouraged the use of drugs.

One need only recall that when Lester Grinspoon of Harvard University wrote his famous apologia on marijuana, "Marijuana Reconsidered," in 1972, the New York Times on page 1 of its book review section touted Grinspoon's work as the "best dope on pot so far," thus converting it into a runaway bestseller.

Today these students are roughly 25 to 45 years old, many of them workers, many of them yuppies, many of them classroom teachers, some of them executives, a disturbing number of them drifters, the great majority of them continuing drug users. During the post-Berkeley period and the 1970s, this sector of our population was heavily involved with marijuana. There was no definitive cut-off in 1979, of course. In each of the succeeding years the high schools continued to add to the general population of pot smokers, albeit at reduced rates.

The scope of the "crack" epidemic begins to make sense in light of the fact that 86 per cent of current cocaine users report that they first used marijuana prior to age 15, that 96 per cent of current users report some use of marijuana and that 78 per cent of cocaine users report heavy regular use of marijuana. In addition, 84 per cent of cocaine users use uppers, 69 per cent use downers, and 74 per cent use other drugs.

To reclaim these millions of young Americans from the drug culture which they embraced many years ago as students is perhaps the most difficult task that confronts us. The recognition that it is in this population area that much of the current drug epidemic is concentrated will help to explain the apparent contradiction between the quantities of drugs coming into the country and the partial but important successes that have been scored in the high schools and in the military.

> *"A winning strategy demands our maximum efforts in the fields of crop eradication, diplomacy, border interdiction, education, urine testing, and law enforcement."*

Not all of the epidemic, however, is confined to this sector of the population. Also involved are the growing number of high school dropouts, among whom drug use is almost universal. Also involved, especially when it comes to the use of crack, are America's many millions of college students.

Finally, the drug culture has recruited heavily from the ranks of young workers and professionals who are on their own and, therefore, not susceptible to the kind of group discipline that can be exercised in the Armed Forces and in high schools, and whose employment is not dependent on any form of drug testing.

Impact of Drug Testing

The anti-drug campaign has, over the past several years, received powerful reinforcement from the social pressures generated by the spread of drug testing—from the Armed Forces to defense industry, to government offices, to industries where public safety is a factor requiring serious consideration, and to industry more generally. . . .

Although the question of general use of drug testing has not yet been ruled on by the courts, there is a consensus that, in certain cases, the use of urine tests to detect drug use is legally valid. There is no question, for example, of the legality of mandatory urine testing in defense industries. Nor is there any question about the propriety of such tests conducted by banks and other institutions where drug use may be incompatible with fiscal responsibility.

No dollar-and-cents study of the impact of drug use among industrial workers on quality control is currently available. But certainly, it has had a baneful effect on the quality of American products and on the ability of these products to compete with comparable items made in Japan and other countries, from automobiles down.

In testimony before the House Select Committee on Narcotics Abuse and Control, Dr. Charles R. Schuster, director of NIDA, said that "marijuana and cocaine use are associated with great job instability and increased job absenteeism." Said Dr. Schuster, "Although an employee has reasonable rights to privacy and confidentiality, an employer has the right to demand a drug-free workplace." . . .

No single approach can win the war on drugs. A winning strategy demands our maximum efforts in the fields of crop eradication, diplomacy, border interdiction, education, urine testing, and law enforcement.

David Martin is a retired staff member of the US Senate.

"Since drug abuse 'cannot be eliminated from society,' it is bad policy to 'spend $6 billion'...in pursuit of an unattainable goal."

The War on Drugs Is Failing

Richard Vigilante

Phil Crane hasn't been heard from much since 1980. For most of the 1970s he was one of the two or three best-known movement conservatives in the House of Representatives. In 1980 Crane was eminent enough to be a fallback presidential candidate in case Reagan faltered. Indeed, the gossip on the eclipse of Crane's career in the Reagan years is that he took his own 1980 run for the nomination a bit too seriously for the tastes of the Reagan people.

He was heard from again when the national press noted that he was the only Republican congressman to vote against the House Omnibus Drug Bill before it was sent to the Senate. If it is ambition that makes our politicians cowards, perhaps ambition denied has the opposite effect. Crane, explaining his vote later, made the obvious and sensible point: Since drug abuse "cannot be eliminated from society," it is bad policy to "spend $6 billion, cut corners on civil liberties, and expand the power of government in ways that we might regret later," in pursuit of an unattainable goal.

In the House debates, people who took that position were denounced as irresponsible drug symps who took abstractions like federalism and civil liberties and the excessive size and power of government more seriously than the lives of children. Rough stuff. Not too surprising, either, given the bad name civil libertarians have given civil liberties. For the past few decades, every time some municipality has shut down a LIVE ON STAGE! SEX SHOW, or allowed a crèche in a public park, or tried to forbid American Nazis from harassing people who outlived the German variety, or suggested that parents be consulted before their children are retrofitted for free love, some civil libertarian has

shown up to cry wolf at the top of his lungs. It becomes easy to dismiss charges of "Police state!"

Nevertheless, Crane was right. Most conservative politicians have behaved irresponsibly on the drug issue, panicking in the face of a media-created crisis, attempting to expand government powers to do for the reckless what they might refuse to do for the poor: protect them from themselves. But though their behavior has been slavishly political, in the long run it may be impolitic. The drug war as it is being waged now violates not merely the abstract symbols of civil liberties beloved of left-wing intellectuals; it violates genuinely important rights in ways Americans have not in the past been disposed to tolerate.

The last drug scare comparable to this one started back in the 1960s and was fused in the public mind with the generation gap, hippies, draft dodgers, cheap sex, revolutionaries, and all the other forces that threatened the fabric of decent society. For a time at least, it was possible to believe drug users as well as drug dealers were the enemy. They were suspect victims, seduced to the dark side, to be feared and fought as well as pitied. It was in this atmosphere that possession of a single marijuana cigarette could earn an 18-year-old ten years in a Texas prison. As late as 1972, *NR [National Review]* senior editor Jeffrey Hart could write that we ought to keep marijuana illegal because the drug laws were a good weapon against the counterculture. Popular opinion was already swinging the other way, but Hart articulated perfectly the view that had made the drug crackdown a conservative cause in those contentious days.

Too High a Price

Punishing users eventually became an insupportable position. Eventually everybody knew some "good kids" who had been busted; it was impossible to think of them as the enemy. It became

Richard Vigilante, "Reaganites at Risk," *National Review*, December 5, 1986. © 1986 by National Review, Inc. 150 East 35 Street, New York, NY 10016. Reprinted with permission.

impossible as well to imagine that an arrest record or a few months in prison would do them less harm than a little dope. Most people still hated the idea of kids or anybody else using drugs, and the evidence of their harmfulness continued to mount. But the price of punishing users seemed too high, and by and large the country gave up on that tactic. In New York, marijuana was decriminalized in 1977, just four years after the Rockefeller drug laws, which, enacted as the drug panic had passed its peak, prescribed up to 15 years' imprisonment for possession of one ounce of marijuana and six years to life for possession of small amounts of narcotics.

In the decade since, the war against drugs has been fought on the supply side, with enforcement efforts focusing on major dealers. As Richard Cowan points out, such high-level enforcement raises profit margins and also favors the most organized dealers, such as the Mafia. Concentrating police resources on glamor prosecutions wherein the defendants can offer millions in bribe money guarantees widespread corruption. And, of course, the supply-side tactics proved to be utterly ineffective. It is impossible, in a free society, to catch any significant percentage of wholesale couriers, who can pick their time and place of entry into the country and then move about with utter freedom once they are here. Though there have been dozens of huge, well-publicized drug busts and enforcement campaigns, yielding billions in confiscated drugs, these campaigns have had no sustained impact on drug abuse. The *French Connection* heroin was stolen, by police, out of an evidence locker and sold on the street.

"The Fourth and Fifth Amendments not only prescribe government actions, they help describe a free society."

Everyone knows this. You can curb drug use only by punishing users as well as dealers—the incentives to use drugs are lower than the incentives to sell them. Singapore shoots dealers and flogs users, and has no drug problem. Criminologists have demonstrated that, on the average, arresting even heroin users significantly deters their future drug use. But if you sensibly decide that punishing users is too high a price to pay, you have to forget about winning the drug war through enforcement. This is what the country began to concede as the Sixties came to a close.

Forgotten Lessons

What has happened in the latest panic is that we have forgotten these hard-learned lessons. We have decided once again to make curbing drug use a major government objective, and in the best management-by-objective style we have chosen to ignore the impediments. No one *decided* to go after users again; had the question been posed so explicitly the new drug crusade might never have gotten off the ground. But the necessity is unavoidable. If you decide to fight a major drug war you are going to have to go after users no matter how loudly you proclaim them victims. That is exactly what is happening.

The centerpiece of user harassment is the drug-testing craze. To his credit, Ronald Reagan shot down proposals from the Justice Department and the office of Personnel Management for wholesale compulsory testing of federal employees. Nevertheless, some federal employees will be tested simply because they hold sensitive or safety-related jobs, even if their behavior on the job is exemplary. Indeed, the government has helped establish a public consensus that not testing in such cases would be irresponsible.

Violation of Rights

It is easy to see how people would take such a position; it is an easy line to step over. Employment is voluntary, and employees already allow employers to violate their privacy in lots of ways. But drug use is a crime; we have a long tradition of forbidding arbitrary searches where crimes are suspected, of presuming innocence where there is no specific evidence of wrongdoing, and of not forcing people to procure evidence against themselves. Employers aren't police, so drug testing is clearly not a violation of the Fourth and Fifth Amendments. But the Fourth and Fifth Amendments not only prescribe government actions, they help describe a free society. The presumption of innocence is as important a social rule as it is a legal rule; nor do we want a society whose members have so little sense of self that assertions of privacy are generally regarded as either eccentric or guilty.

These are not considerations of absolute importance, but they are important enough that we should not dismiss them without good reason. It is rhetorically effective to say that we cannot afford a single air-traffic controller on drugs and therefore we must test them all, even if their performance indicates their innocence. But there is no reason to believe drug use among air-traffic controllers has reached dangerous proportions—no major crash has been linked to drug use. Thus when we compromise what the air-traffic controllers, like most Americans, regard as their traditional rights, we get for that violation no more than an insignificant increase in public confidence and probably no increase in public safety.

Universal testing in sensitive occupations is the hardest case. Yet the Federal Government is encouraging even wider testing. It has promoted the utterly false notion that drug abuse is on the increase and has reached crisis proportions. It has authorized agency heads to require certain federal contractors to test their employees. And it has offered assistance to private employers who wish to do tests. The President and his Cabinet members all had their urine tested. Big business, whose professional managers may be the most fashion-conscious group in the nation, has jumped on the bandwagon. Worst of all, a clear majority of Americans favors widespread testing.

If we are to believe the anti-drug crusaders, more than thirty million Americans use illegal drugs at least occasionally. According to the crusaders' own figures, few of these people are habitual or abusive users, and most use nothing more powerful than marijuana (which shows up better than any other illegal drug in the urine tests). Society has no interest in doling out significant punishments to casual users; we learned that last time. Even if we are convinced that we need to keep drug use a crime, the casual users are the guilty ones we want to get away. They walk like responsible citizens, talk like responsible citizens, and do their jobs like responsible citizens; if they didn't, we would not need drug tests to find them out.

Furthermore, drug tests cannot distinguish between casual use and habitual abuse. Thus even if the results of employee tests are shielded from police scrutiny, these perfectly decent citizens face significant harm, including loss of livelihood and reputation, should drug testing become widespread. Punishing these people to that extent will do more harm both to them and to society than leaving them alone. This is exactly what should be expected when we start looking so hard for criminals that we find them even though we can detect no effects of their crime.

"Democracy depends on a formal commitment to regarding our fellow citizens as equals with us in their rights to govern themselves."

For these reasons, drug testing and other intrusive enforcement measures will not long be tolerated if they are ever widely employed. The baby-boomers in particular, who now make up the bulk of the workforce, will not tolerate in their thirties and forties harassment they rejected in their teens and twenties. Even those who do not use drugs will reject the notion that their friends should lose their jobs because of a minor indulgence.

The Left has been screaming that Ronald Reagan and his right-wing allies are a threat to freedom. The screaming has had little effect because up till now the charge has been absurd. On the whole, the Reagan agenda tends toward a freer society,

especially for people who rank the importance of various freedoms differently from the way left-wing intellectuals do. But a political movement that proposes to make outcasts of thirty million citizens has poor long-term prospects. What for a few months looked like a bandwagon may end up being an overstuffed tumbrel.

A Rejection of Principles

Embracing the drug hysteria requires a rejection of essential conservative principles. In a democratic society, the crucial psychological step in justifying coercion is to become convinced that those who are to be coerced lack the judgment to make minimally sensible decisions about their own welfare. Since this is an ability nearly all people feel they have, those who are to be coerced must be alleged to be unlike us, by virtue either of their abilities or of their circumstances. Yet democracy depends on a formal commitment to regarding our fellow citizens as equals with us in their rights to govern themselves—except in the face of powerful and specific evidence to the contrary. This is the essence of the rule of law. The welfare state, for instance, corrupts democracy and corrodes the rule of law precisely by judging that tens of millions of citizens, with nothing in common but the modesty of their means, should have their lives arranged for them by the poverty warriors.

This same corrosive assertion is crucial to the drug war. Only serious drug addicts, a small percentage of all who use illegal drugs, can be said to be incapable of self-governance. Yet nearly all drug users are implicitly alleged by the crusaders to have surrendered their free wills. The most repulsive instance of this is the tendency of the media to treat millionaire playboy cocaine addicts as victims, as if addiction were a natural catastrophe that befalls the helpless rather than the result of self-indulgence. Similarly, the media tell us that crack is an "epidemic" that "invaded" the ghetto, as if the drug were an insidious agent with a will of its own, ruining otherwise stable and happy lives. Surely it is more likely that crack found a home in the ghetto because it is mostly used by people who take more risks because they have less to lose. It is true that the ghetto poor are in some sense victims, both of racism and of government policies that seek to make them dependents rather than citizens. But to imply that they are utter victims, passive objects of passing plagues, is to surrender to the worst and most elitist fallacies of the welfare state.

Ignoring Real Crises

The image of drug abuse as unwilled catastrophe provides an excuse for ignoring real social crises. The catastrophe model begs the question of why people are willing to overcome great obstacles of cost and risk to use drugs. The anti-drug crusaders aren't surprised by drug abuse, because they have stopped thinking of users as free agents. But we ought to be surprised. We might find part of the explanation in a divorce rate that left more than one million children in broken homes, or in the fact that more than half of American children come from homes in which both parents work. And let's not forget the neuroses of a generation that was persuaded that self-fulfillment was not only a right but a solemn duty. If the good life consists of a succession of personal highs, who can blame the temporarily unthrilled for getting a little chemical help?

If we think about the drug problem in this way, rather than using it as a scapegoat for our larger problems, we will find that we are thinking about ourselves as we really are, not about users and dealers as we imagine them to be, utterly unlike ourselves. That's a lot harder than "declaring war on crack," but it's more honest and it will do a lot more good.

Richard Vigilante is the article editor of National Review.

"A strong demand-side policy...could reduce significantly the number of drug users, and thus the demand for drugs."

Reducing Demand Will Stop Drug Abuse

Jeffrey Eisenach

Despite dramatic increases in resources devoted to tackling the drug problem, the use of illegal drugs in the United States remains widespread. To make matters worse, policies aimed primarily at reducing the supply of drugs are producing such undesirable side effects as crime, corruption, and strained relations with other countries. The cost of the war against drugs is now so substantial, and the results so disappointing, that commentators across the political spectrum—from conservative author William F. Buckley to Washington's liberal mayor Marion Barry—have even called for the radical measure of legalizing some or all drugs.

Calls for legalization reflect the frustration felt by many Americans. The use of drugs in America has reached epidemic proportions. About 23 million Americans, or one in ten, use an illegal drug at least once a month; six million of these use cocaine. Perhaps most disturbing, drug use is most prevalent among young adults.

Costs to Society

Proponents of legalization, however, ignore the costs imposed by drug users on society, costs that would escalate if drugs were made legal. Up to 15 percent of highway fatalities involve drug use, and drugs are a major factor in crime. Studies by the National Institute of Justice find that as many as three-quarters of individuals arrested for a crime in some cities test positive for drugs. And each heroin user, the Institute has found, on average costs other Americans $14,000 in burglaries and other crimes.

Public opinion polls indicate clearly that Americans view drug use with alarm. Drug use is the number one problem identified by high school students and their parents. In a recent survey of "young professionals" published in *Rolling Stone*

magazine, 26 percent of respondents said they were concerned about having someone close to them involved with a serious drug problem.

Polls also find strong support for tough actions to deal with drug use. In contrast with the more relaxed attitude of the 1960s and 1970s, two-thirds of Americans today believe drug possession should be subject to criminal penalties. Furthermore, no state has "decriminalized" drug possession since Nebraska did so in 1978. Indeed, Americans by wide margins support wide drug testing to combat drug use, despite its intrusive nature.

While there is strong support for fighting drugs, there is less consensus on what steps actually would be effective. Should law enforcement focus mainly on trying to prevent drugs from entering the U.S., for example, on the sale and distribution of drugs inside the U.S., or on the drug user herself or himself?

At one time, disagreement over these questions was understandable. Now, however, evidence is mounting that if additional resources are to be committed to fight drug use, the resources best would be used in efforts to reduce demand, rather than on trying to block supply. The record shows that despite dramatic increases in seizures of drugs entering the U.S. and in convictions of drug traffickers, there has been virtually no effect on the availability of drugs on America's streets. Apparently, as long as there is strong demand, enormous potential profits will attract suppliers to serve the market. Efforts to attack supply, though important, thus seem futile unless accompanied by actions to reduce demand. . . .

A strong demand-side policy, based on the zero tolerance principle, could reduce significantly the number of drug users, and thus the demand for drugs. Such a strategy also would reduce potential profits from drug trafficking, and thus limit the crime, corruption, and international problems

Jeffrey Eisenach, "Why America Is Losing the Drug War," The Heritage Foundation *Backgrounder*, June 9, 1988. Reprinted with permission.

associated with current drug control efforts. . . .

That drugs increasingly are related to crime is evident from drug tests applied to serious criminals arrested in Washington, D.C., and New York City in 1984 and 1986. The National Institute of Justice reports that nearly three-quarters of all those arrested in the District of Columbia tested positive for drug use in 1986, compared with 56 percent in 1984. In New York City, the percentage of those arrested who tested positive for cocaine nearly doubled, from 42 percent in 1984 to 80 percent in 1986.

If estimating current levels of drug use is difficult, projecting future trends is even more so. Yet the U.S. Department of Health and Human Services attempts this. Reviewing the data in its 1987 *Triennial Report to Congress on Drug Abuse and Drug Abuse Research*, the Department concludes that "Extrapolating from these data, it is possible that the overall prevalence of use among high school seniors may continue to increase over the next several years."

Societal Costs of Drug Use

Drug use exacts a substantial and rising cost from American society. While some of these costs are related to efforts to enforce the drug laws, the direct costs imposed on America by drug users are also substantial. For example, consider the number of drug-related deaths reported by the Drug Abuse Warning Network (DAWN). The DAWN system draws data from only 117 counties, and does not include deaths from drug-related crime. Yet even with these restrictions, DAWN's data show reported deaths from drugs rose from 2,825 in 1981 to 4,138 in 1986, an increase of 46 percent. The DAWN system also monitors admissions at 744 of the nation's 5,000 emergency rooms. While the overall number of drug-related emergency room admissions remained roughly constant between 1981 and 1986, at about 120,000, the number of cocaine-related emergency room admissions rose by more than five times, to over 24,000.

Other direct costs of drug abuse include increased highway fatalities, workplace accidents, and teenage suicides. The U.S. Department of Transportation estimates that 10 to 15 percent of all highway fatalities involve drug use. Other studies find that drug users are three times as likely to be involved in on-the-job accidents, are absent from work twice as often, and on average incur three times the level of medicine costs as non-users. And virtually all experts see a strong link between teenage suicide and use of illegal drugs.

Unlike other components of the costs of drug use, the link between drugs and crime is well documented. A 1983 National Institute of Justice study found that each heroin user imposes costs on society amounting to an average of $14,000 per year in terms of burglary, theft, and other non-drug crimes alone. And a study by the Bureau of Justice Statistics reports that 20 percent of all convicted murderers admit they were using drugs at the time of the homicide.

Adding together such costs, the Research Triangle Institute, an independent research group in North Carolina, placed the total economic costs of drug abuse on society at approximately $60 billion in 1983. The Department of Justice estimates that figure rose to as much as $100 billion by 1986. These estimates do not, of course, attempt to measure pain and suffering associated with such things as drug-related deaths.

Trends in Policy

Recent federal policy regarding drug use has concentrated on three objectives:

1) Reducing supply by attacking the production, transportation, wholesaling, and retailing system;

2) Reducing demand through education and by influencing public opinion; and

3) Providing rehabilitation and treatment, on a voluntary basis, for drug users.

Resources devoted to all three areas have grown dramatically since 1981, as shown in the table below.

Increase in Federal Drug Policy Outlays, 1981-1988 (in current $ millions)

Category	1981	1988	Percent Change
Drug Law Enforcement	806.0	2,492.5	209
Drug Abuse Prevention	117.0	454.2	288
Drug Abuse Treatment	205.8	370.2	80
TOTAL	1,128.8	3,316.9	194

Source: Office of Management and Budget

At first glance, the strategy of interrupting supplies might seem to be successful. A doubling of Customs Service and Coast Guard outlays between 1981 and 1986 for drug interdiction activities, for instance, resulted in a sixteen-fold increase in seizures of cocaine, which rose from 1.7 tons in 1981 to 27.2 tons in 1986. Similarly, beefed up domestic enforcement efforts have led to a large rise in the number of arrests and convictions for drug offenses. From 1982 to 1986, the number of Drug Enforcement Administration (DEA) drug convictions doubled, from about 6,000 to about 12,000, while the number of FBI convictions rose from just 43 to 2,791. Seizures of clandestine drug laboratories, marijuana eradication, and other indices of drug enforcement success also were up dramatically.

Courts also have been tougher. The average sentence for DEA convictions rose from 51 months in 1982 to 61 months in 1986. The average penalty for cocaine offenses rose by 35 percent, from 48 months to 65 months. Statutory changes contained in the 1984 Comprehensive Crime Act and the 1986 Anti-Drug Abuse Act have resulted in large increases in the confiscation of assets of drug offenders. These rose from $100 million in 1983 to $165 million in 1987, and this year are expected to exceed $270 million.

The strategy of limiting the supply of drugs also has included foreign eradication efforts, such as "Operation Blast Furnace" in Bolivia, and increased "street-level" enforcement by local police, such as "Operation Clean Sweep" in the District of Columbia. Other actions include steps to prevent money laundering and increased penalties for use of minors in drug dealing.

In total, the federal government will spend nearly $2.5 billion on drug law enforcement in fiscal 1988, up sharply from $806 million in fiscal 1981. Yet drugs continue to be widely available throughout the U.S. Foreign eradication efforts have not prevented increases in foreign production. Said the State Department 1987 report on the international drug trade: "narcotics production was up all over the world." Nor have interdiction efforts reduced substantially the amount of drugs entering the U.S. A Rand Corporation study estimates that cocaine imports more than doubled between 1981 and 1985 while marijuana imports remained roughly constant.

Arrests of pushers and street-level efforts also have not made much of a dent in the supply of drugs. A Department of Health and Human Services study concludes that "Substantial evidence exists to suggest that cocaine is becoming more widely available throughout the United States and that its price has been going down while its purity has been going up."

Thus, recent history provides very convincing evidence that efforts to limit supply, by themselves, do not substantially reduce the availability of drugs nor significantly inhibit drug use.

Drug Education

The second area of policy emphasis in recent years has been drug education, designed to persuade young Americans not to try drugs, and to persuade current users to stop. While the evidence is not conclusive, these programs do not appear to have been very effective in reducing the demand for drugs.

Federal spending on drug education and prevention programs rose from $117 million in fiscal 1981 to a projected $454 million in fiscal 1988, a 288 percent boost. . . .

More significant than the rapid rise in spending has been the heightened emphasis on education and prevention. For example, most observers would agree that the "Just Say No" campaign originated by Mrs. Reagan has altered the entire tone of the drug debate by promoting the concept of "zero tolerance." And the Department of Education now plays a central role by disseminating information about drug education programs through such publications as *What Works: Schools Without Drugs.* . . .

Laudable and important as these programs are, the available evidence fails to document that these efforts are reducing drug demand significantly.

"Drug education . . . programs do not appear to have been very effective in reducing the demand for drugs."

A 1987 report by the National Institute of Justice supports this finding, noting that "there is no consistent evidence that drug education programs either decrease or increase the likelihood that students will use drugs." The report also notes that "programs that address only the negative aspects of drug use, especially those that exaggerate these aspects, tend to be disbelieved. The unfortunate result is that young people may become more rather than less likely to experiment with drugs." This 1987 report confirmed a 1980 review of the available studies on drug education which found that "by far the largest number of studies have found no effects of drug education on use."

In these otherwise pessimistic findings, there is evidence that appropriately designed drug prevention efforts, including enforcement of reasonable but strict penalties, can reduce drug use in the schools. The successful programs described in *What Works*, for example, are founded on efforts to detect drug users and a commitment to impose tough penalties for those detected. In Anne Arundel County, Maryland, for example, the school system has put in place a policy calling for greater involvement on the part of the parents, as well as school officials and local police. If a student is found to possess drugs, the police are called and the individual is suspended. To be allowed to return to school, the student, along with his or her parents, must agree to participate in some aspect of the district's Alternative Drug Program. The result has been a 60 percent drop in the number of drug offenses.

Rehabilitation and Treatment

Rehabilitation and treatment is the third key element in today's drug policy. Federal spending on treatment programs has nearly doubled since 1981, from $205 billion to $370 billion in 1988.

But as with tougher law enforcement and increased education efforts, the evidence is persuasive that current drug treatment and rehabilitation efforts are not very effective in reducing drug use. A Rand Corporation study of drug treatment programs in the District of Columbia found that the percentage of drug users successfully completing rehabilitation programs ranged from a maximum of 50 percent for marijuana users to a minimum of 20 percent for heroin users. The study noted, "even those who initially succeed in treatment often slip back into drug use. Nationwide studies indicate that a majority of people treated for either heroin or heavy cocaine abuse were again using drugs on at least a weekly basis within a year after leaving treatment."

While the history of drug treatment programs is not encouraging, there is some hope for treatment approaches currently under development. For example, low-cost, private outpatient programs such as Narcotics Anonymous have shown increased success rates relative to earlier programs, and supervised probation/rehabilitation programs, which rely on urine testing to monitor use, have been shown to be effective in rehabilitating drug offenders. Yet these programs can only help a minority of drug users. Rehabilitation and treatment can reach only those users who choose or are forced to undergo treatment.

Despite the outlook for improvements in these programs, rehabilitation and treatment are by definition only effective in preventing continuing use by current users. As Los Angeles Police Chief Daryl Gates asserted, "There has to be some recognition . . . that rehabilitation has not worked. It will work on some, but it's not going to work on a total of 23 million . . . that's why it's so important that we get to this generation so that that 23 million doesn't expand into 40 million in the next generation, and it could easily."

After nearly a decade of concerted efforts to reduce drug use, there is no sign of America's drug problem being solved. The costs of drug use are large and growing. Current policies, which have sought to suppress supply while offering education and treatment to drug users, have not been effective in reducing drug use.

A careful examination of the impact of federal interdiction programs shows that increased funding during the 1980s has paid off in terms of dramatic increases in the amounts of drugs seized, the number of arrests, and other measures of enforcement success. These efforts, however, apparently have been more than matched by increased smuggling activity. Estimates of the volume of drugs entering the U.S. are rising rapidly.

More, Cheaper Drugs

State and local governments also have stepped up their law enforcement activities, but these, too, have not reduced street-level availability of drugs. The supply is rising while prices are falling.

Efforts to cut demand through education and rehabilitation also do not appear to have met with much success. Despite some evidence that new techniques may be more effective than those used in the past, there is, regrettably, little reason to believe that these programs can ever produce substantial, dramatic reductions in drug use.

Based on these findings, policymakers seem to face two options: adopt a new strategy for winning the war on drugs, or admit defeat and legalize drugs.

Proposals for legalizing some or all drugs amount to an admission of defeat and invite social catastrophe. Even proponents of legalization cannot deny the societal cost of drug use in terms of broken lives; they can only argue that the costs of fighting the war outweigh the benefits. If America's efforts remain no more effective than they are today, the proponents of legalization might well be right.

"Zero Tolerance"

Alternatively, rather than admitting failure in a war that America must win, policymakers should consider adopting a set of policies that could substantially reduce the demand for drugs. Increased law enforcement, mandatory penalties for users, and application of the "zero tolerance" approach in workplaces, schools, highways, and prisons constitute a promising strategy which so far has not been tried on a large scale. . . .

"There is evidence that appropriately designed drug prevention efforts . . . can reduce drug use in the schools."

The evidence indicates that drug use can be cut when reasonably aggressive enforcement efforts are combined with "measured response" penalties against the drug user. Future policy thus should focus heavily on the "demand side" of the drug equation, and not simply beef up interdiction. A carefully designed "zero tolerance" strategy would enable the U.S. at last to turn the tide in the war on drugs.

Jeffrey Eisenach is a US government advisor and a researcher at the Heritage Foundation.

"We can do more to prevent criminals in foreign nations from growing and processing illegal drugs."

viewpoint **64**

Reducing Supply Will Stop Drug Abuse

William J. Bennett and William von Raab

Editor's note: The following viewpoint is comprised of two speeches. The first speech is by William J. Bennett, the second by William von Raab.

I

As Secretary of Education, I have said many times that a society is judged by how well it performs the fundamental task of the nurture and protection of its children. With respect to illegal drugs, we are not doing enough. We are not protecting our children. Let me tell you where this fact leads me, and where perhaps it should lead us as a nation. I realize some may disagree with what I have to say, but this is the way I think it is.

On the one hand, we have seen a fundamental shift in attitudes toward illegal drug use. President and Mrs. Reagan have helped to forge a serious national consensus and commitment against drug use. Many dedicated men and women lay their lives on the line every day in the war against drugs. And this Administration and Congress have worked hard to reduce the drug trade; we have greatly increased the resources devoted to fighting the drug problem; and we have increased seizures, arrests, and prison sentences for those convicted of drug trafficking offenses.

On the other hand, we must face the truth: While we are winning some battles, we are in real danger of losing the war on drugs. While public sentiment has changed profoundly, the drug trade and the drug problem are as serious as they have ever been. What is now needed is a transformation of government policy to match, and build on the transformation of public sentiment. This means that we in government must move beyond the sound but piece-meal and incremental steps that we have so far taken. We

William J. Bennett, "The War Against Drugs: Where We Stand," a speech given to the White House Conference for a Drug-Free America on March 2, 1988.

William von Raab, "U.S. Winning Battles But Losing the Drug War," *Human Events*, December 12, 1987. Reprinted with permission.

cannot win simply by doing more of the same. We must consider a qualitative change in how we conduct our war against drugs.

Foreign Policy

Today we face bumper crops of many illegal drugs. Powerful, billion-dollar drug-producing cartels threaten the stability of several Latin American governments, and threaten to undermine American foreign policy interests in the region. Furthermore, we are interdicting only a small percentage of all drugs shipped to the United States. The drugs sold on our streets today are generally easier to get, cheaper, and more potent.

To cut down on supply, the war on drugs must be a fundamental part of our foreign policy. As the greatest military and economic power in the world, we can do more to prevent criminals in foreign nations from growing and processing illegal drugs. It is to be hoped we can do this in collaboration with foreign governments—but if need be we must consider doing this by ourselves. And we should consider broader use of military force against both the production and shipment of drugs.

We also need to do what it takes to make the shipment of drugs into this country far more difficult, by increasing our ability to search cargoes and mail entering the U.S., by restricting air traffic to specific, constantly monitored, air lanes, and in general by reasserting control over our own borders. I am for reducing demand but, if the country is awash in drugs, lasting reductions in drug use will be very difficult indeed.

In concert with cutting down on the entry of drugs, we must intensify the attack on drug dealing. Today, despite record numbers of arrests, drug dealing is growing in many metropolitan areas. Particularly in the case of crack, we seem to be facing increasingly powerful drug gangs who are ever more willing to use violence and to involve young children in the sale and distribution of drugs. And while the incidence of first-time drug use may be declining among young people generally, this is not true in many metropolitan areas, and the overall consumption of illegal drugs does not seem to be declining significantly.

Getting Tough

Our first priority at home must be this: We must take back our streets from the drug traffickers. Security for law-abiding citizens is the first requirement of any civilized society. We need to commit whatever resources are necessary from all levels of government to secure safety and order for all our neighborhoods. In some cases, the police and courts do not have the legal support and the human and material resources to make real headway against the drug trade. We should pass tougher laws, build more prisons, expand forfeiture laws, and raise fines to cover enforcement, court and jail costs. The costs society imposes on those who try to push drugs should be great and certain. Drug pushers are not paying a high enough price for their crimes.

II

In [the August 16, 1987] New York Times, there was a front-page story about Colombia which should sober even the harshest critics of our anti-drug programs. The article described point by point how Colombian drug lords have neutralized the Colombian Supreme Court, how they have either bought or so frightened the Colombian Congress that anti-drug legislation is now highly unlikely, and how they in effect have actually paralyzed the entire Colombian government.

In Colombia, the drug lords have won this round.

I am hopeful that the Colombian government will fight back—despite the enormous bloodshed it may cause. For if they don't fight back in Colombia, we will see a tidal wave of drugs hit our shores that will make the last four years seem like ripples on a pond.

And if we don't see Colombia make serious efforts to retake control of their nation, events like those taking place in Colombia may work their way north like falling dominoes—through many countries already weakened by drug-induced corruption.

Could you imagine drug-supported guerrillas taking over our Supreme Court building and killing half of our justices? An astounding thought. But that's just what happened in Colombia—resulting in the death of 13 Supreme Court justices.

Just imagine, drug hit men assassinating one of the members of *our* Cabinet. They did it in Colombia.

And just imagine *our* Congress or *our* Supreme Court afraid to act against drug dealers because they have been threatened with death if they do. Not only their own deaths, by the way, but threatened with the death of their entire families!

The threat is real, and our response should be nothing short of total. It happened in Colombia and it is slowly moving up the Central American peninsula.

We are dealing with a ruthless, violent people who won't let governments stand in their way. We must resolve as a nation as never before to stand up and redouble our attack on this menace. The world as we know it is a lot less likely to be destroyed by a nuclear war than by drugs.

Winning or Losing?

Are we winning the drug war? How are we doing? We are winning the battles. We are losing the war. We are losing even though our troops—federal and state and local police—are doing a better job than ever before. Interdiction is 10 times more effective than five years ago—investigations are bringing prosecutions that are filling the prisons and for the first time seizing the assets of the big traffickers.

We are like the U.S. troops sitting on the Yalu River during the Korean War—well-trained, well-disciplined, well-equipped (now for the first time better than the smugglers), facing an enemy that has unlimited resources and safe bases, trying to stem a flood of poison being produced in incredible and increasing amounts in the safe havens of Mexico and Central and South America.

"The world as we know it is a lot less likely to be destroyed by a nuclear war than by drugs."

The United States Customs Service is the lead agency in our country's relentless efforts to keep illegal drugs from crossing our borders. Cocaine and heroin are not grown, or even produced in the United States. They are both imported. Yet these foreign drugs are the cause for much of the crime in our nation and in our cities and towns. . . .

Drugs corrupt—drugs dehumanize—and drugs kill.

I have sometimes been foolishly criticized for my tough stance against inaction by foreign governments, but I believe we must pressure the countries where cocaine and heroin are grown and shipped—to do far more. Our struggle against drug abuse and drug trafficking is a struggle of good versus evil—of life and death—and we won't get a second chance to cut down this corrupting monster. This is our chance, and now is our time to act. . . .

The Customs Service has started an effort to do what we can to combine our resources with [state and local law enforcement] to mount a united front against drug smuggling on our borders.

We have created new organizations and new approaches. We are standing together as never before, and we are trying new ideas in an effort to defeat our common enemy.

It isn't easy to force new ideas on a 200-year-old bureaucracy as rigid as the federal government. But in the past five years many new ideas have been put into place in the field of narcotics law enforcement at the federal level. Numerous federal interagency squabbles have been put to rest. Federal drug enforcement budgets have mushroomed, and the federal government has worked hard to make Americans of all ages increasingly aware of the personal risks involved in taking drugs. Progress *has* been made.

When I became Commissioner of Customs [in 1982], the agency's budget was around $400 million. I am almost embarrassed to say that our [1987] budget was just over $1 billion—a 250 per cent increase—with most of the new money going to drug enforcement.

So much for the fiction that the Reagan Administration has slashed drug budgets. On the southwest border, for instance, over a quarter-billion dollars of federal monies are going to secure it against the threat from Mexico, with the latest in high-tech radar and aircraft.

Total Deterrence Impossible

But despite better cooperation among federal agencies, new funding, and new resources, we still have serious holes in our nation's drug defenses. It became apparent to me that no amount of effort by the federal government alone would ever result in a total deterrent to drug smuggling.

In my opinion, the best use of the federal government's energy and resources is to support joint efforts with state and local law enforcement. The reason is simple. Local law enforcement officers are the primary defense of any American community against crime—*that* is the American way—*that* is the best way.

In Florida, a multi-million-dollar computerized command center was built to support the Blue Lightning Strike Force—a joint effort involving Customs and the U.S. Coast Guard and over 25 police departments and sheriffs' departments along both coasts of Florida. Hundreds of voice-private radios have been handed out, and Customs officers have been placed on local police boats to give broader search powers to the state and local units patrolling the coastal waters there. In addition, hundreds of local police officers and sheriffs' deputies have been trained and cross-designated as Customs officers to exercise the much broader Customs search authority in specific cases.

Encouraged by our early successes in Florida, I announced the establishment of a second command center at Gulfport, Miss. This center will complement the Florida effort to provide coverage along the Gulf Coast of Alabama, Mississippi and Louisiana.

As part of the arrangement in all of these joint interdiction efforts, the state or local enforcement agency involved in a drug interdiction seizes the smugglers' assets for themselves.

"The smugglers . . . are increasing their activities in Texas and across the entire southwestern border, and we have begun joint efforts to meet the threat there."

In 1987, nearly $5 million in currency and assets have been turned over to state and local police by the Customs Service. That's up nearly 50 per cent from [1987]. The result of all these efforts is that water-borne assets available for a coordinated drug interdiction strategy in Florida and in the Gulf of Mexico quadrupled almost overnight, with relatively little expense to the taxpayer. . . .

We know that our efforts in Florida and the Gulf work. They work so well, in fact, that smugglers are trying new tactics to avoid that part of the country. They are increasing their activities in Texas and across the entire southwestern border, and we have begun joint efforts to meet the threat there as well. Now they are bringing their drugs to your doorstep—to *our* doorstep.

Coordinating Law Enforcement

These incidents involved close coordination between federal, state and local law enforcement agencies. And if there was ever any doubt that we have to redouble our efforts, these cases should put those doubts to rest.

The important point of our joint efforts is that even though Customs is providing the resources that you otherwise couldn't provide—huge radar planes and fast jets—the locally run and steering committees in each area provide the critical direction and oversight. They provide the leadership to make the effort work, and in my opinion, that's why our efforts have been so successful. . . .

No one, of course, expects local officials to provide all the boats, planes and cars needed to interdict drugs at the border; the federal government still has to provide and man most of the resources. What the joint border efforts do is draw on the particular strengths of each agency, and mold those strengths into a singular, powerful unit.

This approach to drug interdiction is right. The federal government and the state and local police together form a bond that is greater than the sum of its parts. . . .

We still have other weapons in our arsenal—in fact, probably the strongest weapons we could ask for—the people of the United States.

Today Civil Air Patrol pilots fly spotting missions for Customs off the coast and in the mountains. They are looking for fast boats, mother ships and remote landing strips that smugglers might use.

As some of you may know, the Civil Air Patrol flew submarine-spotting missions in World War II, and when they spotted a sub, CAP pilots would actually drop bombs from their planes *by hand*!

Well, today's mission of the CAP is not that much different from their wartime mission, except that unfortunately I can't authorize them to bomb smugglers—despite the great satisfaction that might be derived by doing so.

Besides the Civil Air Patrol, we have also turned to the public at large to help us in our anti-smuggling efforts. Every citizen in every state can now report what they believe to be drug smuggling, by calling a toll-free hotline, 1-800-BE ALERT.

The call is free, they can remain totally anonymous, and if their information results in a seizure or an arrest, they could receive up to $2,500 for their help.

"Cooperation between federal and local law enforcement is the key to success in drug enforcement, for it is the lack of cooperation on which drug smugglers rely."

Interestingly, most of the people who call the hotline in Florida don't want the money—they just want to help, and that encourages us. . . .

The extent of the drug abuse problem in our country is enormous. Its impact is felt in every city and town in America. Without question, our nation must continue to work to stop drugs at its borders. I know that interdiction itself is clearly not the only answer to stopping drug abuse, but it does represent an outward expression of our nation's resolve to attack and defeat what is inherently evil—and it takes a lot of cocaine off the streets.

Cooperation between federal and local law enforcement is the key to success in drug enforcement, for it is the lack of cooperation on which drug smugglers rely.

William J. Bennett was US secretary of education from 1985 to 1988. William von Raab is US Customs commissioner.

"Working together, we can win the war against . . . the narcotics traffickers of the world."

International Cooperation Will Win the War on Drugs

George Shultz

Editor's note: The following viewpoint is taken from a speech given by George Shultz to a group of Bolivians and members of the press.

The opportunities and the problems presented by this rapidly changing world often transcend national boundaries. No country today can expect to prosper apart from the global economy. Every country today, including the United States, needs the cooperation of allies and friends to deal with mutual dangers. And that is my subject today: how, working together, we can win the war against the new pirates of the 20th century, the narcotics traffickers of the world, who threaten us all.

Bolivia and the United States are two of the many allies in this war. As democracies, we understand the dangers of failing to fight such a ruthless and pervasive enemy. And as the largest single market for illegal drugs, the United States has a special responsibility in this struggle—a very special responsibility. . . .

Many here and elsewhere continue to ask: "Is the United States really doing enough to reduce the vast American demand for drugs at the heart of this trade?" The answer is, we are doing a lot but not enough—not yet. But the answer also is that we are beginning to do what needs to be done—at last.

Americans are slow to anger, but once aroused, we know how to take action. Today Americans are sickened by the sight of young athletes, who should be heroes, throwing their lives away through drug abuse; by children, whose aspirations are perverted to a life of crime; by auto and train accidents, injuring or killing the innocent, because of drug abuse; by evidence of drug use by those entrusted with our health, our safety, and our security; by the

international drug cartels that make the Capone crowd and the old Mafia look like small-time crooks.

Efforts

Americans have finally begun to say "no" to drugs. Drug-taking is now seen increasingly for what it is: death, not life. A crucial psychological change has taken place, especially among young Americans. In the past 8 years, we have seen dramatic reductions in teenage marijuana abuse: today one in 30 students report using marijuana on a daily basis, compared to one in nine 10 years ago. Cocaine use among young people has also declined, dropping by one-third [in 1987]. American students are saying "no" to drugs and "yes" to their future. . . .

Everybody has a job to do—the churches, the workplaces, the government, coaches and athletes. Everywhere the word has to go out: "Don't take drugs, and if you do, we are going to be tough as nails." It is not a matter of choice, and it's no longer a careless attitude of "live and let live." No quantity of drugs, even small amounts once considered "personal possession" levels will be tolerated—*zero* tolerance. Vehicles and yachts are being seized, offenders are being fined, and our enforcement agencies are sending a loud message—no one is above the law.

We are saying to lawyers, to stockbrokers, to doctors: by choosing to use drugs, you are throwing it all away—your possessions, your standing in the community, your freedom. Personal responsibility can no longer be denied.

Our law enforcement agencies and courts are arresting and convicting more drug offenders than ever before. Over 12,000 people arrested by the U.S. Drug Enforcement Administration were convicted of drug crimes [in 1987], roughly twice the number in 1981. In New York City alone, felony drug convictions during the last 4 years more than tripled, from 4,202 to 13,466.

George Shultz, "Winning the War Against Narcotics," an address at La Paz, Bolivia on August 8, 1988. US Department of State, Bureau of Public Affairs, Current Policy No. 1099.

Over the last 10 years, the U.S. Coast Guard has arrested more than 8,500 drug smugglers. In 1983, we formed the National Narcotics Border Interdiction System, led by Vice President Bush, to coordinate Federal, State, and local law enforcement efforts against drug smuggling nationwide. Since the formation of the border interdiction system, annual cocaine seizures have gone up twentyfold.

The Comprehensive Crime Control Act, passed in 1984, helps us put drug dealers out of business by seizing their assets. [In 1987], over $500 million in drug-related assets were seized in the United States. Since 1981, we have tripled the antidrug enforcement budget, and President Reagan has asked for another 13% increase. That would give the U.S. Government $3.9 billion [in 1989] to fight the drug menace.

Our Congress continues its crusade to eliminate drugs from America. The omnibus drug bill reflects the important changes we have seen in American attitudes. Through new legislation, Congress is proposing that more treatment be made available to users who seek it but is insisting at the same time that those who refuse to be treated will be in trouble with the law. Proposals have been made to rescind drivers licenses of young people who are discovered using drugs and to withhold Federal privileges, such as student loans.

"The economy of narcotics prospers, and soon a country's political institutions are undermined."

Strong new penalties against those who deal in illegal drugs—the peddlers of evil—are being developed. Local and Federal law enforcement agencies are being given increased resources and more legal tools with which to fight an already well-equipped enemy. Across the board, Congress and the Executive are proposing a number of measures to augment the order of battle at home and to help our allies abroad.

Anyone who doubts that the American people are serious about eliminating drug abuse ought to take a good look at any opinion poll, any newspaper, and every political speech. Drug abuse is the number one election issue. And the drug trade is the number one enemy.

So that is the news from the north. We are mobilizing fully to wage this war at home; to cut demand. We are going to win.

Challenges for South America

Let me turn now to the situation on this continent—what you face, what you are doing, and how we can help.

Physicians and scientists tell us that drug addiction does not usually result from massive doses but from small amounts. The addict believes that he or she can stop "at any time." Soon it is too late. The poison attacks the brain and the body, and the victim soon loses health, will, and personality.

Similar things can happen to a country. The cultivation of the coca plants or of marijuana for illicit purposes starts small, in isolated places. People say, "It's always been grown here, and it is being used in dangerous ways elsewhere, so how can it harm us?" There is good money in it, and the drug dealers like to behave like Robin Hoods. They buy allies.

The economy of narcotics prospers, and soon a country's political institutions are undermined. Its constitution becomes a scrap of paper, while the guardians of its independence are corrupted—whether they be soldiers or civilians. And everything goes, including self-respect and sovereignty.

Ultimately, drugs destroy the moral fabric of society. That is why drugs and democracy are permanent enemies. Democratic thinkers from Thomas Jefferson to Victor Paz Estenssoro have taught that democracy rests upon certain ethical foundations. Ultimately, self-government in the political sense depends on self-government in the personal and moral sense. There can be no compromises here. A person must say "no" to drug abuse or eventually he will say "no" to life. A nation must say "no" to narcotics or eventually it will say "no" to democracy.

And what could be more destructive to a nation than a systematic attack on its natural resources? Look at Peru. Experts agree that—unless coca cultivation and cocaine processing are stopped soon—the Upper Huallaga Valley could be reduced to a toxic waste dump. Slash-and-burn agriculture is eroding the soil. Hired coca farmers are carelessly using chemicals and fertilizers. Processors have dumped millions of liters of kerosene, sulfuric acid, acetone, and toluene into the valley's rivers and ground water. When the sun hits the Huallaga River at just the right angle, the chemical pollution—a yellow color—can be seen from the air. That's the color of a dying land.

Developments in Bolivia and Colombia

So, the challenges are clear. What is being done in the region about it? I will comment on developments in several countries, but concentrate on two that are very different—Bolivia and Colombia.

Here in Bolivia, despite strong opposition, your Congress has passed a comprehensive antinarcotics law. You have kept your national pledge to the world community to outlaw all coca cultivation beyond that raised in specific areas, in certain quantities, for traditional uses. You have defined the crimes of illicit narcotics production, processing, and trafficking and specified the penalties for breaking the law. You have voluntarily eradicated over 2,000 hectares of coca—fulfilling the letter of your international commitments. You have captured and jailed Roberto Suarez, a leader among the international drug criminals.

All of this has been difficult. The pirates and warlords of the drug business have fought you at every step, with money, intimidation, and violence. But there can be no question that Bolivia has made the right choice. We salute you for that choice.

We have made the same choice. There is no turning back. The traffickers want us to look the other way. The terrorists want us to run and hide. To both I say: "You have picked on the wrong people. The democracies will not be intimidated. Bolivia and the United States will stand together. We will win this war."

When the history of the war against narcotics is written, Bolivia will rank high. Millions who are young, still more millions not yet born will owe you a priceless debt of gratitude.

There are many lessons to be learned from the Bolivian experience. Perhaps the most important is that a country's own strength to act against the drug menace can be multiplied many times more through international cooperation. A number of countries—including, very much, the United States through the State Department's International Narcotics Control Program and using development and other economic assistance funds—have pledged the monies necessary to support the unique Bolivian combination of economic incentive and law enforcement. And your own legislative decisons have mandated that the "Bolivian way" must be made a reality.

The U.S. Congress has looked at your law and your performance with great interest, and I trust that your steady commitment will convince the members of our legislative body of your serious intentions. To sum up, the drug traffickers are in trouble in Bolivia.

Colombia

In Colombia, the country is under siege. Narcotics traffickers and guerrillas, often operating together in criminal conspiracy, threaten Colombian democracy. The Medellin cartel, as evil a bunch as exists anywhere, has murdered many officials and citizens whose sin it was to stand up for the rule of law, the honor of Colombia, democracy, and just plain human decency. They are in cahoots with other evildoers. The FARC [Revolutionary Armed Forces of Colombia] guerrillas protect the traffickers in some areas and produce their own drugs in others. Then there is the M-19, a new "Murder Incorporated," hired by the drug cartels to kill those who oppose them, as we saw in the attack on the Palace of Justice.

The Government of Colombia is fighting back. The Colombian military—in its largest and most successful operation in the country's drug interdiction history—seized over 3,000 kilos of cocaine, a cache of sophisticated weapons, and large amounts of the chemicals used to manufacture the drug. Air force and army units combined to force down two trafficker planes at a clandestine airfield, where the cocaine was seized. . . .

"We in the United States cannot and will not stand aside from this battle. We are going to help . . . win this war."

We in the United States cannot and will not stand aside from this battle. We are going to help give Colombia the tools it needs to win this war. The U.S. Congress is considering passage of legislation to permit the Export-Import Bank to guarantee financing of loans to governments like that of Colombia for the purchase of weapons and other military equipment to use in the war on the traffickers. . . .

Unfortunately, no country in the Western Hemisphere, including my own, has yet been able to control adequately the movement of coca, or paste, or cocaine, or the precursor chemicals which make it all possible. That's a sad but accurate conclusion. We are all fighting this war, and we have made some headway. Yet the fact is that despite the money spent, the laws passed, and the lives lost, there is more cocaine entering the United States and Europe from South America than ever before. We have failed to stop the enemy. *We* are responsible because the demand for drugs still exists, and *you* are responsible because the drugs are still being produced and shipped northward.

As the U.S. National Drug Policy Board recently reported, the pool of people using drugs has diminished, but the pool's drug consumption has risen. Clearly, though we are allies, we have not helped each other enough. And that's the key to it—to increase our ability to act and our will to act through international cooperation. This is an international problem, and we must deal with it on an international basis if we want to succeed.

Future Efforts

Where do we go from here? Let me suggest some directions.

First, do not give up the fight. That's what it would mean if we legalized narcotics. We do not want a nation of addicts. Neither do you. And you don't want to make the drug syndicates even more powerful in your countries.

Second, mobilize more of our resources, our key institutions: the military, as in Colombia; the legislators, as in Bolivia; the media and the private sector, as in the United States; the schools, the churches, the workplaces, the home.

Third, expand international cooperation among the nations cursed by the drug trade. The Toronto economic summit in June [1988] called for more cooperation against "all facets" of the drug trade, particularly production, trafficking, and financing. The summit also supported the adoption of a UN convention on illicit trafficking. This convention is a Latin American initiative, and it is Latin American leadership that has brought rapid progress toward its completion.

Great changes have already been taking place in this hemisphere, once known for its nationalistic border disputes. Direct law enforcement cooperation is becoming the norm—as among Ecuador, Colombia, and Peru; the Andean nations together in their regional antidrug communications network; and the specific agreements that Brazil has concluded with its neighbors. We all recognize the fact that the problem is greater than any individual country, including the United States.

"The war against narcotics can and must be won."

In Washington, a precedent-setting meeting of the leaders of the Andean Parliament and of our own Congress produced a joint declaration symbolic of this sense of regional responsibility and commitment. The declaration recognized "the menace that organized narcotrafficking represents for the security and the continuation of democracy. . . ." It insisted on the setting of specific goals for the complete elimination of both consumption and production of narcotics. It called for concrete measures to combat drug money laundering. And it asked for the development of "an international strategy and inter-American mechanisms of cooperation in the fight against the illegal production, traffic, and use of drugs."

Our Congress . . . championed those goals. [Bolivian] Vice President Garrett was there with his Andean colleagues and can take pride in his role in that effort. And we—the State Department, Justice, Treasury, and Defense—will do our part, specifically:

• We must continue to refine and expand the State Department's International Narcotics Control Program, now contributing some $100 million a year worldwide (almost half of that in South America) to law enforcement and other antidrug efforts.

• We must expand our military assistance programs to those countries where the direct cooperation of the defense establishment with civilian agencies is essential if the war against the traffickers and their allies is to be won.

• We must revise our own laws and procedures which have made it difficult to provide useful assistance to foreign military or police forces. That means doing something about security assistance prohibitions imposed in the 1960s out of fear that such assistance might strengthen dictatorships. How tragic it is that these laws now hamper our help for democracies so urgently in need. Limitations on what kind of credit and guarantees our Export-Import Bank can provide are also part of the problem. . . .

• We must continue to remember that coca eradication has economic ramifications. With the Europeans and others, we should continue to provide assistance to help countries make the transition to a legal economy.

Summing It Up

Let me sum it up. We in the United States are ready to help, and we all need to help each other. We may be looking at the turning point in this war: at a United States aroused at last to discourage consumption, reduce demand, punish the users and the suppliers; at a United States generous and understanding of its allies in this struggle; at allies who, like Bolivia, aim at the total elimination of the illicit crop within a reasonable period of time; at the determined and rapid destruction of the laboratories, of the aircraft and landing fields; at the arrest, trial, conviction, and jailing of the so-called kingpins; at the seizure of the traffickers' assets; at the new hemisphere-wide conviction that a free people, in democratic consultation, can beat its most powerful enemies; in short, at the supremacy of law, the assertion of sovereignty, and the safeguarding of our peoples' health and honor, dignity, and security.

The war against narcotics can and must be won.

George Shultz was secretary of state for the Reagan Administration.

"[Latin American] drug traffic is such that even more earnest, better-funded efforts would be unlikely to effect a significant reduction in volume."

International Cooperation Will Not Win the War on Drugs

Ethan A. Nadelmann

Among the many obstacles that confront the government of the United States in its global battle against international drug trafficking, drug-related corruption of foreign governments ranks as one of the most troublesome. It is present in virtually every country. In many of the less developed countries in Asia, Latin America and the Caribbean, it is pervasive. Not just policemen and customs officials, but judges, generals, cabinet ministers and even presidents and prime ministers are implicated. Corruption in most of these countries is, of course, nothing new—although the temptations posed by the illicit drug traffic are unprecedented. Nor are US diplomats unaccustomed to dealing with foreign corruption. Their experience in this regard dates back to the origins of US diplomacy. But the need to incorporate the drug control objective, and especially its criminal justice dimensions, into their conduct of US foreign policy has presented US government representatives abroad with a rather unique challenge.

This [viewpoint] examines how the US government has dealt with drug-related corruption in Latin America and the Caribbean. Most of the responsibility for this delicate task has fallen to the US ambassadors and to the agents of the US Drug Enforcement Administration (DEA), which has approximately 100 agents stationed throughout the region. Bereft of any sovereign or police powers, these agents have little choice but to rely on their own diplomatic and investigative skills, as well as on the political leverage of the US embassy, in dealing with drug-related corruption. . . .

This article . . . views drug-related corruption as an obstacle to international drug enforcement efforts of the US government.

Ethan A. Nadelmann, "The DEA in Latin America: Dealing with Institutionalized Corruption," *Journal of Interamerican Studies and World Affairs*, Vol. 29, No. 4, Winter 1987-88. Reprinted with permission.

This perspective certainly is not the most important, or most useful, in terms of understanding the nature of drug-related corruption in Latin America and the Caribbean or even the failure of international drug control efforts. In fact, drug-related corruption is one of the less significant explanations for the inability of governments to stem the flow of illicit drugs to the United States. Nor is it possible to generalize broadly from the experience of the DEA in dealing with drug-related corruption. Relatively few other organizations find themselves faced with a similar task. Nevertheless, the subject gains importance in good part because of the light it sheds on a hitherto unstudied dimension of US foreign policy and criminal justice policy.

DEA's Principal Objective

The principal objective of the DEA overseas is not to eradicate drug-related corruption. Rather, it is to "immobilize" drug traffickers and their organizations wherever they are found. Immobilization involves identifying those individuals who engage in crime, finding and arresting them, gathering the evidence necessary to indict and convict them, and—finally—imprisoning them. Corrupt officials can undermine pursuit of this objective in any number of ways, with the DEA agents themselves, and even the US government as a whole, largely powerless to do anything about it. From the US perspective, the principal and only realistic challenge is to view the corruption as a hindrance to be circumvented rather than a problem to be tackled directly.

From the perspective of interstate relations, epitomized by dealings between the US ambassador and high-level officials in the host government, diplomatic efforts aimed at reforming corruption can be particularly frustrating because they involve a form of transnational penetration which diplomacy is ill-suited to accomplish. In many respects, reforming drug-related corruption in foreign governments poses problems that are little different from those involved in trying to reduce human rights abuses. The US government must contend with different criminal justice traditions and *modi operandi*, conflicting political interests, and insufficient power at the top of government to challenge vested interests at lower levels. In some cases, foreign heads of government would like to oblige US demands but lack the capacity to do so. For instance, just as the current presidents of El Salvador and Guatemala lack the political power to punish the government officials responsible for the most egregious human rights abuses, so the presidents of Peru, Colombia, and Bolivia are not powerful enough to prosecute every official known to have been corrupted by the drug traffickers. Alternatively, foreign heads of government may possess sufficient power to accommodate US demands but lack the desire to do so. . . .

Corruption at Every Level

In most Latin American countries, the DEA agent encounters drug corruption at every level of government from the street cop and airport customs official to the police chief, military general, and cabinet minster. The breadth of the corruption tends to reflect two factors. The first is the number of government agencies involved in drug enforcement. The fewer the agencies, the less dispersed the corruption, since there is little need or incentive for drug traffickers to bribe those officials whose jurisdiction does not include them. The second is the pervasiveness of drug trafficking within the country. The more pervasive the traffic, the greater the opportunity for those officials outside of drug enforcement to profit by becoming facilitators and initiators. Thus, in Mexico, Bolivia, Colombia, Peru, Belize, Jamaica, Ecuador and the Bahamas—of which all but the last two are drug-producing countries—drug corruption is widespread at all levels, and many departments, of government from top to bottom. In other countries, whose role is principally that of transit, opportunities to profit from the drug trade are more limited—to top government officials and those involved in law enforcement.

"High-level corruption in foreign governments imposes specific limits as to which cases DEA agents may pursue."

By and large, customs officials are regarded as the most corruptible, perhaps because of their long experience in "regulating" all forms of contraband smuggling. The military, which has stayed out of drug enforcement activities in most Latin American countries, has had the greatest success in preserving

a reputation for clean hands in this area—although there are conspicuous exceptions. . . .

When US officials present information of drug-related corruption in their governments, foreign leaders often respond by asking to see the evidence. More often than not, the US officials decline to provide it, on the grounds that they need to protect their sources. Consider the following 1985 incident, as reported in *The New York Times*:

> The scene was familiar, both to John Gavin, then the U.S. Ambassador to Mexico, and to the Mexican officials he was meeting, including President Miguel de la Madrid.
> United States officials had put together information implicating a Mexican Government official in drug trafficking, and . . . Mr. Gavin wanted to tell Mr. de la Madrid about the case, as he had done with others before it.
> But this time the case involved the son of the Defense Minister, who directs a significant part of Mexico's drug-eradication program.
> Asked how the Mexican officials reacted to his information, Mr. Gavin imitated them with a shrug and a grimace of mock concern.
> In that case and several others, Mr. Gavin said with frustration, "they would say to me: 'Show me the proof. Show me the proof.'"
> "But as they knew," he said, "to show the proof would be the death warrant for my sources."

Another source which US officials have not felt comfortable revealing, for very different reasons, are the telephone, electronic and satellite intercepts provided by the Central Intelligence Agency (CIA), and, especially, the National Security Agency (NSA). Indeed, these have probably constituted the principal source of US information on high-level drug corruption in foreign governments. Often this information is so highly classified that even the DEA is not privy to it. Nor is information derived from such sources usable for purposes of prosecution. Availability of such information has thrust US ambassadors and others into the frustrating position of knowing about drug-related corruption but of not being able to provide the evidence of that corruption either to US prosecutors or to foreign leaders. . . .

Frustration

For DEA agents overseas, high-level corruption in foreign governments is particularly frustrating, in part because it directly undermines their basic instinct of going after, not just the biggest traffickers, but also those people, such as celebrities and politicians, who are most in the public eye. Most agents who spend no more than a few years abroad are reluctant to abandon this operating principle and to accept politically motivated constraints on their operations. This can, of course, lead to friction with US State Department officials in the embassy, whose institutional and occupational predispositions resist viewing foreign officials as criminals. In effect, high-level corruption in foreign governments imposes specific limits as to which cases DEA agents may pursue. In many countries, for instance, they never know when an investigation will lead to the door of an official who is, for all intents and purposes, untouchable.

There are some instances in which corruption has been so pervasive and institutionalized that DEA ability to function effectively has been almost totally undermined. In some cases, such as that of the García Meza regime, the US government has gone public with its protests and withdrawn both its ambassador and the DEA presence—although undercover DEA agents continued to operate within Bolivia. Within the DEA, agents are divided as to the merits of such a policy. Some believe that it is always better to maintain presence in a country, no matter how widespread and high-level the corruption, because, at the very least, it represents something of a deterrent to drug traffickers and can be useful for gathering intelligence. Others feel that there comes a point beyond which it becomes difficult to justify the cost of maintaining the overseas office, and at which the symbolic value of withdrawing the office—and announcing the reason for doing so—is ultimately more valuable.

In such cases, the typical decision is to maintain the DEA presence, provided that (a) a minimum of cooperation is forthcoming and (b) high-level involvement in the drug trafficking is not too blatant. As one DEA agent who worked in Paraguay and Panama put it:

> You can't dwell on drug involvement at the highest levels. There's nothing you can do about it. If you do, you'd just get depressed. What you can do is play on their weaknesses, for instance, their desire for a better international image. And you try to show them why they have an interest in helping you out.

In such situations, the overseas DEA agent recognizes two limits on his activities. He doesn't target the most powerful officials, even though he may gather intelligence on their involvement in drug trafficking. And he doesn't bother trying to get the richer, more powerful traffickers prosecuted within the country. What he can do is secure cooperation in gathering intelligence, arresting drug couriers, seizing vessels and airplanes transporting drugs, seizing shipments of ether and other chemicals used to refine coca into cocaine, collecting evidence for prosecution in the United States, and in getting a few high-level drug traffickers deported or extradited to the United States.

The Untouchables

When a DEA agent tacitly accepts this arrangement, he is, of course, open to the criticism of having acquiesced in the most virulent forms of drug trafficking in return for cooperation in getting the "small fry." The criticism is most acute when traffic within the country is dominated by a few powerful "untouchables," inside and outside the government. DEA willingness to work with, rather than against, such people can be perceived as succumbing to the organizational temptation to build up the number of seizures and arrests while allowing the biggest violators to go about their business unimpeded. In fact, such a strategy can be viewed as a boon to the "untouchable" traffickers because it helps to eliminate competition and increase their control of the traffic at the same time that the corrupt officials are publicly lauded for what limited assistance they offer. Typically, the DEA responds with one of three arguments: (1) that pursuing such a limited strategy is better than the alternative, i.e., closing the office in the country; (2) that, given the constraints imposed by the US State Department, they, in effect, have no choice; and (3) that they are just awaiting the time when the "untouchables" become vulnerable. . . .

"The level of judicial corruption varies widely from country to country."

Elsewhere, DEA agents have encountered problems where the arresting unit in a police agency has undermined the intelligence unit with which the DEA agents have been working. In both Bolivia and Argentina, the DEA developed a very good relationship with a select unit of the national police which had demonstrated ability both to develop, as well as to carry out, sustained drug investigations. However, these units are considered primarily as intelligence units only, and they lack authority to make arrests in drug cases. Consequently, as an investigation nears completion, the drug enforcement unit of the federal police agency must be called in to make the arrest. In both countries, the drug units have demonstrated an exceptional capacity for corruption. On numerous occasions, DEA agents and the collaborating police unit have seen cases, developed only after many months, destroyed shortly after arrest because the target had succeeded in bribing the narcotics unit to eliminate the evidence or otherwise undermine the case. Although DEA has tried to circumvent corruption in the narcotics units and has pressured them to cooperate, so far its efforts have met with scant success. Typically, the honest police units do not report the corruption of fellow officers out of loyalty to the agency of which both are a part.

Even where DEA does have a relatively corruption-free agency with whom it can work, the ultimate objective of putting high-level traffickers in jail for any length of time remains elusive. Any high-level trafficker who is so careless or unfortunate as to get arrested in the first place still has multiple opportunities to gain his freedom. He can bribe other police agencies who may have become involved, or the *fiscal* (prosecutor), or the judge, or, as a last resort, the prison warden. In the absence of overwhelming political and/or public pressure to punish the trafficker, it is a rare criminal of any means who will not be able to avoid a lengthy stay in jail. In exceptional cases, pressure from the US Government and, occasionally, from local media and politicians have managed to keep a major trafficker in prison for a longer period of time. As for those officials who are implicated in drug-related corruption and forced to resign, they almost never spend any time in prison at all. More often than not, they are simply transferred to another district or agency. Some just leave office quietly and maintain a low profile until the storm has passed.

"The most persistent feature of US efforts to eradicate and circumvent drug-related corruption has been the resilience of the corruption itself."

The inability of DEA, and of the US Government in general, to follow through on cases after the arrest stage represents the greatest failing of US efforts in Latin America. Often all the DEA efforts to circumvent police corruption come to naught as soon as high-level judicial officials enter the picture. The extent of DEA contact with *fiscales* usually depends upon how closely *fiscales* in the country work with the police. In Mexico, for instance, police and *fiscales* work fairly closely, so DEA agents tend to become familiar with them. Elsewhere in Latin America, the relationship is often far more distant and formal, in good part because of the strong class divisions that separate them. Even where local police and *fiscales* do work closely together, DEA agents are often reluctant to pursue cases through the courts for another reason. As one New York City police officer put it, regarding the frustration of seeing criminals whom one had arrested go free a short while later: "What happens in the courts is somebody else's business—we teach that in the academy—and if cops allowed themselves to be frustrated, they'd be doing nothing in the streets." Overseas, it may be difficult for DEA agents to alter the mindset of police who regard their job as done once the criminal has been arrested. Even where they do adapt, options for dealing with corruption among prosecutors and judges are far fewer than those available for dealing with it among the police.

The problem with corruption in the higher reaches of the law enforcement system is twofold: (1) it renders futile the efforts of honest police officials who have succeeded in arresting a drug trafficker; and (2) it undermines morale of low-level officials who lose whatever incentive they might have had to remain honest. When police believe that any wealthy or powerful criminal they arrest will be able to gain his freedom by bribing a prosecutor or judge, the incentive to pocket the bribe personally can become not only logical, but irresistible. When the DEA does succeed in obliging its counterparts to resist drug corruption, the chief consequence may only be to shift the financial benefit from the police agent to the judge. The judge must beware of crossing the DEA only in those cases which generate extensive publicity or engender pressure from the United States.

Corruption Varied

Obviously, the level of judicial corruption varies widely from country to country, and even from court to court. In Ecuador, judges reportedly compete—even bid—to hear drug cases, because such cases offer the most lucrative opportunities. In Argentina, it was rumored that the judge who rejected a US extradition request for former Bolivian Minister of the Interior Luis Arce Gómez received half a million dollars for his decision. Similarly, and despite the many honest judges who still exist, judicial corruption has been rampant in Mexico, Bolivia and Peru. In Colombia, where traffickers are known to shoot before offering a bribe, and where the tradition of judicial rectitude is stronger, many judges resist assignment to districts known to have many drug cases. In Colombia, the power of the drug trafficker to intimidate is so great that even the Colombian Supreme Court has succumbed to their threats. After upholding the validity of a US-Colombian treaty which authorized extradition of Colombian citizens, Colombia's Supreme Court saw half its members murdered in 1985, in an attack by the guerrilla group which calls itself M-19 (*Movimiento del 19 de abril de 1970*), which many believe was organized at the instigation of drug traffickers. During the subsequent two years, another justice was murdered and two chief justices resigned in succession when the threats became too violent. The result has been a persistent effort by a majority of the Supreme Court to abdicate any responsibility over cases involving drugs.

The abundant possibilities for securing cooperation through corrupt means are supplemented by the potential provided by legitimate legal procedures. Police in less-developed countries are even less likely than their US counterparts to abide by all the procedures required by law (such as obtaining a proper warrant). In all these countries, as in the United States, high-priced, sophisticated legal counsel is available to take advantage of every legal technicality and loophole to protect a client. In some countries, of course, a drug trafficker may still have to pay a judge to go by the book, but the legal route frequently offers an important option to the trafficker with the means to pay his way through it. . . .

Corruption is not the only obstacle to arresting the drug traffic in Latin America; indeed, some DEA agents would say that underfinancing and poor training of police, throughout Latin America, constitute equally severe obstacles. Nor is corruption responsible for the fact that illicit drugs continue to flow in great quantities from those countries to the United States and Europe. Even if corruption in Latin America were far less severe than it is today, the nature of the drug traffic is such that even more earnest, better-funded efforts would be unlikely to effect a significant reduction in the volume of the traffic. Rather, drug-related corruption is important because of the obstacles it presents to DEA efforts to cripple major drug traffickers in Latin America. Even when the evidence needed to indict has been gathered, traffickers have still been able to elude arrest, and ultimate conviction, by bribing and threatening the right people.

No Improvement

With no more than a hundred agents stationed throughout all of Latin America and the Caribbean, and deprived of any extraterritorial police powers, the DEA has been hard pressed in pursuing its objective. Nevertheless, DEA agents have devised means of working above—and around—the corruption which infects criminal justice agencies throughout the region. They have pleaded, cajoled, threatened, and tricked their local counterparts into cooperating with them. Relying both on the diplomatic leverage exercised by the US ambassador, and on the transnational police subculture which police share the world over, DEA agents have succeeded in immobilizing many top traffickers who thought they had purchased their safety. In many cases, DEA agents have gone well beyond the privileges accorded them as representatives of a foreign police agency. Their diplomatic efforts, if their activities can be so described, most closely resemble those of the CIA and other transnational organizations in their pursuit of a common mission around the world, and in their persistent disregard of sovereign prerogatives.

So long as consumers in the United States continue to demand psychoactive substances produced abroad, and so long as the market for those substances continues to be a criminal one, drug-related corruption promises to persist. It cannot be said that the US experience in dealing with that corruption has improved over time. Success in cleaning out corruption in police agencies abroad and in creating elite drug enforcement agencies has proved, all too often, to be ephemeral. The close relationships between DEA agents and local authorities, so essential to working around corruption, have rarely survived the transfer of one or the other to different assignments. The most persistent feature of US efforts to eradicate and circumvent drug-related corruption has been the resilience of the corruption itself. For DEA agents, the challenge has truly been a Sisyphean task. Few delude themselves into believing that their efforts can measurably reduce the flow of drugs to the United States.

Ethan A. Nadelmann is an author and professor of political science at Princeton University in New Jersey.

"Not only were high Reagan Administration officials aware of contra drug trafficking, but some have . . . directly assisted such illicit activity."

viewpoint **67**

The US Supports the International Drug Trade

The Christic Institute

A major theme of the Reagan presidency in the 1980s has been the 'War on Drugs', both at home and abroad. During her anti-drug crusade, Nancy Reagan has told America's youth to "Just Say No!" to drugs. Meanwhile, President Reagan and his law enforcement agencies have vowed to stem the flow of narcotics across the U.S. border and "control the problem at its source," namely, in the drug-exporting countries of Latin America.

Astonishingly, however, mounting evidence has implicated the U.S.-backed Nicaraguan "contras"—President Reagan's so-called "freedom fighters" attempting to overthrow the government of Nicaragua—and their supporters in large-scale drug trafficking. Contra narcotics smuggling stretches from cocaine plantations in Colombia, to dirt airstrips in Costa Rica, to pseudo-seafood companies in Miami, and, finally, to the drug-ridden streets of our society.

The evidence suggests that not only were high Reagan Administration officials aware of contra drug trafficking, but some have attempted to cover up this fact and have directly assisted such illicit activity. Despite what has already been revealed by the Iran/contra scandal, the contra-drug connection and the potential U.S. government link to it remains one of the most underreported yet explosive stories of this decade. . . .

Guns for Drugs

Much attention has been focused on the secret resupply operation set up by the Reagan Administration to keep the contras armed when such assistance was outlawed by Congress between October 1984 and October 1986. Lesser known is that this resupply operation involved not only sending arms down to the contras, but also bringing

drugs—mostly cocaine—back into the United States. Profits from these drug sales were recycled to buy more weapons for the contras.

The guns-for-drugs operation worked as follows: Planeloads of Colombian cocaine were flown to farmlands in northern Costa Rica owned by an American rancher named John Hull. Hull has been identified as a CIA or National Security Council (NSC) liaison to the contras based in Costa Rica on the "Southern Front" of the U.S. war against Nicaragua. Several sources told Senator John Kerry's staff that Hull claimed in 1984 and 1985 to be receiving $10,000 a month from the NSC. . . . The *Boston Globe* on July 20, 1986 quoted an intelligence source saying that Hull "was getting well paid and did what he was told to do" by the CIA.

The cocaine on these planes came from Pablo Escobar and Jorge Ochoa, two major Colombian cocaine producers and traffickers who dominate the "Medellin cartel" that accounts for about 80% of the cocaine smuggled into the U.S. each year. This Escobar-Ochoa cocaine was off-loaded at ranches owned or managed by Hull, and then trans-shipped by air and sea to the United States.

John Hull and two right-wing Cuban-Americans—Felipe Vidal and Rene Corvo (or Corbo)—collected money from Escobar and Ochoa in return for the facilities and labor they supplied in the transshipment of cocaine. . . .

Pilots' Confirmation

This operation is confirmed by pilots who participated in the guns-for-drugs operation. One such pilot is George Morales, a former kingpin in the cocaine trade who was indicted by U.S. federal authorities in the spring of 1984 for drug trafficking. According to Morales, a few months after his indictment he was approached by contra leaders offering him a deal: if he helped set up a contra drug smuggling operation, his indictment would be

"A Christic Institute Special Report: The Contra-Drug Connection," published in 1987 by The Christic Institute. Reprinted with permission.

"taken care of." One of the contra leaders who approached Morales was Octaviano Cesar, an alleged CIA operative.

Morales accepted the deal and eventually donated $3 million in cash, pilots, houses, and planes to the contra movement. He directed his pilots to fly weapons to Hull's ranches in northern Costa Rica, and return with narcotics. The drug sales went to buy more contra weapons, fueling the guns-for-drugs trade. Morales says Hull was paid $300,000 per flight into his ranches.

"The money was intended to win friends in Washington for the Colombian drug kingpins."

Gary Betzner, one of Morales's pilots, told CBS News about two of his runs to Hull's ranch. "I took two loads—small aircraft loads—of weapons to John Hull's ranch in Costa Rica, and returned to Florida with approximately a thousand kilos of cocaine." Betzner estimates such drug flights eventually netted the contras "around forty million."

A third pilot, Michael Tolliver, tells how he, in March 1986, flew 28 thousand pounds of weapons to Aguacate air base in Honduras, which was off-loaded by contra troops. His DC-6 returned to South Florida carrying 25,360 pounds of marijuana, which he flew freely into Homestead Air Force Base, where the pot was unloaded. Tolliver was paid $75,000 for the trip.

U.S. government officials and some members of the press dismiss Morales, Betzner, and Tolliver as unsavory, convicted drug traffickers whose testimony lacks credibility. However, as CBS journalist Leslie Cockburn writes in her book, *Out of Control*, these pilots "had already been tried, convicted, and sentenced on separate charges entirely unrelated to their contra-related activities. There was no possibility of shorter sentences. Indeed, since they were confessing to a whole series of offenses for which they never had been indicted, they ran the risk of increased sentences for new charges. The best they could hope for was immunity from prosecution for the contra drug runs they were now disclosing." In fact, no such immunity or deal has been made for their confessions.

The Medellin Payoff

Perhaps the most explosive revelation concerning the CIA-contra-cocaine connection comes from Ramon Milian-Rodriguez, a money launderer for the Medellin cartel, who at the same time was a CIA employee carrying funds to U.S.-favored politicians throughout Latin America. Milian told CBS News and a Senate Foreign Relations subcommittee that he arranged to have $10 million of Colombian drug money funneled to the contras. The cash was

disbursed through a network of couriers in Miami, Costa Rica, Guatemala, and Honduras. These payments began in late 1982 and continued through 1985.

According to Milian, the money was intended to win friends in Washington for the Colombian drug kingpins. "The cartel figured it was buying a little friendship," said Milian, according to a congressional source. "What the hell is 10 million bucks? They thought they were going to buy some good will and take a little heat off them. They figured [that] maybe the CIA or DEA [Drug Enforcement Administration] will not screw around so much."

Milian testified that this money pipeline for the contras was arranged by an old friend and longtime CIA veteran Felix Rodriguez (alias "Max Gomez"). Rodriguez arranged the exact money "drops": "Felix would call me with instructions on where to send the money." As he testified in the Iran/contra hearings, Rodriguez worked with Oliver North to help oversee the airdrop of contra supplies into Nicaragua from the Illopango airbase in El Salvador. He received assistance from Vice-President George Bush's office, meeting directly with Bush three times, apparently to discuss, in part, the contra effort. . . .

Drugs and US Covert Operations

As shocking as the contra-drug connection may be to most Americans, scholars of U.S. covert operations over the past 40 years will not be surprised. Covert operations—with their use of large, unaccountable sums of cash, secret bank accounts, dummy corporations, clandestine planes and airstrips, mercenaries, and shady businessmen, all operating under the protection of the U.S. and foreign governments—are a natural breeding ground for illicit activity. There is a striking continuity between past drug-related U.S. covert operations and the "secret government" of rogue agents and operatives who were used by Oliver North to privately conduct the contra war.

The narcotics link to U.S. covert operations goes at least back to the early 1950s, when the CIA gave support to opium-growing, Chinese Nationalist guerilla forces (the KMT) operating in Thailand and Burma to attack Communist China. The CIA used planes from two front companies—Civil Air Transport and Sea Supply Corporation—to drop military and other supplies to the KMT. These planes then flew opium back out to Thailand or Taiwan. CIA backing for the KMT in the "Golden Triangle"—where Thailand, Burma, and Laos converge—contributed to the explosion of the heroin plague in the United States. . . .

A more contemporary example of drug-linked U.S. covert operations is in Afghanistan. That is the scene of the largest and most expensive (over $500 million a year) U.S. covert operation under the so-called

"Reagan Doctrine" of backing "freedom fighters" around the globe. Like the Nicaraguan contras, the mujahideen rebels also help finance their war through drug trafficking. Rebel commanders and soldiers grow opium poppy to support their war against the Soviet and Afghan armies. Afghanistan and the bordering tribal areas of Pakistan are now "the world's leading source of heroin exports to the United States and Europe," according to a State Department report of February 12, 1986.

US Government Connection?

After establishing the many links between the contra movement and drug trafficking, the more disturbing question remains: What did the Reagan Administration and U.S. Government agencies know of contra drug activity? Did they "wink and nod" at such activity in order to keep the contras funded and armed during the Boland Amendment ban on U.S. aid to the contras? Did U.S. officials impede or obstruct investigations and prosecutions of these operations? Did any U.S. officials directly or indirectly—using private "cutouts"—assist or facilitate contra drug trafficking?

The first question is the easiest to answer. Documents released by the Iran/Contra Select Committee reveal that the Reagan Administration was and is well aware of drug trafficking activities by the contras. . . .

There is a fine line between U.S. officials merely knowing of contra drug trafficking and being complicit in such activity. The first charge is damning enough. At a minimum, the Reagan Administration has tolerated association with drug smugglers as a price for backing the contras. At worst, individuals and agencies within the U.S. government can be charged with shielding from justice or actively assisting contra drug trafficking as one more component of the secret program to keep the contras armed and funded when Congress cut off aid.

"The pilots who flew in the 'guns-for-drugs' operation . . . believe the Reagan Administration was fully aware and largely responsible for contra drug activity."

The pilots who flew in the "guns-for-drugs" operation for the contras believe the Reagan Administration was fully aware and largely responsible for contra drug activity. Some of the major players in Oliver North's private network—all of whom are cited as former or current employees or operatives for the CIA or the NSC—are at the heart of the contra-drug operation.

The most important link between the Reagan Administration and contra drug smuggling is John Hull, whose ranch lands served as the center of the arms-for-drugs operation. Hull had several meetings with Oliver North, according to the Tower Commission, and his name shows up repeatedly in North's handwritten notes. Hull has long been called a CIA operative—a charge he denied vehemently until finally admitting to receiving CIA funding. Oliver North's personal liaison to the contras—Rob Owen—worked closely with Hull, the contras, Cuban-Americans, and mercenaries operating on his ranch. . . .

Complicity and Cover-Up Attempts

Individuals flying or shipping drugs into the U.S. would appear to need some help from government agencies. The *Boston Globe* reported in April [1987] that between 50 and 100 flights that "had been arranged by the CIA took off from or landed at U.S. airports during the past two years without undergoing inspection" by the Customs Service. That same month CBS News reported that the CIA directly intervened when Customs detained indicted drug trafficker Michael Palmer on a flight back from Central America. Customs officials were told to drop the issue of Palmer's extensive drug connections.

Whether or not Oliver North or other U.S. officials *directly* assisted the contra–drug operation, it is clear that the Reagan Administration obstructed investigations into, or, at the very least, has been remarkably dilatory in prosecuting contra gun and drug running activities. Attorney General Edwin Meese and the U.S. Attorney in Miami, Leon Kellner, intervened to head off an investigation of illicit contra activities out of Miami. The Justice Department cover-up may have been intended to keep secret derogatory information about the contras and their backers at a time when the Congress was preparing to vote on contra aid in the spring of 1986. . . .

It is self-evident that the Reagan Administration wants to conceal its association with the contra drug trafficking enterprise. Why some members of Congress and the press are hesitant to expose this operation is less clear. Certainly, pressure from the CIA and DEA, among other government agencies which do not want their methods and participation revealed, is one factor. Some members of Congress are cautious about revealing a major skeleton in the CIA's closet: namely, how drug trafficking has been linked to U.S. covert operations over the past 40 years. The pro-contra lobby in Congress no doubt realizes how damning a full-blown drug trafficking exposé of President Reagan's "freedom fighters" would be. Moreover, there is the traditional desire of many in Congress and public life not to face unpleasant truths.

For instance, the Senate and House Select Committees on the Iran/contra affair refused to deal with the contra-drug aspect of the scandal, as reflected in their final report. Indeed, House Committee staff investigator Robert Bermingham sent a confidential memo on July 23 [1987] to co-Chairmen Senator Daniel Inouye and Congressman Lee Hamilton, urging them to issue an official statement saying that an exhaustive investigation by the staff had produced no evidence of contra involvement in drug activity. In fact, Bermingham and his colleagues misrepresented the position of the House Judiciary subcommittee investigating these charges, and never even consulted with the investigator on the Senate Foreign Relations Committee probing the contra-drug link, as revealed in a July 29 [1987] *Boston Globe* article. . . .

Senator John Kerry (D-MA), Chair of the Senate Foreign Relations Subcommittee on Terrorism, Narcotics, and International Operations, continues to probe the matter. Kerry's subcommittee has had to endure sabotage from within. Richard Messick, a Republican staff member, not only passed documents from Kerry's probe to the Justice Department, which referred to Messick as "our spy on the committee," but according to the *Village Voice* of July 14, 1987, relayed misinformation from the Justice Department to discredit witnesses before the committee. Messick was also the source for *Washington Times* stories intended to undercut both Kerry and the investigation.

"Covert operations are the ideal conduit for the drug trade and other criminal activity."

Overall, the major media continue to treat the story of contra–drug links very cautiously. The experience of Associated Press reporters Bob Parry and Brian Barger, who began developing the contra drug story over two years ago, was one of constant refusal of their editors to run the material. AP was pressured by the Reagan Administration to delete some of their story. "A senior White House official called and said [John] Hull had enough problems right now," says one AP staff member. "They very much wanted to keep his name out of the report." . . .

An Issue of Common Concern

In a nationally-televised speech on March 16, 1986, President Reagan told the nation: "Every American will be outraged to learn that top Nicaraguan government officials are deeply involved in drug trafficking." A few days later, the Drug Enforcement Administration disputed Reagan's assertion by saying that it had no such evidence.

The real outrage for America's parents, of course, should come from learning that the Nicaraguan contras are involved in drug trafficking themselves, and that U.S. officials knew about it. Despite this fact, the Reagan Administration has provided hundreds of millions of U.S. taxpayer dollars to help the President's beloved "freedom fighters" attempt to topple the Nicaraguan government. . . .

U.S. government association with drug traffickers is not only the price paid for backing the contras, but, more generally, for engaging in covert operations around the world for the past 40 years. Covert operations are the ideal conduit for the drug trade and other criminal activity. Even when cloaked by patriotic appeals for achieving "freedom" and "democracy" abroad, covert operations invariably undermine our democracy at home. They subvert our values, our need for an open, honest, and accountable foreign policy, and respect for the rule of law.

As Oliver North told the nation during the Iran/contra hearings, covert operations "are at essence a lie." Unfortunately, it is usually Congress and the American people who are being deceived.

Foreign policy and national security are vague categories that most Americans feel more comfortable leaving to alleged, mostly self-appointed, experts. Drugs, though, are something that everyone understands. On this issue—the contra-drug connection—all U.S. citizens, regardless of party or ideology, can unite. We must demand that Congress thoroughly investigate contra drug trafficking—and any U.S. government knowledge of, cover-up, or assistance to it—as well as the history of drug-related covert operations. Only after we investigate and publicly debate these issues can our government credibly speak about preventing or treating drug abuse at home and curbing narcotics trafficking abroad.

The Christic Institute is an interfaith public interest law firm and public policy organization in Washington, DC that filed a lawsuit in 1986 against Oliver North and other key figures in the Iran/contra scandal.

"The Soviet Union with the collaboration of its allies . . . is the initiator and sponsor of major narco-terrorist activities."

viewpoint **68**

The USSR Supports the International Drug Trade

Rachel Ehrenfeld

Drug abuse for most people in this country is still a matter of individual behavior, either a personal character defect or a community social problem. Thus, in spite of the growing negative publicity against drugs, drug trafficking is still justified by many as an entrepreneurial enterprise, which is of course encouraged by Western society, and mainly as fulfilling a demand in the marketplace. Terrorism, on the other hand, is still perceived by some as politically motivated behavior, as a revolutionary reaction to some injustice and, therefore, somehow justified often as a "fight for freedom." There is and always will be someone to call attention to the "cause" that leads "desperate people" to hijacking, bombing, and murder of innocent civilians, in the same way that there will always be those who justify drug trafficking as a quick way to make a lot of money that fills a fast-growing demand. The idea that drug abuse in Western society, especially in the United States, might have other causes than the local demand, such as planned exploitation by foreign forces, initiated by the Soviet Union, is met with disbelief and denial by almost everybody. Many still do not see the link between terrorism and drug trafficking. For those who do see the link, even in the Administration, it is usually perceived as financially beneficial to both sides.

There is little interest in the Administration in presenting the existing evidence about countries supported and controlled by the Soviet Union in connection with drug trafficking. Not only is it too delicate politically, but once it is admitted publicly, the Administration may then have to actually do something about it. This omission is similar to the one that occurred in the Tokyo Summit on International Terrorism last May [1986], where no links were made between the Soviets and international terrorism. Disbelief and denial are probably the reasons. Those who know the facts and who are outspoken about them, such as William von Raab, Commissioner, U.S. Customs Service, and Elliott Abrams, Assistant Secretary for Inter-American Affairs, U.S. Department of State, are not given appropriate publicity. Thus the public is rarely exposed to those facts.

Soviet Subversion

The Soviets and their proxies did not invent drug abuse in the United States, but they definitely know how to exploit an existing phenomenon to their advantage by undermining American society within the government, at the workplace, on the street, and in homes and disrupting the order and changing traditional values within American society. As Humberto Ortega and the Nicaraguan Interior Minister Tomas Borge told Antonio Farach, a former ambassador to Nicaragua: "The drug trade produced a good economic benefit which we needed . . . we wanted to provide food for our people with the suffering and death of the youth in the U.S. . . . the drugs were used as a political weapon because we were delivering a blow to our political enemy."

The problem of creditability regarding the narco-terrorism phenomenon and its threat to democracy lies in the powerful psychological urge to disbelieve an awful truth even about an adversary's intentions. The problem is also one of interpretation and conceptualization rather than lack of information. Above all, there is a problem in the United States Administration in perceiving Soviet foreign policy in terms of Western values. Often when, in the opinion of Americans, including policy makers, Soviet behavior is "unrealistic" or its goals unclear, there is a tendency to dismiss the very existence of this behavior.

Rachel Ehrenfeld, "Narco-Terrorism: The Kremlin Connection," #89 of *The Heritage Lectures*, The Heritage Foundation. Reprinted with permission.

The Soviet Union with the collaboration of its allies in Eastern Europe, Asia, and the Western Hemisphere is the initiator and sponsor of major narco-terrorist activities. The U.S. Administration's efforts to slow down or halt the drug problem will be in vain, unless there is a carefully planned strategy to handle the magnitude of the U.S. domestic drug problem and recognition, understanding, and acknowledgement of the Soviet-backed plan and the consequences of its implementation. The ultimate goal of the Soviet-backed agenda, as we know it, is to undermine the integrity of the U.S. government and to destroy the social and economic organization of American society, as well as to weaken its moral fiber. Maybe using Nikita Khrushchev's own words: " . . . we must state categorically that anything that speeds the destruction of capitalism is moral," would make the Soviet initiative clearer.

Personal Ideologies

One of the reasons that narco-terrorist investigations dealing with political implications still lack total acceptance is because of the heavy personal ideological and emotional investments of the investigators. The Soviet Union and its surrogates—including Cuba, Bulgaria, Nicaragua, and some international terrorist organizations—use the international drug trade as one of many instruments in their overall strategy of active measures against the West. The United States as the leader of Western nations is the primary target and is known as the "main enemy" in the Soviet global strategic plan. Students of Soviet foreign policy know that it has always been based on the achievement of long-term goals and that the achievement of those goals calls for flexible and dynamic changes, not an "either/or" approach. Therefore, the Soviets exploit favorable conditions within the context of their overall objectives. What better example could there be than the exploitation of the drug phenomenon combined with terrorism in the Western Hemisphere? [According to a former Cuban secret police agent,] "Cuban agents are instructed to exploit any type of weakness in American society . . . their task is to make more acute the internal problems that exist, including drug addiction."

The alliance of the Eastern bloc, their surrogates, and organized crime networks inside the United States performs several functions for the overall strategy tied to the Soviets in their policy toward the Western Hemisphere. Some aspects of these strategic relationships were outlined in numerous publicly available congressional hearings, court decisions, and more recently in the report of the President's Commission on Organized Crime: *America's Habit: Drug Abuse, Drug Traffic, and Organized Crime.*

For the Soviets and their allies, the original network provides an intelligence apparatus parallel with and complementary to the local communist party and labor fronts. Part of this Soviet-inspired program is to penetrate directly into U.S. society by utilizing already existing forces and mechanisms of disruption and illegal activities. Among those forces and mechanisms are organized crime: the Cosa Nostra, the Colombian Mafia, the Nigerians (the largest group of individuals to traffic heroin from Afghanistan, Pakistan, and India to the U.S.) and others; self-styled protest movements that are open to foreign influences. Of course, the existing market of drug users in the United States provides them with the opportunity for exploitation and expansion.

"The existing market of drug users in the United States provides [the Soviets] with the opportunity for exploitation and expansion."

In countries in which terrorism and drug trafficking exist, such as several Latin American countries, this systematic interrelationship and penetration indicates that these associations are more than marriages of convenience. The combined forces take advantage of the lucrative drug trade to and in the United States, not only to fund their activities and to provide a reliable source of arms supplies, but to permit the Soviets and their proxies to erode the security establishments in the Latin American countries where they operate. These security establishments are often the only stable institutions of government support in these countries. When such alliances become permanent, the United States is facing and will face increasingly more serious threats to regional and domestic security. Hemispheric economic and social stability are seriously undermined, and the resources of the United States are severely taxed in the attempt to cope with the situation. The recent political and economic drawbacks in Mexico as well as growing tension in Mexico's relation to the U.S. are caused not only by the oil crisis, but other factors as well. [According to US Customs Commissioner, William von Raab,] "Problems with the Mexican economy and corruption are an integral part of the Mexican drug situation." Mexico's deep involvement in trafficking drugs to this country and arms from the U.S. to terrorist organizations worldwide, as well as in providing safe haven to those who encourage and are involved in these activities, helps to erode not only Mexico's economy, but also its relationship with the U.S.

An Example of Narcoterrorism

Drugs generate money—a lot of it—and money corrupts. Because of individuals within the Mexican government, the whole Mexican government is perceived as the archetype of corrupt administration. Colombian, Bolivian, Cuban, Nicaraguan, and other drug traffickers operating in Mexico and elsewhere in Latin America have been distributing small booklets containing Marxist propaganda to the peasants when they collect the drug crops. This is in addition to encouragement and instructions on how to grow poppies instead of, and [which are] much more profitable than . . . cannabis. There is no need to expand on the issues of financial gain related to the connection between drug trafficking and terrorist organizations or states—everyone understands them. But just as an example, they are the agreements between guerrilla movements in Colombia and the Colombian families that control the local cocaine trade, which generated approximately $1.5 billion in 1985. This should be compared to the better-known guerrilla activities of kidnapping and bank robbery, in which, according to U.S. government estimates, the Salvadoran guerrillas accumulated only about $75 million from the mid-1970s to 1981. Or in the case of North Vietnam, Hoang Van Hoan, a former Politburo member disclosed that in 1982 the Central Committee decided that opium production should be used to raise badly needed foreign currency, for example, U.S. dollars. Needless to say, the production was for sale in the U.S. And a direct Soviet involvement in trafficking heroin to the West was exposed in June [1986] in Rotterdam, where the local police seized 220 kilos of heroin shipped from Afghanistan through Riga on the Soviet ferryboat "Captain Tomson." This was probably not a private entrepreneurial endeavor, but according to Dutch sources, there is growing evidence that the Eastern bloc countries are trying to acquire the Western currency they so desperately need by trading in narcotics.

> "The use of terrorism and drug trafficking in relation to and in accordance with Soviet long-term political strategies is clearly documented."

The use of terrorism and drug trafficking in relation to and in accordance with Soviet long-term political strategies is clearly documented in the Soviet Military Encyclopedia Volume 7, 1979, p. 493. There the definition of special reconnaissance is the following: Reconnaissance carried out, with the aim of subversion of political, economic, military and moral potential of actual or possible enemies. It already had been mentioned that the United States is known as the "main enemy" for the Soviet Union, but the Soviets go further. Basic tasks within special reconnaissance include organization of sabotage and

diversionary terrorist acts and conduct of hostile propaganda for these purposes. The recommendation is to use, among others, biological weapons, narcotics, and poisons. The Soviets equate the use of terrorism with the promotion of drug abuse and have put it down in writing. All that is necessary is to study these plans. Unfortunately, very few do, and even fewer are interested.

Just a Diversion

If we look at the strategic planning criteria for Soviet diversionary operations, we will find that the essence of diversion is to disorient the enemy. In military thought of all persuasions, diversion is clearly defined not as being an end in itself, but as a means to the end of overthrowing the enemy. In this context, it is dangerous to think of terrorism and drug trafficking, the major features of this diversion, as the principal international danger to be encountered. For whatever political or other expedient reasons, the perception of terrorism and drug trafficking as the basis for action prompts a diversionary effect in which attention is drawn away from the main danger, which is the collapse of Western society and values.

Here, another aspect of diversion enters, that of provocation, in which the victim is provoked to act against his own interests. Study of Soviet military science shows that the Soviet Union recognizes the strategic character of diversionary operations. Hence, they surely are initiated at the highest political/military level and involve direction and control by the General Staff, the International Department of the Central Committee, the Committee for State Security (KGB), and other appropriate agencies. Diversion is inseparably interrelated with intelligence gathering, and indeed, the Soviets hold it to be one of its most active elements. In the case of drug trafficking and its connection to terrorism, there are similarities between those links and their connection to the Soviet strategic planning against the West. They have existed as an integral part of Soviet military and political strategy since the 1917 revolution when the Communist Party seized control.

International Conspiracy

Today, countries controlled, influenced, and supported by the Soviet Union are playing an important part in trafficking drugs into the United States, to wit Cuba, Bulgaria, Syria, and Nicaragua. Growing evidence is coming to light about the connection between these countries and the training, funding, and arming of terrorist organizations as well as trafficking drugs into the United States and other Western countries, but people who are born and raised and are living in democratic societies find it hard to believe that this is really true. Causing death by bombing or by providing drugs are similarly violent acts, threats against civilian targets, and crossing national borders of a given state for political purposes. They fall outside the normally accepted rules of international diplomacy and war. These acts are committed by individuals or organized groups operating as allegedly independent entities under no official state umbrella and usually wearing no uniforms. The logistical support comes from a sponsor state, and used as a tactic, these acts create a sense of tension, fear and disorder wherever they are applied. Operations of this kind are systematic attempts to undermine a society with the ultimate goal of causing the collapse of law and order and loss of confidence in the state. Terrorism and drug trafficking are a way of subversion and clandestine support for murder on an organized scale, and they add dangerous dimensions to activities that otherwise would be limited to small groups of lunatics or criminals acting on their own.

Theories like these indicating "international conspiracy" do not find attentive audiences, especially not in the United States. This disbelief is promoted with the help of disinformation instigated by the Soviets, which serves to discourage looking for the real sources behind the increased terrorist and drug-related activities in the Western Hemisphere. And although the "Siamese twins of death and destruction"—drug trafficking and terrorism—are recognized, and "their parents" in the Western Hemisphere are known to be the Cuban government and the Sandinista regime, the question remains—why are the Soviets omitted from those allegations?

Rachel Ehrenfeld is a visiting scholar at the Institute for War and Peace Studies at Columbia University in New York City.

"There is a direct correlation between insurgency and drug dollars."

Drug Traffickers Support Marxist Revolution

Lewis A. Tambs

Editor's note: The following viewpoint is taken from a commencement speech given by Lewis A. Tambs in Raleigh, North Carolina.

I would like to talk to you about war, a war against you, your children, and your families. It is also a war against democratic governments in Latin America, a war financed by drug dollars. This is a narcotics war which is destroying the youth, the society, and the productivity of western civilization in the United States, in western Europe, and in Latin America. This is a world-wide war which ranges from the Golden Triangle in Burma to the Bakka Valley in Lebanon, and on to the Eastern *llanos* (plains) of Colombia, as well as to Peru and Bolivia.

It is incidental as to whether this seductive subversion is a conspiracy, whether it is engendered by corruption or by chance or circumstance. It is a fact, and that is all that matters. Colombia, sensing the danger to its institutions, has emerged as a model in anti-narcotics efforts—a role model in educating its young people to the dangers of self-destruction through narcotics, a role model in extradition, and interdiction of narcotics being shipped to the United States, Canada and Western Europe. Colombia, moreover, is eradicating cocaine and marijuana cultivations. Colombia is eliminating drug processing laboratories and Colombians also have made a determined effort, under President Belisario Betancur Cuartas, to terminate money laundering activities through the banks and other international financial institutions.

Colombia used to be noted for Juan Valdes and coffee. Now it is notorious for narcotics. In 1978, cultivation and processing of cocaine commenced in the eastern part of the country. Much of this area was and is controlled by communist insurgents.

Many Marxists-Leninists, however, have a certain strain of Puritanism; that is, they initially tried to resist or eliminate this traffic. But, eventually they came to the conclusion that it could be very profitable and enable them to arm and equip their guerrilla warriors against the democratically elected Government of Colombia. So after a few clashes with the *narco trafficantes* by 1982 the communists and the drug dealers arrived at a *modus vivendi*.

Drug Dollars Finance Rebels

Communist insurgents, either by levying a liberation tax for protection or actually being engaged in drug business, are financing the procurement of weapons and training for their guerrilla fighters to overthrow a friendly, democratic society. Two presidents, both Liberals, President Turby-Ayala and President López-Michelsen—expressed their concern to me about what was occurring in their country. They understood that communist terrorists, financed by drug dollars, were training and arming and infiltrating into a region of the country, —the Media Magdalena—an area which if it became a communist stronghold, would have controlled over 30 percent of the national economy.

Guerrilla forces were increasingly better trained, better armed, better shod, better fed and equipped than the police and the military. Where did the money come from? It came from narcotics. The Colombian government determined to take a strong stand. In March of 1984, working with U.S. agencies, they launched the biggest drug raid in history in the Eastern *llanos* and destroyed, along with seven large laboratories and airstrips, some 14 tons of refined cocaine. At the seventh airfield and drug laboratory, the Colombian Armed Forces found a rifle range, an obstacle course, a soccer field, and a tailor shop, belonging to one of the major communist insurgent groups. The subversives also left behind three names marked for assassinaton: Col. Ramírez of the

Lewis A. Tambs, "A War That Must Be Won," a Commencement Address to Ravenscroft School in Raleigh, North Carolina on June 1, 1985.

National Police Force, my name, and the Minister of Justice. The young Justice Minister's name was Rodrigo Lara. He was in his early 30's. He had a wife and three children. Six weeks later, he was gunned down in Bogota; assassinated by the narco-terrorists. Only two weeks earlier, I was chatting with him in his office. He told me that he estimated that the narco-guerrillas in two areas alone had netted $110 million in one year and that they were using these ill gotten gains to overthrow the democratic government which he served. He paid for his courage with his life. I buried him. Nevertheless, the Colombian government continued its strong stance. But the terrorists were still active. A few weeks after the assassination of Rodrigo Lara, the United States Embassy was bombed twice, as was my own residence. . . .

Insurgency financed by drug dollars continued. In July 1984, the Colombian Armed Forces undertook a major marijuana operation against the [rebel movement] M-19 near the Venezuelan border. Also in July a singular event occurred when one of Colombia's major drug dealers, Pablo Escobar-Gaviria, was photographed loading refined cocaine in Nicaragua for transshipment to the United States. He was aided by a Nicaraguan government official, Federico Vaughan, who worked for the Minister of Interior in Communist Nicaragua, Tomás Borge.

This is not the first time Caribbean communists were involved in narcotics trafficking. In 1981 the Cuban Ambassador to Colombia, Revelo, was expelled from Bogota because he was engaged in exporting narcotics. He, along with six other Cuban officals are under indictment in Miami, Florida on drug related charges.

Cuban and Nicaraguan Influence

Communist Cubans and Nicaraguans are clearly implicated in international drug dealing. Nicaragua is also the scene of a betrayed revolution. The original Sandinistas were composed of Liberals and Conservatives, Social Democrats and Social Christians. But in July 1979, the communist commandants seized power. They had the guns. The military-Marxists have built up a formidable military machine. In Nicaragua, as of June 1985, the military-Marxists have 110 T-55 and 20 T-76 tanks, some 200 armored personnel carriers supported by 30 helicopters including the latest Soviet model counter-insurgency Hind helicopter, the MIG-24, and over 100 field artillery pieces. Additionally the nine of the military-Marxist junta have at their disposal some 64,000 regular troops and another 60,000 armed militia.

In the worst days of Somoza, the tyrant Anastasio Somoza, his National Guard never exceeded 12,000 men backed by three artillery pieces and three World War II vintage tanks. Nicaragua has become an armed camp, and is exporting revolution to its neighbors in El Salvador and to other countries in Central America.

Central America is important to us. It is important to the United States because of the Panama Canal and our strategic Caribbean sea lanes. Moreover, the construction of the airbase at Punta Huete on Lake Managua—an airfield capable of handling the largest long-range Soviet bombers—will give the Soviets the capability of launching reconnaissance missions from Siberia, patrolling the Pacific coast of the United States and refueling and returning from Nicaragua. Soon you may have a similarity with America's Atlantic coast where Soviet aircraft fly along the Eastern seaboard of North Carolina. Basing on Nicaragua, Soviet Bear bombers may soon be doing the same off America's Pacific shore.

Central America's Importance

Central America is important to the development and defense of democracy. There are three constitutional democracies: El Salvador, Honduras, and certainly Costa Rica. Guatemala is moving toward constitutional government. The United States government believes that democracy is essential for the stability of the region. For, in general, democracies do not export revolution. They do not declare war on their neighbors. Under the Jackson Plan, what the U.S. seeks in Central America is democracy, development, demilitarization and the departure of foreign forces. The [Reagan] Administration hopes to achieve this through dialogue. The Sandinista government, the Junta, the Nine, the military-Marxists—and since they always wear uniforms that should tell you something about them—have broken all their prior promises. Promises they made to hold free, open, democratic elections. Promises they made to respect human rights. Promises they made to establish an independent and impartial judiciary. These promises were made to the Organization of American States in July 1979. More importantly they were made to the Nicaraguan people.

"Central America is important to the development and defense of democracy."

[On] foot, people are fleeing Nicaragua. When the communists take over, ten percent of the people leave. Indochina, Afghanistan, Ethiopia, eastern Europe and Cuba are examples. Currently, Central America is pursuing this pattern. There are 25 million people in Central America; 75 million more in Mexico—a hundred million people. And if these poor souls seeking to survive, following freedom, begin to move, the United States is going to be faced with mass migration—which, in the long run, may aid the United States because these refugees are willing to work and are generally anti-communist. Nevertheless, this migration could present grave social and economic problems in the short term. Therefore, there is danger to the South, danger to the democratic states of Central America, and danger to the democratic states of South America, like Colombia.

"We are talking about a war . . . a direct assault on democratic governments in Latin America, like Colombia, financed by drug dollars."

In Colombia, I noted that the United States had worked with the Colombians in the big bust of March 1984. Late [in 1984] there was reactivation of one of the airfields and laboratories. On October 12 Colombian National Police, aided by the military, helicoptered in to destroy the cocaine laboratories which were being rebuilt along with the 120 drums of precursor chemicals which process this death-dealing drug. The first two days Lieutenant Neyra and a paratrooper died from sniper fire. I buried them. The next day Lieutenant Alvarez was killed. I buried him too. But, nevertheless, the Colombians pressed on and finally were successful in winning through. But what did the Colombians find? They found literature and account books, which belonged to a communist insurgent group. Therefore, once again there is a direct correlation between insurgency and drug dollars. Once again, I'm not interested in whether it's conspiracy, whether it's chance, or whether it's corruption, it's a fact.

Attacks against the U.S. mission continued. In November 1984, the narco-terrorists launched a car bomb against the United States Embassy in Bogota. One unfortunate woman was killed. She, of course, was an innocent bystander. But, the U.S. mission stood fast. We were, however, obliged to initiate the evacuation of our women and children.

And then in December 1984, Ivan Mariano Ospina, the military leader of the M-19, a Colombian communist Castroite group, surfaced in Mexico City. He called not only for the assassination of U.S. diplomatic personnel in Colombia, but also clearly stated his desire to collaborate with the drug traffickers in attacking the United States.

Again in January 1985, Carlos Lehder, one of the major drug traffickers, voiced the same opinions. He singled out the President of Colombia, Belisario Betancur Cuartas, for assassination. Nevertheless, the President forged ahead. The threats continued in April and in May. In April on TV in Paris, the leader of the Moscow line insurgent group Manuel Marulanda, *Tirofijo;* stated that he now had 40,000

men that he was preparing to launch against the Colombian government.

Where did the money come from, you should ask. Well, I think you can guess by now.

And then again in May, two Colombian military helicopters were shot down by communist insurgents in an area which has long been noted for its drug trafficking. The Colombians are taking the casualties. But U.S. citizens are taking the casualties too. With regard to consumption of cocaine, most of it occurs in this country in the age group of 28–42. This is the managerial, the entrepreneurial, the economic elite, the so-called productive class; it can afford to buy this debilitating and demoralizing drug.

Do you wonder why U.S. industry may be in trouble if the scientific, business and academic elite is sniffing its minds away up their noses on cocaine? We have the destruction of our youth. And I ask you how much do you think it costs for rehabilitating a person who is a cocaine addict? The minimum is $20,000, if they are salvageable. It may go as high as a $100,000 in some cases. What are we going to do with these zombies? We are a people in the Judeo-Christian tradition. We are going to have to take care of the unfortunates. We are going to have to warehouse them. And that money could be used for other things. It could be used for your education. It could be used for social services. It could be used for research and development or new production facilities.

A Direct Assault

So, therefore, we are talking about a war—a war which involves not only a direct assault on democratic governments in Latin America like Colombia, financed by drug dollars, but also a generalized war against the future. You, the young people are the future of western civilization, and the war is against our managerial skills, our productivity, our creativity, our tomorrow.

We, therefore, are faced with conflict. We are faced with a crisis. And the fact is that basically, it is a spiritual, a metaphysical problem. You should love yourself and your neighbor, because people who love themselves generally do not get involved in narcotics—either as users, abusers, or dealers.

Therefore, I ask you for your sakes, your children's sakes, for your nation's sake, to remember we are talking about war. We are talking about a war, a war which must be won.

Lewis A. Tambs is the former US ambassador to Costa Rica and Colombia.

"The notion of a 'narcoguerrilla' unites what can't be united: Top traffickers are... capitalists.... Marxist rebels want to overthrow capitalism."

Drug Traffickers Do Not Support Marxist Revolution

Merrill Collett

On March 10, 1984, Colombian police swooped down on a jungle drug complex known as Tranquilandia and seized 27,500 pounds of pure cocaine. It was the biggest coke bust in history. A few days later the U.S. Ambassador to Colombia, Lewis Tambs, made a startling announcement: Tranquilandia had been protected by Communist rebels. He dubbed them "narcoguerrillas."

It's now acknowledged that Tambs conjured up a phantom. There were no guerrillas at Tranquilandia. Gen. Miguel Antonio Gómez Padilla, the former head of Colombia's antinarcotics police, admitted in an interview that police did not encounter Communist rebels, their uniforms or even propaganda. "Tambs got ahead of the evidence," a senior State Department official acknowledged. Nevertheless, the narcoguerrilla was projected as reality by the Reagan Administration. A 1985 State Department and Defense Department report on Soviet influence in Latin America warned of an "alliance between drug smugglers and arms dealers in support of terrorists and guerrillas." A 1986 presidential directive raised drug smuggling to the level of a national security threat because of what Vice President George Bush called "a real link between drugs and terrorism." The next year U.S. delegates to the Conference of American Armies, meeting in Argentina, urged Latin American general staffs to unite against "narcoterrorism." Finally, in a report released [in] May [1988], the London-based Institute for Strategic Studies declared that "narcoterrorism" is now "on a par with communism as a threat to western interests in Latin America."

This language is in line with a familiar vision of the United States besieged by foreign devils, but it obscures the essential difference between drug traffickers and Marxist insurgents. The notion of a "narcoguerrilla" unites what can't be united: Top traffickers are hugely successful capitalists bent on boosting their earnings and their social status. Marxist rebels want to overthrow capitalism altogether. These contradictory objectives explain why guerrillas and traffickers are killing each other in Peru and Colombia, and why the Medellín cocaine cartel lurks behind Colombia's dirty war. The narcoguerrilla notion ignores not only these realities but the political impact of Latin America's exploding drug industry. The voracious U.S. demand for cocaine has jolted regional economies, thrusting to center stage a violent new actor in Latin American politics: the narco New Right.

The Narco New Right

The narcos want to get into the establishment, not overthrow it. They see bloodshed as part of the price of admission to the ruling class—a reasonable reading of Latin American history. The introduction of coffee in Colombia at the end of the last century brought on a civil war. Brazil's cacao boom gave rise to the corrupt killers made famous by Jorge Amado in his novel *The Violent Land*. Eventually the captains of coffee and cacao bought and bludgeoned their way into the oligarchy, and the same is almost certain to happen with the rising new stratum of cocaine capitalists.

The narcos seek to legitimize their nouveau riche status through nationalism, and their nationalism infects their investment decisions. Latin American elites traditionally squirrel away their dollars in foreign banks and buy second houses overseas, but traffickers "don't want to go to the south of France," as one U.S. diplomat told me. "They don't speak French." What they do speak is the language of money. Traffickers bring back drug dollars and invest heavily in the national economy. In Colombia they repatriate between $1 billion and $2 billion annually. [In 1987] they "reactivated" the economy,

Merrill Collett, "The Myth of the 'Narcoguerrillas'," *The Nation*, August 13/20, 1988. Copyright 1988 *The Nation* magazine/The Nation Company, Inc.

according to the controller general. The steady devaluation of the Colombian peso makes dollar repatriation on this scale an unsound business practice, but traffickers are moved by more than the profit motive. They want bank accounts in Switzerland, but they want social status in Colombia too. So they accumulate flashy adornments like soccer teams and fighting bulls, and they also make blue-chip investments. "They are in industry, business, finance, agriculture, construction and real estate," says Colombian Senator Iván Marulanda, a businessman who represents the region that includes Medellín. They are Colombia's "largest capitalists, the largest landowners," he says. As if to announce their arrival in the aristocracy, they made the ultimate gesture of noblesse oblige by offering twice to pay, partially or entirely, Colombia's foreign debt.

But all of their drug dollars can't buy them a drink in Colombia's best social clubs, and this rankles the narcos no end. "I don't need those sons of bitches in the clubs," fumed leading cartel member Carlos Lehder on one occasion. The traffickers were in fact well on their way to social acceptance until they murdered Justice Minister Rodrigo Lara Bonilla in 1984, probably in reprisal for the Tranquilandia raid seven weeks earlier. But Lara Bonilla's death made the narcos social pariahs; an embarrassed elite moved to exclude them from high society and deny them an open role in politics. The symbol of this rejection is extradition, a policy executed by presidents from both ruling parties. Extradition enrages the drug lords because it ratifies in Colombia the U.S. definition of traffickers as criminal deviants, not successful businessmen. They have responded by attacking Colombia's ruling elites as holier-than-thou hypocrites. Acting as "The Extraditables," they murdered an attorney general and kidnapped the son of a former president while issuing an indignant manifesto denouncing government, church, press, industrial and financial leaders as "the real mafia."

Bolivia's Drug Class

The emergence of a self-conscious, violent, drug-dealing class is not unique to Colombia. Bolivian traffickers allied with the military ruled their country for a decade beginning in 1971 with the vicious right-wing reign of Gen. Hugo Banzer Suárez and culminated in Gen. Luís García Meza's 1980 "cocaine coup." García Meza brought in Nazis such as Klaus Barbie and put the Interior Ministry under the control of the nephew of Roberto Suárez Gómez, the self-styled King of Cocaine. In the past Suárez rivaled the Medellín moguls in ambition and earnings, and shared their lust for legitimacy. Just like Colombian cartel kingpin Pablo Escobar Gaviria—"Don Pablo" to the slum dwellers of Medellín—Suárez polished a folk-hero image by

doling out money to the poor. And like the Colombian cartel, Suárez once offered to pay off his country's foreign debt.

Suárez is only the tip of the iceberg. The Bolivian drug trade is big enough to have produced a narco newly rich class like Colombia's. And the Bolivian traffickers, like their Colombian counterparts, make themselves big fish in the national pond by repatriating narcobucks even though economic logic tells them to invest their dollars abroad. Ignoring a five-digit inflation rate in the mid-1980s, traffickers faithfully repatriated an estimated $486 million annually.

"In Colombia, no jail can hold a member of the narcobourgeoisie."

Peru is a somewhat different case. The Peruvian drug trade is large, providing a third of the country's foreign export earnings by some accounts, but Peru has no narco national bourgeoisie because the trade is almost entirely controlled from abroad, by the Colombian cartel. Peasants in the Upper Huallaga Valley, where a third to a half of the world's coca leaf is grown, sell their coca paste to seven or eight groups of Colombian middlemen based in the area. These middlemen fly the paste to cartel labs on the Colombian border to be refined and shipped north. It's a classic dependency relationship: The valley is a virtual colony of the cartel. Peruvian peasants are raw-material producers who earn only 0.5 percent of the retail value of the final product. The cartel's dominance is so complete that Colombian *cumbia* music is heard on every jukebox and kids swap the latest slang from Medellín.

Before the cartel consolidated its grip on the Huallaga Valley, Carlos Langberg, a Peruvian, blazed an alternate drug trade route through Mexico to the United States. Following a familiar pattern, Langberg used his illicit millions to buy legitimacy through politics. He eased himself into the upper echelons of the Apra Party by bankrolling its 1980 campaign. But Langberg didn't want to keep behind the scenes; so, like Carlos Lehder in Colombia, he launched a newspaper. He made himself its chief columnist and spewed out a steady stream of right-wing populism in 350,000 copies distributed free every day. His ambition was his undoing. The paper caught the eye of curious reporters, who exposed him as a drug trafficker, and Langberg was sentenced to fifteen years in Lima's Canto Grande Prison. The imprisonment of Langberg and another big-time trafficker, Reynaldo Rodríguez López, reveals the shallow roots of the Peruvian drug trade. In Colombia, no jail can hold a member of the narcobourgeoisie. They are "stronger than the state," says former President Belisario Betancur.

But they are not stronger than the guerrillas. In both Colombia and Peru, Marxist insurgents are an irritating, and often bloody, thorn in the side of the cartel. Traffickers endure the insurgents not out of choice but because they have to face up to a geographic truth: Guerrillas occupy the chief coca-growing regions.

FARC

Twenty-five years ago Colombian peasant rebels joined with the country's Communist Party and formed the Revolutionary Armed Forces of Colombia, or the FARC. Defeated by the army, FARC guerrillas retreated into the sparsely populated southeastern corner of the country and became armed peasant pioneers. They were joined by a steady stream of settlers seeking land in a nation without effective land reform. This trickle turned into a torrent in the late 1970s. The demand for cocaine in the United States had outstripped the supply of coca leaf in Bolivia and Peru, making the low-quality leaves of the Colombian coca shrub a highly profitable crop. The boom was on in Colombia's Amazon jungle and along the riverbanks of the eastern plains.

"Traffickers endure the insurgents not out of choice but because . . . guerrillas occupy the chief coca-growing regions."

Narco-entrepreneurs from Medellín and Cali organized the trade. In some cases they set it up as a cottage industry, selling independent small farmers coca seeds and processing chemicals and buying back their half-processed coca paste. In other cases, the narcos hired day laborers to clear the jungle and sow coca on plantations owned by the traffickers themselves. Whatever the arrangement, the narcobusinessmen tried to keep day wages and coca paste prices down. But the bottom line was drawn by the FARC, which made itself into an armed trade union for Colombia's coca *campesinos*. The guerrillas, who now have at least a third of their forces in coca-growing regions, fix prices for day laborers on coca plantations, agitate to keep paste prices up and prevent abuses by cartel gunmen. "It's a contract arrived at under the threat of force," says historian Alvaro Delgado, a member of the Communist Party's central committee.

Some profits do go to the FARC, which takes a cut of all crops grown in the areas they administer, including coca. They also put the squeeze on cartel middlemen by levying a 10 percent transit "tax" on drug shipments passing through guerrilla territory. (These funds became more important to the FARC after it agreed to stop kidnapping for ransom as part of the 1984 peace accord with Betancur's

government.) But the FARC does not "protect" cocaine laboratories, as Tambs charged after the Tranquilandia raid, and the State Department repeated in its March 1988 report on the world drug trade. After the fall of Tranquilandia the cartel moved its cocaine-refining operations either to ranches in the department of Antioquia or deep into jungles along the Colombia-Brazil-Peru border region. The "labs" occasionally raided by antidrug police in FARC territory are only the crude pits used by peasants to produce coca paste.

MAS Counterattack

The real functional relationship between the FARC "fish" and the "sea" of coca *campesinos* is turned upside down by U.S. analysts yearning to confirm what the U.S. Embassy in Bogotá calls the "FARC-narc connection." In a 1985 article, Mark Steinitz, an officer in the State Department's Bureau of Intelligence and Research, cited Bogotá embassy sources who asserted that the Colombian Communist Party had endorsed "FARC's overall cooperative relationship with Colombia's drug barons" at its Seventh National Congress in 1982. The idea is farfetched: In 1982 the Medellín cartel was carrying out a murderous assault on the left, including individuals associated with Colombia's four main guerrilla groups. On November 12, 1981, three members of the leftist M-19 organization had seized the 26-year-old daughter of Fabio Ochoa Restrepo, patriarch of Colombia's first family of cocaine. The guerrillas demanded $12 million for her return. The Ochoa kidnapping was the latest in a series of guerrilla attacks on rich narcos, and it infuriated them. A leaflet airdropped three weeks later over a Cali soccer game announced that traffickers were fed up with Communists preying on those "like us, who have brought progress and jobs to Colombia," and declared their intention to counterattack with an underground army called MAS (*Muerte a Secuestradores*, or "Death to Kidnappers"). It was a turning point in the political history of the cartel. "MAS represented the [drug] mafia's first organized expression in defense of its economic interests," says Senator Marulanda.

MAS assault teams promptly captured a half-dozen M-19 guerrillas and Ochoa's daughter was released unharmed. MAS then broadened its focus from M-19 in Medellín to leftists throughout the country. MAS death squads carrying identification from the army intelligence service rounded up and shot peasant and union leaders, progressive university professors and attorneys who defended political prisoners. Over the next five years hundreds of political killings would be attributed to MAS, including the murder of Toledo Plata, one of the top M-19 leaders. In February 1983 Attorney General Carlos Jiménez Gómez charged that among those involved in MAS were fifty-nine active-duty military officers. The highest-ranking suspect was Lieut. Col. Alvaro Hernán Velandia, whose case sheds light on the murky narco/military convergence that underlies Colombia's present dirty war.

The Magdalena Region

In 1982, Velandia, MAS, the FARC and the narcos were all active in the middle sector of the Magdalena River basin in the north-central region of Colombia. The narcos were buying up land abandoned by wealthy ranchers fleeing from the FARC. Velandia, an expert in counterinsurgency, was hunting the guerrillas. MAS was hunting guerrilla sympathizers. Ranchers, the military and MAS formed a "triangle of terror," according to Chilean sociologist Ibán de Rementería, who studied the violence in the middle Magdalena region. This three-way alliance has spread to all of Colombia, according to historian Alfredo Molano. When leftists are murdered, "the [drug] mafia supplies the money [to hire gunmen], the military the arms, and members of the local elites an air of legitimacy," Molano told a reporter.

Velandia went on to head the army's highly secret Intelligence and Counter-Intelligence Battalion. He has been named by the leftist Patriotic Union (U.P.), the political party founded by the FARC, as one of the masterminds of Colombia's current dirty war. Velandia can look back with satisfaction on his efforts in the middle Magdalena; the FARC was pushed out of the area. The narcos, meanwhile, settled in. Two czars of the cartel, Gonzalo Rodríguez Gacha and Pablo Escobar Gaviria, own large haciendas in the middle Magdalena, and in May 1988 two enormous cocaine labs were discovered in the area. "MAS wiped out the guerrilla support network and created the conditions for the narcos to live there in peace," says Fabio Castillo, a Colombian journalist and author of the current best seller *The Horsemen of Cocaine.*

"Traffickers decided it was time 'to liberate themselves from the economic impositions of the guerrillas.'"

MAS is dormant these days, but the narcos are still killing FARC sympathizers. There is well-documented evidence that cartel kingpins are involved in the dirty war against the U.P. Nearly 600 party members have been gunned down since the U.P. was launched in 1984, after the FARC-government peace pact. The common thread running through these crimes—none of them prosecuted—is the modus operandi. Unknown assassins arrive, murder their victims in well-planned, smoothly executed attacks and disappear. Such professionalism is the trademark of the *sicarios*, or paid killers, used by the cartel to murder rivals and defiant authorities, but the evidence of narco involvement in the dirty war is more than circumstantial. Government prosecutors contend that Rodríguez Gacha paid a band of six *sicarios* $120,000 to murder U.P. chair Jaime Pardo Leal. The element conspicuously absent from the government's case is the motive.

A Matter of Economics

To explain why a top trafficker would kill Colombia's leading leftist requires a step back. It is a matter of economics. The fixing of wages and prices by the FARC was a yoke around the neck of the narcos. "The mafiosos respected the guerrilla rules, but they didn't like them," says retired Gen. Joaquín Matallana, an expert on both the FARC and the drug trade. The guerrilla burden was bearable when cocaine prices were rising, but in 1986 coca overproduction swamped the U.S. market. The wholesale price of a kilo of cocaine—$55,000 in 1983—had dropped to $22,000 by the end of 1986, beginning a downward slide that still continues. Traffickers decided it was time "to liberate themselves from the economic impositions of the guerrillas," says Matallana, now president of the cattle ranchers' association in the coca-growing, FARC-controlled plains of southeastern Colombia. Matallana says it was here that the narcos linked up with military officers in a clandestine, anti-Communist alliance. Together they set their sights on the FARC's unarmed flank, the Patriotic Union. Eight party members were shot dead, including an alternate deputy to congress and the mayor of the regional capital of San José de Guaviare. The FARC counterattacked by murdering a half-dozen members of the Plata family, which handled the local coca trade for Rodríguez Gacha. This chain of violence finally reached to the top when Rodríguez Gacha allegedly contracted the murder of U.P. leader Pardo.

A similar pattern of violence is starting to characterize the relations between cartel middlemen and the Maoist rebels of Sendero Luminoso ("Shining Path") in Peru's coca-growing Huallaga Valley. Sendero guerrillas moved into the valley in 1984, but it was not until [1987] that they became a major political force there. Interviews gathered during a five-day trip through the valley in May [1988] confirm that Sendero now dominates dozens of tiny villages and strongly influences several large towns. This was achieved by exploiting the contradictions of the drug economy. Some 60,000 families depend on coca cultivation to survive, and U.S. attempts to eliminate the valley drug trade throw these farmers into "a panic," says Hugo Samánez, director of the valley's U.S.-financed coca eradication project. The guerrillas provide a shield against the eradication effort while mitigating the abuses of cartel middlemen and their private armies.

Like the FARC in Colombia, they take a cut of peasant coca production and levy a transit "tax" on the coca buyers. And like the FARC, Sendero has not traded its political goals for drug profits.

An Ideological Bias

The guerrillas are in the Huallaga Valley because its forest canopy offers a secure place to carve out a liberated territory. "They have studied the Vietnam situation closely," says Gustavo Gorriti, a Peruvian journalist writing a book on Sendero, "and they consider the Upper Huallaga like the Mekong Delta. It's absolutely essential in their geopolitical thinking." With so much at stake, the guerrillas are carrying out a systematic campaign of eliminating all competing authority in the valley. The guerrillas, whose ideology is extremely puritanical, have warned peasants that they must eventually phase out coca cultivation, which would pull the rug out from under the cartel. The Colombians have countered with the threat to organize an army against the guerrillas. Tensions erupted in a shootout [in] September [1987], when a hundred guerrillas launched an attack on thirty traffickers holed up in a bunker in the town of Paraíso, according to Gen. Juan Zarate, head of Peru's antidrug police.

"The narcoguerrilla is less an analytical model than a political slogan."

Those who push the narcoguerrilla notion explain such shootouts as passing feuds rather than the first salvos in a war between staunchly opposed social forces. This fallacy derives from an ideological bias. The narcoguerrilla is less an analytical model than a political slogan. Former Ambassador Tambs, a fervent anti-Communist and close colleague of North Carolina Senator Jesse Helms, invented his "narcoguerrilla" only weeks before the Colombian government was to sign the first-ever cease-fire with the rebels there in May 1984. His announcement nearly sabotaged the peace process by giving the military an excuse to escalate the fighting. "This narco-guerrilla alliance is a new threat to democracy," explained Defense Minister Gen. Gustavo Matamoros in March 1984, "and if we don't act rapidly and energetically it could put our constitutional system in danger."

Four years later it can be said with certainty that what endangers the Colombian constitution is not the narcoguerrilla but the "triangle of terror" that first took shape in the middle Magdalena. There are persistent rumblings that this murderous alliance may seek a military solution to Colombia's "leftist problem." If there is a cocaine coup in Colombia, Washington will have some real "narcoguerrillas" to deal with. And the phantom dreamed up by Tambs will have finally come to life.

Merrill Collett is a free-lance author who writes frequently on Latin America.

"The epidemic of 'crack' or 'rock' cocaine has already reached crisis proportions."

Cocaine Abuse Is Epidemic

Tom Morganthau

Cruising the high-crime streets of Boston's Roxbury ghetto, Officers Leo Ronan and Fred Stevens spotted three young men who seemed to be delivering drugs. The courier was carrying a large gym bag; the other two were bodyguards. Ronan and Stevens stopped their car to investigate and the trio took off running. Ronan chased the man with the gym bag, but the suspect got away through the backyards of Roxbury. But the bag, found under a parked car, contained 1,051 vials of crack cocaine worth more than $26,000 and an address list written on the back of a receipt from a five-and-dime store in New York City. The evidence of a New York connection was disturbing and so was the size of the shipment: Ronan and Stevens had stumbled onto the biggest crack bust Boston had ever seen. "We've been lucky so far," said Lt. James Wood, commander of the Boston PD's Drug Control Unit. "But we have to keep it contained or it could blow up like New York."

Or like Los Angeles, Miami, Houston and Detroit—cities where, by every estimation, the epidemic of "crack" or "rock" cocaine has already reached crisis proportions. Crack—smokable cocaine—has suddenly become America's fastest-growing drug epidemic and potentially its most serious. It is cheap, plentiful and intensely addictive, a drug whose potential for social disruption and individual tragedy is comparable only to heroin. Fueled by the 500 percent increase in the amount of cocaine smuggled into this country from South America, the crack craze is spreading nationwide. According to Arnold Washton, a respected drug-abuse specialist who operates a national cocaine hot line, crack and rock are now widely available. Crack has captured the ghetto and is inching its way into the suburbs; its users come from all social strata and

all walks of life. Wherever it appears, it spawns vicious violence among dealers and dopers and a startling increase in petty crime: in New York, where crack is now the top-priority drug-enforcement problem, police believe it is the primary cause of an 18 percent jump in robberies.

A Domestic Vietnam

The police are losing the war against crack, and the war is turning the ghettos of major cities into something like a domestic Vietnam. The analogy is shopworn but apt. The crack trade operates like a guerrilla insurgency and makes an infuriatingly elusive target for police. Dealers—"ounce men," as they are known in L.A.—organize small cells of pushers, couriers and lookouts from the ghetto's legion of unemployed teenagers. They enforce discipline with savage violence, change locations frequently and alter their tactics constantly to foil narcotics agents. Police raids on "crack houses" typically recover too little cocaine to impress prosecutors or the courts: given the logjam in the prisons, most offenders spend little or no time in jail. Undercover investigations aimed at ringleaders often lead nowhere: crack can be manufactured in any kitchen, and the trade in bulk cocaine is highly decentralized. "It's futile," says Det. Ken Wilkinson, a 22-year veteran of the Los Angeles Police Department. "The answer has to be something other than what we're doing."

Like other narcs in other cities, Wilkinson readily compares rock to heroin—and though the two drugs are very different, the comparison is not farfetched. Rock and crack represent a quantum leap in the addictive properties of cocaine and a marketing breakthrough for the pusher. Sold in tiny chips that give the user a 5- to 20-minute high, crack often is purer than sniffable cocaine. When smoked, cocaine molecules reach the brain in less than 10 seconds; the resulting euphoric high is followed by crushing depression. The cycle of ups and downs reinforces the craving and, according to many experts, can produce a powerful chemical dependency within two weeks. While a typical heroin addict shoots up once or twice a day, crack addicts need another hit within minutes—which means that even at $10 a chip, crack addiction can be more expensive than heroin. Heroin, moreover, is a depressant, while cocaine is a stimulant—which means that heroin addicts are lethargic and mostly immobile during the high, while crack addicts are likely to be paranoid and highly active. In Boston, Lt. Wood says, heroin addicts "are scared of this stuff—and when a heroin addict says something is bad, you know it's *bad*."

The In Crowd

West 107th Street in Manhattan is a fringe neighborhood populated by low-income blacks and Hispanics—and one of New York's open-air drug markets. "One-o-seven, you can get anything you want," says Juan, a skinny 19-year-old. "You get crack, coke, herb, heroin. But crack's the thing. That's what's happening now." The street moves to the furtive sound of illicit commerce. At night, particularly on weekends, West 107th Street sees a steady stream of limos, taxis and out-of-state cars. "Sometimes you get the impression we're in New Jersey," says Deputy Inspector Frank Bihler, commander of the NYPD's 24th Precinct; he jokes about blowing up the bridges and tunnels to keep the suburbanites out. But nobody jokes about the neighborhood young addicts. "They're skinny, dirty and totally obsessed with getting crack," says social worker Joe Stewart. "I see young girls in doorways trying to sell themselves" for the $5 it costs to get high.

"The crack business is a cottage industry which needs virtually no technology or central organization."

It could be anywhere. The drug is the same, the hustle is the same and the cops all say the same things. Selling crack is where the money is, where the action is and where the ghetto's inverted social pecking order begins. "Rock cocaine has taken on the social esteem that being a pimp had 20 years ago," Wilkinson says. "Its just the 'in' thing to do, like wearing Fila running shoes. And these people are very, very into the 'in' thing." The ounce men drive BMW's and Mercedeses, the kids who work as runners and lookouts wear $200 designer-label running suits. By the weary estimate of one of Wilkinson's colleagues on the LAPD, Det. Charles Johns, the rock business is now the largest employer in the Los Angeles ghetto. Although law-abiding neighbors still call in tips by the hundreds,

Wilkinson and Johns say the community as a whole is apathetic about controlling the contagion. "You can't expect the police department to stop the tide of rock cocaine when the people aren't policing themselves," Johns says. "Right now they're saying, 'If it's not directly involving me I'm not going to worry about it.' But it does involve them—and their neighbors and their children." . . .

A Cottage Industry

The crack business is a cottage industry which needs virtually no technology or central organization, and which is essentially bound together only by vast amounts of cash. Its raw material, cocaine, is smuggled into this country from South America, often through Colombia and Mexico. Since 1980, according to congressional sources, the influx of smuggled cocaine has risen from approximately 25 tons a year to 125 tons a year. The U.S. Drug Enforcement Administration, which concentrates on major traffickers, believes there is a two- or three-tier network of wholesale distributors. Crack dealers, operating just above the retail level, frequently buy no more than a pound or two at a time.

What happens next is best illustrated by a raid in New York. A police narcotics squad raided a small crack house in a Bronx apartment and found records leading to the drug ring's factory, which turned out to be in another apartment building next door. They got a warrant and surrounded the building. Two Puerto Rican men were allegedly caught in the act of converting cocaine into crack. The suspects had about two pounds of crack worth about $150,000 in the room. They also had more than 16,000 plastic vials that are commonly used in New York to package crack for sale. The only equipment needed was two glass coffee pots, a hot plate, a pair of scales and a case of baking soda; baking soda is used as a reagent in the conversion process. Luckily, the suspects were caught totally off guard—for they had a small arsenal of loaded weapons that included a rifle, four pistols and two machine guns. It was the biggest crack bust in the city's history—but the "factory," police said, probably served no more than a 10-block area.

A city like New York may have scores of underground factories—and only rarely are police lucky enough to find them. Each factory supplies a handful of crack houses. Each crack house keeps only small amounts of the drug on hand. By restocking their salesmen frequently, dealers prevent police from making large-scale busts. Crack houses are well protected by lookouts and fortified doors; if the police stage a raid, the sellers need only a few seconds to flush their dope down the toilet and evade prosecution. "You can raid a house that's filled with people and has a table covered in crack and drug paraphernalia," says John Hogan, chief of the felony section of the Dade County State's

Attorney's Office in Miami. "But the place is usually registered under a fictitious name, and by the time the police get in no one is physically linked to the drugs. You can't charge anyone."

The war between cops and dealers has become an intricate game. In Los Angeles, where police have successfully raided hundreds of rock houses, dealers are sending their sales teams into the streets. Each team consists of a steerer, who screens would-be buyers for security risks, a cashier, who takes the buyer's money, and a third dealer, who hands over the drugs: if a narcotics agent tries the usual buy-bust tactic, the team scatters instantly and leaves the narc empty-handed. "Today you'll find the biggest amount of dealing in rock cocaine is . . . done by street people who are very, very transient," says the LAPD's Lt. Dick Koskelin. "The reason is that we've educated these dope dealers. Every time you make an arrest, they [ask each other], 'How'd you get caught?' So they know the rock-house approach is passé."

There are ominous signs that crack and rock dealers are expanding well beyond the inner city. L.A. police say rock houses are opening up in the San Fernando Valley and in beach-front towns like Venice; in Florida, lawmen report a similar trend. "Every city, county and almost every little town has been hit by the crack epidemic," says John J. Barbara of the Florida Department of Law Enforcement. "It's everywhere, and it crosses all racial, social and economic boundaries." In the Northeast, police are keeping a wary eye on the crack boom in New York, and there are early indications that New York pushers are branching out. In Texas, rock has shown up in Dallas and San Antonio, and a DEA official in Houston says at least some of the dealers operating in rock-infested Houston have migrated down from New York. Houston police got grisly evidence of the New York connection in a double homicide last August [1985]. The victims, both Haitians from Brooklyn, were involved in a Jamaican-run rock operation. "The workers in the dope houses are being recruited from poor Haitian and American black kids in New York," says Houston Police Sgt. Steven Clappart.

Expansion

The most frightening aspect of the crack problem is its exponential growth. Sen. Lawton Chiles convened a meeting of local police officials in Florida to discuss the spread of "designer drugs" and was startled to find his audience largely unconcerned by exotic hallucinogens. "He found that crack was on everyone's mind," an aide says. "Crack is a firestorm issue that is overwhelming them and spreading like wildfire across the state. They want and need help." A survey by the National Institute on Drug Abuse indicates that 4.2 million Americans reported having used cocaine within the previous

month—but the survey, which dates from 1982, made no distinction between sniffable cocaine and crack. . . .

Outmanned and underfunded police officials point to the abundant supply of cocaine as the root of their problem. As the rising tonnage of smuggled cocaine demonstrates, the DEA's interdiction campaign has so far failed to make much headway against major traffickers—and though few local cops blame the DEA for their problems, they are increasingly angry at Washington. The DEA is "inundated just like we are," says L.A.'s Wilkinson. "My personal feeling is that [federal policymakers are] afraid of stepping on the toes of certain leaders of certain countries. It's obvious to us where the cocaine is coming from." In Detroit, Police Inspector Joel Gilliam makes the same point in more dramatic terms. "In 1941 the Japanese bombed Pearl Harbor and we went to war," Gilliam says. "Today, little white packets are being dropped on this country and nobody gives a damn."

A Local Problem

The DEA, meanwhile, tends to regard the spread of crack as a problem for local police. "If you want to call it crack or rock or whatever, it's still cocaine," says Raymond Vinsik, chief of cocaine investigations for the agency. "For DEA it's a matter of getting to the major suppliers and importers and shutting them down. For the local police departments, it is to attempt to limit the availability of cocaine to the street dealers." Another DEA official thinks the media are partly to blame for the crack craze. "We are very concerned about a market being developed because of all the publicity," says special agent Robert O'Leary of the DEA's Washington-Baltimore field office. "We feel it's being accelerated by media hype."

"[Crack]'s everywhere, and it crosses all racial, social and economic boundaries."

The point is plausible if not persuasive: in New York, for example, crack suddenly became the city's biggest drug problem with very little attention from the press. Crack's lurid appeal as a potent high is part of its rising popularity; conversely, heroin use may be declining because of the addicted population's fear of contracting AIDS from contaminated needles. But at bottom, crack and rock are spreading because cocaine is so widely available in the United States and because the justice system has been unable to thwart the cocaine trade at any level. Police in every city where crack is now a major problem argue that the courts are too lenient with drug offenders, and they may be right. In New York, special narcotics prosecutor Sterling Johnson recently argued for mandatory jail sentences even in plea-bargained drug cases—and warned that some neighborhoods now have "more crack stops than bus stops." John Cusack, chief of staff of the House Select Committee on Narcotics Abuse and Control, stresses the role of judicial "gridlock." "We are not thinning out the ranks and making any impact. We are not *deterring*," Cusack says. "As a matter of fact, the opposite is happening. What's the risk? So few are getting caught and the risk of prosecution is so remote that we are encouraging people to traffic."

"Unlike heroin, which creates a specific physiological need in the body, cocaine dependency involves the subtle chemistry of the brain itself."

Art F. was a fortyish San Francisco lawyer when cocaine took over his life. He was both a dealer and an addict. At the peak of his addiction, he smoked $1,000 worth of rock a day. Somewhere along the way he lost his wife, his two children and his Marin County home. "I could see what was happening, but none of it mattered," he says now. "I'd get depressed that I was an addict, but when I'd slip into depression it would lead five minutes later to another pipe. And when I was happy, that would lead to another pipe." It all ended when a San Francisco police narcotics squad kicked down his front door—though even then, his first impulse after being booked was to go home and get high. Today, Art F. is staying straight and trying to rebuild his life. "I only hope the people using it—the kids smoking it—get sick enough that they get into a recovery program," he says. "Otherwise, life is tough and then you die."

A Subtle Dependency

Crack's rising cost to the nation is perhaps best measured by its toll on individuals like Art F. Despite its benign reputation, cocaine is unquestionably addictive—and crack is extremely addictive. Researchers are not entirely sure how the addiction takes hold. Unlike heroin, which creates a specific physiological need in the body, cocaine dependency involves the subtle chemistry of the brain itself; both forms of addiction are reinforced by psychological dependence, which as any cigarette smoker can testify, is also very powerful. In one experiment, says Dr. Richard H. Schwartz, medical director of a Virginia drug-rehabilitation center, monkeys allowed an unlimited supply of intravenous cocaine died of convulsions within five days. "They preferred cocaine to life—that's the bottom line," Schwartz says. Dr. Frank Gawin of Yale University is pessimistic that cocaine addicts can truly eradicate their need for the drug. "The best way to reduce demand would be to have God redesign the human brain to change the way the cocaine molecule reacts with certain neurons," Gawin says. "It produces pleasure. That's a very unfortunate accident, and I don't know how to solve it."

The implications for national policy are clear. Given the widespread societal acceptance of drugs of all types and given cocaine's immense addictive power, the war against crack will not be won by campaigns to reduce public demand. To be sure, that conclusion contradicts the line taken by many in the Reagan administration—and it would require bigger law-enforcement budgets at both the federal and local level. But the alternative, as the frustrated street cops know, is far worse.

Tom Morganthau is a senior writer for Newsweek *magazine.*

"Crack was not the drug of choice for most users ... its prevalence had been exaggerated by heavy media attention."

viewpoint 72

The Cocaine Epidemic Is a Media Creation

Malcolm Gladwell

The Hype began, quietly and unobtrusively, Nov. 17, [1985] on a page of The New York Times. This was not itself a Hype story, of course, only a minor mention, the miniscare that would turn into a megascare, the cherry bomb that would turn into a mushroom cloud. When The Hype ended, or at least when everyone thought The Hype had ended, there would be much discussion about when The Hype had peaked, when the epidemic had seized American journalism most completely. But one thing was never in doubt: when the whole business began.

It began with the first story on crack.

You can look it up. Page 12, column three: "Program for Cocaine Abuse Under Way." Byline? Donna Boundy. Boundy, it seems, was writing of The Recovery Center, a New York drug abuse program, when the words just slipped out: "Three teenagers have sought this treatment already this year . . . for cocaine dependence resulting from the use of a new form of the drug called 'crack' or rock-like pieces of prepared 'freebase' (concentrated) cocaine." . . .

With just that one short mention, crack took on a life of its own. By Oct. 1, [1986] the major media—The New York Times, The Washington Post, the Los Angeles Times, the wire services, Time, Newsweek and U.S. News & World Report—had among them carried more than a thousand stories in which crack and other drugs figured prominently, coverage feeding coverage, stories of addiction and squalor multiplying across the land. CBS's "48 Hours on Crack Street" reached 15 million viewers and became one of the highest-rated documentaries of all time. NBC brought out "Cocaine Country," culminating a six-month stretch in which the network broadcast 429 reports on drug abuse,

according to a Public Broadcasting Service tally, for a total of 16 hours and 51 minutes of airtime.

It is not as if the mainstream media ignored the drug question up until [1986], of course. From 1981 through [1985], Time and Newsweek averaged about one drug abuse cover a year, and NBC, ABC and PBS each produced long documentaries about cocaine. But crack gave the whole drug story a new angle and a new urgency. This was the ultimate high and what expert after expert called one of the most dangerous and addictive drugs ever.

Cocaine, the glamour dust of the late '70s—fast, clean, fun!—has been boiled down to hard and mean little pellets of crack, giver of euphoria, taker of lives. To a nation that espouses self-reliance, drug dependence has emerged as the dark side of the American character, the price of freedom to fail. It is as if America, so vain and self-consciously fit, has looked upon itself and suddenly seen the hideously consumptive portrait of Dorian Gray. (Time, Sept. 15, 1986)

A Glut of Drug Stories

Time ran two cover stories on the larger drug problem, one in March and one in September [1986], and featured "Crack," an article in its Nation section, on the cover in June; U.S. News & World Report's "Killer Drugs: New Facts, New Enemies" ran in late July [1986] as did Sports Illustrated's "Death of a Dream" cover on the cocaine overdose death of basketball star Len Bias; Life magazine's "I Am a Coke Addict: What Happens When Nice Guys Get Hooked" appeared in October [1986]. It is Newsweek, however, that has been the champion of the drug issue. Comparing drugs to the "plagues of medieval times," Newsweek Editor-in-Chief Richard M. Smith has masterminded a series that has encompassed 14 stories over 38 magazine pages, including three cover stories: "Kids and Cocaine," "Crack and Crime" and "Saying No."

Even The Atlantic, normally the paragon of staid

New England journalism, gave in to the pressures of The Hype. James Lieber's cover story about cocaine in the January [1986] issue was not supposed to be a cover story and was not supposed to be about cocaine. "To be honest, I was surprised when they turned it into a cover," says Lieber, a Pittsburgh lawyer. Originally his article was to be much less ambitious, a story about Miami, about the economy of the area, about immigration, and thirdly—but only thirdly—about drugs. But in 1986, the year of The Hype, stories about Miami are not stories about business and immigration. Nor are they to be buried in the backs of magazines. They are cover stories. They are cover stories about drugs.

The Hype

There is, no doubt, a good side to The Hype. It has heightened public awareness of the dangers of drugs; it has helped to create, as Nancy Reagan has wanted, a "new climate of intolerance" toward drug use. "Since 1981, public attitudes toward drugs have turned around 180 degrees," says Carlton E. Turner, [former] deputy assistant to the president for drug abuse policy. The Hype has something to do with that. But as The Hype has waned, as everyone knew it would, there has been increasing talk of its dark side. A little media scare may have helped the War on Drugs, but was it good journalism?

"The place of the drug issue among the problems of society has been exaggerated by the press," says Ben H. Bagdikian, dean of the journalism school at the University of California at Berkeley. "Trends in drug use have been misrepresented. The impression that has been given is that the problem is out of control and growing. That's simply not true."

Adam Paul Weisman, who researched U.S. News & World Report's cover story on drug abuse, confessed in the pages of The New Republic in late September [1986] that he "selectively" used only facts "that made drug abuse sound like an ever-increasing problem, while leaving out the plethora of equally legitimate, mitigating circumstances."

"There is no worsening epidemic. There is only worsening journalism."

Weisman and others have questioned the figure used by Newsweek and Time of 5 million "regular" cocaine users, pointing out that the National Institute on Drug Abuse's figures are for 3 million to 5 million persons who have simply used cocaine, not used it regularly. Also questionable is the common assertion that there is a cocaine epidemic among the country's youth.

The plain fact is that cocaine abuse is the fastest growing drug problem in America for adults and school age children alike. The plain fact is that coke is widely available at low prices—within the financial reach of the young (Newsweek, "Kids and Cocaine," March 17, 1986).

In fact, according to National Institute on Drug Abuse statistics, 17 percent of high school seniors admitted [in 1985] that they had tried cocaine at least once, up one percentage point from 1982, 1983 and 1984 and the same percentage as 1981.

"The answer when it comes to drugs is simple," wrote the liberal columnist Richard Cohen. "There is no worsening epidemic. There is only worsening journalism."

And the crack explosion? Dan Rather held a container of crack up to the camera on CBS's "48 Hours on Crack Street": *This is the typical, tiny bottle for the new, illegal drug of choice in America: crack. Vials like this one are turning up empty and discarded in the streets, in the parks, in the schoolyards around the nation.*

Newsweek? *Crack—smokable cocaine—has suddenly become America's fastest-growing drug epidemic and potentially its most serious.*

Time? *On both coasts, and in Chicago, Detroit, and other cities throughout the U.S. [crack] is an inexpensive yet highly addictive form of cocaine that is rapidly becoming a scourge.*

DEA Reaction

By September [1986] the crack hysteria had reached such proportions that the Drug Enforcement Administration felt compelled to respond. At a news conference announcing a city-by-city study of crack use, agency spokesman Robert Feldkamp said that crack was not the drug of choice for most users and that its prevalence had been exaggerated by heavy media attention. The DEA, he said, considered crack a "secondary, not a primary, problem in most cities," available in a number of cities but concentrated mainly in New York.

Jay Winston of the Harvard School of Public Health goes further. Even in New York "you've got to go into certain neighborhoods to find crack users," he told National Public Radio's "All Things Considered" news show. "It's not a New York problem. It's a Washington Heights problem."

Such revisionism on the subject of crack, however, has been all but ignored by the mainstream media. The DEA report did not make the ABC or CBS news programs on the night it was released; The New York Times ignored the story; The Washington Post buried it on Page 18, and Time was the only newsweekly to make note of it. That doesn't surprise Jacob Weisberg, the Washington writer who began the crack rethinking in July [1986] in the pages of The New Republic. "Look at Newsweek," says Weisberg. "They said that crack was the biggest story since Vietnam. They've made a huge commitment to in-depth coverage. There's no way they're going to back down now."

Indeed, when Newsweek National Affairs Editor Tony Fuller was confronted by Weisberg and CBS anchorman Bruce Morton on the CBS Morning News in August [1986], he stuck to his guns.

FULLER: As to why we're devoting so much energy to [drug abuse], it occurred to us that in the last few years we've done a number of drug covers, that it is a pervasive problem, it's a drain on the national treasury, it has a criminal, medical pathology. It merited the same sort of aggressive coverage that we give AIDS or have given Vietnam in the past or civil rights.

MORTON: Really that—that major? I mean, Vietnam was a, you know, a war in which 50,000 Americans died.

FULLER: Mm-hmmm. And many people die from drugs.

Selling Magazines

Many critics say what really motivates Newsweek is the thought of selling more magazines. It is well-known that Newsweek has suffered heavily over the past two years from declining ad pages; is its "Drug Crisis" series an attempt to regain lost ground?

"Newsweek has vowed to pursue the lonely struggle against crack no matter how much money it makes," is how Weisberg put it in his New Republic article, pointing out that the "Kids and Cocaine" issue sold about 15 percent more than the average issue at the newsstand and that other cocaine covers have sold as much as 35 percent more than normal.

"The drug issue has grown not so much in response to the growth in drug abuse itself but in response to news coverage of the drug issue."

But there may be more here than simply an attempt to sell magazines or gain ratings by hyping the drug issue. Some suggest that the press by nature is inclined to look at a complicated issue like the drug problem in a certain way.

How much of the hyperbole on "48 Hours on Crack Street" was a deliberate policy decision or the inevitable result of being led to the lurid sections of the drug subculture by the power of the camera? The show's producer, Lane Venardos, had said that if the show did no more than heighten one person's awareness of drugs or reform one junkie then his time and effort were worthwhile. Was this reporting or was this a cautionary tale? Certainly within the show itself there were subtle indications of a disposition to sensationalize the drug scene. Much has been made, for example, of the reaction of "Crack Street" narrator Dan Rather to being taken to a so-called crack house.

RATHER (going downstairs): It doesn't look like I thought it might look. Might—don't ask me how I thought it would look, but it doesn't look like I thought it would look.

POLICEMAN: Does it look better?

RATHER: No, it looks worse.

And with that, music began and the ominous words flashed on the screen: "Americans spend almost $220 million daily on illegal drugs."

Time's Sept. 15, [1986] cover story "Drugs: The Enemy Within" showed the same stretch marks when it came to the drug crisis. "Statistics to be released by the National Institute on Drug Abuse this month will show rather surprisingly that the current cocaine epidemic has already peaked," the story went.

Rather surprisingly? Why should it be surprising? "It's only surprising to the people who've been hyping the drug question for the past six months," says Weisberg.

The Hype, as it has continued, has become a conversation within journalism. "The media have become part of the story," says Charles Freund, who writes on the media for The New Republic. "We saw the same thing with [Nicholas] Daniloff," the U.S. News correspondent arrested in Moscow on spying charges.

Self-Reference

The drug issue has grown not so much in response to the growth in drug abuse itself but in response to news coverage of the drug issue. When Time magazine reported on the DEA crack report, it did so in its Press column. Steven Wisotsky, a professor at the Nova University School of Law in Fort Lauderdale, Fla., and an expert on the drug issue, points out that when the Time column asked whether the press had "overdosed" on the drug issue, it was a self-referential question: Just three weeks before, Time had splashed "Drugs: The Enemy Within" across its cover and begun a 10-page spread—"A nation wrestles with the dark and dangerous recesses of its soul"—with phrases that took The Hype to new heights. *Otherworldly pictures on TV: policemen stand before a table displaying sacks of white powders, like babies laid out in their christening dresses. . . . And how can this be happening in America? Or is the question rhetorical in the land of pioneers: How free can you be, Mr. Icarus?*

Later, "The Enemy Within" speaks of how "Cocaine, the glamour dust of the late '70s—fast, clean, fun!—has been boiled down to hard and mean little pellets of crack." But who was it that called cocaine "glamour dust" in the first place? Why, Time, of course, says Wisotsky, referring to its 1981 "Middle Class High" cocaine cover, which featured a martini glass filled with cocaine topped by an olive.

Still, there is more to The Hype than the vagaries of news coverage. Reporters may have been, as Wisotsky claims, pedantic and ritualistic in their coverage, but the fact remains that their attitudes toward the drug issue were not substantially different from those of the U.S. public at large. Well before The Hype peaked, public opinion polls showed Americans just as concerned about drug abuse as Newsweek is.

"The press just responds to things," says David Musto, a medical historian and professor of psychiatry at Yale University School of Medicine. "They can take something and put it in a prism and make it seem more exciting." But, he says, they cannot manufacture a trend.

And on the drug issue, the media have followed a public lead that has been, according to some observers, hysterical at times, volatile at others, and only partially based in fact. "In a lot of ways this drug thing has superseded our feelings toward witchcraft," says Lieber. "It possesses us. We can't be rational about it."

The Pendulum's Swing

It is clear, for example, that periodic public scares like The Hype occur in American society. There was a drug scare just after World War I that resulted in cocaine being banned. Until then, the drug had been freely available in the United States.

Musto, whose 1973 book, "The American Disease," is considered a classic in the field of sociology, sees a parallel between that time and now. There are "two sides of the American character," libertarian and authoritarian, daring and cautious. According to Musto, "These strains don't go away. They just fall in and out of fashion."

"Good intentions in the cause of fighting drugs can go bad."

Now, he says, the pendulum has swung away from the attitudes of the '60s. "In the past five to 10 years we've moved toward reducing risk in our lives. 'Star wars' is risk reduction, taking carcinogens out of our food is risk reduction. We have an increased feeling of vulnerability. People are trying to strengthen themselves, with stronger, cleaner bodies. People have also come to see themselves as part of a network. What you do affects others. There are no victimless crimes." What that means, Musto concludes, is that "we no longer accept the argument in this country that it's my body, my life, I'll do what I want with it. Drug use is now being considered a threat to the entire community."

Unlike many others, Musto does not see The Hype as necessarily a bad thing. It is the logical result, he says, of the drug education Americans have received since the '60s. Instead of increasing tolerance, prolonged exposure to drug use has turned people even more against drugs.

But even Musto admits that, in the end, there is some danger to the heavy current concentration on drug abuse, that there can be overreaction, that people, "while well-meaning, can indulge in overkill." The gist of the argument against The Hype is no more than this: The drug scare is too much of a good thing. Good intentions in the cause of fighting drugs can go bad.

Malcolm Gladwell is a writer for Insight *magazine, a weekly news and opinion publication of* The Washington Times.

*"Carefully controlled studies . . . will
provide sorely needed information."*

Further Studies of Cocaine's Effects Are Needed

American Society for Pharmacology and Experimental Therapeutics and Committee on Problems of Drug Dependence

The problem of cocaine abuse continues to grow despite evidence that abuse of other drugs in the U.S. peaked in 1979 and has subsequently declined slightly. Exact estimates of the number of users of cocaine are difficult to determine, but most experts agree that literally millions of persons use the drug regularly. Many aspects of cocaine abuse are controversial or not well understood. . . .

Cocaine is a powerful stimulant with positive reinforcing actions. With continued use, the qualitative nature of the stimulation changes, leading to a variety of behavioral changes that often are less pleasurable and are characteristic of the cocaine-dependent state. The mechanism for these effects and the sites in the brain are complex and not completely understood. . . .

We need a clearer understanding of the acute and chronic effects of cocaine on the function of the nervous system with special reference to the monoamine systems, including the levels of the monoamines, their synthesis rates, the enzymes involved in synthesis, the turnover of monoamines, and the electrical activity of the catecholamine and serotonin neurons themselves. More information is also needed on the specific alterations in receptor density and function associated with chronic cocaine administration. We need to identify the specific target neurons where increased receptor density develops with repeated cocaine use. The newly established techniques of autoradiography and computer-assisted image analysis of dopamine and other receptors will permit definitive answers to these questions in the near future.

We need to know more precisely what the differential effects of cocaine are on the different dopamine systems which subserve different behaviors. Are there differences in the responses to acute and chronic cocaine in terms of monoamine metabolism, receptor density and electrical activity, in each of the discrete dopamine systems in the brain? . . .

A Better Understanding

A better understanding of the role of GABA [gamma amino butyric acid] neurons in the action of cocaine and in behavioral sensitization, particularly the kindling phenomenon and the enhanced susceptibility to convulsions, is desirable, and may lead to novel approaches to the therapeutic management or prevention of some of these phenomena. In addition, a greater knowledge of the effects of cocaine on neuropeptide-biogenic amine interactions in the brain may lead to additional insights into the actions of cocaine and the management of cocaine abuse. We need to develop a better understanding of the neurobiological basis of reward, of tolerance, and of psychological and physical dependence.

We should learn more about cellular interactions between ethanol and other drugs of abuse and cocaine. Do ethanol or other drugs of abuse a) block acute effects of cocaine, b) facilitate the cellular actions of cocaine, c) block the development of sensitization, or d) block the "sensitized" response to cocaine? Can prior experience with ethanol and other drugs of abuse modulate subsequent sensitivity or responsiveness to cocaine? Is there any kind of drug-reward contingency learning involved?

In order to mimic the adverse patterns of cocaine use among cocaine abusers, these studies must be performed with different protocols and durations of cocaine administration, including both long-term, continuous, and intermittent. . . .

We know virtually nothing about the effects of cocaine self-administered via the inhaled route. This route of administration, which has an onset of action as rapid as the intravenous route, but does not have

"Scientific Perspectives on Cocaine Abuse," *The Pharmacologist*, Vol. 29, No. 1, 1987. Reprinted with permission.

the same problems, is a popular way to abuse cocaine. Carefully controlled studies in humans comparing the effects of cocaine when it is inhaled with the extensive database already available for the intravenous route will provide sorely needed information relevant to treatment.

It is clear that users claim improved performance after cocaine use. Does it, like amphetamine, provide that "small edge", bringing performance deteriorated by boredom or fatigue back to baseline levels? Or does cocaine in fact have a positive effect on performance? Does it distort judgment, providing the user with a false sense of confidence, or does cocaine in fact facilitate performance in ways that have not yet been evaluated? Further research into the performance-potentiating and debilitating effects of cocaine is a most likely area to shed light on why people use this drug, and also may well contribute to our understanding of its toxicity.

Many potentially useful therapeutic interventions have been suggested for the out-of-control cocaine user. In general, justification for their utility has been minimal, based on anecdotal reports of possible antagonism of hypothesized neurotransmitter roles. These potentially useful interventions should be tested under carefully controlled laboratory conditions, using the human self-administration paradigm, where both self-administration behavior and physiological and behavioral effects are monitored, so that careful evaluation of the full range of their interactions can be carried out.

Although an abundance of data exist supporting the extraordinary reinforcing properties of cocaine, little systematic data have been collected comparing cocaine to other drug reinforcers. There are currently minimal data, other than those collected with psychomotor stimulant drugs, validating the predictive power of the complex self-administration procedure and comparing different classes of drugs.

A very limited amount of research has been carried out investigating individual differences in responses to drugs. There are now abundant data indicating that history and current environmental and behavioral variables, as well as pharmacological variables, all play a part in determining drug effect, including both reinforcing properties and toxicity. This is an important area for continued research, both with non-human and human research subjects under a range of laboratory and more naturalistic conditions where both individual behavior and social interactions can be examined. . . .

Cocaine and Pregnancy

It has been clearly shown that cocaine crosses the placenta via simple diffusion and rapid penetration of mucosal membranes due to its high lipid solubility, low molecular weight, and low ionization at physiological pH. . . .

Cocaine's pharmacological actions contraindicate its use in pregnancy. The vasoconstriction, tachycardia, and increased blood pressure caused by cocaine all increase the chance for intermittent intrauterine hypoxia, preterm labor, precipitous labor, and abruptio placenta, followed by hemorrhage, shock and anemia. Data from clinical populations provide further evidence of problems in children born to cocaine using mothers.

More research is essential to further evaluate cocaine's effect upon the perinatal period, the infant and the child. . . .

"It is obvious that we have much to learn about cocaine action and abuse."

Cocaine is the most effective reinforcing drug we know. It produces intense drug taking behavior in all animal species studied, including man. There is a widespread feeling that cocaine produces improved performance. Laboratory studies in animals and man consistently have been unable to confirm this belief, except under conditions where performance decrements occur because of fatigue. Indeed, there is good evidence that cocaine produces a disruption of attention. Furthermore, the elevation of mood of a single dose does not reflect the effects of repeated administration. Chronic use can lead to severe depression and "cocaine psychosis." High doses can lead to seizures. The specific mechanisms involved with cocaine-induced seizures require further investigation. There is evidence that heart damage, such as myocardial infarction, associated with cocaine use is being seen more frequently. Additional research is needed to more fully characterize this phenomena which appears to occur even in healthy young subjects with no prior history of cardiac problems. We have much to learn about the acute and chronic toxicity of cocaine and are recommending a major effort in this regard. This would include the study of effects on organs such as the heart, lungs and brains, as well as possible long lasting behavioral changes, particularly after administering the drug by inhalation. Since there is an increasing use of the drug among young people there is a great concern about the future health of these individuals. Prospective epidemiological studies are needed to follow these young people into adulthood. There is emerging evidence that cocaine taken during pregnancy has adverse effects on the course of gestation and the fetus. Specifically, difficulties in carrying the baby to term and low birth weight are seen. Additional research is needed to determine the extent and consequences of the abnormal problems.

On the more positive side, cocaine is a drug which is proving to be an important tool for scientists involved in investigating the normal and abnormal function of the brain. It is hoped that the rapidly advancing field of neuroscience will provide information which will allow more rational design of effective treatments for cocaine and other drug abuse problems. The same might be said of the rapidly advancing field of drug abuse epidemiology. For instance, the finding that groups such as overly aggressive and/or shy children are more vulnerable to cocaine abuse, will lead to more specific targeting of prevention and treatment modalities. . . .

It is obvious that we have much to learn about cocaine action and abuse. We recognize that the economic rewards of supplying the illicit market make solution of the cocaine problem by interdiction of drug supplies very difficult. This makes it even more important to devote appropriate resources to research and prevention which have an impact on demand. Therefore there is an urgency to learn more about cocaine in order to prevent increased future problems.

The American Society for Pharmacology and Experimental Therapeutics is a scientific society that investigates drugs and their toxicity. The Committee on Problems of Drug Dependence studies the various personal and social consequences of chemical dependency.

"We believe that sufficient studies, costing millions of dollars to the taxpayer, have already been performed on . . . cocaine."

Cocaine Has Been Adequately Studied

Gabriel and Marilyn Nahas

On January 14 [1987] an ad hoc committee of the American Society for Pharmacology and Experimental Therapeutics and The Committee on Problems of Drug Dependence met and formulated a statement, "Scientific Perspectives on Cocaine Abuse." This "Consensus Statement" recommended the continuation of experimental studies in which cocaine is administered to man under controlled conditions. It was argued that such studies would yield "sorely needed information" relevant to treatment of cocaine addicts. The statement was signed by 32 scientists and physicians from prominent universities in the country and by NIDA [National Institute on Drug Abuse] officials.

We must disagree with this "Scientific Perspective" and have expressed our disagreement to the authors. We feel so strongly about this matter that we wish to call it to the attention of the parents of America. We believe that sufficient studies, costing millions of dollars to the taxpayer, have already been performed on human subjects administered cocaine either orally or by the intravenous route. Results of these experiments confirm those performed on non-human primates (monkeys), i.e., that cocaine is spontaneously and repetitively self-administered and that it rapidly induces tolerance (increasing doses are required in order to obtain the desired euphoriant effect). These experiments have taught us little that we did not already know; they are redundant. Furthermore, they might be dangerous.

Indeed, both animal and human studies performed over the past eighty years and observations on man indicate that cocaine administration produces acute cardiac problems including heart attacks. Such occurrences are usually, but not always, produced by very high doses of the drug. However, some people are much more sensitive than others to the toxic

effects of cocaine and so it is impossible to predict individual reactions to it. Thus, the potential risk to the experimental subject may greatly outweigh the hypothetical benefits derived from these kinds of experimental approaches. It has already been well established, in the experimental animal, that cocaine is damaging to the coronary vessels and to the heart. Thus far in the human experiments, subjects have not presented any cardiac accident. But one must not overlook the subtle damage to myocardial and cerebral vessels which cocaine administration may produce. Such damage may not be detectable by the methods of monitoring which are currently used on these subjects (e.g., electrocardiograms or measurements by mood scales). And as for psychological impairment, in one experiment (unpublished), cocaine was administered intravenously to cocaine addicts until they developed paranoia, i.e., acute mental confusion. This study only confirmed the occurrence of symptoms reported in hundreds of observations over many decades. We are told by the supporters of such studies that the older observations were not performed under clinical, controlled conditions. Studies in which paranoia is produced by infusion of cocaine in the veins remind one of those performed on inmates of concentration camps.

Crack Experiments Unjustified

The American Society for Pharmacology and the Committee on Problems of Drug Dependence claim to " . . . know virtually nothing about the effects of cocaine self-administered via the inhaled route . . ." (i.e., crack smoking) " . . . This route of administration, which has an onset of action as rapid as the intravenous route, but does not have the same problems, is a popular way to abuse cocaine. Carefully controlled studies in humans comparing the effects of cocaine when it is inhaled with the extensive database already available for the

Gabriel and Marilyn Nahas, "The Experimental Use of Cocaine in Man: Is It Acceptable?" *Drug Abuse Newsletter*, April 10, 1987. Reprinted with permission.

intravenous route will provide sorely needed information relevant to treatment." However, the studies of Dr. Raoul Jeri from Lima, Peru, published [in 1977], show that rapid physical and mental damage is produced by this form of administration. Dr. Jeri is in full agreement with the objections we have formulated. Later studies by Mark Gold and many others in the U.S. reported similar effects. It has been very amply demonstrated by now that inhaled cocaine is the most reinforcing means of absorbing the drug and the one most likely to produce permanent physical and mental damage. It is therefore unacceptable to perform the suggested experiments on crack smokers. In our opinion there is no scientific justification for administration of cocaine to man in this form. One does not read of alcohol being administered experimentally by the intravenous route to alcoholics in order to find a treatment for alcoholism and yet alcohol is not as reinforcing and damaging a drug as cocaine. Furthermore, all of the experimental studies on man which used another controlled substance, marihuana, have yielded little data on the long-term toxic effects of the drug and have not resulted in useful therapeutic interventions. The subjects selected for these experiments are cocaine addicts—paid cocaine addicts, a point which raises legal as well as ethical problems. Under the law a physician is only allowed to administer controlled substances for the purpose of treating an ailment; in the case of cocaine, it could be legally used only to induce local surface anesthesia. To give cocaine to an addict on the pretext that it will help find a cure for cocaine addiction seems to be a mere rationalization which permits the physician to get around the law. In our opinion, cocaine administration to cocaine addicts for experimental purposes lacks a firm legal basis.

"These studies have little effect on prevention and no impact on demand."

In addition to the legal issue involved for the physician there is an ethical one: how can one justify giving cocaine to a cocaine addict? Provisions for follow-up of these subjects are not always explicitly stated in the experimental protocols. Cocaine is not innocuous and it will further reinforce the addictive behavior which the physician would like to see abolished. The admonition given by Hippocrates over two thousand years ago was, "Above all, do no harm." Therefore, if the physician is not sure that cocaine might be of therapeutic value to a cocaine addict (and that it might be harmful) how can he ethically justify administering this drug to a patient for strictly experimental purposes in an open-ended fashion? One recommendation appears especially controversial: the systematic continuation of studies of cocaine-consuming pregnant women and of their fetuses and surviving offspring.

More Ethical Questions

My wife, Marilyn, will tell you what she feels about this investigation:

> Just to give you something to think about, the American Society for Pharmacology and Experimental Therapeutics knows from past experiments on various animals that cocaine taken by pregnant females will produce death or damage to the offspring. Every time that cocaine reaches the uterine vessels it reduces blood flow to the uterus. The fetus then gets less oxygen. It is certain that cocaine is, therefore, a danger to the fetus. Cocaine is a vasoconstrictor; it causes tachycardia (rapid heart beat), and increases blood pressure. Cocaine also crosses the placental barrier. Cocaine's pharmacology and actions contraindicate its use in pregnancy.
>
> [In 1985], the *New England Journal of Medicine* published a study involving 23 pregnant women who regularly took cocaine. The results showed that some of these women were suffering spontaneous abortions (probably a blessing to the fetus) with much hemorrhaging. Or, if the baby was born alive, it suffered significant neurological impairment. The group that observed these cocaine-taking pregnant women feel that twenty-three observations are not enough so they are asking for more money to follow many more women who take cocaine during pregnancy. They say more studies are needed. But, are they really? Do they expand our knowledge? Are they humane? Are they ethical? These scientists want to study brain development in the cocaine-exposed fetus using ultrasound methods. They can follow, I suppose, the slower, more depressed development of the fetus' neurological system. Is it necessary? I don't think so.

These proposed studies implicitly accept the fact that cocaine use will not abate in our society and that we are saddled with a major consumption of this drug for years to come. In addition, these studies have little effect on prevention and no impact on demand, contrary to what is implied by the "Consensus" document authors.

Experiments involving cocaine administration to cocaine addicts have been performed with the approval of the FDA [Food and Drug Administration] and of ethical committees of the institutions where they are carried out. They have been approved by NIDA's own review committee which funds these studies to the tune of millions of dollars. Institutions which are hard-pressed for money benefit from such grants which allot up to an additional 80% of the grant money for administration and overhead.

FDA has also approved these studies, since cocaine is a schedule two drug which can be used for therapeutic purposes which is the stated purpose of these experiments. Paradoxically, the antidotes to the acute toxicity of cocaine which were developed in our laboratory cannot be administered under present legislation to treat acute cocaine addiction because of

FDA regulation. And yet these compounds have been extensively used in Europe for the treament of man of coronary insufficiency and hypertension.

Cocaine Toxicity Antidotes

Indeed, in my laboratory, with a group of committed young French scientists, especially Dr. Renaud Trouve, we have been able to define antidotes to the acute effects of cocaine cardiac lethal toxicity. We have carried out all of this work on animals, mostly rats, using the rules of classical pharmacology and physiology, which my American teachers Wallace Fenn and Maurice Visscher taught me [in 1952]. Our studies were also carried out at no expense to the taxpayer. These antidotes have been successfully tested on monkeys at the Addiction Research Center of NIDA. They are ready to be tested on cocaine addicts who wish to kick their habit, not take more cocaine. But on account of FDA regulation, this is not yet possible. These studies have allowed us to formulate a new theory of drug dependence: a self-inflicted disease of neurotransmission. . . .

These experimental studies reinforce our opposition to the proposed and on-going experiments in which cocaine addicts are paid to take cocaine. From such experiments we learn nothing. They should be discontinued, in full compliance with the law written by man and which was intended to reflect a much higher one.

Gabriel Nahas is a pharmacologist, professor of anesthesiology at Columbia University, and author of the antidrug book, Keep Off the Grass. *His wife Marilyn is active in the fight against drug abuse.*

"[The coca producers'] main obligation... is to bring under control, in their territory, the unlicensed and illicit production of coca leaf."

Coca Growing Can Be Eradicated

John T. Cusack

We are in a period of transition in man's 76-year effort to control narcotic substances; today we can add the psychotropic substances. These materials existed 4,000 years ago or more. I think in general people accept without question that existence of the opium poppy, the coca leaf and the cannabis plant can be documented back 4,000 years. What is interesting is that with little or no exception, for thousands of those years, these plants and their usage remained where and as they originated. Then around the year 900 AD, we find that the opium poppy and the cannabis plant began to be carried to other parts of the world; traders began moving opium from its origin in Asia Minor into far reaches of South Asia all the way into China, and the cannabis plant was moved into Egypt and Africa and all the way around the rim of Africa as far as Morocco. Curiously, the coca plant was the most "unadventurous." For the most part, it remained in the Andean region that later would include parts of Colombia, Ecuador, Peru and Bolivia.

We also find that up until about the year 900, opium and cannabis were used predominantly for medicinal purposes by Arab medicine people who were the first to devise the scientific application of opium and its potions to treat illness and pain. Use of opium and cannabis was usually controlled by the tribal leadership, and evidence indicates that they were ingested. Ingestion of opium and cannabis creates a less euphoric reaction than if they are taken in other forms. Smoking these substances, for example, enables more of the alkaloids to be extracted. The first form of taking opium and cannabis for their euphoric effects was smoking, which began around 900. Once opium was smoked, it was "Katie bar the door." That's when serious opium addiction began.

Reprinted with permission from "The International Narcotics Control System" by John T. Cusack, in *Coca and Cocaine: Effects on People and Policy in Latin America*, Deborah Pacini and Christine Franquemont, editors. Published by Cultural Survival, Inc. and Cornell University Latin American Studies Program, 1986.

Abusive smoking of opium and its use in primitive medical practices continued on the Asian continent up until the age of discovery, which began about 1450. Then something else happened. With ships and navigators, for the first time, people and trade began to cross the oceans and move to other continents. Of the narcotic substances, it was again primarily opium that reached the other continents, where it continued to be abusively smoked and used in rather primitive medical practices. This movement of people, trade and narcotic substances to the other continents was a slow, gradual development. We know that early in the nineteenth century morphine was extracted from opium; that around the 1850s, the hypodermic needle was developed; that cocaine was discovered shortly thereafter; and heroin shortly after that. By the year 1900, we had three excellent alkaloids for medical purposes: morphine, heroin, cocaine. Medical science did not quite understand at that time, however, these substances' side effects. The principal side effect was addiction. But it wasn't quite understood for what it was. Throughout the world, these narcotic substances were overprescribed medically and used extensively for pleasure, resulting in widespread addiction.

The Opium Scourge

Meanwhile, particularly in Asia, from the Asia Minor coast of the Mediterranean and the Aegean, all the way to the North China Sea, opium was widely produced, trafficked, used medically and greatly abused primarily by smoking it. Opium smoking was the scourge of those areas. Millions were addicted to it. And, I think, history fairly well establishes that it constrained the development of those areas.

Cocaine, heroin and morphine, by the year 1900, were also widely abused in most European cities, in most North American cities, in many of the larger Latin American cities, throughout the Far East and throughout even countries as far away as Australia. All of these substances were manufactured legally in pharmaceutical factories.

By about 1900, medical science, educators and government leaders began to recognize the public health liabilities of these products when not used for medical purposes. Indeed, they concluded that cocaine, heroin and morphine are different from alcohol and should be controlled and limited to medical purposes. These drugs' toxicity and rapid dependence-producing liability make them quite different from alcohol; in effect these substances have no use other than for medical purposes under the supervision of a trained physician.

Treaties To End Trafficking

There is always something that motivates the action that people have been talking about taking; in this case, it was the situation in the Far East. It involved bitter political controversy over the traffic in opium by the British East India Company into China, where thousands of tons of opium annually were moved from India into China. Beginning at the end of the eighteenth century, it flourished throughout the nineteenth century and into the twentieth century. And as you probably know, two opium wars were fought over this issue. The British prevailed in both and maintained their treaty rights to move this substance into China.

"The coca leaf was imported by the United States and countries in Western Europe which processed it into cocaine for medical purposes."

At any rate, the twentieth century was dawning, and I think the world was a little more enlightened. A conference was called together at Shanghai in 1909 to deal with the opium situation and the practice of opium smoking, and at that conference several recommendations were made. The basic recommendation was that opium and its derivatives, morphine and heroin, should be brought under control and their use should be limited to medical and scientific purposes. The delegates went back to their countries where the medical, scientific, educational, religious and government leaders receptively received the delegates' recommendations. There was a broad consensus that opium and its derivatives should be controlled. The leaders asked, "How do we do this?" The experts answered, "It's quite simple, prepare a treaty. You gather the governments together, you write up a document that states what needs to be done, and you do it." So the experts met in The Hague in 1911, and by 1912, they completed the treaty, called The Hague Opium

Convention of 1912. The treaty called for bringing under control opium and its derivatives, and cocaine. In their deliberations in Shanghai back in 1909, the experts had felt control of these substances required international cooperation, because even in those days the raw materials and the finished products, the manufactured narcotic drugs, were produced in a handful of countries. In other words, a handful of countries were producing the coca leaf, the opium poppy and the cannabis plant.

Now here again I should emphasize that the major problem of the time was opium, and, to a certain extent, its derivatives. Morphine and heroin were not as heavily abused in those days as opium, but they would be in time—they were a growing problem, no question of that. Cocaine was also being abused by then and was becoming a serious problem as well. What the experts felt had to be done was that all countries had to agree that first they would control the production of the narcotic crops at the farm levels—license them and limit their production to quantities that would be needed for medical purposes. Secondly, they would limit and control the manufacture of the natural alkaloids—morphine, heroin and cocaine and any other derivatives that might be developed. And thirdly, they would regulate international trade, the movement of these substances, raw materials and finished products between countries. This would have to be done through a system of licenses or import and export permits.

Medical Uses Only

In the early 1900s, one could import morphine from England to the United States or from Germany to England without any form of licensing—it could be traded just like aspirin or any over-the-counter product. The same was true with opium and the coca leaf. As you probably know, the coca leaf was imported by the United States and countries in Western Europe which processed it into cocaine for medical purposes.

When the experts met in The Hague in 1912, they tried to develop an international treaty that would address the three points just mentioned, but failed. So the experts settled for a treaty that required all parties in their own territories, in their own countries, to enact a law that would limit the use of opium and its derivatives, and cocaine solely to medical purposes. After World War I the League of Nations was given a mandate to develop and administer an international narcotics control treaty system. And in 1925, the League successfully developed the Geneva Opium Convention, a treaty that regulated international trade. All raw materials and finished narcotics products had to be licensed in international trade. The treaty was successful to a great extent, but the quantities of narcotics manufactured legally, particularly in Western Europe, were still enormous. They were producing 100 times more cocaine, heroin and morphine than the world needed. The Chinese laborer in Shanghai was using heroin produced in Germany or in Paris. The individual in Mexico City in 1920 was using cocaine that was probably made in Paris. To address this, the experts finally, in 1931, put together a treaty—The Geneva Convention to Limit the Manufacture and Regulate the Distribution of Narcotic Drugs—that limited the manufacture of narcotic drugs by countries to levels approved by an international board which were commensurate with international medical requirements. This was the disarmament, if you will, of the international manufacture of narcotic drugs. Due to the treaty's effectiveness, from roughly 1931 until 1966, the world was not troubled by cocaine problems. Between 1931 and 1965, the amount of cocaine manufactured legally and diverted into the illicit market available decreased world-wide.

"You can never have total unavailability, but when you have a lack of drugs, you have a lack of addiction."

During this period many of the factories legally manufacturing the opium derivatives were shut down to meet medical requirement levels. Because drug traffickers who were working with these factories to make huge quantities of narcotics available for the illicit international traffic could no longer obtain their supplies, they set up their own clandestine laboratories. They set up these laboratories in Paris, because Paris was the center of the underworld in Europe in those days; it was a great railroad center and had access to the ports of Marseilles and Le Havre where the raw materials could be transported by ship. It was a simple matter to take 10 kg of opium and smuggle it into France, where in the clandestine laboratory it would make one kg of heroin. Extracting morphine from opium and then converting it to heroin is a simple process; extracting coca paste from the coca leaf is a bulky and more complicated procedure.

More Treaties

The 1925 treaty prevented clandestine criminals from operating in Western Europe. Here traffickers had the skills to import clandestinely the great mass of coca leaf they needed to make one kg of cocaine. In South America, where the coca leaf existed and could be easily converted into cocaine, the underworld skills did not exist. This situation remained static into the 1950s.

In 1936, another treaty was passed that organized a more effective illicit traffic suppression; it required the treaty nations to cooperate with each other in campaigns against illicit traffic and to assist each other in uncovering evidence and exchanging information concerning illicit traffic activity. Between the early 1930s and World War II, officials focused on curtailing illicit traffic and kept it in check. In the United States, between 1931 and 1965, officials never seized more than 10 kg of cocaine in any one year, except one year, 1949, when they seized 13 kg.

World War II ended world-wide just about any form of narcotic traffic because transportation systems including shipping were disrupted. This event is often used to demonstrate the correlation between availability of drugs and drug addiction. You can never have total unavailability, but when you have a lack of drugs, you have a lack of addiction. At the turn of the century in the United States an estimated one million people out of a population of 90 million were addicted to opium, morphine, heroin or cocaine. By 1920, the estimated number of addicted people dropped to 500,000; by 1930 it was 100,000; by 1940 it was 50,000; by 1945, following four years of war, it was under 10,000. The number of heroin addicts gradually increased to about 100,000 in 1960. Then in 1964, heroin addiction broke into an epidemic which continued until around 1973, when the market from Turkey was cut off. During these years, the number of addicts reached as high as 750,000. Through international action heroin availability and traffic has to a great extent stabilized. It is still a significant problem, however. There are several serious gaps in illicit production in certain countries, but officials are working toward closing them—at least what must be done is understood. The cocaine outbreak, of course, began in the United States around 1965. That year about 16 kg of cocaine were seized. By 1970, we seized slightly over 100 kg. In 1980, we seized our first 1,000-kg quantity. By 1983, we seized over 8,000 kg, and in 1984 about 15,000 kg. In 1980, it is estimated that 25 tons of cocaine came in to the US; by 1984, the estimate was 85 tons. . . . Since 1970, the number of heroin addicts in the United States has steadily increased. Estimates now indicate well over 600,000 addicts. Some 20 million people are thought to have tried cocaine, and somewhere between 8 and 12 million people are thought to be fairly regular users of cocaine. Each day in the US, 5,000 people will try cocaine.

The Opium Protocol

While the manufacture and trade of narcotic substances had been brought under control following World War II, international cultivation remained uncontrolled. Prior to 1950, no country was required by any treaty to regulate, license and restrict the narcotics crop in the field. Cocaine was not a problem in 1950, but opium was because of heroin. So in 1953, the international leadership met in New

York and established the Opium Protocol. This agreement limited the number of countries which could legally cultivate opium poppies. It also required these countries to license the cultivation, set up a government monopoly for its purchase from farmers, insure that the farmer only grows what he's licensed to grow, and that the number of farmers and the quantity of opium which they authorized them to produce was commensurate with the world's medical needs.

In the mid- to late 1950s, international experts and UN officials decided to codify the 1912 treaty, the 1925, 1931, 1936, 1946 and 1948 agreements (the last had to do with synthetic drugs), and the 1953 Opium Protocol into one treaty, which they called the Single Convention on Narcotic Drugs of 1961. About 100 countries convened in New York for three months to participate in that plenipotentiary conference. In addition to amalgamating all the other treaties, they established the same international system of control the 1953 Opium Protocol required for the opium poppy cultivation, for cultivation of coca leaf and the cannabis plant.

The new treaty went into effect in 1964. At this time, basically only two countries were considered coca producers, Peru and Bolivia. Only Peru was involved in the legal trade. Bolivia didn't export; it didn't have the organization to gather the coca and store, package and market it. There was really no need to do so, however, because Peru produced more coca leaf than could be used legally.

In addition to the requirements previously mentioned, the new treaty obliged countries where coca leaf chewing was practiced to phase out this practice within 25 years after the treaty's enactment. In other words, the implication was that these countries should take steps immediately to bring that about. The treaty authorized these countries to produce as much coca as they needed for the coca leaf chewers, but also required them to gradually reduce the amount of coca they were producing for chewing.

"Peru and Bolivia have failed in their efforts to license and control coca production."

Referred to as one of the transitional provisions of the treaty, this stipulation was also applied to countries where opium smoking was permitted, and where the quasi-medical eating of opium was permitted under nonmedical supervision. In other words, just as one could buy coca leaf in Peru and Bolivia for chewing, one could buy opium in India and Pakistan for eating. Although most countries prohibited smoking opium following The Hague

Convention of 1912, some countries tolerated or permitted it. With the enactment of the new treaty in 1964, they were obliged to phase out opium smoking as soon as possible, and opium eating within 15 years. The last country to do so was Pakistan in 1979—right at the wire they finally phased out the practice of opium vendors who sold opium for eating.

Today, the inability of the governments of Peru and Bolivia to phase out the overproduction of the coca leaf is an enormous problem. From the mid-1960s to the early 1970s, little control activity took place. Some administrative efforts were made but they were never implemented. During this time we see both Bolivia and Peru develop the capability to convert the coca leaf to coca paste and to move it out of the country. By 1976, experts in the field estimated that coca leaf cultivation has increased at a rate as high as 30 percent per year. Some people say it's not that high, but between 10 and 20 percent. Others insist an annual growth rate increase of 20 percent is the best estimate. No one questions, however, that at least there has been a quantum increase in the production of the coca leaf in Peru and Bolivia every year since 1976.

Failed Obligations

There is some reason to believe, on the basis of countries' reports concerning their needs for coca leaf chewing, that coca leaf chewing is expanding in the area. Another development in the last two to three years is the incredible and devastating spread of *basuco* (coca paste) smoking, particularly among young people, and the enormous proliferation, particularly in Peru, and now also in Bolivia, of the coca paste pits and the clandestine manufacture of coca paste close to the coca leaf-growing areas.

As the two major producers of coca, Peru and Bolivia have failed in their efforts to license and control coca production. They really have not addressed the problem of coca leaf chewing, and it is a problem that is similar to many of the problems in their territory which they are unable or unwilling to address. It's just another problem, people say. Well, they have so many problems that they have to assign priorities; coca is not a high enough priority. These countries' international obligations under the law today are quite simple. They have an obligation to phase out coca chewing and the coca that is being produced for chewing. And secondly, their main obligation to every nation in the world today, particularly the developed nations that are most severely affected by cocaine, is to bring under control, in their territory, the unlicensed and illicit production of coca leaf.

John T. Cusack is chief of staff of the US House of Representatives Select Committee on Narcotics Control and Abuse.

"U.S. and Latin American efforts to curb the supply of cocaine have failed abjectly."

Coca Growing Cannot Be Eradicated

Rensselaer W. Lee III

U.S. and Latin American efforts to curb the supply of cocaine have failed abjectly. Some 200–300 tons of cocaine may flow into U.S. markets yearly; as University of Michigan researcher Lloyd Johnston notes, "the supply of cocaine has never been greater in the streets, the price has never been lower, and [the] drug has never been purer." The U.S. government supports a number of programs meant to reduce supply in the Andean countries, but these programs amount to perhaps $40–$50 million a year, a pittance when compared to the South American cocaine industry's earnings of $3–$5 billion a year. Yet more resources may not be the answer. Structural barriers block effective drug enforcement in poor countries, and such barriers could well be insurmountable.

Barriers to Enforcement

First, Andean governments worry about the impact of successful drug-control programs. The consequences would be exacerbated rural poverty and new legions of the unemployed, both of which would strengthen anti-democratic or communist movements. Imagine 200,000 coca-growing peasants marching on Bolivia's capital, La Paz. In Peru and Colombia, the war against drugs has proved difficult to reconcile with the struggle against communist insurgency. The threat of eradication alienates coca growers from the government and enhances the appeal of insurgent groups. In the Upper Huallaga Valley, for example, the U.S.-backed eradication effort has doubtless driven many peasants into the ranks of Sendero Luminoso [a communist insurgent group].

Second, many Latin Americans see the economic benefits of drug trafficking. Colombia's controller general, Rodolfo Gonzales, has publicly hailed the contribution of drug dollars to national economic

growth. Leading bankers in Peru talk about the importance of cocaine earnings in stabilizing the country's currency. Bolivia's president Victor Paz Estenssoro remarked in 1986 that "cocaine has gained in importance in our economy in direct response to the shrinking of the formal economy."

Third, Latin Americans tend to see U.S.-imposed drug enforcement measures as infringements on their national sovereignty. According to a poll, two-thirds of Colombians oppose the extradition of drug traffickers to the United States. This feeling may be heightened because some of the leading candidates for extradition, such as Colombia's Pablo Escobar and Bolivia's Roberto Suarez, provide support for charitable activities and so are popular in their countries. Arresting and extraditing such traffickers would be difficult politically. Officials undoubtedly recall the violent anti-American outbursts in Honduras following the April 1988 extradition of Juan Matta Ballestreros, a narco-philanthropist who cultivated a Robin Hood image.

Fourth, governments often exercise little or no control over territories where drug production flourishes, for these are remote from metropolitan centers, relatively inaccessible mountainous or jungle terrains which are patrolled by guerrillas or other hostile groups. In this way, drug traffic encourages territorial disintegration. The Peruvian government, for example, is losing control over the Upper Huallaga Valley, the region which ships its most important export, coca paste, to Colombia and in return receives money, weapons, and some economic leadership. Colombian aircraft maintain this connection by flying in and out of Peruvian airspace with virtual impunity. Colombian middlemen increasingly buy paste directly from peasants in the Valley rather than through Peruvian dealers. The Upper Huallaga is becoming less a part of Peru and more a part of Colombia.

Finally, corruption severely undermines criminal

Rensselaer W. Lee III, "Why the U.S. Cannot Stop South American Cocaine," *Orbis*, Vol. 21, No. 4, Fall 1988. Reprinted with permission of the Foreign Policy Research Institute.

justice systems in cocaine-producing countries. Law enforcement in Latin American countries often represents simply a way to share in the proceeds of the drug trade: the police take bribes not to make arrests and seizures. When the police do make successful busts, the drugs are often resold on the illicit market.

These barriers mean that anti-drug activities in Latin American countries are largely cosmetic. Governments draw up elaborate plans to eradicate coca—the police make a few highly publicized arrests and cocaine seizures, fly around the countryside in helicopters, terrorize villages, and knock out an occasional cocaine laboratory—but with little effect. The core structure of the cocaine industry remains, and the industry's agricultural base continues to expand. Farmers in the Upper Huallaga Valley plant four or five acres for every hectare of coca eradicated, according to a professor at the Agrarian University of Tingo María, the capital of an important cocaine-growing province in the Valley.

At the same time, governments resist the only effective method for controlling coca cultivation, herbicide. Herbicides toxic enough to kill the hardy cocaine bush may also be dangerous to agricultural crops, wildlife, fish, and even humans. The herbicide tebuthiuron ("Spike"), manufactured by Eli Lilly, is [according to an April 16, 1987 *Washington Post* article] "one of a class of toxins that has caused liver damage and testicle tumors in rats." Lilly has refused to sell the herbicide to the State Department, apparently fearing a rash of liability lawsuits stemming from improper use.

As a result, Bolivia has ruled out chemical eradication entirely. In Colombia, [according to a US State Dept. report,] an experimental spraying program has been halted because the government is afraid of "criticism by environmentalists, the political opposition and peasants involved in drug cultivation." In Peru test spraying has been underway since October 1987; however, the Peruvian government's willingness to move toward full-scale chemical eradication seems contingent on assurances "that the herbicide is not harmful to other plants, animals and human beings." Given the publicity surrounding "Spike" and other toxic chemicals, the Peruvian government may opt to remain at the testing stage indefinitely.

The US Policy Dilemma

A 1988 Department of State report noted that Latin American governments do not yet recognize that coca growing and cocaine trafficking "pose serious threats to their own survival." Be that as it may, many Andean leaders are concerned that the suggested cures would be worse than the disease.

To a degree, that concern must also be the concern of Washington, which wants to encourage stable, economically viable governments in the region; to promote democracy; and to suppress leftist insurgent movements. America's war against its drug addiction is not necessarily compatible with these other priorities, at least in the short run. In fact, the argument can be made that the United States and its Latin American allies have a common interest in minimizing the intensity of the drug war. Yet this may be hard for Washington to do.

The Reagan administration is being pilloried by its opponents for not making drug control a top foreign-policy priority. Legislators and local officials demand reprisals against governments that tolerate the narcotics industry; U.S. Senator John Kerry (Democrat of Massachusetts) and New York City Mayor Edward Koch want to send troops to Colombia to root out the Medellín cartel.

"Unfortunately, there may be no useful way to upgrade the war against cocaine that is not counterproductive."

These critics are responding to real public pressures. A *New York Times*/CBS News poll shows that Americans perceive drug trafficking as a more important international problem than arms control, terrorism, Palestinian unrest in Israel, or the situation in Central America. Another poll reports that Americans perceive stopping the drug dealings of anti-communist leaders in Central America as more important (by a vote of three to one) than fighting communism in the region. A third poll notes a public preference for U.S. government policies that reduce the supply of illicit drugs entering the United States over policies that focus on persuading Americans to stop using drugs.

Disadvantages to All Solutions

Nevertheless, the State Department report is certainly correct if it means that the status quo is not in the long-term interests of the Latin American countries. At issue is not so much democracy as the deterioration and de-modernization of political and economic institutions. As U.S. Ambassador to Colombia Charles Gillespie remarked, "The traffickers have already penetrated the fabric of Colombian life. . . . [T]his penetration will lead not to the downfall of Colombia and its institutions but rather to a serious and lasting corruption." Other political problems include the governments' weakening hold on their territories, their deteriorating reputation, and discrimination against their citizens and products.

Unfortunately, there may be no useful way to upgrade the war against cocaine that is not counterproductive. Virtually every prescription under discussion carries major disadvantages.

Enhancement of drug-fighting capabilities in producer countries. Under this proposal, Andean governments would be provided with firepower, transport, communications, and intelligence support to establish their authority in drug-trafficking zones and destroy the cocaine industry's infrastructure. But the prevailing pattern of corruption in Andean countries makes many U.S. observers skeptical of the utility of such buildups. RAND economist Peter Reuter has suggested that better-equipped governments might mean no more than greater payoffs from the drug traffickers.

"Americanization" of the war on drugs. In this approach, the U.S. receives permission to take over drug enforcement that producer countries cannot perform. Examples to date include Operation Blast Furnace, the U.S. Army-supported operation against cocaine laboratories in Bolivia in the summer of 1986, and the trial of Colombian drug traffickers in U.S. courts. Americanization works to a point—Blast Furnace virtually shut down Bolivia's cocaine industry for three months—but such operations carry extreme political risks for host governments. All segments of Bolivia's political establishment condemned the operation and no leader with less stature than Victor Paz Estenssoro could have survived the political fallout. (The Colombian and Peruvian governments have declined U.S. offers of military assistance.) Extradition is widely unpopular in Colombia and anathema in most of Latin America. The Colombian Supreme Court struck down legislation enabling the government to implement the extradition treaty with the U.S.

Crop Substitution

Income replacement. "If we are to make a difference in cocaine control," declares a Department of State report, "a massive infusion of economic assistance will be required." Such assistance compensates countries for the economic and social costs of shutting down cocaine production. Possible measures include hard currency loans to compensate for the reduced flow of dollars and lowering import barriers for legitimate products, such as textiles and sugar.

But what about the hundreds of thousands of small farmers who cultivate coca? A coca farmer in the Bolivian Chapare can net up to $2,600 per hectare per year, over four times what he can earn from cultivating oranges and avocados, the next most profitable traditional crops. Thus crop substitution offers few attractions. The U.S. government is now indirectly paying $2,000 for each hectare of coca eradicated in Bolivia, but the Bolivian government estimates that the social costs of eradication—the cost of redirecting farmers into the licit agricultural economy—would be at least $7,000 per hectare. For Bolivia, where coca grows on 50,000–70,000 hectares, the cost of total eradication would be a mind-boggling $350–$490 million. Even if the money were available, it might be misspent; there are persistent rumors that some coca farmers in the Upper Huallaga Valley and the Chapare have used the cash payments for eradication to underwrite the costs of planting new coca fields in other locations.

Sanctions. Perennially popular with Congress, this course of action includes withholding aid, prohibiting trade, cutting off international lending, and restricting the flow of travelers. Yet the record shows few cases where sanctions have achieved the desired objective. To cut off aid to the Andean countries would probably provoke intense anti-Yankee feeling, poison the diplomatic atmosphere, and reduce the resources available for anti-drug campaigns.

"To cut off aid to the Andean countries would probably provoke intense anti-Yankee feeling . . . and reduce the resources available for anti-drug campaigns."

In addition, sanctions are a blunt instrument for specific problems. Thus, when Jorge Ochoa was released from a Colombian jail on December 30, 1987 (the second such release in sixteen months), the U.S. government singled out Colombian passengers and products for special customs checks at U.S. ports of entry. Yet the Colombian government had no jurisdiction over the criminal court judge who ordered Ochoa's release, and it had taken extraordinary measures to ensure that Ochoa could not escape from jail. Hence, the U.S. sanctions were misplaced—they will not bring Ochoa back to jail, nor will they make Colombia's criminal justice system less porous. Worse, they doubtless added to the unpopularity of the war against drugs. As Carlos Mauro Hoyas, Colombia's murdered attorney general, remarked, "Reprisals against innocent tourists create anger and resentment as well as a sort of solidarity with the drug bosses, not as traffickers but as fellow Colombians."

Negotiation

Negotiating cutbacks in drug production. This approach requires a dialogue with the Escobars, the Ochoas, the Rodríguez Gachas, and the other chief executives of the cocaine industry. The idea of a dialogue has enormous public support in Colombia. Supporters include a number of distinguished figures: a former head of Colombia's State Council (the country's top administrative court), a former acting attorney general, two Catholic bishops (of Popayan and Pereira), and several congressmen and academics. The traffickers themselves made a formal offer to the government in 1984—to withdraw from the cocaine industry, dismantle their laboratories and airstrips, and repatriate their capital. In return, they wanted guarantees against extradition, which would have amounted to a safe haven in Colombia. The Colombian government has said officially that it will not negotiate with traffickers.

Certainly, selective amnesty arrangements for criminals can and have been tried as tools of law enforcement. (The United States has its own witness protection program, for example.) Cocaine chiefs could reveal much about the structure and operations of the international cocaine industry—its supply channels, distribution networks, personnel policies, financing, and the names of corrupt U.S. officials who abet the trade. They could also provide information about guerrilla operations, for the two often use the same territory, the same clandestine methods, the same smuggling channels, even the same overseas banks.

"Curbing the supply of cocaine from producer countries may not be effective, no matter how much money the United States government devotes to overseas programs."

Yet it is hard to see how the proposal would work in practice. One problem is timing: when the traffickers made their original offer to the government, they were under great pressure. Colombia had a functioning extradition treaty with the United States, and traffickers were being tried in military courts, which have a higher conviction rate than civilian courts. Thanks to Colombian Supreme Court decisions, neither of these conditions is operative today, and the Barco government does not have a great deal of bargaining leverage vis-à-vis the country's cocaine syndicates.

Fundamental Problems

Further, monitoring an amnesty arrangement—the repatriation of capital and the shutting down of a multi-billion-dollar industry—would present fundamental problems. How many Colombian and American law enforcement officials would it take to oversee such a program, and who would monitor the monitors? Too, the traffickers might be unable to deliver on their promises. Is the cocaine industry so tightly structured that a few kingpins can command a larger number of lieutenants to order an even larger number of subordinates to stop producing a product that earns so much? Possibly, but an amnesty might constitute little more than a retirement program for the chief executives of the cocaine industry. They would have to make a practical demonstration of their market power—say, by shutting down 80 percent of Colombian cocaine production for a six-month period. Amnesty is at best a futuristic option—the idea has some theoretical merit, but it would be extremely difficult to implement.

These difficulties suggest that curbing the supply of cocaine from producer countries may not be effective, no matter how much money the United States government devotes to overseas programs.

Are there better ways to spend the U.S. drug-enforcement dollar? The options seem to be increased interdiction, stepped-up enforcement against drug dealers and pushers, and such demand-reduction steps as stiffer penalties for users, "Just Say No" programs, and drug testing. Many U.S. experts expect these measures also may not work very well. Moreover, as the national controversy over drug testing indicates, there are political and legal limits to controlling drug consumption, just as there are limits to controlling production in the Andean countries. Short of legalizing cocaine use (which carries the danger of stimulating even more addiction) or changing the habits and preferences of U.S. consumers, there seems to be no way out of the cocaine morass.

The solution, if there is one, lies not in the Andean jungles but in the United States. The six million people who now consume cocaine must be persuaded to change their habits and preferences. Perhaps they will grow tired of cocaine and switch to designer drugs; or perhaps they will find more productive and healthy forms of recreation.

Rensselaer W. Lee III is president of Global Advisory Services, Inc., and an associate scholar of the Foreign Policy Research Institute.

Drug Testing Benefits Society

Dan Haigh

"Drug tests?—Sure, I guess they're OK for people in critical jobs, but I work on an assembly line."

"Why should I be forced to take a drug test? I don't use dope, and I object to my employer suspecting me!"

"Drug tests are an invasion of my privacy! What I do on my own time is my own business!"

"Drug testing violates my constitutional guarantees against unreasonable search!"

"Drug tests are inaccurate. If my test shows a false positive, I'll be fired without cause!"

I'm sure you've heard these comments and many others like them, time and time again. Our employers have begun to use new, sophisticated tools to deal with the absenteeism, accidents, lowered product quality and diminished productivity that result from drug use. . . .

One of the sophisticated methods of dealing with the problem is the use of urinalysis to detect illicit drug use by both new applicants for employment, and by those already in the workforce. Confusion regarding the need for urinalysis, its legality and the accuracy of the tests has resulted in a great deal of controversy about its use. In this viewpoint we hope to clear up some of that confusion, and help you to become more comfortable with this new, effective weapon in our nation's war against drugs.

First, let's look at the need. Do we really need drug testing in the workplace? To understand the need, we first have to understand a few items that are basic to making a free-enterprise society tick. Those basic ingredients are PRODUCTIVITY, WORKMANSHIP & COMPETITION. PRODUCTIVITY is simply the quantity of goods or services produced by an employee paid a given wage during a given period. The QUALITY of those goods or services— the thing that makes them desirable to customers—

we call WORKMANSHIP. It is the combination of high PRODUCTIVITY and excellent WORKMANSHIP that allows a product or service to be COMPETITIVE.

Anything that negatively affects productivity and workmanship also negatively affects the competitive edge, so profitability suffers. When profitability suffers, wages decline, resulting in decreased incentive. That, in turn, causes productivity and workmanship to suffer even more. Your industry gets trapped in a downward spiral that continues to worsen unless you take strong, positive action to pull it out of the nosedive.

Drug use by workers negatively affects both productivity and workmanship. Drug users have higher accident rates than non-users. This results in higher liability insurance costs for the employer. They make more medical insurance claims, resulting in higher medical insurance costs. They are absent from work more often than non-users, and get into disciplinary problems more often. Additionally, drug users produce more inferior products, and are more likely to steal from their employers. All of these factors negatively affect productivity and workmanship.

Downward Spiral

If we do nothing to reverse this trend, our downward spiral will become tighter and steeper, and our economy will continue to get poorer and poorer. As Dr. Carlton Turner, former Director of the White House Office of Drug Abuse, states:

> America is the most drug-pervaded nation in the developed world. No area of the workplace can consider itself immune. If our country does not wake up and address the disastrous and wide-ranging effects of drugs in the workplace, the United States is doomed to become a second-rate power.

People in the age group of 18-25 years of age represent prime candidates for hire by our nation's employers. However, over 27% of this age group

Dan Haigh, "Drug Testing in the Workplace," *Drug Awareness Information Newsletter*, August 1987. Reprinted with permission.

regularly use drugs! Employers need efficient tools to prevent those drug-using applicants from destroying the competitive edge. Additionally, they need an efficient method to prevent employees from beginning drug use. Urinalysis can answer both of these needs. Its value as a deterrent is perhaps best displayed by the experience of the United States Armed Forces. In 1980, 48% of enlisted personnel were using drugs on a monthly basis. Widespread urinalysis was implemented, and in 1986, the figure was down to 4%! In a U.S. Navy survey, urinalysis was identified as the single most effective deterrent to drug use. Do we need drug testing in the workplace? YOU BET WE DO!!

"Encouraging and participating in workplace drug testing is just another way for drug-free workers to display a high degree of responsibility and concern."

But, what about those employees who aren't on "critical" jobs? And, what about employees who have never (and would never) use drugs? Isn't it unfair to require urinalysis of these people?—No, it really isn't! You see, in a free enterprise economy such as we enjoy in the United States, EVERY employee is critical. Every employee is in a position to add to or detract from the success and safety of the workplace. The janitor is as critical as the assembly line worker or floor supervisor—The baggage handler is as critical as the flight mechanic or pilot. Truth of the matter is—we're all in this economy together—employer and employee alike. We all have the right to expect a safe and drug-free workplace. We all have the responsibility of contributing to a successful workplace. We all have the responsibility of contributing to a successful economy. Encouraging and participating in workplace drug testing is just another way for drug-free workers to display a high degree of responsibility and concern. It's another vote for a safe and productive workplace.

Constitutionality

A few words about privacy—What you do in your own home, or on your own time is indeed your business, and nobody else's—PROVIDED, THAT IS, IT'S LEGAL, AND DOESN'T ADVERSELY AFFECT THE LIVES, SAFETY, OR RIGHTS OF OTHERS! Drug use has those negative effects. You see, drugs (and their effects) aren't necessarily gone from the body just because the user no longer feels "high." For example, THC [tetrahydrocannabinol], the psychoactive ingredient in marijuana, is stored in fatty tissues and is released over long periods of time. Its metabolites are detectable for days—even weeks after use. A 1986 study at the VA medical center in Palo Alto, California, was carried out to determine the effects of marijuana after the "high" was gone. Eight experienced pilots volunteered to use marijuana, and were tested twenty-four hours later on flight simulators. Results showed that certain important components of standard landing maneuvers were seriously impaired, even though all eight pilots thought they had done well. If this hadn't been a test, what those pilots smoked "privately" the day before could have affected—even destroyed—the lives of HUNDREDS of other people!

And, by the way, drug testing DOESN'T violate your constitutional rights. Your constitution guarantees you against unreasonable search and seizure by the GOVERNMENT. Drug testing in a private workplace, however, is a matter between employer and employee. The government isn't involved. Your employer does, however, have the responsibility to provide you with a safe workplace and safe working conditions. The use of urinalysis to ensure a drug-free workplace is just one more way your employer will help ensure safer working conditions for all employees. Since maintaining a safe workplace is REQUIRED of your employer, it's really not a negotiable item.

We need to talk at some length about accuracy, because this seems to be the most controversial question surrounding urinalysis. Let us assure you—right up front—that urine testing for drugs IS accurate. Matter of fact, it's EXTREMELY accurate, and we hope to help you better understand why it has such a high degree of reliability.

Step One

First, let's understand that there isn't a SINGLE urinalysis test used in any responsible testing program. There are several tests, each of which uses a different, reliable scientific procedure to reinforce the information received from the test that preceded it. A urine specimen that tests positive for drug metabolites on the first screening test, must also show positive on the tests that follow in order to be used as evidence of drug use. This procedure effectively eliminates the possibility for "false positives" and unwarranted incrimination.

The first test that is usually performed on a urine specimen is an IMMUNOASSAY. Syva Company developed an immunoassay which they call EMIT (Enzyme Multiplied Immunoassay Technique), and the Biomedical Division of Hoffman-La Roche developed one which they call ABUSCREEN. Although each of these tests uses a slightly different method to measure results, they both depend upon the same technology to detect drug metabolites. That technology is the use of antibodies. Antibodies are VERY specific detectors of compounds or classes of compounds. A particular antibody will only react with and bind to a compound or class of compounds for which that antibody is specifically designed. It's a lot like a lock and key arrangement. Once the antibody is "locked on" to the drug metabolite, its presence is detected and measured by very accurate and precise scientific methods using either enzymes or radioisotopes. With these techniques, one can reliably screen for the presence of cocaine, the cannabinoids (from marijuana), amphetamines, the hallucinogens, barbiturates, opiates, PCP, benzodiazepines (such as Valium), etc. You'll notice that we said SCREEN.

That's exactly what this first test does, and it does it extremely well. It can detect the presence of drug metabolites at from 97% to 99% accuracy when set up to produce detection limits normally used for workplace drug testing. If a specimen tests "clean" by this method, no additional testing is required—the employee is assumed to be drug-free. But what happens if the presence of drugs IS detected in the specimen? If that's the case, the specimen goes on to step two.

Step Two

As we mentioned earlier, the immunoassay is an excellent detector for the presence of drugs, and it can be very specific for drugs like marijuana and cocaine. And, although it will detect the presence of barbiturates, amphetamines, benzodiazepines, etc., it can't properly determine which SPECIFIC barbiturate, etc. might have been used. That's where GC (Gas Chromatography) comes into play. In GC, the sample is injected into a machine that contains a very narrow, very long, hollow column. The inside of the column is coated with special materials that help to separate chemical mixtures into their individual components. As the sample is swept along this column by a gas such as helium (the carrier gas), the individual chemicals in the mixture separate, and exit the column at specific times called the ELUTION time. The presence of these individual chemicals is detected by a special detector which notes both their elution time and concentration on a recorder. When the result is compared to a standardized GC record containing known drug metabolites, individual drugs in the urine specimen can be accurately identified and measured. You might be interested to know that GC is one of the techniques used to measure water quality, and it can reliably measure and identify some pollutants in levels as low as one part per billion parts of water!

Satisfied? Well, many drug-testing companies still aren't at this point! Even though there is virtually NO chance for error when a specimen tests positive by both immunoassay and GC (and in most reputable urine testing programs it MUST show positive in both tests to be considered "dirty"), there is one final test that can be used to confirm the results.

The step three test is called Mass Spectrometry (MS). Remember the pure compounds that exited from the GC machine in step two? Well, those compounds can be individually and automatically fed into a mass spectrometer for a final identity check.

Inside the mass spectrometer, the compounds are broken down into charged particles called IONS. The machine then sorts and identifies those ions according to their mass. The MASS SPECTRUM that is produced is a record of the numbers of different kinds of ions—the relative numbers of which are characteristic and specific for each compound. The mass spectrum is essentially another identifying "fingerprint" of the compound.

You can certainly see that with a series of sophisticated tests like this in the hands of highly qualified analytical scientists, the chance for error and erroneous incrimination is essentially nil! The myth of drug test inaccuracy is just that—A MYTH!

One important factor to keep in mind when you are asked to submit a sample for urinalysis: Although urinalysis tests are very accurate, they can't tell the difference between a particular drug obtained by prescription, and that same drug taken illegally. So, if you have taken ANY medication within a reasonable period prior to submitting the sample, be sure to let your employer know what you have taken. . . .

"We submit to these tests . . . because we know that they benefit us and benefit our society as well."

Don't consider urinalysis an accusation, it isn't! Instead, consider it a minor inconvenience—your contribution to a safer, more productive workplace. We undergo such inconveniences daily for the good of our society and our way of life. We happily submit to baggage searches in airports to ensure safe air travel. We take blood tests before marriage to confirm that we are free of venereal disease. We are tested for, and vaccinated against many dangerous diseases. The blood that we donate is screened to ensure that it is safe and free from the deadly AIDS virus.

Drug testing in the workplace is another contribution to a safe and productive society. Cooperate with your employer and encourage participation in an accurate, comprehensive drug testing program for YOUR workplace. It's another positive contribution to safety, productivity and workmanship.

Dan Haigh is a writer and an anti-drug activist in Michigan.

"In today's hysterical climate, one bad urine test can and has ruined many careers—as did suspicion of communism during the McCarthy period."

viewpoint **78**

Drug Testing Harms Society

Arnold S. Trebach

Urine testing is now flooding through every major institution, impelled by the same type of rationality that spawned the loyalty oaths during the McCarthy era and the religious oaths of belief during the prosecution of Puritan dissenters in the Star Chamber of seventeenth-century England (as well as the more recent attempts of the Reagan administration to commence random lie detector testing of federal employees on grounds of national security). In the armed services, in law enforcement, in private industry, in the Olympics, and (is nothing truly sacred that deserves to be treated as sacred and exempt from such madness?) in major league baseball and football, leaders are lining up in patriotic phalanxes to be the first to say, Hand me a bottle, I'll take one right now, why shouldn't everyone else? To be opposed to such tests is seen, in some circles, as being opposed to a virtuous attempt to save the soul of America from chemicals. When I spoke in 1985 to a seminar of police chiefs at the FBI Academy, nothing I said evoked such emotional reactions as my observation that mass urine testing, even of police officers, raised serious issues of constitutional rights and invasions of privacy. One chief actually declared, I'll take one right now!

Like all procedures for detection of chemicals within bodies, there are positive functions for urinalysis. It is perfectly appropriate, for example, to say to a drug addict who has entered a treatment program under the care of a physician: a condition of staying in the program is periodic, unscheduled testing of your urine. Because prisoners have a special legal status, it is also appropriate in many cases to demand urine samples from them. Difficulties would arise, however, if an addict in

treatment were automatically imprisoned on the basis only of a urine test—or if, as proposed by such experts as Drs. Gabriel G. Nahas and Thomas J. Gleaton, suspected addicts were put into quarantine for forced treatment when they flunked a urine test. More legal difficulties would occur when people suspected of no offense were required to take urine tests on a mass basis, thus raising the specter of mass violations of the rights to be free from unreasonable searches and seizures and from being compelled to incriminate oneself. And that, of course, is what is happening today to millions of American employees.

Fatal Flaws

In a nutshell, the fatal flaws in mass urine testing are that they take the fatal flaws of the anti-drug crusade of the last seventy years and drive them to further absurd extremes. The tests assume that there are rational distinctions between the legal drugs as a group and the illegal drugs as a group. The tests ignore the legal drugs—particularly tobacco and alcohol—and assume that traces of the illegal drugs—especially marijuana—in the urine should be taken as the sign of an impaired employee, or as a sign that the workplace is not drug-free, as all agree, including me, that it should be. At its most benevolent, the policy of the employer would then call for rehabilitation as a next step. But for what? The tests do not measure impairment. Yet a trace of any illegal drug is labeled "abuse." The absurdity is that it would follow that the employee would then be treated for the disease of drug abuse, which he or she might not have.

More often than not, however, the suspect would not be put into treatment but into limbo, into disgrace, and into unemployment. In today's hysterical climate, one bad urine test can and has ruined many careers—as did suspicion of communism during the McCarthy period. As happened then, the legality of the tests is highly suspect. While the Supreme Court has not issued definitive rulings on them, many lower courts have blocked mass urine tests of public employees as violations of constitutional rights. Because the constitution does not apply so directly to private employers, the rights of their employees are less protected and the legalities are still being debated. Yet the essential irrationalities of the tests—and their scientific unreliability—may produce new legal doctrines and negotiated labor contracts that will erect new protection in the private workplace. . . .

The Tests

In the American workplace, the most popular current test seems to be the EMIT system developed by the Syva Company of Palo Alto, California. It was the first relatively inexpensive, rapid, and seemingly accurate urine-screening test put on the market and intended for commercial use. A basic system cost approximately $3,500 and each test $6 in the early Eighties. Since it was first promoted nationally in 1981, the EMIT test for marijuana has been a huge commercial success and was a large contributor to Syva's healthy gross sales of $100 million in fiscal 1983. The test measures delta-9 THC metabolites in the urine, that is, by-products of the process by which human beings break down and excrete marijuana in their systems. It also may be configured to test for a wide variety of other drugs, including heroin and cocaine. Syva literature states that the test measures only the presence of drugs, thus indicating "recent drug use," but warns customers that "no urine test method . . . can determine intoxication."

"The notion of peeing in a bottle to obtain or keep a job which has nothing to do with that particular function is, after all, somewhat ludicrous."

Syva also claims that its tests have proven to be at least 95 percent accurate, whether indicating negative or positive recent drug use. Nevertheless, the company literature also warns users that "positive results should be confirmed by an alternative method." One more comprehensive and reliable method is known as the gas chromatograph mass spectrometer test, which takes more time and costs from $60 to over $100 for each use. In many cases, the responsible officials do not order any second, alternative test but instead simply repeat the EMIT process, or they quietly take action on the basis of the first positive finding. The problems of both administering the tests and making decisions on them are aggravated by the fact that the

number of people subjected to them keeps rising every year, with perhaps five million Americans taking them now in connection with their employment either in civilian or military life.

The Urine Gulag

Until I forced myself to review some of the stories of these ordinary human beings caught in the bizarre workings of the new urine Gulag, I confess that I had dismissed the problem as a relatively unimportant irritation, even something of a joke. The notion of peeing in a bottle to obtain or keep a job which has nothing to do with that particular function is, after all, somewhat ludicrous. Now I see nothing funny at all. The manner in which the tests have actually operated under the Reagan administration—remember, mass testing only began in 1981, the first year that Mr. Reagan arrived in the White House—demonstrates that they may create more victims of the drug war than any other single irrational weapon in this fundamentally irrational crusade. . . .

One example of the terrible dangers in the new chemical Gulag was brought to my attention by Dr. Arthur McBay in 1986. He sent me a notice he had received from the Syva Company advising users of EMIT that the company had discovered that three widely used medicines could come up positive for marijuana. One of those drugs was ibuprofen, taken for years by millions of people in Motrin, Nuprin, and Advil. "Cannaboid assay has been on the market for over five years. . . . This was discovered by accident this year. Who knows how many other substances might do the same?" Dr. McBay observed. Who knows, I ask, how many careers have been ruined by such small quirks of chemistry unleashed?

Dr. McBay also raised questions about the level of accuracy of the tests. He told me that 95 percent accuracy was the highest claimed by the Syva Company, and that was achieved when done by their own personnel. "It's like Babe Ruth saying, 'Here's a bat that hit .300' . . . and then handing it to me!" When Syva or any company hands its test kits out to less skillful technicians, the accuracy rate drops sharply to 90 percent, to 80 percent, and below.

If there *were* a false reading rate of 10 percent, with half false positives and half false negatives, this could mean that 5 percent of the approximately 5 million people tested this year in America were accused improperly of being drug users. Thus, there is a good chance that 250,000 employees were placed under suspicion or had their careers ruined for no reason.

The Impairment Myth

Many clinical chemists are also greatly distressed over the most destructive myth attached to the new wave of chemical searches of American body wastes—that these tests measure impairment and thereby allow managers of major institutions to screen out potentially bad or dangerous employees. To those who will only take the time to hear their words of warning, the objective clinical chemists of the nation are saying, no, it simply is not true. The tests do not measure performance, past, present, or future. Of course, they know that Syva literature contains a caution in one paragraph about not measuring intoxication but they also know that much of the remainder of the promotion material on EMIT negates that warning. Even when an EMIT test is done properly, "You cannot gauge or judge impairment from a positive urine analysis of marijuana," stated Michael Peat, the co-director of the Chemical Toxicology Institute, Foster City, California. The high from marijuana may last a few hours, while traces could be in the urine for weeks or months.

However, the drug warriors are in the political saddle now and they are seeking to ride roughshod over all of the opposition, whether the objections are based on fairness, civil liberties, or science. . . .

The one good result from the epidemic spread of mass, random urine tests has been that they have helped create a spark of opposition to drug-war extremism in the solid center of American society. The first sign of that opposition was found in the general disapproval that greeted many of the recommendations of the report of the President's Commission on Organized Crime in March 1986. The commission took the most extreme ideas that have been floated during the Reagan era and gave them the imprimatur of a recommendation by a major presidential commission: greater use of the military; increased electronic surveillance; drug testing for virtually all employees, starting with government workers and those on the payroll of federal contractors; a prohibition on any government funds to programs that advocate the idea of "responsible" drug use; the repeal of all state laws which decriminalized marijuana; and large-scale prosecutions not only of sellers but also of users of drugs.

War

The commission made it explicit that this really was a "war on drugs—a phrase worn by use but nevertheless the only accurate description of what must be done." The presidential report continued, "We must identify the enemy." Included in that group were "friends, relatives, colleagues, and other 'respectable' people" who were small users of drugs and thus "the driving force behind the traffickers' assault on the country."

To me those words had a nightmarish quality. It was as if the presidential commission had read this in advance and was trying to make its most

frightening predictions come true. Deliberately, leading American judges and legal officials were calling for a war on our neighbors and children, just as I had been arguing. On us.

Even though some experts have argued that the war on drugs is not really a war in the American historical tradition of armed conflicts, it is clear that many leaders want to make it so—and are prepared to commit seemingly unthinkable acts, such as imprisoning hundreds of thousands of decent Americans, young and old alike, simply because they use disapproved chemicals. At least for a while, it looks as if the drug warriors have gone too far.

"The drug warriors are in the political saddle now and they are seeking to ride roughshod over all of the opposition."

For the first time in recent history, a government report urging tougher drug-control measures was met with almost universal opposition, even from public figures who rarely speak out on such controversial issues. For example, on the NBC-TV "Today Show," host Bryant Gumbel asked a leading commission official, Rodney Smith, why the group adopted "this police-state mentality." Newspapers across the political spectrum from left to right castigated the commission for its extremism and callous disregard for constitutional rights. When I appeared on one of those Sunday television talk shows (CNN's "Newsmaker Sunday") with Mr. Smith, I pointed out to him that the commission report had produced more energetic unity in the sane center of American society for drug reform than all of my efforts in the past 14 years. (The clean-cut young lawyer took that as a compliment.)

Heated Opposition

It was the call for mass urine testing that produced the strongest reaction to the report of the high-level commission. On March 18, 1986, for example, Mr. Smith appeared before a congressional committee which was looking into the commission's recommendation of random drug testing for virtually all federal workers. Rep. Gary L. Ackerman (D-N.Y.), chairman of a House subcommittee dealing with human resources, shocked Mr. Smith by suggesting that he take a test before testifying. The congressman held up a small plastic jar, stated "I think a specimen is worth 1,000 oaths," and invited the federal official to go into the men's room right then and produce a sample "under the direct supervision" of a staff member, in line with the currently accepted degrading procedure for such searches. Rep. Ackerman informed the leading drug warrior that arrangements had been made with a laboratory to test the sample immediately. The crime commission official refused, later angrily calling the request a ''cheap shot.'' After Mr. Smith's refusal, the congressman stated, ''I thank you for very eloquently proving the point that we have set out to prove.''

Heated opposition to mass random urine tests, without reasonable suspicion, continues across the country. Generally conservative unions are bringing suit after suit to stop them. Taking a lead role in this widespread opposition has been the National Treasury Employee's Union which, in an ironic twist of history, represents customs agents, the most intrusive group of body invaders in the country. It remains to be seen, however, if these sparks of centrist opposition to the interminable drug war can be fanned into a major reform movement in the years ahead.

Arnold S. Trebach is a professor in the School of Justice at American University in Washington, DC, and the founder of the Institute on Drugs, Crime, and Justice of Washington and London.

Drug Testing in the Workplace: An Overview

Janice Castro

U.S. employers have decided to strike back at the drug plague. In high-rise office towers and sprawling factory complexes, in bustling retail stores and remote warehouses, companies are cracking down on workers who get high on the job. Supervisors are watching closely for telltale signs and confronting workers who seem impaired. Employees caught with drugs are often fired on the spot, and suspected users are urged to enter rehabilitation clinics. Hundreds of companies are setting up programs to combat drugs, providing psychiatric counseling for employees, resorting to urinalysis to identify users, and in a few cases going so far as to install hidden video cameras or hire undercover agents.

A measure of the inroads drugs have made on the U.S. workplace came when the President's Commission on Organized Crime took the extraordinary step of asking all U.S. companies to test their employees for drug use. In an initial report based on a 32-month study, the commission also urged the Government not only to test its own workers but to withhold federal contracts from private firms that refuse to do the same. "Drug trafficking is the most serious organized-crime problem in the world today," said the commission, which argued that the Government and private companies can play a vital role in curbing demand for drugs.

The recommendations immediately stirred a fire storm of controversy. Said Representative Peter Rodino, a New Jersey Democrat who chairs the House Judiciary Committee: "Wholesale testing is unwarranted and raises serious civil liberty concerns." Agreed Democratic Representative Charles Schumer of New York: "Trying to stop organized crime's multimillion-dollar drug business by creating a police state in federal office buildings

would be virtually ineffective and would create one crime to stop another."

But many business leaders have concluded that the threat posed by drugs on the job can be answered only with tough measures. Dr. Michael Walsh, chief of clinical and behavioral pharmacology at the National Institute on Drug Abuse, notes that the number of corporations that ask him for advice on how to get drugs out of the workplace has increased dramatically in the past few months. Says he: "The momentum is very, very strong at this point.". . .

No one knows precisely how pervasive drug use on the job is. But there is no doubt that during the past couple of decades, illegal drugs have become deeply ingrained in American life. Federal experts estimate that between 10% and 23% of all U.S. workers use dangerous drugs on the job. Other research indicates that people who take drugs regularly, some 25% of the population according to Government calculations, are likely to use them at work or at least sometimes be on a high when they arrive at the workplace. In a 1985 study conducted by the 800-COCAINE counselors, 75% of those calling the hot line reported that they sometimes took coke while on the job, and 69% said they regularly worked under the influence of cocaine. One-fourth said they used cocaine at work every day.

Marijuana was once the most common drug in the workplace, but cocaine may now have become No. 1. According to estimates by the National Institute on Drug Abuse (NIDA), the number of Americans who take marijuana at least occasionally declined between 1979 and 1982, the most recent years for which statistics are available, from 22 million to 20 million. During the same period, the ranks of cocaine users increased from 15 million to 22 million. The problem seems to be most prevalent among young adults. NIDA estimated that nearly two-thirds of the people now entering the work force

Janice Castro, "Battling the Enemy Within," *Time*, March 17, 1986. Copyright 1986 Time Inc. All rights reserved. Reprinted by permission from TIME.

have used illegal drugs and 44% have taken them. . . .

Until recently, many companies have been slow to respond to their growing drug dilemmas. They did not realize how widespread the abuse was and had no idea how to combat it. Managers were not sure how to recognize the signs of drug use and were often afraid to confront workers who appeared to be high. Many executives doubted that the problem was serious enough to warrant a crackdown that might generate bad publicity.

But the smoking, snorting and dealing on the job eventually became so blatant and the results so tragic that companies could no longer afford to ignore what was going on. New York-based Capital Cities/ABC woke up to its drug troubles in 1984 after an employee collapsed at work, and subsequently died, from a cocaine overdose. Shortly thereafter, Capital Cities, which later acquired ABC, discovered organized drug dealing in one of its divisions. According to Dr. Robert Wick, corporate medical director for American Airlines, a computer operator who was high on marijuana failed to load a crucial tape into a major airline's computer reservations system. Result: the system was out of service for some eight hours, costing the company about $19 million. Says Wick: "That was an awfully expensive joint by anybody's standards."

Such revelations have broken down corporate resistance to taking a strong stand against drugs. Psychiatrist Robert DuPont, a former director of the National Institute on Drug Abuse who now helps companies set up antidrug programs, says that employers "have gone through a mental barrier that was blocking them before. What was that barrier? The barrier was that it was a private matter. The barrier was that it was not very important. The barrier was that there was not anything to be done about it anyhow. The barrier was that it was a societal problem and not a work-related problem. There was a whole series of barriers that kept the companies from moving, and they are all falling down."

Employee attitudes toward drugs are slowly changing as well. Workers have long been reluctant to turn in their colleagues for drug use. They have been afraid of ruining their co-workers' careers and of being ostracized for snitching. In addition, they could not be sure that management would believe them or back them up. But more and more employees are becoming fed up with working along-side people who are stoned. Says a news correspondent for a major New York City TV station: "After all, you work for days sometimes to make a story the best you can, and then some drug-abusing idiot pushes the wrong button when you're on the air. Why should I put up with that?"

Once companies acknowledge and confront the drug threat, their first task is to establish a consistent policy that is both firm and fair. Typically, companies decide to dismiss workers caught taking or selling drugs on the job but also offer a helping hand to users who voluntarily admit their problem.

To help put impaired workers on the road to rehabilitation, about 30% of the FORTUNE 500 largest industrial corporations have established in-house employee-assistance programs, commonly known as EAPs. Many of these programs were set up during the 1970s for workers suffering from alcoholism, and have since been expanded to include drug abusers. The motivation behind the EAPs has been economic as well as humanitarian. Says Drug Consultant Miriam Ingebritson: "It's much easier to help a person who has been on the job for nine years than it is to hire and train someone to replace him."

Mobil's drug-treatment program is fairly typical. Employees with a problem can call or stop by the medical departments at any of the oil company's facilities around the world. Supervisors who spot unusual behavior that is affecting job performance can encourage workers to contact an employee-assistance counselor. After initial medical examinations and counseling sessions, patients are generally referred to a hospital or outpatient drug clinic for treatment, which may take from four to six weeks. During that period the employees are given sick leave with pay, and their status is kept confidential. Company health-insurance benefits pay all the treatment costs. Once employees return to the job, they are allowed to attend follow-up counseling sessions during work hours. Says Dr. Joseph M. Cannella, Mobil's medical director: "We like to identify people, get them treated and back to work." He claims that Mobil's rehabilitation efforts have been 70% to 75% successful.

"Though employee support for antidrug programs is growing, some workers feel that their companies are going too far."

Many companies, including Capital Cities/ABC, Xerox and Dean Witter, have made it easier for employees to seek help by setting up nationwide hot lines with toll-free 800 numbers that workers and their families can call to get advice on drug problems. The service offers a guarantee of privacy to employees who are reluctant to approach their bosses or stop by medical departments. Once the drug user is on the phone, the hot-line counselor can encourage him to get help through an EAP or local clinical program.

While helping current employees to quit taking drugs, many companies are working to make sure that they do not take on any additional drug users. More and more firms are requiring job applicants to submit to new, sophisticated laboratory tests that can detect traces of narcotics in urine samples, and before long, companies may also be testing hair.

The list of corporations that ask all job applicants to undergo urinalysis is like a roll call of the largest and most prestigious firms in the U.S. Among them: Exxon, IBM, Lockheed, Shearson Lehman, Federal Express, United Airlines, TWA, Hoffmann-La Roche, the New York *Times*. On March 1 [1986], Du Pont became the newest name on the list. And this spring [1986], AT&T, which already tests applicants at plants where volatile chemicals are handled, will start screening all potential employees at its manufacturing facilities for drug use. About one-fourth of the FORTUNE 500 companies now screen applicants for drugs. . . .

The corporate battle against drugs is a bonanza for dozens of small companies that provide the weapons. Private laboratories that perform drug tests, for example, are growing rapidly. So are security firms that supply undercover agents. Professional Law Enforcement, a five-year-old Dayton firm, has doubled its business in the past year. Says President William Taylor III: "Companies are starting to recognize that they have to attack the problem in a different way. You can't send a standard security guard or a management person out there to handle a person dealing in drugs."

Because narcotics abuse spawns stealing, companies that specialize in investigating employee theft are much in demand. A Baltimore firm called Loss Management provides its clients with a national hot line and has solved cases with the help of office tipsters who report theft at their place of work. In one case, a clerk called the hot line when the invoices she was processing did not add up correctly. As it turned out, three top managers at the company were embezzling money to buy cocaine.

Though employee support for antidrug programs is growing, some workers feel that their companies are going too far. At the Kansas City *Star* and *Times*, two newspapers owned by Capital Cities/ABC, employees were stunned when management proposed to use narcotics-sniffing dogs as part of an experimental antidrug effort. Though newsroom wags passed around dog biscuits, most employees were in no mood to laugh. They felt that using the dogs would be an implicit accusation and an unwarranted and heavy-handed action. After heated staff protests, Capital Cities/ABC backed down and called off the experiment.

Much of the criticism of corporate antidrug efforts focuses on the growing use of urinalysis. Opponents charge that urine tests are a particularly invasive and humiliating method of determining whether a worker has used drugs. Says Bus Driver Randy Kemp, whose employer, Seattle Metro, requires employees who appear to be impaired to submit blood and urine samples: "You've got to have a

search warrant to search my house. Well, my body is a lot more sacred than my home."

Some executives agree. Hewlett-Packard and McDonnell Douglas, for example, do not ask job applicants or employees to take drug tests. Says Hewlett-Packard Spokesman Gene Endicott: "It's an invasion of the employee's privacy."

"Company officials point out that a strong stance against drugs is basically humanitarian because it ultimately benefits workers who use them as much as it does the firm."

Another objection to urinalysis is that companies are trying to control what workers do in their private time as well as during working hours. Because the tests do not reveal when a drug was used, workers could be penalized or fired for what they do in the evening or at weekend parties. Workers' rights advocates maintain that corporate antidrug policies can be particularly unfair in the case of marijuana, which has been virtually decriminalized in some states and cities. Says Los Angeles Labor Lawyer Glenn Rothner: "Termination for marijuana use, or worse, for simply having minute traces of marijuana in the body when tested is sentencing these employees to the equivalent of corporate capital punishment for an offense that would only merit a $100 fine in California."

The reaction of organized labor to antidrug efforts has been mixed. Unions generally support corporate drug-rehabilitation programs, but opposition to urinalysis is growing. Says Douglas Maguire, director of the labor assistance program for the Los Angeles County Federation of Labor, AFL-CIO: "Labor is not supporting testing in the workplace. As part of a physical exam for new employees, it is acceptable, but otherwise there are problems of violating civil rights." Some unions also fight against firings of workers with drug problems. Rockwell's Frankel quit as the company's medical director in 1983 partly because, he says, management repeatedly gave in to union demands that drug abusers be reinstated in their jobs.

Many executives are becoming increasingly impatient with the objections of labor leaders and civil libertarians. Says Peter Cherry of Cherry Electrical: "We have a right to say how you behave at the workplace. You don't bring a gun to work. You can't come to work naked. You're not allowed to yell 'Fire!' in the middle of the factory. We're just asking people to be fit while they're on the job."

Because drug use by workers can result in shoddy, unsafe products and accidents in the workplace, executives argue, individual rights must be subordinated to the broader welfare of fellow employees and customers. "We're not on a witch hunt," says Personnel Manager John Hunt of Southern California Edison. "Our No. 1 concern here is safety. We also have a responsibility to our customers. Our meter readers go into people's homes." Independent experts share the executives' concerns. Says Peter Bensinger, a former head of the Drug Enforcement Administration who is now a leading consultant on corporate drug problems: "Companies do have a right and responsibility to establish sound working conditions. We're talking about people and their safety, and our own individual rights to work in a safe environment." Company officials also point out that a strong stance against drugs is basically humanitarian because it ultimately benefits workers who use them as much as it does the firm.

Janice Castro is a staff writer for Time *magazine.*

Drug Testing in the Workplace Is Warranted

Richard K. Willard

The use of illegal drugs has become pervasive throughout the nation and has created problems of epidemic proportions. Corporations are recognizing the tremendous losses that drug abuse brings to the workplace. Today, virtually all professions and occupations are affected in some manner by the use of illegal drugs, and the use includes top executives as well as blue-collar workers.

According to the North Carolina-based Research Triangle Institute, use of illegal drugs cost the U.S. economy $60 billion in lost productivity in 1983. It is estimated that the cost in lost productivity for 1986 ranged from $70 billion to $100 billion. If the use of illegal drugs—like cocaine—continues to escalate at its present meteoric rate, we can expect productivity losses to be even greater. . . .

Another by-product of illegal drug use is violent crime. Drug addicts have an incessant motivation to commit violent crimes—robberies, thefts and muggings. Nineteen-eighty-six arrest studies for Washington, D.C., show that about 65 per cent of people arrested were high on one or more serious drugs, either cocaine, heroin or PCP, at the time of their arrest.

An even more startling recent NIJ study of arrests in New York City revealed that eight out of 10 people arrested showed traces of cocaine in their system. The rate of serious drug use by these predatory criminals was so astounding that the study didn't even bother to measure for so-called "lesser" drugs such as marijuana and alcohol. Street crime "victimizes" everyone, but especially the elderly, the poor, those living in public housing and those living in our nation's cities.

Let us all understand that when the so-called "recreational user" claims his habit harms no one

and that drug use is a victimless crime, he is ignoring the reality that he is a link in this monstrous criminal chain.

Drug Use in the Workplace

Illegal drug use, on or off duty, also has debilitating effects on our workplace. It drains our nation's productivity, strangles the economy, and hinders our ability to compete internationally against an ever more disciplined foreign workforce.

Consider the following facts. Drug users in the workforce:

• are three times more likely to be involved in on-the-job accidents,
• are absent from work twice as often,
• incur three times the average level of sickness costs, and
• are only two-thirds as productive.

On average, compared with their non-drug-using counterparts, substance abusers consume three times the medical benefits, are five times as likely to file workers' compensation claims, experience seven times as many garnishments and are repeatedly involved in grievance procedures. It is important to remember that this is not a problem that affects just one group of workers. The problem of illegal drug use cuts across every segment of the workforce, from the assembly line to the board room. Its debilitating effects are being felt at every level of our society.

A few examples will help illustrate how, in addition to lost productivity, drug abuse incurs disastrous social costs. In one harrowing case, an airline pilot for a major international carrier called a drug hotline, complaining that he was feeling exhausted and paranoid after snorting cocaine for three days straight. He was scheduled to fly a passenger jet to Europe that night, but he told the counselor he "was sure that he could stay awake and alert if he just kept taking drugs." The counselor

Richard K. Willard, "Achieving a Drug-Free Workplace," *Human Events*, May 2, 1987. Reprinted with permission.

who took the call never learned whether the pilot called in sick, as he suggested, but noted that these types of calls were typical. Obviously, that man's cocaine use was neither victimless nor recreational.

In another incident, a computer operator high on marijuana failed to load a crucial tape into the computerized airline reservation system causing the system eight hours of "down time" at a loss to the company of almost $19 million. As a company official noted, "That was an awfully expensive joint by anybody's standards."

Of course, the dangers of illegal drug use increase in industries where mistakes cost lives. One can imagine the dire consequences of illegal drug use among men and women working in nuclear power facilities, or as air traffic controllers or aviation mechanics. The industries and the occupations where illegal drug use has the potential to harm lives goes on and on. Our society is set up in a way that requires us to depend on one another in critical ways. Hardly any occupation is so isolated that an error in judgment caused by drug use does not have the potential to seriously hurt other people. . . .

"The workplace is an excellent place to start to reduce the demand for illegal drugs in this country."

Recognizing the importance of a drug-free workplace, numerous private employers have already instituted some sort of drug testing program to deter illegal drug use, identify substance abusers and help them get treatment. An October 1985 survey found that almost 20 per cent of 180 Fortune 500 companies, including Ford Motor Company, IBM, Alcoa Aluminum, Lockheed, Boise Cascade and the New York *Times* had instituted urinalysis drug detection programs. Another 19 per cent indicated a 50-50 chance or better that they would institute such programs within two years (by October 1987). Testing programs such as these, which can be tailored to the nature of the job and the prevalence of illegal drug use, have been enormously successful, resulting in increased productivity, fewer on-the-job accidents, and improved employee morale. Consequently, their use is growing. It is estimated that an additional 20 per cent of Fortune 500 companies will institute drug testing programs. The success of these programs gives us real cause to hope that a carefully implemented program of drug testing can lead to real progress in the war on drugs.

The practical effect of a drug testing program can best be seen in the nation's military, where drug use has been brought under control since a comprehensive testing program was introduced in 1981. Since instituting drug testing, the military has experienced a 67 per cent across the board decrease in drug use. In 1985, less than 9 per cent of the nation's 2.1 million servicemen used drugs, down sharply from 27 per cent in 1980. These sharp declines are the result of tough—but fair—mandatory drug testing programs.

Education and Rehabilitation

Many critics of drug testing believe that the drug problem can be alleviated by costly educational and rehabilitation programs or by splashy celebrity endorsements. Unfortunately, the facts do not bear this out. One prominent behavioral scientist concluded that educational and celebrity programs designed to control adolescent drug use simply don't work. "Such programs assume that children use drugs because they are ignorant of the dangers. Unfortunately, there is a wealth of evidence that mere knowledge of the facts does not affect behavior directly, particularly if social influences contradict the facts." In 1973, the National Commission on Marijuana and Drug Abuse conceded that "no drug education program in this country, or elsewhere, has proven sufficiently successful to warrant our recommending it." Similarly, a 1980 study reviewing over a hundred drug programs reported that "by far the largest number of studies have found no effects of drug education on use.". . .

Where employees are put on notice in advance that drug use is unacceptable, we can expect to see a significant decline in illegal drug use and, therefore, a reduction in addiction rates in future years. In addition, once identified and held accountable for his actions, the drug user is more likely to accept treatment and rehabilitation. Treatment experts agree that the most effective way to treat drug abuse is by requiring personal accountability by the drug user. That means the drug user must learn that drug use has a consequence. Since personal denial is the *sine qua non* of the addicted personality-profile, the issue of accountability usually doesn't arise until the addict gets caught. This is why testing only for "probable cause" is not sufficient. Often, there may be no easily detectable signs of drug use—especially to the untrained eye of supervisors. . . .

Our survival as a democratic nation is threatened when we allow ourselves to be drawn into increasingly decadent pursuits of chemically induced pleasures. Illegal drug use is tearing our nation apart, destroying families and careers and hindering our ability to compete in an ever more competitive world market. The workplace is an excellent place to start to reduce the demand for illegal drugs in this country.

Richard K. Willard is the assistant attorney general for the Civil Division of the US Department of Justice.

"In no case does a urine test establish that your work has ever been impaired by drugs, much less that you're a drug-addict."

Drug Testing in the Workplace Is Inappropriate

The New Republic

Most people who smoke half a joint at a Friday-night party don't have to worry that they'll get caught in a surprise urine test at the office Monday morning. At least, not yet. But the number is growing. Take, for example, anyone who works at the Department of Health and Human Services as an animal caretaker. That's one of 350,000 federal positions that the administration recently deemed "sensitive"—so critical to "public health and safety or national security" that its occupant will soon be subject to unannounced drug tests. As government documents note, drug use by an animal caretaker "could result in death or injury to valuable research animals or cause irreparable harm to experiments and jeopardize the results of research."

One could reasonably ask for a bit of elaboration on the connection between public safety and the prospect of some dope-smoking civil servant's absent-mindedly sticking a laboratory rat in the microwave. But to dwell on the government's overly broad definition of "sensitive position" would be to miss the larger point. For the White House's drug-testing program is essentially a red herring. Though Ed Meese's adrenaline may flow more freely at the thought that one-eighth of the federal work force will now have to stay on the straight and narrow, the administration's ultimate aim is much broader. Concerned, apparently, that only a fraction of American companies now give workers random drug tests, President Reagan is determined, as he put it in the executive order creating the program, to "show the way towards achieving drug-free workplaces." Meese seconded the motion, insisting that "most areas of work" should have drug testing. Reagan and Meese are less interested in using drug tests to keep the government workplace safe and productive than in using the non-government workplace to enforce drug laws.

If you start throwing around phrases like "police state" to describe Reagan's ideal America, administration spokesmen will hasten to straighten you out. The government is not, they stress, acting as policeman when it commands workers to pee into a jar, because catching lawbreakers is not its aim. Though test results are considered just cause for disciplinary action, urine will never be gathered for use in criminal proceedings. The government is simply acting as a concerned employer, intent on keeping the workplace safe and efficient and getting workers with drug problems the counseling they need.

Paternalistic Government

Well, if the government is playing paternalistic boss and not authoritarian cop, why is it testing only for illegal drugs? Is it any scarier to have a pot-head behind the wheel of a government bus than a drunk? If we're going to invade the privacy and compromise the dignity of our workers in the interest of health, safety, and national security, let's do it right: breathalyzers after lunch for everyone.

Actually, breathalyzers would be *more* defensible than urine tests. At least they establish whether you're under the influence of a drug while at work. Urine tests only determine—with hazy certainty—whether a drug has been in your system recently. How recently? Depends on the drug—weeks for marijuana, days for cocaine. In no case does a urine test establish that your work has ever been impaired by drugs, much less that you're a drug addict or have a long-term problem. Pity the weekend pot smoker who has to sit through the counseling mandated by the government until he finally breaks down and agrees that he's in the "denial" phase and won't get better until he admits the depth of his problem.

It's worth asking why employers *don't* bother to give breathalyzers after lunch. The answer is that they don't have to. If drinking gets to be a workplace problem for someone, any reasonably perceptive boss will know it. And if drinking doesn't get to be a workplace problem, any boss who isn't a pathological meddler won't care. It's a hallowed American tradition that, so long as you do your job, nobody will gripe about how you spend your spare time. This isn't Russia, after all. And it's not Fascist Italy, where the government turned private companies into surrogate overseers. In fact, this isn't even modern Japan—which, though hardly fascist, has a more symbiotic link between professional and personal life than Americans are used to. Though we admire Japan's stark efficiency, we'd just as soon admire it from afar.

The Old-Fashioned Approach

The old-fashioned approach to workplace monitoring (keeping an eye out for screwups) can handle all the drugs the government's program focuses on—marijuana, cocaine, amphetamines, opiates, and PCP, the powerful hallucinogen also known as angel dust. If daily dope smoking is making someone lethargic, fire him for lethargy. If coke has a worker alternating between intense but shabby work, mindless chattiness, and sloughs of despond, fire him on all three grounds. As for PCP, the oddest inclusion on the list of target drugs: Why waste money on lab work when you can just be on the lookout for workers who ask the Xerox machine out to lunch? Among the dubious data brandished by advocates of drug testing is the estimate that workers with severe drug and alcohol problems have 16 times the average rate of absenteeism. Well, you shouldn't need a chemist to tell you to fire somebody who spends ten or 20 weeks a year in bed.

Obviously there are cases where you don't want to wait for a drug abuser's incompetence to manifest itself before doing something: air traffic controller, train engineer, espionage agent, White House astrologer. For positions of such responsibility, the degradation of random drug testing may be justified. But the same cannot be said for "most" American workers, as Meese would have it, or even for most of the 350,000 federal workers targeted by the administration.

"Turning every CEO in the country into a de facto deputy just isn't the American way."

The constitutionality of the administration's drug-testing program is far from clear. As you may recall, the Fourth Amendment grants Americans the right "to be secure in their persons, houses, papers and effects, against unreasonable searches and seizures,"

and dictates that searches be based on "probable cause." The courts are getting lots of paperwork about the testing program from employees unions and the ACLU [American Civil Liberties Union], and the Supreme Court has already agreed to hear a parallel case involving the Customs Service's existing program for testing workers.

Short-Circuiting the Constitution

But even an adverse ruling won't necessarily squelch Reagan's vision of a better America. . . . Administration staffers are already advising corporations on how to collect and analyze urine efficiently. So by the time a Supreme Court decision comes down, the government's showcase program may well have spawned clones all across the private sector. And since the Bill of Rights applies only to the government, not to private employers, the administration will then have the best of both worlds: a pervasive, invasive deterrent to drug use, but a deterrent that isn't subject to constitutional constraints on law enforcement.

If the drug problem is really so pernicious that comprehensive on-the-job urine tests are worth contemplating, let's debate the possibility, see how the average worker feels about it, and then leave it for Congress to take action—including any required revision of the Bill of Rights. But there's no need to short-circuit the Constitution. Turning every CEO in the country into a de facto deputy just isn't the American way.

The New Republic *is a weekly journal of opinion.*

viewpoint 82

Anabolic Steroids: An Overview

Christina Dye

The whole world was watching.

Canadian sprinter Ben Johnson, who captured the world's imagination and a gold medal in the 1988 Olympics' 100-meter dash, became the target for universal scorn when a post-race test showed traces of anabolic steroids in his urine.

It was only the most recent in a long list of controversies involving steroids. But it surely won't be the last.

Because the incident merely served to remind us that steroids—hormones that stimulate growth and weight gain and which have been a fixture in professional sports for some 20 years—have today become a standard, and increasingly visible, part of collegiate and even high school sports programs.

Critics and Advocates

Critics of steroid use say the drugs are unsafe and unethical. As evidence, they cite the following:

• In 1986, six U.S. athletes died of problems—including liver tumors and heart disease—linked to long-term steroid use.

• More than a million American athletes currently take steroids without medical supervision.

• Among professional body-builders, an estimated 99 percent of men and 20-30 percent of women use steroids.

Advocates argue that steroids simply even the odds between opponents, since so many athletes already use hormones. And since the chemicals work best as a supplement to an intensive exercise program, they argue that steroids merely enhance the benefits of hard work and natural athletic ability.

The truth seems to lie somewhere between the extremes.

In this [viewpoint], we'll examine steroid use in sports today, and review current research into the chemicals' effectiveness and the lengthening list of risks tied to their use.

We hope you'll stay with us. Because the issues in the debate go further than the simple winning and losing of medals. They go to the heart of what winning and losing *really* is.

The Steroid Solution

Anabolic steroids are lab-made versions of the male sex hormone, *testosterone.*

Naturally secreted by the pituitary gland and the testes, testosterone triggers the growth spurt that turns boys into men during puberty, providing such "secondary" sex characteristics as a lowered voice and increased body and facial hair.

Such hormones are a main factor in the body process known as *anabolism*, in which nonliving material is converted into living cellular tissue, hence the name anabolic steroids.

Anabolic agents were developed in the early 1950s in a search for a testosterone-like drug that would trigger general body growth without the strong masculinizing effects of the male hormone.

They are prescribed medically to treat anemia, breast cancer, osteoporosis, and, following careful medical evaluation, some cases of dwarfism and delayed puberty.

Steroids promote rapid synthesis of protein in the body by speeding up the genetic machinery of cells that produce ribonucleic acid, which in turn manufactures protein.

In healthy adults who do not exercise, steroids may simply increase appetite and feelings of well-being with no effect on muscle size or strength. But in athletes in heavy training, the steroids dramatically increase muscle size and body weight.

Other claims for the performance-boosting effects of the steroids include:

• Reduces excess body fat so that musculature is more clearly defined.

- Boosts red-blood cell concentration and blood volume to improve endurance.
- Lowers muscle recovery time from training and overall fatigue.
- Speeds up muscle healing time.
- Increases feelings of mental intensity and aggression.

While some experts doubt the effectiveness of anabolic agents despite glowing testimonials on their use, steroids clearly do *something* that athletes see as desirable, even necessary, to achieving the winning edge.

Doping and Stacking

From sprinters and weight-lifters to linebackers, steroids seem to offer an easy answer for anyone seeking a shortcut to athletic fame and fortune, or who simply want to add a few inches and pounds to a skinny teenaged frame.

Steroid supplementation of training spread so quickly in the 1960s that the International Olympic Committee Medical Commission banned anabolic "doping" in 1974.

Nonetheless, use of steroids has continued to spread.

Two gold medalists and one silver medalist were disqualified at the 1976 Olympics when steroids were found in urine tests. In 1983, 14 athletes from 10 countries were sent home from the Pan American Games for steroid "doping."

In the most celebrated recent case prior to the 1988 Olympics, Oklahoma linebacker Brian Bosworth was banned from the 1987 Orange Bowl when urine tests detected steroid use.

Experienced users typically take steroids in a complicated "stacking" regimen intended to maximize effects while minimizing potential health risks and avoiding possible detection.

"Stacking" involves progressively increasing dosage and types of steroids beginning 3-4 months before competition, and typically involves dosages 10-40 times greater than those prescribed therapeutically.

Doses are tapered off weeks before an event to avoid detection. Some athletes use "masking" drugs to hide steroid traces. Two such drugs—probenecid (which lowers steroid excretion rates) and Lasix™ (which dilutes the urine)—are now banned by the IOC.

Still, there is no medical evidence that supports steroid "stacking" as a more effective means of achieving maximum anabolic action.

In fact, some experts question the ability of steroids to improve athletic performance at all and wonder whether side effects *can* be avoided.

Most studies (and the self-reports of users) indicate that anabolic steroids do, in fact, increase body weight and muscle size, but whether they do so consistently is still a topic of medical debate.

While the personal testimonials of users almost unanimously reflect improvements in both performance and strength, research is split almost evenly between positive and negative results.

To date, controlled studies involving steroids indicate that the following changes occur:
- *Body Weight and Muscle Size.* Increases (averaging 2.2 kg) can be attributed in part to higher water retention in body tissue.
- *Muscle Mass.* Increases (averaging 2-3 kg) in muscle fiber do occur, but inconsistent research results make predicting the extent or probability of change difficult.
- *Muscular Strength.* About half of all animal and human studies have demonstrated improvement in muscle strength with steroid therapy above the effects of resistance training alone.
- *Aerobic Capacity.* Most studies indicate that steroids have little positive effect on aerobic work capacity.
- *Dose-Response.* Most studies have not demonstrated that greater growth effects come with higher doses of steroids.

Controlled research on the performance-enhancing effects of steroids is still inconclusive.

> *"Controlled research on the performance-enhancing effects of steroids is still inconclusive."*

Some researchers attribute the inconsistency of test results to individual differences in metabolism and natural athletic ability.

Recent investigations also point to a powerful psychological action of steroids.

Users report surges in self-esteem, energy, and sex drive, along with increased appetite and aggression, and a lowered tolerance to pain.

In addition, users may feel less able to control their emotions, particularly anger, and exhibit a generally lowered tolerance of frustration or poor performance.

Some observers believe the psychological effects of steroids may simply drive athletes to train harder and longer.

Health Effects

While only half of all controlled studies support performance-enhancing capabilities, a growing body of evidence indicates that steroids can pose serious risks to health.

Immediate dangers involve their effects as synthetic versions of testosterone.

In women, this involves a range of "masculinizing" reactions, including growth of facial and body hair, deepening of the voice, menstrual irregularities, and enlargement of the clitoris.

In men, enlargement of the breasts (gynecomastia) and a decrease in sperm production are common.

Long-term effects of steroids can include:
• Atrophy of the testes, prostate cancer, impotence
• Severe acne and early baldness
• High blood pressure, heart disease
• Liver tumors and failure of liver function
• Stunted growth and permanent short stature in children and teenagers.

The psychological fall-out is no less troubling.

First, steroids can cause psychological dependence with regular use.

And since the chemicals slow natural testosterone production, ex-users may continue to suffer withdrawal symptoms—including depression, fatigue, and impotence—weeks or months after stopping use.

A 1988 study also linked use to a "steroid psychosis," marked by hallucinations, delusions of grandeur, and violent mood swings.

Of 41 bodybuilders studied, 12 percent reported symptoms considered "overtly psychotic"—including severe paranoia and auditory hallucinations—while another 10 percent were described as "subthreshold psychotic." . . .

Although reports of severe or life-threatening effects of steroids are rare, experts warn that major problems may not become evident for 20 or more years following use.

Still, medical evidence of serious long-term reactions to anabolic steroids remains inconclusive.

The Superstar Syndrome

The possibility of becoming a world-class athlete is powerfully compelling. And that urge lies at the heart of the current moral debate over use of steroids and other hormones.

Is it fair to use artificial means for building the body and fine-tuning performance? On the other hand, is it fair *not* to when opponents in other countries or other schools may be using growth chemicals?

"Although reports of severe or life-threatening effects of steroids are rare, experts warn that major problems may not become evident for 20 or more years following use."

Proposed solutions to the problem have thus far come in various shapes and sizes, ranging from total bans backed up by severe penalties to rescheduling the compounds under federal law as controlled substances.

That's the tack the U.S. Congress took in October 1988, in passing tough new laws that impose fines and set jail terms for sales of the drugs. And both the National Collegiate Athletic Association and the National Football League have begun testing programs to identify steroid-using players.

Clearly, resolving the questions surrounding steroid use will involve many more tough choices and hard decisions.

Because in a world that likes its sports heroes bigger than life—and in some cases, as large as refrigerators—steroids represent an apparent means to one of the most potentially-profitable ends available for millions of yet-uncheered heroes and superstars.

And many don't mean to miss their chance.

Christina Dye writes for the Do It Now Foundation, an organization that publishes and distributes educational materials on drugs.

"Steroids can be used safely. Just be smart about it."

Steroid Use Can Be Justified

Steve Courson and Ron Hale

Editor's note: The following viewpoint is in two parts. Part I is by Steve Courson. Part II is an adaptation of an interview of Ron Hale by USA Today.

I

My first encounter with anabolic steroids . . . was in 1974. After my freshman season I wanted to get stronger and was frustrated that I couldn't gain weight on my own. I began taking an anabolic steroid, Dianabol, and gained 20 pounds in 30 days and increased my bench press by 70 pounds.

I never took steroids again while I was in college, but I used them often in my nine years as an offensive guard in the NFL [National Football League]. In a story in [Sports Illustrated in 1985] I talked about my taking of steroids and their widespread use in the NFL. At that time the league's commissioner, Pete Rozelle, and the director of the players' union, Gene Upshaw, claimed that steroids weren't a significant problem. But I knew differently, and after the 1985 season the Tampa Bay Buccaneers dropped me. I still wonder if that article had something to do with my being cut and the subsequent refusal of any NFL team to touch me.

Steroid Hypocrisy

There is great controversy—and hypocrisy—about steroid use in sports. In the NFL, management long turned its back on steroids, claiming ignorance of the subject. Now Rozelle says that about 6% of the players are on anabolic steroids and that the league is really concerned. Who is he kidding? My educated guess is that close to 50% of the linemen use steroids, which right there would be about 15% of all players. And I have to laugh at NFL officials' talking about the health risks, using that as a scare tactic, as if football isn't filled with health risks.

It is not the use of steroids that I object to, it's the way that usage is dealt with. Why is it always the athlete who is chastised for using steroids when it is the system that compels him to do so? The answer: It is easier to blame the athlete, who does what he feels he has to do to survive in this era of chemically enhanced competition, than it is to do something constructive. What's a nosetackle supposed to do when he knows his coach expects him to weigh 295 pounds and bench-press 600 pounds? Those numbers are not attainable by most men without the help of steroids.

It is time to get realistic about steroids. A decade ago the American College of Sports Medicine lost credibility with athletes when it stated that anabolic steroids do not enhance performance, a position it didn't reverse until recently. Athletes had found out that they did enhance performance. So why would they listen when the medical community cautioned about steroids' deleterious side effects? The health hazards associated with steroid use should be put into perspective. Others . . . disagree with me, but I question whether it is really unethical to give steroids to healthy people such as football players. What about painkillers, which players use even more heavily? What about sleeping pills, Valium, diet pills and birth control pills—all are widely accepted. How are they different from steroids?

Ban Impossible

It would be great if sports were pure and steroids weren't a factor. It would be great also if we lived in a world without nuclear weapons. But can pro football be played today without steroids? If you're talking about maintaining present levels of aggression and strength, the answer is no. And it is naive to think that we can go back to the presteroid days.

By pretending that is possible, the NFL is treating the issue as no more than a p.r. problem. But it is actually getting itself into a p.r. dilemma. Publicity about steroid use has given the NFL a black eye. But it is apparent to me that the majority of sports fans are more interested in being entertained than in worrying about whether players are taking steroids.

The NFL recently announced that it will test all players for steroid use in preseason. But tests can be beat. Until a completely reliable testing methodology is developed, you will never get steroids out of sports. I believe we should recognize that players are going to take steroids, and we should establish procedures for monitoring that use for possible ill effects. Have the athletes watched by physicians trained in sports medicine, and administer everything from heart and liver tests to regular eye exams. The player would get his information from doctors instead of some guy on the street or at the gym.

Monitor Use

I think athletes would welcome this change. At South Carolina I received my Dianabol on a prescription from a team doctor, and although that may sound sensational today, remember that steroids were less of an issue back then. At least the doctor who wrote that prescription took my blood pressure and checked me over before doing so.

II

I first heard about anabolic steroids in 1965, when I found out some guys on the West Coast were using them.

I was told they could be dangerous if not taken under a doctor's care, and I wasn't particularly interested in using them anyway, because I was progressing pretty well at the time without them. I was 25 years old, and that year I won the Indiana state power-lifting title.

A year later, I changed my mind, and now, after 20 years as a steroid user, I can confidently say two things:

• Never, ever, should teenagers use these drugs. They can stunt your growth and cause other damage.

• But any adult should be able to use them under a doctor's care. For most, small or moderate doses are safe.

Reasons Against Steroid Ban

I feel that way for several reasons.

The first is my own experience. I have undergone every possible medical test, including heart catheterization, and they show no ill effects.

Second, communist countries give them to athletes, so if we don't use them, we are at an unfair disadvantage.

Last, I just don't think sports organizations have the right to tell me what to do to my body.

Look at this thing with the NCAA [National Collegiate Athletic Association] suspending [football linebacker] Brian Bosworth. I think the Constitution allows Bosworth to do what he's doing. He's an outstanding athlete taking steroids for an injury problem. But even if he weren't, steroids aren't uppers, they're not downers, they don't alter the mind, and it's not a habit that can't be broken.

If he feels they help his performance, that's his business. To look at him on television, he's a model of what we need in America. The NCAA should let him go and worry about testing for marijuana.

The same goes for my sport.

"Used properly, they are no more of a threat to an adult than liquor is."

Even though I was a state champion, I started taking steroids because I thought my progress was slowing.

I was 5 feet 5 inches tall and weighed 155 pounds. I could lift a total of 1,150 pounds in the three lifts the event requires.

Three years later, weighing 165, I won the U.S. senior power-lifting title with 1,425 pounds.

In all, I've won nine state titles, and I think I'd probably have won most of them without steroids. But there's no way I could have won that national title without them.

Used properly, they are no more of a threat to an adult than liquor is. I've known many people who've used them, and except for one national champion who took very large doses I don't know anyone who's had trouble.

I wouldn't let my son, who's now 12 years old, take them until he's fully grown. But if he comes to me 10 years from now and asks if he should take them, I'll say yes, as long as you do it under a doctor's care.

As for me, I've been off steroids for nine months while I take a break from competition, but I plan on returning, and if I go against people who are using them, I will, too.

Steroids can be used safely. Just be smart about it.

Steve Courson played football as an offensive lineman for nine years with the Pittsburgh Steelers and Tampa Bay Buccaneers. Ron Hale is a former US power-lifting champion.

"The immediate solution to chronic steroid abuse in this decade is to make the drug illegal unless there is a specific medical indication."

Steroid Use Cannot Be Justified

A.L. Strickland and Stephen Chapman

I

Joe Coley is a sophomore at All-American University. Realizing that in order to play the defensive line in major college football, he has to be heavier and stronger because his opponent usually outweighs him by 35 pounds and can bench-press 50 pounds more. To build his strength, he strenuously works long hours in the gymnasium. Despite his efforts, he can only bench press 300 pounds. Rumors around the campus are that a miracle drug called "steroids" may help him to add weight and strength. Such drugs are often obtainable from some physicians who will prescribe medication to treat a fictitious ailment such as "for rapid healing of a sprained ankle." Since he achieved the desired weight gain and strength after two months' consumption of the drug, he is now a confirmed believer in the benefit of steroids for competitive sports. He continues the ready access to the drug through a local black market.

What Are Steroids?

What are steroids? The term "steroids" includes a group of compounds with different classes having entirely different effects, despite having a similar nucleus of three benzene rings composed of six carbon atoms each and one with only five. The main class is the glucocorticoids with 21 carbons. Cortisone and cortisol are the chief examples of this class and are the true "steroids." Cortisone is among the most frequently used drugs in medicine. Androgens (male sex hormones), estrogens (female sex hormones), and progesterone (also a type of female hormone) are also loosely termed "steroids" because they are derived from cholesterol through the same chemical pathways as cortisol. The steroids

used by athletes are androgens, such as testosterone (the natural androgen made in the testes) or synthetic androgens. The latter are derivatives of testosterone with side-chain substitutions, such as an alkyl radical (methyl group—CH_3) at the 17th carbon. This substitution enhances the effect of the compound by prolonging the half-life through resisting degradation by liver enzymes. These synthetic forms can also be taken orally rather than parenterally. The substitutions make these drugs more anabolic (protein sparing) rather than androgenic (effects on body hair growth, libido, acne, voice change, i.e. characteristics of maleness). The anabolic and androgenic effects haven't been fully separated, however, since all synthetic androgens retain undesirable side effects of androgens and are not therefore purely anabolic. . . .

The most common oral steroids used by athletes are oxandrolone, fluoxymesterone, and stanozolol. The FDA (Food and Drug Administration) requires a warning in the *Physician's Desk Reference* as follows: Warning: "Anabolic steroids do not enhance athletic ability." Replacement dose of the two oral androgens for hypogonadal men is five to 10 mg per day, but athletes often take 50 to 100 mg per day.

What Steroids Do

Researchers have shown that anabolic steroids stimulate the growth of muscle by increasing protein in each muscle fiber, thereby adding weight (hypertrophy), but not necessarily strength. It would appear that even when placebo pills are given to athletes, they often gain weight and strength. The placebo appears to induce psychological effects that help them to eat more, work harder, and feel better. Because women normally have a much lower testosterone level than men, the effect of anabolic steroid is more pronounced in women. In males, who natually possess significant levels of testosterone, the effect is not so apparent because

A.L. Strickland, "Steroids: Do They Enhance Athletic Performance?" *The Journal of the South Carolina Medical Association*, Vol. 84, No. 2, pp. 59-62. Reprinted with permission.

Stephen Chapman, "The NFL's Oversized Problem," *The Washington Times*, December 11, 1986. Reprinted by permission: Tribune Media Services.

hypertrophy of muscle fibers can only increase so much.

Therefore, acute side effects are readily seen in the female, but are not so readily apparent in the male. In the female, these include weight gain, acne, clitoral enlargement, menstrual irregularity or cessation, voice change, breast shrinkage, hirsutism, male pattern baldness, and perhaps an increase in libido as well as infertility.

Harmful Effects

Aside from the question of possible advantage given the athlete in sports events, why are physicians so reluctant to give androgens to athletes? When androgens are used in the growing child, they speed up the rate of linear growth, but unless they are given in exact proper doses, they may close the child's growth plates (epiphyses) and actually make the child a shorter adult than he was destined to be. Androgens may create or worsen acne, increase or decrease libido, add weight, cause headaches, gynecomastia, alter liver function, alter thyroid metabolism, increase aggressiveness, decrease testicular size, and cause nausea and dizziness. Chronic high doses have been associated with primary liver cancer (oral forms), hyperinsulinism, abnormal glucose tolerance leading to diabetes, and most significantly there is a strong suggestion that it leads to coronary atherosclerosis. Atherosclerosis may possibly result from the fact that androgens lower the high density lipoprotein cholesterol levels which are thought to be a protective factor against coronary artery disease. "Body-builders" psychosis is a new entity now thought to result from chronic excess anabolic steroids in up to 10 percent of users. They can become unusually aggressive and display symptoms of manic-depressive psychosis. These users appear to have a self image problem (i.e. the reverse of anorexia nervosa) in which they consider themselves too thin or small.

"Those young athletes who ingest steroids in high doses for more than two years probably have to look forward to congestive heart failure between the ages of 40 to 60."

Those young athletes who ingest steroids in high doses for more than two years probably have to look forward to congestive heart failure between the ages of 40 to 60. When muscle fibers hypertrophy to their maximum size they stretch under contraction and relaxation to their peak strength according to Starling's law, i.e. they produce maximum strength at a specific tension beyond which the strength with stretch decreases. When steroids are discontinued,

the muscle is hypertrophied beyond its natural state and eventually becomes weaker as the athlete decreases his exercise and activity with age. Since the cardiac muscle is the largest muscle in the body and has to work continuously, it becomes flabby and weaker with age, creating a condition which predisposes the individual to earlier onset of heart failure than if steroids had never been used. This is potentially the greatest hazard to chronic androgen use.

The steroid issue in athletes is most likely settled, at least for the short term. The International Olympic Committee has advised against steroid use and is now testing athletes to enforce a ban. The NCAA is also spot testing in major college events, such as the major football bowl games, and likely will eventually increase the frequency to include all college sports. Colleges will soon get the message. Alabama has taken the first step to become the first state in the U.S. to make steroid use in athletes illegal. In Britain, the use of androgens is now completely banned.

Another sidelight to the abuse of steroids is the development of amyotrophic lateral sclerosis (ALS or Lou Gehrig's disease) in three (out of 40) San Francisco Forty-Niner football team members from the 1960 team. Gary Lewis and Matt Hazeltine recently died and the health of Bob Waters, the coach at Western Carolina University, is deteriorating slowly. One of the common factors involving these men is their use of steroids. Bob Waters is currently seeking to find out how many others of the 1960 team also took steroids and if they may be having symptoms. Other common factors may also be found to have a link with this disease. The usual expected incidence of ALS is 1/100,000 which makes 3/40 a highly significant finding.

What Should Be Done

The controversy regarding chronic androgen abuse continues. Double-blind testing with human volunteers is probably unethical because it takes 20 to 40 years or more to determine the final results. Therefore, we may never have a definitive answer, but the immediate solution to chronic steroid abuse in this decade is to make the drug illegal unless there is a specific medical indication.

II

Professional football used to be a game for large men. No more. Those who are merely large would feel small in a National Football League locker room. Football has become a coast-to-coast freak show, dominated by two-legged mastodons created in a chemistry laboratory.

The NFL, which for years has ignored this development, now says it will include anabolic steroids in its drug testing of players. Steroids are synthetic versions of male hormones, which are used to increase both weight and strength. Though they pose a danger to both the user and the non-user, the league didn't mind as long as they didn't cost the owners any money. But when two insurance companies cited steroids as one reason for their decision to stop writing some policies for football players, it finally was moved to act.

"It's much easier to justify testing for steroids than testing for drugs like marijuana and cocaine."

Twenty years ago, an NFL lineman as heavy as 250 pounds was rare. Today a lineman that light is rare. The Chicago Bears' interior offensive line, not notable for its size, *averages* 268 pounds. Some of the growth of the typical NFL player can be ascribed to advances in nutrition and weight training, but much of it is due to steroids.

Potent Reputation

Although scientists disagree about whether steroids actually improve performance, the athletes clearly think they do. So potent is their reputation that these drugs have found their way into college locker rooms—and even high schools.

The question is not whether NFL players use them; the only question is how many. They are supposed to be dispensed only by prescription, and only for comparatively rare conditions, but active players quoted in a *Sports Illustrated* story . . . estimated that from 40 percent to 90 percent of their colleagues use steroids. Former Tampa Bay guard Steve Courson, who as a player was open about his use of steroids, guesses that 95 percent of NFL linemen have tried them: "You've got to get on drugs to survive."

That's the rub: once steroids are established, even players who don't want to use them have little choice. A 250-pounder armed with only the advantages provided by hard work and ample meals is mismatched against a 280-pounder bursting with artificial hormones. Says Courson, "It's very easy for people outside to criticize. But it's different when it's your livelihood, when it's your job to keep a genetic mutation out of your backfield."

Risking the Side Effects

Professional necessity is the only way to explain why players are willing to risk the side effects of these drugs, which include cancer, liver and kidney damage, impotence, atrophy of the testicles, high blood pressure, and increased aggressiveness.

Steroids also are blamed for some on-the-field injuries, the result of loading too much weight onto bones and joints. Not only that, but the larger and stronger the players, the greater the risk of harm when they collide. The rise of steroids has coincided with a sharp decline in the length of playing careers.

For several reasons, it's much easier to justify testing for steroids than testing for drugs like marijuana and cocaine. One is that steroids clearly are affecting the outcome of games by enhancing the performance of players—and by fostering injuries. Another is that, to the extent they work as intended, steroids tend to force players to use them, with willing users driving out abstainers.

By causing irritability and belligerence, steroids also exacerbate the game's inherent violence. *The New York Times*'s Pulitzer Prize-winning sportswriter, Dave Anderson, says the popularity of steroids is one reason that "more and more, NFL games are projecting the image of two street gangs in a violent brawl."

Infallible Tests

Finally, the test generally used for steroids, unlike the ones used by the NFL for other drugs, is virtually infallible.

Testing for recreational drugs like marijuana is more a public relations gimmick than an effort to deal with a real problem. But testing for steroids is important to preserving the integrity of the game. Left alone, steroids have the potential to destroy the public appeal of the game—or to turn it into a grotesque caricature of sport, fit only for those willing to risk disease and death by turning themselves into "genetic mutations."

The NFL took too much time to confront the problem, but better late than never. Football ought to be a sport for large men, not the war among Frankenstein's monsters that it threatens to become.

A.L. Strickland is a physician at the Spartanburg Regional Medical Center in Spartanburg, South Carolina. Stephen Chapman is a nationally syndicated columnist.

"The use of anabolic steroids by females . . . is especially dangerous."

Steroids Harm Female Athletes

Bob Goldman, with Patricia Bush and Ronald Klatz

Steroids scare me for what they can do over the long term. And for what they can do to women.

Professor Arnold Beckett
University of London

You've seen her standing on the blocks at the end of a pool waiting for the starting gun, or running down the field, or into the spin that hurls her discus farther than the others, or standing at rest at the side of a track with a javelin in her hand, or walking away from you in her running shoes and warm-up suit. And you've said to yourself, "My god, is that a woman? Look at those great hulking shoulders and those arms. Why, she looks more like a man than half the men I know."

If you had seen her earlier—a month, six months, a year, three or four years, or more—in the privacy of her locker room at her home gym, you would have seen her drinking a white powder mixed in juice or swallowing tablets or taking an injection in her behind.

If you had asked her what she was taking, she might have been able to tell you, but she was more likely to answer, "Oh, just some powder to make me stronger. All the girls take it."

"Just some vitamins that the coach gave me."

"Some growth stuff that all the East German girls are taking."

If you had suggested that she was taking a drug that might be harmful, she would probably have dismissed your concern.

"I know that, but I need it so I can break the record," or "win in Mexico," or in wherever the next major competition was scheduled, or

"Well, maybe. But I'm going to stop taking it when I retire and then I'll be O.K.," or

"I don't think my coach would give me anything that would really hurt me, and besides, it's worth it. Do you know I've taken nearly three seconds off my time since I started taking those drugs?" or

"I get a lot of exercise and I don't drink or smoke or take birth-control pills, so I don't think I'll get any bad effects from this stuff. It's only helping me get stronger like steak or supervitamins or something," or

"Listen, when everybody gives up booze and Valium, come back and tell me about it."

The participation of women is the newest and most exciting aspect of bodybuilding competition. My first exposure to real, honest-to-goodness female competition was at George Snyder's Best in the World contest, where the women competitors were all taken very seriously by the audience and the judges. The evidence of the hours of hard work, dedication, and physical excellence shone forth from these exceptional female specimens of health and fitness.

As I sat in the audience, troublesome thoughts entered my mind. Shades of past Olympics— incidents where sex tests and chromosome tests had to be performed to fully identify the sexual gender of the competitors. Visions of the seven-foot-four-inch woman basketball player from the Soviet Union—the East German swimmers with the deep voices, and the facial hair and massive arms of the Bulgarian female shotputter. I began to worry that the drug bastardization of the female form could also enter and destroy the beauty of this new area of competition. . . .

Women at Greatest Risk

"Giving male hormones to a male may not be a very nice thing to do, but at least you are giving him more of something his body produces naturally. But if you start giving a female that same male hormone, it's going contrary to her whole endocrine make-up,"

Bob Goldman, Patricia Bush, and Ronald Klatz, *Death in the Locker Room.* Tucson, AZ: HP Books, 1984. Reprinted with permission.

said Dr. Clayton Thomas of the Harvard School of Public Health, and a member of the U.S. Olympic Committee's Sports Medicine Committee, in an interview given to *The Washington Post* in 1979. Thomas went on to say, "I don't think you could do this for an extended length of time without running a great risk of doing permanent damage to her endocrine normality as well as her long-range potential for childbearing.

"I think you even run the risk of causing neoplasms [abnormal growths] or cancers in some part of her body that would not have developed if she hadn't taken these steroids. That may be a rather free-wheeling statement, but I feel strongly about it—particularly in light of the problems we have seen with a female hormone that was widely used and thought to be completely safe; the oral contraceptive pill."

Women's bodies produce many steroids normally. Steroids are responsible for growth and metabolism, and some of a women's sex hormones, the estrogens, are steroids too. The problem with women taking anabolic steroids is that they are synthetic derivatives of the strongest androgen, the strongest male sex hormone, testosterone.

It is true that women's own bodies produce small quantities of testosterone naturally, and it is generally conceded that testosterone is responsible for a woman's sex drive. A woman's natural testosterone is in a delicate balance with her own estrogens that govern her reproductive cycle and feminine characteristics—breasts, distribution of body hair, and adipose tissue.

Women are not as big or as strong or usually as sexually aggressive as men because of the dominant relationship of their estrogens relative to their androgen, their testosterone.

Freaks

Said Pat Connolly, former women's track coach at UCLA, "It's sad, because the use of [anabolic] steroids does—I hate to say this, but it's true—it makes freaks out of women. Women are beautiful creatures the way God made them, and they can do a lot of things tremendously well. We don't even have any idea of how well we can do some things because we haven't been trying very long. But by taking a male hormone, a woman is really changing what she is all about.

"I've seen some women who have been taking them, and their personalities change. It's just really sad and depressing that steroids are part of the scene, and that a woman instead of perfecting her body the way God gave it to her, has to make herself into some creature that's not really a woman and not really a man."

Anabolic refers to a substance that promotes growth or repair. *Androgen* refers to steroids that produce or stimulate male characteristics. An androgen produces male sex characteristics and has a second major effect, body building. Androgens are in a biological antagonism with estrogens. In men, androgens develop men's sex organs, beard growth, skin thickness, body hair, and depth of voice. Androgens also develop weight and muscle mass by increasing protein assimilation. There is no such thing as a strictly anabolic steroid, meaning a strictly bodybuilding drug. Anabolic steroids are androgenic and are masculinizing. All affect sexual processes and characteristics. When a woman takes an anabolic steroid, she is taking a masculine growth substance that is antagonistic to her own estrogens. She is a female turning male.

"The risks that women take are especially great because there has been little research into the effects of anabolic steroids on women's bodies."

And she is taking a very great risk.

When the American College of Sports Medicine issued its position paper on anabolic steroids in 1978, it said:

> The use of anabolic steroids by females, particularly those who are either prepubertal or have not attained full growth, is especially dangerous. The undesired side effects include masculinization, disruption of normal growth patterns, voice changes, acne, hirsutism and enlargement of the clitoris.
>
> The long term effects on reproductive function are unknown, but anabolic steroids may be harmful in this area. Their ability to interfere with the menstrual cycle has been well documented.
>
> For these reasons, all concerned with advising, training, coaching, and providing medical care for female athletes should exercise *all precautions available to prevent the use of anabolic steroids* by female athletes [emphasis added].

The risks that women take are especially great because there has been little research into the effects of anabolic steroids on women's bodies. There have been dozens of investigations into the effects of anabolic steroids on males, and although much remains to be studied, something is known about what happens to men when they take moderate doses of these drugs. But scientists believe that the potential of anabolic steroids to harm women, both short- and long-term, is so great, scientists will not even take the risk of performing experiments to see if anabolic steroids improve women's athletic performances.

Going Against Nature

Any biologist, any physiologist, any endocrinologist, any pharmacologist knows that he is giving directly against nature if he gives a woman an anabolic steroid, i.e., a male growth hormone. Any team physician, coach, or trainer worthy of the title knows it too, and every female athlete and parent of a budding female athlete ought to know it.

The dangers of anabolic steroids to women are especially great in adolescent women and in those women who are also taking oral contraceptives. It is difficult to imagine a greater assault on a woman's natural hormonal system than the double whammy of synthetic estrogens (oral contraceptives) and synthetic androgens (anabolic steroids).

The risk of getting breast cancer in the normal population of women is 10 percent. Anabolic steroids will increase this risk many times. It is true that certain steroids are used in cancer therapy, but in most cases they are more likely to induce a cancer than cure or prevent one, especially in a healthy individual.

If you want to get an idea of the risks of women taking anabolic steroids, all you have to do is read one of the manufacturer's inserts that is sold with each package, Dianabol for example, and reprinted in the *Physician's Desk Reference*. It states in the section called "Contraindications":

"1 Carcinoma of the breast in females;

2 Masculinization of the fetus;

3 In females: hirsutism, male pattern baldness, deepening of the voice, clitoral enlargement.

THESE CHANGES ARE USUALLY IRREVERSIBLE EVEN AFTER PROMPT DISCONTINUANCE OF THERAPY AND ARE NOT PREVENTED BY CONCOMITANT USAGE OF ESTROGENS."

Female athletes on oral contraceptives have been excused from the doping tests because the persons responsible for the testing have sometimes been unable to distinguish between the metabolic products of these two kinds of drugs in the urine. Thus there is a strong incentive for women taking anabolic steroids also to take oral contraceptives. It all comes down to an incredible risk.

Effects of Anabolic Steroids

Metabolism is the sum of all chemical and energy processes, those that build up and those that tear down, in reference to living cells and their exchange of energy. It is the working of life from the smallest to the largest of living things. It represents an interlocking network of cellular functions.

Anabolic steroids have a variety of effects on female metabolism. They regulate the protein in connective tissue and bone. They inhibit the pituitary gland's ability to produce the hormones that stimulate the ovaries into producing estrogens. They affect the development of internal and external female organs. If a woman, pregnant with a female child, takes anabolic steroids, these drugs will have a masculinizing effect on her unborn baby. A female baby still in the uterus whose mother takes anabolic

steroids will develop some male traits, extra hair, and clitoral enlargement.

Even in an adult woman, these undesirable effects can be irreversible. Many of the Soviet and East German women who took anabolic steroids and developed low voices and beards are stuck with them.

The effects of anabolic steroids on a woman's reproductive system and secondary sexual characteristics are in addition to those which also occur in men. In both men and women, anabolic steroids increase the body's normal insulin activity, upset the body's enzyme systems, break down genetic patterns in the nuclei of the body's cells, affect the absorption of calcium in the bones, stop bone growth in young persons who have not reached their full height, cause the body to retain water, produce the typical "moon-faced" appearance, produce acne, and destroy the kidney and the liver whose job it is, among others, to detoxify alien synthetic chemicals such as anabolic steroids.

Because of the potential damaging effects of anabolic steroids on the genetic material in the nuclei of the cell, many women athletes who took anabolic steroids are now afraid to have children. Says twenty-five-year-old Renate Vogel Heinrich, who nine years ago was a champion East German swimmer and who was brought up on anabolic steroids: "I would love to have children, but I am afraid that I would bring them into the world handicapped."

"Many women athletes who took anabolic steroids are now afraid to have children."

Warned Dr. Thomas, a consultant on human reproduction at the Harvard School of Public Health, "Supplying such drugs [anabolic steroids] to women may in the future be reclassified from unethical to criminal."

Despite warnings from concerned doctors like Dr. Thomas, anabolic steroid use is reported to be on the increase among women competing at top international and collegiate levels. Many women have been caught doping and disqualified in the last few years, and many women have "taken and told."

Even Women Get Caught

At the Winter Olympic Games in Lake Placid in 1980, doping tests were administered to two athletes picked at random from every team event, the first four finishers in every individual event, and every athlete whose performance was much better than expected. The women were not excepted. They too gave about two ounces of urine to the Olympic drug watchdogs who were looking for athletes who had taken stimulants, narcotics, anabolic steroids, and other banned substances.

Said Olgo Fikotova Connolly, a 1956 gold medal winner who has participated in five Olympic Games as a discus thrower, "There is no way in the world a woman nowadays, in the throwing events—at least the shot put and the discus—I'm not sure about the javelin—can break the record unless she is on steroids. These awful drugs have changed the complexion of track and field.

"It's a terrible thing, but it's true. Once a girl has developed her natural powers to the utmost, she has to start taking something that will alter her natural endowments of strength in order to continue the quest for a world record. She sees these big balloons competing, and she thinks she must become a balloon too."

But with all the testing, how do they get by with it? Well, doping tests are not done at all sports events. And sometimes, as mentioned before, women have not been tested because they said they were on the pill, and the tests were not sensitive enough to distinguish between anabolic steroids and oral contraceptive steroids. Then it's possible to take anabolic steroids and go off them in sufficient time before a sports competition so that they won't show up in the urine.

> *"Doping is a methodical, covert practice in the state-supported training camps of East Germany."*

But not all women have got by with it. In 1979, seven top women were banned from Olympic competition *for life* by the Amateur Athletic Federation because they were caught taking anabolic steroids. This means that the top three 1,500-meter runners of 1979 could not take part in the 1980 Moscow Games, even if their sentences were commuted to the eighteen-month disqualification period that commonly results from an appeal.

Banned for life were two Romanians—Natalia Maracescu, who holds the world mile record for women, and Ileana Silai, the 1968 Olympic 800-meter silver medalist—and a Bulgarian—Totka Petrova, who won the World Cup for 1,500 meters in Montreal in 1979. Also penalized were two junior discus throwers from the Soviet Union.

Dr. Tony Daly, a member of the International Amateur Athletic Federation, said he had been unaware before the banning that middle distance women runners were using anabolic steroids. . . .

It is generally believed that the most recent group of banned women athletes got caught because their trainers had not realized that the tests for anabolic steroids had become more sensitive and specific.

Athletes used to believe they could stop taking the drugs two to three weeks before a test, but now sophisticated equipment can detect anabolic steroids taken as far back as two months.

Some cynics believe that catching Ileana Silai doping will increase anabolic steroid use by track and field women athletes. At thirty years of age, Silai broke four minutes in the 1,500 meter race, a feat that is seen by many as proving that steroids work and that if women want to break records they had better climb aboard the drug bandwagon.

Renate's Story

Now when Renate Vogel Heinrich looks at pictures of herself, during her competitive years, she says, "I get sick. We never really noticed what we looked like, because swimmers were always kept together. It didn't hit me until an old friend said, 'Wow Renate, you speak like a man, and you've got those unbelievably broad shoulders.'"

Renate was relatively lucky. Her weight has dropped from 155 to 130 pounds well distributed over a five-foot-eight-inch frame, and her voice has risen to its normal pitch. Renate managed to flee from a training environment where anabolic steroids were handed to her like morning orange juice. "It was just given to us along with the vitamin pills," she relates.

Ms. Vogel Heinrich is not so confident about the long-term effects that taking anabolic steroids for so many years may have had on her body and freely admits her fear of having children. Concerned about her husband who is still behind the iron curtain, she does not freely admit how she escaped to Stuttgart in West Germany in the late summer of 1979. When she left, her husband, Volker Heinrich, was immediately arrested by the East Germans.

Now Renate spreads her story about East German training camps and drugs, a story that has done more than catching a few athletes taking drugs, to convince sports authorities that doping is a methodical, covert practice in the state-supported training camps of East Germany.

In 1974, Renate Vogel held the world record for women in the 100-meter breaststroke. She was a national heroine, which meant that she enjoyed privileges denied to most East Germans: a luxury apartment, choice goods, and foreign travel. It was the foreign travel that opened her eyes to the intellectual restrictions of the East German Communist Party. Renate, like many tourists, enjoyed taking photographs on her trips, but when she returned to her home land, she found her slide shows were censored. Said Renate, "They let me show my slides of Hiroshima but not of Disneyland or Hollywood."

Renate quit the drugs—and perforce her training— but when she defied the authorities, she lost a special privilege. She was not able to participate in the program run by medical specialists that slowly decelerates an athlete who is coming off training and training drugs. Renate went "cold turkey," which worsened her already bad health.

"When I stood up," she says, "I often lost consciousness. If I moved my head too quickly, I blacked out." Her health and the social censure and ostracism in her native country were finally too much, and Renate went AWOL to provide us with a firsthand account of programmed athletic training in Eastern Europe where "success is as exactly planned as is production out of a nationalized factory."

Dosage

Most women in the West who try to increase their strength and endurance with anabolic steroids know that they are corrupting their natural hormone systems, and they are concerned about "the right amount," which they believe is an amount that helps them win without permanently damaging their health.

"There are no 'right doses' of anabolic steroids for women."

In general, women athletes who dope do so in lower doses and for shorter periods of time than their male counterparts. Said Pat Connolly:

> Women who start with a very small dose for four or six weeks, train on it, and then go off the drug and let their bodies get normal again still have the benefit of that training. They have taught the muscles to do new things, and the know-how remains. They can continue to compete at a higher level even though they're off the drug.

I think women coaches feel a lot differently about it than males who coach females. There are some highly principled male coaches who don't want their girls fiddling with that stuff, but there are others who let their egos get in the way. All they care about is performance, and when that happens, there doesn't seem to be any ethics anymore.

> Very few of the girls taking steroids have good medical supervision. No doctor would prescribe them for a woman. A few "understanding" doctors say that, while they are "unaware" a patient is on steroids, they will do regular blood, liver, and urine checks to watch for abnormalities.

What these "understanding" physicians should also be doing is explaining that by the time these so-called abnormalities show up, the female athlete who has taken anabolic steroids may have irreparably, irreversibly, damaged her body. These "abnormalities" are often signs of permanent underlying damage to the body's metabolic and excretory systems. In addition to menstrual irregularities and masculinization, there is no doubt that a woman who takes anabolic steroid drugs risks severe long-term effects—tumors, cancer, and babies born with birth defects.

There are no "right doses" of anabolic steroids for women, and no amount of medical monitoring by "understanding" physicians can make it so. There is no amount of informed consent that can make it all right for women to risk so much for athletics. There is no time in a woman's athletic career when taking anabolic steroids is worth it.

Some coaches believe that if women take anabolic steroids they should do it after ten to fifteen years of training, at the peak of their careers, and during their middle twenties. Although the side effects of anabolic steroids are somewhat less devastating at this age than during the growth period when bones are not fully developed, suggesting that it is better to take anabolic steroids at this time of a woman's life is rather like saying that lung cancer alone is better than cancer and tuberculosis.

No coach, no physician, should in any way, tacitly or otherwise, appear to condone anabolic steroids. Every parent of a young woman who is on a team should make certain that drugs are not a part of her training, and that she knows the special danger of anabolic steroids. Any woman who has taken anabolic steroids in the past should have her hormone levels checked and should have liver- and kidney-function tests.

Everyone (fans, athletes, and health professionals) should support an educational campaign to make certain that female athletes and female potential athletes know the special long- and short-term dangers that anabolic steroids pose to women.

Bob Goldman is a former competitive athlete who has done extensive research on steroid use in athletics. Patricia Bush is a professor at the Georgetown University of Medicine. Ronald Klatz is staff physician at the Chicago College of Osteopathic Medicine.

"Because no-one really knows how a highly trained female athlete should look people are often suspicious of a woman who does not conform to our stereotype."

viewpoint 86

Steroid Use Among Female Athletes Is Exaggerated

Tom Donohoe and Neil Johnson

That is not a normal physiological female body. I've treated Olympic female athletes in 34 countries but I've never seen a body like that. I can truthfully say that I think there is something chemically different about her physical make-up and it hasn't come from weight-lifting.

Dr. Leroy Perry, Los Angeles chiropractor, talking about Czech middle-distance runner Jarmila Kratochvilova.

This statement embodies the thoughts of many people when they first see muscular women athletes like Kratochvilova. However, there is a growing school of enlightened opinion which views this as Victorian resistance to the relentless upsurge of women in sport. Successful female athletes often have physiques that put many men to shame. The fact that they do makes most of us defensive, yet there is no reason why women should not have a powerful physique. We should ask whether our social constraints regarding the female 'ideal' be allowed to dictate the development of women's sport. Instead of questioning the physical and chemical make-up of Jarmila Kratochvilova perhaps Dr. Perry should have scrutinised his own male chauvinism. Having said this, there is something about the bodies of women such as runner Kratochvilova and weightlifter Bev Francis which tests the mettle of even the most liberal-minded people. . . .

Women are rapidly pushing through physical and psychological barriers to become a real force in modern sport. Women's athletics records are being set at a much faster rate than those of men. If trends continue then women's marathon times will equal those of men by the end of the century.

Women currently swim at speeds comparable to those of men in 1970 and their middle-distance running times are now on a par with those of men of the 1930s. According to Dr. Paul Wade, consultant to the US Olympic Committee Elite Program, the women's high jump world record has improved by 40 per cent over the last 60 years compared with only 29 per cent by men in over 100 years. As Dr. Wade points out, this discrepancy cannot continue. Women's sport is still in its infancy and only undergoing phenomenal advances in performance because women are learning to train in a way that was previously denied them; perhaps quite soon their rates of improvement will fall to those of men. Ultimately, sheer physical strength will mark the difference between male and female athletic capability, although several endurance events may favour the woman's more efficient fat-burning processes and her ability to control body temperature without excessive water loss through sweating. Given appropriate encouragement and facilities women should eventually compete on equal terms with men in those events where greater total strength is not important.

The New Female Athlete

Inevitably, our male-dominated Western societies will be forced to welcome a faster, stronger woman who may not embrace our vision of the female physical 'ideal'. The problem for these women is that they first have to convince society that they have not acquired their muscular physiques through the use of drugs. Because no-one really knows how a highly trained female athlete should look people are often suspicious of a woman who does not conform to our stereotype. Beauty-conscious female American swimmers seem to have a history of narrow-mindedness in this respect. When they were thoroughly beaten by their dedicated East German opponents at the 1976 Montreal Olympics there

Tom Donohoe and Neil Johnson, *Foul Play*. New York: Basil Blackwell, 1986. Reprinted with permission.

were the usual complaints about Communist steroid abuse; thankfully, a level-headed section of the American public put their sportswomen in order. Letters to the *New York Times* said:

> Perhaps the East German women take their skills more seriously and are capable of viewing themselves as attractive, sexual women, not by their measurements, but because of who they are as human beings.

In contrast to the verbal assault on Eastern countries there is now a growing realisation that the United States has an enormous influence on drug use in sports. At a conference on drug abuse in early 1985, Sir Arthur Gold, President of the European Athletic Association, rebuked other officials for specifically attacking East Germany: 'I ask you to look West to the United States. . . . Much of it [drug abuse] would stop if athletes were not having to keep up with the American Joneses'. Of course, the East Germans are not angels. At Montreal, when comments were made about their masculine physiques and deep voices the East German coach said 'we have come here to swim, not sing'. There are many stories about the organised abuse of steroids by the East Germans. Some of these are probably exaggerated but others have a little more credibility. The 1974 100m breaststroke world record holder was Renate Vogel. When she defected to the West in 1979 she told how steroids were handed around 'along with the vitamin pills'. While official involvement in doping is often attacked as State control by Western critics, and certainly cannot be condoned, there are probably many American or European athletes who would welcome the medical backup that accompanies tacit approval of drug abuse. This is not to say that the East achieves results through its use of doping agents; these female athletes have a reputation for hard work and discipline, something which, until recently, set them apart from women in the West. Dr. Paul Wade is convinced that the fear of 'getting big' prevents our female athletes from stepping over the line into the weights room, yet this is exactly what they must do in order to compete effectively with the Communist bloc women who have more dedication to their sport than to their figures. Resistance to strenuous physical training amongst Western women goes back a long way. Eleanor Holm who won the 100m backstroke event for America at the 1932 Los Angeles Olympics was regarded as a 'Venus of the Waves'. After setting a new Olympic record she probably did a great disservice to the future of women's athletics by saying: 'The moment I find swimming makes me look like an amazon, I'll toss it aside. My appearance is more important to my life as a woman than any championship'. Her lack of commitment became obvious on the 9-day voyage to Germany as part of the 1936 Olympic team. Once on board, her drinking and, for the time,

unrestrained behaviour caused a scandal. Before reaching Hamburg she was expelled from the team by members of the American Olympic Committee; despite protestation from the press and some of her fellow athletes she was not reinstated.

Women and Steroids

Having established the extent of the bias against muscular women in sport it might be possible to approach the question of drug abuse more objectively. Not all 'big' women use anabolic steroids but some certainly do. A spate of disqualifications and bans occurred in the late 1970s as a result of tests for these drugs. The first Olympic track and field athlete ever to be disqualified was a woman. Danuta Rosani of Poland qualified for the final of the discus in 1976 but failed the steroid test before having a chance to compete. In 1977 the East German shot-putter Ilona Slupianek lost her gold medal at the European Cup, while Nadyezhda Tkachenko forfeited her pentathlon gold a year later at the Prague-held European Championships. Despite these early warnings, no fewer than seven Olympic class women were banned for life after being caught using steroids in 1979. Part of the reason for these 'scoops' was that the detection methods changed slightly to enable scientists to distinguish between anabolic steroids and the closely related oral contraceptive steroids which had previously interfered with the radiommunoassay stage.

"[Communist bloc] female athletes have a reputation for hard work and discipline, something which, until recently, set them apart from women in the West."

Although women produce their own androgenic steroids from their adrenal glands, these are not synthesised in amounts large enough to cause masculinising effects. A man taking anabolic steroids is simply adding to his own high levels of anabolic/androgenic hormones and usually looks no more than a bigger, more muscular version of what he was before. Women, on the other hand, by taking anabolic steroids, shift the balance of their appearance so that it resembles that of a man. Their normal menstrual cycle is often suppressed and certain masculine features may appear. For example, the clitoris, which is a penis equivalent, may start to grow (clitoral hypertrophy) to embarrassing proportions; the vocal cords may lengthen to deepen the voice and a masculine pattern of hair growth and baldness may begin. All three of these problems are usually irreversible even after the anabolic steroids are discontinued and the inclusion of 'female' hormones (oestrogens) will not prevent their appearance.

Another problem that worries cheating female athletes is the possibility of birth defects as a result of steroid abuse. The foetus is much more susceptible than the adult to the effects of many drugs but anabolic steroids present a unique and frightening problem. Research has shown quite clearly that exposing female animals to androgens, at certain so-called 'critical' periods in their development, can cause masculinisation. In humans the critical period occurs while the baby is still in the uterus and if the pregnant mother is given androgens it can cause a condition in the foetus called 'pseudohermaphroditism' where male sex organs partially develop on an otherwise female body. The danger of giving birth to such babies is very real if high doses of anabolic/androgenic steroids are taken *during* pregnancy. Few women would find themselves in this position since pregnancy usually means a temporary curtailment of competitive athletics. . . .

Sex Tests and Femininity

Although women are closing the gap on men's records they still have a considerable amount of work yet to do. Not surprisingly, to maintain fair play in women's events it has been necessary to introduce sex tests to ensure that successful women are the gender they claim to be. At one time this was done by purely physical examination, the female competitors queuing up in the medical officer's waiting room dressed in only a towel. This procedure was embarrassing for officials and competitors alike, so more sophisticated methods were devised. Current sex tests use methods which detect the differences found in cells as a result of having male (XY) or female (XX) chromosomes. Thus, femininity is now determined by demonstrating the existence of the so-called Barr bodies that are present in 20 to 50 per cent of a woman's cell nuclei; men have none at all. This sort of test can be performed on skin cells from inside the mouth (a buccal scrape) or from the root of a hair.

In 1975 Dr. Daniel Hanley, the US representative to the IOC's Medical Committee described sex testing as 'an expensive overreaction to a remote possibility', mainly because a man has never been caught impersonating a woman at the Olympics. This is only true now because of sex tests which, at the time of their introduction, caused a flurry of incidents that more than justified their necessity. At two consecutive Olympic Games the mighty Tamara Press, from Georgia in Russia, dominated the field events. At Rome in 1960 she won the gold medal in the shot put and the silver in the discus; 4 years later at Tokyo she went one better and won the gold in both events. Tamara's sister Irina came sixth in the shot put and it seemed that both women were set to clean-up at Mexico City in 1968. However, when sex-testing was introduced in 1966 the two 'sisters' dropped out of competition, never to return. Exactly the same thing happened with the Romanian world champion high-jumper Iolanda Balas and two more Russians: long-jumper Tatyana Schelkanova and former 400m world record holder Maria Itkina. Whether these athletes were really men or just women dosed with anabolic steroids was never discovered. Another celebrated case is that of Erika Schineggar, the women's downhill ski-racer of 1966. She had her male identity revealed by the advent of chromosome tests in 1967. It was later alleged that 'her' male sex organs had been hidden inside her body since birth. She changed her name to Eric, married a woman and became a father. . . .

"Not all 'big' women use anabolic steroids but some certainly do."

Suspicions have been raised about the femininity of Jarmila Kratochvilova, the powerful middle-distance runner from Czechoslovakia. She holds world records for the 400m and 800m and won both gold medals at the 1983 World Championships at Helsinki. She was later voted European Sportswoman of the Year. After a long battle to finally beat Marita Koch in 1981, Kratochvilova now dominates the track at major competitions. To Western eyes her gaunt, muscular appearance is far from feminine, but in her quiet village home in Bohemia she claims 'I am just a country girl'. According to her coach Miroslav Kvac this tough upbringing, together with her punishing training programme, is the real secret of her success. Sports journalist Rob Hughes has witnessed her training routine and says:

> The intensity of training is unequalled by any I have witnessed by any other woman and all but a handful of boxers and male athletes in two decades of sports watching.

Almost 20 years of Kvac's programme have turned Kratochvilova into a powerhouse of a woman with a motivation to win that matches her strength. She is a certified woman, according to the sex chromosome test, and regards accusations about her gender as ridiculous. Although insinuations concerning advanced hormone substances are rife, particularly amongst disgruntled Western coaches, some people see Kratochvilova's success as the product of training. The American women's Olympic track coach Brooks Johnson insists that his proteges stop regarding Kratochvilova as a freak: 'They have to be willing to train as hard or her accomplishments will never seem attainable'.

The quote that opens this [viewpoint] forces us to take sides in the issue of changing female physiques. If we accept that women can never be physically confused with men, no matter how much training they undergo, then we must also accept that 'superwomen' athletes are the product of an artificial process.

Bev Francis is an Australian weightlifter and bodybuilder who weighs nearly 13 stones (85kg) and has a 42 in. (1.2m) chest of solid muscle. Unlike many young women she would not resign herself to a lifetime of dieting; instead she used her natural bulk to best advantage by taking up weightlifting; in her own words she resolved to 'make myself stronger and really achieve something in sport'. She has certainly done that. Bev Francis is probably the strongest woman in the world with squat and deadlift records of over 440 lb (200kg).

"There is no physiological reason to assume that the only way for a woman to become muscular is by abusing male hormones."

Together with other, similarly shaped, women Mrs. Francis has achieved negative results in tests for anabolic steroids but many people are still suspicious of her physique. However, any doubts about the femininity of such athletes could simply be due to a natural bias away from tough, hardworking women. There is no physiological reason to assume that the only way for a woman to become muscular is by abusing male hormones; hard training alone can do it. After all, a woman's breasts, universally accepted symbols of the female gender, are mainly fat, the first thing to go when strenuous exercise burns off excess adiposity. The thick necks and flat chests of these women may stretch the bounds of credibility but perhaps these will become the hallmark of the modern sportswoman.

Western resistance to the physical development of women could seriously hinder the advance of women's athletics such that it never realises its true potential, though hopefully we have now straddled the more difficult social barriers. As more women cross the dividing line between male and female sexual dimorphism the 'he-woman' will achieve more acceptance in a culture which expects women to be nothing but grace and charm.

Tom Donohoe is a research scientist at the Institute of Neurology in London. Neil Johnson is a researcher in pharmaceutics.

"The family has a lot at stake; it is the entity that often is hardest hit by the drug abuse problem—sometimes even devastated."

Family Therapy Can Provide Effective Treatment

Arlene Utada and Alfred S. Friedman

Each year hundreds of thousands of families in the United States are challenged, distressed, and sometimes torn apart by a teenage family member using drugs. Parents, adolescent substance abusers, and the other family members are caught in a desperate situation that may escalate into a major crisis in the life of the family. Many of these families may be confronted with recurring crises over a period of years. What is perhaps most disconcerting about this situation is the likelihood that the parents themselves unwittingly contributed to the development or the escalation of the drug problem.

Although the fact that there are many harmful illicit drugs readily available to young people makes possible the drug abuse problem, the problem cannot be explained solely by this fact. One might say that even with the availability of the substances young people should be more enlightened or exercise more self-control or, at the least, should have been frightened away or deterred from use of these harmful substances. There is also the role of the family to consider in the development of this problem: Why have the parents not been effective in raising children or adolescents so that they do not become involved in substance abuse? The family has a lot at stake; it is the entity that often is hardest hit by the drug abuse problem—sometimes even devastated—when it happens to an adolescent member of the family. Some parents may actually experience more suffering from the youngster's involvement in drug abuse than the adolescent abuser experiences himself or herself.

The parents unfortunately are in the front-line trenches in this battle against drug abuse and usually have the main responsibility for dealing with and solving the problem. Why this is so needs further explanation. The parents may feel that they

didn't create this problem but that it was imposed upon them: if it were not for the fact that their youngster came under the influence of the wrong friends; if it were not for the government's failure to adequately control the large-scale trafficking in drugs; if it were not for a deterioration in the social and moral values of our society. . . . On the other hand, if the problem is explained by the fact that this has become a drug-using society, and that using drugs has become a rite of passage for all adolescents, why have half the adolescents not tried drugs at all, and the majority who have experimented with drugs have only used them infrequently or occasionally at a party? Why have only approximately 10 percent become so seriously and heavily involved in regular substance abuse or addiction that it has become the central theme in their lives, and has negatively affected their development and careers, and the lives of their families? It is reasonable that the effort to understand the problems of this 10 percent should include not only the study of the adolescents as individuals, but the study of the families, and certain situations and conditions in the histories of these families, and the histories of the particular child growing up in these families.

No Single Cause

Thus, blaming the peer group, or blaming the larger society, the schools, the churches, or the drug enforcement agencies, is not very realistic. No one or any single cause is to blame; not the parents, not the grandparents, not the peer group. All are caught up together in a complicated situation and the solutions are not easy to find. In many cases the ways that the parents have contributed to the development of the problem are subtle and hard to see. Was it just that they did not listen to the youngster in an understanding enough way, or they didn't pay enough attention, or were rejecting, or too strict or controlling, or not firm enough, or too permissive, or too indulgent? The parents need the help of someone not directly and emotionally involved in the family situation, who can perceive objectively what happens in the family, is skilled and wise and experienced, will listen with understanding and discernment, and will intervene in constructive ways that the family can accept and respond to.

"For the future welfare of the child it is essential that parents become involved in whatever treatment process is recommended."

Even relying on a psychiatrist or on the expertise of a specialized drug treatment program to solve the problem is not sufficient. The family almost inevitably has to be actively involved in the solution, since it may well have been part of the problem. The problem needs to be understood within the framework of the family, and in terms of the dynamics of the system of relationships and interactions that have developed in the family. Every family is unique in regard to the constellation of interrelationships that have developed during its history, and these relationships operate at more than one level. For example, one family can be described as having "pseudo-mutual" relationships: the family members appear on the surface to get along with each other, to be loyal and unified, to defend each other against outsiders; but this is partly a facade kept up at the price of suppression of resentments and hostilities felt toward each other. Another family may be openly argumentative and conflictual, but with deeper ties of affection and love than the first family. Given this and even greater degrees of complexity of each family's system, it requires time and understanding on the part of a skilled family counselor or therapist to enter into the various levels on which the family interrelationships are operating. From such empathic understanding one may find some clues for helping the family change its pattern of interactions or some of the attitudes and feelings that the members have toward each other.

There is a growing awareness that parents are not only inextricably involved, but that for the future welfare of the child it is essential that parents become involved in whatever treatment process is recommended. Adult drug abusers have more independent control of their life situations than young drug abusers. Most youngsters, even after successfully completing an inpatient or residential treatment program, must return to their families and the living conditions they were in when they used drugs.

Some adolescents abuse drugs to gain attention in a family that otherwise ignores them. Family therapists who specialize in treating substance-abusing young people have found that the families of their patients often are conflictual or disengaged, or lack open communication, mutual respect, reasonable organization, and close, loving relationships. The parents and children often are alienated and the parents may be poor models, or may be overly controlling. In such cases, expert assistance may be needed. The drug use itself is of deep concern but cannot be treated outside the context of these other factors.

Researchers found that initial use of illicit drugs by adolescents is related to parent-child relationships. Adolescents who feel close to their families are less likely than others to begin using illicit substances. Conversely, the children of parents who are perceived as maintaining strict controls and parents who tend to disagree about discipline are more likely to begin using illicit drugs. Use of drugs by parents has also been found to be an important predictor of adolescent drug use.

Family Factors

Findings produced by the National Youth Polydrug Study show the relationship between family factors and adolescent drug abuse:

> Adolescents whose parents had drug problems, alcohol problems, psychiatric problems, or problems with the law are more heavily involved in drug abuse than adolescents whose parents were not reported to have such problems.
> There is a significant positive correlation between the number of problems reported in families and the number and types of drugs used by the adolescent offspring.

High school students who use drugs spend more time with peers who have similar drug use behavior patterns and are more likely to be estranged from parents and other adults than students who do not use drugs.

Absence of parent, lack of parental closeness, unconventional parents, excessively passive mothers, lack of perceived closeness to parents, and drinking and drug use patterns of parents have been positively correlated with drug use.

Families of adolescent drug users differ significantly from families in which the adolescent offspring either do not use drugs or have used marijuana only experimentally. In contrast to experimental drug users or nonusers, adolescents with serious drug problems come from families with certain characteristics:

> Parents are perceived as having relatively less influence than peers. Both parents are perceived to be more approving of drug use.

Offspring perceive less love from both parents, particularly fathers.

Less shared authority and poorer communication characterize the family.

Less spontaneous problem solving occurs in structured family interaction tasks. . . .

Today, most adolescent drug treatment programs (outpatient, residential, and hospital settings) provide family services. Increasingly, programs have come to realize that adolescent substance abuse impacts severely on the family and that the whole family may need assistance to cope with the problem.

The Main Problem

Most families who come with or bring an adolescent member for drug abuse treatment see this adolescent as the only or main problem in the family. Their attitude is that the adolescent needs to be treated or controlled so that the family can get some relief from the problem, but not that the whole family needs treatment. If they agree to attend any family sessions they are likely to see their role as providing information about the behavior of the young client to the client's therapist. The family therapist however may view the adolescent drug abuser as an integral part of a dysfunctional, disturbed, or disorganized family. It follows from this view that the family needs to change. In some families it appears that the drug abuse behavior of the adolescent may serve the function, whether intentionally or not, to maintain the family homeostasis or status quo. For example, if the parents are in a state of emotional divorce, or have a very conflictual marital relationship, it may appear that the parents need to stay together to cope jointly with the continuing family crises posed by the adolescent's drug abuse problems. This deflects the parents from facing the problem of their relationship, and avoids the greater danger of the family breaking up. Or in another family it may appear that a parent needs to keep an adolescent dependent in such a way that the adolescent does not become self-sufficient and independent enough to move away from the parents. A mother may believe that she continues to give her adolescent child money to buy drugs so that he or she does not steal, and thus to avoid the risk of the child's going to jail. At the same time this parental behavior may operate to keep the child tied to the parent.

Even if it is assumed that the family was not significantly involved originally in the development of the adolescent's drug problem, the family can, with expert guidance, help the drug abusing youngster to overcome the problem. This may develop into a long-term endeavor, in the more severe cases, requiring patience, firmness, persistence, and tolerance of frustration on the part of the parents. For this reason the parents often need the support of a professional during the process.

A central concept of family therapy is to work with and attempt to change the family system rather than the individual family members. The family, rather than the identified drug-abusing client, is the main focus of treatment. In some cases, the emotional atmosphere is so consistently negative or pathological in the family that it is necessary to treat teenage drug users in a different living milieu, away from the family. Inpatient or residential treatment may also be needed by young clients who require a maximum degree of structure and control for their drug abuse and other problem behavior. The parents themselves may welcome the separation from the youngster, since it promises temporary relief from recurrent crises and behavior that they may feel helpless to control. In situations like these, the adolescent client is treated separately until it is determined that family interaction should begin. Where possible, programs have youngsters and their families participate in the same sessions, to help prepare them for the youngster's return home.

"A central concept of family therapy is to work with and attempt to change the family system rather than the individual family members."

Not every family is available to participate in family therapy, and some are not willing to be involved. There are some families who are afraid of what might be exposed. In a recent case in our drug abuse treatment clinic, it was difficult to get the mother and the 15-year-old daughter, the drug client, together for a session. The mother showed up alone for the first scheduled family session, and stated that she was afraid to meet together with the daughter. She was very angry at her daughter's behavior, and was concerned that if she expressed her anger, it would be harmful to her daughter and would complicate the situation further. The daughter had started in individual counseling and was cooperating with the treatment. But she was adamant about not having joint sessions with her mother. It turned out that the mother had undergone major surgery several months earlier, and the daughter was afraid that if the anger between her and her mother were allowed to surface it could conceivably kill her mother. In such a situation the family is not ready for family therapy. Often family members need professional help and support on an individual basis before they are ready to face joint family sessions. It is possible that, in the case example cited, the mother and daughter could, after adequate preparation, have several joint sessions in which they could reach a better mutual understanding and a more satisfactory relationship.

Many adolescent drug abuse clients resist the idea of involving their parents and other family members in treatment. They want to be in control of what is talked about in the therapy or counseling sessions, to tell their side of the story or to withhold information about their questionable behavior. They are often also afraid of confrontation with their parents. Thus, they need to be reassured that the therapist is not going to side with the parents against them. Parents are also afraid of what the adolescent might reveal in the family therapy sessions: a parent's questionable behavior, a family secret, or problems in the parents' marital relationship.

It is important to get the parents working together to reinforce the family's generational hierarchy. At the same time, it is necessary to find appropriate ways to join and support the adolescent. Each side should be helped to recognize what is legitimate in the other's position.

Family Problems

The therapist looks for possible ways that the family problems, the negative aspects of the family system to which the adolescent drug abuser is reacting, can be changed so that the more positive and functional tendencies of the adolescent can emerge and be facilitated. Also, the therapist looks for potential assets and strengths that can be developed and actualized in each family member, and facilitates the adolescent's developmental need for individuation and differentiation.

One of the family situations in which it is easiest to see how the parents have contributed to the development of the problem is where they have been poor role models, particularly if one of them has been a substance abuser himself or herself (most often an alcoholic father). This inevitably has caused a serious problem in the history of the family and in the childhood development of the adolescent. . . .

While the parents of the majority of adolescent drug abusers who come to treatment may not be users of illicit drugs themselves, or have alcohol problems, a number of other characteristics are seen in many of the families of adolescent drug abusers:

1. The family is split (the parents are divorced or separated).

2. The father has been abusive to the adolescent child.

3. The father has shown rejection of the adolescent.

4. The father displays impulsive and aggressive behavior.

5. The emotionally immature mother displays ambivalent feelings toward the adolescent (concerned about her, caring for her in some ways and trying to hold on to her, but resenting her and feeling inadequate as a mother and overburdened by the responsibility for her).

6. There is a lack of open, honest communication and trust between the mother and father, and between each parent and the adolescent child.

7. There is a lack of adequate understanding between the mother and child.

8. There is a breakdown of communication between the parents regarding the child, a lack of a unified approach to dealing with the child, and a lack of reasonable, consistent, and controlled discipline for the child. . . .

Parents are likely to need a considerable amount of understanding, empathy, and support from the treatment team to help them with their difficult family situation. . . .

Sullen Adolescents

Many young clients are very noncommunicative at intake. . . . The adjective "sullen" captures the adolescents' response style. Since this response is so typical, therapists must develop strategies for coping with the client's silence. Regarding this point, one older therapist explained his approach in this way. "I talk about the adolescent experience directly with the kid and some of my own adolescent experiences. There's no point in denying the reality of our helplessness feelings. When the youngster sees that the treatment situation is not one of judged and blamed, he begins to talk, and things begin to happen."

"Parents are likely to need a considerable amount of understanding, empathy, and support from the treatment team."

A younger, more streetwise therapist may ally him or herself with the adolescent client in a variety of ways. The therapist may use humor, commiserate with the client about how "awful" it is to be taken to treatment when one doesn't want to go, or demonstrate his or her ability to speak the language of the adolescent. Once the therapist is established in the client's eyes as a non-enemy, he or she can usually be a powerful factor in helping the client to see that significant adult "others" are not enemies either.

The young client typically has great difficulty stating the problem, but most frequently, he or she may say: "I want to get my head together," or "I'm okay; my problem is that my parents are on my back." Commonly, however, the adolescent is denying a very real, serious, and acute problem.

The feelings and emotional state of the parents of a youth who is entering drug treatment are very telling for the treatment process, and therefore, must be explored, clarified, and understood. They themselves have most likely experienced a degree of emotional upheaval comparable to that of their child and have lived through the child's rebellion and antisocial and/or self-destructive acting-out behavior. Consequently, the emotional "baggage" and disturbed feelings that they carry to the first treatment session may be even heavier than those of their child, since they include the weight of their own problems as adults and often the feeling of having failed as parents.

In describing the parents of adolescent clients at treatment entry, drug counselors report that the parents' feelings and attitudes are often muddled, confused, and in conflict within themselves. Also, conflict between the two parents is often apparent. They have been so emotionally exhausted by the events leading to treatment that they present a sense of hopelessness and willingness to give up. At the same time, they are described as overinvested emotionally in the problematic situation and as desperately seeking guidance and direction. From the therapist's viewpoint, the first task is to engage the adolescent client and the parents and attempt to establish some connection and rapport. Without such a connection (on a level of understanding, empathy, identification, or sympathy for the family) the therapist can have no real therapeutic effect. Different therapists approach the task differently. It seems natural that a young therapist would interrelate better with the adolescent client and that an older therapist would interrelate better with the parents. For this reason, if a program can afford it, it is often best to have a cotherapy team composed of an older and a younger therapist to work with the case, with the younger therapist providing the individual therapy to the adolescent client and the cotherapy team conducting family therapy sessions with the whole family. It also adds another useful dimension for the cotherapy team to be "heterosexual," and for the younger therapist who sees the adolescent client individually to be the same sex as the client. In some cases, the mother responds better to an older female counselor. The average drug treatment program, however, cannot afford to tailor the treatment team composition that is ideal for each case.

Almost all programs use the vehicle of the psychosocial history at the intake session for obtaining the necessary information, and as the first step in engaging the client and family in treatment. When this procedure includes meeting with the family members together in addition to interviewing them separately, it also allows the treatment team to obtain their first view of the nature of the family interaction and relationships.

Treatment Admission

A brief description of what the client and family will be asked during this treatment admission (intake) session follows:

The events and situations that led up to the application to treatment.

Basic demographic information about the client (age, sex, race, educational history, vocation history, hobbies and interests, living arrangements).

Reason(s) for applying for treatment.

Family background (parents' occupation, outline of structure of client's nuclear family, person(s) responsible for raising the client, siblings, birth order, a description of the quality of the client's family life, any alcohol or drug abuse history of other family members).

Information regarding the client's development and early childhood, particularly any disturbances/abnormalities in the client's birth, sleep patterns, unusual behavior, and so on.

Other notable features of the client's personal history (behavior problems, psychological problems, running away, physical or sexual abuse).

Medical history.

The history of the client's drug use and his or her perception of the effects of drug use: how it affected his or her life and functioning in school, at work, in the family, and so on.

Legal history, including the client's arrest record, details of his or her most recent brush with the law, and the client's probation/parole officer.

Previous treatment experience, if any.

In the history-taking session interactive family situations naturally emerge from the standard questions that are being asked. Some common parent-child interaction patterns noted by therapists are that a parent will identify the problem by reporting the child's bad behavior: "He's failing in school," "He breaks the rules," "He stays out all night and only comes home to shower and eat," "He's destroying the house," "She steals money," "He wrecks the cars," "She's acting out sexually.". . .

"The family therapy approach has as good a chance as any other treatment approach."

While treatment philosophies, approaches and policies may vary from program to program it has become widely accepted that the family therapy approach has as good a chance as any other treatment approach to help solve the adolescent drug abuse problem.

Arlene Utada is the coordinator of the Family Therapy for Adolescent Drug Abuse Demonstration at the Philadelphia Psychiatric Center. Alfred S. Friedman is the director of research at the Philadelphia Psychiatric Center.

"The therapeutic community (TC) brand of drug-free therapy offers the most comprehensive response to social, educational, and economic deficits."

viewpoint 88

Therapeutic Communities Can Provide Effective Treatment

Mitchell S. Rosenthal

Of all treatment alternatives for drug abusers, the therapeutic community (TC) brand of drug-free therapy offers the most comprehensive response to social, educational, and economic deficits and the maladaptation of clients. It brings a variety of resources to bear in a setting tailored for social learning. Within the closed environment of the TC, client behavior, attitudes, values, and skills can be observed and modified, and treatment can respond to specific emotional, educational, and vocational needs.

While treatment provided by the TC is appropriate for a great many drug abusers, it is not appropriate for all. The therapeutic community offers an established route of recovery from dysfunction that results from abuse of all classes of drugs or the use of psychoactive substances in various combinations (i.e., "polydrug" abuse). It is capable of treating successfully clients with a considerable range of emotional disturbance—including even profound character disorder. There also exists the possibility, in certain circumstances, of TC treatment for clients whose mood or thought disorders require adjunctive chemotherapy as part of a comprehensive treatment plan. . . .

Suitability for Admission

The following criteria are employed by most traditional therapeutic communities to determine suitability for admission.

Drug use should be chronic. More important, it should be considered by the client as an essential means of managing life situations and dealing with emotional discomfort or stress. Thus, some degree of psychological dependency should be present. While physiological dependency may also exist,

Mitchell S. Rosenthal, "Therapeutic Communities: A Treatment Alternative for Many But Not All," *Journal of Substance Abuse Treatment*, Vol. 1, 1984. Reprinted with permission.

detoxification is generally required before admission to the program.

Legal involvement must be considered, for treatment candidates frequently have been involved in drug-related crime—most often nonviolent "property" crime—and such involvement is viewed as behavior that can be addressed within the therapeutic community. A history of violence, sexual abuse or arson, however, is generally considered grounds for exclusion, since such behavior would prove disruptive to the general community and would require special management. Clients who have been convicted of a crime and certain to serve a jail or prison term rarely are admitted, although this may occur when treatment is an option mandated or under consideration by the court.

Social, interpersonal, family, vocational, and educational functioning are all aspects of behavior that should be assessed before admission. Candidates whose drug use continually disrupts their ability to sustain intimate relationships or to fulfill work or educational requirements, or who are involved in regular criminal activity as a result of drug involvement are highly suitable for TC treatment. Signs of social dysfunction, antisocial behavior, dysfunctional family relationships or inability to maintain interpersonal relationships also can indicate suitability for TC treatment. In addition, an adolescent or preadolescent response to peer rejection is a characteristic common to many appropriate candidates, as is acute or chronic dysfunction in the workplace or in mainstream educational settings (e.g., truancy, expulsion, or dropping out), where such dysfunction is drug-related.

Adolescent candidates pose special problems. Determining their suitability can be far more difficult than making the same determination for an adult and may be based upon far less obvious manifestations of drug abuse. Those youngsters whose abuse has become more of a problem than either their schools or their families are capable of handling must be assessed with particular care. Levels or patterns of drug use may be less significant than motivation and circumstances. For example, adolescents who invariably use drugs to cope with the stress of social or educational situations are demonstrating characteristic signs of progression towards increasingly compulsive use. Frequency and patterns of use must also be considered within a context that includes family ability both to set and to enforce standards of behavior. Where the home situation is chaotic or has been disrupted, and there is little parental presence and monitoring of behavior, drug involvement of youngsters may require potent intervention. On the other hand, whenever possible, the adolescent drug abuser should not be removed from a supportive family environment. Indeed, many youngsters whose drug abuse appears quite substantial may be well served by after-school programs that require sustained parental participation. Several of these model intervention programs have been developed in recent years. They employ fundamental TC processes and concepts and often serve as adjuncts to such other forms of intervention as psychotherapy and family counseling.

"TC clients . . . are significantly improved over pretreatment status."

Psychological/psychiatric status is often the basis for exclusion for TC treatment candidates. Most TC clients who do enter treatment are measurably depressed, anxious and have a characteristically low self-esteem. Psychological measures tend to be in the deviant range. In general, appropriate treatment candidates appear impulsive and exhibit character disorder with acting-out behavior symptomatic of underdeveloped psychosocial skills. Frank clinical illness (e.g., psychosis or suicidal depression) has been typically recognized as a cause for exclusion and referral, and candidates should be carefully screened for delusions, hallucinations, incoherence, loose associations, and inappropriate affect. Although a pattern of behavior dangerous to the client or to others, refractory hallucinations, or the inability to sustain a single topic of conversation would preclude admission, the presence of some thought or mood disorder need not necessarily bar a candidate from TC treatment. Where such disorder is manageable with adjunctive chemotherapy and a candidate is capable of meeting the demands of treatment in a therapeutic community, there is the possibility of admission. Clearly, an individual treatment plan with specific behavioral goals and frequent evaluations would need to be developed for such a client.

Outcome studies have revealed the immediate and long-term posttreatment status of TC clients (both those who remain in treatment for the optimal period of time and those who do not) are significantly improved over pretreatment status. The Drug Abuse Reporting System (DARP) studies, based on opiate, non-opiate and alcohol use, arrest rates, additional treatment, and employment, showed maximum or moderately favorable outcomes for more than half of the sample of "completed" clients and dropouts. Similar findings are reported in the program-based studies of Phoenix House and elsewhere. Both the DARP and Phoenix studies found favorable treatment outcome directly related to time in treatment. In addition, the Phoenix studies showed a significant relationship between outcome and psychological status, with those successful clients who remained in treatment for the optimal period registering the greatest improvement.

Attempts to determine client characteristics indicative of subsequent treatment success, however, have not proven very revealing. No clear client profile of success or retention emerged from a study of the Phoenix sample of completed clients and dropouts, although this might well reflect no more than the relative homogeneity of the drug abusers in this sample. The few predictors that were obtained suggested that successful clients are more likely to be opioid rather than nonopioid abusers, with relatively little criminal involvement, to have better social relations (fewer drug-using associates) at the time of admission, to be less defensive and more willing to disclose their personal dysfunction.

Since success is determined in large measure by length of treatment, indicators of retention are also important. A review of program-based research found certain client characteristics consistently have correlated with length of treatment, although the predictive power of these characteristics has not been corroborated in replicated study designs. Nevertheless, these studies have found nonopioid abusers, Hispanics, and clients with longer and more severe lifetime criminal histories have shorter durations of stay in therapeutic communities; clients under legal pressure at the time of admission and those whose health, lifestyle, drug use or criminal activity had worsened during the period immediately preceding admission have somewhat longer durations of stay, as do those with a pronounced desire to change their deviancy. In addition, several studies indicate that early dropouts reveal higher levels of psychological dysfunction than do clients whose durations of stay are longer.

Treatment Referral

Referral to a therapeutic community should be based upon both recognition of client need and an understanding of the nature and demands of TC treatment. Although there is today great variety among programs operating under the TC designation, the majority tend to share a similar structure, purpose and view of rehabilitation. They have common antecedents in such self-help groups as the Oxford Group, the Washingtonians, and Alcoholics Anonymous, and almost all draw on the experience and the practices of Synanon, the first TC to treat drug abusers, as well as such older traditional programs as Daytop Village, Phoenix House, and Gateway House.

Structurally, the TC is a 24-hour-a-day residential program with a primary treatment staff most often composed of paraprofessionals. More traditional programs consider the optimal length of treatment to be at least 15 months, although there have been experiments with shorter stays of 2-9 months. The goal of treatment, as recognized by all TCs, is the integration of the client into the larger society as a drug-free and productive individual. To that end, TCs view rehabilitation as global and involving efforts to remedy chronic deficits in social and economic skills and other effects of social disadvantage, family disruption, or individual maladaptation. Drug abuse is perceived as a disorder of the whole person, and rehabilitation is based upon the recognition of motivation, social learning, and self-help as significant aspects of recovery.

> "Because treatment . . . is a brief episode in the client's life, it must be able to overcome all the influences that preceded it."

It is important to recognize, when referring candidates for TC treatment, that some form of pressure—intrinsic or external—is usually needed before a drug abuser is willing to enter a TC and remain long enough to succeed. Intrinsic pressure can stem from a candidate's recognition of substance abuse as a factor in the deterioration of lifestyle, but is more likely to result from a "crisis" event— rejection by a spouse or loved one, loss of employment, or a similar traumatic incident. While such crises may provide the impetus to seek help, they rarely generate sufficient motivation to ensure that clients remain in treatment, and it is most often necessary for the TC staff to reinforce the initial insight—the role of substance abuse in the client's admitted deterioration.

External pressures are generally more tangible and their effects could be more sustained. These pressures include legal requirements (conditions of probation or "diversion" from the criminal justice system) or requirements imposed by employers as conditions of further employment. Family pressure too may be brought to bear and is often particularly

effective in influencing clients.

Because treatment, even long-term traditional treatment, is a brief episode in the client's life, it must be able to overcome all the influences that preceded it and be sustained in the face of the influences that follow it. For this reason, negative "outside" influences are minimized during the period of TC residence when treatment is high impact.

The acquisition of a new lifestyle demands a social learning situation, for recovery depends not only upon what is learned but also upon where and how it is learned. Negative patterns of behavior are not acquired in isolation. Neither can they be changed in isolation. In a TC, learning is accomplished by participation in the TC regime. Socially responsible attitudes are acquired by acting responsibly (initially, simply because such behavior is demanded). Treatment staff and clients who have progressed in the program serve as role models and also reaffirm the client's changing perspectives of both self and society. Self-help is the mechanism of change, and while clients cannot provide their own treatment, they must be willing to accept and participate in the interaction between the individual and the treatment process.

Emotionally Demanding

TC life is intense. The daily regime is emotionally demanding, and therapeutic confrontations, although supervised, are relatively unmoderated. A full and varied schedule fills at least 12 hours each day and includes a variety of learning experiences—seminars, formal classes, special meetings and training—as well as group therapy, work and recreation. This regime produces an orderly environment for clients, many of whom come from chaotic and disruptive settings, and also facilitates management of the community. It minimizes boredom and allows few opportunities for negative associations or the preoccupation formerly associated with drug abuse. . . .

Clearly, TCs vary not only in the optimal length of treatment they recommend, but also in size, professional support, and ancillary services. While size is rarely a determinant of quality (effective programs can exist with treatment populations as small as 35), the variety and quality of ancillary services do have an impact on treatment outcome, as does the extent to which families of clients and significant others in their lives are involved in the treatment process.

Mitchell S. Rosenthal is the president of the Phoenix House Foundation in New York. The Phoenix House provides counseling for drug abusers.

*"Recovery is a process of self-mastery
that expands out forever and stops only
when we do."*

viewpoint **89**

Focusing on the Self Can Provide Effective Treatment

Jim Parker

Knowing ignorance is strength.
Ignoring knowledge is sickness.

—Lao Tsu

It's a different world out there today. It is, at least, if you're making your way back from a problem with chemical dependency, and if you compare things with the way they were a few short months or years ago.

You can probably see it most clearly in your decision to stop using a substance or substances—whether alcohol, marijuana, cocaine, or something else—that had been a pretty large part of your life.

Your personal life probably seems a lot more up in the air as a result.

It may be in shambles, it may not be. But the pieces of your life seem more precariously balanced than before. You're probably facing questions now where there had been only answers, and confronting uncertainty in a life grown comfortable—or at least predictable—with the rhythm of routine.

Your future probably seems equally up for grabs. You may be rethinking directions that weeks or months ago went without question. And suddenly, you feel an obligation to think through where you're going from here—and just as important, *how* you're going to get there.

That's what this [viewpoint] is about: *How* you're going to get to where you're going. We can't tell you where you ought to go with your life, but we *can* provide some tips on ways you can get yourself there, keeping yourself whole—and your recovery intact—in the process.

We'll do it by introducing you to some concepts that, weeks or months ago, might have struck you as a little weird or, at least, unnecessarily difficult. . . .

We'll also make suggestions for activities you can easily incorporate into your life to make your recovery less difficult and more satisfying—both for yourself and the people you care about.

That's the real purpose of this [viewpoint]: to help you put the pieces of your life back together in a way that both makes sense and makes permanent recovery possible.

And it *is* possible. In fact, it's going to be the very best part of your life. . . .

Inside Yourself

So where do you start to stop an addiction?

The best place is inside yourself. You have to believe you can (and know you should) get off chemicals before you can get anywhere.

So in case you haven't done it yet, or in case you're still thinking about it, or in case you've done it for a while but are thinking about it as a temporary sort of change (you may even already be looking forward to a week or a month or a year from now when you can stop not-doing it), we have good news and bad news:

You really *do* need to quit doing drugs and alcohol. For good.

If that isn't obvious to you by now, maybe you don't have a drug or alcohol problem. Because if you did, you'd know the simple truth that you need to quit—now—and stay off whatever you've been on.

If you haven't quit, do it. If you have, keep doing it. If you're thinking about it, stop thinking about it and refer to the first sentence in this paragraph.

It's as simple as this: If you don't quit, you won't know if drugs and alcohol are your main problem. And at this stage of your life, you really need to know.

If you realize later that chemicals have been (and continue to be) a problem for you, you'll know what to do. (In fact, if you paid attention to the paragraph before last, you'll already be doing it.) If chemicals

Jim Parker, *Total Recovery: A Guide to Lifestyle Management in Recovery.*
Copyright 1988, Do It Now Foundation, Phoenix, AZ. Used by permission.

aren't your problem (and for some people, they're not), you'll know that, too, and can act accordingly.

If you're wondering *how* to quit, realize that there's really only one way: Altogether, all at once.

And while there are potential problems you should be aware of if you're strung out on alcohol, downers, or minor tranquilizers—including the risk of seizures (which means you should be under some form of medical supervision)—for any other sort of addiction, all you need to do is quit, pure and simple. . . .

And once you get it done, keep it done. Make staying sober or straight what your life is about. Don't panic, thinking you'll never be able to do it— or never want to stay that way—for the rest of your life. Just take care of today's business today.

And don't wobble. Tomorrow will take care of itself. . . .

The simple fact of the matter is that quitting is the *easy* part of recovery.

Keeping Them Off

If you stop and think about it, you'll realize how simple it is to get someone to quit something. All you have to do is tie them up and lock them in a room. They'll get off whatever they've been on—at least for as long as you keep them locked up. The trick is keeping them off when the door's open.

It's the same for any recovering person.

Because addiction is as complicated as each of us, and operates on a number of different levels simultaneously.

Whatever you were on—and the specific chemical or combination isn't all that important, whether heroin or booze, pills, pot, or cocaine—chemicals affected you the way they affected you through an interplay of factors inside you that are as unique as your thumbprint and as individual as your social security number.

Some factors are physical—a tendency toward low-blood sugar, for example, or an inherited intolerance for alcohol. Others are psychological—whether you see yourself as basically competent, for example, or whether you often feel anxious or depressed. Still others are more spiritual or existential in nature, and touch on your personal philosophy of God and experience of yourself.

"You're not going to be 100 percent you *again until you pick up all the pieces of your life."*

It gets complicated—because we are.

And that's why any program of recovery that's going to have any chance of working has to address itself to all the different parts of you.

Because *all* of you was affected when chemical dependency got its hooks into your body and mind

and soul. And until you get serious about getting *all* of you into the recovery picture, you're likely to keep on having problems.

Not that you won't be able to stay off what you were on. That's possible. But you're not going to be 100 percent *you* again until you pick up all the pieces of your life, and that involves doing more than just giving up drugs and alcohol.

It's a lot like trying to put out a fire in part of a building when the whole structure is burning out of control. You might cool things off for a while, but you're not going to cool things off for long. To do it right, you've got to do it all.

That's why we say the most important step after stopping is to seriously commit yourself to a plan of total recovery, a plan that includes simultaneous work on your body, mind, and spirit. Because the simple truth is that, until all of you gets involved in recovery, all of you ain't gonna get well.

And as long as any part of you is messed up, you're potentially *all* messed up.

Understanding Addiction

Before we go any further, we first need to review some basic notions about what addiction is—and what it isn't. That's necessary because research breakthroughs in recent years have revolutionized our understanding of how and why psychoactive drugs affect the brain, even shedding light on how the brain itself works to generate consciousness. And *that* has far-reaching implications for your trip through recovery.

We also need to define some basic concepts and terms. For starters, we should point out that we'll use the word *addiction* to describe all types of dependence.

We won't make a distinction between physical and psychological dependence, mainly because we think splitting hairs about "addiction" and "dependence" is basically beside the point.

Too often, people make too much of words, reading into them things that really aren't there— or shouldn't be. The language of addictions is a case in point.

To too many people, the term "physical dependence" means something a lot more serious and potentially life-threatening than "psychological dependence," which is often used as if it describes something minor, or even imaginary.

The fact is that *any* addiction is a serious matter, as anyone who's gone through one knows.

Similarly, we're not going to waste time sorting through theories of addiction, for the simple reason that it doesn't matter much in the context of where we're going in this [viewpoint]—and hopefully where you're going with your life.

Let's just say that you used chemicals for the reasons that you used chemicals and I used them for the reasons I used them.

We had a problem and chemicals covered it up. Then *chemicals* became the problem.

There *is* an aspect of addiction science that we should spend a little time with, though. It involves recent research into a group of body chemicals known loosely, if a little erroneously, as "endorphins." They may just turn out to have *everything* to do with why some of us become addicts and some of us don't.

And even more importantly, endorphins may tell the some of us who *do* how we can reverse the process of addiction and accelerate the process of recovery.

Discovered in a research lab in Aberdeen, Scotland in 1975 by researchers John Hughes and Hans Kosterlitz, endorphins are molecules produced by the body that were found to "turn on" our own internal system of pain relief during times of stress and injury.

The existence of such a system had only been guessed at previously. Earlier researchers had argued that the body *must* contain receptor sites for specific drugs for the chemicals to exert any influence in the body at all. One researcher even predicted how the system would fit together: like locks and keys.

Hughes and Kosterlitz found the key—at least the first one. What they discovered were short chains of amino acids, organic molecules sometimes referred to as the "building blocks of life." They named the first one "enkephalin" from the Greek words for "in the head," where the substance was produced.

Later, more complex molecules were identified, including Beta-endorphin (a contraction for *endogenous*—or internal—*morphine*). Endorphin captured the most early attention, because of the variety and desirability of effects—including everything, apparently, from pain relief to relaxation—it seemed involved in.

In recent years, investigators have expanded their understanding of endorphins, and now include more than simple relief from pain and tension as by-products of the chemicals.

"Saints and swamis have been saying the same thing for centuries: Know yourself."

Today, evidence links neuropeptides with the foundations of consciousness itself. From pain to pleasure, appetite control to analgesia, it now looks as though the chemicals play a main part in many of the events that shape our lives—or, at least, that shape our perceptions and feelings about our lives.

Most interesting about *that*, from a recovery perspective, is recent research which shows we can directly influence levels of endorphins by increasing

levels of activities that stimulate their production—that we can, in effect, "grow our own" endorphins by doing the things that make them happen.

And *that* brings us to the very interesting notion that *we can change our feelings by changing our actions*—a situation that has important implications for anyone recovering from a chemical dependency problem. . . .

Lifestyle Changes

Almost anyone can see the need for body-oriented changes in recovery.

You don't have to be particularly insightful to suspect that your body *had* to be affected by the chemicals you spent months or years swallowing, snorting, smoking, or shooting. Or that the best way to begin cleaning things up there is through fundamental nutritional and lifestyle changes on a physical level.

Similarly, most everyone will agree on the need for a basic shift in the way we've got our minds wired up if we're going to stay away from chemicals for any length of time and avoid the problems that lead to wanting *just one* drink, joint, line, or fix in the future. . . .

A key element at any stage of recovery is recognition—seeing the need for change as fundamental to our interests. Now we need to expand that idea a little by saying that the key to recognition is *observation*, and a main part of our approach to generating deeper changes is simply expanding our ability to observe the mind in action.

It's not as complicated as it sounds. In fact, saints and swamis have been saying the same thing for centuries: Know yourself.

It's almost the first law of being a person, but few of us practice it as if our lives really depended on it. And the reason we fail—in life and in knowing ourselves—is because we're so good at identifying with our minds that we don't question its assumptions about itself and the rest of the world. Even more than that, we think it's *crazy* to think that we are—or could be—anything else.

Well, we've got good news and bad news about that. First, the good news: We're not our minds. Now the bad news: We have to figure out who we are on our own.

One of the best ways we know of for figuring out who we are is through the process of meditation.

There are as many different forms of meditation as there are people to practice them, but all revolve around one basic goal: stopping, at least temporarily, the flood of thought, commentary, and self-talk that flows through our minds.

Meditation has been studied extensively for years and offers all kinds of benefits—lowered heart rate and blood pressure, increased self-esteem and confidence, and expanded interpersonal effectiveness, among other things.

But the reason we think so much of it in the context of recovery is that it works so well in both filling up the time formerly set aside for addictive behaviors and in reversing the psychological stress and depression that can trigger relapse.

Don't know how? Don't worry about it. Meditation is one of the simplest things in the world to teach or learn.

If you'd like formal meditation training, you can contact any of a number of organized groups to arrange it. Prices, as in most things, can vary from a little to a lot, but unlike most things, when it comes to meditation you don't necessarily get what you pay for. You get what you create—every day, twice a day.

Transcendental Meditation

A basic approach to meditation that seems to include all the essentials is passed along by Dr. Herbert Benson in his book, *The Relaxation Response*. According to Benson, all approaches to meditation accomplish the same basic goal in the same way, gradually reducing electrical activity in the brain and central nervous system.

Benson himself became involved at Harvard Medical School in the early 1970s, studying the physical and psychological changes associated with one approach to meditation, Transcendental Meditation (TM).

The basic TM process that Benson originally studied involves the silent repetition of a word (often a Hindu name for God) called a *mantra*, accompanied by deep relaxation of the body. The technique worked—very well, in most cases.

But Benson didn't stop there. He kept looking at his data, at the lowered metabolic rate and decreased anxiety levels of TM meditators, and wondered if the results reflected something specific to TM or more properly true about meditation in general. To find out, he repeated his experiments with a group he taught to meditate using the word "one" as a mantra, rather than the Sanskrit word specified by the TM instructor.

The results were clear-cut. "One" seemed to work as well as the meditator's mantras, at least in eliciting a deep state of body/mind relaxation. Benson immediately dubbed the state the "Relaxation Response."

Benson believes that deep relaxation is an inborn human capacity that's gradually fallen into disrepair over the centuries. That's happened because to survive in a hostile world, we've had to adapt a hair-trigger approach to sorting out potential difficulties in our minds by constantly creating different "what-if" scenarios that typically boil down to two basic choices: fighting or fleeing.

Nothing wrong with that, according to Benson, except that gradually we've lost the ability to relax fully and we need to re-learn it.

How do you teach yourself?

Easily enough, as it turns out. Begin by finding a quiet place. Ideally, it should be comfortable (since you're going to be sitting in one basic position for about 20 minutes) and distraction-free, since interruptions can both break your concentration and make 20 minutes seem like a long time, indeed.

After a while, though, comfortable and quiet aren't even prerequisites. Experienced meditators meditate wherever they are—whether on a crowded commuter train or in their office between appointments. Still, for starters, it's best to find a reasonably quiet and comfortable place.

"For most of us, relaxed, focused awareness is the only thing all our best moments have in common."

But not *too* comfortable. Try an armless straight back chair, but see that you're able to keep your spine straight and your muscles relaxed.

Begin by closing your eyes. Take a breath, relax, and start to feel the tension flow out of your body. If you have a tough time with this (and many do), systematically tense and relax the main muscle groups of your body.

Starting with your feet, flex your toes and relax. Then tense and relax your ankles. Do the same in your calves and knees and thighs and hips and pelvis and abdomen and chest and back, upper arms, forearms, and fingers. Feel the tension in your body dissolving as you bring it up to conscious awareness.

After you've become relaxed, begin to pay attention to your breathing. Nothing fancy here, just notice the rhythmic in-and-out flow of breath, and silently say the word "one" (or "Aum" or "calm" or any other one- or two-syllable word that seems to fit) to yourself as you exhale.

This is where you'll begin to notice the incredible tangle of disconnected thoughts that ordinarily command so much of our attention—all the things we didn't say or could have done, all the events we felt good/bad/indifferent about, all the slights and omissions dispensed and received, all the trivia that endlessly runs through our minds, that in fact forms a major part of who most of us consider ourselves to be.

When stray thoughts intrude (and they will), just notice them and, without getting angry at yourself for "not doing it right," simply go back to repeating the word you've chosen as a mantra.

Sound boring? It can be, sometimes. But it can also be inspiring, invigorating, and just plain fun.

Variations on the meditation theme can include closed-eye visualizations, in which you form mental images to role-play your way through a problem, for example, or focus attention on a specific goal. But the basic premise is the same: Stop the endless flow of self-talk in our minds and all sorts of possibilities open up.

And that's all that meditation is about. Because in spite of the mystical overtones often associated with the practice, meditation is merely a technique to help focus awareness. If you're wondering what good *that* is, just think back to some of the best moments in your life. For most of us, relaxed, focused awareness is the only thing all our best moments have in common.

What are you waiting for? Meditation is just like needlepoint, bowling, gourmet cooking, or anything else we've ever heard of. The only way to get good at it is through practice—preferably twice a day, every day.

You *can* settle for less. The only problem is that you get less if you do.

Expanding Ability

All the changes we've talked about thus far have been aimed in the same direction: expanding our ability to be responsible for ourselves and our thoughts, feelings, and actions.

Still, there's a further place that we can get to. Because while it's fine to accept ourselves exactly the way we are, we usually think it's better to take responsibility for making ourselves exactly the way we want to be.

The problem is that change can't be forced. That touches back on one of the basic principles of personality—that whatever we resist persists.

So how do we change? How do we override the programs that have gotten us stuck and led us down the path of chemical abuse and dependency?

This issue is one that's intrigued human beings as long as we've been human beings, and something that's likely to hold our attention a good while longer.

But consider: No matter what we ultimately *do* to make ourselves change, real transformation only comes from shifting our awareness—by re-focusing our attention, and becoming conscious of the often-unconscious mental machinery that runs our lives.

This is important stuff. Because in the act of observing our mental processes we create another layer of attention—a level beyond ordinary awareness, one that allows us to become increasingly mindful of the conditioned responses, reflexes, and fears that till now have really run our lives.

And in generating this layer of awareness, we literally create possibility out of impossibility, which is the first step in transforming our lives.

The next step is to act.

Fear—of one kind or another—is a basic issue that most of us get to confront sooner or later in the recovery process.

In fact, recent studies show that at least 40 percent of all alcoholics drink to relieve symptoms of anxiety. And when you hold something down for as long as some of us have been holding down fear, it's bound to bounce back—often with a vengeance.

In recovery, fear might come bounding back in the form of white-knuckled panic focused around specific situations or things (a fear of failure at a particular task, say, or an unease in meeting new people) or as a more general apprehension and dread.

But no matter what lights up the fear in your belly (and something does, for each of us), living with fear *can* be uncomfortable—particularly when we've shut ourselves off from our favorite fear-dampening abusable substance.

As you might expect, lots of rationalizations and justifications surround the items we fear most. And equally unsurprising, mastering fear can be a tricky process, particularly when it rears its ugly head in the middle of the vulnerability and uncertainty that takes place in recovery.

So where do we go with our fear and anxiety? Any number of places.

For one thing, it's important that we tell the truth about our feelings to ourselves and allow things to be the way they are.

It's literally true that the things we resist the most persist the most, so until it's all right with you that certain things can trigger an occasional case of the jitters or downright cold sweats, chances are good that those things will continue to run you—whether you like it or not.

So begin by accepting, without judgment or self-criticism, yourself exactly the way you are. Don't beat yourself up because of your limitations—or you'll only end up investing that much more energy in them.

"We literally create possibility out of impossibility, which is the first step in transforming our lives."

The next step is to take responsibility for whatever you're afraid of.

Don't buy into the "poor me" scripts that you've unconsciously memorized all your life about how things aren't your fault—or that they're so much your fault that you'll never be able to set things right.

The fact is that while your problems *aren't* your fault, they most definitely *are* your responsibility once you open your eyes in the morning. So take full responsibility for being how you are, where you are. Don't resist. Just accept your life—all of it—the way that it is, the way that you've made it. Then if you really want things to be different, take responsibility for having them be another way.

There, we said it—the magic word in any program of recovery from anything: Responsibility. When we believe in it and act on it we literally produce magic in our lives. Fail to accept it or do anything about it and we watch the parade go by without us.

Often, taking responsibility for our lives leads us in the direction of fear itself. That's because we intuitively know that the only thing in our lives stronger than fear is courage, and the only way to summon courage is to create it by defying fear. In his essay "On Courage," Emerson put it this way: "Always do what you are afraid to do."

Believe it.

Conquering Fear

Because it's the only way that it's done: We conquer fear by conquering fear. We don't do it by waiting until we feel stronger or until we think circumstances are better: We do it now or we don't do it at all.

Why not begin confronting your fears right now? Take a few minutes and list the situations that inspire the clammiest hands or the driest throat in *your* life. Then look over your list and rank the items in order of the fear they trigger. Then come to terms with them. Don't resist them or hate them or come up with a "What, me worry?" sort of artificial optimism. Just acknowledge that, yes, they sure do look familiar and, yes, they sure have run your life for a long time.

Then decide if you really want to come to grips with them. Maybe you don't want to (and maybe you don't even *need* to). If you decide you do, make another list—this time of commitments you're willing to make to increase your ability to cope with whatever it is you haven't been coping with.

"If you want to change your thoughts and feelings, change your actions. Get out and do something."

Then *do something*. If you're afraid your marriage is falling apart, do something to fix it or to at least focus your ability to see the problem. If you're afraid of leaving your house or apartment, commit to some activity that will force you out, even if it's only to keep an appointment with a therapist. If you're afraid of speaking up in public, sign up for a public speaking course at a local community college.

Whatever it is that we want to change requires only that we do something now. Fear scatters in the presence of honest, committed courage the same way that darkness vanishes when we turn on a light.

Just remember: Life-controlling fears and worries never just "go away." We beat them or they beat us.

Handling depression in recovery is a lot like tip-toeing through a minefield, so you'd better do it right.

Advance planning can help. Because when you're depressed, you don't always recognize depression for what it is. You get so used to feeling down or defeated that depressed feelings just look like Business As Usual.

That's what makes depression so potentially deadly. You don't even know it's there. You think it's just the way things are. Or you think other people are doing it to you again. So you bite your lip or slump in front of a TV or just sit on the hurt or anger or disappointment, and unconsciously chip away at the foundations of your recovery.

What else is there to do?

Well, for starters, you can begin to be aware of depression for what it is and beware of it for what it can be. Don't stand still and wait for it to grab you. And if it's already got you, make it turn you loose.

Here's the secret we always forget when we're down:

If you want to change your thoughts and feelings, *change your actions*. Get out and do something—but not just anything. Consciously select what most needs doing in your life right now and do that. If your sink's full of dirty dishes, and you don't feel like doing them, do the dishes anyway. Need clean clothes but hate to do laundry? Do your laundry. Feeling tense or depressed but too tired to do anything about it? Pull out your running shoes and put in a few miles.

In recovery, we have to make a conscious point of reminding ourselves that there is no reality that matters as much as the one we create for ourselves.

So create away.

Because the basic law of taking control of your life is to realize that we are what we do.

And if we don't do anything, what does that make us?

Choosing This

The five colors blind the eye.
The five tones deafen the ear.
The five flavors dull the taste.
Racing and hunting madden the mind.
Precious things lead one astray.

Therefore the sage is guided by what he feels
    and not by what he sees.
He lets go of that and chooses this.

—Lao Tsu

Lao Tsu's words are simple, deceptively so. Because even though choosing this—whatever is here, now—seems an obvious, effortless path to personal freedom, it usually doesn't turn out that way. In fact, "choosing this" can seem downright impossible sometimes.

Nowhere in life is the difficulty more clear-cut than during recovery.

In one way or another, your life has come down around you. You may be in jail, in a hospital, an unemployment line, or a divorce court, but you're probably in trouble, in one way or another, wherever else you might be.

Because a basic truth about recovery is that most of us don't do it without feeling we have to do it.

We either lose something (a marriage, a job, freedom, "sanity") or feel ourselves about to lose something equally major before the cloak of denial we wrap ourselves in starts to slip away. Then, by the time we get around to actually doing something about our problems with chemicals, we usually have a stack of *other* problems to contend with—problems that can make "choosing this" that much harder.

Still, to borrow an ancient metaphor, a journey of ten thousand miles begins with a single step, and the single step we need to start with in recovery is in choosing where we are right now. Because if we haven't taken responsibility for being who we are, where we are, we're not going to get anywhere.

So take a moment now and choose this—whatever your *this* is.

As soon as you finish this paragraph, try closing your eyes and looking at your life exactly the way it is, with whatever problems and possibilities you've created for yourself. As soon as you're *sure* that you've *chosen this* exactly the way that it is, and when you're positive about who's in charge of making things change, open your eyes.

Choosing this is closely linked with a secret of happiness that saints and sages have known throughout the ages: that contrary to what most of us think most of the time, happiness is *not* about getting what we want. It's about *wanting what we get*. And every time we choose *this*, the way things are, we move closer to wanting what we get, which is where happiness resides.

And the closer we move to true happiness, the closer we get to who we really are.

Self-Mastery

After you've gotten off what you've been on and incorporated some of the changes we've talked about so far, you may be tempted to think that you've taken recovery about as far as it can be taken.

Don't believe it.

Because recovery is a process of self-mastery that expands out forever and stops only when we do.

What all the processes and activities that we've talked about are designed to do is to expand awareness: the awareness of chemical dependency as an opportunity rather than an obstacle; the awareness of the relationship between body and mind, thought and action; the awareness that our intentions can override our feelings as the primary factor in determining the quality of our lives.

But that's not as far as you can take recovery—not at all.

Because the ultimate challenge is to make personal transformation what we're about all the time. And that's more than the ultimate challenge in recovery—that's the ultimate challenge in life. Because if we can begin to see the truth in the proposition that we're not our minds and our opinions and our limitations, we begin to glimpse the deeper reality that no one else is, either.

"The ultimate challenge is to make personal transformation what we're about all the time."

And when we see *that*, we begin to understand that relating to people inside the walls of reaction and fear and anger and pain that we usually operate inside of in our interactions with each other is as ultimately false and unsatisfying as relating to ourselves from the web of perfectionism, stress, and depression that we lived inside when we were addicted.

Want to step outside those walls? It's easy.

Look for opportunities to expand yourself *beyond* yourself. Do things that, before you got yourself straight, you wouldn't have even *wanted* to do.

If you're still not sure what that is, just look around.

See what needs doing and do that. Pick up a broken bottle or a candy wrapper on the sidewalk in front of your home. Make it your responsibility to make life easier for the people you see every day and to make the world a better place for people you don't even know. Find opportunities to share who you really are—and not just what you think or how you feel about whatever was on television last night.

Just pull your attention off yourself and your thoughts and feelings and start focusing in on others—and making a difference in their lives.

Because the final lesson in recovery is the ultimate lesson in life: We become ourselves the most the times that we most give ourselves away.

Maybe that means that we're really here for each other.

Or we're not really here at all.

Jim Parker is an author for the Do It Now Foundation. The Do It Now Foundation works to prevent drug abuse and to educate the public about issues that affect health.

"There have been major advances in the treatment of substance abusers... with the development of effective pharmacotherapies."

viewpoint **90**

Medication Can Provide Effective Treatment

Jeffrey S. Rosecan and Edward V. Nunes

The use of medications in the treatment of substance abusers is controversial, and most alcohol and drug treatment programs proscribe rather than prescribe them. There are several reasons for this. First, the clinician does not want to give alcoholics and drug abusers the message that their problems can be "solved by a pill." This attitude often led them to seek alcohol or drugs in the first place. L. Wurmser has proposed that drugs are used by addicts to protect against painful feelings (rage, shame, and loneliness) that they were psychologically unable to cope with because of defects in their ego defenses. E.J. Khantzian has taken this observation one step further and has proposed that drug abusers "self-medicate" not only painful emotional states, but also psychiatric disorders. Using this rationale, cocaine abusers may be medicating themselves for mood disorders (depression, manic-depression, cyclothymia) or behavioral disorders (attention deficit disorder). Preliminary diagnostic studies of cocaine abusers support this view.

Another reason that most alcohol and drug rehabilitation programs discourage the use of medication is tradition. Alcoholics Anonymous (AA), the largest and most influential provider of substance abuse treatment in the United States, has been dogmatically opposed to the use of any mood-altering substance, including psychotropic medication, since its founding in 1935. Narcotics Anonymous (NA), Drugs Anonymous (DA), and Cocaine Anonymous (CA) are similar self-help organizations based on the 12-step model of AA, and all share its antimedication views.

Many substance abuse programs, however, have combined the AA model with other modalities, including medication treatments. We feel that there

Jeffrey S. Rosecan and Edward V. Nunes, "Pharmacological Management of Cocaine Abuse," from *Cocaine Abuse: New Directions in Treatment and Research.* New York: Brunner/Mazel, Inc., 1987. Reprinted with permission from Brunner/Mazel, Inc.

have been major advances in the treatment of substance abusers in the past generation with the development of effective pharmacotherapies. To the extent that addictions have a physiological basis, appropriate pharmacological interventions are rational. Furthermore, the tremendous addictive potential of cocaine, as demonstrated in laboratory animals and humans, suggests that pharmacological interventions might be applied.

Freud used cocaine himself beginning in 1884 as a curiosity, as a research interest in experimental pharmacology, and probably as a self-medication for his own depressions. He also used it therapeutically in the treatment of morphine addiction after reading reports of successful treatments by physicians in the United States. Freud administered cocaine to his friend and colleague Von Fleischl, who had become addicted to morphine, and who, to Freud's horror, proceeded to develop the first case of iatrogenic cocaine psychosis ("a delirium tremens with white snakes creeping over his skin"). Freud subsequently moderated his views on the effectiveness of cocaine as a treatment for morphinism.

Dr. William Halsted, the renowned surgeon who discovered nerve block (local) anesthesia with cocaine, unfortunately became addicted to it in the process. Ironically, Halsted "cured" his cocaine habit by becoming addicted to morphine, a dependence he continued for the rest of his long and distinguished surgical career.

These two historical examples point out a clear danger in the treatment of drug dependence with another drug; the substitution of one dependency for another. This is a rationale for the antimedication tradition of AA and other self-help organizations.

Pharmacological Approaches

Several pharmacological approaches to the treatment of substance abusers are already accepted in clinical practice. In these examples, medications appear to be helpful only if used as an adjunct to a comprehensive treatment program.

Disulfiram (Antabuse), although technically not a psychoactive medication, has been used by many alcoholism treatment programs and individual practitioners worldwide, although not without controversy. The principle behind disulfiram treatment is that patients taking the medication have an unpleasant and often aversive reaction to alcohol. Disulfiram works by inhibiting alcohol dehydrogenase, an important enzyme in the metabolism of alcohol, causing the buildup of acetaldehyde in the body. This produces the flushing, nausea, and vomiting that are characteristic of the alcohol-disulfiram reaction. Although disulfiram is not the panacea that was initially hoped for when it was introduced in Denmark in 1948, it remains an important adjunct in the treatment of alcoholism when used in conjunction with AA or individual or group psychotherapy. Many clinicians find that disulfiram taken on a daily basis complements AA's credo of "one day at a time," with the spiritual values and group support of the latter augmenting the external control of the former.

"Medications . . . appear to be useful in the treatment of alcoholism, opiate addiction, and cigarette smoking."

Methadone maintenance has been a major advance in the treatment of opioid (mainly heroin) dependence since it was introduced into clinical practice in 1964. Methadone, a long-acting (once-a-day dosage) opiate, reduces the heroin craving and euphoria when given in adequate doses. Methadone maintenance programs have been helpful for addicts in several ways. For one thing, the need for illicit opiates is negated, and the criminal behavior associated with their procurement is often reduced. The methadone maintenance patient is capable of socially productive behavior. Although he is still addicted to an opiate, the addiction is medically and socially controlled.

A major recent advance in the treatment of opiate addiction involves the use of nonopiate medications. Clonidine (Catapres), an α-adrenergic receptor agonist, has been used successfully to suppress the opiate withdrawal syndrome. This is often followed by maintenance treatment with naltrexone (Trexan), a long-acting opiate antagonist. The advantage of this medication combination is that an opiate-free withdrawal and maintenance is possible for motivated addicts. Naltrexone, like disulfiram, is often used in conjunction with a self-help group or individual or group psychotherapy.

Cigarette smoking produces a physical dependence on nicotine, which often makes stopping unpleasant and hence difficult. Nicotine chewing gum (Nicorettes) has recently been introduced to help smokers stop smoking by alleviating the nicotine withdrawal. Again, nicotine gum seems to be most effective when combined with a comprehensive smoking cessation program incorporating behavioral or other psychotherapeutic strategies.

Useful Medication

The medications described appear to be useful (to a greater or lesser extent) in the treatment of alcoholism, opiate addiction, and cigarette smoking. Are there medications that are useful in the treatment of cocaine abuse? Cocaine has only recently been reconceptualized as a physiological as well as a psychological dependence. In addition, it has only been in the [1980s] that cocaine abuse has reemerged (after a relatively quiescent period of 70 years) as a major public health problem in the United States. For these reasons, the use of medication in the treatment of cocaine abuse is in its infancy, although the medications to be discussed have been used for various medical and psychiatric illnesses for decades.

There are several guiding principles for the pharmacological management of cocaine abusers. First, medications should always be used as an adjunct to a comprehensive cocaine abuse treatment program. We have found that they can be effective when combined with individual psychotherapy, group psychotherapy and self-help groups, family and marital therapy, and inpatient treatment. Second, the treatment must be tailored to the individual patient. Preexisting or coexisting psychiatric disorders that may require psychotropic medication should be identified by careful diagnostic interview. Patient and family member attitudes toward medication should be assessed to ensure that magical expectations regarding medication and idealization of the medication giver are minimized. Patients and their families often think of medication as a "cure." This is usually a combination of misinformation and denial. It is important for the clinician to emphasize that cocaine abuse can be a lifelong problem requiring a commitment to total abstinence from cocaine, and that a "cure" in the traditional medical sense is not possible.

Medication is indicated in the treatment of preexisting or coexisting psychiatric illness. Chronic cocaine abusers appear to have a greater prevalence of affective disorders (depression, manic-depression, and cyclothymia) than other substance abusers. However, it is often difficult to make an accurate diagnosis of affective illness in the patient who is actively using cocaine or withdrawing from it. To further complicate this issue, it is our clinical impression that chronic cocaine use can intensify preexisting affective illness, especially depression, and appears to be depressogenic for some patients.

The neurochemical changes produced by chronic cocaine use appear similar to the changes found in depression. Further studies are clearly needed to clarify the clinical and biochemical interrelationships between cocaine abuse and affective illness. . . .

Tricyclic Antidepressants (TCAs)

TCAs have been used empirically by clinicians for years in the treatment of cocaine abuse since depression is so prominent in many of these patients. This in itself is an important rationale for the use of TCAs in this setting, since self-medication of underlying depression may fuel cocaine addiction.

Another theoretical rationale for the use of TCAs is that in laboratory animals and in preliminary human studies, they appear to reverse some of the neurochemical effects of chronic cocaine administration. The presynaptic and postsynaptic actions of TCAs can be looked at separately.

Presynaptically, both cocaine and TCAs block the reuptake of the neurotransmitters dopamine (DA), norepinephrine (NE), and serotonin (5-HT), possibly at the same presynaptic sites. Cocaine does this within minutes, TCAs within hours. It is possible that TCAs antagonize cocaine by displacing it presynaptically or by blocking a putative cocaine receptor. Although it is theoretically possible that TCAs may potentiate the actions of cocaine presynaptically, we are not aware of case reports of adverse sequelae to the TCA-cocaine combination.

"Chronic cocaine use can intensify preexisting affective illness, especially depression."

Postsynaptically, chronic cocaine administration produces a supersensitivity ("upregulation" or proliferation) of the DA, NE, and 5-HT receptors, which may result as a compensation for the neurotransmitter depletion also resulting from chronic cocaine administration. As noted previously, neurotransmitter depletion and receptor supersensitivity may be the neurochemical basis for cocaine craving. TCAs produce receptor subsensitivity ("downregulation" or reduction in number) and may reverse the cocaine-induced receptor supersensitivity. This effect occurs over several weeks along the same time course as the antidepressant action of TCAs.

To date, there have been several uncontrolled and two controlled studies of TCAs in cocaine abusers. All of these studies have been on outpatients. F.S. Tennant and Rawson reported that desipramine (DMI) helped 14 cocaine abusers become abstinent. However, 11 of these patients were on medication for less than a week, and follow-up was limited. J.S. Rosecan reported that imipramine (IMI), in combination with the amino acids L-tryptophan and L-tyrosine, helped 12 of the 14 cocaine abusers become abstinent over 10 weeks. Seven of the 12 noted, in addition, a reduction in cocaine craving and an attenuation of the cocaine euphoria. Rosecan and D.F. Klein also found a blocking of cocaine euphoria after a double-blind challenge with cocaine in four patients on IMI, L-tryptophan, and L-tyrosine. In addition, the expected elevations in pulse and blood pressure were blocked in three of four patients. F.H. Gawin and H.D. Kleber found prolonged abstinence (greater than 12 weeks) and diminished craving for cocaine in a six-patient trial with DMI. In the latter study, DMI was effective in depressed as well as nondepressed patients. Gawin, R. Byck, and Kleber have recently completed a placebo-controlled, double-blind study of DMI in nondepressed cocaine abusers. They found that DMI was significantly more effective than placebo in promoting abstinence and reducing cocaine craving. In both the Rosecan and Gawin studies, the reduction in craving and/or blocking of euphoria occurred over two to four weeks, which is the usual time course for the antidepressant effect of TCAs. In addition, the TCAs in these studies were administered in antidepressant doses (i.e., 150-300 mg). A double-blind study of DMI by Tennant and Tarver failed to show a superiority of DMI over placebo in promoting abstinence or reducing cocaine craving. However, in this study both the average duration of treatment and the average dose of DMI were probably subtherapeutic. Perhaps the attenuation of cocaine euphoria reported by Rosecan and Klein with IMI is a reflection of IMI's serotonergic actions which DMI does not share.

Based on these preliminary data, it appears that TCAs may be effective adjuncts in the outpatient treatment of cocaine abusers, whether or not they are depressed. It is our clinical impression that cocaine-abusing patients who have significant cocaine craving are those who are most helped by TCAs. Although the use of TCAs in the treatment of cocaine abuse without depression is not FDA-approved, it is probably justified in carefully screened treatment-resistant cases. As noted, there have been no reports of adverse effects of the cocaine-TCA combination in any of these studies, and in one study, the tricyclic antidepressant amitryptyline protected laboratory animals from sudden cardiac death from cocaine. Clearly, further research is needed in this area to determine when and for whom TCAs might be helpful. . . .

Physiological Addiction

Cocaine abuse has recently been reconceptualized as both a physiological and psychological addiction, and several medications are showing promise as adjuncts to cocaine abuse treament. . . .

We conclude with a word of caution. The medication treatment of cocaine abuse is still in its infancy and is still to be considered experimental, even though the medications proposed have been safely used by physicians for decades in the treatment of various medical and psychiatric illnesses. Since cocaine abuse is now epidemic in the United States with no present sign of abating, the prevention and treatment of this problem should be given our highest national priority. The medication treatments reviewed deserve further study based on these promising early results.

Jeffrey S. Rosecan is assistant clinical professor of psychiatry at Columbia University in New York and is director of the Cocaine Abuse Treatment Program at the Columbia-Presbyterian Medical Center. Edward V. Nunes is an instructor of clinical psychiatry at Columbia University and is director of research at the Cocaine Abuse Treatment Program at the Columbia-Presbyterian Medical Center in New York.

Holistic Methods Can Provide Effective Treatment

Richard Leviton

"It has been my experience in the treatment field that, even at its most difficult, getting off drugs is infinitely easier than *staying* off," Richard Seymour is saying. The fifty-year-old, lightly bearded Seymour, who is director of education and public information at the Haight Ashbury Free Medical Clinic in San Francisco, is talking with me at the corner of Haight and Clayton Streets. With his hand he gestures to the infamous neighborhood, The Haight, always an epicenter of drug use and experimentation, from flower child psychedelics to nightmarish crack. And with his sweeping gesture Seymour, who has been with the Clinic from its beginnings in 1967, also takes in the five buildings, pastel-colored Victorian homes scattered inconspicuously throughout the interlinking blocks, that now form the Clinic's extended complex.

Since it was founded by Dr. David Smith, now president and medical director, the Clinic has been devoted to providing effective, alternative, and free outpatient medical and counseling aid for the local population. In the last two decades, during which time the Clinic's reputation as a renowned research and outreach establishment has spread worldwide, its offices have clocked some 700,000 patient visits, mostly from street addicts, the working poor, and low-income local residents.

Thus the publication of its landmark recommendations in *Drugfree: A Unique, Positive Approach to Staying off Alcohol and Other Drugs* is all the more impressive for the personal commitment that backs the multiple and innovative suggestions.

Following Mahatma Gandhi's inspiring example to personally abstain from using sugar before he advised a young child to do similarly, Seymour notes, "I stopped using any chemical substance for its psychoactive qualities. I have been able to write

Richard Leviton, "Staying Drugfree Naturally," *East West*, March 1988. Reprinted with permission from *East West: The Journal of Natural Health and Living*. All rights reserved.

this book with the courage of conviction that abstinence truly is an opening of doors. Over these past three years, I've used many of the alternative therapies that you find in this book, and I'm happy to report that they do work." Such a refreshingly authentic approach, in which the medical advisers actually embody the model of healthy, sustained abstinence from self-destructive addictive substances, may very well be precisely what's required to help lift the pall of chemical dependency and its toll of personal and social disruption from the minds and bodies of millions of Americans. It is also characteristic of the growing trend, though one not as yet widely reported, towards holistic, positive, sustainable, and ultimately healing approaches to this insidious problem.

The Addictive Milieu

It is an understatement to describe alcohol and drug addiction, clinically called "chemical dependency" as pandemic to America. The number of people affected and the cost in disruption and treatment is staggering.

It is estimated that 18 million Americans have serious drinking problems, although one study reports that alcohol consumption has declined by 5 percent since 1981. Approximately 3 million people are narcotic or cocaine addicted while 20 billion doses of psychoactive drugs are distributed legally each year. How many more doses are circulated clandestinely on the streets is anybody's guess. In 1982 the National Institute on Drug Abuse estimated that at least 33 percent of Americans older than twelve had experimented with one or more of a cornucopia of psychoactives including marijuana, mescaline, LSD, "Ecstasy," cocaine, heroin, and various prescription amphetamines, barbiturates, and tranquilizers. Moreover, some 5 million teenagers have drinking problems, a condition that in some cases reaches back in age as early as fourth grade.

The drug addiction phenomenon spans the demographic range from street addicts and the medically indigent to middle class and upwardly mobile professionals and encompasses every racial and ethnic minority. "We no longer have a drug-using subculture," Smith and Seymour point out. "We are a culture that uses drugs."

For many today, the drug addiction problem seems utterly intractable, an insoluble web of self-destruction, poverty, pain, and alienation.

While the addictive milieu seems to be blossoming like a poisonous mushroom plume across the country, the mainstream medical and media establishments seem to be foundering for effective treatment approaches. Although *Time* announced in a cover story that, "Changing attitudes and new research give fresh hope to alcoholics," the most promising signs they could point to were of the familiar medicine-as-savior mode. Citing new research into the neurochemical bases of addiction and suggesting that a genetic predisposition might allow for a simple and definitive cure, *Time* concluded, "There is hope that medicine may make the course to sobriety less perilous."

Medical treatment centers for alcoholism, for example, have proliferated in the past two decades to 7,000 nationwide, with a 65 percent increase in the past six years alone. As *Newsweek* noted in a mid-1986 article on crack addiction, "There is big money to be made in the drug rehabilitation business and enterprising corporations are setting up chains of profitable centers." Conifer Park, a thirty-two-acre wooded estate in upstate New York, costs $8,300 for thirty days. Comprehensive Care, a Fortune 500 national chain of Care Unit centers, charges $16,000 for a typical six-week residency at its 103-bed rehabilitation center in southern California, while another program in Houston costs $21,000 for the same time period.

Despite the dizzying costs of guided recovery from addiction, the actual inpatient medical protocols are remarkably conventional, essentially the same "drying out" therapies first developed at Hazelden in Minnesota, a pioneering clinic in the 1940s. Substitute drugs and chemical antidotes (tricyclics, bromocriptine, Antabuse) in conjunction with some counseling are standard. The usual "alternative" for heroin addiction withdrawal remains methadone (a synthetic opiate) although fentanyl, Demerol (mepridine), Talwin (pentazocine), and Darvon (propoxyphene) are also used widely.

The nationwide Alcoholics Anonymous (A.A.) organization, founded in the 1930s, and now with numerous spin-off groups, stands at the borderline between conventional and alternative treatment. Central to the A.A. protocol is what's called the Twelve Step Program, a kind of behavioral catechism and "blueprint for recovery" that leads one into an appreciation of the transpersonal and the role of Grace in healing. This approach, relied on by thousands, has spawned related treatment groups like Cocaine Anonymous, Narcotics Anonymous, Nar-Anon, Al-Anon, and other family-oriented modalities, reflecting the multifaceted co-dependency of the problem. Al-Anon, founded in 1951, now has 26,000 regional chapters, while the Adult Children of Alcoholics group was launched in 1983 to benefit an estimated 30 million American offspring of chronic drinkers.

Treatment Options

Yet with this plethora of treatment options, the recidivism rates remain high. The best estimates are that only 12–25 percent of recovered patients remain abstinent for three years. Some California drug treatment authorities place relapse at 90 percent. And only 15–20 percent of chemically dependent alcoholics ever receive treatment at all. Something clearly is missing from the conventional approaches. As Smith and Seymour observe, "It is life *after* drugs that's the real hurdle. We estimate that in the next five years approximately 20 million people will try to quit their drug of abuse. Of those, only about 2.8 million will still be clean one year later." The other 17 million will relapse into drugs because both abusers and those around them "simply don't know how to deal with abstinence."

"Only 15-20 percent of chemically dependent alcoholics ever receive treatment at all."

Similarly, many medical experts are only now beginning to appreciate the depth and intricacy of a chemical dependency situation. It was only in 1960, with the publication of E. M. Jellinek's then radically provocative *The Disease Concept of Alcoholism*, that the medical community was prepared to grant that the problem of drug addiction might have roots beyond absence of free will or psychological mettle.

"The most current definition," state Smith and Seymour, "describes addiction as a disease entity with its own psychopathology characterized by compulsion, loss of control, and continued use in spite of adverse consequences. Addiction is progressive, potentially fatal if untreated, and incurable but remissible through abstinence and recovery."

Smith and Seymour also subscribe to the more holistic, multi-dimensional definition devised by Chuck Brissette, associate director of Azure Acres, a recovery-oriented program in Petaluma, California. Brissette characterizes addiction as a three-headed dragon, with physical, psychological, and spiritual aspects. Thus on many levels of one's being, the addictive process claims one's autonomy. "The attitudinal or spiritual basis for addiction," notes Smith and Seymour, "is a deep-rooted conviction that alcohol and other drugs are good and provide temporary relief from emotional discomfort without negative effects."

The drug addiction problem has grown so enormous and pervasive that nonmedical social critics have begun offering their analyses to help place the matter in perspective. Drug abuse represents an evolutionary crisis of spiritual starvation, suggests Dr. Michael Grosso, author of *The Final Choice: Playing the Survival Game.*

"Throughout history psychochemicals have been used to open the mind to hidden dimensions of reality for periodic contact with alternate realities," explains Grosso. The drug problem won't go away because "the drive toward self-transcendence won't go away," he notes.

Feminist psychotherapist Anne Wilson Schaeff also places a major share of responsibility on society for promulgating the addictive milieu, a vast and negative thought-form overshadowing the contemporary world. In her *When Society Becomes an Addict* Schaeff posits that our entire society functions as an addictive system.

"More people are getting into drug-free alternatives."

"The fact of the matter is we live in an addictive system. Our society has all the characteristics and exhibits all the processes of the individual alcoholic or addict." For Schaeff the definition of addict is broad, taking in both familiar substances (caffeine, nicotine, sugar) and obsessive processes (perfectionism, work, sex, relationships, compulsive spending, religion). In short, "Anything we feel *tempted* to lie about, anything we are not *willing* to give up, anything that keeps us unaware of what is going on inside us, that dulls and distorts our sensory input."

This, then, is the addictive milieu into which alternative, holistic therapies must move. "The drug problem is getting worse," admits David Smith, "but there's more acceptance of the drug-free alternatives. The good news is we're understanding it better and more people are getting into drug-free alternatives. The bad news is that the problem population is getting younger with more polydrug abuse."

Counterculture History

Once countercultural history was made here but today the Haight-Ashbury district is an architecturally unsettling mixture of the unkempt and seedy with yuppie pretension. The Free Medical Clinic, says Richard Seymour, was born "at an epicenter of drug experimentation and treatment," in a neighborhood with "the densest alcoholic population of the entire city." The Clinic is thus strategically nestled right in the unhappy heart of this drug-intense neighborhood. It is poised for providing free and immediate relief for the 10,000 who walk in from the streets every year for general medical aid as well as for the 3,600 who voluntarily walk into 529 Clayton Street's Drug, Detoxification, Rehabilitation and Aftercare out-patient clinic or to the Haight Ashbury Alcohol Treatment Services section (HAATS) at 1658 Haight.

The Clinic's five buildings are all old, homey, converted residences with interior corridors anachronistically decorated 1960s' style—Grateful Dead posters. Yet despite the Clinic's modest, folksy decor, it is a nationally respected facility, with a paid staff of fifty and over 200 professional volunteers. It has been at the forefront of delivering alternative modalities since its inception. However, since it has never charged for services, relying instead on government and private sector grants, the Clinic's scope of services fluctuates with the tides of funding. For ten years the Bill Pone Memorial Acupuncture Clinic used its Oriental needles to ease the pain of drug withdrawal but in 1985 this section was reluctantly terminated and acupuncture is now provided through referrals.

Even so, with its multiple aftercare modalities, the use of initial non-narcotic symptomatic medications, nutritional and psychological counseling, and copious referrals, the Clinic remains a beacon of inspiration in the neighborhood. "We're working here on the front lines of immediate detoxification," says Seymour, from his second floor office. "We are dealing with immediate casualties, bringing them through withdrawal, then passing them on through gentle persuasion into the developing continuity of supported recovery. The key here is that the Clinic is one component in a larger array of available treatments in the community."

One such community outreach program is the Clinic's own HAATS Drop-in Center, founded in 1984 with a staff of two (both in recovery themselves). HAATS provides information and referral, and group and individual therapy for people in beginning alcohol recovery.

"We provide a place where people can experience not-drinking safely," explains co-director Diana Nordbrok. "We work in groups to break the isolation. Clients are less resistant if peers are advising them to stop. It's all multiple addictions now. There is no such thing as a specialist in addiction anymore.

"Recovery is only possible when people feel safe without drugs. Drugs are really an attempt to self-medicate, to cry for help, to attempt to change their life," comments Nordbrok. "We work with people in the early phase of recovery, the first year of being drug-free, which is a no man's land for people after a twenty-year drug history. We show them how to survive drug-free. Like our clients, we define success by the phrase 'One day at a time.'"

Seymour, who also teaches courses in the physiology and pharmacology of substance abuse in Bay Area colleges, explains that the general program for chemical dependency treatment involves intervention (recognition of the dependency), detoxification (physiological systemic cleansing), and recovery (prolonged abstinence). It is at the recovery-aftercare phase, usually characterized by what Seymour vividly calls "white knuckle sobriety," that the greatest difficulties and recidivisim occur. But it's also precisely here that the most innovation is required, self-help modalities that can permanently re-channel psychoemotional energies into non-addictive streams of activity.

As Seymour and Smith, and many other alternative practitioners have found, *free* also means "a freedom to work beyond the confines of conventional medicine in finding answers." The drug-free recovery strategy that Smith and Seymour chart in their new book is built on a cornucopia of alternative, consciousness-enhancing practices that "empower individuals to discover [that] their use of drugs is superfluous." These include yoga, meditation, exercise, aerobics, lucid dreaming, biofeedback, acupuncture, hypnotism, hydrotherapy, massage, and creative expression.

In *Drugfree* and at the Clinic, Smith and Seymour extoll the benefits and details of each modality and urge clients to experiment with them in the greater San Francisco-Berkeley community. The idea is that the quality of consciousness (euphoria, inspiration, detachment, rapport) sought in the drugs can be attained, and without any physical or familial debilitation, through such practices.

"With minds, bodies, and spirits clear of drugs and their effects," state Smith and Seymour, "we can come to appreciate the psychoactive qualities of many activities that we may have taken for granted." Implicit in this program is the insistence that a client assume the major share of his or her life responsibilities, throwing off the mantle of negativity and rerouting his or her temporarily derailed development. The client has to make what both the Buddha and Richard Seymour describe as "a turning-about in the deepest seat of consciousness."

The Addictive Physiology

One of the community resources the Haight Ashbury Free Medical Clinic calls on is the forty-eight-bed in-patient Merritt-Peralta Chemical Dependency Recovery Hospital in nearby Oakland, where Dr. David Smith is research director.

At Merritt-Peralta Smith's research team is studying various non-narcotic nutritional and biochemical supplements to facilitate painful withdrawal and detoxification. In addition, Smith is looking at brain chemistry and "the addictive physiology," the use of high doses of amino acids for withdrawal, the use of naltrexone (a long-lasting opiate-receptor antagonist) in relieving opiate addiction, as well as family research, nutrition, exercise in relation to recovery, and the spiritual aspects of A.A.'s program. The results so far are most encouraging.

"Free means 'a freedom to work beyond the confines of conventional medicine in finding answers.'"

"We've found that with cocaine addiction and withdrawal there is a severe depletion of neurotransmitters in the brain, primarily nor-epinephrine and dopamine," says Smith, who sees some 500 drug-abusing patients yearly. "The amino acid L-tryptophane builds up these depleted neurotransmitters so we're using it in little pills for cocaine withdrawal."

Merritt-Peralta is one of the leaders in the new field of benign, nonaddictive nutritional supplements to ease the physical withdrawal process. This field is also one of the major areas of expansion in other clinics, says Smith. "The biomedical field is an extremely fertile area and one of the most promising. We believe drug-free is abstinence from any major mood-altering drugs. Thus the use of a nutritional supplement does not violate a chemical-free philosophy."

Since 1973 Dr. Michael Smith and colleagues at the Acupuncture Clinic of the Lincoln Medical and Mental Health Center in the Bronx, New York, have achieved remarkable and consistent success in sedating withdrawal symptoms through acupuncture treatments on the outer ears. Advantages include physiological relaxation, a reduction of drug craving, and modification of appetite swings and depressive states. Smith's clinic, which has received considerable attention in the mainstream media, handles over 200 addicts daily.

The treatment procedure is disarmingly simple. Walk-in patients, treated in an open communal room, receive three-to-five short thin needles on outer ear points for forty-five minutes. Altogether 80 percent of detoxification clients report a favorable response. Other more comprehensive response studies confirm the positive reception that withdrawing addicts have to an otherwise unusual protocol.

In a report issued in May 1987, based on a three-month study of 105 female crack addicts, Smith described the results as "among the most impressive

I have seen in my professional career." After three months of acupuncture and counseling, 42 percent showed no further traces of cocaine in their urine, which means continuing abstinence. Another study of forty-six pregnant "crack mothers" revealed that 50 percent showed a continuous pattern of drug-free behavior during a two-month period. "The quick and effective acupuncture treatments calm patients, giving them breathing space from their chronic drug hunger and consumption, and making them accessible to counseling and eventually rehabilitation."

Ear acupuncture seems to work because it stimulates the renewal of endorphin production, which the opiate addiction had shut down. Severe physical withdrawal symptoms occur, as David Smith and Richard Seymour explain, because, "There are neither opiates nor endorphins there to protect the cleaning-up addict from all the pain of regaining a systemic balance."

Acupuncture Efficacious

Acupuncture is also efficacious in remedying alcoholic recidivism, as a May 1987 study released by Dr. Milton Bullock at the Hennepin County Detox Center in Minneapolis indicates. Bullock's investigation centered on "a randomized trial of acupuncture on a group of fifty-four hard-core alcoholic recidivists." The results were very encouraging, Bullock reports. "Patients in the treatment group expressed less need for alcohol and had fewer drinking episodes and admissions to the Detox Center." The majority of the patients who received acupuncture felt that it had "a definite impact on their desire to drink."

Smith, who had just returned from the World Congress of Acupuncture and Natural Medicine in Beijing, where he presented a paper on acupuncture and AIDS, is very optimistic about the possibilities of acupuncture for addiction. "I don't know many other alternative treatments for drug addiction that have any serious input," he told *East West* recently. "Acupuncture treatment simply has a better record of treatment for cocaine and alcohol abuse in detoxification than any other treatment that's ever been tried. Without any question, the statistics are much better."

As president of NADA, the National Acupuncture Detoxification Association, Smith has spread his well-founded optimism far afield from the Bronx clinic. Lincoln Center's success has inspired many other public agencies and treatment programs to try acupuncture. These include Hennepin County Medical Center (Minneapolis), Los Angeles County Sheriff's Department (seventy patients daily), Hooper Center (Portland, Oregon), Kings County (N.Y.) Hospital (forty patients daily), Project Recovery (Pine Ridge, South Dakota, a Sioux Indian reservation), Nagyfa Hospital (Szeged, Hungary, with a 60 percent

success rate in the first six months), and Turnaround in downtown Los Angeles.

Practitioners at the public clinic of the John Bastyr College of Naturopathic Medicine in Seattle describe a different protocol from acupuncture, one that is based on botanicals and the facilitation of natural healing processes.

"Acupuncture treatment simply has a better record of treatment for cocaine and alcohol abuse in detoxification than any other treatment that's ever been tried."

According to clinical and faculty member Jane Guiltinan, sugar is the primary addiction people suffer from, beginning a process that can accelerate into further addictions to caffeine, nicotine, alcohol, cocaine, and other substances. "Alcohol is basically looked at as a sugar by the body," Guiltinan comments. "Cocaine, though it's not a substance with calories and is not metabolized as a carbohydrate, has effects on the adrenal glands, liver, pancreas, and central nervous system, all organs that directly affect blood sugar."

Guiltinan delineates four stages in the naturopathic style of treating drug addictions. The first is identification of the problem through counseling and patient education in order to develop motivation and a commitment to resolve the situation. Drug use must be curtailed while the physician provides a view of what emotional-psychological support systems will work for the client.

Detoxification comes next and might involve either a cleansing diet or actual fast, and generally extends for five to twenty-one days. "In my practice a cleansing diet is high in complex carbohydrates, such as brown rice, millet, and whole grains, organic fruits and vegetables, and low-to-moderate protein to rest the liver, which usually is not functioning well after a long-term addiction. I would keep the protein low unless the person is debilitated or wasting away. Absolutely no sugars or refined carbohydrates, and almost no processed foods would be served."

Guiltinan then applies megadoses of vitamin C for cleansing, up to 10,000 mg in divided doses during the day. "Vitamin C is a potent antioxidant which scavenges free radicals and toxins from the body, and stimulates the immune system."

The much-abused liver is fortified with several botanicals, including chenionanthus, choline, and inositol (nutritional supplements), and beets and artichokes (containing silymarin). For the sleeping disorders and nervous agitation that accompany alcohol withdrawal, mineral combinations like calcium-magnesium in liquid form, or *Valerian passiflora* or hops given as teas, are effective, in addition to lukewarm baths with Epsom salts. For cocaine withdrawal symptoms, stimulating support for the adrenal glands is provided by teas of licorice root, ephreda, and peppermint, and vitamin B_6 pills.

The emphasis in the detoxification stage is to eliminate through all four eliminative organs. Thus copious amounts of water are consumed to flush the kidneys and bowels, while sweating is induced through exercise or saunas, along with deep breathing, to move toxins out through the skin and lungs.

The third phase of naturopathic treatment is a nourishing protocol to refortify the devitalized and drained tissues. This may last up to three months but usually takes four to six weeks, says Guiltinan. Acupuncture, Chinese herbs, or homeopathic medicines might be used to deal with the body's subtler electromagnetic imbalances. Licorice root, pantothenic acid, and vitamin C will nourish the adrenal glands. For the pancreas, the blood sugar level must be stabilized so that the customary drastic upsurges and troughs which lead to either food or drug craving can be avoided; the pancreas is fortified with B vitamins and chromium. The liver is given "building herbs" like silymarin and "tonifyers" like *Avena sativa* (oats, in powdered form)—also good for the nervous system—as well as nettle, Siberian ginseng, and red raspberry leaf teas.

The Final Phase

The final phase, which lasts in its intense form for three to six months but which is otherwise ongoing, is rebuilding-restrengthening. A balanced diet with more non-animal protein, and ample, live, nourishing fresh foods, multivitamin supplements, and vigorous outdoor exercise are all components, says Guiltinan.

"Air, light, and water are probably the most powerful healing and spiritually rebuilding agents we have," Guiltinan suggests. "I encourage my patients to end their showers at home with a blast of cold water for a full minute. This immensely strengthens their body's vitality and durability. Then we provide any further psychological or emotional support, either through us or referrals, that they might need to make the real core changes in their lives to keep from falling back into the same patterns."

At the National College of Naturopathic Medicine, also located in the Pacific Northwest (in Portland, Oregon), a small outpatient clinic treats addicts. Like its colleagues at John Bastyr, the Portland naturopathic public clinic hasn't been properly tested to date for large-scale treatments, due to inadequate funding, insurance reimbursement restrictions, and lack of awareness by addicts of this option, explains Dr. Guru Sandesh Singh Khalsa, professor and clinical physician at the school.

Few Portland addicts seek out naturopaths for treatment, even though sliding-fee scales are offered.

"In this medicine you have to take an amount of responsibility for yourself in changing your lifestyle and orientation," explains Khalsa. "For a lot of these people, it's touchy even to get up and fix a meal."

Despite the problems, naturopathy holds promise for treating addictions successfully. "If you would combine the things we do with the vocational rehabilitation and counseling, there would be a higher success rate," says Khalsa. "By removing the physical problems that underlie addiction, by improving nutrition, increasing the elimination of toxins, and making people feel better physically, there would probably be far fewer people dropping back into addiction." . . .

> ### "Naturopathy holds promise for treating addictions successfully."

Emily Dickinson once wrote, "Narcotics cannot still the tooth that nibbles at the Soul." Her sense of the truth behind addictions from 125 years ago rings true today, that addictions are self-destructive, self-numbing developmental detours, with a biochemical dependency component certainly, that a person takes on the way to somewhere else, to wholeness. As we've seen, chemical dependency with all its psychoemotional ramifications, is reversible. Even the darkest of personal situations can be turned around with commitment and a little outside encouragement.

This affirming sense of miraculous turnaround is what David Smith and Richard Seymour extoll both in *Drugfree* and at their Haight Ashbury Free Medical Clinic. "We believe that there are positive alternatives, ways of living a life of pleasurable and rewarding recovery."

Smith and Seymour believe that primary prevention among young adults is of paramount importance. "We're working now on the development of a comprehensive school drug and alcohol prevention program based on the ideas in the book," says Seymour, "that will run from kindergarten through high school." Yet Seymour prefers the term "life enhancement" over prevention, because it better describes a process "whereby people work together for mutual growth. What is needed by young people—by everyone, for that matter—is not limiting but expanding, not curtailing freedom but increasing it by providing opportunities for growth and development that make the use of drugs superfluous."

Richard Leviton is a senior writer for East West.

"People will stop using drugs as soon as they find something better."

Drug Education Should Stress Alternatives to Drug Use

Allan Y. Cohen

"Why would you want to use drugs?" asked the psychologist. His client looked him straight in the eye and asked back, "Why not?"

A lot of time and money has been spent trying to find out why people use drugs. . . . You begin to get the idea that there are all kinds of causes for drug abuse—social and economic problems, personality difficulties, family hassles, boredom, curiosity, escape, excitement, pressure from peers, and many, many more. We realize that people have been raised in different environments. They have different needs and different motives, and they may grow up with different attitudes about taking chemical substances—whether cigarettes, alcohol, prescription medicine, or illegal drugs.

Americans use an incredible amount of legal and illegal drugs. Adults seem to prefer abusing the legal variety—alcohol, tranquilizers, nicotine in tobacco, or stimulants (like diet pills). Somehow people seem to have lost respect for the natural efficiency of their own bodies and minds. When they feel sick or mentally worried, the first thing they think of is "medicine." Billions of doses of dangerous mind drugs are prescribed by doctors, sometimes because the doctors don't know how to handle normal psychological problems, sometimes because the patients demand some kind of medication. Most researchers estimate that more than half the American adult population has a serious problem with the abuse of mind drugs.

Social scientists have almost given up some of their pet theories about the "weird" drug user. It now seems clear that we are in the midst of a drug-using society, a civilization that considers drug use natural and looks to external aids for the solution of internal problems. The use of mind drugs is a *style*, a style reinforced by adult behavior, by

pharmaceutical company media advertising, and by the idea that all medical problems should be cured by drugs.

Drug users range from those who are just curious experimenters to those who are completely hooked. Most of the publicity in the early 1970s centered on heroin addiction, on the narcotic-dependent "junkie" often involved in crime to support the demanding habit. But heroin use is merely the tip of an iceberg. Other mind drugs might not be as dramatically addicting, but their effects can be dangerous, partly because they can also be subtle. New findings on the effects of THC (their principal active chemical) suggest that "grass" and "hash" may have accumulative negative effects on the nervous system and especially on the personality and mind. Heavy users, who smoke more than once a week, may have some cumulative effects. Since these effects occur gradually, they never suspect that the cause is marijuana or hashish.

Alternatives to Drugs

People continue to take drugs even when they are aware of unhealthful side effects. The classic case is cigarette smoking—the "mature" adults in our society have shown a remarkable resistance to giving up cigarettes, knowing the health hazards involved.

This type of behavior helps us to understand a "mystery" about drug abuse that may point the way to some solutions. The secret is an observation often overlooked because it is merely common sense: *people use drugs because they want to.* They get some enjoyment from drugs, even if the enjoyment is temporary. People use drugs in the hope of feeling better, whatever that might mean for each individual. Unfortunately, most drugs seem to exact a more precious price than the "high" they give, the fun they provide, or the relief they temporarily produce.

Allan Y. Cohen, "Now the Good Part Begins: Alternatives to Drug Abuse" in *Mind Drugs*, editor Margaret O. Hyde. Reprinted by permission of Dodd, Mead & Company. Copyright © 1986 Dodd, Mead & Company, Inc.

Psychologists and educators say to drug users, "You know that drugs are bad for you, physically and mentally! You've seen the damage that drugs have done to friends of yours! But you keep doing it. How can we convince you to stop?" The young person takes it all in and quietly challenges, "Show me something better!"

This tells us a lot about preventing drug abuse before it destroys a person's chance to make a life for him- or herself. People *will stop* using drugs as soon as they find *something better*. People are not as likely to *start* serious drug abuse if they have *something better going for them*. The "something better" is what we might call an *alternative to drugs*. The common denominator of all successful drug abuse prevention and treatment programs is their ability to provide the potential users, the experimenter, or the addict with meaningful and satisfying alternatives.

> *"The common denominator of all successful drug abuse prevention and treatment programs is their ability to provide . . . meaningful and satisfying alternatives."*

When we talk about "alternatives" to drugs, we do not mean the same thing as "substitutes" for drugs. One crutch is not necessarily better than another. A young heroin addict might give up "junk" in order to join a violent street gang; this might be a substitute, but it is not a very constructive alternative. Another thing to realize about alternatives is that no one alternative is relevant for everyone. There is a pertinent saying in the drug field: "Different strokes for different folks." We know that people abuse drugs for different motives and needs. Sometimes these motives and needs come from *deficiency*, from serious problems. But other times there are *positive* needs causing drug experimentation, like the desire for adventure, curiosity, or the urge to explore oneself. Since people have varying needs and aspirations, the alternatives replacing drugs must also vary.

Generally, alternatives must be stronger as drug dependency gets stronger. The hard-core heroin addict has to be faced with a very involving alternative. Many successful former addicts have undergone deep spiritual conversions. Others have been rehabilitated through a tightly controlled residential therapeutic community where they could neither obtain drugs nor kid anybody about who they were.

When children first start out in school, it is possible to provide them with much subtler alternatives—like a real joy for learning, respect for themselves and their bodies, and the ability to understand and enjoy other children. The more people have good feelings about themselves, the better they can appreciate and relate to others; the more they know what is important in their lives, the less attraction the drug experience will have for them. It is not so much that drug-free people are afraid of drugs—educators have not been successful in *scaring* students out of drug use—it is more that they have better things to do than getting "stoned" with chemicals. . . .

Types of Alternatives to Drugs

There is one primary step in promoting this new approach to the drug problem—getting people to think about alternatives and to apply the principle to themselves. A parallel trend we see is a new appreciation of the natural environment. The beauty and desirability of unspoiled air, water, and open space is increasingly a matter of concern. Ever since the 1960s, Americans have become more and more alert to the necessity for avoiding and reducing pollution. The same consciousness has been turning to the purity of foods and the undesirability of artificial and perhaps dangerous ingredients. Today, more and more people are becoming aware of "health pollution" and are trying to be moderate in drug use as well as avoiding other toxic chemicals.

Before mentioning other types of alternatives, it might be good to mention one alternative rarely discussed—the discontinuance of drug use. Many moderate drug users find that they feel much better (physically and mentally) after they stop their drug use. Even long-term users of marijuana report rather dramatic improvements (according to their own judgments) three to twelve weeks after they stop using mind drugs.

Of course, the structure of our social institutions has much to do with whether or not many kinds of alternatives are available to the general public. Part of the more general cause of the drug-use explosion has been the inability of government and society to meet adequately individuals' legitimate aspirations. These same deficiencies in society make the application of viable alternatives very difficult and slow. A good example of this is our elementary and secondary school systems. With some real exceptions, school is likely to be an uninspiring and sometimes meaningless experience for many students. In many places, the school curriculum is built around the world of students of twenty years ago. Most schools still stress competition and the importance of grades; this interferes with the joy of learning. Much of the material covered in the classroom has little application to the practical problems encountered by students. Many old-time teachers are very reluctant to explore the area of students' *feelings*; and yet, the emotional and mental state of students is critically important to them when decisions about drug use have to be made.

In a true "alternative school" situation, teachers are allowed to innovate and get "turned on" by the subject, thereby transferring this enthusiasm to students. Since teachers are possible models, they would, ideally, be relatively free from drug dependency and be able to communicate the feeling of the "natural high." Students would be given feedback, but not graded—especially in so-called extracurricular areas like art, music, physical education, manual arts, homemaking, drama, etc. After all, students should be able to develop real interests in leisure or career activities, freed from the debilitating pressure and anxiety that comes from worrying about how good one is at a particular subject. If a person finds something valuable in his or her life, whether it is a hobby, a talent, a purpose, other people, etc., the lure of drugs loses its luster.

Examples of Natural Alternatives

In order to be more specific, let us look at examples of natural alternatives. One way of categorizing alternatives involves *areas of experience*. These areas of experience—from physical to spiritual—correspond to the kinds of gratification people seek when they use drugs. There is a lack in some area of experience and people try to use drugs to fill that deficiency.

One level is the *physical*. Here the person may use drugs to try to improve his or her sense of physical well-being. Examples of alternatives (there are scores more for each level of experience) might include the following: dance and movement training; physical recreation, e.g., athletics, exercise, hiking, and nature exploration (for *fun*); relaxation exercises, physical (*hatha*) yoga, and proper training in the martial arts, e.g., aikido, karate, judo.

Some people use drugs to gain satisfaction in the *sensory* area—involving the desire to enhance or stimulate sight, hearing, touch, or taste. Examples of alternatives include such things as: training in sensory awareness (balance, coordination, small-muscle control, etc.); visual exploration of nature; and the learning and practice of responsible sexuality.

One of the areas most commonly stressed in the study of drug abuse is the *emotional* level of experience. Here people might turn to drugs to gain relief from psychological pain, in an attempt to solve personal problems, or to eliminate anxiety or gain some measure of emotional relaxation. Natural alternatives in this area might include: getting a trusted professional to give counseling or psychotherapy; educational instruction in the psychology of personal development; and emotional awareness exercises, e.g., learning "body language," self-awareness, and psychological awareness.

A key area of alternatives is the *interpersonal*. It is no secret that many use drugs to try to gain acceptance and status from friends and peers or to break through interpersonal barriers of one kind or another. Natural alternatives include a whole host of possibilities, some being: getting into a group of friends who are not serious drug users; experiencing well-run group therapy or counseling sessions; family life education and training; emotional tutoring, e.g., big brothers and sisters helping younger people; and creation of community "rap centers."

A rarer type of gratification sought by drug users involves the *mental* or *intellectual* level. They try to escape mental boredom, gain new understanding in the world of ideas, to study better or satisfy intellectual curiosity. Drug-induced insight is rarely enlightening—the author knows of a respected scientist who made an incredible "discovery" under LSD; for weeks afterward he walked the streets telling everyone he saw that "two plus two equals four." There are more natural possibilities, e.g., intellectual excitement through reading, discussion, creative games and puzzles; training in hypnosis under qualified teachers; creativity training; and memory training.

In the 1960s there was quite a bit of talk about the *creative* or *aesthetic* level of experience related to drugs. People tried to enhance their experience or productivity in the arts. (Some people still cannot stand to go to a concert unless they are high.) Yet natural alternatives work out better for the artist or appreciator of art and music. Alternatives might include: nongraded instruction in the performing or appreciation of music; creative hobbies, e.g., crafts, sewing, cooking, gardening, and photography; and experience in communications skills such as writing, public speaking, conversation, etc.

"If a person finds something valuable in his or her life, whether it is a hobby, a talent, a purpose, other people, etc., the lure of drugs loses its luster."

Another subtle level might be called *stylistic*. Here the user is caught up in certain styles, e.g., the need to identify through imitation of adults or the desire for achieving things instantly. Alternatives can include: exposure to others who are meaningfully involved in nonchemical alternatives; parents agreeing to cut down on their own drug use; and exposure to the philosophy of the natural, appreciating the great possibilities of inner human resources.

An area often overlooked but with great potential for dissatisfied drug experimenters is the *social*, including the notion of *service to others*. Some may be desperate about our social and political situation and try to forget it or rebel against it through the fog of drugs. The alternatives are not only more constructive, but can be very fulfilling on a personal level. In the political area, people can be involved and work for particular candidates or in nonpartisan political projects, as in lobbying for environmental groups. One of the most powerful sets of alternatives, available to almost everyone, consists of getting involved in social service—helping others. This could include: helping the poor; providing companionship to the lonely; helping those in trouble with drugs or family problems; or helping out in voluntary organizations (like YMCA and YWCA, Girl Scouts, Boys' Clubs, Big Brothers and Sisters, etc.).

Another experiential level, the *spiritual* or *mystical*, attracted many users of psychedelics. Psychologists and sociologists are beginning to discover that they underestimated the power of the drive for spirituality. Some people hoped that drugs would give them direct spiritual experience, going beyond the limits of orthodox religion; they hoped to get a vision of God. For these people drugs can be very seductive because certain chemicals can induce illusory religious experiences that seem very real to the user. Even though a user may be temporarily inspired, too often she chases after this mirage and cannot apply what she thought were profound mystical insights. In contrast, growing in popularity are nonchemical methods for spiritual understanding and experience. These include such approaches as: study of spiritual literature; meditation and yoga; contemplation and prayer; spiritual song and dance; and increased exposure to different techniques of applied spirituality. In the spiritual area as well as the other areas not every alternative offered is of the highest quality. As we become more sophisticated about alternative means of inner growth, we shall become better able to discriminate the really helpful approaches from the hollow or misleading ones.

"Growing in popularity are nonchemical methods for spiritual understanding and experience."

The examples given above do not cover every level of experience; indeed, some readers might like to categorize alternatives in very different ways. There are some examples that we might call *miscellaneous*. These relate to other needs such as the need for risk-taking and danger, the desire for adventure or exploration, the need for economic success, and combinations of various other motives. Here one might think of alternatives such as: sky diving,

scuba diving, and "Outward Bound" survival training; vocational counseling leading to meaningful employment; and the possibility of gaining school credits for actual work experience in the community.

Hints for the Alternatives Seeker

The use of mind drugs demands that people be *passive* and *uninvolved*. The lure of chemical intervention is that you can get something for nothing—by swallowing, smoking, or injecting you get happiness at a low price. But the evidence shows the contrary. When someone possesses the drug style, it possesses him back. But it is not always fair to criticize the drug user. After all, he is merely falling for the cultural line; he is going along with the prevailing philosophy that deep down, people are not really worth that much and have to be enhanced by some outside agent.

But times are changing. A few years ago, in many circles, it was more hip to use drugs; now it is beginning to be more hip to go beyond drugs. But how does one choose the way of going beyond? For some, it is no big problem—drugs are not that attractive; life is involving and meaningful, if not always easy. Other searchers may not be getting much help from their families, schools, or communities—they may not recognize the need to assist in the provision of alternatives.

The individual searcher must be alert. If she wants to be happier and more fulfilled, she must *try*. A great alternative in itself is the *process of putting energy into finding alternatives*. There are other guidelines that may be helpful. Be optimistic. If you have used drugs, ask yourself what you enjoyed about the drug experience; ask what areas in your life need work and fulfillment. Then *seek*, particularly in the areas of your highest interest. That means asking about different alternatives you hear about or read about. Follow up leads, investigate possibilities. One useful way is to discover the secrets of those you really admire— whether friends, peers, or heroes—in order to find out what turns *them* on. It can help to ask anyone who might know about interesting avenues of exploration, especially former drug users. Look for help and ask for help if you need it. Stay off drugs as much as possible while looking; it will help you to evaluate the alternatives. Get others to join you in the search. Have faith in yourself and the possibilities of natural alternatives.

Allan Y. Cohen is the executive director of the Pacific Institute for Research and Evaluation, a social science research center specializing in substance abuse. He is also a practicing clinical psychologist.

"The solution is not more values clarification and situation ethics, but factual instruction backed up by a no-nonsense school policy."

Drug Education Should Stress Abstinence

Malcolm Lawrence

The American people are, quite frankly, growing weary of a problem that has plagued us for two decades. There is a real job to do. We must all face in the same direction and destroy an annual 100 billion dollar industry that threatens the moral fiber and economic base of our society.

A major contributing factor to the tolerance of illicit drugs and narcotics in America is that many of our schools are sending out weak and confusing messages. Since the early 1970s, educators have been brainwashed by permissive pundits and curriculum developers to believe that scare tactics and facts about drugs are counter-productive and that the solution to the drug abuse problem for students is to use a values clarification approach, apply compassion, give counseling, set up hot lines, and at all costs avoid using the word "don't" when discussing drugs. The fashionable approach in drug education has been to let the children examine all aspects of their feelings, attitudes, values and societal pressures and then make their own decisions about whether to use drugs.

In point of fact, our schools never really did use scare tactics or give adequate factual information about the serious effects of drugs on the body, the brain and the genes. Those who say that scare tactics and facts have failed are usually the ones who make the ridiculous argument that law enforcement has failed, the implication being that we have to give up law enforcement and try something else. As any sensible person in the drug battle knows, we need all the help we can get.

In my 17 years of experience in dealing with the drug problem, I have read much drug curriculum and talked with many parents. I have yet to come across any good, solid, effective education. I have,

Malcolm Lawrence, "Drug Abuse Prevention," a speech presented to the Joint Hearing on the Problem of 'Crack' Cocaine, held by the House Select Committee on Narcotics Abuse and Control and the House Select Committee on Children, Youth, and Families in Washington, DC on July 15, 1986.

however, become acquainted with some poor curriculum. Let me cite some examples.

Heading the list of wrong-headed education is the values clarification approach exemplified by the widely used but highly controversial kindergarten through 12th grade curriculum called, "Here's Looking at You, Two." This misguided package dwells on stress, fear, anxiety and unpleasant situations, but does not teach about the real dangers of illicit drugs or that taking drugs is wrong.

Missing the Mark

Another curriculum that misses the mark is called "Ombudsman," which was developed with funds from the National Institute on Drug Abuse. "Ombudsman" has very little information about drugs, but exposes 5th through 10th graders to such things as role playing, encounter activities, feelings charades, warm fuzzies, love lists, self portraits, personal questionnaires, the trust fall, the human knot, who shall survive exercises, gravestone statements and death notices.

Even children in grades 1 through 6 have to suffer through a values clarification course called, "The Me-Me Drug Prevention Education Program," developed 11 years ago with U.S. Office of Education Title III funds. Little 6 and 7 year-olds learn all about their full potential, self concepts, decision making, peer pressure, Mr. Yuk, and developing positive feelings toward their teachers. Unfortunately, "Me-Me" and "Ombudsman" are still being promoted by the National Diffusion Network of the U.S. Department of Education.

There are elementary level drug courses that classify all kinds of substances into the harmful basket category—coffee, tea, soft drinks, aspirin, tobacco, cough syrup, beer, marihuana, heroin, cocaine, pills of all sorts, etc.—conveying the notion that the differences are minor. To a small child, if something is bad, it is bad. This type of education presents a real problem for the 7 year-old who may tend to equate drinking a cup of coffee with shooting heroin.

Some schools give 2nd and 3rd graders an assignment to explore the family medicine cabinet and take inventory of what they find. It is amazing how curriculum developers try to encourage curiosity in children well beyond their maturity levels. It is even more amazing that school boards approve such curricula. Showing a small child where mom's sleeping pills are can be the same as handing him a loaded gun.

About the most asinine approach I have come across is from the 7th grade drug curriculum in my own community, Montgomery County, Maryland, which opens as follows:

> Currently, community concern regarding drug misuse is centered on today's youth. They are growing up in a world full of problems for which they see no immediate solutions. Young people in adolescence undergo bodily changes with related emotional pressures. Superimposed on this is peer pressure, accompanied by the 'fad syndrome.' It is not surprising, therefore, that many young people are seeking an escape through drug experimentation.

Stupid Rationale

This message implies that earlier generations did not experience bodily changes, emotional pressures, fads and peer influences and were able to solve all of their problems. Therefore, those people didn't need drugs. Such rationale is not only stupid, but is an open invitation for 12 year-olds to enter the drug culture.

It is no small wonder that drug abuse education in our schools is getting such a bum rap. It is also no small wonder that there are 20 million persons admitting to using cocaine, five million regular cocaine users and up to one million cocaine addicts, as well as half a million heroin addicts and countless millions of abusers of marihuana, PCP, and other illicit drugs. Will crack get as strong a hold on our youth as marihuana has?

My observations may be limited, but I have reached the conclusion that our wishy-washy approach on the demand side of the drug problem has been a major contributing element to addiction and death among our youth. In a word, our schools are not tough enough. The solution is not more values clarification and situation ethics, but factual instruction backed up by a no-nonsense school policy. . . .

Drug abuse prevention is, of course, a blend of education and enforcement. On the enforcement end, the controls include international and bilateral agreements negotiated by the U.S. Department of State to curtail the flow of drugs and narcotics into our country, border inspections by the Customs Service, interstate control efforts by the agencies of the Justice Department, and the enforcement

facilities of the state and local police. This down-the-line control is carried out by official organizations which we maintain through tax dollars to keep illicit substances from reaching the end-users who constitute the effective demand. Why?

We do it because it has been determined that the abuse of certain drugs is dangerous, insidious, and a menace to society and that steps must be taken to restrict the traffic in the interest of the public welfare. In other words, as a nation, through those agencies charged with the maintenance of law and order, we are saying "The abuse of illicit drugs is harmful and, therefore, wrong."

"There is no need for a pro-and-con debate. Drug abuse is bad."

It seems clear to me that the reasons for the enforcement measures in the area of drug abuse should form the basis of our educational approach. Indeed, the message to be emphasized in the home, in the schools and by the media should be the straightforward extension of the findings of the medical and chemical experts as well as the justifications for the laws.

A massive supply of drugs and narcotics has slipped into our midst within the past two decades, but this does not mean we should in any way foster the notion promoted in our schools that each person be permitted to make an independent analysis and decide whether or not illegal drugs are the thing for him. It cannot be viewed as a civil right and a privilege for any individual to dabble in such substances and in the process drag others with him down the road to addiction and crime. It is nothing short of ridiculous to devote so many of our resources to cutting off the supply of drugs and at the same time carry on with a soft, compassionate approach at the demand end.

We are not trying to curtail the supply simply to give enforcement officials something to do. There is a much better reason, and that is to keep the drugs and narcotics from the end-users. If the abusers and the prospective abusers do not understand this, then perhaps the message should be put across much more emphatically than it has in the past. We should stop teaching the reasons why children take drugs and instead teach them the very basic and perfectly clear reason children should not take drugs. The message should go to young and old alike; the young do not have a monopoly on self-abuse.

The Practical Truth

Drug abuse education can only be effective if it is done correctly, if it tells the practical truth. There is no need for a pro-and-con debate. Drug abuse is bad. It can destroy the mind and kill the body. In a word, it is stupid. This is a very simple truth, a sad one reported daily in the newspapers. Hence, we should moralize about the subject. We should say it is wrong to abuse drugs and to abuse yourself. We should say, "Don't!"

Let's face it. A large percentage of our youth has been suckered into a drug-oriented cult, whether on a street corner, in a school yard or at a rock festival. At the same time, many otherwise clear-thinking adults have been duped into believing that a vast range of social and psychological pressures has forced children to rely on a crutch to soothe their natural and normal growing pains, a crutch which is preventing a portion of our youth from maturing, facing reality and earning a decent place in society. . . .

Since children spend almost half of their waking hours, five days a week, involved in school activities away from home, the schools constitute the most important focal point for the youth of the community and should spearhead the drive against drug abuse. The public schools are a multi-billion dollar infrastructure working for parents and taxpayers. They are well placed to do the job. The selection of the school system does not in any way imply that the schools are the source of the problem, but is merely a plan to unite the community as a whole toward a solution to the drug problem. The opportunity to assume leadership should be readily acceptable to any correct-thinking school board or administration; to refuse this responsibility would be an error of omission. The local board should be pressured to move toward a position of leadership. The parent-teachers associations and the network of business, professional, social and neighborhood civic organizations should rally to the cause and support a consolidated campaign, rather than conduct a splintered program.

"The schools constitute the most important focal point for the youth of the community and should spearhead the drive against drug abuse."

Dealing with the drug problem in the schools calls for much more than "busting" students and throwing them out of the system. Rather, every board of education should formulate a Policy Statement on Drug Abuse which for all practical purposes should apply to the middle school through senior high levels. The Policy Statement should be a community education document. Thus, sufficient copies should be printed and disseminated to parents, students, religious leaders, civic clubs, and other interested groups.

The Policy Statement should condemn the abuse and distribution of drugs and narcotics as defined under the law and implement a constructive action program to combat the problem during school hours and on school property. Specifically, it should do the following:

1. Outline the scope and dangers of drug abuse;
2. Define the penalties under county, state and federal laws for the abuse and distribution of drugs and narcotics, including the penal procedures for juvenile offenders;
3. Identify the principal types of drugs and narcotics as well as the symptoms to look for in persons under or suspected of being under their influence;
4. Spell out the administrative measures to be implemented by school authorities on an area-wide scale to curtail the illegal use and transfer of drugs and narcotics on school property, including school vehicles;
5. Indicate the precise procedures to be followed by school personnel when drugs and narcotics are found on school property and when students are determined to be or suspected of being under their influence.

In developing the administrative measures for inclusion under item 4, school officials should, of course, make a careful study of the conditions contributing to the abuse of drugs by students. They should take into consideration the adverse influences of such things as:

—Inadequate security against unauthorized persons on school grounds,

—Off-campus escapades by students during lunch and other free periods,

—Roll-taking procedures,

—Carelessly administered smoking regulations,

—Presence of publications and student organizations glorifying and advocating the use of illicit drugs, and

—Harboring of drug abusers by school personnel serving as confidants.

Other Factors

Should these or any other factors be contributing to the drug abuse problem, counter-acting regulations should be incorporated as component sections in the Policy Statement and rigorously enforced by the school authorities.

Whatever else might be included in the Statement, there must be a provision calling for absolute and complete cooperation on the part of school administrators with the local police department to eliminate the sources of supply in the area and prevent the casual experimenters from moving on to other drugs and possible addiction. Indeed, the withholding of information concerning the illegal sale and possession of drugs and narcotics is in itself an offense under the law and can be prosecuted.

A logical way of maintaining drug abuse control in the district would be to designate a senior official at each school—ideally the principal or assistant principal—to serve as the central reporting point for all instances of use, sale or transfer of illicit drugs and narcotics on school property. If the system works, such officials would be able to gauge the extent of the problem in their schools and through simultaneous notification of the police and parents could quickly bring about corrective action. While a student offender's name would be turned over to the police, he would not necessarily be taken into custody or "booked." Rather, the police could schedule an appointment for the parents to bring the child in for a discussion.

If it should be the student's initial experience with drugs, it would be far better for him to receive guidance from a police official in the presence of the parents rather than have his problem covered up and withheld from parents by a school staff person under a state confidentiality law. Differences in the qualifications and attitudes of teachers, counselors, nurses and other school employees tend to yield variations in the guidance offered. Moreover, it is most unwise to cover up a situation which should be reported to the parents if to no one else. Should the child be a repeated abuser, there is all the more reason for his practice to be reported to prevent him from continuing on a path to self-destruction.

In any event, consultation with police officials would impress upon the child the harmful effects of drugs as well as the seriousness of criminal arrests and serve as an excellent deterrent against further experimentation with trouble via the drug route. In short, he will have been adequately and officially informed and warned. If he abuses or in any way gets involved with drugs again, he does so in defiance of the law. If and when apprehended, he should be appropriately disciplined. Obviously should the offender be addicted to cocaine, heroin or some other narcotic, he should be removed from the school system and committed to a rehabilitation center.

"There should be no glamorization of the topic of drug abuse, no soppy mysticism and no soul-searching seminars."

I wish to re-emphasize that the Policy Statement on Drug Abuse should go to all school personnel, parents and students so that everyone in the system is aware of the rules.

In addition to its regulatory function, the school's Policy Statement should provide the basic thrust for the drug abuse curriculum in the classroom.

Instruction should be factual, uniform and uncomplicated. It should be included in routine fashion with the treatment of other health hazards such as alcohol and tobacco and handled in a matter-of-fact way as a component part of the health education instruction. Students should be tested on their knowledge of the subject matter to ensure proper understanding. There should be no glamorization of the topic of drug abuse, no soppy mysticism and no soul-searching seminars on the deep-rooted causes and significance of the drug phenomenon in our society. There should be an absolute minimum of films, and those shown should be selected with the greatest of wisdom.

Overdone Education

I am firmly convinced that if drug abuse education is overdone, it will not only bore the students, but will expand the base of the problem. Student exposure to all aspects of drug abuse on a kindergarten through 12th grade basis would not represent a panacea; it would instead only increase curiosity and lead to greater experimentation with drugs and narcotics. School authorities would do well to keep the instruction within the limits of an informative message and not treat drug abuse as a behavioral science by putting it on a psychological altar. In my view, the 6th grade would be the appropriate starting level for most school areas.

Let me say in closing that the adoption of a constructive policy by the school system of each community in our nation would have a profound influence on the local population in the following ways:

—The subject of drug abuse would be placed in proper perspective, and the current cloud of frustration that tends to mark the reliance on drugs as a predestined curse on the young would drift away.

—The healthy, hardy, fun-loving "in" groups of abusers would be ostracized by their peers and would no longer be considered either fashionable or tolerable.

—The youth of the community would become far too wise to serve as legal guinea pigs for the older libertines and libertarians who dedicate themselves to the worship and use of marihuana, LSD, PCP, cocaine, heroin and other illegal substances.

—The cop-out mentality would disappear because the children would realize that whatever they might want to do, they could do it better without drugs.

Malcolm Lawrence is the former special assistant for International Narcotics Control Matters in the US Department of State.

Stressing Abstinence Will Not Work

Michael D. Newcomb and Peter M. Bentler

The use and abuse of psychoactive chemicals, including not only illicit drugs but also such widely available substances as cigarettes, alcohol, and prescription and over-the-counter medication, has become recognized as a major national—indeed, international—problem that affects all segments of society. While enough anecdotal evidence on the devastating effects of drug abuse on health, social, and personal functioning exists to merit strong efforts at clinical intervention, as well as prevention, scientific evidence on such consequences in relatively normal and unselected populations is really quite meager. In addition, because abuse of a variety of drugs rather than only a single substance tends to be a common occurrence, evidence for the differential consequences of use of particular substances tends to be even more scarce. This represents a pioneering attempt to evaluate the effects of general and specific drug use during adolescence on young adult functioning. . . .

We report a series of integrated analyses based on our unique study of a large sample of young adults whose personal and social development has been followed in our research program. The goal is to examine the impact or consequences of teenage drug use on the transition into young adulthood, the acquisition of normative role responsibilities, and social integration. While controlling for tendencies toward deviance or lack of social conformity, we assess the influence of using various substances during early and late adolescence on the ability to acquire and perform effectively in a variety of adult roles as young adults. Such roles or behaviors include family formation (i.e., marriage, children), as well as difficulties with this (i.e., divorce) or alternatives (i.e., cohabitation), employment, livelihood, and job stability, reliance on public

assistance (welfare, food stamps), sexual behavior, deviance (arrests, criminal activity), educational pursuits, mental health status (i.e., depression, suicide ideation), and social integration (i.e., loneliness, social support). . . .

Teenage Drug Use

Drug use among adolescents and young adults has become quite widespread during the past 25 years, with many characterizing the increase as epidemic in proportion. For instance, in a recent national survey, 92% of high school seniors reported using alcohol some time in their life, whereas 54% reported marijuana use, and 40% reported using some other type of illicit or hard drug. Although it is not too surprising that many teenagers have experimented at some time with various drugs, problems and concerns begin to arise when this experimental use becomes regular use or even abuse. In this same national survey, 37% reported at least one instance of heavy drinking (five or more drinks) during the past two-week period. In addition, 26% reported use of marijuana within the past month and 5% reported daily use. Thus, for many teenagers, drug use is more than an experimental behavior or simply the result of curiosity. For many adolescents, ingestion of various drug substances has become an important facet of their life-style. It is critical to determine how this behavioral life-style of drug involvement affects a teenager's social and psychological development beyond the years of adolescence.

The transition from high school (adolescence) to young adulthood is one of the most important and difficult passages faced by everyone in his or her life. Changes in social environment (high school to college, job, military, or marriage), role responsibility (dependent high school student to independent spouse, parent, coworker), intimacy needs (as lover, spouse, or romantic attachment), community integration (adherence to laws and social norms),

Michael D. Newcomb and Peter M. Bentler, *Consequences of Adolescent Drug Use.* Copyright 1988 by Sage Publications, Inc. Reprinted by permission of Sage Publications, Inc.

and psychological climate (self-feelings, emotional status, stress) can be quite pronounced during this period of development. In fact, one frequently mentioned defining feature of adolescence is the rapid and far-reaching changes occurring in virtually all aspects of life and the resultant high-level stress and disequilibrium. These challenges are related directly to the developmental tasks confronted by adolescents, such as individuation from parents, establishment of one's own socioemotional support system, and career preparation. Of course, these psychological changes occur in conjunction with aspects of biological maturation.

Upon graduation from high school (or leaving high school should the student fail to graduate), many decisions must be made and life directions set. For instance, the young adult may choose to continue living with parents, or leave home and choose a new living arrangement or environment, such as living alone, with roommates, in a dormitory, with a spouse, or cohabitation. At the same time, essential decisions are made regarding life pursuit or livelihood activities, reflecting changes in role responsibility and practical demands. For some, who are financially able and academically inclined, continuing education in college may be a desired life pursuit. Others may choose to engage in part-time or full-time employment, join the military, become a housewife/mother, or perhaps do nothing.

Thus, during this transition from adolescence to young adulthood, the individual is moving from a rather uniform and stable social environment (attending high school and living with parents) to a world that is increasingly differentiated and diversified in regard to new types of peer relationships (coworkers, roommates), personal responsibilities (career, family, livelihood), options for autonomous functioning, and different sanctions for certain behaviors (cigarette and alcohol use become legal, the right to vote is acquired).

"One frequently mentioned defining feature of adolescence is the rapid and far-reaching changes occurring in virtually all aspects of life."

The transition to adulthood is also characterized by a normative succession of social roles, typically progressing from school to work to marriage and family. Each of these new and differing social roles includes varying degrees of traditional (or nontraditional) expectations for attitudes and behavior. As a consequence, the process of entering into these new social role participations and social environments will exert pressure to conform to the existing values of the role, resulting in varying

degrees of role socialization. Role socialization can be observed in changes in behavior or attitude upon entry into the role or environment. For example, if a preexisting behavior is at odds with a new role participation, the individual can either socialize to the role by changing the behavior, or retain the behavior by selecting another role more consonant with the behavior. The desired outcome is to participate in a role that is consistent with attitudes and behavior, by either changing the attitudes and behavior or changing the role.

These are some of the normative processes that characterize the developmental period from adolescence to young adulthood. It has not been determined, however, if, or in what manner, use of drugs in the teenage years affects this adaptation and accommodation to adult responsibilities and behavior. . . .

Prevention and Treatment Implications

Education, prevention, intervention, and treatment of drug abuse have become top priority national issues. Heavy use or abuse of drugs clearly has destructive effects on the individual, social relationships, and society. In our analyses, we have demonstrated this in regard to a wide range of different types of substances over several critical areas of life functioning. We have also shown here and elsewhere that drug use is a relatively common occurrence among today's teenagers. In fact, not experimenting or at least trying tobacco, alcohol, and cannabis as an adolescent can be considered unusual and deviant behavior, because use of these drugs is so widespread. Adolescence is a period of experimentation with new and different attitudes and behaviors, and for good or ill, drug use has become a part of this natural curiosity.

When viewed from this perspective and with appreciation for the nature of adolescence, it would seem that eliminating the trial use of drugs among teenagers is neither an easy nor a high priority goal. Delaying the onset of experimentation as long as possible would most likely have the beneficial effect that experimental drug use would not be as easily transformed to severe drug use, because general coping patterns will have been further developed. Completely avoiding experimentation with drugs, however, seems unlikely in today's society. Thus it would seem that an emphasis must be placed on reducing the abuse, regular use, and misuse of drugs among teenagers. The typical youngster who has a beer or some marijuana at a party is not the one who is going to develop long-term damage as a result of their drug use. It is those teenagers who develop a life-style of drug use to relieve emotional distress and other life stressors (including the natural discomfort of adolescence) who will suffer long-term negative consequences of their use. Such consequences include those that have been identified in our analyses. The negative effects we have found for teenage drug use are not the result of very occasional or infrequent use, but are based on frequent and committed drug use as a teenager over a four-year period from early to late adolescence. It is these youngsters who need to be the focus of prevention and treatment efforts, and not the occasional user who indulges in substance use within social situations.

Peer Influences

An implication of this notion that has been substantiated in research findings is that peer influences tend to motivate nonproblematic experimental use of drugs typically in a social setting. The real concern should not be directed toward eliminating experimental drug use as often generated in peer settings, but toward preventing abuse or problematic use of drugs, which has many other causes aside from peer pressure. While peer pressure is an important and subtle phenomenon, that can no doubt have the effect of enhancing pseudomaturity as emphasized in our precocious development theory, it may not be destructive unless combined with a psychological difficulty. The psychological causes for abuse of drugs are many, but can include emotional distress, lack of self-esteem, low self-efficacy, family problems, inherited vulnerabilities, dysfunctional coping styles, and other stressors faced by the teenager. Dealing with these issues—for example, by personal and social skills training—and showing that drug use does not solve these problems, should be one important message in drug prevention programs. Focusing simply on handling peer pressure, such as the "just say no" approaches, may placate concerned but naive parents, teachers, and funding sources, but is an incomplete approach to confronting the task of preventing drug abuse among this nation's youth.

"It has not been determined if, or in what manner, use of drugs in the teenage years affects adaptation and accommodation to adult responsibilities."

It must also be remembered that alcohol, cannabis, and hard drugs are not the only substances used by adolescents. Cigarettes are the second most frequently used substance by teenagers, with only alcohol being more prevalent. The vast destructive effects of cigarette smoking have been well documented and greater effort must be directed at preventing regular use of this extremely hazardous substance among teenagers. The effects of smoking in adolescence on respiratory impairment are obvious within a few years and, in fact, in the quantities used by teenagers in our sample, cigarettes had greater physically destructive effects over a four-year period than alcohol, cannabis, and hard drugs. The recent increase in smokeless tobacco use among teenagers, especially males, is also alarming. Increased emphasis should be placed on always considering tobacco products when focusing on drug education, prevention, and treatment among teenagers. Such emphasis is a natural concomitant of an emphasis on health promotion.

Etiological Studies

Although the best source of information regarding drug prevention comes from etiological studies, and the best information about drug treatment is found in intervention studies, data from our analyses can also be useful for these tasks. Unfortunately, there has not been a strong tendency to incorporate results of empirical research into education or prevention programming, which may account for the less than successful impacts of such programs. Although many programs have been proposed, rarely do they take into account the multidimensional nature of teenage drug use and the need to integrate a range of divergent approaches.

Although the strictly scare tactics of previous decades are less a part of contemporary intervention effort, virtually all substance use education, prevention, and treatment programs directed toward adolescents emphasize the negative and undesirable consequences of ingesting drugs. It is in this area that the current results can best be utilized in such programs. We have been able to establish that certain types of drugs are related to specific kinds of negative outcomes for the teenager. Information regarding such consequences can be incorporated into programs to convey the possible eventual results of abusing drugs as a teenager. It must be remembered, however, that information-only approaches to drug use education and prevention have not been very effective, but need to be linked to other interventions such as coping skills training and alternatives appreciation.

Present Results

Another distinct implication of our present results for prevention and treatment programs is the fact that drug use among teenagers is one component of an integrated life-style involving attitudes and other behaviors. Thus a strict focus on teenage drug use will be too limited for effective prevention or treatment. At an individual level, the surrounding and correlated aspects of drug use must also be carefully considered and integrated in programs, as, indeed, at the social level, the general community climate must be considered.

Finally, the theoretical hypotheses advanced to help understand the consequences of teenage drug use are quite interesting and potentially useful in and of themselves. They provide important perspectives on how drug use influences adolescent psychosocial development. . . . Many of the propositions make intuitive sense and could help guide program development. They may help provide a richer background against which to understand drug use among teenagers.

In sum, we have been able to provide some new information regarding the impact of teenage drug use on later psychosocial outcomes as young adults. We have attempted to integrate these results into available theories and provide implications for prevention and treatment of drug abuse. Our innovative methodological approach has permitted us to separate out effects of general drug use from types of specific substances, so that a very detailed picture of drug use consequences emerged.

"Although many programs have been proposed, rarely do they take into account the multidimensional nature of teenage drug use."

The study of consequences of teenage drug use represents not only an empirical challenge, but also a challenge to the natural integration of adolescent development theories with theories on the life-span consequences of developmental patterns. This is an old topic in psychology, going back to Freud at least. In contrast to the global consequences of early childhood experiences, which remains a most difficult and abstract area to study, the effects of adolescent drug use would appear to be more narrow in nature and more empirically verifiable. Furthermore, such effects have potentially important consequences in modern society and merit study because drug use is an integral aspect of growing up as a teenager in American society. Consequently, the dynamics of drug involvement and outcomes of drug use are important aspects of maturational or developmental processes occurring between adolescence and young adulthood. . . .

This represents one of the most comprehensive series of studies on consequences of teenage drug use to date. Of course, we have not been able to answer all of the crucial questions. We have, however, been able to provide some clear conclusions that should be useful to a wide range of professionals. Continued research will help bolster and supplement our initial attempts, and yield an even more complete picture of the consequences of teenage drug use. Several research projects have appropriate long-term data to address these vital issues from different perspectives and we must await analyses from these data sets to substantiate or challenge our current findings.

Michael D. Newcomb is adjunct associate professor and associate research psychologist at the University of California, Los Angeles. He is also associate professor in the counseling psychology department at the University of Southern California. Peter M. Bentler is professor of psychology at the NIDA/UCLA Drug Abuse Research Center.

"In a society rooted in strong families, schools and religious institutions...such a drug epidemic could hardly have reached its current proportions."

Returning to Traditional Values Can Prevent Drug Abuse

J.A. Parker

There is a widespread view at the present time that the United States is not winning the war against drugs and drug dealers, either at home or in those foreign countries which are the major sources of narcotics which are shipped into the U.S.

The wholesale price of cocaine is now at its lowest point in years and the nation's consumption of crack and cocaine has more than doubled since 1982. Heroin, despite the fact that there is a growing risk of contracting AIDS from sharing needles, is also making a comeback. The number of drug-related homicides in cities such as Houston, Washington, D.C. and New York is soaring.

In Washington, in the first 40 days of 1988, 410 weapons were seized; more than 25 per cent were automatic and semi-automatic. There were 44 homicides, 77 per cent of them drug-related. "These cases remind me of Wild West shoot-outs," said Police Chief Maurice Turner, Jr. "Drug dealers are terrorizing the city. It's a matter of time before an innocent person is killed." . . .

There appears to be a growing consensus that while efforts to stem the supply of narcotics from abroad must be strengthened, the most important part of the battle is in drying up demand within the U.S. Columnist William Raspberry writes that, " . . . for me, the most encouraging news is what is happening in some of this city's (Washington, D.C.) most drug-ridden neighborhoods. Worried parents and preachers, vulnerable teenagers and concerned community leaders have declared their own war on drugs. They have served notice that they will no longer tolerate the infiltration of pushers into their communities. They have pledged to help police close down 'crack houses' and other places known to be dealing drugs. They won't argue with the president's pledge to do something about the international

menace of drug dealing, but they recognize their own need to do something about the enemy agent nearer at hand: the big-spending dealer bent on recruiting or poisoning their children."

The Larger Question

In much of the discussion about the proliferation of drugs and how best to combat them, the larger question of why our society has become such fertile ground for narcotics has been largely ignored. In a society rooted in strong families, schools and religious institutions—a society which holds individuals responsible for their actions and has a well-defined understanding of the difference between right and wrong, between acceptable and unacceptable behavior—such a drug epidemic could hardly have reached its current proportions.

In our society, quite to the contrary, drugs have been promoted by television and Hollywood as a sophisticated and "liberated" lifestyle. Prior to the 1960s, those movie characters who used drugs—such as Frank Sinatra's "Man With The Golden Arm"— were portrayed as hopeless junkies. More recently, however, drug use has been presented in a far different manner. The 1969 film "Easy Rider," a box office hit among young people, featured the casual use of marijuana, cocaine and LSD. Actor Paul Newman, who lost a son to drug abuse, states that he is "shocked" by the favorable depiction of drug use in films. "I think some people are irresponsible, some people are unconscious, and some just don't care," he declared.

In 1986, President Reagan focused public attention upon Hollywood's role in glorifying the use of drugs. In an interview with NEWSWEEK, Mr. Reagan criticized the music world for its attitude about the use of drugs, making "it sound as if it's right there and the thing to do . . . Musicians that young people like . . . make no secret that they are users."

With regard to the lifestyle of many in Hollywood, the President lamented that drug use was widespread.

J.A. Parker, "Ending the Drug Epidemic Is More Than a Matter of Supply and Demand," *The Lincoln Review*, Spring 1988. Reprinted with permission.

He noted that the motion picture industry "has started down the road they'd been on before once, with alcohol abuse." Hollywood, he said, "is at a level of society where . . . they have a dinner party and feel they have to put the drug out on the coffee table, as at a cocktail party." One result, he said, is that some recent films have included scenes of drug use "that made it look kind of attractive and funny, not dangerous and sad."

Abandoned Children

Because Americans have, in large numbers, abandoned their responsibility of child-rearing many of our young people are particularly vulnerable to the inducements of the drug culture.

Dr. Lorenzo Merritt of Project HEAVY West, a nonprofit counseling center in Los Angeles that tries to help children stay out of jail, said that they join gangs and the drug culture "fundamentally because of a need for acceptance and identity. It generally means an absence of a cohesive . . . family life where there is a sense of belonging and respect."

Divorce has become rampant in American society. One out of every two of today's marriages will end in divorce making the U.S. divorce rate the highest in the industrial world. Millions of children are now living in one-parent families. Dr. Lee Salk, professor at Cornell University Medical College and president of the American Psychological Association's division of child and youth services, argues that children are less valued than they used to be in the American society. He states: "Society is finding more and more ways of separating children from their families. We are expending more and more money outside the home on child care instead of providing funds to help families function as a social unit. Children are being viewed as a burden. Increasingly, they are regarded as unimportant. In part, this is a reflection of the growing self-centeredness of people . . . It's irresponsible to bring children into the world and then turn them over to someone else to raise. If a person bought a dog and then turned it over to a veterinarian to raise and had a dog walker every day, we'd say that was cruel. But somehow or other we tolerate that for our children."

In her book, "Children Without Childhood," Marie Winn argues that we have entered an anti-child era that lacks clear generational distinctions, a time in which children grow up and become sharp, savvy, self-assured mini-adults before they are out of grade school.

Collapse of the Family

Testifying before the Senate Caucus on the Family, Father Bruce Ritter, a Franciscan priest and executive director of Covenant House in New York City, which aids homeless and run-away children, stated: "The traditional American family is an awesomely strong and resilient institution, but it has probably never been closer to collapse than it is now. For example, from 1970 to 1980, the number of married couples with children under 18 declined, while the number of single-parent households doubled. The divorce rate has tripled since 1960. Of the children who come to Covenant House, less than a quarter have been raised in two-parent homes. In counseling our kids and working with their parents we see day after day the overwhelming emotional and economic burdens that single parenthood imposes."

"Young teenagers today exercise more control over their own lives than any previous generation and are given far more freedom than they can handle."

It is Father Ritter's view that, "Ours has become a deeply materialistic, even hedonistic culture—a society of consumers. One of the great minds in federal tax policy—Henry Simons—has said that children are 'a form of consumption' for their parents. That is, he believed the birth of a child into a family should be treated for tax purposes no differently from the purchase of a new boat or car or any other luxury. Distinguished advertising firms carefully manipulate children to develop their consumer mentality, then cynically turn around to use children in seductive, sexually suggestive campaigns to sell produce to adults . . . Surrounded by a culture which regards children more as objects than as developing human beings, it is hardly a shock that many parents treat them as objects, too."

Millions of children are completely unsupervised after school ends each day. A recent Louis Harris poll discovered that 25 per cent of the parents of children in elementary school said their youngsters were often alone from the end of the school day until dinner time. A majority of teachers in a survey of parents and teachers say that the major reason children have difficulty in school is their isolation and lack of supervision after school. Fifty-one per cent of the teachers cited this problem, ahead of poverty and other social ills. Public libraries across the nation are increasingly being used, and librarians say abused, by parents who drop off their children for many hours on a regular basis. As a result, Flagstaff, Arizona has adopted a policy prohibiting parents from leaving children under the age of 10 unattended in public libraries. In Atlanta, signs have been posted in libraries warning parents they could face criminal charges of child abandonment for abusing library privileges. A policy statement in the headquarters of the Montgomery County, Maryland public library system warns that it considers it a "form of child neglect" for children under 13 to be left in the library "unattended for long periods of time on a regular basis or not picked up at closing time." According to a survey of libraries in Los Angeles, between 1,500 and 2,000 unattended children were using the public library each day as a refuge.

Teenagers

Young teenagers today exercise more control over their own lives than any previous generation and are given far more freedom than they can handle, according to Professor Tony Campolo, chairman of the Sociology department at Pennsylvania's Eastern College. Writing in YOUTHWORKER, Dr. Campolo observes that young Americans now "do things in their early teens that a generation ago were reserved for older high schoolers." The primary reason for this "transformation of junior highers," he believes, is the "diminishing presence of parents" in the lives of young adolescents. Because many of them live in single-parent homes or in two-income families where both parents are "out of their homes much of the time," young teenagers are "left with the freedom to do what they want to do." Dr. Campolo reports that many young teenagers become "emotionally disturbed and psychologically disoriented" when given personal autonomy prematurely.

Who is taking care of the nation's children? Almost half of mothers with children under age 1 and 67 per cent of women with children under 3 are working, while 53 per cent of all mothers with children under 6 are working. All too often, the children are largely overlooked and ignored. . . .

Must Rebuild Standards

With regard to drugs, the developing debate is centered partly on whether the emphasis of the anti-drug effort should be on the foreign supply or the domestic demand. Clearly, both of these problems must be addressed, as must the need for tougher law enforcement and harsher penalties for drug dealers.

We must, however, not view the drug problem in a vacuum, as if supply and demand can be properly understood without assessing the atmosphere of today's American society in which the proliferation of a drug culture has been permitted. Unless we address the larger problems of the collapse of family life, the indifference so many exhibit with regard to child-rearing, and the moral climate in which anything goes and to be "judgmental" is viewed by many as the cardinal sin, we will continue to fail in our efforts.

Only a decadent society would be indifferent to the proliferation of drugs. Sadly, until recently, America was not only indifferent but many elite groups—such as those in the media—were actively promoting a permissive attitude toward narcotics. The fact that there is now a public outcry against drugs is hopeful. Yet, understanding that a serious problem does indeed exist is only a first step. Unless we reconstitute the structure of our families, communities and moral standards, our battle against drugs is unlikely to succeed. In this sense, the drug epidemic is only a symptom of our larger societal problems, problems which we have found it difficult to confront.

"Unless we reconstitute the structure of our families, communities and moral standards, our battle against drugs is unlikely to succeed."

The time is late and the drug problem has reached unprecedented crisis proportions. Perhaps this is what has been needed to bring the American society to its senses. Let us hope that we will not permit this question to become a matter of partisan debate rather than mutual commitment and resolve to move forward and to defeat an enemy which, if victorious, would destroy us all, black and white, liberal and conservative, Republican and Democrat.

J.A. Parker is editor of the Lincoln Review, *a conservative black journal.*

"The idea that young people themselves create the drug culture because of weaknesses in family upbringing and school education is thoughtless and superficial."

viewpoint 96

Returning to Traditional Values Cannot Prevent Drug Abuse

Giuseppe di Gennaro

The increase in drug dependence among young people is creating exacting new problems for educators, who need to grasp the true nature and scope of the phenomenon in order to carry out their duties.

The non-medical use of drugs has always existed, but in forms which have little in common with drug dependence among young people as we know it today.

Historical and anthropological research has shown that in the past drug-taking was almost always confined to adults. Adolescents were never involved. Drugs were taken sporadically for mystical, religious or ritual purposes, and only by certain groups and in certain circumstances. The important thing about the practice and purpose of these forms of drug-taking was the absence of dependence.

Later, when morphine, heroin and cocaine began to be used, there were cases of addiction among adults, but until the mid-1960s the numbers involved were so small that the phenomenon never reached a socially significant scale and on the whole attracted little attention.

It was not until the late 1960s that drug abuse began to make inroads among young people and children and eventually became a world problem, as uncontrollable waves of epidemic proportions swept from continent to continent.

Mistaken Assumptions

It is therefore both mistaken and dangerous to assume that the present situation is simply the continuation of the past. It is mistaken because only today have drugs become a culture which everyone must face. It is dangerous because it makes people less vigilant and encourages passivity and acceptance. We expect that the damage will be limited and that the community will continue to take things in its stride as it has done over the centuries.

Educators must take stock of the dangers that drugs represent for children and adolescents today, foresee possible future developments, understand the causes of the situation and the forces underlying it, and introduce appropriate remedial measures into the educational process. This is an arduous task, as can be seen from the persistence and increasing gravity of drug dependence in spite of the determination of many educators and the hard work they have done in the last twenty years.

The subject has been exhaustively discussed. Whole libraries of books have been devoted to it, written by specialists in every branch of knowledge; research has been carried out by highly qualified authorities and organizations; innumerable conferences and meetings have been held, both local and international; but the guidelines for reliable and effective educational defense measures have still not been clearly and unequivocally defined.

It is thus vital to continue our efforts to understand the situation and deal with it more effectively. The purpose of this [viewpoint] is to stimulate critical reflection about certain widely held beliefs. There is a risk that such beliefs may be considered to be absolutely true, although they are not, and be taken, wrongly, as a basis for educational theory and practice, now and in the future.

These beliefs all stem from the assumption that drug dependence among young people is due to factors caused by the changes and tensions of modern society. In accordance with this assumption various situations have been singled out and blamed for the spread of drugs. An exhaustive list of these situations would be extremely long and is unnecessary for our purpose. We shall merely point out certain widely accepted allegations.

The first comes under the heading of "youthful

Giuseppe di Gennaro, "How Should We Attack the Drug Problem?" Reprinted from the *Unesco Courier*, July 1987.

protest". It has been maintained that young people at a certain stage refused to be dominated by the adult culture, which in their view was entangled with profit-making and the status quo, and reacted against the idea of being excluded from the construction of the future society in which they would have to live. This reaction turned into confrontation and struggle, and the anger that in some countries culminated in the disturbances of 1968 was accompanied by the development of a general attitude of rejection of adult behaviour and values. Drug abuse was essentially a deliberate insult and provocation on the part of young people towards adults.

The correlation between the spread of drug dependence and youthful protest seemed convincing because the connection appeared to be logical and because the two phenomena occurred at the same time. Youthful protest lost its impetus within a few years and was inevitably followed by a general feeling of defeat, resignation and disengagement from society. This second phase was also accompanied by drug dependence. Specialists have stressed the importance of detachment and the flight from reality in drug abuse, and have proposed another causal hypothesis without paying much attention to the fact that it is the antithesis of the first.

Meanwhile, in some societies an extreme form of consumerism was developing at a time of general social well-being—and at the same time drug dependence among young people assumed greater proportions. Again the two phenomena were seen by some to be related; this paved the way for the theory that drug dependence was due to well-being and excess. It was only later that underdevelopment, poverty and drugs came to be associated, and sparked off a search for other causes.

Various theories continued to be put forward. Some assertions were so general as to be irrefutable since they were impossible to verify empirically. One was the claim that drug dependence is the result of the collapse of traditional values.

Blaming the Family

Other theories based on the simultaneous occurrence of spreading drug dependence and certain forms of social change were refuted by the observation that the same social conditions did not always give rise to similar phenomena. One of the most important of these theories claimed that there was a relation between the loosening of family ties and drug dependence. This theory, of course, originated in highly industrialized countries, where the family has been affected by the demands made by the level of organization and by the tensions of industrialized society.

The family and especially the parents were blamed for this tragedy. Today, many people question their

culpability, having seen situations in which the epidemic of drug-taking on the part of young people has appeared in a context characterized by social and economic immobility and the stability of family structures.

Lastly, the idea that there is a causal link between unemployment and drugs has recently been disproved by the spread of drug dependence among workers.

"For more than twenty years we have seen a feverish succession of prescriptions and measures intended to tackle a wide variety of different 'causes.'"

Logically enough, whenever one of these theories was put forward, those concerned with the prevention and treatment of drug dependence took action against the supposed causes of the phenomenon. In consequence, for more than twenty years we have seen a feverish succession of prescriptions and measures intended to tackle a wide variety of different "causes". Everyone agrees that education is an essential tool in combating drug dependence, above all as a means of prevention. However, it has lost its bearings and is now at the centre of a heated argument that is fed by alternating aetiological "credos".

The inability of the family and the school to perform their respective educational functions has been castigated by the supporters of these different theories, who maintain that certain factors are the cause—or at least contribute to the cause—that corresponds to their particular theories. The following remarks are intended to help these two great forces which are under accusation—the family and the school—to rediscover their bearings and to perform their difficult task successfully, each in its own sphere of responsibilities and each applying its own methods.

Family and School

Although family upbringing and school education have much in common as regards their dynamic and their aims, there are important differences between them.

By family upbringing we mean the natural process by which parents and other members of the family nucleus transmit to their children a number of messages, by word, action and behaviour. Such messages give, more or less directly, an indication of what "should be"—in other words, guidance for living and an idea of the behaviour that is expected of young people.

School education, on the other hand, is an institutional process designed to integrate the process of family upbringing. In school education trained professionals transmit messages which are meant to inform their pupils and influence their behaviour by means of the values and ideals that they assimilate.

The process of family upbringing is largely unconscious, and in the mechanism whereby messages are transmitted and received the emotional or affective element is usually more potent than the intellectual or cognitive element. School education, on the other hand, is a conscious process, although the emotional or affective element may play an important part in it.

The two educational processes, for all their differences, have one thing in common: they interact with a series of influences originating in the circumstances of the young person's life. It is clear that the effect of identical educational processes will vary as a result of different external influences. It is generally realized that the influence of friends, or the "peer group", is extremely powerful in this respect, especially at certain stages of adolescence.

If the influence of the peer group conveys the values of an alien or hostile culture, it will encourage and strengthen attitudes of confrontation and opposition to the authority of parents and teachers, together with rejection of the culture to which the family and the school owe allegiance.

Instead of being a part of the growing-up process, when adolescents assert their own personalities and attempt to throw off the bonds of parental authority, this stage may on the contrary become an opportunity for messages from alien and hostile cultural sources to enter their minds. The young person's personality becomes a battlefield, in which the more powerful influences can be expected to prevail.

What Causes the Drug Culture

How does the peer group transmit the messages of the drug culture while the school and the vast majority of families belong to a different culture? To answer this question, we need to know where the drug culture comes from and what sustains it.

The idea that young people themselves create the drug culture because of weaknesses in family upbringing and school education is thoughtless and superficial. Reliable research findings now indicate that the drug culture is the outcome of shrewd manipulation by the many persons who work for the barons of the drug traffic. These powerful figures possess very considerable financial resources and highly efficient and far-reaching organizations. Just as the great fashion centres and the producers of other consumer goods create and impose a culture that aspires to the acquisition of such products, so those who control the vast drug market create and impose a culture that leads inevitably to drug abuse and the spread of drug dependence. In this market, young people are not active agents; they are conditioned customers.

If this is true, it is false and unjust to blame the family or the school, and it is pointless to look for causal factors among social phenomena or tensions. Drug dependence springs from the drug culture, which, in its turn, is created by drug traffickers and their battalions of propagandists.

"It is false and unjust to blame the family or the school. . . . Drug dependence springs from the drug culture, which, in its turn, is created by drug traffickers."

The family and the school should realize this; they should stop feeling guilty and should understand that, in the present state of affairs, if they wish to protect young people they must do more than generate and transmit traditional positive influences.

Drug abuse will not be beaten unless the drug culture is beaten too, and this means waging a determined struggle against illicit drug production and trafficking and against the powerful criminal syndicates that grow rich in this way.

Of course the family and the school have a role to play, but their efforts will be inadequate if not fruitless unless government institutions and the resources of the community are mobilized to defeat those responsible for the scourge of drug dependence.

Giuseppe di Gennaro is an Italian jurist who has been the executive director of the United Nations Fund for Drug Abuse Control since 1982. He is also a former chairman of the UN Commission on Narcotic Drugs.

"Prevention starts with . . . the parent."

Parents Can Prevent Teen Drug Abuse

Beth Polson and Miller Newton

If you're like most parents, you'd give anything to hear that the scientific community had come up with a cure for kids on drugs. Wouldn't it be great if you could turn on your television and see Dan Rather say, "Good evening. Tonight's top news story . . . the drug epidemic has ended. Government sources today announced a shutdown of all illegal drug trafficking in this country."

Well, sorry, but this isn't likely to happen. There are no magic elixirs out there. The government hasn't been able to stop illegal drug trafficking. And drugs are no more likely to disappear from a teenager's environment than Big Macs, french fries and pizza.

It would be nice if this [viewpoint] could provide you with some assurances. "If your child is _____ or _____, you don't have a thing to worry about." The sad truth is: THERE ARE NO GUARANTEES. There are no vitamins that, if taken daily, are going to prevent the disease. And there's nothing about your child that makes him invincible in the face of drugs.

So the best you can hope for is your own not-so-magic elixir, a family potion, a kind of prevention that, while it still will give you no guarantees or immunities, will give you fighting strength. It's being prepared to wage a war you hope you never have to fight. It's called Prevention.

Prevention is a safety measure. It's like keeping matches away from small children, locking up poisonous substances and putting nonskid mats under rugs. It's something you do to provide your family with the happiest and safest environment possible. But prevention against drug use is not easy—especially when psychological and sociological experts are talking about the failure of the family in our precarious times. It's hard for the family to stand as a bulwark against the ever increasing influence of school, peers and the media.

You've learned that families are the basic unit of loving and caring, of strength and stability. That, while families may bounce aimlessly around when family members have problems, they can also be resilient, like super rubber balls, if other family members understand and reach out to stabilize the disturbance, rather than grabbing balance by finding new family roles. You've learned that family members working together can rebound. And you've learned that healthy families are the best prevention.

Parental Patterns

Prevention starts with you, the parent. Parents teach the infant his first learned reactions—smiling, laughing, and cooing. It is parents who set the learning pattern, and that pattern continues into adulthood.

But we don't mean to imply that parents and family systems cause kids to become involved with drugs. As we've said repeatedly, *kids* make the decision to try drugs the first time and to use drugs with their friends again and again before they finally lose control and become dependent. What *is* true is that certain issues can cause communication problems within a family, thereby lessening the influence of parents at the times when kids are most susceptible to the lure of drugs. Kids also learn patterns of coping with life from parents that either help them resist peer pressure or make them more vulnerable to it. But, again, there's no magic formula: Many kids who've been protected from peer pressure by their parents still become involved with drugs, and many unsupervised kids somehow manage to say no to drugs. But let's look closely at what parents can do anyway.

Kids' "beauty marks" as well as their "warts" come from the parents. Parents like to claim the strengths and pass on the weaknesses. A mother will say her son gets his bad temper from his father. Or a father will say his daughter gets her stubborn streak from her mother. If it's a pleasant personality or musical talent, suddenly everybody is willing to lay claim to it. The fact is, parents are role models for both the strengths *and* the weaknesses in their children. Consciously and unconsciously, parents pass on family values and behavior.

Parents knowingly hand down their values—family traditions, strong feelings about how children should act, what schools they should go to, what professions are admirable ones, what their life values should be, what spiritual beliefs they may have and so forth. Moms and dads live, speak and act out their conviction in these values every day. A child may willingly accept some of them, and may see others as enormous pressures. Dad may really want his son to follow in his footsteps and go to Yale. The child may end up spending most of his school years just wondering if he can measure up and be accepted at his old man's alma mater. But the parents don't want the child to be pressured. They simply want him to have strong religious beliefs. They want him to go to college. They want him to carry on family traditions. Their intentions are usually the best. But unknowingly, they pass along just as many negative traits from the growing-up war chest as positive ones. They may unknowingly pass along an unspoken fear of touching or hugging. Or the inability to say, "I love you." Parents are pattern-makers. Don't forget it. . . .

One of the keys to stopping a drug problem in your family is clearly defining the boundary between parents and kids. That is, parents should be parents and kids should be kids. And never the twain should meet.

An Important Factor

This is also an important factor in prevention. Before a drug problem rears its ugly head, you need to clarify who's in charge in the family, who sets the rules, who draws the bottom lines and why. Parents set a model of authority, privilege and power that will take charge, set limits, and protect kids from the lethal consequences of immature decisions. Once the kids have proven sufficient maturity to take their places as adults in society, they can aspire to the parental model.

In the meantime, kids should be dealt with on their own terms. They should be given kid—not adult—responsibilities. They should be talked to as the kids they are, given guidelines and consequences from a sensitive and authoritative adult. This means that you as a parent have to take the time to realize that a problem that may seem trivial to you is all-consuming in the kid world. Don't dismiss as childish or irritating anything that your kid comes to you about and asks for help with. Determine if it is a real problem in his view, not in yours.

Don't apply adult solutions to kids' problems. You need to listen to an eleven-year-old in terms of eleven-year-old problems, a fourteen-year-old in terms of fourteen-year-old problems. Your child may be worried about school or a friend who drinks, or a friend's parents getting a divorce, or his or her own sexual identity. Each problem needs a specific, thoughtful, age-oriented answer, and the answer should allow the child to make his own decision based on the guidelines you have given him. Give the child sufficient time to explain the problem and give him sufficient time to understand the guidelines you are giving him. Don't make snap decisions. And don't expect your child to come to you with his problems if you're not able to deal with his problems *in kid terms* as a fair, understanding, loving, caring parent—not a judge. . . .

Honest and Open

Prevention will be most likely to work when you can be honest and open with all aspects of your lives and all the lives of members of the family. It means everybody knows and understands the family values and rules. It means anybody can talk about anything within the family love circle.

Families ought to provide an atmosphere in which all family members feel valuable, worthwhile. No matter if they are short or tall, fat or thin. Each person is valued for who he or she is as an individual and what he or she brings to the family.

"Before a drug problem rears its ugly head, you need to clarify who's in charge . . . and why."

Families have two messages that need to be communicated to their members. The first is the accepting kind of love message we talked about. No matter who you are and what you are, you are valued and loved because you are a member of this family. The second is one of bottom lines. Depending on the family value system, certain kinds of behavior are acceptable and rewarded and other kinds of behavior are unacceptable and penalized. But applying consequences when that value system is violated does not mean that the individual is any less loved. Every member of the family needs to understand that the two family messages do not contradict each other, that in fact it is *because* the individual is valued and worthwhile that bottom lines are drawn. Bottom lines exist because parents care about their children, children care about their parents, parents care about each other and children care about each other. Bottom lines are part of the accepting love message. If a bottom line is violated, the security of the family atmosphere is threatened. . . .

Because ours is a mobile, multimedia society, teenagers find ways to avoid being part of the family. By the time children reach twelve or thirteen years old, they no longer think it's cool to be seen with their parents or a brother or sister. The child's withdrawal from the family is usually attributed to "that strange period kids go through." Daughters no longer want to go shopping with their mothers. Sons don't want to be hugged after the winning game. Or kissed when they are heading off on the class trip. Teenagers often do not even want to share meals with the rest of the family. They'd prefer to eat in their rooms, in front of the television, at a friend's house or just say that they're not hungry. These are all signs of a weakening of the family ties. How does a parent regain those ties with a teenager and not lose them with younger children?

First of all, it is the parents' responsibility to insist upon family activities. Again, this is a bottom line. It is not something about which children have any say. There will be certain meals that the family has together, no matter what the dance classes, baseball practice or social schedules demand. For example, Sunday night can be family night. It might be a night for popcorn and television after dinner. It may be a night that the family sees a movie together. Or it may be the night chosen for family forum. In any case, parents need to designate some mealtimes, some evenings, some activities that keep the family operating as a family. Attending church or synagogue or visiting grandparents should not be events that children are allowed to give up when they become teenagers. They must remain family activities.

Some people suggest that making demands on teenagers only reinforces their stubborn rebellion. The fact is, all teenagers test the adult world's limits and expectations. It's a normal part of the growing up process. The kids who find no boundaries, as a rule, become very distressed and disturbed in their development. Teenagers feel most comfortable when, as they test family boundaries, they find secure limits and expectations. They find that their parents care enough to say, "You really belong." Often when a parent has been too permissive and suddenly changes the game, it takes time for the teenager to accept the change and become comfortable. That's okay. It's worth the effort.

Family Activities

To encourage a teenager's willingness to join in family activities, use your dinner discussions or another family gathering to have each family member suggest what he might like the family to do together. Perhaps a teenager would like his family to take skiing lessons together. Or if the child has some special interest in a subject, he might like the family vacation to include a stop at a museum or Dodger Stadium or a ride on a steamboat down the Mississippi. There are things close to home that a teenager might be pleased to have his family join him in, even though it may take some coaxing. A swimming meet, an antique car show, a dirt-bike race—most teenagers just won't volunteer to invite their parents unless they are encouraged.

"Prevention is the easiest step to take in the drug war. And the most valuable."

Sometimes the family should do things alone; other times, family members should be allowed to bring along friends. The more pride a teenager takes in his family, the less likely he is to violate the family's value systems. Getting together with other families will give the child a wider field in which to experience his self-worth, acceptance and value as a human being. Including other generations of the family also gives the child a larger foundation of people who feel good about him. Older family generations, grandparents, aunts, uncles, reinforce the family system as a strong, ongoing, determining structure. The activities a family shares should be balanced by each member's *individual* activities. Dad may belong to a service club. Mom may volunteer at the hospital twice a week. A daughter could enjoy gymnastics or a son might love baseball. Members can support each other through their individual activities and then join together in family activities.

If your family is drug free, put prevention practices to work at once. If you see a cloud on the horizon, reach out for your kids as you've never reached out before. Reach inside yourself as you've never reached. And reach inside your family and touch every member with loving, caring honesty.

Instill in your kids the idea that life is learning about themselves and the world. It's about setting goals and feeling good about themselves without any need for chemicals. Encourage them when they do well. Redirect them when they get confused and make mistakes. And find them when they get lost and reset their compasses. Use compassion and firmness. Prevention is the easiest step to take in the drug war. And the most valuable.

Beth Polson produces television specials and documentaries focusing on youth chemical abuse. Miller Newton is a clinical drug therapist.

"Proper guidance, . . . combined with the affirmation and support of a loving Christian community, help to develop and foster a responsible attitude toward alcohol and drugs."

viewpoint 98

Churches Can Prevent Teen Drug Abuse

The New Jersey Bishops

Our Holy Father John Paul II, in his remarks pertaining to substance abuse, has stated:

"Among the inviolable human rights is the right to a dignified existence, one in harmony with one's condition as an intelligent and free being. This right, viewed in the light of revelation, takes on an unsuspected dimension: Christ, by his death and resurrection, freed us from the radical slavery of sin so that we could have full freedom through the liberty provided for the sons of God. . . . As free people whom Christ called to live in freedom, we must fight decisively against new forms of slavery which subjugate so many people in so many parts of the world, especially the young" (Cartagena, Colombia, July 6, 1986).

Our freedom is being threatened every day by drug and alcohol abuse. This threat permeates every stratum of society: the young and old, rich and poor, the homemaker, the professional, the student, the priest and the parishioner. No individual, no family and no church is exempt from the potential harm that exists within a society where drug addiction and alcoholism are on an alarming increase.

Since the dawn of human existence, our Creator has reached out lovingly to us with open arms, inviting us to appreciate our innate goodness and to participate in the continuing act of creation. In light of our God-given potential, we are called to grow and mature in a movement that is harmonious with nature and congruous with grace. The Son becomes the most vivid sign of the Father's love and the means of human redemption. His death and resurrection establish a new covenant, which provides us with the freedom necessary to live and grow in accordance with our human potential and God's loving plan.

New Jersey Bishops, "Pastoral Statement on Substance Abuse," *Origins,* June 23, 1988.

The process of growth is never without stress and often involves confusion, fear and pain. However, despite assurances of God's constant love and help, people are sometimes drawn by a promise of instant relief or the pleasurable escape offered by the abuse of drugs and alcohol. The result is an experience of disengagement from the natural process of living. Hoping that these chemicals will permanently relieve painful feelings or provide artificial happiness, people find that the effects of the substance are not the answer to their needs, but in fact exacerbate their problems.

Such Feelings

Such feelings as worthlessness, helplessness, anxiety, fear, anger and desperation become complicated by guilt over the misuse and abuse of alcohol or drugs. The addict then becomes trapped in a dehumanizing pattern of living which affects his or her total being. For the intravenous drug dependent person, moreover, the threat of AIDS presents a further danger. Physical, emotional, psychological and spiritual health are all violently interrupted and the person ceases to thrive. This inhibits the addict from responding to the fullness of life and love to which God has called each of us.

As if this scenario were not dreadful enough, the suffering is imposed unavoidably on family members and those who share the daily life of an addict. Research has shown that for each individual who is chemically dependent, at least four other persons' lives are directly impaired as a result of their relationship to that person. These people are our neighbors, parishioners and coworkers. They are children who lie in bed at night crying and praying that the fighting will stop. They are parents who fear the trauma of hospital emergency rooms and police investigations stemming from car accidents caused by their addicted son or daughter. They are spouses whose daily existence is fraught with feelings of guilt, inadequacy, fear, anger and frustration as a result of their futile efforts to control the alcoholic behavior of their loved ones. The list of examples is endless.

In recent years we have witnessed drastic societal changes. We now live in a culture full of conflicting moral messages and inconsistent values, particularly as portrayed by the media. The unified value structure that in times past was supported by extended families, neighborhoods, churches, schools and government has all but disappeared. The resulting confusion, coupled with widespread denial concerning the diseases of alcoholism and drug addiction, has contributed to the urgency of the current situation.

Alcoholism and drug abuse are treatable family diseases. Early detection and help are essential and produce the greatest chance for recovery. We encourage families to seek assistance when a problem first becomes apparent.

We applaud the treatment programs and facilities being offered both under church auspices and in the secular domain. Our gratitude is also directed to the individuals whose professional lives are dedicated to meeting the needs of those seeking help in the recovery process and to the countless volunteers who offer their time and life experience to implement the Twelve-Step programs such as Alcoholics Anonymous, Al-Anon, Alateen, Narcotics Anonymous and Adult Children of Alcoholics. In addition, we call for consistent public funding for treatment, prevention and education, especially to support programs for those without access to adequate private resources.

"We have the tools to offer support for people who are experiencing pain in the growing process of life."

Let us keep in mind that we are not alone in our concerns. We urge and support cooperative efforts among all churches and secular groups. Our role as church is not to duplicate or replace, but to enhance and enrich existing services. We have the tools to offer support for people who are experiencing pain in the growing process of life. The Holy Spirit offers us the gifts of understanding and compassion, which can be utilized for sensitive support and genuine spiritual direction. This focus on the spiritual growth of each person enables us to live out our faith.

It is within this context that we offer the following as possibilities for more consciously moving into a pastoral model for addressing the realities of alcohol and drug abuse today.

The eucharist is indeed the source and the summit of our parish life, from which flow our mission and ministry as a people of God. The gathering of the church around the table of the Lord becomes the paramount expression of our relatedness to one another with the Father, Son and Holy Spirit. If isolation and despair are to be overcome by compassion and affirmation, then let our efforts emanate from the love, unity, strength and sacrifice that we celebrate at the eucharist.

The Liturgy

During the Liturgy of the Word, the Scripture readings reveal God's infinite mercy and love. The homily breaks open that word so that the faithful may experience the richness of the good news and feel a deep sense of participation in God's loving plan. A supportive, positive message helps everyone to embrace the struggles of the human condition with confidence and hope. The Gospel challenge of unselfishness and self-sacrifice need not be presented in a counterproductive atmosphere of condemnation that serves only to entrench an addict in feelings of guilt and inadequacy. What we preach is the good news of hope and healing.

The church, as the community to which Christ has called us, can be a real source of affirmation, thereby providing each of its members with healthier coping mechanisms. The parish at large, as well as each subgrouping within it (Renew group, Altar Rosary Society, Holy Name Society, senior citizens group, young adult group, committees and clubs), can supply a viable community experience that promotes growth, maturation, support and compassion for each of its members.

The local church should be aware of services and resources for alcohol and drug prevention and treatment. Through parish social concerns committees, knowledgeable persons may be identified to facilitate the process of referral or treatment as specific needs arise.

On the parish level, education regarding drugs and alcohol and programs to help addicts and their families are responses to Christ's mission of bringing the fullness of life to all people. Families struggling with contemporary concerns can be enriched greatly by parish-based experiences offering personal growth, family enrichment and support in times of crisis. Many groups can conduct seminars, discussions and workshops relating to parenting skills, stress management, and alcohol and drug abuse. The use of parish facilities should be extended to those who provide programs that aid in the recovery process. Parishes providing these opportunities serve an important human need and participate in the healing ministry of Jesus.

Although the moderate social use of alcoholic beverages may be enjoyed in its proper place, pastoral leaders should be sensitive to the needs of alcoholics and their families. It is important, for example, that when alcohol is served at parish gatherings, it is not the only beverage available.

Substance abuse is a family problem. Families can be challenged and encouraged to participate in education, counseling and Twelve-Step programs. Each member of the family can be empowered to:

—Understand the nature of substance abuse as a treatable disease.

—Recognize the roles of "enabler" and "addict."

—Build self-esteem.

—Accept responsibility for the consequences of their behavior.

—Improve communications skills.

—Develop healthier relationships.

—Handle problems more constructively.

—Find or renew faith in God.

—Experience serenity and self-acceptance.

The social climate in which our young people live often involves intense peer pressure, accessibility of drugs and alcohol, and promotion of their use through the media. This situation presents a special challenge to the whole church and specifically to our young people. Rather than being influenced by others whose ideals are lacking, they are called to be an influence for good upon their peers. In addressing youth, our Holy Father said: "Dear young friends, I pray that your faith in Christ will always be lively and strong. In this way, you will always be ready to tell others the reason for your hope; you will be messengers of hope for the world" (Teleconference With Young People, Los Angeles, Calif., Sept. 15, 1987).

The Catholic Mission

The mission of Catholic schools is both educational and formational. Through their curricula and community atmosphere, our educational institutions must address the problems of alcohol and drug abuse from the physical, psychological, intellectual and spiritual dimensions. Academic endeavors, sports programs, extracurricular activities and clubs, campus ministry programs and retreats, chaplains, guidance counselors and support groups all converge to assist the student in the development of:

—An appreciation of God's love and each individual's unique role in the plan of creation.

—An understanding of Christian values.

—Self-esteem.

—Socialization skills.

—Healthy coping skills.

—A sense of support and affirmation by both peers and faculty members.

—An awareness of the problems caused by drug and alcohol abuse.

In addition, schools should develop enrichment programs for their faculties to renew their sense of Christian mission and the responsibility they have to provide prudent counsel and appropriate role modeling for the students. Our schools should provide them with educational opportunities and counseling resources.

Moreover, we need to unite our efforts and improve our ability to face the problems of drug and alcohol abuse, responding to their victims with understanding, compassion, challenge and hope.

"Our educational institutions must address the problems of alcohol and drug abuse from the physical, psychological, intellectual and spiritual dimensions."

Contemporary education theory and studies in faith development conclude that the tenets of our religion are best understood when placed in the context of relevant experience. Catechetical leaders should be aware of the drug and alcohol education programs offered in local public schools. Religious education curricula can then be adapted so as to include discussions of drug and alcohol abuse as a context for the teaching of faith as a loving response to a loving God. Further, religious educators and catechists should not underestimate their ability to share the faith that emanates from God's love and the power to influence youth through word and deed.

Two Primary Goals

"The Vision of Youth Ministry" (National Conference of Catholic Bishops, 1976) proposes that the two primary goals of youth ministry are to assist the youth of our church in their spiritual and personal development, and to invite them to a deeper participation in the life of the church. Addressing the evils of drug and alcohol abuse is most assuredly in line with these goals. Proper guidance, education and role modeling, combined with the affirmation and support of a loving Christian community, help to develop and foster a responsible attitude toward alcohol and drugs. The parish youth group should be a place of both support and enrichment, providing educational opportunities enfolded with Christian values.

The appropriate diocesan departments should be engaged in drug and alcohol education, referral and treatment since they have an essential role in providing support and direction to parishes, institutions and diocesan staff. Typically this will involve the following ministries on a diocesan level:

—Social concerns.

—Catholic Charities/community services.

—Family life.

—Department of schools.

—Religious education/catechetics.

—Youth ministry.

—College campus ministry.

—Young adult ministry.

Activities with which these offices may become involved include:

—Training parish and school leadership.

—Sponsoring educational symposiums and workshops.

—Acting as resource and referral centers.

—Coordinating efforts toward education. . . .

Our theological hope supports and affirms the basic goodness of life. Invoking the Spirit of love which binds us together and makes us one, we ask God's blessing on all our efforts to share this hope and to live in the freedom to which Christ has called us.

The New Jersey Bishops issued a pastoral statement on substance abuse on June 23, 1988.

"If every young person pressured by his or her peers to use drugs would 'Just Say No,' there would be no 'drug problem.'"

viewpoint 99

The "Just Say No" Campaign Can Prevent Teen Drug Abuse

"Just Say No" International

"Just Say No." Could the answer to the vexing and complex problem of drug abuse be so simple?

In theory, yes. If every young person pressured by his or her peers to use drugs would "Just Say No," there would be no "drug problem," no need for treatment programs or massive interdiction and law enforcement efforts to stem the flow of drugs to our nation's streets and schools. But not everyone says No.

Most young people today at some point find themselves tempted by friends to drink or take drugs. Statistics show that the *majority* of them say Yes at least once; millions go on to become occasional or habitual users. The key to winning the war against drug abuse lies in persuading young people not to take the first sip, puff, snort, or injection.

To accomplish that, it is necessary to understand why some children and teenagers use drugs and others do not. What determines how a youngster will respond when pressured to drink or use drugs? That is the question The Just Say No Foundation asked when embarking on the task of developing a program for use by "Just Say No" Clubs.

A generation of research and clinical experience gives us considerable insight into factors that contribute to drug abuse. Our understanding of the roots of the problem, though far from complete, allows us to identify character traits, experiences, and circumstances that put some people at greater risk than others for becoming drug abusers.

A 1986 study by the California attorney general's office suggests that some young people—about 50 percent of the 7th graders in this particular survey—may be "immune" to drug use. They say No without prompting, and are not susceptible to pressure from

peers to use drugs. The author of the study, Dr. Rodney Skager, speculated that these youngsters eschew drugs not for "extrinsic" (external) reasons such as fear of punishment or losing friends, but for "intrinsic" (internal) reasons, i.e., drug use violates their principles and does not fit their self-image.

Any program designed to keep young people from drinking and using drugs must take these factors into account. If we can provide the information, skills, and support typically lacking in drug abusers, perhaps we can help the "susceptible 50 percent" develop self-concepts incongruous with drug use, while at the same time reinforcing the drug-free self-image of nonusers. . . .

The "Just Say No" Program

The "Just Say No" program represents a balanced and comprehensive approach to preventing drug abuse. The program:

• Reaches young people at the time of life when they are most vulnerable to peer pressure, the middle and upper elementary and junior high years.

• Incorporates the most promising prevention strategy yet devised, teaching kids "refusal skills"— how to say No.

• Focuses on the "gateway" drugs, alcohol and tobacco. These are the drugs most people use first, and the "gate" through which the great majority of abusers enter the world of illicit drug use. (Club materials can be adapted for use in communities where other drugs, such as marijuana, cocaine, "crack," and inhalants, are used by Club-aged children.)

• Reinforces the "nonuse norm." During the elementary school years, most young people don't use drugs; not using drugs is said to be the "norm." As children approach and enter adolescence, the balance shifts and drinking or using drugs becomes the norm. The "Just Say No" program seeks to reinforce the nonuse norm that exists at the grade school level and extend it into junior high or even high school.

- Promotes friendships with drug-free peers.
- Involves non-Club members in Clubs' recreational and service activities, thus bringing other children into contact with children who are committed to leading drug-free lives.
- Provides structured activities for after school, weekends, and vacations. A recent study found that young people who are involved in clubs and similar organized activities are less likely to use alcohol and other drugs than those who are not.
- Exposes members to positive adult and teenage role models who share and support their commitment to remain drug-free.
- Involves Club members' parents. Parents are the single greatest influence in the lives of most children, and various Club activities seek to strengthen the parent-child bond and to provide parents with the information they need to reinforce the "Just Say No" message in the home.
- Teaches responsibility to self and others through educational and service activities.
- Provides endless opportunities to learn new skills and explore personal horizons.
- Promotes the values of friendship, helpfulness, responsibility, and service.

"The 'Just Say No' program represents a balanced and comprehensive approach to preventing drug abuse."

"Just Say No" Clubs are groups of children, 7-14 years old, united in their resolve to say No to drugs. Through a variety of educational, recreational, and service activities, the Clubs support and strengthen members' determination to lead drug-free lives. They reinforce the message that drug use is wrong. Members learn to stand up for what they know is right—and feel good about themselves for doing so.

Club members encourage their friends and classmates to join them in their commitment to say No to drugs. Suggested activities keep the Clubs— and the "Just Say No" message—visible in the school and community. Club members learn, and communicate to their peers, that it isn't necessary to use drugs to make friends and have fun.

What began as a single "Just Say No" Club in an inner-city Oakland grade school in January 1985 has grown into an estimated 15,000 today—and new Clubs are launched every day.

Phenomenal Acceptance

Why the phenomenal acceptance of "Just Say No" Clubs?

Children flock to the Clubs because they are afraid—afraid for themselves, afraid for their friends.

They don't want to drink alcohol or use drugs, and they don't want their friends to, either. Recognizing the formidable power of peer pressure, young people join "Just Say No" Clubs for the mutual support they offer. They know that together they can generate a new kind of peer pressure—peer pressure to remain drug-free. Kids join also for the fun, the excitement, the chance to make a positive difference.

Drug abuse consistently rates among the principal concerns of parents, educators, and the general public. Adults too are afraid—afraid for their children, their schools, their communities. At the same time, they are drawn by the deceptively simple "Just Say No" message. They are encouraged by the overwhelming response to the "Just Say No" Clubs by the youth of America. They see young people expressing *their* deep-felt concern about drug abuse, and rallying together in unprecedented numbers behind the "Just Say No" slogan.

"Just Say No" program activities fall into five categories:

Educational Activities, including exercises to help foster friendship among Club members; to help them appreciate their families and be clear about family rules; to help them develop a sense of personal responsibility; and to provide them with information about drugs and drug abuse.

"Saying No to Peer Pressure," a five-session sequence of activities that examines peer pressure and teaches Club members how to resist pressure to use drugs or do other things they know are wrong.

Recreational Activities teach cooperation and strengthen interpersonal skills.

Service Projects that enable members to help others in direct and meaningful ways.

Outreach Activities in which the "Just Say No" message is carried into the school and community, and other children are invited to participate in the Clubs' recreational and service activities.

The "3 Steps To Say No"

The cornerstone of the educational component of the "Just Say No" program is this simple technique to help Club members resist peer pressure. By practicing the "3 Steps" in the safety of the Club meeting, supported and encouraged by fellow Club members and their adult and teen leaders, young people become confident of their ability to say No in real-life situations.

Step 1—Figure out if what your friend wants to do is OK.

Sometimes this is easy ("Let's go smoke this cigarette"), sometimes it requires a little "detective work" ("Let's go down to the train tracks"). Sometimes you have to ask your friends questions ("Are we allowed to be there?", "What will we do there?") and yourself questions ("Would my parents allow me to go there?") to help you decide if what your friend has suggested is all right.

Step 2—If it's wrong, say No.

As soon as you or your friend gives an answer that lets you know that what has been suggested is wrong, stop asking questions and state firmly, "No, thanks." Then explain your reasons for saying No.

Step 3—Suggest other things to do instead.

After saying No, suggest alternate activities that are legal, safe, healthy, and fun.

Once members have learned and practiced the "3 Steps," Clubs teach them to other youngsters through skits and plays at school assemblies, at presentations before other youth groups, and at other school and community events.

"Recognizing the formidable power of peer pressure, young people join 'Just Say No' Clubs for the mutual support they offer."

The "Just Say No" Pledge is a simple but powerful statement of the principles of the "Just Say No" movement. Every time children recite the Pledge, they are reaffirming their commitment to those principles:

I pledge to lead a drug-free life. I want to be healthy and happy. I will say No to alcohol. I will say No to tobacco. I will say No to illegal drugs. I will help my friends say No. I pledge to stand up for what I know is right.

"Just Say No" International, formerly The Just Say No Foundation, was begun with the help of former First Lady Nancy Reagan, the honorary chairperson.

"America has a huge drug market because many Americans like to do drugs."

Drugs' Popularity Makes Drug Abuse Prevention Impossible

Cait Murphy

Illegal narcotics trafficking may be the last bastion of unbridled free enterprise on earth. Unencumbered by health regulations, safety laws, minimum wage requirements, or conscience, drug lords are free to do exactly as the market dictates. For the past 20 years, the market has demanded more and better drugs; and traffickers have been happy to supply them. Creating a "drug-free society" then, as President and Mrs. Reagan have called for, is not just a matter of law enforcement. The question is: how does one stop others from doing something they clearly want to do?

Americans are eager consumers of narcotics; according to a report published by the Institute for Social Research at the University of Michigan, which conducts an annual drug use survey of U.S. students, young Americans "show a level of involvement with illicit drugs which is greater than can be found in any other industrialized nation in the world." We spend $110 billion a year to buy illegal drugs, and lose perhaps $46.9 billion more in hidden costs to the economy, according to the Research Triangle Institute, a North Carolina think tank.

Some 22 million Americans have tried cocaine, 10 million in the last year, three to five million in the last month. Cocaine deaths have increased every year, reaching a new peak of 613 in 1985. There are half a million heroin addicts, and heroin-related deaths have increased by a third since 1983. The President's Commission on Organized Crime estimates that a quarter of all Americans have tried marijuana, and that 20 million use the drug at least once a month. Fifty-four percent of high school students have tried pot at least once. By their mid-20s, 75 to 80 percent of young Americans have tried an illicit drug.

"High Times in America," by Cait Murphy, is reprinted from *Policy Review* issue number 39 (or fall 1987), the quarterly publication of The Heritage Foundation, 214 Massachusetts Avenue NE, Washington, DC 20002.

The good news is that—with the possible exception of cocaine—drug use is actually declining. (Cocaine use is increasing among high school students. At the college level, cocaine has stabilized; for the general public, the number of users has leveled off, but consumption is up.) The use of pot, heroin, PCP, LSD, Quaaludes, amphetamines, and barbiturates has declined steadily since 1980 and shows no sign of an upturn. As Carlton Turner, director of the White House Drug Abuse Policy Office said last October [1986], "It's not an epidemic now. It *was* one in 1981."

Five years after the epidemic, Congress discovered drug abuse. The *Wall Street Journal* had warned of "Congressional resistance to major budget increases for the war on drugs." It seemed that even if Dr. Turner wanted more money, he would not be able to pry it from Congress.

A New Derivative

Then a new cocaine derivative, crack, hit the streets; two prominent athletes died from cocaine overdoses; and President Reagan sent troops to Bolivia to interrupt cocaine production. Congressmen of both parties began to compete to see who could put together the biggest, toughest, meanest, most expensive drug bill. The death penalty, military surveillance, changing the exclusionary rule, and mandatory drug testing—each of these was pondered by Congress. Remarked Barney Frank (D-MA) of the House effort, "I am afraid that this bill is becoming the legislative equivalent to crack. It is going to give people a short-term high, but it is going to be dangerous in the long run to the system and expensive to boot."

Frank's warning went unheeded: the short-term high is gone already, but the country is stuck with the $2.4 billion Drug Enforcement, Education, and Control Act of 1986, which President Reagan signed into law on October 26. The bill follows the classic four-part pattern of American drug policy established by President Kennedy's Prettyman Commission in 1963: treat the user, educate the potential user, punish the trafficker, and intercept the drugs.

As a plan, it seems sensible. The only problem is that it does not work—and it makes little sense to address drug abuse by simply intensifying the failed policies of the past generation. If these four strategies are so valuable, why did drug abuse explode *after* the Prettyman Commission?

"The only way to decrease drug abuse is for people to decide they don't want to do it."

The principle of narcotics interdiction, for example, is sound: destroy the drugs before they get to anyone. Congress appropriated about $572 million for aircraft, radar systems, and Customs Service personnel for the purpose. But so much dope is grown in so many different places, that while drug enforcement agents seized more drugs than ever before in 1985, the street prices of drugs—the clearest indication of decreased supply—did not rise at all. Says William F. Alden, public affairs officer at the Drug Enforcement Administration, "We have all these good statistics—arrests are up, seizures are up, intelligence is better than ever. But there's as much or more drug use today as there's ever been." . . .

Limited Strategies

Other parts of American drug strategy are also severely limited. Curing addiction is almost impossible; rates of recidivism are high in virtually all drug treatment centers. International programs have the same sad results. Methadone maintenance has not worked in Britain, where the number of heroin addicts has tripled in the last decade. Nor do Thailand's Buddhist temple programs work very well: 80 percent of the addicts who go through the program go back to heroin within six months. A number of scientific studies have proved that the "cold turkey" approach is ineffective, as well as excruciating to the addict. In short, nothing seems to stop addicts from wanting to go back to their drugs. The exception to this dismal record might be treating opium addiction; in both Egypt and Sri Lanka, programs that treated the symptoms of opium withdrawal, combined with group therapy, worked well for highly motivated opium addicts.

But this can teach the United States nothing. Most hardcore American drug addicts abuse more than one drug. So while methadone, for example, might help to alleviate the craving for heroin, it does nothing to treat alchoholism or prescription addiction. Second, even if the treatment does seem to work, the pressures of adapting to drug-free life—

finding a job, a place to live, new friends—are often too much for newly released addicts, who escape from their new difficulties by returning to their old drug habits.

Other Countries

A look at other countries' drug policies shows that the relationship between the severity of drug laws and the rate of drug abuse is unpredictable. Neither harshness nor leniency can guarantee an end to drug abuse.

Despite its liberal drug policy—coffee bars legally sell hashish and marijuana—the Netherlands has a much lower abuse rate than many countries, including the United States. Only eight percent of all Dutch students have tried marijuana, compared with over 60 percent of American students, according to the Foundation for the Scientific Study of Alcohol and Drug Use. Yet the Netherlands has not been able to effectively contain heroin and cocaine use—though its levels are still far lower than in the United States—and Amsterdam is widely known as a drug mecca. Street crime has increased tenfold since 1974. . . .

In Japan, drug laws are less stringent than in the United States but there is no drug problem to speak of. There is some concern about a growing heroin problem: the number of cases of suspected heroin possession in Tokyo rose from 29 to 36 [in 1986]. Until 1985, India also had lenient drug laws, but unlike Japan, drug abuse became a serious problem. The Indian government toughened the laws, but it is too early to tell if there are any effects.

On the other extreme, Malaysia has among the harshest anti-drug laws in the world—and one of the most serious drug problems. Prime Minister Mahathir Mohamed has publicly estimated that 500,000 Malaysians are heroin addicts—the same number as the United States—out of a population of 13 million. Seventy percent of the addicts are under 30. Draconian narcotic laws for trafficking, including unlimited detention in prison and the death penalty (two Australians were hanged for suspected trafficking, the first Westerners to die under the new law), have made only minimal progress in curtailing supply and use. . . .

The American Way

In the United States, law enforcement has partially succeeded in controlling heroin, PCP, and Quaaludes. Heroin abuse tends to be localized, almost always taking place in poor, inner city neighborhoods. Therefore, intensive anti-heroin police actions like "Operation Pressure Point" in New York City in 1983-84 can have an immediate, discernible impact on the heroin culture. In the last 10 years, the number of heroin addicts has fallen from over 700,000 to about 500,000.

Quaaludes were second only to marijuana in popularity in the late 1970s. Now they are virtually off the market. Quaaludes are composed of methaqualone and had been prescribed legally as a sleeping pill, but Colombian traffickers were acquiring the chemical, and converting it into high-dosage tablets. By limiting the manufacture of the chemical, and then breaking up the supply lines by targeting the licit factories that manufactured methaqualone, the governments of the United States, Europe, India, and Colombia were together able to stop the traffic.

The story of PCP is similar. By enforcing tight controls on piperidine, an essential ingredient, governments effectively limited the supply of the drug. Also, PCP was not a "feel good" drug. Most people who tried it didn't repeat the experience. In the United States, PCP deaths have fallen every year since 1983, though Washington, D.C. and Los Angeles continue to have serious problems.

"Society is the one that ends things. It does so by changing its attitude and removing its support."

What these three examples of drug enforcement share, other than a degree of success, is the fact that the overwhelming majority of Americans were solidly behind the efforts. Absolutely no one argues that heroin is good for you; and the wild violence of some PCP druggies was enough to scare off many potential users. In this respect, these drugs differ from marijuana and cocaine, the two most popular illegal drugs.

Some 60 million Americans have smoked pot; it is by far the most socially entrenched illegal drug, almost a rite of passage for adolescents and a natural party adjunct for many young adults. In California, Hawaii, and parts of the south, marijuana agriculture is so important to the local economy that prosecutors have difficulty getting convictions for large planters. Law enforcement officials simply cannot deal with this kind of overwhelming defiance: what city cop is going to arrest every pot smoker he sees? If these drug laws are not going to be enforced on the street, it might make sense for the D.E.A. and the Justice Department to cut down on spectacular multi-helicopter anti-marijuana campaigns and concentrate their resources on harder drugs.

Cocaine use has not yet reached the same dimensions as pot, but 22 million Americans have tried it—among them, of course, a considerable proportion of our sports and entertainment elite. Middle class abuse of cocaine, says Rudolph Giuliani, the U.S. attorney in Manhattan, "creates a runaway, impossible problem for law enforcement to deal with." . . .

What, then, is the solution? The simple answer is that there isn't one; to look for magic bullets in an omnibus drug bill is a waste of time and money. America has a huge drug market because many Americans like to do drugs. Therefore, the only way to decrease drug abuse is for people to decide they don't want to do it. President Reagan referred in a speech on drugs to "an overwhelming change in consciousness that is taking place in America." So far, this is an exaggeration; rates of drug use are declining only modestly, albeit steadily. But it *is* true that such a shift in attitude is the key to reducing drug abuse. People have to *want* to "just say no."

The Limits of Law

Legal sanctions can, of course, influence private behavior. No doubt there are some people who have buckled up their seatbelts or refused to smoke a joint simply because the law told them to. But without a social consensus that verges on unanimity, laws seldom work; police can only deal with a limited number of violators. On the other hand, when such a consensus does emerge, the social pressures it generates are far more powerful than any law.

Cocaine was not illegal in the United States, for example, until the Harrison Act of 1914; by that time, hardly anyone was using it anymore. But in the 1880s and 1890s, cocaine was the drug of choice. Sigmund Freud wrote approving essays on its qualities, even sending the magic powder to his fiancee. Arthur Conan Doyle had his famous detective, Sherlock Holmes, take cocaine in several of the earlier stories; after the turn of the century, it never appears again. Vin Mariani, a wine drink containing cocaine, had such a cult following that its manufacturer put together a dozen volumes of testimonials, including endorsements from three popes. And Coca Cola contained cocaine until 1903; a common order for the beverage was, "Give me a dope." But as the dangers of cocaine became more widely known in the early 1900s, cocaine use steadily declined. By the time the states started restricting access to the drug and the federal government outlawed it, the problem was already under control.

In modern times, two of our most dangerous legal drugs—alcohol and nicotine—are too entrenched to be outlawed, but social pressures are effectively reducing their abuse. Only 32 percent of American adults smoke cigarettes today, down from 43 percent in 1965. And while alcohol is still the most common drug—92 percent of all high school students will have tried it before they graduate—the worst effects of liquor, drunk driving fatalities, dropped to 23,500 in 1985, from 26,000 in 1980.

Historically, as public awareness of the danger of a drug increases, use decreases. This was true of opium, laudanum, ether, morphine, heroin, and particularly cocaine in the 19th and early 20th centuries. The reverse is also true: when a drug comes to be considered innocuous or even beneficial—i.e. pot and LSD in the 1960s, cocaine in the 1970s, "Ecstasy" most recently—expect consumption to increase.

So, for example, when the misperception arose in the early 1970s that cocaine was non-addictive and not particularly dangerous (reversing the turn of the century consensus), consumption immediately went up. In a typical remark of the period, Peter G. Bourne, who later served as President Carter's drug adviser, wrote in 1974 that cocaine "is probably the most benign of illicit drugs currently in widespread use." Now that such drug experts are no longer trumpeting cocaine as a harmless high, use will probably begin to go down.

New research on pot may play the same role. A poll of Californians indicates that the recent decline in pot use was attributable to smokers' health concerns, not to legal sanctions. By 1985, some 70 percent of high school seniors believed marijuana use to be harmful, according to the National Institute on Drug Abuse; this is almost certainly a factor in the drop in use among students. The same holds true for the declines in heroin and PCP. Research into the physical effects of drugs is, therefore, an effective, if long-range means of controlling drug abuse.

Education

Second, education programs might be a useful, if limited, preventive measure. Unfortunately, there is no consensus on what kinds of education programs succeed in preventing students from using drugs. In fact, there is some evidence that indicates that the more kids learn about drugs, the more likely they are to try them. New programs that emphasize helping students to cope with social pressures show promise, but require special skills of the teachers who must direct them and are too new to have a proven track record.

So before spending $700 million over three years—the amount the drug bill authorized—we should figure out what works and not repeat the mistakes of the past. In particular, the scare tactics that characterized many drug programs in the 1970s have proved ineffective. At a time when almost 60 percent of high school seniors have tried dope, telling them simply that "drugs kill" is not going to make much of an impression. Of course drugs *can* kill, but students also know that it is possible to do drugs and live, and will not take such dire warnings very seriously.

Nor should drug education implicitly sanction drug use. A 1979 textbook entitled *Responsible Drug and Alcohol Use* advised students: smoke dope only with friends, clean out the seeds, don't smoke and drive, and don't drop ashes. Not exactly a hard-hitting prevention program.

The goal of drug education should be to make drug use so socially undesirable that kids won't even want to try it; it might be better to say that drugs are not just dangerous, but *gross*. The smoking analogy could be useful; probably more kids quit smoking because it made their breath smell and hurt their basketball game than because it causes lung cancer. Despite its limits, better drug education is a reasonable direction to go in. Since it is impossible to stop the supply of drugs, efforts to control demand make sense.

But the "war on drugs" will not be won by these measures. No government program, no matter how sensible and well-meaning, can stop Americans from doing what they want to do. As one D.E.A. official put it in a 1985 book, *International Drug Trafficking*:

> There has never been an illegal activity that was reduced or ended by laws themselves as long as the public condoned it. Society is the one that ends things. It does so by changing its attitude and removing its support. And that's the way it's going to be with [drug] traffic. Only when the world has gotten thoroughly fed up with today's abuse problem and has reached the day when it can say 'enough is enough' will the traffic truly find itself crippled.

Cait Murphy is assistant editor of Policy Review, *a quarterly journal of social policy.*

glossary

acetaldehyde substance produced by alcohol breaking down in the body; more toxic to the body than alcohol; affects the heart and may affect the brain and liver; plays a part in **Antabuse** reactions

alkaloids organic chemicals usually extracted from plants; examples are morphine, cocaine, nicotine, and caffeine

anabolic steroids artificial hormones taken by athletes to increase strength and muscle size

analgesics drugs that reduce or eliminate pain

androgen male sex hormone

anhedonia inability to enjoy what is usually pleasurable

Antabuse commercial name for a drug used in the treatment of alcoholism; causes a toxic buildup of **acetaldehyde** and so induces nausea in a person who drinks alcohol while taking it

atherosclerosis disease associated with hardening of the arteries and obstructing the flow of blood; smoking is one of several possible contributing factors to the disease

barbiturate drug with sedative (calming) effects; popularly known as sleeping pills or "downers"

basuco coca paste which is smoked in the South American coca-producing countries

benzodiazepine prescription tranquilizer; most common brand is Valium

biogenic amine nitrogen-containing chemical produced in the body

campesino South American peasant farmer

cannabis generic name for marijuana

catecholamine neurotransmitter in the central nervous system

Chapare chief coca-growing region of Bolivia

coca leaves from the coca plant; the raw material from which cocaine is made

coke slang for cocaine

Controlled Substances Act enacted in 1970 to control the classification, distribution, sale, and use of illegal drugs; consolidated all federal drug laws since the **Harrison Narcotics Act of 1914** and adopted by most states

crack potent, smokable form of cocaine; also known as "rock"

crack house makeshift "laboratory" where cocaine is made into crack

DEA Drug Enforcement Administration, agency of the Department of Justice; investigates and prosecutes organizations and individuals who grow, manufacture, or distribute illegal drugs

decriminalize eliminate criminal penalties for certain drug offenses

designer drugs unlicensed substances that duplicate the effects of certain illegal drugs; differ chemically from the original drugs, enabling the user and supplier to evade prosecution for possession of an illegal drug; legislation is being proposed to classify them as illegal

dopamine neurotransmitter in the central nervous system

drug interaction when two or more drugs are taken together, the combined action increases the effect of each drug

(the) DTs delirium tremens; a serious condition of withdrawal from alcohol or **barbiturate**-type drugs; considered a medical emergency; symptoms may include hallucinations, uncontrollable trembling of hands, confusion, restlessness, nausea, fever, and abnormally rapid heartbeat

emphysema disease of the lungs making it difficult to exhale; most commonly associated with smoking

endorphins proteins with potent **analgesic** properties that occur naturally in the brain

environmental tobacco smoke combination of **sidestream smoke** and the fraction of exhaled **mainstream smoke** not inhaled by smokers

epidemiologic survey comprehensive look at the incidence, distribution, and control of disease in a population

eradication destruction of narcotic-producing plants

estrogen female sex hormone

ethanol grain alcohol

euphoriant drug that produces a feeling of well-being

Fairness Doctrine policy mandated by the Federal Communications Commission requiring broadcasters to grant equal time to present an opposing viewpoint to one already aired

field sobriety test tests imposed by police in an on-the-spot check to determine if a driver is drunk

freebase smokable form of cocaine; to smoke cocaine in this form

free basing process of refining cocaine for use in smoking

GABA gamma-aminobutyric acid; one of the principal **neurotransmitters** in the central nervous system

gas chromotography/mass spectrometry drug test which can detect and identify particles of drugs in the urine

generic drugs families of closely-related drug compounds having essentially the same biological effect; usually cheaper than commercial counterpart

Golden Triangle Asian region where the borders of Laos, Burma, and Thailand converge; supplies most of the world's heroin

hallucinogen drug or other chemical substance that causes hallucinations; for example, LSD

Harrison Narcotics Act of 1914 first law in the US to regulate narcotics; designed primarily to channel the flow of opium and **coca** leaves and to make their transfer a matter of record

hypoxia low level of oxygen in the blood

immunoassay type of drug test that uses antibodies to detect the presence of drugs in the urine

interdiction prohibiting illegal drugs from entering the country

lipids fats and fatlike substances such as cholesterol

M-19 *Movimiento del 19 de abril de 1970*; Colombian guerrilla organization

mainstream smoke smoke drawn through the cigarette during puffing

Medellin cartel drug-trafficking syndicate in Colombia

Media Magdalena chief Colombian **coca**-growing region

metabolites chemicals in the blood or urine left over from drug use; can be detected by drug tests

methadone maintenance substitution of one drug (methadone) for another (heroin) to avoid withdrawal symptoms

monoamine **neurotransmitter** in the central nervous system

narcoguerrilla or **narcoterrorist** member of a rebel force financed by drug trafficking

narco trafficantes South American drug traffickers

neurons cells that conduct impulses to the nervous system

neuropeptides protein-like molecules found in brain tissue

neurotransmitter chemical that is released in the body from a nerve ending; excites or inhibits other nerve cells

Omnibus Drug Bill comprehensive drug abuse legislation enacted by Congress in 1986; increases penalties for most violations of the **Controlled Substances Act** and sets a mandatory minimum sentence of twenty years in prison for drug-related offenses resulting in death or serious injury

opiate drug derived from the opium poppy; for example, heroin or morphine

OSHA Occupational Safety and Health Administration, agency of the Department of Labor; sets up and enforces health and safety rules for employees

passive smoking inhaling the tobacco smoke of others

PCP phencyclidine; drug that produces hallucinations; also known as "angel dust"

pharmacology study of drugs and their effects on the body

physiological dependence accommodation of the body to continued use of a drug; withdrawal of the drug causes pronounced physical reactions (withdrawal symptoms)

placebo substance without medicinal properties which is administered for psychological benefit or as a test in controlled experiments on the effects of another substance

Prohibition period of US history from 1919 to 1933 when the sale of alcohol was prohibited by the Constitution and the Volstead Act

psychoactive drug drug affecting the mind or behavior

psychological dependence emotional desire or need to continue using a drug

psychomotor muscular (motor) activity that results from mental commands

psychotropic drug see **psychoactive drug**

Quaalude non**barbiturate** drug with sedative (calming) effects; prescribed for patients with sleeping difficulties; removed from the market in the early 1980s because of its widespread abuse

receptor cell or group of cells that receives stimuli

receptor agonist binding of a drug to a cell to initiate a response in the cell

secondhand smoke see **passive smoking**

serotonin hormone produced in the body and affected by LSD; **neurotransmitter** in the central nervous system

sidestream smoke smoke which escapes from the tip of the burning cigarette between puffs

speed slang for amphetamines (**stimulants**); produces an aroused, excited state

steroids general name for substances occurring naturally (sex hormones, cholesterol, cortisone) or produced artificially; see **anabolic steroids**

stimulants drugs that increase the activity of the nervous system

tachycardia rapid heartbeat

THC (delta-9-THC) tetrahydrocannabinol; a compound found in **cannabis** or made artificially; the primary intoxicant in marijuana; its effects vary depending on the strength and amount consumed; physical effects may include reddening of eyes, increased heartbeat, drowsiness, and muscular incoordination; psychological effects may include mild euphoria and alteration in judgment; acute intoxication may induce hallucinations, anxiety, depression, and mood changes

Tranquilandia large cocaine-processing plant raided by Colombian police in 1984

Upper Huallaga Valley chief **coca**-growing region in the Peruvian Andes

vasoconstrictor agent that narrows blood vessels

Volstead Act federal prohibition act, passed in 1919 to enforce the Eighteenth Amendment prohibiting the manufacture, sale, and transportation of alcoholic beverages

Zero Tolerance federal policy which does not allow any use of illegal drugs in any quantity by any person; also, policy of seizing the vehicles of drug smugglers entering the US

organizations

Action on Smoking and Health (ASH)
2013 H St. NW
Washington, DC 20006
(202) 659-4310

ASH calls itself the "legal action arm of the anti-smoking community." Founded by John Banzhaf III, the lawyer behind the ban on cigarette commercials, it has fought to obtain no-smoking sections on all major airlines, as well as for other rights for nonsmokers. It publishes the newsletter *ASH Smoking and Health Review.*

Al-Anon Family Groups
PO Box 862, Midtown Station
New York, NY 10018-0862
(212) 302-7240

Al-Anon's members are the family and friends of alcoholics. They offer support to other members but do not counsel or advise. They publish brochures including *What Do You Do About the Alcoholic's Drinking?* and *So You Love an Alcoholic.* Al-Anon is affiliated with and can provide information about Alateen, a support group aimed specifically at teenagers.

Alcoholics Anonymous (AA)
Box 459, Grand Central Station
New York, NY 10017
(212) 686-1100

AA is an international self-help group for recovering alcoholics. Members share their experiences and offer their support in achieving sobriety. AA publishes a monthly magazine, *AA Grapevine,* and many books, including *Twelve Steps and Twelve Traditions* and *AA Comes of Age.*

American Atheists' Addiction Recovery Groups (AAARG!)
PO Box 6120
Denver, CO 80206-0120

AAARG! was formed as a "non-religious, scientific alternative" to Alcoholics Anonymous. It questions the feasibility of abstinence and calls for the legalization of all psychoactive drugs. It publishes a newsletter for members.

American Civil Liberties Union (ACLU)
132 W. 43rd St.
New York, NY 10036
(212) 944-4064

The ACLU champions the rights set forth in the Declaration of Independence and the Constitution. It objects to drug testing because it believes such testing violates the individual's right to privacy. It publishes a *Briefing Paper on Drug Testing* and also distributes a packet of materials on drug testing.

American Council on Alcoholism, Inc. (ACA)
8501 Lasalle Rd., Suite 301
Townson, MD 21204
(301) 296-5555

ACA focuses on prevention through education. It provides a network for corporations, treatment centers, and individuals, offering speakers, literature, and a National Resource Library. The *ACA Journal* covers new developments in law, research, and educational programs as they relate to alcoholism.

American Lung Association (ALA)

ALA is an association of doctors, nurses, and individuals concerned about respiratory diseases and the hazards of smoking. It publishes the *American Review of Respiratory Diseases* monthly. Contact your local chapter for more information.

American Medical Association (AMA)
Department of Media and Information Services
1101 Vermont Ave. NW
Washington, DC 20005
(202) 789-7419

The AMA is a professional organization for people who work in the health care field. It has initiated and supported legislation prohibiting media advertising of tobacco products. The AMA attempts to persuade newspapers and magazines to voluntarily refuse tobacco advertisements. It publishes the *Journal of the American Medical Association* and *American Medical News* weekly.

American Pharmaceutical Association (APA)
2215 Constitution Ave. NW
Washington, DC 20037
(202) 628-4410

The APA is a professional society which works to establish standards for prescription drugs, to provide information, and to help prevent adulteration of drugs. It maintains a library at its headquarters, the American Institute of Pharmacy in Washington, DC. It publishes the *Pharmacy Weekly,* the *Journal of Pharmaceutical Sciences, American Pharmacy* and many other periodicals and booklets, as well as the *Handbook of Nonprescription Drugs.*

Americans for Nonsmokers' Rights (ANR)
2054 University Ave., Suite 500
Berkeley, CA 94704
(415) 841-3032

The organization is largely concerned with the dangers of secondhand smoke for the nonsmoker. They support legislation which would allow communities to limit tobacco advertisements. They publish educational literature and a newsletter, the *ANR Update.*

Center of Alcohol Studies
Rutgers, The State University of New Jersey
Smithers Hall, Busch Campus
Piscataway, NJ 08854
(201) 932-2190

The Center contains a large library on alcohol-related topics, and provides clinical services and information services. It publishes bibliographies on topics such as the psychological, social, and physiological aspects of alcoholism.

Children of Alcoholics Foundation
31st Floor, 200 Park Ave.
New York, NY 10166
(212) 351-2680

The Foundation works to lessen the suffering and anguish of children of alcoholics. It provides materials to teachers as well as businesses and communities in the hopes of preventing alcoholism. It also makes available the *Directory of National Resources for Children of Alcoholics* and numerous brochures for children.

Coalition for 100% Drug Reform
Box 392 Canal St.
New York, NY 10013
(212) 677-4899

The coalition, founded by Dana Beal, former Youth International Party (YIP) spokesperson, works to legalize all drugs. It believes a drug-free America is an unrealistic goal. Legalizing drugs will ensure that the drugs on the street are as safe as possible. It supports giving clean needles to drug addicts. It also endorses a boycott on crack and promotes marijuana as the safest of all illegal drugs. The coalition is developing a newsletter.

Committees of Correspondence, Inc.
57 Conant St.
Danvers, MA 01923
(508) 774-2641

The Committees were formed out of the concern that books used to teach about drugs in schools contain "at best, confusing mixed messages and, at worst, are virtual commercials for illegal drug use." They publish a handbook of recommended materials to prevent drug abuse, as well as the monthly *Drug Abuse Newsletter*.

Do It Now Foundation
2050 E. University Dr.
Phoenix, AZ 85034
(602) 257-0797

The Foundation, founded in 1968, offered one of the first drug-abuse hotlines in the country. It publishes pamphlets on chemical dependency, such as *Valium, Librium, and the Benzodiazepine Blues* and *Everyday Detox: A Guide to Living Without Chemicals*, as well as on other topics such as AIDS and eating disorders.

The Health Connection
Narcotics Education, Inc.
6830 Laurel St. NW
Washington, DC 20012-9979
(202) 722-6740

The organization distributes magazines, audiovisuals, and other materials that warn about the hazards of drug abuse. It publishes several magazines aimed at children, including *The Winner*, for ages nine through twelve, and *Listen*, for teenagers.

International Commission for the Prevention of Alcoholism and Drug Dependency (ICPA)
6830 Laurel St. NW
Washington, DC 20012-2199
(202) 722-6729

ICPA educates for the prevention of alcoholism and other drug dependencies. They publish *101 Things To Do for Prevention*, with practical ideas for teachers, parents, and community leaders.

"Just Say No" International
1777 N. California Blvd., Suite 210
Walnut Creek, CA 94596-4112
(800) 258-2766

The program provides "positive peer pressure for a drug-free America." It created an anti-drug television program, *The Flintstones Kids "Just Say No" Special*, and coordinated a drive to get schoolchildren to take the "Just Say No" Pledge.

Legal Action Center
153 Waverly Place
New York, NY 10014
(212) 243-1313

The Center is a nonprofit organization dedicated to preventing and combating discrimination on the basis of a person's history of drug or alcohol addiction, past criminal convictions, or risk of developing AIDS. It has mounted test cases challenging many employment practices, including drug-screening programs. It publishes a bimonthly newsletter, *Of Substance*, and several books, including *Confidentiality*, about the federal regulations protecting the records of those treated for drug or alcohol addictions, and *AIDS: A Guide to Legal and Policy Issues*.

Libertarian Party
1528 Pennsylvania Ave. SE
Washington, DC 20003
(202) 543-1988

The Libertarian Party's goal is to ensure respect for individual rights as the precondition for a free and prosperous world. It advocates the repeal of all laws prohibiting the production, sale, possession, or use of drugs. It believes law enforcement should stop violent crime against persons and property—not prosecute people with peaceful but unpopular personal lifestyles. It publishes *Libertarian Party News* and many books, including *Restoring the American Dream* and *Winning Through Intimidation*.

Mothers Against Drunk Driving (MADD)
669 Airport Freeway, Suite 310
Hurst, TX 76053
(817) 268-6233

MADD supports strict laws against drunk driving and aids victims with a Victim Outreach Program, which takes victims through the court proceedings step by step. It conducts research, provides information, and maintains an extensive library. It publishes *MADD Chapter Bulletins* and *MADD National Newsletter*.

The Narcotic Educational Foundation of America
5055 Sunset Blvd.
Los Angeles, CA 90027
(213) 663-5171

The Foundation sends "drug educational-warning materials" to every sheriff's and police department in the country, as well as to all secondary schools and many colleges. Such materials include a handout for students entitled *A Very Potent Drug: Ethyl Alcohol* and a brochure, *Drugs and the Automotive Age*.

Narcotics Anonymous (NA)
PO Box 9999
Van Nuys, CA 91409
(818) 780-3951

NA is an organization of recovering drug addicts who meet regularly to help each other abstain from all drugs. It publishes *NA Way Magazine* and *Newsline* monthly.

National Association for Children of Alcoholics
31582 Coast Highway, Suite B
South Laguna, CA 92677
(714) 499-3889

The Association serves as a resource for children of any age whose parents are or have been alcoholics. It works to increase public awareness of the problem as well as to offer support. It publishes a newsletter, *Network*, and other publications such as the *Children of Alcoholics Handbook* and *Children of Alcoholics: A Guide for Professionals*.

National Clearinghouse for Alcohol and Drug Information
PO Box 2345
Rockville, MD 20852
(301) 468-2600

The Clearinghouse provides educational literature and a reference and referral service. It publishes a bimonthly newsletter, *Prevention Pipeline: An Alcohol and Drug Awareness Service*, to report the newest data on alcohol and drug abuse.

National Council on Alcoholism
12 W. 21st St.
New York, NY 10010
(212) 206-6770

The Council provides educational materials and supports strict measures against drunk driving. It also believes the media should realistically portray the dangers of alcohol. It publishes many brochures, including *Who Says Alcoholism Is a Disease?* and *What Are the Signs of Alcoholism?* and issued a policy statement on the effects of alcoholism on women.

National Council on Patient Information and Education
666 11th St. NW, Suite 810
Washington, DC 20001
(202) 347-6711

The Council consists of pharmaceutical manufacturers, health care professional organizations, and consumer groups. It provides information on the use of prescription drugs and calls for increased discussion between doctors and patients regarding prescribed drugs. It publishes the *Directory of Prescription Drug Information and Education Programs and Resources*.

National Federation of Parents for Drug-Free Youth
1423 N. Jefferson
Springfield, MO 65802
(417) 836-3709

The Federation began REACH, Responsible Educated Adolescents Can Help America Stop Drugs, to train high school students to help educate younger children. It also coordinates the Red Ribbon Campaign to increase public awareness. It publishes a newsletter quarterly as well as the *Parent Group Starter Kit*, *Press/Media Guidelines*, and the *Anti-Paraphernalia Kit*.

National Institute of Justice
PO Box 6000
Rockville, MD 20850
(800) 851-3420

The Institute serves as a clearinghouse for information on the causes, prevention, and control of crime. Among the publications available are *Alcohol Use and Criminal Behavior* and *Probing the Links Between Drugs and Crime*.

National Lawyers Guild
853 Broadway
New York, NY 10003
(212) 966-5000

The Guild is a progressive organization made up of lawyers, law students, and legal workers. It opposes government efforts to impose widespread drug testing. It publishes the monthly *Bulletin* and a biennial *Referral Directory*.

National Organization for the Reform of Marijuana Laws (NORML)
2001 S St. NW, Suite 640
Washington, DC 20009
(202) 483-5500

NORML fights to legalize marijuana and to help those who have been convicted and sentenced for possessing or selling marijuana.

They publish a newsletter, *Marijuana Highpoints*, on the progress of legislation concerning marijuana throughout the country.

Public Citizen Health Research Group
PO Box 19404
Washington, DC 20036
(202) 293-9142

Public Citizen is a lobby group for consumer interests founded in 1971 by Ralph Nader. Its monthly newsletter, *Health Letter*, has included articles on quitting smoking and on prescription drug abuse. The director of the organization, Sidney M. Wolfe, has published several books on drugs, including *Pills That Don't Work* and *Over the Counter Pills That Don't Work*.

The Rand Corporation
Publications Department
1700 Main St.
PO Box 2138
Santa Monica, CA 90406-2138
(213) 393-0411

The Corporation publishes the results of its research in the fields of national security and public welfare. Its publications include *Alcoholism and Treatment*, and *The Course of Alcoholism: Four Years After Treatment*.

Smoker's Rights Alliance, Inc.
20 E. Main St., Suite 710
Mesa, AZ 85201
(602) 461-8882

The Alliance challenges anti-smoking legislation and discrimination against smokers. It feels disputes over smoking should be worked out by individuals, not regulated by the government. It publishes a newsletter, *Smoke Signals*.

Tobacco Growers' Information Committee, Inc.
PO Box 18089
Raleigh, NC 27619
(919) 848-4920

The Committee consists of tobacco growers and farm leaders who do not lobby but do provide information on tobacco-related issues. It publishes *The Tobacco Primer*, which disputes the assumption that smoking causes disease to smokers or nonsmokers, as well as other common beliefs about tobacco.

The Tobacco Institute
1875 Eye St. NW
Washington, DC 20006
(202) 457-4800

The Institute is the major national lobbying organization for the tobacco industry. It argues that the dangers of smoking have not been proven and opposes restrictions on smoking on airlines, in restaurants, and in public buildings. It also publishes many brochures and booklets like *Environmental Tobacco Smoke and Health: The Consensus*.

Tobacco Products Liability Project
Northeastern University School of Law
400 Huntington Ave.
Boston, MA 02115
(617) 437-2026

The Project believes tobacco companies should be held responsible for deaths caused by cigarette smoking. It helps those who have been harmed by smoking to file suit against tobacco companies. The Project publishes the monthly *Tobacco Products Litigation Reporter*, which summarizes decisions in recent liability cases, and *Tobacco on Trial*, a newsletter which reports on current litigation.

Wisconsin Clearinghouse
1245 E. Washington Ave.
Madison, WI 53703

(608) 263-6884

The Clearinghouse provides publications and video tapes on drug and alcohol abuse. Titles include *Drugs and Drug Abuse: A Reference Text* and the *Making Prevention Work Kit*.

Women for Sobriety, Inc. (WFS)
PO Box 618
Quakertown, PA 18951
(215) 536-8026

The organization was the first national self-help group specifically for women alcoholics. WFS was developed in the belief that women alcoholics have different psychological needs than male alcoholics and thus need a different treatment program. Its newsletter, *Sobering Thoughts*, appears monthly. It also publishes a collection of questionnaires called *Self-Analyzers*, and other brochures such as *Self-Esteem* and *Relationships: Trying To Make Them Work*.

bibliography

Addiction

William Ira Bennett	"Patterns of Addiction," *The New York Times Magazine*, April 10, 1988.
Bob Brewin	"So, What About Booze?" *The Village Voice*, September 30, 1986.
Winifred Gallagher	"Boy Could I Use a . . . ," *Mademoiselle*, October 1987.
Richard Goldstein	"The New Sobriety," *The Village Voice*, December 30, 1986.
Timothy F. Kirn	"Drug Abuse: More Help Available for Addicted Persons, but Main Problem Continues Unabated," *Journal of the American Medical Association*, October 21, 1988.
Molly Malone	"Dependent on Disorder," *Ms.*, February 1987.
Tom Morganthau, et al.	"Kids and Cocaine," *Newsweek*, March 17, 1986.
Stephen J. Morse	"Drug Problem Seems To Be Bearable," *Los Angeles Times*, July 1, 1987.
Craig Nakken	*The Addictive Personality.* Center City, MN: Hazelden Foundation, 1988.
Stanton Peele	*The Diseasing of America: How the Addiction Industry Captured Our Soul.* Lexington, MA: Lexington Books, 1989.
Stephen E. Schlesinger and Lawrence K. Horberg	*Taking Charge: How Families Can Climb Out of the Chaos of Addiction and Flourish.* New York: Simon & Schuster, 1988.
Lindsy Van Gelder	"Cross-Addiction," *Ms.*, February 1987.
Eric A. Voth	"Addiction as a Primary Disease," *Drug Awareness Information Newsletter*, September 1987. Available from Committees of Correspondence, 57 Conant St., Room 113, Danvers, MA 01923.
Ben Whitaker	*The Global Connection: The Crisis of Drug Addiction.* London: Jonathan Cape, 1987.

Alcoholism

Margaret Bean-Bayog and Barry Stimmel, eds.	*Children of Alcoholics.* New York: Haworth Press, 1987.
David Berenson	"Alcoholics Anonymous: From Surrender to Transformation," *The Family Therapy Networker*, July/August 1987. Available from The Family Therapy Networker, 8528 Bradford Rd., Silver Spring, MD 20901.
Dan Calahan	*Understanding America's Drinking Problem.* San Francisco: Jossey-Bass, 1987.
Morris E. Chafetz	"The Third Wave of Prohibition Is Upon Us," *The Wall Street Journal*, July 21, 1987.
Mona Charen	"Is Alcoholism a Disease or a Weakness?" *Conservative Chronicle*, May 11, 1988. Available from the *Conservative Chronicle*, 9 Second St. NW, Hampton, IA 50441.
Eli Coleman	*Chemical Dependence and Intimacy Dysfunction.* New York: Haworth Press, 1988.
Lily Collett	"Step by Step," *Mother Jones*, July/August 1988.
Herbert Fingarette	*Heavy Drinking: The Myth of Alcoholism as a Disease.* Berkeley, CA: University of California Press, 1988.
Charles Leerhsen and Tessa Namuth	"Alcohol and the Family," *Newsweek*, January 18, 1988.
Joan Libman	"The Drinking Trap," *Los Angeles Times*, December 27, 1988.
Lewis J. Lord, et al.	"Coming to Grips with Alcoholism," *U.S. News & World Report*, November 30, 1987.
Arnold M. Ludwig	*Understanding the Alcoholic's Mind: The Nature of Craving and How To Control It.* New York: Oxford University Press, 1988.
Joseph M. Queenan	"Too Late To Say, 'I'm Sorry,'" *Newsweek*, August 31, 1987.
Don Sloan	"Alcohol in Our Lives," *People's Daily World*, November 29, 1988. Available from *People's Daily World*, 239 W. 23rd St., New York, NY 10011.
Larry M. Thomas	"Alcoholism Is Not a Disease," *Christianity Today*, October 4, 1985.
David S. Wilson	"Drunken Drivers Visit the Morgue," *The New York Times*, September 21, 1988.

Athletes and Drugs

Peter Alfano and Michael Janofsky — "A 'Guru' Who Spreads the Gospel of Steroids," *The New York Times*, November 19, 1988.

Pete Axthelm — "Using Chemistry To Get the Gold," *Newsweek*, July 25, 1988.

Glenn D. Braunstein — "Anabolic Steroids: To Race Against Risk," *Los Angeles Times*, October 9, 1988.

William F. Buckley, et al. — "Estimated Prevalence of Anabolic Steroid Use Among Male High School Seniors," *Journal of the American Medical Association*, December 16, 1988.

Rudolph Chelminski — "The Shocking Stain on International Athletics," *Reader's Digest*, August 1988.

Virginia S. Cowart — "Athletes and Steroids: The Bad Bargain," *The Saturday Evening Post*, April 1987.

Edward F. Dolan — *Drugs in Sports*. New York: Franklin Watts, 1986.

Tom Donohoe and Neil Johnson — *Foul Play*. New York: Basil Blackwell, 1986.

Marty Duda — "Do Anabolic Steroids Pose an Ethical Dilemma for US Physicians?" *The Physician and Sportsmedicine*, November 1986.

Norman Fost — "Ben Johnson, World's Fastest Scapegoat," *The New York Times*, October 20, 1988.

William Gildea — "Life—and Drugs—in Sports' Fast Lane," *Reader's Digest*, January 1988.

Eleanor Grant — "Of Muscles and Mania," *Psychology Today*, September 1987.

Gary Alan Green — "Drugs and the Athlete," *Delaware Medical Journal*, September 1987.

Jonathan Harris — *Drugged Athletes: The Crisis in American Sports*. New York: Four Winds Press, 1987.

Michael Janofsky — "US and Soviet Union Approve Plan on Drug Testing of Athletes," *The New York Times*, November 11, 1988.

Michael Janofsky and Peter Alfano — "System Accused of Failing Test Posed by Drugs," *The New York Times*, November 17, 1988.

Malini Johns — "The Inside Dope," *Runner's World*, September 1988.

William Oscar Johnson — "Sports and Suds," *Sports Illustrated*, August 8, 1988.

William Oscar Johnson — "Steroids: A Problem of Huge Dimensions," *Sports Illustrated*, May 5, 1985.

William Oscar Johnson and Kenny Moore — "The Loser," *Sports Illustrated*, October 3, 1988.

Frederick C. Klein — "Purging Steroids from Sport," *The New York Times*, November 25, 1988.

Tony Kornheiser — "Ben Johnson's Olympic Disgrace—and Ours," *The Washington Post National Weekly Edition*, October 3/9, 1988.

Jacob V. Lamar — "Scoring Off the Field," *Time*, August 25, 1986.

Mike Lupica — "The Alcohol Rub," *Esquire*, June 1988.

Roger W. Miller — "Athletes and Steroids: Playing a Deadly Game," *FDA Consumer*, November 1987.

Sandy Padwe — "Symptoms of a Deeper Malaise," *The Nation*, September 27, 1986.

John Papanek — "Athletes or Role Models?" *Sports Illustrated*, June 15, 1987.

Rick Reilly — "When the Cheers Turn to Tears," *Sports Illustrated*, July 14, 1986.

Anne C. Roark and Steven R. Churm — "Steroids' Lure: A Way To Look Good," *Los Angeles Times*, December 26, 1988.

Carl Rowan and David Mazie — "The Mounting Menace of Steroids," *Reader's Digest*, February 1988.

William N. Taylor — *Hormonal Manipulation: A New Era of Monstrous Athletes*. Jefferson, NC: McFarland & Company, Inc., 1985.

Rick Telander — "A Peril for Athletes," *Sports Illustrated*, October 24, 1988.

Jean D. Wilson — "Androgen Abuse by Athletes," *Endocrine Review*, May 1988.

Cigarette Advertising

Murray Bring — "Cipollone Jury Decision: Its Meaning and Its Impact," *Philip Morris Magazine*, Summer 1988. Available from Philip Morris USA, 120 Park Ave., New York, NY 10017.

Simon Chapman — *Great Expectorations: Advertising and the Tobacco Industry*. London: Comedia Publishing Group, 1981.

Jean Cobb — "Clearing the Air: Should All Cigarette Advertising and Promotion Be Banned?" *Common Cause Magazine*, March/April, 1986.

David Gidmark and Christina Nichols — "Tobacco on Trial," *Environmental Action*, May/June 1986.

James J. Kilpatrick — "'The Devil Made Me Do It' Syndrome," *Conservative Chronicle*, June 29, 1988. Available from *Conservative Chronicle*, Box 29, Hampton, IA 50441.

Stephen Koepp — "Tobacco's First Loss," *Time*, June 27, 1988.

Tibor R. Machan — "Smokers Stand Alone in Blame," *Los Angeles Times*, March 5, 1988.

Morton Mintz — "The Artful Dodgers," *The Washington Monthly*, October 1986.

Multinational Monitor — "The Tobacco Trap," July/August 1987.

The Nation — "A Symposium: Cigarette Ads and the Press," March 7, 1987.

Martin H. Redish — "Statement Before the Subcommittee on Health and the Environment, House Committee on Energy and Commerce," July 27, 1987. Available from The Tobacco Institute, 1875 I St. NW, Washington, DC 20006.

Harold Smith — "A Colossal Cover-up," *Christianity Today*, December 12, 1986.

Washington Legal Foundation — "Keeping an Open Mind: George Will and the Ad Ban Controversy," *Legal Backgrounder*, October 16, 1987. Available from Washington Legal Foundation, 1705 N St. NW, Washington, DC 20036.

Charles O. Whitley — "Statement Before the Subcommittee on Health and the Environment, Committee on Energy and Commerce," July 27, 1987. Available from The Tobacco Institute, 1875 I St. NW, Washington, DC 20006.

Cocaine

Jerry Adler — "Crack: Hour by Hour," *Newsweek*, November 28, 1988.

Trevor Armbrister — "We *Can* Conquer Cocaine," *Reader's Digest*, February 1987.

Gilda Berger — *Crack: The New Drug Epidemic*. New York: Franklin Watts, 1987.

Jane Brody — "Cocaine: Litany of Fetal Risks Grows," *The New York Times*, September 6, 1988.

Mark Buechler — "Why Not Ban Falling in Love?" *Reason*, March 1988. Available from the Reason Foundation, 2716 Ocean Park Blvd., Suite 1062, Santa Monica, CA 90405.

Ebony — "How To Deal with the Cocaine Scourge," October 1986.

Paul Eddy, Hugo Sabogal, and Sara Walden — *The Cocaine Wars*. New York: W.W. Norton & Company, 1986.

Patricia G. Erickson, et al. — *The Steel Drug: Cocaine in Perspective*. Lexington, MA: Lexington Books, 1987.

Lester Grinspoon and James B. Bakalar — *Cocaine: A Drug and Its Social Evolution*. New York: Basic Books, Inc., 1985.

Peter Kerr — "Addiction's Hidden Toll: Poor Families in Turmoil," *The New York Times*, June 23, 1988.

Nicholas J. Kozel and Edgar H. Adams, eds. — *Cocaine Use in America: Epidemiologic and Clinical Perspectives*. NIDA Research Monograph 61. Rockville, MD: National Institute on Drug Abuse, 1985. Available from the Superintendent of Documents, US Government Printing Office, Washington, DC 20402.

Jacob V. Lamar — "Kids Who Sell Crack," *Time*, May 9, 1988.

James Lieber — "Coping with Cocaine," *The Atlantic Monthly*, January 1986.

Peggy Mann — "Breakthrough Against Cocaine," *Reader's Digest*, April 1987.

Cardwell C. Nuckols — *Cocaine: From Dependency to Recovery*. Bradenton, FL: Human Services Institute, 1987. Available from HSI, P.O. Box 14610, Bradenton, FL 34280.

Office of Substance Abuse Prevention, US Department of Health and Human Services — *Cocaine/Crack: The Big Lie*. DHHS Publication No. (ADM)88-1427, 1988. Available from Superintendent of Documents, Government Printing Office, Washington, DC 20402.

Alan Riding — "Cocaine Billionaires: The Men Who Hold Colombia Hostage," *The New York Times Magazine*, March 8, 1987.

Tina Rosenberg — "Colombia: Murder City," *The Atlantic Monthly*, November 1988.

Marc A. Schuckit — "Cocaine: An Update," *Drug Abuse & Alcoholism Newsletter*, June 1988. Available from Vista Hill Foundation, 3420 Camino del Rio North, Suite 100, San Diego, CA 92108.

Robert Stone — "A Higher Horror of the Whiteness," *Harper's*, December 1986.

Arnold M. Washton and Mark S. Gold — *Cocaine Treatment: A Guide*. New York: The American Council for Drug Education, 1986. Available from 136 E. 64th St., New York, NY 10021.

Peter T. White — "Coca: An Ancient Herb Turns Deadly," *National Geographic*, January 1989.

Elisabeth Wynhausen — "Cracked Out," *Ms.*, September 1988.

Drug Testing

American Bar Association — "Drug Testing on the Job: What Are the Legal Limits?" *Your Law*, Spring 1988. Available from the ABA Division of Public Education, 750 N. Lake Shore Drive, Chicago, IL 60611.

American Federation of Labor and Congress of Industrial Organizations (AFL-CIO) — *Drug & Alcohol Testing on the Job: Safety with Personal Dignity*. Publication No. 177, May 21, 1986. Available from 815 16th St. NW, Washington, DC 20006.

Business Week — "Drug Testing: A Delicate Balance," October 13, 1986.

Janice Castro — "Battling Drugs on the Job," *Time*, January 27, 1986.

Jeffrey Chamberlain — "Legal Aspects of Employee Drug Testing," *USA Today*, May 1988.

Congressional Digest — "Reagan Administration Drug Testing Program: Pro & Con," May 1987. Available from Congressional Digest Building, 3231 P St. NW, Washington, DC 20007.

Harper's — "Foiling the Urine Police," March 1987.

John Hoerr — "The Drug Wars Will Be Won with Treatment, Not Tests," *Business Week*, October 13, 1986.

Abbie Hoffman — *Steal This Urine Test: Fighting Drug Hysteria in America*. NY: Penguin Books, 1987.

C. Holden — "Doctors Square Off on Employee Drug Testing," *Science*, November 6, 1987.

Jet — "Black Federal Workers Oppose Drug Testing," June 22, 1987.

Barbara Kantrowitz — "Bringing Home the Drug-Test Dilemma," *Time*, July 21, 1986.

John Kaplan — "A Positive Check on Crime," *Los Angeles Times*, March 16, 1988.

John Kaplan — "Taking Drugs Seriously," *The Public Interest*, No. 92, Summer 1988. Available from 1112 16th St. NW, Washington, DC 20036.

Jefferson Morley — "Our Puritan Dilemma," *The New Republic*, December 1, 1986.

The New Republic — "The Right Spirit," September 8, 1986.

A.M. O'Keefe — "The Case Against Drug Testing," *Psychology Today*, June 1987.

Syva Company — *Emit Drug Abuse Assays: How Accurate Are They?* 1986. Available from Syva Company, PO Box 10058, Palo Alto, CA 94303.

Michael Waldholz — "Drug Testing in the Workplace: Whose Rights Take Precedence?" *The Wall Street Journal*, November 11, 1986.

The Legalization of Drugs

Gary S. Becker — "More People Are Saying 'Yes' To Legalizing Drugs," *Business Week*, June 27, 1988.

Gary S. Becker — "Should Drug Use Be Legalized?" *Business Week*, August 17, 1987.

David Boaz — "The Legalization of Drugs," *Vital Speeches of the Day*, August 15, 1988.

Taylor Branch — "Let Koop Do It," *The New Republic*, October 24, 1988.

William F. Buckley — "Koppel's Drug Bust," *National Review*, October 28, 1988.

David Glidden — "Legalizing Dope: A Life-Threatening Idea," *Los Angeles Times*, September 24, 1988.

Marc Leepson — "Should Drugs Be Legalized?" *Common Cause Magazine*, July/August 1988.

Tom Morganthau — "Should Drugs Be Legal?" *Newsweek*, May 30, 1988.

Pacific Research Institute for Public Policy — *Dealing with Drugs: Consequences of Government Control*. Lexington, MA: Lexington Books, 1987.

Reason — "America After Prohibition," October 1988.

Vermont Royster — "Some Lessons from a 'Noble Experiment,'" *The Wall Street Journal*, June 1, 1988.

Kurt L. Schmoke — "Let's Declare Defeat in the War on Drugs and Legalize Them," *The Washington Post National Weekly Edition*, May 23/29, 1988.

Joseph F. Schuster — "The Not So Seamless Web: Some Thoughts on 'Victimless Crime,'" *Journal of Contemporary Justice*, February 1987.

Jerome H. Skolnick — "Drugs: More or Fewer Controls?" *Los Angeles Times*, June 22, 1988.

Cal Thomas — "Don't Give Up on Drug Users?" *Los Angeles Times*, May 19, 1988.

Marijuana

Steve Chapple — *Outlaws in Babylon: Shocking True Adventures on the Marijuana Frontier*. New York: Long Shadow Books, 1984.

Miriam Cohen — *Marijuana: Its Effects on Mind & Body*. New York: Chelsea House Publishers, 1985.

Alan M. Dershowitz — "Drug-User Witch Hunt Exposes the Hunters, Unmasks the Hypocrisy," *Los Angeles Times*, November 27, 1988.

Robert Edwards — "The Modern Moonshiner," *Newsweek*, October 27, 1986.

Ramsey Flynn and Steven D. Kaye — "Collision at Gunpow," *Reader's Digest*, May 1988.

Winifred Gallagher — "Marijuana: Is There New Reason To Worry?" *American Health*, March 1988.

Jon Gettman — "Why Marijuana Should Be Legalized," *High Times*, March 1988.

James K. Glassman — "The Money Culture Gone to Seed," *The New Republic*, August 25, 1986.

Herbert Hendin — *Living High: Daily Marijuana Use Among Adults*. New York: Human Sciences Press, Inc., 1987.

Michael Isikoff — "Snuffing Out the Pot Producers," *The Washington Post National Weekly Edition*, July 11/17, 1988.

Helen C. Jones and Paul W. Lovinger — *The Marijuana Question*. New York: Dodd, Mead & Company, 1985.

Michael Kinsley — "Glass Houses and Getting Stoned," *Time*, June 6, 1988.

Geoff Lowe — "High and Housebound," *Psychology Today*, September 1987.

Peggy Mann — *Marijuana Alert*. New York: McGraw-Hill Book Company, 1985.

Newsweek — "A Bumper Crop of Hothouse Marijuana," August 15, 1988.

Lori Oliwenstein — "The Perils of Pot," *Discover*, June 1988.

USA Today — "Marijuana and Pilot's Performance," August 1986.

Rick Weiss — "Take Two Puffs and Call Me in the Morning," *Science News*, February 20, 1988.

Prescription Drugs

American Medical Association — *Guide to Prescription and Over-the-Counter Drugs*. New York: Random House, 1988.

Thomas S. Baker — "Commentary: Prescription Addiction," *New Jersey Medicine*, August 1987.

Uriel S. Barzel — "Brand-Name Drugs Are Safer than Generics," *The New York Times*, August 31, 1987.

FDA Consumer — "Myths and Facts of Generic Drugs," September 1987.

Tricia Gallagher — "Treating Prescription Drug Addictions," *DARE Magazine*, vol. 2, no. 3, 1987. Available from OSAM/DARE, 1011 First Ave., New York, NY 10022.

Erica E. Goode — "Medicine-Chest Roulette," *U.S. News & World Report*, May 9, 1988.

C.K. Gutman — "Treating Stress with Drugs," *Current Health*, October 1988.

Frank E. James — "Approved Drugs Find Unapproved Uses," *The Wall Street Journal*, July 12, 1988.

Frank E. James — "Doctors Don't Tell All on Drugs' Effects," *The Wall Street Journal*, May 20, 1988.

Robert W. Lee — "Just Say No to Ritalin," *The New American*, November 7, 1988.

James T. Mulry and Joan Stockhoff — "Drug Use in the Chemically Dependent," *Postgraduate Medicine*, April 1988.

New England Journal of Medicine — "Advertising of Prescription Drugs," August 4, 1988.

Barbara Ogur — "Prescription Drug Abuse and Dependence in Clinical Practice," *Southern Medical Journal*, September 1987.

Jim Parker — *Valium, Librium, and the Benzodiazepine Blues*. Phoenix, AZ: D.I.N. Publications, 1985. Pamphlet available from Do It Now Foundation, 2050 E. University Drive, Phoenix, AZ 85034.

Sam Peltzman — "By Prescription Only . . . or Occasionally?" *Regulation*, nos. 3/4, 1987.

John Schwartz — "Now, One-Stop Medicine?" *Newsweek*, May 25, 1987.

Harold Silverman and Gilbert Simon — *The Pill Book*. New York: Bantam Books, 1986.

Ellen Switzer — "Overmedication: Health Hazard of Our Time," *Vogue*, March 1986.

P. Tyrer — "Dependence as a Limiting Factor in the Clinical Use of Minor Tranquilizers," *Pharmacology & Therapeutics*, vol. 36, issue 2/3, 1988.

Rick Weiss — "Take Two Puffs and Call Me in the Morning," *Science News*, February 20, 1988.

Sidney M. Wolfe — "The People's Doctor," *Multinational Monitor*, June 1988.

Prevention

Ken Barun and Philip Bashe — *How To Keep the Children You Love Off Drugs.* New York: The Atlantic Monthly Press, 1988.

Barry Bearak and Richard E. Meyer — "Drug Furor: Overdue or Much Ado?" *Los Angeles Times*, October 20, 1986.

Mark Bregman — "Fast Lane to Nowhere," *Futures*, Spring 1987. Available from *Futures*, 730 Broadway, New York, NY 10003.

Education Update — "Stopping Drugs in Schools: Tough Policies Work," Fall 1988. Available from The Heritage Foundation, 214 Massachusetts Ave. NE, Washington, DC 20002.

Barry Glassner and Julia Loughlin — *Drugs in the Adolescent Worlds: Burnouts to Straights.* New York: St. Martin's Press, 1987.

The Heritage Foundation — "Strategy for a Drug-Free America: A Symposium," *Backgrounder*, September 12, 1988. Available from The Heritage Foundation, 214 Massachusetts Ave. NE, Washington, DC 20002.

Chris Lutes — "Positive Peer Pressure: A New Weapon Against Drugs," *Christianity Today*, February 20, 1987.

Michael D. Newcomb and Peter Bentler — *Consequences of Adolescent Drug Use.* Newbury Park, CA: Sage Publications, 1988.

William Pollin — "Drug Abuse, U.S.A.: How Serious? How Soluble?" *Issues in Science and Technology*, Winter 1987.

Phyllis Schlafly — "Drug Education," *The New American*, April 7, 1986.

Janny Scott — "Debate Resurrected Over Risks of Casual Drug Use," *Los Angeles Times*, August 10, 1988.

Time — "Campus Dryout," June 6, 1988.

U.S. News & World Report — "Keeping Prime Time Clean and Sober," September 12, 1988.

Public Smoking Laws

Alan Blum, ed. — *The Cigarette Underworld: A Front Line Report on the War Against Your Lungs,* Secaucus, NJ: Lyle Stuart Inc., 1985.

William U. Chandler — "The Devastating Costs of Tobacco Addiction," *USA Today*, July 1986.

Marcelle Clements — "Why I'm So Angry with Myself for Quitting Smoking," *Utne Reader*, November/December 1988.

Nancy C. Doyle — *Involuntary Smoking—Health Risks for Nonsmokers*, December, 1987. Pamphlet available for $1.00 from Public Affairs Pamphlets, 381 Park Ave. S, New York, NY 10016.

Glen Evans — "Stub Out Antismoking Zealotry," *The New York Times*, May 7, 1988.

Barry Glassner — "Why Smoking Bans Are Dangerous," *The New York Times*, February 9, 1988.

Dexter Hutchins — "The Drive To Kick Smoking at Work," *Fortune*, September 15, 1986.

Richard Lacayo — "Smoke Gets in Your Rights," *Time*, April 18, 1988.

Myron Levin — "Big Tobacco Buying New Friendships," *Los Angeles Times*, May 22, 1988.

Susan Milligan — "Eyes on the Lies," *The Washington Monthly*, June 1987.

Tobacco Growers' Information Committee — *The Tobacco Primer.* Available from the Tobacco Growers' Information Committee, PO Box 18089, Raleigh, NC 27619.

The Tobacco Institute — *An Assessment of the Current Legal Climate Concerning Smoking in the Workplace*, July 1988. Available from The Tobacco Institute, 1875 I St. NW, Washington, DC 20006.

The Tobacco Institute — *Indoor Pollution: Is Your Workplace Making You Sick?* May 1988. Available from The Tobacco Institute, 1875 I St. NW, Washington, DC 20006.

Robert D. Tollison — *Clearing the Air: Perspectives on Environmental Tobacco Smoke.* Lexington, MA: Lexington Books, 1988.

Alice Walker — "Slavery on Tobacco Road," *In These Times*, March 11/17, 1987.

Kenneth E. Warner — "What Would Happen If Nobody Smoked?" *Journal of the American Medical Association*, October 16, 1987.

Tobacco and Health

B. Bruce-Briggs — "The Health Police Are Blowing Smoke," *Fortune*, April 25, 1988.

Mona Charen — "Smoke and Mirrors and Misconceptions," *Conservative Chronicle*, June 8, 1988. Available from *Conservative Chronicle*, Box 29, Hampton, IA 50441.

Alexander Cockburn — "The Great American Smoke Screen," *The Wall Street Journal*, June 16, 1988.

Tom Ferguson — *The Smoker's Book of Health.* New York: G.P. Putnam's Sons, 1987.

Jonathan E. Fielding and Kenneth J. Phenow — "Health Effects of Involuntary Smoking," *The New England Journal of Medicine*, December 1, 1988.

Erica E. Goode — "How To Stop Smoking—and Stick with It," *U.S. News & World Report*, August 1, 1988.

Christine Gorman — "Why It's So Hard To Quit Smoking," *Time*, May 30, 1988.

Leon Howell — "Smoke Gets into More than Your Eyes," *Christianity and Crisis*, August 1, 1988.

Walter B. Jones — "Inconclusive Evidence on the Harmful Effects of Smoking," *Congressional Record*, February 18, 1987.

C. Everett Koop — "Non-Smokers: Time To Clear the Air," *Reader's Digest*, April 1987.

Charles A. LeMaistre — "Lung Cancer in Perspective," *Vital Speeches of the Day*, July 1, 1987.

J.P. Pierce, et al. — "Trends in Cigarette Smoking in the United States: Projections to the Year 2000," *Journal of the American Medical Association*, January 6, 1989.

National Research Council — *Environmental Tobacco Smoke: Measuring Exposure and Assessing Health Effects.* Washington, DC: National Academy Press, 1986.

Robert J. Samuelson — "The Assault on Smoking," *Newsweek*, March 23, 1987.

Roberta Sandler	"Blowing Smoke," *Harper's Magazine*, August 1987.
Peter Schmeisser	"Pushing Cigarettes Overseas," *The New York Times Magazine*, July 10, 1988.
Martin Tolchin	"Surgeon General Asserts Smoking Is an Addiction," *The New York Times*, May 17, 1988.
Robert D. Tollison, ed.	*Smoking and Society: Toward a More Balanced Assessment*. Lexington, MA: D.C. Heath, 1986.
Steve Weinstein	"The Question," *Philip Morris Magazine*, Spring 1988. Available from Philip Morris USA, 120 Park Ave., New York, NY 10017.
Larry C. White	*Merchants of Death: The American Tobacco Industry*. New York: Beech Tree Books, William Morrow and Company, 1988.

Treatment

Stephanie Brown	*Treating Adult Children of Alcoholics: A Developmental Perspective*. New York: John Wiley & Sons, 1988.
Charles Bufe	"AA: Guilt and God for the Gullible," *The Match!*, November 11, 1987. Available from *The Match!* An Anarchist Journal, Box 3488, Tucson, AZ 85722.
Toby Cohen	"Why Subsidize Expensive Drug Care," *The New York Times*, June 6, 1988.
Norman Denzin	*Treating Alcoholism*. Newbury Park, CA: Sage Press, 1987.
Griffith Edwards	*The Treatment of Drinking Problems: A Guide for the Helping Professions*. Boston: Blackwell Scientific, 1988.
Elpenor	"A Drunkard's Progress," *Harper's Magazine*, October 1986.
Ellen Herman	"The Twelve-Step Program: Cure or Cover?" *Out/Look*, Summer 1988. Available from *Out/Look*, Box 460430, San Francisco, CA 94146-0430.
Kathryn Hudson	"Parents Detect Kink in Straight Drug Program," *The Washington Times*, December 6, 1988.
Peter Kerr	"Acupuncture Seems to Ease Crack Addiction, Study Says," *The New York Times*, September 30, 1988.
Mary Ellen Mark	"Turning Kids Off Drugs," *The New York Times Magazine*, May 24, 1987.
Roger Owen	"Getting Better," *Encounter*, September/October 1987.
Andy Plattner and Gordon Witkin	"Drugs on Main Street: The Enemy Up Close," *U.S. News & World Report*, June 27, 1988.
Nan Robertson	*Getting Better: Inside Alcoholics Anonymous*. New York: William Morrow & Co., 1988.
Anne Wilson Schaef	*Escape from Intimacy*. New York: Harper & Row, 1989.
Ed Storti and Janet Keller	*Crisis Intervention: Acting Against Addiction*. New York: Crown Publishers, 1988.

The War on Drugs

David Boaz	"Let's Quit the War on Drugs," *The New York Times*, March 17, 1988.
Lee P. Brown	"The Illegal Use of Drugs," *Vital Speeches of the Day*, September 15, 1988.
Angus Deming	"Guns, Drugs and Politics," *Newsweek*, July 28, 1986.
Ted Gest	"Soldiers Can't Beat Smugglers," *U.S. News & World Report*, May 30, 1988.
Anthony Henman, Roger Lewis, and Tim Malyon	*Big Deal: The Politics of the Illicit Drug Business*. London: Pluto Press, 1985.
James A. Inciardi	*The War on Drugs: Heroin, Cocaine, Crime, and Public Policy*. Palo Alto, CA: Mayfield Publishing Co., 1986.
Jo Ann Kawell	"Peasants To Pay the Price for U.S. War on Drugs," *In These Times*, July 8-21, 1987.
David Kline	"How To Lose the Coke War," *The Atlantic Monthly*, May 1987.
Edward I. Koch	"An Arsenal for the Federal War on Drugs," *The New York Times*, July 18, 1986.
Louis Kraar	"The Drug Trade," *Fortune*, June 20, 1988.
Jacob V. Lamar	"Where the War Is Being Lost," *Time*, March 14, 1988.
James Mills	*The Underground Empire: Where Crime and Governments Embrace*. New York: Doubleday, 1986.
Thomas Molnar	"Exporting the Drug War," *National Review*, May 22, 1987.
Tom Morganthau	"Going After Hollywood: Critics Call for the Deglamorization of Drugs," *Newsweek*, August 11, 1986.
Robert M. Morgenthau	"We Are Losing the War on Drugs," *The New York Times*, February 16, 1988.
The New Republic	"The Quack Epidemic," November 14, 1988.
The New York Times	"A Hemisphere at Risk from Drugs," February 20, 1988.
The New York Times	"Too Soon To Back Down on Drugs," April 14, 1988.
Viveca Novak	"The War on Drugs Gets Serious," *Common Cause Magazine*, July/August 1988.
Peter Ross Range	"The Demand-Side Drug Fix," *U.S. News & World Report*, March 14, 1988.
Peter Reuter, Gordon Crawford, and Jonathan Cave	*Sealing the Borders*. Santa Monica, CA: The RAND Corporation, 1988. Available from 1700 Main St., PO Box 2138, Santa Monica, CA 90406-2138.
Alan Riding	"A Drug Problem for All the Americas," *The New York Times*, July 31, 1988.
Jacqueline Sharkey	"The Contra-Drug Trade Off," *Common Cause Magazine*, September/October 1988.
Lester C. Thurow	"US Drug Policy: Colossal Ignorance," *The New York Times*, May 8, 1988.
Ben Whitaker	*The Global Connection: The Crisis of Drug Addiction*. London: Jonathan Cape, 1987.
Steven Wisotsky	*Breaking the Impasse in the War on Drugs*. Westport, CT: Greenwood Press, 1986.

index

addiction
  consequences of, 4, 23, 33, 415-416
  definitions of, 31-33, 36, 386-387
  endorphins and, 36, 375
  is a chemical imbalance, 35-38
  is a disease, 29-33
    myth of, 21-22, 39-40
  is a lack of self-discipline, 39-44
  is contagious, 4
  is epidemic, 1-4, 11-14, 303-306
    myth of, 5-9, 15-19, 264, 307-310
  media's view of, 3-4
  reasons for, 1-4, 23-24, 30, 31, 36, 387
  research on, 6-7
  treatments for, 30, 37-38, 43-44
    are ineffective, 269-270, 340
  types of, 5-6, 374
  see also drug abuse; prevention;
    treatment
alcohol
  as gateway drug, 419
  dangers of, 18
  effects on brain of, 47
Alcoholics Anonymous (AA), 63, 381, 386,
  416
  is effective, 63-65
    myth of, 67-70
  religious nature of, 67-70
  twelve steps of, 65, 67
alcoholism
  and the law, 52, 71-72, 73-74
  genetic factors in, 47-48, 57
    are inconclusive, 60
  is a disease, 45-49, 55-57, 64
    myth of, 39-40, 51-54, 59-61
  medical costs of, 46, 51
  stages of, 48-49, 52, 55-56
  statistics on, 18-19, 55, 198, 385-386, 425
  treatments for, 52-53, 416-417
    acupuncture, 389
    Alcoholics Anonymous (AA), 56-57
    are ineffective, 53-54, 61
    holistic, 389-390
    medication, 382
  see also drunk driving crackdowns
Alden, William F., 11, 424
American Council on Science and Health,
  109
American Nonsmokers' Rights Foundation,
  163
American Society for Pharmacology and
  Experimental Therapeutics, 311, 315, 316
anabolic steroids. See steroids
Anslinger, Harry, 244
Avorn, Jerry, 93, 95

Banzhaf, John F. III, 181
Barnett, Randy E., 201
Barry, Marion, 189, 197, 267
Benham, L., 102, 107
Bennett, William J., 212, 261, 271
Bentler, Peter M., 399
Betancur Guartas, Belisario, 293, 295, 298
Biernson, George, 225
Borge Thomás, 289, 294
Brickfield, Cyril F., 87
Buckley, William F., 190, 197, 219, 259, 267
Burger, Alfred, 97
Bush, George, 207, 286, 297
Bush, Patricia, 353

Castro, Janice, 335
Chapman, Stephen, 211, 349
The Christic Institute, 285
Christopher, James, 67
Church, George J., 187
cigarettes. See smoking
cocaine
  abuse of
    is epidemic, 303-306, 335-336, 423
      myth of, 307-310
  availability of, 305-306, 322, 323, 425
  dangers of, 315
    in pregnancy, 312, 316
  eradicating
    is possible, 319-322
      myth of, 323-326
    methods of, 322, 324-326
  is addictive, 22, 198, 306, 381
    myth of, 195
  on the job, 13-14
  research on
    dangers of, 316-317
    is needed, 311-313
  teenagers and, 13, 308
  traffic in, 12, 304-305, 325-326
  treatments for, 313, 317, 382-383, 390
Cockburn, Leslie, 217, 286
Cohen, Allan Y., 391
Cohen, Eric P., 105
Cohen, Richard, 15, 197, 308
Cohen, Sidney, 79
Collett, Merrill, 297
Committee on Problems of Drug
  Dependence, 311, 315, 316
Connolly, Pat, 354, 357
Consumer Reports, 171
Courson, Steve, 347, 351
crack, 12-13, 19, 259
  effects of, 303-304, 316
    are unknown, 311-312
  is addictive, 303, 304, 306
Cusack, John T., 306, 319

Dalterio, Susan, 227, 232
Den Uyl, Douglas J., 177
Dewey, Martin, 153
Donohoe, Tom, 359
drug abuse
  among teenagers, 399-402, 405
  and morality, 193-194
  as harmful, 198, 267, 268, 339-340, 423
  causes of, 265-266, 381, 391, 401
    collapse of the family, 404-405
    drug culture, 409
    family relationships, 363-367
    in movies, 403-404
    poor education, 396
    society's failure, 392-393, 403-405
      myth of, 407-408
  definitions of, 26, 41-42
  statistics on, 2, 6, 12-14, 194-195, 198,
    259, 385-386, 423
  symptoms of, 8, 27-28
  versus drug use
    can be responsible, 7-8, 27-28, 42
    myth of, 21, 22, 215-216
  see also addiction; prevention; treatment
drug enforcement
  failure of, 192, 211-212, 217-218, 246,
    251-252, 253, 264, 267-268, 305-306,
    424
    myth of, 221, 259
  harms of, 192-193, 201-202
    breeds corruption, 204-205, 218, 246,
      323-324
    invades privacy, 203-204, 218, 246
  legalization would harm, 221-223
    myth of, 217-219, 252
  should be increased, 208-209, 270,
    271-272, 306
    myth of, 201-205, 211-213, 425
  successes of, 424-425
  see also war on drugs
drug prevention. See prevention
drugs, illegal
  and crime, 202-205, 207-209, 211-212,
    215-216, 339
  are addictive, 21-24
  effects of, 23, 26-27, 196, 230-253,
    303-304
  history of, 222-223, 319-322
  in the workplace, 13-14, 335-336,
    339-340
  should be legalized, 191-196, 201-205
    benefits of, 187-188
    con, 197-200, 207-209, 215-216,
      221-223, 253
    harms of, 22, 189-190, 222
  withdrawal from, 23
  see also cocaine; heroin; marijuana; war
    on drugs